CHILDHOOD AND DEATH

CHILDHOOD AND DEATH

Edited by

Hannelore Wass

University of Florida, Gainesville

and

Charles A. Corr

Southern Illinois University at Edwardsville

HEMISPHERE PUBLISHING CORPORATION
Washington   New York   London

DISTRIBUTION OUTSIDE THE UNITED STATES
McGRAW–HILL INTERNATIONAL BOOK COMPANY
Auckland   Bogotá   Guatemala   Hamburg   Johannesburg
Lisbon   London   Madrid   Mexico   Montreal
New Delhi   Panama   Paris   San Juan   São Paulo
Singapore   Sydney   Tokyo   Toronto

CHILDHOOD AND DEATH

2 3 4 5 6 7 8 9 0   B C B C   8 9 8 7 6 5

Library of Congress Cataloging in Publication Data

Main entry under title:

Childhood and death.

(Series in death education, aging, and health care)
Bibliography: p.
Includes indexes.
1. Children and death. 2. Terminally ill children—
Psychology. 3. Bereavement in children. I. Wass,
Hannelore. II. Corr, Charles A. III. Series.
BF723.D3C54 1983   155.9'37   82-23365
ISBN 0-89116-320-4
ISSN 0275-3510

To Our Spouses, Harry and Donna,
Whose Encouragement and Tolerance
Have Smoothed the Often Rocky Path to the Completion of This Volume

and

To Our Children, Brian, Kevin, Karen, and Susan,
Who Have Contributed Much
to Our Motivation and Understanding

Contents

IV
SUICIDE

V
DEATH EDUCATION

Contributors

DAVID W. ADAMS, M.S.W., Director, Social Work Services, McMaster Division, Chedoke-McMaster Hospital, Associate Clinical Professor, Department of Psychiatry, McMaster University, Hamilton, Ontario, L8N 3Z5 Canada

MARYLOU BEHNKE, M.D., Assistant Professor, Department of Pediatrics, College of Medicine, University of Florida, Gainesville, Florida 32610

PATRICIA CARLSON, R.N., M.S., Senior Staff Nurse, Children's Special Care Unit, University of Minnesota Hospitals, Minneapolis, Minnesota 55455

UTE CARSON, M.A., Teacher and Writer, 2875 Dominique, Galveston, Texas 77551

LAURA CASON, M.A., Educational Psychology, College of Education, University of Florida, Gainesville, Florida 32611

FREDERICK W. COLEMAN, M.D., Medical Director, Psychiatric Nursing Clinic, University of Wisconsin Hospitals and Clinics, Madison, Wisconsin 53702

WENDY S. COLEMAN, M.D., Clinical Pediatrician, Jackson Clinic, Madison, Wisconsin 53703

CHARLES A. CORR, Ph.D., Professor, School of Humanities, Southern Illinois University, Edwardsville, Illinois 62026

DARRELL CRASE, Ph.D., Professor, Department of Health and Physical Education, College of Education, Memphis State University, Memphis Tennessee 38152

DIXIE R. CRASE, Ph.D., Professor of Child Development, Department of Home Economics, College of Education, Memphis State University, Memphis, Tennessee 38152

GLEN W. DAVIDSON, Ph.D., Professor and Chairman, Department of Medical Humanities, Professor of Psychiatry and Chief of Thanatology, Southern Illinois University School of Medicine, Springfield, Illinois 62708

ERNA FURMAN, B.A., Assistant Clinical Professor, Department of Psychiatry, Case Western Reserve University Medical School and Cleveland Center for Research in Child Development, Cleveland, Ohio 44106

WILLIAM F. HENRY, M.A., Director, Trustee Education, Programs in Hospital and Health Care Administration, University of Minnesota, Minneapolis, Minnesota 55455

IDA M. MARTINSON, R.N., Ph.D., Professor and Chairperson, Department of Family Health Care Nursing, School of Nursing, University of California, San Francisco, California 94143

JOAN N. McNEIL, Ph.D., Professor, Department of Family and Child Development, Kansas State University, Manhattan, Kansas 66506

PAULETTE MEHTA, M.D., Assistant Professor of Pediatrics, College of Medicine, University of Florida, Gainesville, Florida 32610

MARGARET SHANDOR MILES, R.N., Ph.D., Professor of Nursing and Medicine, College of Health Sciences and Hospital, The University of Kansas, Kansas City, Kansas 66103

JAY MONTGOMERY, M.P.H., Health Consultant, Minneapolis, Minnesota 55455

KATHY MONTGOMERY, R.N., B.S., Health Consultant, Minneapolis, Minnesota 55455

JOHN A. NACKASHI, M.D., Resident in Pediatrics, Department of Pediatrics, College of Medicine, University of Florida, Gainesville, Florida 32610

RICHARD A. PACHOLSKI, Ph.D., Professor and Chairman, Department of English, Millikin University, Decatur, Illinois 62522

ED PAKES, M.D., Assistant Professor, University of Toronto, Senior Psychiatrist, Hospital for Sick Children, Toronto, Ontario, Canada

MICHAEL PECK, Institute for Studies of Destructive Behaviors, Suicide Prevention Center, Los Angeles, California 90053

CYNTHIA R. PFEFFER, M.D., F.R.C.P.(C), F.A.P.A., D. Psych., Assistant Professor of Psychiatry, Cornell University Medical College, Chief, Child Inpatient Unit, New York Hospital–Cornell Medical Center, Westchester Division, White Plains, New York 10605

MARSHA D. RAULERSON, M.D., Resident in Pediatrics, Department of Pediatrics, College of Medicine, University of Florida, Gainesville, Florida 32610

PAMELA M. SCHULER, M.D., Resident in Pediatrics, Department of Pediatrics, College of Medicine, University of Florida, Gainesville, Florida 32610

MARIAN SIMACEK, R.N., M.S., Investigator, Health-Law Division, Attorney General's Office, State of Minnesota, Minneapolis, Minnesota 55455

M. L. S. VACHON, R.N., Ph.D., Research Scientist, Associate Professor, Department of Psychiatry, University of Toronto, Toronto, Canada

EUGENIA H. WAECHTER, R.N., Ph.D., Deceased

HANNELORE WASS, Ph.D., Professor of Educational Psychology, Foundations of Education, College of Education, University of Florida, Gainesville, Florida 32611

MORRIS A. WESSEL, M.D., Clinical Professor of Pediatrics, Yale University School of Medicine, New Haven, Connecticut 06520

Preface

Some years ago, when we conceived the idea of preparing a volume in which all facets of death involving children would be examined, a number of friends and colleagues discouraged us from proceeding with such a project. "How depressing"; "how morbid," they said. "Who would want to read such a book?"; "don't you think it would be too heavy a dose of death?"; "why would you want to work on such an emotionally taxing subject?" These and similar comments did in fact discourage us for a time. "Why indeed," we asked ourselves. What did we hope to accomplish? Certainly we did not want to publish a morbid and depressing book. However, after some months, during which we interacted further with children, parents, and caregivers, we became convinced that we should go ahead with the project. Coming through the pain and despair we all feel when death is associated with children are the deeper aspects of human love, faith, and meaning that find expression in this context and that we share in our common humanity.

Death is a fact of life. It is real whether we like it or not. Children do come in contact with death. Some of them experience it as a personal threat or even as a personal reality. Dying is a frightening prospect for most people, and children are no exception. They need love, care, and reassurance as much as or more than adults. For parents the loss of a child through death is surely one of the most tragic events that could happen. It can be devastating to them and to surviving family members. The death of a child can also disrupt a classroom or a school. For caregivers in our health system, death is almost always frustrating and emotionally taxing. Even people with deep faith need much comfort and support in such a situation.

For a person in the formative years, to lose a parent is a traumatic event that can threaten, in the mind of the child, the continuation of his or her own life, and can make the child feel lost and abandoned in a world that has become frightening because the familiar anchor that held fast is suddenly gone. Even the child who is not directly affected by death needs help in dealing with the idea and especially with the many fears and anxieties that accompany it.

We have talked with many children—some dying, some bereaved, and many as yet untouched by these experiences—and we have talked at length with parents, psychologists, and caregivers. In different ways and in different words they all told us the same thing: "We need help." How, for example, can parents and caregivers cope with the fact that child suicide is a growing problem? Admittedly, no book, no matter how excellent, can replace the warmth and depth of love that comes from caring personal contact. But we are convinced that *Childhood and Death* will be of help to many who provide that personal contact, for, to be helpful, one needs understanding of the processes involved in trying to cope with death. Helpers also need understanding of their role, their capabilities and their limitations in the helping relationship. To be frank, helpers want to know what to say, how to say it, when to be silent, and when to talk. Although there are no easy recipes for difficult situations, this book sets forth guidelines that can help the helpers in specific as well as in general ways.

We owe a great debt of gratitude to our contributors, who freely share in the chapters of this book not only their valuable expertise but also their personal experiences and their compassion. This kind of sharing will be a most important aid to readers as they strive to become more effective caregivers and helpers, to those who seek in these pages guidance and comfort in the face of the personal tragedy of having a dying child, to those who seek to help a bereaved child or to deal with their own bereavement upon the death of a child, as well as to those readers who confront the easier, but important, task of helping a healthy child cope with thoughts and fears of death.

The University of Florida and Southern Illinois University at Edwardsville have helped in many practical ways with our work on this book. Our publisher has been most tolerant and cooperative. Our spouses have constantly encouraged us in this undertaking. But none deserve our gratitude more than our own children, Brian, Kevin, Karen, and Susan.

Hannelore Wass and Charles A. Corr

I

DEATH

The basic questions adults have been asking about children and death are these: Are children interested in death at all? Is death a concern to them? Are thoughts and fears of death something that is normal and healthy or should we view them as a sign of an emotional disturbance? Answers to these and similar questions are critical to all who live, work, and interact with children. For those who are familiar with the available research on the subject or those who have been observing and listening to children in their families or in nearby surroundings, the answers are obvious. Of course children are concerned about death. Children have a basic need to make sense of the world and of themselves in it. In their own way they seek answers to existential questions much as we adults do. Children are curious about all aspects of life. Death, with its many manifestations, is among those aspects. Sometimes the ways in which death presents itself and is interpreted are powerful, strange, and confusing; at other times they are casual, familiar, and clear. But we should not doubt that death is a part of the child's world. To believe otherwise means that we greatly underestimate the motivations and capacities of our young. To ignore these facts may cause us to leave many children with distorted views and understandings and with fears that threaten the child's basic sense of security.

To discover what children think and feel about death, we must ask them, which poses difficulties for the researcher. One problem is that the child's world of thoughts, fantasies, and feelings is probably far richer than he or she is able or willing to communicate. Further, our modes of eliciting information from the child may influence the answers we receive, and thus tend to bring into question the conclusions we draw.

Despite these and other difficulties, however, psychologists have over the past 50 years attempted to enter the world of children's perceptions, thoughts, and feelings about death with the goal of obtaining insights into help the child may need from adults. Most often studies have been conducted in relative isolation and without a clear link to any theoretical framework. In general, questions related to the development of children's thoughts of death have been studied more extensively than those concerning the impact of environmental factors. The results have seemed inconsistent with respect to these two types of foci. Often cognitive aspects have been explored independently from affective considerations or vice versa. Thus, a considerable body of research on this subject does exist, but up until

1

now it has lacked integration. Previous reviews of the research literature have sampled rather than synthesized the available reports. Clearly, we need to achieve more and better knowledge about the formation of death-related thoughts and feelings in childhood if we are to understand the concerns of children and if we are to be able to interact with them and help them more effectively.

In Chapters 1 and 2, Hannelore Wass and Laura Cason provide the thorough and comprehensive assessment of this subject that has long been needed. For purposes of discussion, thinking and feeling are treated in separate chapters, but their organic unity in children is never out of sight. First Wass briefly summarizes Jean Piaget's theory of intellectual development in children. This widely-respected outlook has been most influential in enhancing appreciation of the uniqueness of cognitive processes in childhood. Here it serves as a background to an exposition of research concerning concepts of death at various stages in childhood development. Numerous studies and many examples are cited to support the major claim that findings are indeed consistent. There is an orderly sequence in the development of children's concepts of death. Though variations as to rate of development and some other factors do exist, consistency between theory and data is the overriding point, and is confirmed by an exploration of what children say about religious beliefs.

In Chapter 2 Wass is joined by her coauthor for an analysis of children's fears and anxieties about death. In the affective realm no single conceptual framework dominates as does Piaget's in the cognitive order. Instead, four major viewpoints are considered in turn and each is credited for what it has to offer in guiding our understanding of children's feelings about death. In the course of this discussion, a broad range of experiential and other factors underlying such feelings is acknowledged. Special kinds of death-related experiences, such as personal encounters with death and how the child and those around deal with these experiences and how we can help to achieve more effective coping, are discussed in the remaining chapters. Chapters 1 and 2 provide the base by placing before us as full an exposition of the child's world in relationship to our subject as is consonant with existing research and theories.

1

Concepts of Death

A Developmental Perspective

Hannelore Wass

If we adults want to help the child cope with death, it is essential that we know something of the child's world of thoughts and feelings. For discussion purposes we shall consider thinking and feeling as separate dimensions and deal with them separately, knowing, however, that the two processes are inseparably intertwined in the real flesh-and-blood person. In the final analysis, death remains a mystery, yet people have concepts, knowledge and understandings about death and dying. We are not born with these concepts, knowledge, or understandings. Rather, they develop and are learned. How this occurs is our topic of discussion.

The development of an understanding of death is best viewed in the broader context of the child's general intellectual development. Such a context is provided by Jean Piaget, the famed Swiss developmental psychologist who has designed the most comprehensive theory of cognitive development to date. Piaget's work spans nearly half a century and has resulted in over 200 articles and over 30 books, most of them now available in English translation. Piaget's theory is generally supported and confirmed by many replication studies in various countries, including the U.S.A. Although Piaget himself has not specifically studied the question of how the understanding of death develops, his theory and findings on conceptual development in general can be readily applied to the development of the concept of death. We shall review a number of studies that explored the development of death concepts and use Piaget's formulations as the theoretical basis for explaining and interpreting findings.

It is not necessary for our purposes here to present a summary of Piaget's monumental work. Rather, we will discuss those aspects of his theory that we consider most relevant to our topic.

To begin with, in Piaget's theory children's thoughts, perceptions, judgments, and reasoning are seen as qualitatively different from those of adults and are believed to develop in an orderly and hierarchical sequence eventually to become identical with those of adults as the child's underlying cognitive structures develop and change.

PERIODS OF COGNITIVE DEVELOPMENT

Over the years, Piaget has offered somewhat divergent organizations of these developmental sequences. In his most recent formulations Piaget (1) views intellectual development as a succession of *three major periods*, each of which integrates and extends the preceding one, reconstructs it on a new and higher level, later to be surpassed to an even greater degree. These periods are divided into subperiods or stages some of which are further divided into substages. Together these periods, subperiods, and substages form a complex system of cognitive development spanning a child's life from birth to approximately 15 years of age. A simplified outline of the system is presented in Table 1.

The first major period in Piaget's system is a novel conceptualization. Unlike psychologists before him, Piaget suggests that intellectual development begins at birth with sensory and motor actions and that during infancy these actions, through repetition, become established as schemata or behavioral sequences that form the basis for later intellectual structure and function. But infants are believed unable to think and form concepts; they possess little or no language, and they are just becoming aware of themselves as entities apart from the world. For example, after the required mobility is attained, the infant, through exploration and manipulation, discovers that toes are not toys that roll away or fall out of reach, but that they are permanently attached.

The second major period in Piaget's system is viewed as an intermediate period which prepares and organizes concrete thinking which, in turn, prepares for the final period of formal thinking or operation. This period includes the child from early childhood to adolescence and will be of special interest to us.

The period of formal operations during adolescence is the integration and culmination of previous periods in which the mature adult level of cognitive structure and function is obtained.

Put very simply, Piaget views intellectual development as growing from undif-

Table 1 Piaget's system of cognitive development

Period and stage[a]	Life period[b]	Some major characteristics
I. Period of sensorimotor intelligence	Infancy (0-2)	"Intelligence" consists of sensory and motor actions. No conscious thinking. Limited language.[c] No concept of reality.
II. Period of preparation & organization of concrete operations		
1. Stage of preoperational thought	Early childhood (2-7)	Egocentric orientation. Magical, animistic, & artificialistic thinking. Thinking is irreversible. Reality is subjective.
2. Stage of concrete operations	Middle childhood/ preadolescence (7-11/12)	Orientation ego-decentered. Thinking is bound to concrete. Naturalistic thinking. Recognizes laws of conservation and reversibility.
III. Period of formal operations	Adolescence and adulthood (12+)	Propositional and hypo-deductive thinking. Generality of thinking. Reality is objective.

[a]Each stage includes an initial period of preparation and a final period of attainment; thus, whatever characterizes a stage is in the process of formation.

[b]There are individual differences in chronological ages.

[c]By the end of age 2 children, on the average, have attained a vocabulary of approximately 250-300 words.

ferentiated to differentiated, from simple to complex, from ego-centered to ego-decentered, from concrete to abstract, from action to thought, from subjective to objective, and from non- or pre-logical to logical.

The first fundamental component in Piaget's theory is that of organic growth or *maturation*, including the maturation of the nervous system and the endocrine system. Maturation determines the unvarying order in the sequence of the child's intellectual development. However, the social and physical milieu play an important role, and *experience* or practice is the second major factor necessary and essential for cognitive development (2, pp. 154-155). Thus, mental growth happens in constant and close interaction between child and environment. It is worth noting here that Piaget focused his attention almost exclusively on intellectual development occurring in an *optimum, constant* environment. The effects upon the child's mental development of extreme environments have been studied by others.

As indicated before, in the first period of cognitive development, the infant typically does not have concepts. The third period of cognitive development characterizes the kinds of thinking capacities and structures that are believed to have reached adult status. Therefore, our focus will be on the second period of cognitive development. It best describes the evolution of thinking and extends from early childhood to adolescence. This period consists of two stages, termed preoperational thought and concrete operations (see Table 1). We shall discuss these stages in turn.

The Stage of Preoperational Thought

An operation is defined as a thought that follows rules of logic whereas preoperational thought does not follow such rules. Central to the understanding of the young child's thoughts and perceptions during the preoperational stage is his or her egocentric orientation. Egocentricity refers to the lack of differentiation between the internal world and the physical world around, between the child's own point of view and that of others. This lack of differentiation leads to at least three kinds of thinking and conceptions of the world that are unique to the child at this stage. They are animistic thinking, participation and magical thinking, and artificialism.

Animistic Thinking

Animism is the attribution of life and consciousness to inanimate objects. For example, Piaget (3) reports from conversations with his own children:

Jacqueline at age 2;7 (was looking for her lost spade) asked: "Shall we call it?"
At 3;3 J. explains: "The clouds go very slowly because they haven't any paws or legs."
Lucienne at 3;7 (when the family missed the train): "Doesn't the train know we aren't on it?" (251-252).

Similarly, the child believes that "stones can be young, old, happy, or afraid, walls hit and hurt people, trees cry and sleep, the car knows what to do, the clouds know when it's cold, the sun knows it gives light, the wind knows it is blowing, etc. Initially, all objects that move, such as sun, moon, clouds, bicycle, car, stones, and river are described as being alive. At a later phase of development within this stage only objects that move *spontaneously*, such as clouds, sun, river, but not bicycles, cars, or stones, are endowed with life. It is only during the stage of concrete operations that the child will have clearly learned to attribute life correctly only to people, animals, and plants (4).

A number of studies replicated Piaget's observations of animistic thinking. Klingberg (5) reports the responses of Swedish children to the question "Is it living?" listed in Table 2.

It is striking to note the large proportion of children up to ten years of age who report the objects "watch" and "car" as living. Even when the researchers rephrased the question and asked "Does it have life?" the percentages were only slightly smaller; approximately 20 percent of the children believed that watches and cars have life. However, this study dates back to 1957. It would be interesting to see how contemporary American children would respond. Whatever the results might be, certainly one would not expect older children, teenagers or adults to have animistic notions. Yet, how are we to explain the large number of words in our language denoting objects that are associated with the word "dead," seemingly signifying an animistic notion that they were once alive? Here is a sample: dead end, dead battery, dead motor, deadline, dead air, dead bolt lock, deadpan, dead-lock, deadweight, dead letter, dead zone, dead time, and dead center. Of course, one can come up with a variety of speculations about this usage, and certainly one cannot assume a direct causal relationship between language and thought. But could there be remnants of animistic thinking in adults? Why do we kick the table leg after we have stubbed a toe on it?

Participation and Magical Thinking

Objects are also thought to have intentions, wills, and forces of their own as well as being subject to such wills, intentions and forces (6). Thus, things both command and obey. Children also command and obey. They need and demand food, shelter and other means of survival, they demand love, attention, space, freedom to explore, and answers to satisfy their curiosity. They learn to obey and to acquiesce in many things. It would probably surprise many parents of young children to find how frequently their child has to follow parents' orders without understanding them but which the child explains through primitive causal thinking because it is the only reasoning available at this stage. For example, you have to wash your hands because supper is ready, use the spoon because it wants to be used, and take a bath because the water is in the tub.

Objects and events are believed to make other objects and events obey. Thus, the wind pushes the clouds, air comes from the leaves in the tree, the sky makes the clouds stick to it, etc. Things also act for the benefit of people, e.g., the moon

Table 2 Responses of children to the question, "Is it living?"

	7–8 Year-olds		9–10 Year-olds	
	Living (%)	Not living (%)	Living (%)	Not living (%)
Dog	94	4.5	97	3
Stone	5	91	3	97
Tree	88	12	100	0
River	37.5	61	23	70
Pencil	12	85	3	93
Bicycle	21	77.5	10	90
Moon	67	27	43	50
Watch	37.5	62.5	33	67
Car	33	67	23	73

walks with people so they can see in the dark, the sun shines to give us light or to make us warm. People can participate in this magic by their own actions. For example, Piaget (3) reports that at age 4;5 Lucienne was in a small boat with him and after it had not moved for several minutes she said urgently: "Row, Daddy, row fast, the boat is going to fall." Then she pressed her feet against the bottom of the boat: "I'm putting my foot so that it doesn't fall." Jacqueline at 5;6 is over-heard in the garden talking to herself: "I'm making the daylight come up" (with a gesture of raising something from the ground). A year earlier she had stamped her foot on one occasion declaring: "I am stamping because if I don't, the soup isn't good enough. If I do, the soup's good" (pp. 258-259).

Just as children believe they can make objects obey by their actions, they also believe they can do so by thought. Lucienne at 3;2 heard a wagon on the road at right angles with the one the Piagets were traveling in and was frightened: "I don't want it to come here. I want it to go over there." The wagon went by as she wished. She said: "You see, it's going over there because I didn't want it to come here" (3, p. 258). Such notions of magical causality are of particular interest and importance in relation to the child's fears of death as we shall see in the next chapter.

It may seem odd, but magical and other pre-logical thinking removes all mystery, all surprises from the child's world. There are no random events. Everything is caused. In fact, as Piaget notes, in phenomenistic causal thinking the appearance of two events together in space and time are sufficient to make them causally re-lated. This may appeal to the child's need to make sense out of the world and to discover an order in it. On the one hand, it seems that an orderly, magically ex-plainable world is reassuring. On the other hand, a world in which everything is possible, in which even the young child is endowed with magical power, can be very frightening. It is interesting to note that at this stage fairytales are especially attractive because they demonstrate, tale after tale, not only that magic works, but that, fortunately for the protagonists, it works for their benefit. In this orderly world, life is a natural phenomenon and death has no place in it. But when coming face to face with death the child's curiosity is set in motion "precisely because if every cause is coupled with a motive, then death calls for a special explanation." The child will then seek to discover what differentiates life from death which will lead him or her to replace magic pre-logical explanations (7, pp. 205-206).

Older children, seemingly as a joke, often engage in various magic practices, such as holding their breath while passing a cemetery or avoiding stepping on the cracks in the sidewalk. Even adults "knock on wood," or may feel momentarily irritated when a black cat crosses their path. Adults can laugh off these silly super-stitions but for the young child magical practices are a serious matter. Most small children have at one time or another wished their mothers, fathers, or siblings were dead. Sometimes, when a parent or sibling actually dies, the child may carry a heavy burden of guilt believing that he or she has actually brought about the death; psychological counseling is often necessary to help dissipate these ideas. Children gradually abandon this kind of thinking as they come to recognize and conceive the idea of physical constraints, that is, the idea that objects and events obey physi-cal laws.

Artificialism

Artificialism is the belief that all objects and events in the world are manufac-tured to serve people. This kind of thinking is in direct opposition to animistic thinking, but the child is unconcerned about this contradiction, and both kinds of thinking exist side by side. Jacqueline says at 2;11 (as daylight begins): "Now they've put on the light outside" (3, p. 246). At age 5;6 she asks: "Mummy, what did they do to fill the lake?" Mrs. P. Do you know? J: "Yes, they use watering cans" (p. 247). Piaget reports the following dialogue between a research associate and child Blan at 6;0:

> What do you do to get trees?
> B: "You sow seeds."
> (And to get seeds?)
> B: "You buy them in the shops."
> (And the shopkeeper?)
> B: "He makes them."
> (What with?)
> B: "With other seeds."
> (Where did they come from?)
> B: "The shop" (4, p. 335).

Artificialism and the Beginning of Life

Of special interest are the child's notions concerning the beginning of life during this stage. Jacqueline is 3;3 when she asks her first question about birth: "Daddy, where did you find the little baby in the cradle?" (it is Nonette, her new baby sister). Piaget answers that Mummy and Daddy had given her a little sister. At 3;6 J. asks: "How are babies made?" At various times in the next 6 months she makes the following statements: "She (her baby sister) came out of the wood." "That little baby was bought. They found her in a shop and bought her. Before that she was in the wood. I don't know all the rest. . ." "How are grannies made?" Touching her grandmother's eyes, nose, etc., she asks "Did you make yourself?" At age 4;10 J. declares that babies come "from the clinic . . . All the babies in the clinic have the same mummy. This mummy gets them ready and they grow. They have teeth and a tongue put in them." At 5;3 referring to new kittens J. discovers behind the woodpile, she states: "These babies were bought in a factory." At 5;4 she asks: "What are you before you are born?" P: Do you know? J. laughs: "An ant? Are you dust before you're born, are you nothing at all, are you air?" At 5;5 J. to her mother: "Where do babies come from?" Mrs. P. What do you think? J: "From inside you . . . They are bubbles of air . . . They are very tiny . . . But there must be something in the air that babies are made of . . ." (3, pp. 246–247).

In light of these observations, it is not surprising that the little boy whose dog has been killed urges his father: "Daddy, hurry, take him to the doctor. He can fix him up." Perhaps the paradox between artificialistic thinking about the origin and maintenance of life may not be such a paradox after all when we consider current medical and technological advances that enable us to replace parts of the human body with artificial parts. We already manufacture artificial hands, feet, limbs, jaws, shoulders, hips, breasts, joints, eyes, larynx, bronchial tubes, stomachs, and experimentation is underway to produce artificial blood and an artificial heart!

The Stage of Concrete Operations

The major accomplishment at this stage is the children's ability to free themselves of their egocentric orientation. However, this is a slow and gradual process and some traces of egocentric orientation may be retained in the period of formal operations during adolescence and even in adulthood. As we have seen, this egocentricity was responsible for the lack of differentiation between the internal and the external world where reality was construed with the self as model and referent. Now animistic, magical and artificialistic thinking decrease and will eventually disappear. The process of decentering begins as children become conscious of their subjectivity. Through interaction with their environment children discover the existence of their own thought and thinking as distinct from the world of objects and from other people, and they discover the existence of words and names as distinct from the things themselves. For example, at the preoperational level Jacqueline could not view her ideas as independent. At age 6;7 she was looking for her doll and was asked:

> *You've no idea where you put it?*
> J: *"No, I've no more ideas in my tummy. My mouth will have to give me a new idea"*
> *(3, p. 256).*

However at the stage of concrete operations, children responded as follows:

> *Where is thought?*
> Visc, 11;1: *"In the head."*
> *If the head were opened, could you see it?*
> Visc: *"No."*
> *Touch it?*
> Visc: *"No."*
> *Can the eye see inside the head?*
> Visc: *"No." (4, p. 54).*

It is similar with words and names. The following child is at the preoperational level:

> *(Stei believed that the name of the mountain Saléve comes from the mountain itself.)*
> *How did people know what it was called?*
> Stei: *"Because it's a big mountain."*
> *How did the teachers know?*
> Stei: *"Because they had seen it."*

At the stage of concrete operation, on the other hand, the children respond as follows:

> *Did the sun exist before it had a name?*
> Mey, 10: *"Yes, men gave it its name."*
> Veil, 9;6: *"It was already there."*
> *What was it called then?*
> Veil: *"It hadn't yet got a name." (4, pp. 67-68).*

When previously children considered their own views as absolute and shared by all, they now come to realize the *personal* nature of their views. At this stage children are increasingly able to use language as a bond between thought and word. Verbal skills are refined, vocabulary increases dramatically, and thought becomes more socialized as children learn to communicate it (7).

Piaget termed this stage "concrete operation." In his theory, *operations*, as we have seen, are cognitive acts or thoughts that are characterized by rules of logic as opposed to thoughts that are governed by magic, for example. The child's thinking becomes logical as he or she discovers and applies the laws or rules of logic, such as the rules of arithmetic, geometric, temporal, mechanical, and physical operations, and the rule of reversibility, that is, the rule that every thought or series of thoughts can be reversed or negated. At this stage, also, the child acquires the major concepts of conservation, space, time, rate, etc. The concept of conservation, also referred to as permanence or invariance, includes segmenting, partitioning and reunion and adding, and displacement by spreading out or concentration, all with respect to matter. These major concepts are necessary to the understanding of physical objects and events. The question of the child's ability to "conserve" or to understand the concept of conservation, is one that Piaget and his associates studied extensively. Piaget designed certain tasks to determine whether or not a child can conserve. Well-known is that of the water level. The experimenter places two identical beakers filled to exactly the same level with water in front of the child and asks whether the amount of water in the two beakers is the same or whether one has more water than the other. The child observes and replies: "They are the same." Now the experimenter, in full view of the child, pours the water from one beaker into a tall tube, then asks the same question as before. The child who states that the tube has more water in it, is basing his or her reasoning on the misleading perception of the difference in containers. When the water is poured back into the beaker, this child will declare that now they are the same again. This child has not yet attained the concept of conservation. On the other hand, the child who *knows* that the amount of water *has* to be the same since no water has been added or taken away, has discovered the concept of conservation. These concepts and rules are discovered over a period of years, and not only are some of these concepts more difficult to obtain than others for children in general, but individual differences are so large that some children may be adolescents and still in the stage of concrete operations, whereas some very young children may be fully functioning at this level.

Piaget terms this stage *concrete* operations because the child is interested in real objects or objects he or she can easily imagine. Thus during this stage children's thinking is more concerned with the concrete than with abstractions, and with the actual more than the hypothetical. So too the reasoning of the child is connected with actual belief that is based on direct observation so far as possible. For example, during the preoperational period of development, the young child believed that bicycles are alive; they move because they want to or because we want them to, there is an engine in the wires (spokes), the pedals make the wheels move, or you put a current in the tires. Thus, as far as causality is concerned, anything can be the cause for its working. The child who has progressed to the stage of concrete operations has carefully observed bicycles, is able to identify all of its parts, and produce the correct mechanical explanation of how it works (6). At this stage the child's thinking is no longer tied to the rigid and static thinking of the previous stage, it now becomes more flexible and mobile. However, the child as a rule does not yet generalize beyond what is finite, visible, and tangible. It is not surprising, then, that the child at this stage is primarily interested in the details of "how," the mechanisms, and techniques of objects and events in sharp contrast to the preoperational child who was preoccupied with the "why" of things. As children learn more about the objective physical world, discover laws concerning natural processes and seek natural explanations, animistic, magical, and artificialistic thinking are gradually replaced by concrete thinking. Children discover that many of their experiences cannot be accounted for by magical explanations. This is the case when the child is confronted with death. It may be the death of an animal or a person in the child's family or neighborhood. The child now knows that animals and people do not die because a magic spell has been cast upon them that can be lifted. Because of the emphasis in the child's thinking on the concrete, natural and observable, the child now seeks to discover what it is that differentiates death from life.

We have described the major characteristics of thinking at the preoperational stage and at the stage of concrete operations embracing the ages from approximately 2 years to 12. It is important to bear in mind that even though Piaget clearly identifies periods and stages of development, he does not believe this evolutionary process is rigidly divisible. Nor does he believe that children leap into and out of stages, or that the chronological ages he suggests are correct for all children. Developmental changes are gradual rather than abrupt. For example, magic, animistic, or artificialistic thinking do not disappear overnight. They may extend over a long period of time, indeed years. The process of concrete operations, for example, is an evolution in which children grope for natural explanations, but during these gropings, they hold on to earlier beliefs, they may oscillate from stage to stage over time and may, therefore, show occasional reversals of the sequence (4, pp. 189-190).

During the third period, that of formal operations in adolescence and extending into adulthood, previous cognitive structures and functions are integrated and full intellectual capacities and structures are now achieved. In this period the young person is able to formulate generalizations far beyond what is based on experience or what *can* be experienced, and he or she can state propositions and hypotheses and reason deductively. The young person should now be able to deal effectively with the world of abstract ideas as well as with reality.

Let us now look at studies dealing with the development of the concept of death in the framework of Piagetian theory, specifically, his formulations about that phase of development that spans the period from early childhood to adolescence.

STUDIES OF DEATH CONCEPTS AND PIAGETIAN THEORY

If we accept that children's concepts develop in an orderly sequence, and further, if we recognize that though the *sequence* is the same, the *rate* of development may vary, i.e., children may differ widely in the ages at which they move through the sequence, then we should expect findings in various studies of death concepts in children to be reasonably consistent. A review of the literature shows that to be the case. In fact, there are striking similarities in the protocols resulting from interviews conducted by Schilder & Wechsler (9) with American children in 1934, by Nagy (10) with Hungarian children in the 1930s (her research was not published in English until 1948), by Anthony (11) with English children in 1940, by Gartley and Bernasconi (12) with American children, by Koocher (13) with American children in 1972, and by Wass et al. (14-18) with American children during the period 1975-1978. We shall discuss these studies below.

Death Concepts at the Stage of Preoperational Thought

At this stage, the child may know the words "dead" and "death" but understand little or nothing of their meaning. The young child has no answer to the question "what is death?" We must recall that at this stage everything is alive and death is totally foreign to the child's world. When the child *does* observe death, it is a puzzle that he or she often solves with a magical or other pre-logical explanation. Many young children respond to the questions "what is death?" or "why do people die?" with "I don't know," or they parrot what they have heard from adults. Some offer stunning misinterpretations related to their pre-causal thinking. Here are some examples:

> *Schilder & Wechsler (9, 1934)*
> J. H., 5, explains, "My grandfather died by eating too much dinner." (p. 34).
> *Anthony (11, 1940)*
> T., 5;5, "If people don't go out for a walk they die." (p. 52).
> A., 5;8, "Hadn't had no dinner." (p. 53).
> *Wass & Rogers (15, 1977)*
> N., 3;5, (People die) . . . "because they eat too much candy . . . lollipops."
> B., 3;9, . . . "because they have to go to jail."
> L., 3;4, . . . "because the nurse gives them a pill."

The following are examples of responses young children give in various studies to the question: "What happens when people die?"

> *Anthony (1940)*
> D, 4;8: "It don't go on."
> C, 5;5: "To go asleep." (11, p. 52).
> *Schilder & Wechsler (1934)*
> S. R., 6: "They put him in a grave. He stays there until Saturday, then he may come out."
> G. M., 6: "Boys don't die unless they get run over. If they go to a hospital I think they come out living." (p. 421).
> *Nagy (1930s)*
> S. T., 4;8: "It can't move because it's in the coffin."
> B. I., 4;11: "He lies there. Scratches the earth to come up. To get a little air."
> T. P., 4;10: "He would like to come out but the coffin is nailed down." (10).
> *Wass & Rogers (1977)*
> Ni, 3;5: "They fall and their eyes get poked out."
> *What happens then?*
> "They get up and eat."
> No, 3;11: "They can't get up."
> *What do they do with somebody who can't get up?*
> "They help them up. Lay them in the truck and take them home. Then they put them to bed."
> *And what happens after that?*
> "They wake up in the morning and then he's all better."
> B, 3;9: "He goes to the hospital."
> *Then what happens?*
> "That's it."
> M, 4;5: "They be dead. People be killing them."
> *What happens then?*
> "Their mama has to come and get them."
> *Then what happens?*
> "They be better."
> T. A., 4;5: "Big birds come and eat you."
> H, 5;1: "Sometimes they go to heaven, and sometimes they throw them in the ocean."

What happens then?
"They drown."
And then?
"They get a new body. I don't know any more than that." (15).

The results of these diverse studies and a number of others reviewed elsewhere by Stillion and Wass (19) show that children at the preoperational stage of intellectual development have erroneous or incomplete understandings of death. Death is conceived as a *reversible* event such as sleep, or as a temporary state of restraint and deprivation. One notable difference between children in the early studies (Schilder & Wechsler, Nagy, Anthony) and recent studies with American children at this stage is that children in the early studies more frequently report accurately on funeral practices. In the early part of the century, life expectancy was considerably shorter, and contact with death was a more common experience in the young child's life. Young children were more likely to have participated in funerals than are young children of today. However, the experience of having observed funeral proceedings does not in itself enable the young child to comprehend "death." This is clearly shown by the responses of the children in Nagy's study. It is not difficult to conclude from these responses that the children considered putting people in coffins and in the ground a rather cruel thing to do.

This lack of comprehension of the meaning of death in the very young child has important implications for adults' behavior toward the child when a death has occurred. Adults who are not in tune with the young child's world may be distressed to find the child indifferent to the news of the death of a loved one. A young acquaintance of the author was upset and angry with her three-year old daughter for her apparent unconcern over her father's sudden death. After being told that Daddy died, the little girl asked if she could go out to play now. The child was sent to relatives until "it was all over" and enjoyed her stay tremendously. It was only after she had returned home, that the child asked casually: "When is Daddy coming back?" The mother's answer, "Daddy is gone forever, he isn't coming back," brought on symptoms of shock, disbelief, distress, and tears expected earlier. The question of providing explanations of death that the child can grasp is discussed in detail in other chapters. Here we would stress the importance of reassuring the child that he or she will not be abandoned but will be loved and taken care of as before.

Death Concepts at the Stage of Concrete Operations

At this stage, the child's thinking has shifted to the logical and naturalistic. The primary concern at this level is with the concrete physical and mechanical aspects of the world. The child now knows that only people, animals, and plants are alive, and that what lives also dies. Death is now understood as an irreversible event. The child will say: "When you are dead you are dead," and the only possibilities of coming back to life are through resurrection, reincarnation, or else the child may believe in some kind of immortality such as the transmigration of souls, as the 9-year old girl does who states: "I believe your soul goes into the next baby born." At this stage children do answer the question "What is death?" In two extensive studies with over 250 children ages 9 to 12 we found that approximately 65 percent of the children provided logical-semantic definitions of death, such as death is . . . "the end of living," ". . . when you don't live anymore," ". . . the opposite of life," etc. Approximately 15 percent of the children defined death as the cessation of physical functions, such as death is ". . . when the body stops functioning." The rest of the children provided either egocentric-affective definitions, such as "death is a scary thing," ". . . something I don't like," ". . . very sad," ". . . something that hurts, I wish it never happened," or religious definitions, such as death is ". . . when you go to live with the lord" (17, 18).

Concrete and Other Explanations

When asked the question "Why do people die?", children at this stage most frequently give *concrete* explanations. They now focus on physical causes. Concrete explanations can be divided into two categories, 1) external explanations, such as assault, accident, or disaster, and 2) internal explanations, such as disease and old age. The following are examples of responses:

External Explanations for "Why Do People Die?"

Schilder/Wechsler, Anthony	Gartley & Bernasconi, Koocher, Wass et al.
(1934-1940)	(1967-1978)
"They kill him."	"They get killed by rat poison."
"They get poisoned."	"They get shot or stabbed in the back."
"They die from fire."	"You could shoot yourself or hang yourself."
"They get run over."	"Sharks kill them."
"His head gets cut off."	"They die in a car wreck."
"They stick a knife in their heart."	"They get attacked by a tiger."
	"They fall off buildings or mountains."

What seems surprising in these examples is the striking similarity of responses from studies carried out over 30 years apart. From the developmental perspective, however, these findings are to be expected. The child at the beginning of this stage, approximately between seven and nine years of age, is more likely to view death as an unnatural event than later on during this developmental span. Death is believed to be brought about by external forces, which presumes a strong element of luck if one escapes these forces, or of misfortune if one does not. Thus death is capricious. These children list a number of external explanations, some of them quite fantastic, as causes of death. Children who have progressed further at this stage list external events less frequently. Now illness and old age are most often mentioned.

Internal Explanations of "Why Do People Die?"

Schilder/Wechsler, Anthony	Gartley & Bernasconi, Koocher, Wass et al.
(1934-1940)	(1967-1978)
"They get sick of pneumonia."	"They have heart attacks."
"They die by throat disease."	"They die of cancer."
"They get old."	"You could die with ulcers or maybe appendix."
	"They get old."

A number of older children offer non-concrete explanations. In two of our studies (17, 18) approximately one-fifth of the older children at this level provided explanations that fall into the category of *general law of nature explanations*, such as "everybody has to die sometime, nobody can live forever," "death is part of the life cycle," "they have to or else the world population would be too much." About 15 percent of the children provided *theological explanations*, such as "it is God's will," "because God thinks you have served your purpose," "because God wants you with Him," "God strikes them dead." Similar findings are reported in other studies (12, 13).

Personification of Death

Supernatural explanations other than God's will or plan, are reported in Nagy's study of Hungarian children in the 1930s. Nagy found that of the children she interviewed in Budapest, those ages five to nine explained death as murder and mutilation of the body by the "death angel," "bone skeleton," "white skeleton," etc. which was described as a "man-like" creature who lives in the graveyard and hates people. Based on these statements, Nagy believed that the personification of death constitutes an intermediate stage in the development of the concept of death. However, no other study early or recent, has produced any similar finding. This has puzzled researchers. Anthony (11) offers a plausible explanation for the discrepancy. She reports that the Hungarian language has different roots for the words "death" and "dead," and that younger children did not use the former term, and further, at the time of Nagy's study, before World War II, pictorial presentation of death as "a reaper in white" was common, and older children personified the abstraction (p. 75), thus leading to the very culture-specific responses. In fact, one of Nagy's children, H. G., 8;5, said: "I think it [death] is only a picture . . . It has a white cloak on, a scythe in its hand, as one imagines it in a picture" (p. 22). In light of these findings and considerations, we can conclude that death personification is not a stage in the development of death concepts as Nagy suggests but a cultural and linguistic artifact.

Childers and Wimmer (21) studied the understanding of the concepts of *universality* and *irrevocability* of death in children ages four to ten. Of the four year olds, 11 percent recognized that death is universal, of the five year olds it was 20 percent, and by the age of nine, 100 percent of the children viewed death as a universal event. The pattern was less clear with respect to the concept of irrevocability. Sixty-three percent of the ten year olds gave affirmative responses to the question "Can people come back to life?" whereas 27 percent responded negatively and ten percent were undecided. From these findings the authors conclude that a large proportion of the children lack the concept of irreversibility of death. In our findings (17, 18) over 36 percent responded with "yes" to the question "Can dead people ever come back to life?" and approximately 10 percent said "maybe." However, most of the children who responded with "yes" or "maybe" spontaneously elaborated or did so when questioned further. From the elaborations it became apparent that these children did not lack comprehension of the concept of irreversibility but they responded to the question in terms of theological beliefs such as resurrection or reincarnation, that is, they stated that through intervention of a superior power, God, the dead can live again.

The question "What happens when people die?" is answered at the *preoperational* stage with the reversal or undoing of whatever caused someone to die. For example, the child at the earlier stage will say that people "get better," "get up and eat" etc. The child at the stage of concrete operations answers this question by accurately describing what is done with the body and what happens to the body physiologically. For example:

Schilder and Wechsler (9)
    V. O., 10, "They go 6 feet under, then stay in the ground. Then after 5 or 6 years they are only bones." (p. 437).
Wass et al. (14, 15)
    C., 7;10, "They put you in a casket and you get buried in the graveyard. Then you start rotting and you rot until all there is is a bunch of soil. Maybe the coffin rots too, and all that soil turns into part of the ground."
    L., 9;2, "The body is put in a casket and the casket is put in the ground in the ceme-tery. The body just lies there and disintegrates."
    S., 11, "They lay in the ground and then their skin rots away, then there is just bones."
    B., 12, "They decay into the ground."

Typically, children first describe funeral procedures or decay of the body, the state that the soul goes either to heaven or hell. In Koocher's (13) study 52 percent of the children he interviewed referred to burial and 21 percent mentioned going to heaven or hell or hinted at some kind of afterlife.

Thus, naturalistic explanations about why people die and concrete physiological descriptions of what happens when people die, seem to predominate at this stage. This is completely consistent with Piaget's theory. The child who has fully ad-vanced in his or her cognitive development to the level of concrete operations, views death as a natural, universal and irreversible event. However, this event is seen as being in the very distant future. One 12-year old boy states:

"Well, to me death is a natural thing. Everybody has to die sometime. Nobody can live forever. I know that my mother and father will die sometime. I just hope it's not soon. Then, later, I myself will be threatened by this natural thing called death" (20).

This boy's statement represents the thinking of the child late in this stage as well as the adolescent who has entered the stage of formal operations. It is pro-bably what adults typically think. Since researchers tend not to confront the child bluntly with his or her own *personal* death, it is difficult to make definitive statements about children's concepts of personal death. Wass and Scott (16) asked children ages nine to twelve to write down what they imagine it feels like when someone dies and what happens afterwards. Analysis of these free stories revealed that most children in a sample of 85 did refer to their own deaths, and in many cases, they expressed concern and anxiety related to their own death. Here are some examples:

"I think when someone knows they are going to die they are very scared. I would. I hope I never die."
"I get scared and I don't want to die."
"When I think about death I get all spooked out. I don't know about you, but I'm going to Heaven" (22).

It seems that while death is understood as a natural event, there is at the same time an anxious reluctance to consider it as a possibility for oneself.

It is the older adolescent who appears to view the universality of death with less anxiety. Below are two typical responses of teenagers:

R., age 16: "I am not concerned with death. I plan to live a long life, and if I think about dying at all, it won't be until I am old. I am not worried about death but I am worried about living a dull life."
M., 17: "Death for me is a long way down the road of life. Right now I am more concerned about what I am going to do with my life than how I am going to terminate it" (14).

In the framework of Piagetian theory, the cognitively advanced adolescents who have reached the final period of formal operations fully comprehend death. They know that death is irreversible, natural, and universal. In this period they can also view death as an abstract idea. Because adolescents in this period have acquired a more accurate concept of time than the child in the earlier periods, they can derive a sense of comfort from the expectation of a long life yet to be lived. However, the recognition that death is universal implies the understanding that it is inevitable and thus *personal*. This recognition, as we have seen, is threatening to the older child. Kastenbaum and Aisenberg (22) have suggested that adolescents experience heightened concern about death because death conflicts with and threatens the young person's emerging individual identity (p. 34). In order to cope with such a threat, the adolescent, similar to the adult, tends to shut the thought of death-as-a-personal event out of his or her mind and deals with death safely in the abstract.

We have reported findings from a number of studies of children's concepts of death that are consistent with Piaget's theory of cognitive development. In fact, it seems that this theory offers cohesive explanations and interpretations of these results. Findings of additional studies (23-28) further support our conclusions. We think that concepts of death develop in an orderly sequence from ignorance to limited understanding to accurate comprehension with advancing growth from infancy to adolescence. There is little variation in the *sequence* provided the environment is constant but as with all growth, children vary in the *rate* of cognitive development; that is, children differ widely in chronological ages at which they reach higher cognitive levels of understanding, including the understanding of death. Further, cognitive development is an ongoing process, and Piaget, as well as other developmental theorists, stresses the variability inherent in such a process. A brief outline of the stages in the development of the concept of death in the framework of Piagetian theory is given in Table 3.

DEATH CONCEPTS AND RELIGIOUS BELIEFS

Although one would assume that a child's religious beliefs concerning death would be strongly influenced by the church, the research literature does not support this assumption (11, 12, 16, 26-28). This does not necessarily mean that such influence is absent. It merely means that it has not been discerned by investigation. When children do express certain beliefs, one has then to determine whether these beliefs have actually been incorporated and represent real personal conviction or are merely the "parroting" of what has been taught. This is a difficult question to answer. We can approach the question from Piaget's developmental perspective. If Piaget is correct in his theory of a sequence of cognitive development, we should expect that beliefs about life after death, the meaning of death, the purpose of death, etc. should be closely related to the ability to grasp such beliefs *intellectually*. The validity of this expectation should be established before we even ask whether or not the child truly accepts a certain belief. In an attempt to answer this question

Table 3 Development of death concepts

Predominant death concepts	Piaget's period/stage of cognitive development	Life period
1. No concept of death	Sensorimotor period	Infancy
2. Death is reversible: a temporary restriction, departure, or sleep	Stage of preoperational thought	Late infancy Early childhood
3. Death is irreversible but capricious; external-internal physiological explanations	Stage of concrete operations	Middle childhood Late childhood or preadolescence
4. Death is irreversible, universal, personal, but distant; natural, physiological and theological explanations	Period of formal operations	Preadolescence Adolescence Adulthood

we will review a number of studies and see what children at various developmental levels from childhood to adolescence reveal about religious beliefs.

The Young Child at the Stage of Preoperational Thought

Piaget (5) observed that the majority of young children he and his associates questioned only bring God in to explain the world and its origin when they can find nothing else. The young child tends to attribute to *parents* the perfections later attributed to God. Elsewhere, Piaget states: "If the child is puzzled by the problems of death, it is precisely because in his conception of things death is inexplicable. Apart from theological ideas which the child of 6 or 7 has not yet incorporated into his mentality, death is the fortuitous and mysterious phenomenon par excellence" (7, p. 178).

As we have seen the young child at the level of preoperational thought views death as reversible. Even so, most children at this level are told about God and Heaven and Hell. But when young children adopt these concepts, they make them consonant with their own experience and understanding. In the early studies, young children much more frequently reported accurate funeral procedures than did children in more recent studies, as mentioned earlier. Nagy's (10) children, for example, frequently commented that dead people wanted to come out of their graves but couldn't. It is here that religious beliefs become readily adopted and may provide a solution to a dilemma. G. P., age 6, one of the children in Nagy's study, stated that a person lies in the grave for four days. Why four days?

> G. P.: *"Because the angels don't know yet where he is. The angels dig him out and take him with them. They give him wings and fly away." (p. 14).*

Similar responses were given by children in our studies (15): What happens after a person dies? H. C., 8;1: "They get buried." And then? "They go to heaven." How do they get there? "By angel. An angel picks them up and then she puts you down in heaven."

Schilder and Wechsler (9) report how one child reconciles being buried in the ground and getting to heaven:

G. M., 6: "The hole that they put people in is near heaven, right next to it."

Another child in the same study said the following:

E. D., 6: "God makes them come up by magic. He puts his hand down—he comes up. When God says 'presto' they come up to him." (p. 424).
P. C., 6: "A little boy died—I saw the casket."
Where is he now?
"He has fun with God."

However, not all children are able to make their observations consonant with religious belief.

E. C., 7: "I saw my mother and father dead . . . I think they are still under the dirt . . . How should I know they are in heaven? I am sure they are under the ground. I saw them" (p. 420).

Parents frequently have no idea of their children's notions and beliefs about death. This is well illustrated by a case reported by a minister-friend of the author:

Seven-year old Ron's cat was run over by a car near his home while he was at school. The parents quickly removed the cat's body and traces of blood. After Ron had been home from school for a while he asked: "Where's my cat?" His parents haltingly and with considerable discomfort, replied: "Ronnie, your cat—is in Heaven with God." The boy looked from one parent to the other with a puzzled frown. Then he asked in an astonished tone of voice: "But Mom, Dad, what would God want with a dead cat?"

The young child at the stage of preoperational thought typically views God as a male (as is the common notion) and a person very much like a father, except taller, bigger, older, with a beard, and larger hands and eyes. This personification of God is reinforced by pictorial representations as well as written and verbal religious teachings and often persists into adolescence and adulthood.

Heaven is viewed by the young child as a place, in or above the clouds, that is familiar to the child's personal experience or is an interpretation of what he or she is told. Some children view heaven as a very pleasant place, whereas others believe it is rather restrictive. For example, Gartley and Bernasconi (12) interviewed 60 Roman Catholic children ages 5-1/2 to 14. Among the questions they asked were these: What do you understand of heaven and hell? What does a dead person do in Heaven? In Hell? They report that children ages 5 to 7 gave responses such as these:

What do you do in Heaven?
G. M., 5;5: "Close your eyes and live with God."
M. G., 6;7: "You can talk to the other angels but you can't play hopscotch because you're supposed to do what Jesus says and angels aren't supposed to play." (pp. 74-75).

The above researchers also asked children if it was possible to come back to earth from heaven:

M. C., 7;5: "No. Because you'd be up there and there's no ladder in heaven."
L. C., 7;1: "You couldn't get out. There is no door and God wouldn't let you out."
(p. 76).

Schilder and Wechsler (9) also asked the question "What does a dead person do in heaven?" Here are some illustrations from their sample:

A. R., 7: "He flies around with the wings . . . They eat whatever God gives them."
And Hell?
R. M., 7: "The devil does not give food."
E. D., 6: "The devil eats them all up." (p. 421).

G. P., a boy age 6 in Nagy's (10) study offered the following answer to what happens to people in heaven: "If it's a woman, she does the cleaning. If it's a man, he'll be an angel." The same child also suggested that he is going to bake cakes the whole year, that each angel has his own stove, that there are lots of houses with lots of children who play hide-and-seek in the clouds" (p. 14-15).

The Older Child at the Stage of Concrete Operations

As we have seen, the child at this stage tends to provide naturalistic-physiological definitions of death. Few children offer theological definitions. Theological *explanations* are more common. Approximately 15 percent of the older children offered such explanations (see page 15 of this chapter). When asked what happens after people die, more than half the children in two of our studies (17, 18) mentioned heaven and hell after having described funeral and decay. But there was no spontaneous elaboration as to how this is accomplished. The statements tended to be laconic, stereotypic, and in some cases expressed doubt. Below are some examples of such statements.

D. W., 11: ". . . Hopefully my soul will go to heaven."
E. S., 12: ". . . If you are good you go to heaven and if you are bad you go to hell."
C. D., 12: ". . . then I'd go straight up to heaven."
B. W., 11: "When you die you slowly begin to fade away. Then you're dead and that's it (no afterlife)."
J. G., 11: "After you die I don't have any idea what happens to you and if you did go to heaven what would you do there?"

Gartley and Bernasconi (12) also noted the frequency of stereotypic or "I don't know" responses.

What would you do in heaven?
M. M., 10;2: "Adore God."
Do you think you'll enjoy that?
"I don't think it'll be much fun at all."
P. M., 12; 3: "Praise God . . . I haven't been there so I don't know for sure."
S. S., 11;5: "I was never there to tell you the truth, but when you get there you have eternal happiness with God."
Could you play games?
"I don't have the faintest idea."
What would you like to do in heaven?
M. D., 10;8: "Play hockey."
Do you think you will be able to do that?
"No. God probably won't let me."

The older children's notion about hell were found to be similarly stereotyped:

What is hell like?
S. S., 11;5: "It's a place where you suffer for the rest of your life and you can never go to heaven."
D. S., 12;6: "You see all sorts of devils. They are getting burnt and hollering for the mercy of God."

It has already been stated (pp. 13-14) that a large proportion of the older children in two other studies (17, 18) gave theological responses to the question: Can dead people ever come back to life? Below are examples of such responses.

A. A., 9: "They can but not on earth."
M. J., 9: "Yes. But only in heaven."
S. R., 9: "If God wants to he can give you a new body."
B. T., 10: "Yes, in heaven people may come to life with a new body but I don't know how."
T. O., 10: "Yes, if God performs a miracle . . . I don't think it happens very often."
G. D., 11: "In a spiritual sense but not in body form."
L. P., 10: "Yes, but not in the same form."
T. F., 12: "Yes, but not the way we are living."
R. F., 11: "I don't know, I have never died . . . Well, actually if there was reincarnation I might have died and come back, who knows?"
D. P., 11: "I believe after you die you have another life and you might come back from anything like a cockroach to a royalty."

The Adolescent at the Period of Formal Operations

It appears that though religious convictions begin to emerge at the stage of concrete operations, the beliefs seem vague and poorly developed. We believe that this results from the child having difficulty in dealing with abstract ideas and ideologies at this stage. It is during the period of formal operations, in adolescence, that religious positions are clearly established. Only now has the child the intellectual capacity to grasp abstract meanings. Below are some representative excerpts from protocols of a study of 45 senior high school students. The question asked was: What is your view on death?

J., 17: "My interpretation of death is clearly from a Christian's point-of-view. I believe in an eternal life after death without human fault or sin. I believe that all souls will eventually be in heaven, heaven being defined as true inner peace within yourself and God."
C., 17: "Death is the ultimate demise of every human that inhabits the earth. Death has been made into more than just an inevitable biological process. All religions that people hold dear are mainly to provide some security about after death. I accept death as the final termination."
K., 16: "I plan to lead a full, useful, and satisfying life knowing that my life (in the present form at least) will end some day. I believe that some form of afterlife will exist for me and I have a certain curiosity as to what the nature of this will be."
M., 17: "To me death is part of living that holds no terror for me. I do not consider myself as very religious, and I don't believe in an afterlife" (14).

Thus it seems clear that children's religious beliefs are in accord with Piagetian theory and parallel the development of their concepts of death.

CONCLUDING REMARKS

We have made a case in this chapter for the developmental view in considering children's understanding and thoughts of death. Piaget's model seems to provide a good fit for interpreting findings from various studies on the subject. However, many questions remain. For example, in Piaget's view infants do not conceptualize even though they "act" intelligently by using their senses and motor capabilities to perceive and to explore. Whereas these ideas have been supported experimentally by Bower (29), Bower has also elaborated and clarified them. He and others (30) have found that infants are much more advanced in their cognitive development than Piaget believed. Although it has not been determined yet through systematic study if this is true for infantile understanding of death, it is possible that infants have some kind of pre-awareness, that they may "sense" or in some way "experience" death at a period in their lives when subjective and objective reality are still fused as Lonetto argues (31, p. 6). Such early experiences may indeed leave a mark or impression later to be assimilated or accommodated to a cognitive system and perhaps retrieved as a memory (or forgotten). Experiences of this sort may very well be accompanied or preceded by affective states. Such "premonitions" may occasionally become apparent to an adult observer. This may have been the case with the little 16-months old boy who saw a caterpillar run over and sadly said: "No more," as Kastenbaum reports (32, p. 116). It is quite possible that adults typically are not tuned in to such early communications.

We also know little about the extent to which words that young children utter adequately represent their thoughts and thinking processes. It appears that a child's world of thoughts, fantasies, and feelings is far richer and more extensive than he or she communicates. There is evidence suggesting that young children communicate non-verbally among themselves and that attempts to communicate this way with adults are made by children.

A final word about the developmental approach to dealing with children's death concepts. It would be a mistake to consider development as strictly limited to maturation. A human being does not develop in a social vacuum. We cannot neglect the many factors in the environment that influence a child's cognitive, affective, social, and physical development. Obviously, both maturation and environment combine to influence development. The divergence between the results of studies that have focused on the child's responses to parental death (33) or on the thoughts of dying children (34) on the one hand, and those of the non-bereaved, non-dying child on the other hand, need not be viewed as conflicting. The core of the divergence is the chronological *age* at which mature understandings occur. Piaget's theory does not address the question of variable environmental conditions. It is, therefore, not inconsistent with the Piagetian view to find large differences in the *rates* at which children pass through the stages of cognitive development. Viewed this way, the conflict is more apparent than real. This view is supported by others. For example, in his recent definitive work on loss Bowlby (35) has suggested that our understanding of children's responses to separation and loss can be best understood from the systematic work of developmental psychologists, particularly the work of Piaget and has reinterpreted the studies of loss in childhood on the basis of the Piagetian framework (pp. 425-439).

Finally, we would like to emphasize that generalized knowledge of the kind we have presented here is important and can be helpful to parents, teachers, and counselors as a basic background, a frame of reference, or a general guide. However, it should be complemented with understanding, insight, sensitivity and responsiveness to the individual child with whom one interacts. A particular child has many characteristics and circumstances in common with other children but there are some characteristics and circumstances a child shares with no others thus making the child unique. This uniqueness applies to all aspects of growth and development including understandings, perceptions, and concepts of death.

REFERENCES

1. Piaget, J. *The child and reality—problems of genetic psychology.* New York: Grossman, 1973.
2. Piaget, J. & Inhelder, B. *The psychology of the child.* New York: Basic Books, 1969.
3. Piaget, J. *Play, dreams and imitation in childhood.* New York: Norton, 1951.
4. Piaget, J. *The child's conceptions of the world.* C. K. Ogden (ed.), Totowa, New Jersey: Littlefield, Adams, 1965.
5. Klingberg, G. The distinction between living and not living among 7-10 year old children with some remarks concerning the so-called animism controversy, *Journal of Genetic Psychology, 90,* 1957, 227-238.
6. Piaget, J. *The child's conception of physical causality.* New York: Harcourt, Brace, 1930.
7. Piaget, J. *The language and thought of the child.* New York: Harcourt, Brace, 1926.
8. Piaget, J. *Six psychological studies* (translation edited by D. Elkind). New York: Vintage, 1968.
9. Schilder, P. & Wechsler, D. The attitudes of children toward death. *Journal of Genetic Psychology, 45,* 1934, 406-451.
10. Nagy, M. The child's theories concerning death. *Journal of Genetic Psychology, 73,* 1948, 3-27.
11. Anthony, S. *The discovery of death in childhood and after.* New York: Basic Books, 1972.
12. Gartley, W. & Bernasconi, M. The concept of death in children. *Journal of Genetic Psychology, 110,* 1967, 71-85.
13. Koocher, G. P. Childhood, death, and cognitive development. *Developmental Psychology, 9,* 1973, 369-375.
14. Wass, H. Children's concepts of death. Audiotaped Interviews, University of Florida, 1975 and 1976.
15. Wass, H. & Rogers, D. Children's death concepts. Videotaped Interviews, University of Florida, 1977.
16. Wass, H. & Scott, M. Middle school students' death concepts and concerns. *Middle School Journal, 9,* 1978, 10-12.
17. Wass, H., Guenther, Z. C., & Towry, B. J. United States and Brazilian children's concepts of death, *Death Education, 3,* 1979, 41-55.
18. Wass, H. & Towry, B. Children's death concepts and ethnicity. *Death Education, 4,* 1980, 83-87.
19. Stillion, J. & Wass, H. Children and death. In H. Wass (ed.), *Dying—Facing the Facts.* Washington: Hemisphere, 1979, 208-235.
20. Wass, H. & Shaak, J. Helping children understand death through literature. *Childhood Education, 53,* 1976, 80-85.
21. Childers, P. & Wimmer, M. The concept of death in early childhood, *Child Development, 42,* 1971, 1299-1301.
22. Kastenbaum, R. & Aisenberg, R. *The Psychology of Death.* Concise Edition. New York: Springer, 1976.
23. Melear, J. D. Children's conceptions of death. *Journal of Genetic Psychology, 123,* 1973, 159-160.
24. Swain, H. L. The concept of death in children. Unpublished doctoral dissertation, Marquette University, Milwaukee, Wisconsin, 1975.
25. Elkind, D. The child's conception of his religious denomination: I. The Jewish child. *Journal of Genetic Psychology, 99,* 1961, 209-225.
26. Elkind, D. The child's conception of his religious denomination: II. The Catholic child. *Journal of Genetic Psychology, 101,* 1962, 185-193.

27. Elkind, D. The child's conception of his religious denomination: III. The Protestant child. *Journal of Genetic Psychology, 103*, 1963, 291–304.
28. White, E., Elsom, B., & Pravat, R. Children's conceptions of death. *Child Development, 49*, 1978, 307–320.
29. Bower, T. G. R. *The development in infancy.* San Francisco: W. H. Freeman, 1974.
30. Gratch, G. Review of Piagetian infancy research: Object concept development. In W. F. Overton & J. H. Gallagher (eds.) *Knowledge and development, Vol. I.* New York: Plenum Press, 1977.
31. Lonetto, R. *Children's conceptions of death.* New York: Springer, 1980.
32. Kastenbaum, R. J. *Death, society, and human experience.* St. Louis: C. V. Mosby, 1977.
33. Furman, E. *A child's parent dies: Studies in childhood bereavement.* New Haven, Connecticut: Yale University Press, 1974.
34. Bluebond-Langner, M. *The private world of dying children.* Princeton, New Jersey: Princeton University Press, 1978.
35. Bowlby, J. *Attachment and Loss, Vol. III, Loss—Sadness and Depression.* New York: Basic Books, 1980.

2

Fears and Anxieties about Death

Hannelore Wass and Laura Cason

Children's feelings about death cover a broad range and arise from many sources. Throughout their development children define and redefine their ideas about death as has been illustrated in the preceding chapter. However cognitive in nature, these definitions and redefinitions are accompanied by feelings. Often experiences that contribute to an understanding of death also lead to curiosity and bewilderment which may become complicated by fear and anxiety. Fear and anxiety about death are of great practical concern to adults who relate to children in any capacity. They are the focus of discussion in this chapter.

In psychology a distinction is sometimes made between fear and anxiety. Anxiety refers to a state in which danger or threat that may be vague or unknown, is expected. On the other hand, fear refers to a feeling about a known object or event of which one is afraid. We will not strictly adhere to this distinction. We *will* distinguish between major theoretical viewpoints regarding children's fears and anxieties about death. We present such viewpoints hoping thereby to contribute to an understanding of these feelings in a way that assists in the interpretation of research findings and clarification of the complexity of the issues.

Four points of view will be developed from theories that have focused on different aspects of children's feelings, perceptions, and behavior. The first is based on the work of Sigmund Freud which is recognized as the core of the psychoanalytic tradition. Formulations relevant to our discussion and studies based on these formulations are primarily concerned with the genesis, causes, and nature of feelings. The second view focuses on how children's thoughts and their interpretations of events come to bear on their feelings and draws heavily on Jean Piaget's theory of cognitive development. The third view considers a particular process by which children's experiences influence their ideas and feelings and is anchored in the social-learning theory of Albert Bandura. A fourth view is based on several theories here called humanistic psychology, notably those of Rogers, Combs and Snygg, and Maslow and discusses the role of perceptions or personal meanings and how the family and significant others influence them. We shall discuss each of these views in turn.

PSYCHOANALYTIC VIEW

The most formidable attempt to describe the causes, genesis, and nature of feelings in children and adults was made by Sigmund Freud during the late 19th and early 20th century. Through the method of psychoanalysis which involves recording and analyzing patients' reports of their thoughts, feelings, and dreams, Freud tried to understand the character and origin of mental illness in his patients. These patients' expressions formed the basis upon which Freud developed his complex theory of personality. It assumes that all pathology can be viewed as uncontrolled or maladapted functioning of normal personality. We will briefly describe Freud's concepts of the basic instincts, the components of mental life, and the nature of fears and anxieties to provide a background for the psychoanalytic view of children's fears and anxieties about death. We will then review studies and clinical observations based on this view.

The Importance of Instincts

Freud believed that all behavior is motivated by basic physiological instincts. (Freud used the German term "Triebe" which would be better translated as "drives" rather than instincts.) They are energies which, transformed from the physiological, provide the link between body and mind, needs and wishes, and have the ultimate aim of achieving pleasure and avoiding pain (1). Freud did not speculate about the number of instincts but he believed that no matter how many, they can all be grouped into two major conflicting instincts, one sexual, the other destructive. These he later termed Eros (Greek for love), the wish to live and to love, and Thanatos (Greek for death), the wish to die or to kill. Freud never fully developed his notions about the death wish but he believed all human beings have a wish to die or a self-destructive instinct to return once again to the state of inorganic matter from which life is believed to have arisen (2). However, the wish to live asserts itself more strongly. In one essay (3) Freud states: ". . . at bottom no one believes in his own death . . . in the unconscious every one of us is convinced of his own immortality" (p. 305). The self-destructive instinct is also turned against others thereby becoming the wish to kill. In the same essay Freud writes: "In our unconscious we daily and hourly deport all who stand in our way, all who have offended or injured us . . . Indeed, our unconscious will murder even for trifles" (p. 314). The notion of the death wish apparently preoccupied Freud more during the years when his fame had grown and with it the vehemence of his critics. Further, over a period of 16 years Freud underwent 33 operations for a cancer and suffered almost continuous pain. These and other adverse experiences may have influenced his thinking.

Components and Functions of Mental Life

Although instincts are the basic units of personality providing it with energy, motivation, and direction, they are not part of our awareness. Freud asserted three levels of consciousness, the *unconscious* comprising the largest segment of the mind in which all drives and wishes reside, the *preconscious* which stores all memories, perceptions and thoughts of which we are not presently aware but which can be brought into awareness, and the *conscious*, consisting of all feelings, thoughts, memories, etc. of which we are fully aware at any given time. The unconscious also includes thoughts and feelings which have been in the conscious, are now repressed but continue to influence ideas and behavior (4). In later writings Freud (5) introduced the concepts *id, ego,* and *superego* to describe the three realms of mental life. The id corresponds closely to the unconscious that is filled with conflicting drives and wishes all constantly exerting pressure toward release. In contrast, the ego represents the power of perception, memory, and judgments, is rational, interprets the external world to the id and determines when and how instincts can best be satisfied within the boundaries of what is socially acceptable. The superego (conscience) is the arbiter of morality that monitors the ego. Like the id it is cruel and relentless in exerting pressure for perfection, although its goal is different. The ego, then, functions as a mediator between two powerful systems of forces. Freud believed that these mental structures develop sequentially. He thought that an infant's "mental life" consists entirely of the unconscious or id. Through early experiences the child develops the ego, and through internalization of parental and societal demands, the superego. Both ego and superego are thought to be established by the age of six. However, we must remember that the powerful unconscious impulses and wishes of the id exert their influence throughout life. And as mentioned before, the unconscious also includes repressed thoughts, feelings, and fantasies that continue to influence behavior.

Thus, in the psychoanalytic view a child's feelings—fears, pleasures, anxieties— may be understood in terms of an experience in the present, as well as past experiences especially with respect to the gratification and fulfillment of basic needs and wishes. The assumption of basic instincts that underlie all activity implies a continuity of mental life, i.e., all mental events are related to one another and all are determined by the pressure of the instincts and by past events. In this view fears, anxieties and memories of early experiences continue to influence the feelings children have later in life.

Fears and Anxieties

In Freudian theory anxiety is a critical aspect of an individual's life at any age. It is a signal of impending danger or threat and activates responses that are vital to effective coping. Anxiety fulfills first a physiological function. Here it is a reaction to some condition of danger and is manifested physiologically by rapid changes that prepare the organism for "fight or flight," changes that will do away with the danger or serve as a protective shield against it. Anxiety also fulfills a psychological function. Here the anxiety response is by the ego and derives from the conflicts between instinctual wishes and external demands; it involves the use of unconscious psychological methods that serve to avoid the danger situation (6). They are known as mechanisms of defense.

In psychoanalytic theory birth is seen as the origin of anxiety. Freud's disciple Otto Rank asserted that the "birth trauma" is the "prototype" of all anxiety. Freud agrees that birth is traumatic, threatening to overwhelm the organism. It thrusts the infant into a new environment full of noise, harsh light, contact, and coldness, bombarding him or her with these stimuli. The physiological anxiety reaction of the infant typically is increased heart rate, gasping, crying, wiggling, etc. What makes this event a "prototype" is that certain stimuli that by themselves would not bring about anxiety may now do so. Thus, when older children and adults experience traumatic anxiety or a threat to their self or integrity, they may be reduced to the state of total helplessness similar to that experienced in very early post-natal life. More significantly, whatever mechanisms were used to protect the infant from this overwhelming stimulation may be used continuously in later anxiety-provoking situations.

Death anxieties and fears in children and adults are thought to be derivatives of other anxieties and fears that develop in early life, beginning with birth as we have noted. Prominent among these are separation anxiety, the related fear of object loss, and the fear of castration. While Freud himself made little reference to death anxieties, their relationship with these fears and anxieties were explored in subsequent psychoanalytic studies.

Fears and Anxieties Related to Death

From the moment of birth the infant embarks on a journey of development that requires many adaptations to separation and loss. With the separation from the mother at birth the infant enters a phase in which his or her survival and fulfillment of needs depends on the presence, proximity, and responsiveness of a separate human being. Growing up from infancy through adolescence entails giving up the security of total dependence and adapting to a much lesser degree of dependence. Any threat of non-gratification generates an anxiety response (7). In *The Problem of Anxiety* (8) Freud asserts that infantile anxieties are all reducible to *one* feeling, loss of the person that is loved and longed for. Being left alone, being in the dark, finding a stranger in the place of the one the child trusts are events provoking such anxieties.

An important addition to Freud's concepts of the nature of separation anxiety are those of John Bowlby (9) which evolved out of his studies of young children's responses to the separation from the mother or other primary caregiver. Both agree that anxiety is evoked by separation but Bowlby believes that the anxiety results from the activation of instinctual response systems that underlie what he calls attachment behaviors such as crying, following, and clinging. When these responses are activated and remain so by prolonged separation, an anxiety response results that consists of three successive phases: protest, despair, and detachment. Other experimental studies and clinical observations have supported the notion that death fears and anxieties are intimately linked with separation anxiety (10-13), with the fear of abandonment (14), and with infantile fears of physical immobility or of the dark (15).

Freud and other psychoanalysts have also postulated a close relationship between death anxiety and castration anxiety. Castration anxiety arises from sexual yearnings for a parent during the child's psycho-sexual development. It involves feelings of guilt, and fears of punishment, retaliation, and aggression related to the development of the superego. During the early years children internalize parental and societal standards of right and wrong and good and bad as the superego which imposes judgments from within not only on the child's actions but also on wishes and thoughts. In fact, a "verdict of guilty" by the superego for a thought or a wish may be as severe as that for an action. Young children's beliefs about their thoughts, wishes, and reasoning processes in general influence their fears of punishment and retaliation. As Wahl (16) points out, young children tend to reason by the so-called Law of Talion according to which "to think a thing is to do a thing; to do a thing is to ensure an equal and similar punishment to the self" (p. 24). For example, the angry or frustrated child's exclamation "I wish you were dead!" may not only result in fear that the wish may actually cause the death but such a wish is also a threat to the child's own life. Several authors suggest a close interplay between the young child's feelings of guilt and fears about death (16, 17). The young child may also interpret certain religious concepts and practices in a way that the fear of death becomes closely related to the fear of punishment for one's sins (18).

However, children are not preoccupied solely with their wishes and thoughts. They are concerned with action and, as physical coordination progresses, with assertive and aggressive action. In interaction with siblings and peers, in games such as "Cowboys and Indians" and various war games, and through exposure to violent contests between heroes and villains in the media, children come to terms with aggressive acts and their consequences. Whether through imagination or experience, aggression and the concept of death become related. This was shown in research by Anthony (10). Her findings suggest that two types of death anxiety are generated by the fear of aggression, viz., *chronic* and *critical* death anxiety. Chronic death anxiety is characteristic of the young child, is seen as a reaction to the child's own aggressive impulses, and does not depend on a clear conception of death. Critical death anxiety, on the other hand, appears when the child recognizes that he or she is an independent being and therefore can die.

Children express death anxiety in various ways. Anthony (10) notes that around the age of ten, children enter a phase in which physiological aspects of death appear extraordinarily "funny" to them. At this time they may recite with glee rhymes such as this:

"Little Willie's dead
Jam him in the coffin
For you don't get the chance
Of a funeral of'n" (p. 76).

Many of the readers may well remember the rhyme that starts with the lines:

"The worms crawl out, the worms crawl in,
They crawl all over your mouth and chin."

Counting rhymes of this kind are:

"Twist his neck and hit him on the head
Throw him in the ditch and he'll be dead."

or

"Oranges and lemons
Say the bells of St. Clemens...
Here comes the candle to light you to bed
Here comes a chopper to chop off your head." (19).

This kind of irreverence is also reflected in children's humor, such as in this moron joke:

"Why did the moron jump off the Empire State Building?
Because he wanted to make a smash hit on Broadway."

One of the authors recently shared some of these rhymes and jokes with a group of freshmen at the University of Florida. She was informed that they were more than mild compared to the ones they knew. With embarrassed giggles two of the students related some so-called "dead baby jokes" apparently current among older children and teenagers. They are disconcertingly morbid. What makes such rhymes, chants, and jokes "attractive"? Are they expressions of a kind of "gallows humor"? From the psychoanalytic perspective one can argue that morbid materials are really disguises for expressing forbidden aggressive-destructive impulses. At the same time, they may serve as means for releasing anxieties related to death. Anthony (10) suggests, further, that during the younger years death may have been frightening and private, with the older child it becomes public, and although the child may still have anxieties, there is comfort in defying and mocking death in the company of other children. The survival of chants and rhymes with death-related content through the generations seems to make these explanations plausible.

In concluding this section we should mention a frequently cited study of death anxiety. Alexander and Adlerstein (20) measured death anxiety in two controlled experiments, using a word association test and galvanic skin response. They found that response time to death related words was significantly larger than to neutral words in each of the three age groups they used, the youngest a group of children ages 5-8, the middle group children ages 9-12, and the oldest group adolescents ages 13-16. However, the experiment using the galvanic skin response failed to show corresponding results. Instead, the youngest and the oldest age groups showed a significantly higher response (decrease in skin resistance) to death related words than to neutral words, whereas the middle group did not. The researchers explained these results in terms of the relative growth and changes in ego strength suggesting that the 9-12 year olds are in a kind of complacency period with respect to self and anxiety about death.

Undoubtedly death anxiety and fear take on various forms just as death has many meanings. It is the cessation of biological life. It entails separation and loss, and it is also the result of aggression and violence. Our understanding of children's death fears and anxieties must take into account these various meanings and related fears. In addition, as the child develops new concepts and interprets experiences in light of these concepts, death fears and anxieties may arise as a direct consequence of these cognitive activities as we shall see in the next section.

COGNITIVE VIEW

In Chapter 1 we discussed Piaget's descriptions of the development of children's thinking and their conceptions of the world. Understandings of death can be viewed as consisting of two different aspects. One concerns the process of dying and its consequences, involves questions as to why and how death occurs, and results in explanations that reflect underlying kinds of causal thinking. The other aspect has to do more specifically with the consequences of dying, namely with death itself. It involves questions that are concerned with what death "is like" and reflects notions about the nature of the state of death. Both kinds of understandings may influence the development of anxieties and fears concerning death.

Causal Thinking and Death Anxieties

Piaget explored the evolution of children's causal thinking that leads to an understanding of physical causality within the period of preoperational thought. Of 17 types of causal relations he identified, three appear relevant to fears and anxieties concerning death in early childhood. They are phenomenological, magical, and psychological causality. Phenomenological causality refers to the young child's tendency to relate causally two events that occur together in time and space. Examples of such explanations of death are listed on page 12 in Chapter 1. Closely related is magical causality (magical thinking) discussed in detailed in Chapter 1. This kind of causal thinking is particularly important in considering the child's fears of death. In one of his writings (21) Piaget observed that children who are haunted at night by fears of death may perform some action or mental operation believing that thereby they can actually prevent death. He relates the recollections of a collaborator who at the age of about 6 to 8 was terrified by the thought of not waking up in the morning. He would feel his heart beating to assure himself that he was all right. Then he would count quickly between each heartbeat and if he was able to count to a certain number before the next beat, he would feel saved. The qualities of phenomenological and magical causality may result in a large number of death fears and anxieties that would be inexplicable to an adult and that may remain largely undisclosed by the young child. The third type of causality, psychological causality, refers to the tendency in young children to perceive a psychological motive as the cause for everything. For example, Piaget reports young children's belief that ". . . God or men send us dreams because we have done things that we ought not have done" (21, p. 258). Theological explanations that involve the "will of God" reflect psychological causality (see p. 15, Chapter 1). In childhood and adulthood as well, these beliefs may alleviate fears concerning death. On the other hand, they may also lead to fears related to the omnipotence of a supreme power. Children's understanding of the "what" of death can also influence their feelings about the subject.

Concepts of Death and Their Relation to Death Fears and Anxieties

Findings of studies that have explored children's concepts of death are discussed in Chapter 1. They indicate that concepts of death develop throughout childhood and that differences exist in the death concepts held by children at different developmental levels. Because children seem to have different concepts of death at different developmental ages, it is reasonable to assume that fears of death may be influenced by the changing concepts of death.

During infancy, Piaget's sensorimotor period, there are no indications that death is conceptualized. This is not to say that infants do not or cannot respond emotionally to the death of a pet or a person. However, at this early age the response is probably to loss rather than to death. Beginning in late infancy and during early childhood children do appear to have concepts they can verbalize. In this period, the stage of preoperational thought in Piaget's system, children conceive of death as a temporary departure, a sleep-like state, or a state of restriction as discussed in Chapter 1. One might imagine that such conceptualization would prevent the development of fears concerning the finality of death. However, other equally intense feelings may emerge as a result of this concept and the young child's exposure to burial practices. For example, if the child believes death to be reversible and a temporary state, he or she may become very anxious about how the dead person will get out of the coffin and out from under the ground. Indeed, there is evidence to suggest that young children have just such fears (22).

Findings show that children's thoughts and concepts of death do in fact influence their death-related fears and anxieties. It is also plausible to assume the reverse, that death fears and anxieties influence children's thoughts and beliefs about death. It is acknowledged that in different cultures and civilizations certain belief systems about death and afterlife have evolved out of basic dread and anxiety concerning death and these have helped people to derive some comfort in the face of their mortality. Why should children not do likewise? There is, indeed, some indication that children "invent" ways for the dead to get out of their graves. By doing so, children may be able to handle their fears about being trapped. For example, a child invents a certain "bearable" length of stay for the body in the ground. One child in Nagy's study declared that a dead person lies in the grave for four days (22, p. 14); one six-year old in the Schilder and Wechsler study explained: "They put him in a grave. He stays there until Saturday, then he may come out" (23, p. 421), and another six-year old explained: "The hole they put people in is near heaven, right next to it" (p. 424). Such early fears of being trapped in the grave may persist in one fashion or another into adult life. The comment made recently to one of the authors by a twenty-year old woman is illustrative. Despite her knowledge of the general practice of embalming, she reported that her greatest fear about dying was that she would be buried "alive" and not be able to get out of her coffin. A funeral director reported to one of the authors that occasionally a member of the family or a friend of a deceased person will place something in the casket with the body. One man recently placed a fifth of bourbon in the casket by his friend explaining to the director jokingly and somewhat apologetically: "If he wakes up and discovers where he is, he will need it. It's the least I can do for him."

The concept of death attained during middle childhood and preadolescence at the stage of concrete operations includes the understanding that death is an irreversible event. As discussed in Chapter 1, early in this stage children tend to provide external explanations for death, such as violence, disaster, or accident. One would assume that much fear may be associated with these types of explanation. One may be lucky and escape these external forces of destruction, but then one may not. This makes death rather capricious. In this view, some of the magic practices of children, such as holding their breath when passing a cemetary, may be more serious than they care to tell adults. Children in Nagy's study (22) who had attained the concept that death is irreversible, tended to report fear and dread of the powerful Lord who could bring about one's death. The idea of capriciousness tends to disappear as children begin to provide natural and logical explanations for death. The child at the stage of concrete operations may continue to fear death in terms of separation but may also experience some of the dread that comes with the recognition that death is a permanent loss. In a study by Wass and Scott (24) children spontaneously reported fear and concern along with their explanation of the irreversibility of death. In the same study it was found that children's feelings about death are significantly related to concepts and beliefs they hold about life after death. Children who did not report any position or belief had more death anxiety than those who did. Among the children who expressed beliefs, those who believed in heaven or hell had more death anxiety than those who believed in some other kind of immortality, such as reincarnation, transmigration of souls, conversion to other forms of life or energy.

Studies show consistently that children at the stage of concrete operations tend to describe in detail not only the procedures of funeralization but also the process of decomposition and decay. It is possible that decay is a fearful concept for children that is not publicly admitted. Certainly the apparent preoccupation with the unpleasant details of the physiological consequences of death seem to indicate such a fear. One might also speculate that detailed description of the death processes may be a way to cope with such fears.

By late adolescence the young person typically has come to conceive of death not only as irreversible but also as universal and personal. The notion of personal death, however, is immediately placed in the context of the distant future. In this way death loses its threat as an actual force in the present. Other studies (25, 26) support this interpretation.

SOCIAL LEARNING VIEW

Without question the environment contributes an important share to the child's feelings, understandings, and actions. It should play an important role in the learning of fears and anxieties about death as well.

Learning through Observation

In order to look more closely at the influence of the environment on the development of children's death-related fears and anxieties, we have chosen a theoretical perspective that is concerned with the importance of specific types of experiences in childhood and with ways they influence feelings, thoughts, and behavior. Such a perspective is provided by the social learning theorist Albert Bandura (27). Bandura's social learning view departs substantially from other recent behaviorist theories, particularly Skinner's, in two ways: First, it acknowledges that whereas direct reinforcement learning has proved successful with animals, it is inadequate for explaining the vastly more complex aspects of human interpersonal behavior. Bandura agrees that much human learning does occur as a result of external reinforcement or by trial and error; at the same time, he stresses that almost all types of learning can be acquired, often more efficiently, without any reinforcement. Secondly, Bandura notes that Skinner's theory of learning disregards any phenomena not accessible to direct observation, such as internal states of fear and anxiety. Thus it offers no help in investigating these phenomena.

Bandura's social learning view differs significantly from the psychoanalytic view in that it does not assert a set of basic instincts or motives that persist through childhood and adulthood although they manifest themselves differently in behaviors. Bandura's view simply assumes that seemingly diverse behavior is controlled by diverse causes. The most important contribution Bandura's social learning theory makes is the view that behavior, attitudes, and feelings can be learned without direct experience by observation through modelling, sometimes called observational learning, a process that requires no reinforcement. Thus, the reactions of other persons to the idea or event of death to which the child is exposed, may influence the development of particular attitudes and feelings about death. Although social learning theorists have not investigated this possibility, other researchers have. For example, studies have been done to see if children's feelings about death are influenced by those of their parents. Findings do indeed indicate such a direct influence and may thus be used in support of the modelling view.

Studies by Lester (28) and Lester and Templer (29) indicate that death fears and anxieties in children resemble those of their parents. These and other studies contradict the findings of Alexander and Adlerstein cited earlier, but as has been pointed out often, most recently by Lonetto (30), inconsistency in findings on death fear and anxiety may be due to differences in methodology, sampling procedures, and analytic strategies. A number of studies on child-rearing practices and discipline techniques also come to mind. They report positive relationships between parents' aggressiveness and that of their children and may support the notion of aggressive imitation (31–33).

Many persons besides the parents are significant others in the lives of children, especially as they grow older and their social world expands. Siblings, particular peers, entire peer groups, teachers, a favorite relative all may serve as models. Very little research has dealt with the influence of these various persons on the child's death fears and anxieties, but there are some things adults know from direct observation. Other siblings and peers are frequently providers of "information" about death that can be truly frightening. Siblings and peers can be observed being cruel to animals that can cause anxieties. On the other hand, they can also be a comfort when one can share one's anxieties with them. Teachers are known to be influential models. At present, it is difficult to know how teachers deal with various death-related situations that occur in the classroom. It is still the minority of schools that have death education as an integral part of the curriculum and in which teachers have confronted some of the questions related to death and are prepared to use a "teachable moment" to help children deal with a death-related incident.

Bandura has pointed out that social learning comes about not only through observation of real life models, but of symbolic models as well. In the following sections we will consider a few sources of symbolic models to which developing children are exposed.

Television Violence

Bandura's early work has been instrumental in initiating a great many studies, extending over more than a decade, that have investigated the effects of filmed and televised violence. While these studies have not been conducted in the theoretical context of death anxiety and fears, their findings are certainly applicable to this concern.

An estimated 98 percent of American households with children contain at least one television set. In one study 45 percent of the parents kept an additional set in their bedroom, and 10 percent of the children had their own sets (34). Young children are the heaviest users of television, spending approximately two to three hours a day in front of the television set and more on weekends (35). Such extensive exposure suggests that television is an important force in the socialization process. It is, therefore, not surprising that the impact of this particular medium on children has been a concern of psychologists, parents, teachers, physicians, government officials, and the television industry itself (36). What has been disturbing to many individuals and groups is the very high amount of violence shown on television. Seventy percent of the leading characters in action programs are involved in some form of violence, mostly as the aggressor (37). Children's cartoons contain even more violence; about six times as many violent episodes are contained in one hour of cartoons as in one hour of adult programs. No wonder that well over 100 studies have been undertaken to determine what effects television violence has on children. A review of these studies reveals that most were concerned with effects on *behavior*. Basically, it was found that children learn aggressive behavior from aggressive television models (38, 39), that they retain much of what they learn (40) and that they actively imitate models' behavior, especially boys of working classes (41, 42). Young children are particularly prone to aggressive imitation (43). Content analyses of popular television programs show that violence is the most frequent and successful method for achieving goals (37).

On the other hand, there is evidence that television violence does *not* lead to aggressive behavior in non-aggressive children (44).

The research cited does not summarily support the notion that television violence leads to increased aggressiveness in children. A number of studies used a methodology whereby after having viewed aggressive behavior by filmed models children were given dolls, bozo clowns, and similar toys, and increased aggression was defined as increased aggression toward these toys compared with children who had not viewed aggressive film models. In these instances it could not be determined if children would act more aggressively toward other *children*, rather than toys. It would be difficult to prove that television is the single villain that causes aggressive behavior. More likely television violence combines with other factors, most importantly the family, and the child's perceptions, to make its impact.

The social learning view of modelling implies that television violence is harmful to children and a negative force in the socialization process. Not so according to the psychoanalytic view, however. We will remember that in Freud's thinking the young child is filled with aggressive-destructive drives and wishes that press for release and indulgence. By watching television violence, say psychoanalytically-oriented psychologists, children are provided an opportunity to "act out" vicariously their own violent fantasies and instincts, thus, television violence serves as a substitute for overt aggression and therefore is of benefit. In fact, according to Freud, the repression of basic impulses should be kept to a minimum because too much blotting out of unconscious urges leads to neurotic behavior. So one could conclude that the more violence the child can act out vicariously, the healthier. A simpler explanation would be that television violence allows for "letting off" of pent-up anger and frustration.

In social learning theory the influence of television violence is not limited to aggressive behavior. It extends to *feelings* as well. Bandura (28) states:

"Although emotional responses often are learned from direct experience, they also are frequently acquired observationally. Many intractable fears arise not from personally injurious experiences but from seeing others respond fearfully toward, or be hurt by, threatening objects." (p. 65)

These premises are extremely important in considering the development of fears about death in childhood. In our times children's *direct* experiences with death are relatively limited in scope compared to earlier times, while *indirect* experiences with others' attitude and feelings about death occur more frequently than in the past, especially through the media. For example, through the extensive television coverage of President John F. Kennedy's assassination in 1963, particularly at the early stage when no definite information was available and reporters and newsmen were still unable to control their own shock and anxiety, and again during the coverage of the funeral proceedings where millions of children vicariously participated in a funeral for the first time in their lives, children could witness the emotional pain and grief on the part of the persons associated with the events.

Far fewer studies have focused on the effects of television violence on children's feelings and beliefs. One of the main reasons for this lack is probably the methodological difficulty of establishing a direct causal relationship between televised violence and subsequent viewer fears. Fears are difficult to assess in any case. Children may not share them with adults, or they may be unable to articulate them. Nevertheless, television violence appears to have a strong impact on children's death fears and beliefs. Television gives a distorted picture of reality with respect to death caused by violence. For example, homicide accounts for only a fraction of one percent of the crimes committed in real life, whereas it is the most frequent television crime. However, children, particularly aggressive children, those from poor families and from minority groups, tend to believe that television violence accurately reflects real-life violence (45, 46). Prolonged and repeated exposure tends to desensitize young viewers; that is, they become emotionally indifferent both toward aggressive acts and the victims of such acts (39, 47). Television assault and killing often occur without visible pain and blood thereby making them more acceptable (48). Unusual violence and violent episodes that show negative consequences result in exaggerated fears and suspicions as well as increased anxieties (39, 44).

Television provides a distorted view of death. Thus children "incidentally" may learn myths rather than facts. Most deaths on television are violent. Seldom do children see programs in which people die naturally. And seldom do television characters really die. Though shot and killed time and again, the actors reappear very much alive on later shows. Reruns often feature actors who may have died many years before. This does not surprise the young child since magical and animistic thinking prevent the comprehension of death, as we have seen in Chapter 1. However, the young child needs an optimal environment to progress to a realistic understanding of death. Extensive exposure to the distorted portrayal of death on television can have the effect of retarding this development.

Television also has created superhuman beings, creatures that seem to be indestructable. Whereas in previous years such creatures had at least some features that distinguished them from human beings, such as attached wings in Superman or Batman, more recently such characters as the Bionic Man and the Bionic Woman look in every respect like human beings, thus intimating immortality for ordinary people.

Observational learning occurs not only through watching other persons live or on film. It occurs also by observing the physical environment, various events in this environment, and by *symbols*, such as words. Records of the written word are an important aspect of a highly developed culture. Human learning depends to a large degree on cognitive processes. Our educational system is based on this fundamental premise. Reading and hearing what others think, feel, and do is presumed to modify the understanding and attitudes of the readers or listeners.

Children's Books

Though empirical study generally has not been concerned with this question, at least one study by Bandura and Mischel (49) did explore it. They report that reading about the behavior of others is strikingly potent in altering attitudes. This finding is extremely important in considering children's attitudes toward death because there is an extensive, ever-increasing literature of children's books, both fiction and nonfiction, that deals with various aspects of dying, death and bereavement, and its role in providing vicarious death experiences and in developing certain attitudes must be recognized.[1] However, as in television, the critical intervening variable is the parents. First, it is they who through their own interest provide a model for the child. Then, it is the parents who bring the young child to the books or the books to the child. Parents perform an important function in judging the quality and suitability of particular reading materials for their child. For the very young, parents have to do the actual telling or reading of the book and may be engaged in considerable dialogue along the way. In an open supportive family environment, older children often discuss such books with their parents, sometimes for clarification, sometimes for comfort, and often because they are interested in their parents' viewpoints on these matters. In other words, books may have the potency as claimed by Bandura and Mischel, but the parents are necessary and helpful mediators by providing access to the books, and they can greatly reinforce the influence of the reading material by being involved in it with the child.

Fairy Tales

Fairy tales have long been an important part of the young child's literature and contributor to his or her enjoyment. Original fairy tales, especially those collected by the Grimm brothers were told by soldiers and sailors for mutual entertainment. They were bloody tales of murder, sex, and sadism. As they were passed on by word of mouth to mothers and grandmothers, much of the offensive material was dropped or couched in innocent terms. Despite these efforts, many fairy tales still describe horror, suffering, and brutal punishment. Yet they have survived through the years, and children love them. But is the fairy tale fare desirable for children? In terms of observational learning based primarily on live and filmed or televised models, one would assume that fairy tales negatively affect children's feelings about death. Social learning theorists have not explored this question experimentally. However, psychoanalytically-oriented psychologists offer answers based on clinical observations, as we shall see.

Disregarding for the moment either theoretical viewpoint, we can consider positive and negative aspects of the fairy tale. On the positive side we find a close affinity of thinking between the young child and the characters in the fairy tale. This thinking is magical and animistic. Good fairies wave magic wands and fulfill every wish. The world of the fairy tale is enchanted, a world of beautiful castles and kingdoms, charming princes and lovely princesses, incredible riches, gold and silver, all available to the young, poor, and downtrodden. In this world mirrors talk, mountains obey orders, and trees give off beautiful gowns and dancing shoes. Death for the young child is a temporary state, so, too, is death in the fairy tale, for the protagonists. They wake up from a 100-year sleep, die from a poisoned apple and come alive again, turn into frogs, swans, ravens, stones, and return after a time to their human form, and are eaten by a wolf and later jump out of his belly intact. Most fairy tales immediately establish the distance of the events either in time or space from the world of the young listener. For example, fairy tales typically begin with "once upon a time," "a thousand years ago," or "in a faraway land." Thus the child is given to understand that whatever happens in the

---

[1] For an extensive annotated bibliography on children's and adolescents' books on death the reader is referred to the book by Wass and Corr, *Helping Children Cope with Death: Guidelines and Resources, Second Edition*, 1984, Hemisphere, and Wass et al., *Death Education: An Annotated Resource Guide, II*, in press, Hemisphere.

fairy tale is in a different world and cannot threaten the child no matter how frightening the events may be. The fairy tale portrays a simplistic notion of justice. Like the fairy tale, the young child views people or situations as either good or bad. This kind of thinking provides clarity but most importantly, justice always prevails. The good, kind, and innocent are rewarded and the evil forces are punished. Thus, suffering is never in vain, and there is always a happy ending for the protagonists, which alludes to the absence of death, as in the common ending: "and they lived happily ever after."

On the negative side, violence, suffering, and cruel punishment by death are explicit. And the distancing mentioned above may well fail for many young children who cannot playfully enter this fantasy world, but, instead, become immersed in it. There are parents in the fairy tale who leave their children in a forest to die because there is not enough food for all (Hänsel and Gretel). There is a wicked stepmother who orders the young princess killed and demands her heart as proof (Snow White). There is a bad wolf disguised as Grandmother who devours the little girl (Little Red Riding Hood). These are terrifying happenings even though the children later are saved from certain death. The punishment for the evil characters is even more frightening because it is cruel and final: the witch is shoved in the oven to burn (Hänsel and Gretel), the wicked stepmother has to put on hot iron slippers and dance until she drops dead (Snow White), and the false bride is put in a barrel lined inside with sharp nails and rolled until she is dead (The Goose Girl). The fairy tale knows no mercy. According to social learning theory, these behaviors and events ought to result in heightened anxieties and fears of death.

This cruelty that has led many parents to avoid fairy tale literature for their young. However, some psychologists defend fairy tales and view even the cruelties as positive factors. The best known and most articulate advocate of the fairy tale is Bruno Bettelheim. In a recent book (50) he suggests that the fairy tale not only entertains and stimulates the imagination but is essential for the child's healthy personality development. Representing the psychoanalytic view. Bettelheim suggests that anxieties arising from the fairy tale are wholesome because they provide form for the child's own unconscious impulses and anxieties and point at ways to overcome them. This process of "working through" is essential. Thus, the fairy tale can be therapeutic for the child. As we have seen previously, in psychoanalytic theory early childhood is a period in which unconscious wishes, instincts, internalized demands, and anxieties are pitted against one another in fierce contest. These internal pressures often overwhelm a child. Bettelheim suggests when these pressures take over, the only way a child can hope to regain control over them is by externalizing them to a degree. To do this, the child needs help. Fairy tales offer such help. For example, the child's destructive impulses get embodied in the evil witch, wishful thinking in the good fairy, and fears in the voracious wolf. It is fascinating to read Bettelheim's interpretations of individual fairy tales such as Hänsel and Gretel, Snow White, Little Red Riding Hood, Cinderella, and others in terms of their symbolic meanings within the framework of psychoanalytic theory. He finds in these tales numerous examples of separation anxiety, castration anxiety (anxieties that have been associated with death anxieties), fixations, complexes, narcissism, and so on, all conflicts and anxieties that are normal problems during development in early childhood. Anthony (10) generally supports the child's exposure to fairy tales. She notes that cruelty is by no means alien to the child and death certainly plays an important role in the child's fantasy. However, she advises against adults' offering fairy tale material to children, specifically those of Central European origin (Grimms'). She suggests that such offerings may encourage a sadistic disposition in the child and cites some clinical case studies to support her point.

Thus, whether we believe fairy tales to be beneficial or harmful depends on the particular theoretical viewpoint we adopt. However, we may remember that various views agree on the importance of parents in the child's affective development. With fairy tales, as with other children's books, parents function as mediators. Parents who know their children well are sensitive to their needs and feelings and quick to notice unusual anxieties. At that point parental intervention is critical. We would underscore Anthony's warnings above. Because of the child's dependency and the power it gives to parents, they should be careful not to sanction cruelty, sadistic action and killing whether this be in the home, on the street, in film or television, or in a fairy tale.

HUMANISTIC PSYCHOLOGY

The term *humanistic psychology* is used here as an inclusive term for several different theoretical orientations that go by various names such as *third force* psychology, *self* theory, *phenomenologic, perceptual, existential* view and others. Each view offers specific concepts or insights, but all share several basic assumptions that justify grouping them in this way. Further, these basic assumptions are divergent from the psychoanalytic view and offer alternative explanations about feelings, thoughts, and behavior. Major representatives of these views are Gordon Allport (51), Carl Rogers (52), Arthur Combs and Donald Snygg (53), and Abraham Maslow (54). We will outline some of the major components of humanistic psychology dealing with the basic nature of human beings, the importance of personal perceptions, and the influence of childhood experiences. In so doing we will concentrate on factors that we believe are relevant to our discussion. Few studies of children's death fears and anxieties are based on humanistic psychology. However, this theoretical perspective offers a great deal of optimism, suggests the need for emphathetic understanding of the child's feelings about death and offers guidelines for helping children deal with their feelings.

Human Nature

Freud believed that human beings are motivated by powerful instincts, that all of the instincts are unconscious, all persist throughout life, and many are antisocial and destructive; that a perpetual battle rages between conflicting instincts, wishes, needs, and demands, blocked by feelings of anxiety and guilt. In this battle unacceptable wishes and fantasies persistently threaten to surface from the "dark cellar." It takes enormous amounts of energy to keep the lid on the id, so to speak. In this view human beings, in the final analysis, are irrational, controlled by basic forces of which they are largely unaware. In contrast, humanistic psychology holds that human beings are good by nature, rational, and free to make choices. They are not born with aggressive-destructive instincts. Whatever aggression they display is learned; aggression is always a response to external deprivation or threat. There is considerable evidence in anthropological literature that some cultures are aggressive whereas others are not. Such findings refute the notion of innate aggressive instincts.

Ashley Montagu (55), an anthropologist, suggests that, in fact, all available evidence by reputable scientists leads to the conclusion that human beings are born without any trace of aggressiveness. While humanistic psychology agrees that human beings *re*act to biological needs and that they *re*act to external stimuli, there is an additional uniquely human "third force" namely to *pro*act, a need or motive for self enhancement, self-actualization, and self determination. Another basic assumption distinguishing humanistic psychology from others is the perceptual-phenomenologic view which asserts that the behavior of individuals is best understood from the point of view of the individuals themselves. Conscious experiences and perceptions of self, others, and the world constitute an individual's personal meanings. They are of primary concern. Subjectivity of experience is acknowledged as the legitimate basic datum for understanding human beings. It is a person's perceptions at the moment rather than unconscious instincts and repressed wishes that determine behavior. Humanistic psychology views human beings optimistically, as persons motivated toward healthy forward growth which they actively initiate and choose rather than having to inhibit undesirable impulses.

The Importance of Needs and Perceptions

According to Combs and Snygg (58) all behavior is a function of a person's perceptions of personal meanings. Perceptions include not only sensory experiences but also the processes of knowing, understanding, and valuing. Perceptions are believed to be interwoven into a complex organization termed the perceptual field, also referred to as the experiential field. It is a person's subjective reality; in other words, the same objective stimuli are perceived differently by different individuals, and thus we know the world only through our perceptions. Perceptions are influenced by need and beliefs. Humanistic psychology postulates *one* single need or motivational force. Although named somewhat differently by different theorists, there is essential agreement as to the nature of the phenomenon they denote. Rogers (52) states: "... The organism has one basic tendency and striving—to actualize, maintain, and enhance the experiencing organism" (p. 487). Maslow (54), although identifying a hierarchy of needs beginning with basic needs for survival, security, love, etc., believes the highest and truly human principle is the need for self-actualization. Allport (53) labels this need "proprium" considering it to be the root of a basic self-consistency in goals, and values. Combs and Snygg (53) call it the need to maintain and enhance self. They state: "... From birth to death the maintenance of the phenomenal self is the most pressing, the most crucial, if not the only, task of existence ... we express maintenance and enhancement as two different words, but both relate to the same function—the production of a more adequate self" (p. 45).

From these statements it is apparent that in humanistic psychology self and the perceptions one has about oneself are the core of a person's perceptual field, the "I," "me," "myself" or what we call personality. These perceptions are considered to be the most important determinants of behavior. In contrast, Freud considered the ego as the part of our personality that is constantly trying to appease and mediate between inner conflicts and those between the person and the external world. Thus the ego merely responds to and coordinates psychological functions. It cannot engage in any unencumbered self-observation or self regard.

In the humanistic view, in order to understand another person's feelings or behavior it is necessary to try to discover what the person's perceptions are, particularly those of the self; that is, one must put oneself into the other person's place. According to Combs, effective helping relationships, indeed all effective human relationships, require such an emphatic process whether these relationships involve parents, teachers, physicians, ministers, nurses, employers, wives, husbands, lovers, friends, or politicians.

The Impact of Childhood Experiences on Fears and Anxieties

Both psychoanalytic and humanistic psychologies stress the importance of childhood in the development of fears and anxieties. In both perspectives parents are the most significant persons in the child's early life. The primary role of parents is the fulfilling of the child's basic needs for health, safety, security, and comfort. The two views differ with respect to the relative permanence of parental impact. Freud believed, as we have seen earlier, that adult personality is shaped completely during the first six years of life. Any emotional maladjustment in adulthood can be traced historically to unresolved conflicts, phobias, complexes, fixations, traumata, etc. arising in early childhood. This view of human development dismisses as insignificant any environmental influences during later childhood and the course of adult life. It assigns to parents a most powerful role and involves them as primary objects in the child's battle with instincts, wishes and impulses and external demands. These impulses are sources of anxiety but they are unconscious. This is particularly true for the very young child whose ego is still weak and whose defenses against instinctual impulses are not well developed. Because impulses and anxieties are barred from conscious awareness, they cannot be expressed, so that typical parents may have no idea about the inner turmoil their children experience and the role they have in it. For example, castration anxiety is unconscious; it is experienced as free floating, deep-seated anxiety for which the child has no label. According to the psychoanalytic view it seems that such neurotic problems are unavoidable, and it is up to child and parents to resolve them somehow. But how are parents to know when such impulses and anxieties exist in the child? Even more importantly, how can they help their child overcome them? Answers to these questions are not provided by Freud except through psychoanalysis. Humanistic psychology views childhood as far less problematic and anxiety-riddled. In this view the unsocialized, self-centered nature of human beings during infancy and early childhood is recognized, as is the dependency of the child upon adults to satisfy basic needs of health, safety, and security. In addition, humanistic psychologists emphasize the need for unconditional love, affection, and esteem. Problems in normal development arise only to the degree to which the environment is inappropriate or hostile and thus thwarts a child's basic goodness and leads to hostility, aggression, etc. Although in humanistic psychology unconscious processes are not denied, they are not emphasized. Combs et al. (56) suggest that the development of self-awareness begins at birth with the interaction between the child and the environment and becomes progressively more differentiated. They believe that while traumatic events such as birth, death, or divorce bear on a child's perceptions of self, their impact has been overvalued by psychoanalytic theory. In their view the child's everyday interactions with parents and others are of far greater significance. This seems reasonable when we consider the enormous amount of communication, verbal and nonverbal that occurs between parent and child in the course of a day, a week, a month, a year, many years. Millions of messages are conveyed to the child concerning his or her worth, acceptance, approval, or disapproval, and feelings of love or rejection or ambivalence are continuously communicated. In humanistic psychology the development of perceptions of oneself as adequate and worthy are the central function of socialization. In this view, anxieties are caused not by any instinctual impulses or drives but by persons, situations, or events that endanger or threaten the maintenance and enhancement of self. Rogers (57) suggests that each person has a need for positive regard. By positive regard he means acceptance, love and approval from others. This need is learned. It is learned in infancy and is pervasive and persistent. If positive regard is not given the child by parents, the tendency toward actualization and self enhancement are threatened. Parental disapproval of a child's behavior, for example, is perceived as disapproval of the total child or self unless the child has learned that the parents give their *unconditional* positive regard; that is, the child perceives sufficient over-all approval and love on the part of the parents, even though specific behaviors meet with their disapproval. The attitudes of important others, especially parents, become internalized. As a consequence, positive regard given by parents, for example, gradually comes from within as positive *self* regard. On the other hand, when parents' love and approval are *conditional*, children learn that parents value them under certain conditions and reject them under others. Parental manipulation of love and affection, then, is detrimental to the child's emotional development. Any inconsistency causes insecurity and anxiety according to Rogers.

Applying the notions of humanistic psychology to children's fears and anxieties about death one would expect that in an environment of care, love, acceptance, and esteem children tend to grow up relatively unencumbered by the kinds of anxieties related to separation, abandonment, loss of love, and fear of punishment. This is not to suggest that children do not experience fears and anxieties. They do. It is suggested, however, that children's selves are less threatened in a nurturing environment that considers them as worthy, able, and unique.

Furthermore, in such an environment fears, worries, and anxieties can be verbalized and shared in an atmosphere of open communication and freedom of expression. Thus parents can help children by reassurance, by reaffirmation of their love, by providing accurate information, and by sharing their beliefs. Open communication with children about such subjects as death requires that parents themselves have relatively low anxieties and fears concerning death, that they are willing to confront such issues and encourage their children to *ex*press their fears rather than to *re*press and deny them (58).

There is a tendency among some humanistic psychologists to romanticize childhood and, in fact, life. It may be a worthwhile goal to raise people to be free from anxieties but it may be quite unrealistic and impossible to achieve because of the very tenets of this view. For, the more one stresses the uniqueness and the subjectivity of self, the more one points at the individual's separateness and essential loneliness. Existential philosophers have struggled with these concepts, agreed with the condition but arrived at opposing solutions. For Jean-Paul Sartre, the human condition leads to anguish, abandonment, and despair and results in hopelessness and nihilism. For Martin Buber on the other hand, there is salvation for existential loneliness—love of self and others. Perhaps the experience of *some*

Daseinsangst, i.e. existential anxiety, such as loneliness, is an essential part of one's human-ness. Perhaps infantile fears of separation and loss of those on whom one depends are a part of this existential anxiety. An interesting study of the relative persistence of childhood fears was done by Jersild and Holmes (59). They found that although many childhood fears wane, some persist into adulthood. The most intense among them are the fears associated with loneliness and threat to the physical self.

It is interesting that few empirical studies have used humanistic psychology as a theoretical base for exploring death fears and anxieties in children. One likely reason is that this particular psychology focuses on healthy personality and positive emotional growth rather than on problems. Another probable reason is that psychological tradition in this country has been anchored in psychoanalytic or behavioristic theories. There are, however, numerous findings in the research literature on death anxiety that support the assumptions of humanistic psychology. Some of these are described on pages 33-34 of this chapter. Bluebond-Langner (60) has suggested that the self concept may relate importantly to children's management of death anxieties. This hypothesis was supported in results of a study by Wass and Scott (24) showing the reported self concepts of 11 and 12-year olds to be inversely related to their death anxieties, that is, the higher their self concepts, the lower their death anxieties.

The empirical and clinical studies related to separation anxiety, fear of abandonment, loss of love, cited in the previous section could also be cited here along with many others. These findings are undisputed. What differs are the theoretical explanations.

We have presented four theoretical perspectives for considering children's death fears and anxieties and cited numerous studies along the way. We have seen that death fears and anxieties can be differently explained and interpreted with respect to origin, causes, and development. We have identified several sources for death fear and anxiety in children, among them the child's understanding, the family, especially the parents or other caregivers, and the media. One major source for fear and anxiety that we have not presented here is the child's own personal experience with death. Without question, personal experience with death presents the most direct, immediate, and powerful threat to the child's self or life and thus the most frightening. Personal encounter with death and how the child and those around cope and how we can help toward more effective coping is the subject matter for the remaining chapters.

REFERENCES

1. Freud, S. Instincts and their vicissitudes. In E. Jones (ed), *The Collected Papers of Sigmund Freud.* Vol. IV. London: The Hogarth Press and the Institute of Psychoanalysis, 1953, pp. 60-83.
2. Freud, S. Anxiety and instinctual life. In J. Strachey (ed), *Basic Works of Sigmund Freud.* Franklin Center, Pennsylvania: The Franklin Library, 1978, pp. 567-592.
3. Freud, S. Thoughts for the times on war and death. In E. Jones (ed), *The Collected Papers of Sigmund Freud.* Vol. IV. London: The Hogarth Press and the Institute of Psychoanalysis, 1953, pp. 228-317.
4. Freud, S. The unconscious. In E. Jones (ed), *The Collected Papers of Sigmund Freud.* Vol. IV. London: The Hogarth Press and the Institute of Psychoanalysis, 1953, pp. 98-136.
5. Freud, S. The dissection of psychical personality. In J. Strachey (ed), *Basic Works of Sigmund Freud.* Franklin Center, Pennsylvania: The Franklin Library, 1978, pp. 545-565.

6. Freud, A. *The ego and the mechanisms of defense.* New York: International University Press, 1946.
7. Freud, S. *Inhibitions, Symptoms and Anxiety.* E. Jones (ed), London: The Hogarth Press, 1949.
8. Freud, S. *The Problem of Anxiety.* New York: Norton, 1936.
9. Bowlby, J. Separation anxiety. *The International Journal of Psychoanalysis, XLI,* 1960, pp. 89–113.
10. Anthony, S. *The discovery of death in childhood and after.* New York: Basic Books, 1972.
11. Hug-Hellmuth, V. H. The child's concept of death. *Psychoanalytic Quarterly, 34,* 1965, 499–516.
12. Maurer, A. Maturation of the conception of death. *Journal of Medical Psychology, 39,* 1966, 35–41.
13. Miller, J. B. M. Children's reactions to the death of a parent: A review of the psychoanalytic literature. *Journal of the American Psychoanalytical Association, 19,* 1971, 697–719.
14. Rochlin, G. The dread of abandonment: A contribution to the etiology of the loss complex and to depression, in *The Psychoanalytic Study of the Child.* New York: International University Press, Vol. XVI, 1961, 451–470.
15. Harnick, J. One component of the fear of death in early infancy. *International Journal of Psychoanalysis, 11,* 1930, 485–491.
16. Wahl, C. W. The fear of death. In H. Feifel (ed), *The Meaning of Death.* New York: McGraw-Hill, 1959, 16–29.
17. Zilboorg, G. The sense of immortality. *Psychoanalytic Quarterly, 7,* 1938, 171–199.
18. Caprio, F. S. A study of some of the psychological reactions during pre-pubescence to the idea of death. *Psychiatric Quarterly, 24,* 1950, 495–505.
19. *The Oxford Dictionary of Nursery Rhymes.* Oxford: Clarendon Press, 1955.
20. Alexander, I. E. & Adlerstein, A. M. Affective responses to the concept of death in a population of children and early adolescents. *Journal of Genetic Psychology, 93,* 1958, 167–177.
21. Piaget, J. *The child's conceptions of the world.* C. K. Ogden (ed), Totowa, New Jersey: Littlefield, Adams and Co., 1965.
22. Nagy, M. The child's theories concerning death. *Journal of Genetic Psychology, 73,* 1948, 3–27.
23. Schilder, P. & Wechsler, D. The attitudes of children toward death. *Journal of Genetic Psychology, 45,* 1934, 406–451.
24. Wass, H. & Scott, M. Middle school students' death concepts and concerns. *Middle School Journal, 9,* 1978, 10–12.
25. Kastenbaum, R. Time and death in adolescence. In H. Feifel (ed), *The Meaning of Death.* New York: McGraw-Hill, 1959, 99–113.
26. Gartley, W. & Bernasconi, M. The concept of death in children. *Journal of Genetic Psychology, 110,* 1967, 71–85.
27. Bandura, A. *Social learning theory.* Englewood Cliffs, New Jersey: Prentice-Hall, 1977.
28. Lester, D. Relation of fear of death in subjects to fear of death in their parents. *Psychological Record, 20,* 1970, 541–543.
29. Lester, D. & Templer, D. I. Resemblance of parent-child death anxiety as a function of age and sex of child. *Psychological Report, 31,* 1972, 750.
30. Lonetto, R. *Children's conceptions of death.* New York: Springer, 1980.
31. Glueck, S. & Glueck, E. *Unraveling juvenile delinquency.* Cambridge, Mass.: Harvard University Press, 1950.
32. Bandura, W. & Walter, R. H. *Social learning and personality development.* New York: Holt, Rinehart & Winston, 1963.
33. Martin. B. Parent-child relations. In F. D. Horowitz (ed), *Review of child development research.* Vol. 4. Chicago: University of Chicago Press, 1975.
34. Lyle, J. & Hoffman, H. R. Explorations in patterns of television viewing by pre-school age children. In R. Brown (ed), *Children and television.* Beverly Hills, Calif.: Sage, 1976, 45–61.
35. Murray, J. P., Nayman, O. B., & Atkin, C. K. Television and the child: A comprehensive research bibliography. *Journal of Broadcasting, 26,* 1972, 21–35.
36. Cowan, G. *See no evil.* New York: Simon & Schuster, 1979.
37. Gerbner, G. Violence in television drama: Trends and symbolic functions. In G. A. Comstock & E. A. Rubinstein (eds), *Television and social behavior.* Vol. 1. *Media Content and Control.* Washington, D.C.: Government Printing Office, 1972, 28–187.

38. Bandura, A., Ross, D., & Ross, S. A. Imitation of film-mediated aggressive models. *Journal of Abnormal and Social Psychology, 66*, 1963, 3-11.
39. Gerbner, G. & Gross, L. Living with television: The violence profile. *Journal of Communications, 26*, 1976, 173, 194.
40. Hicks, D. J. Imitation and retention of film-mediated aggressive peer and adult models. *Journal of Personality and Social Psychology, 2*, 1965, 97-100.
41. Lefkowitz, M. M., Eron, L. D., Walder, L. O., & Huesmann, L. R. Television violence and child aggression: A followup study. In G. A. Comstock and E. A. Rubinstein (eds), *Television and social behavior*. Vol. 3. *Television and adolescent aggressiveness*. Washington D.C.: Government Printing Office, 1972, 35-135.
42. Feshbach, S. & Singer, R. D. *Television and aggression: An experimental field study*. San Francisco: Jossey-Bass, 1971.
43. Bandura, A. Influence of models' reinforcement contingencies on the acquisition of imitative responses. *Journal of Personality and Social Psychology, 1*, 1965, 589-595.
44. Noble, G. The effects of different forms of filmed aggression on children's constructive and destructive play. *Journal of Personality and Social Psychology, 26*, 1973, 54-59.
45. McIntyre, J. J. & Teevan, J. J., Jr. Television violence and deviant behavior. In G. A. Comstock and E. A. Rubinstein (eds), *Television and social behavior*. Vol. 3. *Television and adolescent aggressiveness*. Washington, D.C.: Government Printing Office, 1972, 383-435.
46. Greenberg, B. S. & Dervin, G. *Use of mass media by the urban poor*. New York: Praeger, 1970.
47. Cline, V. B., Croft, R. G., & Courrier, S. Desensitization of children to television violence. *Journal of Personality and Social Psychology, 27*, 1973, 360-365.
48. Hartman, D. P. Influence of symbolically modelled instrumental aggression and pain cues on aggressive behavior. *Journal of Personality and Social Psychology, 11*, 1969, 280-288.
49. Bandura, A. & Mischel, M. Modification of self-imposed delay of reward through exposure to live and symbolic models. *Journal of Personality and Social Psychology, 2*, 1965, 698-705.
50. Bettelheim, B. *The uses of enchantment—the meaning and importance of fairy tales*. New York: Vintage Books, 1977.
51. Allport, G. W. *Pattern and growth in personality*. New York: Holt, Rinehart & Winston, 1961.
52. Rogers, C. R. *Client-centered therapy*. Boston: Houghton Mifflin, 1951.
53. Combs, A. W. & Snygg, D. *Individual behavior: A perceptual approach to behavior*. New York: Harper & Row, 1959.
54. Maslow, A. H. *Motivation and personality*. 2nd ed. New York: Harper & Row, 1970.
55. Montagu, A. *The humanization of man*. Cleveland, Ohio: World, 1962.
56. Combs, A. W., Richards, A. C., & Richards, F. *Perceptual Psychology: A humanistic approach to the study of persons*. New York: Harper & Row, 1976.
57. Rogers, C. R. A theory of therapy, personality and interpersonal relationships, as developed in the client-centered framework. In S. Koch (ed), *Psychology: A study of a science*. Vol. 3. New York: McGraw-Hill, 1959, 184-256.
58. Stillion, J. & Wass, H. Children and death. In H. Wass (ed), *Dying—Facing the Facts*. Washington: Hemisphere, 1979, 208-235.
59. Jersild, A. T. & Holmes, F. B. *Children's fears*. Child Development Monographs No. 20. New York: Teachers College, Columbia University, 1935.
60. Bluebond-Langner, M. Meanings of death to children. In H. Feifel (ed), *New Meanings of Death*. New York: McGraw-Hill, 1977, 47-66.

II

DYING

The dying of a child is one of life's most tragic events and one of the most difficult to deal with for the child and perhaps even more so for the adult. Many people still believe or desperately want to believe that terminally ill young children are not aware of the seriousness of their condition, do not grasp its meaning, and feel little or no anxiety about it. This belief, when held by professionals, is largely based on studies of the development of death concepts in *healthy* children. It has provided the rationale for not telling young children and even older children about their impending deaths. And when children remain silent about their own diagnosis and prognosis, their worries, fears, and terror, these behaviors are often used as further proof of ignorance on the part of the child and as support for shielding the child from the harsh reality of the situation. However, all this is erroneous. From careful observation and research we know that what may hold true for healthy young children is dramatically altered for children who encounter death as a personal threat or actuality in their lives. In fact, many clinical practicioners have commented on the unusual level of maturity "far beyond their years" often achieved by dying children. But what happens all too often is that for adults the dying of a child is most difficult to accept. Not only does it seem untimely and inappropriate, it frequently creates enormous amounts of guilt and anxiety in parents, health caregivers and others who are condemned to stand by helplessly watching a child die. But silence really protects no one. Adults and healthy people seeking to safeguard their sick loved ones or patients in a well-intentioned but misguided way feel little relief from such an evasive maneuver. If we adults want to help a dying child cope with this awesome reality, we must acknowledge the available evidence and stop playing the game of pretense. For all too often children, even young ones, are keenly aware of their parents' or caregivers' inability to cope with the impending death and so dying children, in an ironic role reversal, go along with the game of pretending that all is well in order to protect the very people whose support they need. In doing so a dying child may have nowhere to turn for help in dealing with the depression, despair, and anxieties that often overwhelm and that add an unnecessary burden to the tragedy of premature death.

Each human being is marked by his or her experiences, by the knowledge that he or she has acquired, and by his or her feelings. Each of us is sensitive to the moods of others, and each attempts to cope with events encountered in life. More often than not, these events are less fearful in actuality than are the demons conjured up by our anxieties. That is why we should listen carefully to the particular child, drawing out his or her concerns and sharing together a process of exploration and resolution. And that is why it is far better to link hands in a shared effort to cope with life-threatening illness and dying, than to withdraw and condemn each other to struggle alone without the support of those who love and care.

Eugenia Waechter was one of the first researchers to explore systematically what has since been called "the private worlds of dying children." In Chapter 3 that opens this section, Waechter reviews previous efforts by herself and others to study in depth the real concerns of dying children about bodily integrity and death, and adds a report of a more recent investigation to determine whether things have changed in the past ten years or so. Results show that fatally ill children do differ from their peers in many ways and Waechter is able to lay out in detail specific fears and concerns that are likely to be found in the pre-school child, in school-aged children, and in adolescents.

Next in Chapters 4 and 5 Marylou Behnke, and her colleagues in Florida, and David Adams, writing from Canada, explore appropriate roles for physicians and non-physicians in providing comprehensive care for children with life-threatening illness and for their families. If in no other kind of health care, it must be eminently clear that caring for children cannot merely be a physiological or biomedical process, and that seeing the ill child as a total entity demands attention to the family context as well. Both of these chapters are sensitive to the professional and human limitations of caregivers, but both also call upon caregivers to meet responsibilities to those whom they serve by preparing themselves in advance, addressing needs realistically, and responding in a thoughtful and imaginative way. These chapters are rich in experience and practical insight for those who work with or seek to assist dying children.

At the close of Chapter 5, Adams notes the value of the home environment as an alternative to institutionalization for those families who can and wish to care for a dying child in the last phases of illness. That possibility is developed in detail in Chapter 6 by Patricia Carlson and her colleagues. Under the leadership of Ida Martinson, the Home Care Project at the University of Minnesota School of Nursing has demonstrated the feasibility and value of this method of offering support to some children and families. Here the authors focus on the problems faced by such families and on home care as one promising way to mitigate difficulties within the family unit. Obviously this is not the only constructive approach, but it does show positive benefits from drawing upon latent strengths in family members themselves. The central principle is that professionals must give support through the family wherever possible, thereby enhancing rather than preempting parental, sibling, and other familial roles. Two parent coauthors, Kathy and Jay Montgomery, who have participated in this program through the death of their child testify to its effectiveness, numerous examples illustrate its application, and a series of structured interviews suggests implications for bereavement up to two years after death.

Chapters 7 and 8, the final two chapters in this part, discuss in detail problems faced by staff members and by siblings or other children who may be involved with a dying child. Caregivers who work with many seriously ill and dying children experience many sources of stress. Mary Vachon and Edward Pakes identify common sources of stress associated with typical pediatric illnesses or situations, show how stress is mediated by a variety of factors, and correlate its manifestations with a variety of preventive or coping techniques. Their work is the fullest treatment so far available of this important subject. No less significant, but certainly not as well recognized, are problems experienced by siblings and peers of a dying child. Noting the limited research on this subject, Frederick and Wendy Coleman set directions for clinical practice and future study by outlining a framework in systems' theory for understanding the issues involved and by identifying areas of concern for intervention. The resulting typography and illustrative vignettes demonstrate the sensitivity that is required of adults and the broad range of individuals encompassed by the phrase "other children." Once again, we see that preparation, thoughtfulness, and attention to detail can enable professionals and non-professionals alike to achieve an increasingly higher standard of support and care for all those who are touched by problems of dying in childhood.

3

Dying Children

Patterns of Coping

Eugenia H. Waechter

INTRODUCTION

Until ten years ago, no systematically controlled research had been done directly with children to determine their awareness of a life threatening condition. Former conclusions about the impact of illness on children were based on observations of them and their parents and on indirect evidence drawn from anecdotal data provided by hospital personnel. Although there was general agreement that adolescents were aware of the potential outcome of their illness, and were anxious and concerned about body integrity, it was assumed that children under the age of ten years were not aware of their diagnosis or prognosis and had little or no anxiety about their bodies or the future. This conclusion was based on previous research concerned with the development of the concept of death in normal, well children which indicated that a mature concept of death is not formed in children until after the age of nine years (1, 2). These findings were based on a Piagetian framework. The reasoning then followed that children do not have concerns about future body integrity until they have reached this age of understanding. Therefore, professionals working with children with life threatening illnesses assumed that the findings with healthy children also applied to their patients and reasoned that if adults did not discuss the seriousness of their illness with them, they would experience no anxiety. This concept was somewhat supported by the fact that young children rarely questioned their caretakers directly about death.

THE DYING CHILD'S AWARENESS OF DEATH

Early Assumptions

Based on these studies and the derived reasoning, a widespread closed clinical approach was advocated by physicians during the 1950s and 60s to the effect that disruptions of this natural order for readiness to deal with feelings of death would be harmful to the child (3, 4). Physicians widely counseled parents to maintain a sense of normality in the family and shield children from the realization of the seriousness of their illness, and assumed a cheerful manner that things would soon be well (5, 6).

Other clinicians, however, contested the practice of shielding children from knowledge of their illness giving rise to a "to tell or not to tell" controversy. It

Eugenia Waechter died tragically on Jan. 12, 1982, in a fire at her home.

was their contention that maintaining silence was an unrealistic burden for parents which would result in greater problems for the child, since he would be able to sense this withdrawal by parents and lose trust in them.

Vernick and Karon (7) were among the first to challenge the protective approach in their observational study of older school-aged children in a leukemia ward. They suggested that all their patients were afraid and anxious despite lack of specific knowledge. They further suggested that children sense adults' discomfort with the topic of death and learn not to ask disturbing questions. This lack of trust in the veracity of caregivers in their view led to further anxiety, withdrawal and need for greater emotional support. They were convinced that, "Every child who is lying in bed gravely ill is worrying about dying and is eager to have someone help him talk about it. If he is passive it may only be a reflection of how freely the environment encourages him to express his concerns" (p. 395).

From his clinical experience, Solnit (8) also disagreed with the closed approach and observed that his young patients invariably sensed what was happening, even when deliberate attempts were made to shield them from this tragic and frightening situation. He suggested that adults are blinded to the fears of dying children because of their own anxiety.

As a result of clinical interactions with young leukemia children and their parents, Binger et al. (9) agreed with the contentions of Vernick and Karon, and reported that, "Most children above 4 years of age, although not told directly of their diagnosis, presented evidence to their parents that they were well aware of the seriousness of their disease and even anticipated their premature death" (p. 415). They suggested that these young patients attempted to communicate their concerns through behavior and symbolic questions.

First Systematic and Controlled Studies

The first direct, systematic and controlled study of children with life threatening illness was conducted by Waechter (10). In order to elicit expression of the child's concerns about present and future body integrity, Waechter studied 64 children between the ages of 6 and 10 years inclusive through the use of a projective test and anxiety scale. These children were divided into four groups: 1) children with chronic disease for which death was predicted, 2) children with chronic disease with a good prognosis, 3) children with brief illness, and 4) non-hospitalized, well children. Children between groups were matched as to sex, age, race, social class and family background. Children within the fatal group fell into four categories by diagnosis: 1) leukemia, 2) other neo-plastic disease, 3) cystic fibrosis, and 4) progressive septic granulomatosis.

The study was carried out while the first three groups were hospitalized for treatment or diagnosis. The children within the fatal group were matched with subjects within the other three groups for sex, age, race, and social class.

A set of eight pictures was shown individually to each child and stories requested in order to elicit fantasy expression of the child's concern regarding present and future body integrity and functioning. Four of the pictures were selected from the Thematic Apperception Test and four were specifically designed for the study depicting hospital situations involving children and caretakers.

The stories were scored with attention to content related to threat or fear of death, body mutilation or loneliness, to the methods used in the story to cope with threat and to the problems anticipated in the reduction of insecurity. The measurement of fear was based on the same general rationale utilized in the scoring of other motives under the view that fear of bodily harm is a motive.

The General Anxiety Scale for Children as designed by Sarason and associates (11) was administered to each hospitalized child in the study. Previously determined normalized scores for well children were used for comparison with the scores received by the hospitalized groups.

A tape recorded, semi-structured interview was held with the parents of each hospitalized child in the study. The purpose of the interview was to elicit information regarding the following variables deemed significant to the amount of death anxiety expressed by the child: 1) the amount of verbal interaction with the ill child as to his diagnosis and prognosis, 2) the child's previous experience with illness and death, 3) the religious training which the child had received, and 4) the warmth of the mother-child relationship.

Analysis of the data from the General Anxiety Scale for Children indicated that the mean score for fatally ill subjects was almost double that of the two comparison groups of hospitalized children and three times the score of healthy children as presented by Sarason. This finding supported the prediction that children aged 6 to 10 years with a diagnosis for which death was predicted expressed significantly more $(p > 0.01)$ generalized anxiety than did children who did not have a poor prognosis.

Analysis of the children's stories also supported the prediction that the dying children would express significantly more anxiety specifically related to death, multilation and loneliness than other ill children. A χ square test of significance between proportions of the groups telling unrelated stories was found to be greater than 0.01. These findings indicated that the subjects were more preoccupied with threats to body integrity even though only 2 children within the fatal group had been told of their diagnosis.

The test of significance of differences of proportions of subjects using fear-related imagery in their scoreable stories indicated that the children with fatal illnesses used both loneliness and death imagery more frequently than all comparison groups at a significance level of 0.001. It seemed possible therefore that the concern with loneliness was also related to the concern about death.

Judgments were made on the basis of the maternal interview regarding the opportunities the child had had to discuss the nature of his illness with parents or professional personnel. Most parents felt very strongly about this question. A few felt that their child should know as much as possible about his illness, whereas most went to great lengths to insure that the diagnosis would not be mentioned to their child by hospital personnel. Many parents felt unable to cope with the feelings which a frank discussion about the possibility of imminent death would arouse. As previously indicated, only 2 children with fatal illness had discussed their imminent death with their parents, six had received little realistic information regarding their illness, and the remainder had been informed that their illness was temporary or trivial.

The dichotomy in the degree of awareness on the part of the child as inferred from his imagination stories and the parents' belief as to the child's awareness was often striking. Although only the two subjects had discussed their concerns about death with their parents, the percentage of death imagery in stories containing threat was found to be 63 percent. Many of the children who had not been told their diagnosis nevertheless indicated awareness of knowledge of the diagnosis or symptoms in their imaginative stories. In all of the protocols, the degree to which the characters in the story were given the subject's personal diagnosis and symptoms was striking.

The correlation between the child's opportunity to discuss his illness, and the anxiety score on the projection test was found to be $r = 0.633$ which was significant at the 0.01 level. This finding indicates that those children with fatal illness who had had a greater opportunity to discuss their fears and concerns about their future and present body integrity expressed *less* specific death anxiety. This finding supported the hypothesis that understanding acceptance or permission to discuss any aspect of his illness may decrease feelings of isolation, alienation and the sense that the illness is too terrible to discuss.

The findings of this study indicated that despite efforts to protect children from knowledge of their prognosis, they had considerable preoccupation with death in fantasy when given the opportunity, along with feelings of loneliness and isolation and a sense of lack of control of the forces impinging on them. It was suggested that the child perceives the threat through the altered affect in his total environment and from parental anxiety communicated in non-verbal ways. The data also suggested that adults may be blinded to the child's anxiety because of personal fears and concerns and a sense of helplessness related to the diagnosis. Further, even though the child may not have achieved a mature concept of death, the threat to body integrity was nonetheless communicated.

A study by Spinnetta et al. (12) was conducted to test Waechter's conclusion about the higher level of anxiety in fatally ill, hospitalized children. This study also utilized a control group of non-fatally but chronically ill children—the two groups being matched for frequency and intensity of hospital experiences. In the study, 25 children aged 6 to 10 with a diagnosis of leukemia were matched in age, sex, race, grade in school, seriousness of the condition, and amount of medical interaction with 25 children with such chronic illnesses as diabetes, asthma, congenital heart disease and renal problems.

The children were asked to tell stories about each of the four pictures designed by Waechter, and about each of four figurines (nurse, doctor, mother, father) placed in a three-dimensional replica of a hospital room. Each child was also given a brief anxiety questionnaire sorting out hospital anxiety from home anxiety.

This study supported the Waechter findings in that the leukemia children related significantly more stories that indicated preoccupation with threat to, and intrusion into their bodies, both in the stories relating to the pictures and the stories told about the placed figurines. The children with fatal illness also expressed more hospital-related and non-hospital related anxiety than did the chronically ill children.

Although the parents of these children maintained that the children did not know their illness was fatal, as was the case in Waechter's study, there was a significant difference in the level of anxiety that was present from the very first admission to the hospital. Spinetta also concluded that despite efforts to keep the child with fatal illness from becoming aware of his prognosis, he somehow feels a sense that his illness is not ordinary, but very threatening.

In a later study (13), Spinetta investigated the question, "Does awareness of the seriousness of their illness persist with the fatally ill children when they are not in the hospital?" Using the same instruments as in the previous study, he tested 32 children between the ages of 6 and 10 years attending outpatient clinics for treatment of leukemia and other non-fatal chronic illnesses. Again, he found a significantly greater pre-occupation with loneliness and with threat to body integrity and functioning than did the control group of chronically ill children. He also found that the younger chronically ill children had a level of anxiety relative to the outpatient clinic that diminished with age, whereas the leukemia childrens' anxiety relative to those attending the outpatient clinic increased with age at a significant level.

Newer Treatment Developments

Since the early Waechter study however, the definitions and prognoses of fatal illness have altered considerably. The diagnosis of cancer no longer automatically means impending death. Because of major successes in medicine in treating some kinds of childhood cancer, more and more children with this disease have the chance to become adults. At least half of the 6000 children expected to develop cancer in the United States next year are likely to survive many years, thanks to improved radiation and chemical therapy.

These illnesses which were once acutely fatal, have now become chronic life threatening conditions. However, despite the positive success of increased life spaces, new problems have emerged in relation to the quality of life which concern parents and professionals engaged with them and their children. Parents face much ambiguity and uncertainty related to making treatment decisions, integrating the ill child into the mainstream of the community, and the child's education. Maintaining constructive peer relationships has become increasingly important as has the long term effects of treatment on the child's physical and psychosocial development. Parents are encouraged to devote their energies toward the issues of life and to hope for prolonged remission or cure. On the other hand, they must be told that death is also a possibility and that which of the two alternatives will occur may not be known for a number of years. These parents and children now sit under a modern sword of Damocles, which is, understandably, a powerful source of stress.

Despite the greater openness in our society related to death, the social stigma of cancer does not seem to have altered substantially in the past ten years. Cancer is still seen as a mysterious, often fatal disease. Parents often complain of the treatment they receive from former associates and their children are often shunned by former playmates. Such responses are still sometimes due to a fear of contagion. More frequently, they are due to a continuing unease with "what to say" and the child's uncertain future. Confrontations with life threatening illness also often evoke personal fears of mortality.

Current Studies

In a current study, Waechter and her associates interviewed the parents of 56 children between the ages of 4 and 10 years who were under outpatient treatment. All but a few of these parents responded that they felt they should be open with their children. All reported discussing aspects of treatment with their children, although some parents, particularly those with very young children were more guarded in discussing the prognosis. However, if the child asked questions about death, no parent stated that they avoided or refused to discuss them. Most of these children were under medical care which espouses the open approach and many were included in the conferences physicians held with their parents.

Almost all parents stated that their children over five years of age also learned much about their illness from other children and from professionals on the wards and outpatient clinics. The amount learned and the quickness of learning appeared to be related to age, the acuteness of the illness, and the degree of openness espoused by the particular medical setting. Older children with an illness having a faster course treated in an open setting were able to answer the most questions in greater detail about tests, symptoms and diagnosis. Most of this knowledge stemmed from the induction phase of the illness. These children, however, did not necessarily also speak freely about their prognosis. Some children talked openly about their possible deaths, whereas others stated that they would rather not know too much about the future since it would cause them to worry more. Almost all children over six years of age stated that their mothers worried about them, whereas only a few felt that they could or should share all their worries freely with their parents.

Some children as young as four years of age indicated awareness of the seriousness of their illness. Although children of this age may not ask as many questions of their parents regarding causality, diagnosis and prognosis, many give behavioral clues of fears and concerns. Most mothers of four- and five-year-old children described changes in their child's behavior after the diagnosis was made even though the child was physically doing well. One mother of a four-year-old who felt unable to talk with the medical team or to her child reported, "He seems so scared to ask questions. He's so terrified. He's got this funny laugh now. He says, 'Mommy, don't look so sad.' " Another mother of a five-year-old girl described her daughter's unruliness and their initial tolerance of her behavior after a diagnosis of leukemia had been made: "I think she really thought to herself, 'I must be pretty sick if I can get away with this kind of behavior.' You have an urge to do everything possible you can right now and the hell with anyone else, but as soon as you see the changes aren't good—bah, she was horrible."

In an effort to discover whether the greater hope given to parents at the time their child was diagnosed as having a life threatening illness would reduce the child's preoccupation with body integrity, the children in Waechter's current study were asked to tell stories in response to eight pictures. Four of these pictures were drawn from the Thematic Apperception Test and four were designed for the study.

In addition to eliciting attitudes and concerns about treatment procedures, the stories also contained much imagery relating to loneliness, mutilation and death. Those children with life threatening illnesses told stories containing such imagery significantly more ($p = 0.001$) than did the matched children with other chronic illnesses. Thus it appears that despite the greater hope offered to parents, and the greater communication they report that they have with their children, the children were still greatly concerned about the integrity of their bodies in the present and for the future.

CONCERNS AND COPING PATTERNS OF CHILDREN WITH LIFE THREATENING ILLNESS

Concerns communicated by children, either verbally or through their behavior are related to their cognitive perceptions of events as well as to the relationship between illness and treatment effects and the developmental tasks of the period. Concerns may also be related to the specific diagnosis and its implications and the severity of the illness. Coping patterns are also related to the child's developmental capacities as well as to innate individual differences and prior experiences.

The Preschool Child

Causality of Illness

Although young children rarely ask why they have become ill, they often have their own convictions. Because of immature concepts of causality, they often assume responsibility for their illness and may feel guilt in addition to their many other fears and concerns. This was supported in the author's current study as children under six years of age tended to assign the cause of illness to some aspect of their own behavior, either of commission or omission related to obeying parental mandates.

Young children are convinced that nothing happens by chance, and that retribution follows as swiftly for "bad behavior" as it does for breaking a physical law of nature. They are also convinced that if they have been punished, it was justified by their bad behavior or thoughts. It is a small step from the concept, "I have been bad" to "I am bad." Certainly nothing can seem more punishing than abandonment and rejection by parents in the frightening, new world of the hospital and some of the procedures with which they are confronted. This is illustrated in a story told by a four-year-old: "That's a little boy just sitting there. Somebody killed a bird. He's thinking about the dead bird. The bird got killed because the bird was bad. The boy is a bad boy too—so something is going to happen to him."

Where these internal convictions are unvoiced, they may be inadvertently reinforced by adults. In attempts to protect the child from knowledge of the possible future and the purpose of painful treatment which seemingly continues indefinitely, adults convey to the child a quality of punishment which strengthens the belief in his or her own unworthiness.

When hospitalized, therefore, young children tend to blame themselves for this rejection and may respond with guilt, sadness and withdrawal. In rejection of their own angry thoughts, they see professional personnel as also hostile to them. Young children also believe that others can read their thoughts as they themselves can, and therefore expect retaliation in further punishment. This also extends to their parents in that they are angry at them for their desertion despite their need for them.

Because of their feelings of guilt and self-blame for the punishment "I deserve," some young children will keep their feelings inside themselves and become even more withdrawn from others. It is also frightening to be angry at people on whom they depend and cannot do without. Other children may direct the anger they feel toward their parents, to other children or adults in their hospital environment. This may earn them avoidance or disciplinary measures which confirm their wickedness.

Preschool children who are hospitalized need their parents to cope with these emotions. They must have reassurance from their parents that they have not been abandoned or rejected. Parents must also emphasize that they are not angry with the child and miss him when they cannot be with him. The child needs confirmation of his parents' love in order to regain a sense of worth.

The young child cannot cope constructively without the physical and emotional support of his parents. He is cognitively unable to understand the cause and effect relationship between his illness and treatment procedures. Nor is he able to comprehend all of the alterations in his former patterns of living and the pain he is forced to endure. Only with the support and presence of his parents will he be able to openly express his anger and resentment. It is the secure child, and self-confident child, who can express such feelings. Children who are uncertain of parental love are unable or afraid of verbalizing such feelings because of the threat of further loss of love.

Anger must be accepted and understood and the child should be reassured that such feelings are not indications of his wickedness. At the same time, the child cannot be allowed to abuse either his parents or professional staff. He will require help in channeling his resentment productively by pounding a peg board or other aggressive play which does not endanger others.

Concerns about the Body

Threat to body image may also cause distress to young children at a time when they are beginning to form a concept of self. Whereas healthy children are now becoming comfortable with the functioning of their bodies, the bodies of ill children are under constant assault. The flaws in their own body are also constantly in their attention and they may also need to deal with the side effects of treatment.

Even very young children may be quite concerned about obesity resulting from steroid therapy and loss of hair resulting from chemotherapy. Because of the egocentricity and lack of empathy of children at this age period, their playmates and other children may respond to them in a negative manner which is painful. In an interview the mother of a four-year-old boy commented, "Kids can be cruel sometimes. Like Gene for quite a while was awfully bloated. His stomach was bloated way out and his cheeks were puffed out. He looked like he had perpetual mumps. We took him to the zoo one day and he started to play on a certain toy and there was a little girl there and she said, 'No, go away you fat little boy. You can't play here.' And Gene was really hurt. He started to cry and run to Mommy. It was hard for him."

Loss of hair may be taken in stride by some four year olds, although other children in the later preschool years may be very concerned. Others may not verbalize their feelings, but withdraw from former contacts. It is also possible, that although concerns about body image may not be overtly expressed at ages three to four, such concern may surface at a later date. A mother of a $5\frac{1}{2}$-year-old girl reported, "Lately things have been coming up, although she isn't bald now. She'll say, 'Don't stare at me.' She wasn't concerned about being bald a year and a half ago—it's funny—like she'll be in a grocery store and there will be some girls over in the corner laughing and she'll come back to me and say, 'It's 'cause I don't have any hair.' When she did get obese and lose her hair, she was four, she wasn't too concerned about it. But now she sees pictures of herself as she was then and I know she felt a lot of people staring at her. I asked her, 'Well, if you saw somebody bald, wouldn't you look at them?' And she said, 'No, that would make them sad.' I felt, 'Wow, she must have felt bad, although I didn't know it at that time.' " Such children may be forced by such circumstances to move beyond egocentrism at a relatively early age.

Whereas some children cope with hair loss matter-of-factly, by showing their head when they are questioned, parents of other children must prepare their children, to anticipate such confrontations. Providing them with a reply often restores their confidence in meeting playmates.

Concern about Treatment Procedures

Most very young children do not appreciate the therapeutic intent of professional personnel and view procedures as hostile and punishing. Because of their own feelings of anger, they also attribute such feelings to those caring for them. With their viewpoint of adults as all powerful, much of what is done to them may appear as merely the whim of the administrator of the treatment. In the current research, previously cited, young children gave significantly fewer stories where the administrator of the treatment felt positively toward the child, and more where the child in the story saw the treatment as an attack. Further, young children told significantly more stories where the child did not know the goal of treatment, and where the child had no choices in the matter.

Young children, because of lack of knowledge as to the purpose of treatment, may fantasize the specifics of a personal attack. One four-year-old boy told the following story after seeing a picture of an intravenous infusion. "This boy has a blood problem. It's a very bad thing and he's not feeling good. The doctor put the tube in. To drain out his blood. He took a whole lot of blood. The boy dies. He gets buried. He feels unhappy because he did not want to die. He is mad at the doctor. He dunno why the doctor did that to him—'cause he wants his blood to test." In this illustration, the child's immature conception of death is also apparent—the child dies but does not cease to exist.

Young children also have vague ideas of internal body functioning, and do not realize things adults often take for granted, such as that their bodies are capable of generating more blood. Repeated withdrawal of blood may imply to them that there will soon be none left. Urgent requests for a bandaid may have the dual purpose of "keeping the blood where it belongs" and of restoring a sense of body wholeness.

Diagnostic and therapeutic procedures may become the battle ground for the child's expression of his feelings of helplessness regarding the entire series of events since a diagnosis of life-threatening illness was made. One mother of a four-year-old boy who fought everyone like a tiger when a procedure was done explained, "I think, personally, that there's so much that he's not had a say about that he uses this time to bring it all out. I think it gets bottled up inside him and he just takes it out on everybody that way and gets rid of it. I think that is it, because he's so young and he didn't have much to say. So this is the way he gets back at everybody—he's fighting the whole thing right there." A child who has developed such a pattern of coping could be described as a "defier, non-complier."

Other children, realizing the inevitability of the procedures, despite their protest, may become passive conformers, though this may increase their sense of helplessness and hopelessness. Their feelings may also surface in indirect ways. One mother of a five-year-old girl who described her daughter as "just lying down and taking bone marrows—very relaxed and calm," later also related "There is a lot under the surface with her—a lot. The other day she had a bad dream about mosquitoes and Dr. Grout sometimes teases her and says, 'I'm going to give you a mosquito bite' when he's giving her a shot. Well, she had this dream about hundreds of mosquitoes. I know there is a connection there somewhere . . . they were just all around her trying to bite her. Imagine how terrifying!"

Other children may make a "differentiated protest." Though seemingly defiant at the beginning of the treatment, they realize (consciously or unconsciously) that they are dependent on the administration for assistance and survival, and place boundaries around their behavior. Though they may scream, "I hate you" to their physician while he is engaged in the procedure, they may make attempts at amends when the procedure is completed. One mother described her four-year-old's behavior: "But afterwards, they are friends and he still wanted Dr. Kuay to carry him back to his room and tuck him in and give him his teddy bear and sit and talk to him for a couple minutes. Even though he knows Dr. Kuay has to hurt him once in a while."

Parental expectations, of course, greatly influence a child's response to painful procedures. Such expectations are conveyed to children consistently after initial procedures are done on diagnosis. Some parents are more tolerant of their child's protest, seeing it as natural and expected in terms of the child's age. For example, the mother of the four-year-old who fought like a tiger commented, "Oh, I think its all right to get mad. I don't want him to hurt anybody, but I think this is good for him."

Other parents convey expectations for more conforming behavior. Not only does their child's behavior reflect on them as parents; but they *must* trust the medical team, and particularly, the physician to ease some of their anxiety about their child's survival. Behavior which might be seen as alienating the administrator can be threatening to parents.

Some children, as young as four years of age, cope with the procedures, their feelings of helplessness and their parents' expectations through developing a pattern of "conforming-controlling." This adaptive pattern is enhanced when professional personnel allow children whatever measures of control are possible in the situation; and when parents are perceptive in timing their preparation of the child for what is to come.

Many parents describe how even very young children prepare themselves through rehearsals, through talking and asking questions and through gathering knowledge of "what is going to happen next." One father of a four-year-old girl related, "She wants to know what days she has to come in for treatment and what days she has off. She sort of prepares herself." A mother of a five-year-old boy described even greater initiative in this process of information gathering. He stated to his parents, "We've got to have a talk and you tell me exactly what they are going to do and what's going to hurt and what to expect."

Many parents have also found, however, that because of the young child's immature concept of time, they have needed to pace the timing of informing their child about coming procedures in order to eliminate extensive periods of worry. Shorter periods of time allow the child to mobilize resources without great elaboration of fears with fantasy.

The manner in which the first extensive diagnostic procedures were done at the child's first hospitalization often sets the stage for what is to follow—for better or worse. If the first experiences were excessively traumatic and restricting, each new procedure may reactivate feelings of terror and helplessness. One mother related that her five-year-old daughter "was stuck four times before they could get any blood—they wrapped her in a sheet so she couldn't move. This whole kind of control thing was crammed down her throat before she met Dr. Knox. She was terrible with procedures after that. It was a totally different thing with Dr. Knox and he gave her a lot of room and she was working with him and it *worked*!" Another mother of a five-year-old stated, "Well, the first time they gave her a spinal, they tried to put her under, and that was a disaster. She was half-conscious, really terrified—but anytime she feels sort of in control . . ." Other mothers have confirmed that when time is taken with the child during the period of diagnosis and first hospitalization to explain the procedures with patience, truth, and empathy at the child's level of understanding, the child is able to develop trust and a greater sense of adequacy.

The need to trust and the need to control are frequently mentioned variables in the child's response, and increasingly so as the child matures. In parents' words, "Knowing they have something *involved* in it—they don't feel so helpless." Control over sites of injection, timing, assisting in the procedures whenever possible and permission to express feelings often help enable the very young child to master excessive anxiety and to lessen convictions that the procedures are punitive. Further, the enhancement of the child's self-esteem may assist in coping with other painful experiences in the future.

Following procedures many young children can use some of the equipment in play in order to express their anger and frustrations and to master the feelings of helplessness through personal contact. One mother of a five-year-old related, "He loves to play doctor at home, and they'd let him take the disposable syringe home and practice on his teddy bear. Well, sometimes Pooh isn't good enough and he has to try it on Mommy, because Pooh didn't say 'ouch.' He'd shove that thing at me—boy he'd really let out his frustrations."

Fears of Dying

Although as previously mentioned, many young children do not overtly speak of their own possible death, they may nevertheless have fears and concerns. Although preschool children have an immature concept of death as incomplete and reversible, by the age of four years they nevertheless are aware that other living creatures have become nonexistent. With their frightening convictions related to guilt for past misdeeds, some children may fear that even greater retribution is to follow; that they may not go to Heaven, or that they may be left alone to face the ultimate.

Though preschool children may avoid speaking of death and seem outwardly unworried, they may show their concern in their behavior. Many parents report that their children, though not asking about death, may have nightmares or other behavioral changes, such as greater play aggressiveness, or concern about the death of others. One mother of a four-year-old stated, "I believe that she thinks a lot more than we know." Another mother of a five-year-old boy reported, "He's so terrified. He's never asked me, but he's got this funny laugh now."

Many other young children may not allow themselves to think of non-existence and not ask questions, suppressing their feelings. For them this is necessary until death is very near. Regression to more infantile behavior then allows them to become very dependent on their parents. At that time, they need the reassurance that they will be cared for and not left alone to face the unknown without support.

The School-Aged Child

The school-aged child has many more resources with which to cope with threat. He can communicate his thoughts and feelings verbally to a much greater degree.

Although still operating very much in the here and now, he has grown cognitively and can solve problems by thinking as well as by action. He has learned about rules, and is much better able to see cause and effect relationships. He has increasing self-control and is learning cooperation in achieving a goal. Although still in need of parental support, the attitudes of his peers are of great importance and influence his behavior.

Awareness of self has become much more stable as has self assertion. Although still dealing with a sense of inadequacy, problems can be seen as a challenge which he can master with support from peers or adults. This sense of mastery increases self-esteem. On the other hand, he is vulnerable when the problem seems overwhelming, such as disease of his body, which threatens defeat.

With a sense of time as flowing from past to future, he can also imagine an unpleasant future. He is learning about death, and some healthy children become preoccupied with the meaning of this concept. Many have been taught about a hereafter, but this may not be comforting to the child who must look forward to possibly going to Heaven alone and without parental support.

Communication of Concerns about the Future

Most parents now are advised to discuss their child's questions with him as they arise; particularly at the larger medical centers. Parents reported that almost all of the children between the ages of 6 and 10 in the current study cited earlier asked questions about their future at some time. This generally occurred at the time of diagnosis or relapse and much less often during periods of remission, when the topic was most generally avoided. Some communicated their thoughts and concerns openly, some indirectly, and a few reportedly did not question their prognosis. The amount of direct communication which occurred was related to the openness of the parents to such dialogue and to the relationships within the family. One eight-year-old boy repeatedly asked his parents to tell him if and when he was going to die so that he could prepare himself. At one time he commented to his mother, "Mom, I wouldn't mind dying and going to Heaven, but I'd like to come back." At another time during a conversation with his father who had sensed his concern following a clinic visit, he commented, "I don't want to worry you, Dad. You know Dad, I won't mind dying, but I know you and Mom will miss me so much."

Other children may not be so direct in discussing their thoughts, but seek information indirectly with questions such as Dean voiced after several years of treatment for leukemia, "Am I ever going to get well?" Others speak of death jestingly to test the healer's reaction. When joshed about his talkativeness by his physician, Mark quipped, "Well, you know doctor, there's just so much you have to say in this world before you die."

With increased cognitive capacities, many children question why they were singled out for this calamity. Although some may still express self-blame and guilt for the illness, many others now are able to see external circumstances as the causation factor when the matter is explained honestly. Nevertheless, the specter of punishment still hovers near. Eight-year-old David who had had a bone marrow one day followed by a spinal tap the next day cried, "Mommie, why is God punishing me?" Later he questioned, "Mommy, why did God give this to me? You said God does everything." His mother answered, ". . . maybe, because He knew you were a big and a strong boy and could take it." At this, David cried and replied,

"But Mommy, I'm not a big boy. I'm just a baby." This comment also illustrates a sense of vulnerability and the fear that his abilities might be unequal to the coping tasks ahead. In talking with their children, some parents have been able to elicit concerns about death in order to help their children. The mother of a seven-year-old girl stated that she was talking with her daughter, Gina, one day when her daughter said, weeping, "Momma, if I die and go to Heaven, when you come to Heaven you'll be old and I won't recognize you." The mother replied, "Honey, I'll call your name." And Gina smiled and said no more.

Spinetta and Maloney (13) studied communication patterns in school-aged children with cancer, and its relationship to successful coping. They defined coping as successful attempts on the part of the child to master troublesome situations relative to the illness, a nondefensive personal posture, closeness to parental figures, happiness with oneself and the freedom to express negative feelings within the family. It was an assumption that communication of the child's thoughts and concerns, both happy and painful, was healthier than silence. They hypothesized that the child with more open communication would score as less defensive, express closeness to family members, express happiness with the self, and be more free to express negative feelings. Parents were scored on a 4-point scale as to how much communication occurred within the family. All of the items characterizing successful coping correlated significantly with amount of communication except for freedom to express negative feelings and there was a strong trend in that direction.

Spinetta and Maloney concluded as did Waechter (10) that the choice for silence can lead to denial, and lead to a feeling of rejection and isolation in the child. In contrast, open communication can at the child's own request lead to mutual support among family members. However, Spinetta and Maloney caution that a forced openness too soon for some families can be destructive in that the additional stress may cause maladaptive behavior.

Education and Social Relationships

With the increasing survival rate in the past ten years, the focus of parental concerns regarding the time the child missed from school has changed from providing normality in the child's life to the child's need for education itself in an uncertain future. The importance of school is also stressed as school is the main arena for the child's social relationships.

The need for long term medical supervision in inpatient and outpatient settings results in the loss of four to six weeks of school time within a year for many children. Academic difficulties imposed by this loss of time may be compounded by the child's reluctance to attend school because of negative changes in appearance imposed by treatment and at times, by the fear of separation both on the part of child and parents.

Although there may be teasing and negative response to the ill child by peers, this is not as evident in school-aged children who have the ability for empathy and who are assisted in understanding the reasons for physical changes. However, the changed behavior of the child after diagnosis may induce problems in former peer groups. Deasy (14) found significantly different behavior in children with cancer as opposed to their healthy classmates. These children had difficulty in concentrating, in initiating activities, in attempting new things and in participating in ongoing activities. They were also more lacking in energy, more self-conscious, and worried more. More of these problems were seen in children receiving treatment and in relapse.

Teachers require help and support in dealing with the ill child in the classroom. This experience is generally a new one for the teacher who may not know how to deal with the situation or how to respond. Information about the illness and the particular child's activity patterns is necessary in order to smooth the child's transition back into the classroom. Without information, the teacher may create dual standards for the child as opposed to his peers, thus enhancing the child's sense of inadequacy.

Problems of reintegration after a prolonged absence may be particularly difficult. Many parents are now counselled about the positive value of school in the child's overall adjustment to the illness. Yet their need to protect the child, both physically and psychologically may be in conflict with this goal. In schools where psychological consultation is available, children have less difficulty. In these instances, reintegration of the child can be facilitated by involvement of the school, the parents and the child in preparation of his return.

Body Image

The increased emphasis placed on the child's involvement with peers and school often compounds the child's concern about his appearance. More vigorous, aggressive therapy now utilized also often produces side effects of a more drastic nature than was seen formerly. Loss of hair, jaundice, stunted growth, obesity or amputation are sources of great distress for the child.

The isolation of children with cancer is a major concern of parents and helping professionals. In the author's current study, four out of five children were isolated to some extent and some were severely withdrawn to the point where they had little contact with peers and others in the community. What this can mean for emotional and social development is obvious.

Children however can and do learn to cope with social concerns in a variety of ways. Learning to live with baldness can be most difficult, particularly with girls, yet many children do find ways to deal with their classmates' curiosity. Heffron and associates (15) report that one boy who had been given a wig discovered a technique for preventing the teasing of classmates. He would take off his wig and play catch with it! In the author's study, a grandmother described her seven-year-old grandson's response to his loss of hair and how she helped him cope. "Monday, his hair started coming out. The next day there was more and by Wednesday morning, he was completely bald, and believe me, that was trauma! That really was! So we decided a little wig would help a lot, you know. Of course, after we explained to him that it would grow back and when he saw that it didn't show too much under the cap, it wasn't too bad. But then he didn't want us to see him when I put him to bed. He didn't want Grandpa to see him. So I said, 'You know, Mark, that Grandpa will not love you any less without your hair.' And then I explained to him, 'You know, Mark, if you will not take off your cap and show the kids, they're going to call you Baldy. You just take off that cap right away and show it to him and then you tell him that it was because of your radiation and your illness and so on and he'll never ask you again.'

"Well, the funny thing was, he's got these two little boys next door that he plays with and he just loves them. One is about two years older and the other is about two years younger. So he was playing with them and had his little cap. So when he came in to eat his dinner, he said, 'Grandma, I showed Mike and Jeff my head.' I said, 'What did they say?' He said, 'They didn't say anything. They wanted to know how come I was bald and I told them it was because I had leukemia.' "

Some children may use their illness to become manipulative with peers and teachers, as well as with parents and siblings. Parents always have concerns about disciplining their children with life threatening illness. Previously, when life expectancy was relatively brief, parents could rationalize indulging their ill children with the argument that they wished their child to be as happy as possible in the short time available. Even then, however, they encountered problems with their other children who tended to get caught in the cycle of jealousy and guilt, which was exacerbated when relatives bestowed special presents and favors on the ill child.

Currently, when life expectancy is much more ambiguous, parents are regularly counselled at the onset of the illness to maintain normalcy for the child in order to support the child's positive view of the future, to prevent sibling problems, and to avoid creating a "social tyrant" who will have trouble in relating to others in the future.

This is a difficult area for parents, since the young cancer patient tends to be manipulative with parents because of hospital experiences and may be difficult to discipline. This difficulty is increased because of the parents' sense of guilt for the illness. Most parents are able to deal with this period of self blame. Others, however, unable to resolve their guilt and engrossed with anticipatory grief, may abdicate this parental responsibility. Severe family problems are usually inevitable. In a recent retrospective study, Gagan and others (16) reported that five or more years after diagnosis of cancer in a child who is still alive, problems with siblings included intensified rivalry, inappropriate feelings of guilt and a sense of exclusion from a significant family crisis.

In the author's current study, all but two parents reported problems with disciplining their ill child. Of those children who had siblings, all parents except one reported sibling problems ranging from mild to severe. These problems ranged from somatic complaints to difficulties with school, peers, family and other relationships. Obviously these deteriorating sibling relationships also negatively affect the fatally ill child.

Further Concerns about Hospitalization and Procedures

School-aged children, though gaining increasing independence from parents still need them when ill and are lonely, frightened and sad when hospitalized. However, with support and with increased resources, most are able to cope. They may be angry and direct this hostility toward the treatment team, but when treated with respect and honesty, they are usually able to control themselves and cooperate in the treatment regime. When unable to trust, however, they may become depressed and withdrawn.

School-aged children are still frightened by procedures and many are supported by the presence of their parents or other familiar adults. Control over the situation as much as possible is almost a coping requirement, as is becoming familiar with the environment and equipment. The mother of a seven-year-old girl reported, "She tells them which finger she wants pricked, she sets up her own tray, goes right through the lab and looks at the microscope." Children of this age may also be much more assertive than preschool children in verbally communicating their opinions on the matter. The mother of the same girl reported on another occasion, "She was not about to have it in her arm, and she let them know it in no uncertain terms, and there was a fight." The administrators of the procedures are also often evaluated as to how much pain is inflicted, and one administrator may be preferred over others. After many repetitions of a procedure, some children seem to acquire the nonchalance of a veteran and will walk into a laboratory stating, "Do you want to use my finger or my arm?" Successful coping in the fact has led to a sense of mastery and enhanced self-esteem.

When hospitalized, many children have the additional concern of loss of status in the peer group, particularly if the absence is to be prolonged. They can be greatly cheered by cards, letters, and visits from their friends and reassured that they are cared about and not forgotten. Often they place these on the walls about their beds, for constant visual assurance of their importance to their friends.

The Adolescent

There is still much room for research regarding the concept of death during adolescence. Most developmentalists assume that by early adolescence most individuals have reached a level of cognitive growth at which the finality and inevitability of death are comprehensible, though they may not be accepted emotionally. This is true for many adolescents, particularly for those in the middle and late stages of the developmental period. However, it is not true for all. Many individuals have not reached the level of formal thought described by Piaget (17). Others may have had previous experiences with death which have led to a distortion of the concept. For some, death may still be seen either as a redeemer or as an avenger that punishes for sins committed (18). For many adolescents, who already have a tendency to feel guilty as they attempt to separate from parents, death may be seen as a confirmation of essential badness. This is reinforced by the inevitable breaking of many family and cultural rules as they test their independence.

The Sense of Isolation

In addition to guilt and depression, the adolescent with life threatening illness is also bitter, angry and bewildered. He may know that he has broken many rules, but he is deeply shocked at the magnitude of the punishment which also implies rejection. Because he is resentful toward those people whom he still depends on and cares for deeply, his quiet depression and helplessness deepen. Many dying teenagers feel that no one can understand them, and they face death lonely and alone.

Such a sense of isolation is also a result of separation from the peer group, which has become all-important as the ties to parents and family loosen. This is particularly difficult for those adolescents who have disrupted family bonds abruptly or drastically. Teenagers who have felt deprived or rejected by parents during childhood may, of necessity, become extremely dependent on peers for direction, for support, and for the comfort of companionship. These teenagers are extremely vulnerable when faced with life threatening illness, for the group may be of little help. The serious illness and possible death of a friend is threatening to them in that it points up their own vulnerability and frailty. When body image is a major concern, they are uncomfortable with illness, mutilation or disfigurement. In order to cope with feelings they have not had to face before, they must withdraw from former close relationships.

Dying adolescents also contribute to the loosening of such ties. In defending themselves against the threat of abandonment by friends, they often deny their need for them by emphasizing their own self-sufficiency and independence. Fearing rejection by friends, they may repulse friendly overtures. Feeling very different, they set themselves apart to prevent exclusion and to avoid pity they do not want. If the teenager turns to his parents in his loneliness and need for understanding, he may feel that he is surrendering and returning to a former, outgrown, child-like state. Wanting attention desperately, he may cut himself off from all warmth.

The Body and the Future

The young adolescent wants to live. Acutely aware of his body, he senses its deterioration. At a time when the whole world is opening up, he learns there is nothing for him. Understandably, the young adolescent is bitter and resentful and asks, "Why me?" "To whom can I assign blame?" Keenly living life, he can appreciate losing everything in dying. He has just come to realize what life can hold when the visions and dreams are snatched away. Not knowing where to direct his anger and bitterness, he often struggles on alone.

Death can only mean defeat for the adolescent on the threshold of mastery. The 16-year-old youth is well aware that death will take away all his physical and mental powers, will strip him of his competency and of his future. The 16-year-old young woman often, in addition, faces the deterioration, deformity, or disfigurement. It is not surprising that young people who are undergoing such major alterations of body image and destruction of hopes have self-doubts and low self-esteem, or that they withdraw from contacts with others. This is cruel reality, and the adolescent will reasonably react with anger, bitterness, and helpless rage at the futility of life, because the adolescent at this age has tasted mastery and self-achievement, the deprivation is the greater.

Coping with Threat

Those adolescents, however, who have become more secure in their own individuality may not need to reject their parents as violently as does the young, troubled teenager. With greater self-confidence, they no longer need to defend themselves as strenuously against ease and comfort lest they become children again. Even though they feel bitterness and rage, the need is less intense to direct such feelings against parents, particularly when communication lines have been maintained and concerns can be discussed openly. When such communication lines are closed, however, and the young person is not allowed to disclose feelings, bitter episodes of fighting between the adolescent and parents may occur until the adolescent finally becomes severely depressed and withdrawn. Neither side knows how to break the silence, which may last to the end.

When communication is open, the adolescent's rage may periodically erupt against his family, but usually the older teenager will attempt to control and direct these feelings elsewhere. Explosions are usually triggered by changes in treatment procedures, lack of proper explanations, or threats to the adolescent's sense of independence—for example, not allowing him to have a voice in the decisions which concern him. When the adolescent is the last to know about a new therapy which is being considered, he rightly explodes and considers it unfair, for, after all, it is his body "they're doing it to." Though angry and hurt, he may continue to smile at hospital personnel for fear of being further excluded from decision-making processes in the future.

In coping with the intense threat of premature death, adolescents use much denial, which often permits them to live with their illness. As time progresses, both the adolescent and his family may begin to grieve in anticipation of death. This "grief work" often allows the adolescent to accept, at last, the inevitability of his own death. As death approaches, the world of the adolescent narrows to his bed and to a few loved members of his family. Even the young adolescent is able to accept the caring of warm and loving relations. He can allow himself to be babied, as death grows nearer, as long as he is not treated disrespectfully.

In the terminal phase, adolescents usually select one or two adults to share their thoughts and feelings. Some younger adolescents may resist to the end, lonely and proud, but this is relatively rare. In many cases, as death nears, adolescents show amazing strength, comforting their parents who are in pain and providing meaning to this tragedy by teaching others the value and ideals of living.

REFERENCES

1. Nagy, M. H. The child's theories concerning death. *Journal of Genetic Psychology, 73*, 1948, 3–27.
2. Kubler-Ross, E. *On Death and Dying*, New York: MacMillan, 1969.
3. Green, M. Care of the child with a long-term, life threatening illness: Some principles of management. *Pediatrics, 39*, 1967, 441–445.
4. Natterson, J. M. & Knudson, A. G. Observations concerning fear of death in fatally ill children and their mothers. *Psychosomatic Medicine, 22*, 1960, 456–465.
5. Evans, A. E. "If a child must die . . ." *New England Journal of Medicine, 273*, 1968, 138–142.
6. Toch, R. Management of the child with a fatal disease. *Clinical Pediatrics, 3*, 1964, 418–427.
7. Vernick, J. & Karon, M. Who's afraid of death on a leukemia ward? *American Journal of Disease of Children, 109*, 1965, 393–397.
8. Solnit, A. & Green, M. P. The pediatric management of the dying child, Part II. The child's reaction to the fear of dying. In A. Solnit and S. Provence (eds.), *Modern Perspectives in Child Development*. New York: International Universities Press, 1963.
9. Binger, C. M., Ablin, A. R., Feuerstein, R. C., Kushner, J. H., Zoger, S., & Mikkelsen, C. Childhood leukemia: Emotional impact on patient and family. *New England Journal of Medicine, 280*, 1969, 414–418.
10. Waechter, E. H. Children's awareness of fatal illness. *American Journal of Nursing, 71*, 1971, 1168–1172.
11. Sarason, S., Lighthall, F., Davidson, K., Waite, R., & Ruebush, B. *Anxiety in Elementary School Children*. New York: Wiley, 1960.
12. Spinetta, J. J., Rigler, D., & Karon, M. Anxiety in the dying child. *Pediatrics, 52*, 1973, 841–849.
13. Spinetta, J. J. & Maloney, L. J. Death anxiety in the out-patient leukemic child. *Pediatrics, 56*, 1975, 1034–1037.
14. Deasy, P. The role of the school in the life of the child with cancer. Paper presented at Symposium, *Living with Child Cancer*, San Diego, Calif., Feb. 2, 1980.
15. Heffron, W. A., Bommelaere, K., & Masters, R. Group discussions with parents of leukemic children. *Pediatrics, 52*, 1973, 831–840.
16. Gagan, J. Treating the pediatric cancer patient: A review. *Journal of Pediatric Psychology, 2*, 1977, 42–46.
17. Inhelder, B. & Piaget, J. *The Growth of Logical Thinking from Childhood to Adolescence*. New York: Basic Books, 1958.
18. Reigh, R. & Fineberg, H. The fatally ill adolescent. In Feinstein, S. and Giovacchini, P. (eds.), *Adolescent Psychiatry*, vol. 3. New York: Basic Books, 1974.

4

The Pediatrician and the Dying Child

Marylou Behnke, John A. Nackashi, Marsha D. Raulerson,
Pamela M. Schuler, and Paulette Mehta

INTRODUCTION

There is a time for everything,
And a season for every activity under heaven:

A time to be born and a time to die,
A time to plant and a time to uproot,
A time to kill and a time to heal,
A time to tear down and a time to build,
A time to weep and a time to laugh,
A time to mourn and a time to dance,
A time to scatter stones and a time to gather them,
A time to embrace and a time to refrain,
A time to search and a time to give up,
A time to keep and a time to throw away,
A time to tear and a time to mend,
A time to be silent and a time to speak . . . (Ecclesiastes 3:1-7)

We are taught from our earliest days that there is a time for everything, including "a time to die." This chapter explores some of the complex interpersonal skills that must be used by the physician during that stressful and sensitive time, the death of a child patient.

The physician's role especially needs to be clarified, because it becomes increasingly multi-faceted when a child patient is dying. Many physicians are highly competent in the role of healer. They are less comfortable but acquainted with the role of the physician as news bearer of the impending death of a child. At times it is expedient for the physician to take the unfamiliar roles of mourner, counselor, consultant to the family of the patient. All of this requires forethought and training.

For many years, dealing with the dying patient in these ways has been a neglected aspect of the physician's work. Often instead of concentrating on how to better prepare their patients, the patients' families and even themselves for the death, physicians have been immersed in the medical aspects of patient care, providing only minimal psychological support for the terminal period. In recent years, however, there has been an awakening of interest in death counseling and a sharpening of the physician's skills in dealing with dying patients and their families.

Dealing with children is a unique experience. Physicians deal with young people who are alive, they help them grow and be healthy, and they deal with patients who respond to sensitive care. Pediatricians often guide and protect the child, sometimes

I would like to gratefully acknowledge the efforts of Martha Peacock who contributed long hours of her personal time to help edit this paper. I would also like to thank Marian Murchison who was responsible for contributing her personal time in the initial typing of this manuscript.

even against parents and authorities. The death of a child is contrary to everything for which a pediatrician strives. As Easson (1) states: "While all doctors face their own particular anguish when their patient dies, the pediatrician more than others may have a heavy emotional burden when he has to deal with the dying child. He has sought the special joys that come in dealing with the young; he must accept the special agonies also."

This chapter includes a presentation of several case reports followed by the physician's analysis of various practical ways to help dying children cope with their "time to die." Also, this chapter discusses the parents' role in the dying process of their child in order to help the physician meet their needs.

SOCIAL FACTORS AFFECTING THE PHYSICIAN'S VIEW OF A PATIENT'S DEATH

In many instances, physicians personally have a difficult time dealing with death. But why should this be so? Part of the explanation lies in society's expectation of physicians. They are traditionally seen as members of the most trusted professional group in society. They are viewed as healers, and therefore they see achieving a complete cure as the emphasis of their therapy almost to the exclusion of counseling the patient about ways to handle the problems that accompany illness. Early in their careers, most physicians begin to apply to themselves the high expectations they, and society, have of the medical profession. There is, therefore, great frustration on the part of physicians when faced with an incurable patient, because they are tempted to perceive themselves as failures (2, 3).

Another factor which influences physicians is the idea that they must appear at all times to be energetic, competent and healthy. It is not uncommon for physicians to believe subconsciously that they are immune to their patients' diseases. This is evidenced by a lack of conscientiously following ward isolation policies. Also, they are notoriously reluctant to seek help when sick, as well as to follow up on their own health care. This type of thinking has allowed physicians to be manipulated into the position of viewing themselves as omnipotent. They reason that if they have control over their own health, then surely they must have control over that of their patient's. This, of course, will again cause frustration on the part of physicians who continue to be reminded that they only have limited control over their own and their patients' health (2).

Also to be considered is the direction medicine has taken in modern times toward concentrating physicians' efforts on the technical aspects of health care. Because of the time and skill involved in the technical features of patient care, the tendency is to overlook the emotional needs of the patient (2).

In addition, with this increase in emphasis on technology (4), death becomes the enemy that is unconquerable, and its positive aspects are no longer valued. Life is still unpredictable in spite of increased technology, and answers are hard to find in such a setting.

PERSONAL FACTORS AFFECTING THE PHYSICIAN'S VIEW OF A PATIENT'S DEATH

It should be noted further that although a physician's life is usually arduous and stressful, it is particularly so when dealing with the death of a child. Physicians in one study considered the death of a child much more anxiety-producing than the death of an adult (2). In another study, a varied sample of 366 American and British subjects viewed the death of a child as the most upsetting life event that could happen to them out of 61 different choices (5).

The idea that some patients will die is something medical students come to accept, however the roles they will need to assume under those circumstances are rarely discussed or clarified. Therefore, the physician is thrust into the family's grief and the dying child's needs without a clear picture of the extraordinary assistance a person in that unique role can give.

Most physicians, indeed most people, deal with death in one of several different ways. Some physicians have spent considerable time trying to understand and accept the death of their patients but are unable to resolve the issue within themselves. In order to keep a tolerable emotional distance from death, physicians in this situation begin to see patients as interesting clinical problems instead of as human beings who are dying. They may lose interest in a dying patient and show this by quickly passing the patient by on rounds or by being unavailable to mourning parents. This defense mechanism can be so effective that the physician might idly wonder why a patient's death presents no great personal conflict. In this condition a physician is unable to help the patient or the family to cope.

Other physicians find death too distasteful to really think through its ramifications, so they ignore the fact that they will have patients that die. When a physician in this frame of mind is confronted with a dying patient, emotional chaos takes place. The physician may go to the extreme of being withdrawn, angry and minimally involved or to the extreme of being overinvolved. Either way the physician is unable to cope effectively with the situation.

Yet other physicians are able to resolve the issue of death for themselves, either through religious and/or secular training. Because these physicians have answered the question of death personally, they are better able to deal with the stressful situation when a child patient dies and to provide support for all involved.

THE PHYSICIAN'S NEED FOR TRAINING IN DEATH COUNSELING

The ability to give counsel to a dying patient and the family can not be thought of as solely an innate talent. While this might be the case to a certain extent, communication skills can be sharpened, wisdom can be learned, and concern can be cultivated to make even a good physician better.

It is easy to fall into the trap of believing that technology and increasing ability to cure are incompatible with the interpersonal skills necessary to help the dying child. The increasing technology and organization of medicine should, in fact, free physicians to be more available to personally interact when needed.

According to Hans Mauksch (6) we need an educational process that conveys respect to students so they in turn may convey respect to their patients. Along with this, there must be a change from producing strictly technically capable physicians to producing doctors who have the ability to deal with their own feelings and the training to use those feelings in a deliberate, sophisticated way in the counseling process.

Mauksch also points out that the skill necessary to deal with a dying patient is not something which can be turned on and off and used only with the dying. "The skills, the relationships, the attitudes, and the behaviors which are implicit in these needs must be fundamental to the total network of relationships with all patients."

With this obvious need for specific training what, if anything, is being done to help physicians prepare themselves to deal with the dying patient? In 1976, a review of death education in 107 of America's 113 medical schools was quite revealing. According to the report only seven medical schools had a full term course on death, 42 had a lecture or two, 44 had a mini-course, and 14 had no course at all (7).

In 1979, a study was published which evaluated the extent to which interpersonal skills were being taught in U.S. medical schools. This study showed that at least 68 percent of all medical schools in the U.S. had specific courses for teaching interpersonal skills. It also showed that these courses were fairly recent additions to the curriculum, and medical students graduating before 1975 had little or no training in this area. While this study is encouraging, it should be pointed out that counseling on death and dying specifically was only available in 28 percent of the 79 responding medical schools (8). So, while the trend of including death counseling courses in the general medical school curriculum is encouraging, the goal of educating all physicians in this vital area is still a long way off in the future.

In regard to children, certain distinct areas of training are helpful. The physician should be familiar with the developmental stages a child goes through so that conversations can be geared to the child's level of understanding. In this decade a study by Swain (9) analyzed the concepts of the finality, inevitability and personal nature of death. He took into consideration age, sex, religious influence and level of parental education and found age to be the only significant variable of the four. This topic is discussed fully in E. H. Waechter's chapter, "Dying Children: Patterns of Coping."

Training in certain interpersonal skills better prepares the physician for the task of counseling. Listening, responding and observing are characteristics that can be developed by physicians in an effort to improve communication with patients.

Also helpful to the physician would be an awareness of the grief processes people go through and the bereavement processes they experience after the child's death.

THE PHYSICIAN'S RESPONSE TO THE DYING
CHILD AS A LIVING PERSON

In considering a physician's reaction to the dying child and the child's family, it is helpful to divide the problems that occur along the way into three time periods: impact, battle and defeat (10). Each has its special problems.

The period of impact is experienced by the physician, the patient and the family. The physician is the first to experience the impact of a tragic diagnosis and prognosis and must then tell the parents. It is best for parents to be told by the physician in whom they have the most confidence. Both parents should be told together so they can support one another during this family crisis. Another meeting should be arranged within one to two weeks to answer any questions that have arisen, giving the parents time to understand what they were told initially. Often parents find this period of time more difficult than the actual death of their child. This is a crucial time for the physician to provide support for the family and help the parents plan for the future by putting the prognosis into a general time frame and by explaining future therapeutic regimens.

An important decision that has to be made by the physician during the period of impact is how much to tell the child. Once the parents know, the child will be aware that something upsetting is happening because of the significant change in the parents' attitude. So, the question should never be whether or not to tell the child, but *how much* to tell the child. The only indicator that can be used to know how much to tell the child is the individual child, and the only judge as to how much to tell is the sensitivity of the most significant person in the child's life. This person could be a parent, a friend, a close sibling or the physician. The physician should encourage the child to communicate and should be available both to the child and parents to answer questions during this period of time.

The second period, or battle phase, encompasses the time up until the child is in the final stage of illness. During this time the emotions of everyone involved are brought to the fore, particularly anger and guilt. However, it should be remembered that anger, guilt, grief, and depression may be present in all three phases at various times.

Anger may be present not only in the child and the parent, but also in the physician. The child is angry at the personal loss of a future as well as the loss of independence, the mutilation of the body, and the unfairness of the whole situation. The parents may be angry at the physician because they subconsciously consider physicians to be omnipotent, and they may feel their child's prognosis could be changed if the physician so desired, if he or she would just make the extra effort for their child. Also, they may be angry at the child because the impending death threatens their parental immortality. "To bury a child is to see a part of yourself, your eye color, your dimple, your sense of humor, being placed in the ground" (11).

The physician, however, may also experience anger at a child's death because it threatens the imagined omnipotence. Anger may also be expressed as a substitute for depression. Also, doctors may turn their anger inward, feeling they have failed the patient somehow. Sometimes physicians even vent their anger toward their patient or the patient's family, which leads to outbursts that impede the effectiveness of therapy. If physicians understand that they may often feel angry while a patient is dying, then they can find ways of channeling the anger constructively. This includes such activities as research, lecturing to increase public awareness of the disease, or fostering financial support for research (1).

Guilt is commonly present in each person involved, especially during the battle phase. Children may feel guilty because they believe that something in their personality, behavior or thinking made them sick. The parents may feel guilty and need to be constantly reassured that they did nothing to cause their child's illness. The physician may also feel guilty because the prescribed treatment or counseling isn't working. Guilt must be carefully dealt with because it can lead to many problems, including overpermissiveness with the child, rejection of the child or denial of the child's impending death.

The final period is that of defeat, when it becomes evident that there is nothing more that can be done to keep the child alive. The most common reaction of physicians during this period of time is to emotionally withdraw from the situation and reinvest time and energy in other patients. Although this is a natural part of anticipatory mourning, it should not be done abruptly or comprehensively. Also, the physician should make every effort not to withdraw from the family at a time when they need optimum support. The physician has the responsibility to be involved with the dying child as long as necessary to fulfill the child's needs. The physician does not have the emotional freedom to withdraw completely, in order to facilitate personal mourning, until the child dies (1).

Although an extended period of defeat causes emotional strain on physicians and other staff members, the enthusiasm used in extending the patient's life during the terminal phase should be based on the wishes and needs of the family and the patient rather than on those of the physician.

VARIOUS MODELS TO HELP THE PHYSICIAN EVALUATE GRIEF

Certain processes of grief are experienced by those who have adequate warning of their impending death. It must be remembered, however, that although these processes of grief do take place in children, allowances must be made for each individual child's psychosocial and cognitive levels and for each child's ability to verbalize and communicate emotions. Also to be remembered is that the various stages of grief a particular patient goes through may last for varying lengths of time, exist side by side, be skipped entirely or replace each other. Thus, physicians or anyone else taking care of the child may not observe all of the various stages of grief being verbalized by a particular patient, but every effort should be made to help the child work through each set of emotions. It is of primary importance to create and maintain a positive atmosphere for communication when the child is ready and able to communicate.

Now we can go on to discuss grief processes which must be worked through, not only by the dying child, but by the parents and to some extent the doctor when confronted with the child's certain death.

The Death-Trajectory-Phases Model, as put forth by Pattison, suggests that patients anticipate their probable lifespan. This "potential death trajectory" is then divided into two segments by the "knowledge of death," which alters the initial trajectory. The first segment includes normal expectations concerning death after living a full life. The second segment is known as the "living-dying interval" and extends from the "knowledge of death" to the actual "point of death." This interval is further divided into three clinical phases. The "acute crisis phase" is the phase during which anxiety peaks because of the knowledge of death. The next phase is the "chronic living-dying phase" during which the patient meets directly the issues and fears relative to dying. The "terminal phase" is the time during which the dying patient withdraws and prepares for the end (12).

The next model to be discussed is the Personality-Repetitive Alternation Model. In this model the patient's personality determines the various coping mechanisms used to face death. If the patient has dealt with stressful situations in the past by using denial or by becoming depressed or through overactivity, then these types of behavior will be exhibited when the patient faces the stress of death. Also, instead of progressing through various stages, the patient alternates between several different coping mechanisms for varying lengths of time, all of which is again determined by the patient's personality. Thus patients typically alternate between acceptance and forms of habitual coping or defense mechanisms (12).

Elisabeth Kübler-Ross has outlined the Stages Model which she has observed in dying patients: denial, anger, bargaining, depression and finally, acceptance (13). Although her case studies were mainly adults, an understanding of these various stages of grief is helpful when trying to deal with everyone involved with the dying child, including the child.

Kübler-Ross describes the first stage, denial, as a buffer which allows the patient to become collected, and with time, mobilize other defenses. Denial is also a defense that is not only used initially but also from time to time during the course of the illness.

When denial can no longer be consistently maintained, anger, the second stage Kübler-Ross observed, emerges with feelings of rage, envy and resentment at impending death. The child may manifest anger toward anything or anyone in the environment, including the family. It is important to recognize the child's anger as an attempt to cope. The physician needs to help the parents to interpret the anger accurately and not to take it as personal rejection.

A third stage observed by Kübler-Ross, bargaining, is usually brief and can be helpful to the patient. The patient bargains with God for an extension of life, attempting, in this way, to postpone the inevitable. Experience has taught that a reward may be granted for good behavior, so with promises to do good, a deal is made with God.

According to Kübler-Ross, a fourth stage is depression which takes place in two forms: reactive and preparatory. Reactive depression includes a sadness for *past* losses such as loss of school time and social activity because of illness, loss of family possessions which were sold to pay for medical care, or sadness over the scars of surgery. Preparatory depression deals with the *impending* loss of everything and everybody the patient loves. Children after six years of age begin to have the cognitive ability to mourn the loss of their future. It would be tragic not to recognize these feelings in children and thus force them to pretend that they are not suffering the greatest loss of all. In dying, children lose everything from possessions to self, and it is right for them to grieve over this loss (14).

Preparatory depression facilitates a final stage of acceptance, a time void of feelings, when the struggle is finally over. Even though a child may have accepted death, the child's parents may not have achieved acceptance yet. They may require more support than does the child during this period of time.

It is interesting to note at this point the similarities between the models of Kübler-Ross and Pattison. Pattison's "acute crisis phase" overlaps with the stages of denial, anger and bargaining in Kübler-Ross' model while her observed depression and acceptance stages are similar to Pattison's "chronic living-dying phase."

In concluding our discussion of the various models of the grief process, it should be re-emphasized that observed stages and coping mechanisms may last for different lengths of time, exist in tandem or replace each other. The one thing, however, that usually is consistent throughout all of these models is the patient's hope that eventually all of the tragedy will have meaning, and the suffering will pay off if one can only hold on. It is important for physicians to recognize the hope that their patients have and not to convey hopelessness to them by mentally writing them off as dead. Hope can often be conveyed to the patient by showing interest in a patient's ability to draw, write or perform other creative activities. It can also be conveyed by encouraging the patient to complete such unfinished endeavors. It is equally as important, however, that neither the physician nor the family force hope upon the child patient who is ready to die.

THE PHYSICIAN'S RESPONSE TO PARENTAL GRIEF AND BEREAVEMENT

As the parents attempt to provide support for the child, they personally go through several processes of grief. Physicians need to be aware of these processes so that they can counsel and reassure parents that what they are experiencing is normal and necessary for good mental health. It is also important for physicians to be familiar with these normal processes so that they can be aware when parents are responding abnormally, requiring psychiatric intervention to resolve their grief. Lastly, in order to insure comfort, support and understanding in an extremely stressful situation, it is important for physicians to understand which emotions and behavior of dying patients and their families are signs of healthy grieving so as not to regard such actions as a personal attack on themselves or their profession (15).

Besides going through the various processes of grief as discussed above, parents often undergo anticipatory mourning during which emotional attachment to their child is relinquished over a period of time. This involves the steps of: 1) acknowledgement of the inevitable death, 2) grief over the impending loss of their child, 3) reconciliation to the fact of their child's death, 4) detachment, at which point the parents gradually withdraw their emotional investment from their child and, finally, 5) memorialization, a process the parents work through to idealize the mental image of their child, constructing a complex memory which they will cherish after the child dies (14, 16).

After the child dies, parents begin a process of bereavement, the complex set of reactions that survivors experience after the death of someone close to them. There are several symptoms common to bereaved individuals, and these include: somatic distress such as tightness in the throat, shortness of breath and weakness; a preoccupation with images of the dead child in familiar places; feelings of guilt because of failure to prevent the child's death; disorganization in daily activities; hostility in personal relationships, and an inability to complete tasks (16, 17). It is these reactions that physicians should be aware of so that they can reassure parents who experience such normal problems.

The following five case histories define some of the special problems, needs and responses of the dying child, as well as those of the physician and the child's parents. Possible effective procedures will be suggested, and the role of the physician will be clarified wherever possible.

Case 1

Baby Boy G. was a premature infant who weighed 1400 grams at birth. The pregnancy was complicated by an abnormal amount of amniotic fluid, and an examination by ultrasonography revealed a gastrointestinal obstruction in the fetus. The baby was delivered by Caesarean section in order to maximize his chances of survival. At delivery the baby was noted to be in respiratory distress and was placed on a ventilator to facilitate his breathing. Also, the child was noted to have a deformed left hand and right leg, both of which were felt to be surgically correctable. During the first week of life the child underwent a surgical procedure to correct the gastrointestinal obstruction. Also at this time, the child underwent surgical correction of his right diaphragm which was thought to be the etiology of the child's persistent respiratory problems. Throughout all of this, however, the child showed no evidence of neurologic or other medical problems.

At three weeks of age the child was continuing to have respiratory distress. Examination of the baby was highly suggestive of a patent ductus arteriosus, a type of congenital heart disease. Subsequent laboratory studies were normal and did not substantiate the diagnosis of a patent ductus arteriosus. However, based on solid clinical evidence, the child was scheduled for surgery to correct what was thought to be a minor heart defect. It was hoped that this procedure would solve the baby's major problem of respiratory distress. Unfortunately, during surgery a previously undetected heart defect was found and was felt to be inoperable. The family was notified immediately, and a decision was made to continue life support as long as the family desired it. At eight weeks of age the child had an acute decompensation that resulted in his death.

Discussion

Grief, unless it becomes a way of life, is not a pathologic process. In fact, it is a normal process and it should be understood as such so that physicians can both work through their own grief and help their patients and parents do the same. As has been said, if physicians do not work through their own grief effectively, then they will be unable to help those within their care in an optimal way during their time of need. In the case of the physician, this process does not necessarily require a great amount of time, only recognition and thoughtfulness. Whether the grief is consciously worked through or not, it will be experienced. If grief reactions are not consciously dealt with, the physician may avoid or reject the grieving family, ignore pathologic reactions by the family to their child's death, or discourage the family's normal show of despair. Also, physicians in this situation may be tempted to treat the physical symptoms of the family's grief with tranquilizers or mood elevators without addressing themselves to the cause of the physical symptoms (18).

The three time periods that problems of care can be divided into were exemplified in this particular case. Because of the previous encouraging prognosis, everyone involved with this baby was shocked at the news about the inoperable heart problem (period of impact). The physician who dealt with the family the most consistently was shocked. His role as healer was impinged upon, and he needed to deal with the attachment he had developed to the baby. In this psychological turmoil he had to tell the family about the prognosis and deal with their initial reactions of shock and grief.

During the period of battle, the physician often feels anger and guilt and struggles with the reality of personal fallibility. This physician felt guilty for not having discovered the problem sooner, thus putting the baby through the suffering of unnecessary surgery. Also, he felt as if he had built up the family's hopes, making it harder for them to cope with the seriousness of the child's heart problem. His grief and depression were compounded as he compared this patient to his healthy newborn son.

The period of defeat, when the child was terminally ill, was another stage of inward searching on the part of the physician. During this time the family wanted heroic measures to maintain life in their child. The physician, recognizing the inevitable outcome, found it difficult to do painful procedures to the child because he didn't want him to suffer needlessly. The physician felt helpless. He was caught between recognizing that the baby would die and that life support would need to be continued because of the parents' wishes. Slowly the physician withdrew, knowing that if he were to exhibit his previous level of interest in the baby's treatment, it might convey false hope to the parents (10). He did, however, remain involved with the family and continued to be of assistance to them.

The physician has three major tasks to perform for the parents when they undergo the loss of a newborn baby. These include: 1) helping activate normal grief reactions in both parents, 2) helping the parents understand their loss and making it real for them, and 3) meeting whatever individual needs certain parents may have (18, 19). These three tasks were performed by the physician in this case.

The parents of this baby were in their early 20s, and they had one healthy little girl at home. They were religious people, and with the support of their religious beliefs, they were willing to accept their baby with his various deformities. Indeed, the baby was thought to be normal neurologically and would be able to compensate for his physical deficiencies without too much difficulty. The parents were intelligent, and appeared to be very capable individuals. They had a great desire to care for their baby, and it was felt that with these loving and conscientious parents, the child could live a life very close to normal. With all of this in mind, the child was vigorously supported, and the parents were reinforced in their desire to care for him.

The announcement that the child had an inoperable congenital heart defect was devastating to the parents because they had been given positive reinforcement up until then of a good outcome for their baby. The child had already undergone two surgical procedures to save his life. This had all added to the parents' love for the baby and helped them to readily accept his physical abnormalities.

At this time a decision was made to continue life support to allow the parents time to deal with their feelings. The parents appeared to have accepted the diagnosis and were not angry about it. They did bargain with God, however, and begged for a miracle to save their baby's life. Although they fully recognized that a miracle might not be God's will, they remained hopeful.

Throughout all of this the family was encouraged to visit their child frequently, which they did. This is one way to help parents understand the reality of the situation in which they are involved. After the child dies, parents should be allowed to see and hold their child if they wish. This provides a good time for the parents to say good-bye. Many parents are better able to work through their grief when they have faced the reality of the situation by holding and seeing their dead child (20). Other parents find this part of mourning unacceptable, and of course, their personal preferences should be respected.

When dealing with a stillborn or an unseen newborn baby, parents need specific, and if acceptable, firsthand information about their dead child. Without that information they will mourn on the basis of fantasy, always wondering whether the baby was the child of their dreams or the monster of their nightmares.

A formal ceremony of some sort is also helpful in achieving closure and helping parents to say good-bye. Often in the case of a newborn this is not encouraged, or even thought of by the physician because of the practice of hospital cremation, but it is a very practical way of helping the family to work through the grief process (19). Having something concrete to share with other people and to cry over provides memories that facilitate normal mourning processes. Physicians should be able to help the parents make the most of what is readily available and can be remembered (21).

At the time of the death, all parents will need some help in making even minor decisions. They often look to the physician for this help. We, as physicians, should be prepared to help parents with decisions about such matters as how to explain the death of a sibling to another child (18, 22-26), how to make funeral plans (22, 24), and, of course, how to work through their grief (16, 17, 22, 24, 25, 27).

Klaus et al. (28) suggest that the physician see the parents three times after the death of an infant. The first meeting with the physician is at the time of death to help the family make decisions and to discuss their anguish with them, explaining that their feelings are normal. The next meeting should be within two or three days to talk over the process of grief again but in more detail with the family. They should be helped to understand the normal types of reactions they will be having so that they will not be shocked by them. This meeting is important because many parents will not remember much of what was said at the first meeting because of their state of shock at that moment. The third meeting should be in three to six months to review the autopsy findings if one was done and to make sure the parents are approaching acceptance and beginning to plan for the future. Often these meetings after the death of a child are not arranged. However, when they are, they are of great benefit to the family to help them finalize the death of their child. In a study by Rowe et al. (29), it was found that physician follow-up after a child's death resulted in better parental understanding of the events surrounding the death and increased satisfaction with the information they received.

At the time of Baby Boy G's death, both physician and parents were relieved that the child would not suffer any more. All people involved appeared to have worked through the process of pain to the point of acceptance, which is a goal we should continually strive to achieve with ourselves, as physicians, and with the families with whom we deal.

Case 2

L. D. was an 8-year-old girl who had been healthy until one week before her first hospital admission. Some twenty-two days later she would be dead.

L. D. presented to her pediatrician with fever, headache, cough, and blurred vision. She then developed extreme weakness and was admitted to her local hospital. Her evaluation included various blood tests and a bone marrow aspiration that suggested a diagnosis of acute myelogenous leukemia. At this time she was transferred to our tertiary care center for treatment.

Physical examination upon admission to our hospital was remarkable for extreme pallor, fever, bilateral retinal hemorrhages, a massively enlarged spleen and bruised lower extremities that were tender to touch. A peripheral blood smear showed predominantly lymphoblastic cells with a high white blood cell count compatible with the diagnosis of leukemia.

Because of the extremely high number of leukemic cells present and the risk of intracranial hemorrhage, radiation therapy to the central nervous system was started on the day of admission and continued every day throughout her first hospitalization.

During her first hospitalization, L. D. had no appetite or energy. She required transfusions with various blood products and complained of pain in her legs, back and chest. After one week in the hospital, L. D. and her family went to a nearby motel where she could be out of the institution but easily return for radiation and chemotherapy. They went home for the weekend, but L. D. was readmitted a day later with numerous mosquito bites, fever and a very low white blood cell count.

This time when L. D. was admitted, she had red lines on her face which marked the radiation points. Blood was crusted in her nose, her lips were ulcerated, and she had white patches of oral candidiasis inside her mouth. Her hair was falling out, and bald spots were visible. She received antibiotics for seven days, and during this time, the nurses noted that she was irritable and uncooperative. She had difficulty sleeping and had nightmares accompanied by screaming and moaning.

On the ninth day of this hospitalization L. D. again became febrile. Antibiotics were restarted, and her trip home was cancelled. The next day she developed diarrhea and abdominal pain and was thought to have a viral gastroenteritis. Cultures of her blood and stool were negative.

The night before she died, her father came to see her and brought her a cute blond wig, but L. D. wasn't interested because her stomach hurt. During the night she developed bloody stools, tachycardia and mild respiratory distress. In the morning, she was awake and very alert, but her color was ashen, her pulse was 160, her blood pressure was dropping and her respiratory rate was 30. She then began to hemorrhage from the rectum but was still alert. She talked with her parents during this time, but they left after five minutes when she began hemorrhaging from the mouth. Within another five minutes full resuscitation measures were in progress. Shortly after this L. D. died.

By the next day blood cultures were positive for Pseudomonas aeruginosa, and stool cultures were positive for Salmonella enteritidis. The autopsy showed leukemic infiltrates virtually everywhere in the body, and the bone marrow had scattered lymphoblastic cells with no normal marrow.

Discussion

L. D. was in middle childhood. It is difficult to know whether children who are terminally ill at this age can conceptualize their own death, but it is thought that, although they personally may not be able to talk about it, they are aware of the seriousness of the illness (30). It is important to remember that children in this age group are in a transitional stage and still have vestiges of magical thinking prior to the total development of an adult concept of death (31), although they do see death as permanent (9, 32).

When L. D. was first seen in the clinic, she appeared sad and frightened, and whimpered throughout her physical examination. After being told her diagnosis and its meaning in very simple terms, L. D. remained subdued, and the only concern she expressed was to wonder when her hair would fall out. During the next few days she continued to remain frightened, rarely venturing from her bed and always wanting her mother close by. Death would mean loss to her, and that idea of loss produced a separation anxiety.

During her second hospitalization, L. D. appeared to be experiencing anger and depression. As she grew more demanding (an expression of her anger) and pathetic (an expression of her depression), her mother withdrew from her instead of supporting her.

Minutes before her death. L. D. asked that penetrating question, "Am I going to die?" L. D. was not looking for a direct answer to the question. What she was really asking was, "Will I be all right? Will this hurt? Will someone I love be with me?" It was these questions that the physician attempted to answer by staying with L. D., and trying to relieve her anxiety by her presence and loving, reassuring words.

Not every child who says the words "Am I dying?" really wants to know the answer to that specific question. The physician should strive to differentiate between children such as L. D. who have deeper questions they need answered than the one verbalized, and children who are seeking genuine answers to their questions, both in concrete and philosophical terms, that will enable them to make sense out of the situation in which they find themselves.

The behavior of L. D.'s parents brings up some interesting issues. At the time of L. D.'s diagnosis, her attending physician talked to her parents about the gravity of the situation. She told them of the possibility of death during the induction phase of the chemotherapy and indicated that, at best, L. D. would live only a few years. L. D.'s mother was a tiny dark-haired lady with lined face who constantly smoked thin brown cigarettes, looking older than her 36 years. Her father appeared younger and was blond and tanned. They seemed not to hear the doctor's words and exhibited classic denial. "When can we take her home?" they asked, seemingly not concerned about, or acknowledging, the gravity of her illness. "We don't want this to dominate our lives, as we have a 9-year-old son and don't want him to be affected by this," they added. To punctuate this attitude, the parents, because of a promise they made to their son, took L. D. and her brother to a stock car race during her first weekend at home. L. D., however, was too weak and too tired to enjoy herself and was rehospitalized the next day.

These parents, as sometimes happens, used almost total denial to cope with their feelings of shock and disbelief about their child's fatal diagnosis. Their continued denial resulted in a lack of cooperation with the medical staff. Parents may initially act as if their child is not ill, but usually they will begin to accept the diagnosis intellectually and cooperate with the physician. Intellectual acceptance is followed by acceptance of the diagnosis emotionally as parents say, "It finally hit me." It is this acute emotional impact that often heralds the beginning of anticipatory mourning (25).

In regards to anticipatory mourning, L. D.'s parents appeared to reach the stage of detachment too early. As L. D. become more demanding, her mother retreated more and more to the parents' room to smoke. Grandma came to help and seemed to comfort L. D., but her father stayed home, 160 miles away. Although detachment is vital to the mental health of the survivors, the timing must be right. If the detachment is completed too early, then the child will be left to die alone, unsupported emotionally by those who should be the closest (1, 14, 33).

Although it appeared that L. D.'s parents were working their way through the grief process relative to her poor prognosis, they were not ready for her sudden death, which occurred over a period of hours. When her death was made known to them by the physician, they cried out in anguish, totally unprepared.

Parents whose children die unexpectedly are noted to have a surge of intense, intolerable feelings because they have no time to psychologically prepare for the death. After an unexpected death, the parents experience extreme sadness, depression, loneliness, and all the symptoms that accompany these problems. Anxiety is present because the death reminds the parents of their own mortality and their own helplessness. Anger is also present, and it may be directed at anyone: at God, at the child; or at the physicians, a living sibling, a spouse or anyone else who was involved with caring for the dead child (34). Physicians should be aware of these types of reactions so that they can be prepared to reassure parents that they are not "losing their minds" as many parents in this situation feel they are doing.

In this case, L. D.'s family had difficulty working through the grief process. Now one year later, her mother sits alone for hours at a time, unable to function and still asking "Why?" Her brother has stomach aches at school and has to come home frequently. When grief feelings are delayed or repressed, as happened in this case, the person tends to remain poorly functional for perhaps years. Some bereaved parents become involved in uncharacteristic, hedonistic social lives. Others become fearful and overprotective of their other children. Still other parents create enshrinements to the deceased, such as preserving the dead child's bedroom intact. They also may experience imagined physical complaints, remain depressed or withdraw from society, all of which are situations that prevent a normal life from going on around them (16). It is assumed by most professionals that this inability to function can be prevented (34). Several ways are described in case 4.

Several other useful processes to work through in an attempt to prevent poor functioning include incorporation, substitution and denial. Incorporation is an attempt to turn the supposed feelings of the deceased person inward to speak to oneself: "Susie was a happy child; she wouldn't want me to cry." Substitution occurs when something or someone is chosen to replace the dead child: another child, a toy, a piece of clothing that belonged to the deceased. Adoption is not recommended under these circumstances as an effort to provide a substitute for the lost child. Denial appears in the form of shock and disbelief that occur at the time of death. This type of behavior is useful during the months that follow to help the parents work through their grief. After that the parents may begin various types of searching activity, looking in familiar places for their child. These processes allow them to gradually detach themselves from the deceased (34).

Each of these three mechanisms has proved useful to parents in learning to accept the death of their child, especially when it occurs suddenly, and to escape the trap of a daily life-style of intense grief for a prolonged period of time. When a parent reacts as L. D.'s mother did, professional help should be encouraged by the physician to prevent his or her total immobilization.

Problems with L. D.'s brother could be due to unresolved fear, guilt that he did not die instead of his sister, or anger in regards to his sister's death. His mother was so overwhelmed by her own unresolved grief that she was not able to emotionally support her son. His stomach ache and his need to be close to his mother suggest that he has not received the emotional support he needs from an adult to help him work through his own grief effectively (22, 33), Although a poor prognosis had been given, there was little time to prepare this family, or L. D., for the suddenness of her death. However, when time allows, the physician should encourage involvement of siblings in the process of bereavement. This would allow the other children to better understand their parents' behavior and the significance of the death to the parents (18, 24-26).

Because L. D.'s death was so sudden and the family's reactions atypical, the physician felt inadequate in trying to help them deal with their grief. She had not been trained to deal with denial or with a family's failure to accept the death once it had occurred. Also, the physician did not know how to deal with her own grief and shock, and she found herself psychologically unprepared to help someone else. She realized her inadequacy was due to poor training in interpersonal skills and bereavement counseling as well as her own lack of personal reflection on the subject of death.

Case 3

J. D. was a 14-year-old male whose presenting symptoms consisted of sore throat and enlarged lymph nodes. He had both a negative throat culture and a negative infectious mononucleosus test. He continued to have enlarged lymph nodes in the neck and was treated with penicillin after his pediatrician noted infected areas on his tonsils. When the lymph nodes did not resolve and increased anorexia was noted, the child was admitted to his local hospital. There he was noted to have an increased white blood cell count and was transferred to our tertiary care center for further evaluation.

On admission J. D. was noted to have massively enlarged lymph nodes in the neck. A mass was noted in the posterior aspect of the nasal septum. The tonsils were large and met in the midline of the throat. An enlarged liver and spleen were present on abdominal examination. The remainder of the physical examination was normal.

The patient was initially evaluated for the presence of an infection somewhere in the body. A bone marrow aspiration was performed in the course of his evaluation for an infection, and it was interpreted as lymphoblastic lymphoma. The patient was immediately transferred to the oncology service and started on chemotherapy while his metastatic work-up was being completed.

J. D. had a very complicated course following his induction chemotherapy. He required central nervous system chemotherapy, with spinal taps performed every three days. Three days after his first dose of medications, he went into acute renal failure from the massive tumor breakdown and required peritoneal dialysis in the intensive care unit for two days. He was able to return to the floor by the fifth day, but at that time his blood counts began dropping and he started having bleeding from his nose and rectum. Also, at that time, he had diarrhea, vomiting and a high fever. He was started on antibiotics and blood and platelet transfusions, but it was difficult to control the bleeding. Five days later J. D. had a massive hemorrhage into his lungs and died suddenly, only weeks after his initial diagnosis.

Discussion

J. D. was at the beginning of the adolescent period of development, during which most children are more concerned with the external effects of their disease and necessary treatment on their body than they are about their disease and its implications of mortality. During this time of life, the child understands death to be a personal, permanent event and often uses denial in trying to cope with the anxiety produced by the thoughts of dying (13, 31). It is important in dealing with a child this age to recognize the complex emotions involved in the grief process. If the disease can be explained properly from the beginning (35), then a positive atmosphere for communication can be established, and there may be a better chance to help the child work through some feelings, verbalize needs, and thus, free up energy that could be spent in positive ways.

In this case, J. D. was told at the time of his diagnosis that he had a type of cancer of the lymph nodes. He was told that there was treatment available, and the kinds of drugs to be used were explained to him. It was explained that the treatment would result in the loss of his hair and possibly in vomiting for a few hours after the medicines were given. He was also warned of the chance of infections throughout the course of his chemotherapy. J. D. accepted all of that information and asked a few questions, most of which were concerned with his body image and the loss of his hair. Mutual trust was established between J. D. and the physician as a result of these talks (33).

For the next few days J. D. was extremely sick. He expressed anger and evidenced periods of depression. Both these complex emotions are typical of the grief process. Someone was always around drawing blood, doing a spinal tap, giving medications, or giving him his radiation therapy. He would express anger at each interruption and sometimes cry in anger, but none of it was taken personally by the physician, as she had learned that his anger was not at her personally but was an expression of his feelings of "why did this have to happen to me?" During this time J. D. was supported emotionally, made to feel important as a human being and encouraged to ask questions. Gradually he withdrew and became very depressed (12, 13, 33).

Death was not an issue that was directly discussed with J. D. because throughout his illness he never indicated, either directly or indirectly, that he wished to discuss the topic. The physician should always remain sensitive to the patient and learn to interpret non-verbal cues (such as unattributable anxiety) or disguised verbal cues (such as superficial questions with deeper implications) that indicate a need for the patient to talk. However, the issue should rarely be forced (13).

J. D., nevertheless, sensed the possibility of death. This was especially true just prior to his being intubated. At that time he acknowledged that he knew he was dying, by offering comfort to the doctor, saying he knew she was doing everything possible for him. J. D. was not unusual in doing this, as the consolation of others by dying patients is something that is observed frequently when death is close at hand.

J. D.'s mother stayed close to him throughout his entire illness. She knew from the beginning that he was going to die, as the physicians had all been quite frank with her in regards to his prognosis. She appeared to be working her way through her own personal grief process but was coping by means of denial up until the day prior to his death. At this time he acutely worsened, and she could no longer deny the inevitable. From that time on she began to work her way through the process of anticipatory mourning, rather quickly going from acknowledgement to grieving. It was at this point in time that J. D. died. Since then the mother has continued to work through her grief, and when seen two months after J. D.'s death, she was able to sit with his physician, talk about J. D., look at his baby pictures, and review his life. She had apparently reached the stage of memorialization, the fashioning of an ideal memory of the deceased loved one, a very human response to that most permanent of losses (14). Emily Dickinson articulates a memorialization out of her past grief:

> If anybody's friend be dead,
> It's sharpest of the theme
> The thinking how they walked alive
> At such and such a time . . .
>
> How warm they were on such a day;
> You almost feel the date,
> So short way off it seems; and now,
> They're centuries from that . . .

. . . when was it, can you tell,
You asked the company to tea,
Acquaintance, just a few,
And chatted close with this grand thing
That don't remember you?

J. D.'s mother appeared to have successfully worked through her grief to a point of acceptance. Physicians should keep in mind when trying to help parents reach this goal that acceptance does not suggest that the parents feel their child's death is fair, just or reasonable. It does, however, mean the development of appropriate coping mechanisms, as in the case of J. D.'s mother, to combine the finality and reality of the death with the pattern of one's own personal life (20).

The physician in J. D.'s case was faced with experiencing her first patient death. Her initial thoughts when she met J. D. were how much she was going to enjoy following him over her next three years as a resident. This thought was soon shattered by his sudden death.

As J. D. grew sicker, the physician felt helpless, realizing she could not cure him. She experienced guilt and agonized over whether she was missing something that could help him. She was attempting to go through her own grief process as J. D. was dying. She stood appalled during his cardiac arrest, experiencing personal sorrow. After his death she dictated charts until she lost her voice, trying to distract herself instead of working through her pain over J. D.'s death in a constructive way. The next morning, she was very bitter, full of self-accusation and anger which she directed everywhere: at the attending physicians, nurses, and fellow residents and even physically striking the crash cart. As is sometimes the case, this physician was not trained in school or during her residency to deal with death and did not understand the emotions she was experiencing. She, therefore, thought of herself as an ineffective physician rather than an untrained physician.

Case 4

R. A. was an 11-year-old boy who had been healthy and active all of his life until nine months prior to his death when he was diagnosed as having acute lymphoblastic leukemia. He received induction chemotherapy and went into remission only to relapse several months later. At that time he underwent a second course of induction chemotherapy, and remission was once again achieved. One week before his death R. A. was sent to hematology clinic by his local pediatrician because of a mildly elevated white blood cell count. A few days earlier the patient and his sister had both suffered a viral illness, but at the time of the clinic visit that had resolved. On that day a peripheral blood smear showed a few atypical lymphocytes but no lymphoblastic cells. Two weeks previously, a bone marrow aspirate showed no evidence of a leukemic infiltrate. It was felt that indeed the patient was merely recovering from a viral illness, and he was sent home from the clinic. Several days later R. A. was admitted to the hospital gravely ill with massive enlargement of the liver and spleen, fluid in the abdomen, and enlarged lymph nodes in the neck and chest. The initial laboratory studies confirmed a relapse.

The attending physicians were divided in what they suggested. One physician recommended heroic measures, including making use of intensive care, peritoneal dialysis and experimental chemotherapy. All of this would have required that

R. A. be physically separated from his family. The rest of the team, including resident physician, nurse practitioner and family, felt that supportive therapy in a private room would be best. Then R. A. could have his family and close friends with him.

R. A. was put in a private room and lived for four days prior to his death.

Discussion

This particular case exemplifies some important points relative to children who are facing their own death and to their families. R. A. had gone through personal grief from denial to acceptance prior to his last days in the hospital. The week before his death he was his usual "wise-guy" self, teasing his doctors as they drew his blood and examined him. This was the first time he met the resident physician who cared for him up until the time of his death.

The second time R. A. was seen by the resident he was critically ill. He was intermittently incoherent and appeared frightened. The father, at this time, appeared to be fully aware of the graveness of the situation. The expression on his face, as well as his words, told us his question, "This is the final replase before he dies, isn't it?" Because the parents were aware R. A. would die, that it was just a matter of time before the cancer would take his life, the resident could nod quietly in response. Often in such a situation little actually has to be said. Just the physician's presence and willingness to answer questions expresses involvement and concern to the parents. Indeed, when effectively trained, the physician may be the only individual who can emotionally tolerate listening to the family express their distress, and just being available may be helpful (24).

As was pointed out earlier, during the period of defeat when the child's death is inevitable, the parents' wishes may conflict with the physician's. The parents' wishes should be abided by, no matter how painful this is for the physician in the role of healer (10). In this case the parents did not want medical postponement of R. A.'s death. They were ready for it. Prolonging the time before R. A. died would have caused the child unnecessary suffering and created more anguish for the family.

Information gathered from a recent study (15) that centered around terminally ill neonates appears to relate to older children as well. The study suggested that parents who participated in making decisions about withdrawing supportive care from their terminally ill children enhanced the resolution of their grief. It was suggested that this might be true because helping to make the decision to terminate care provided the parents time to grieve before the child's death. Also, when physicians included parents in the decision-making process it elevated the parents' self-esteem and helped reduce their feelings of helplessness and lack of control over their child's care. That is, the family could feel like they had provided their child with the best possible care but at the same time they had protected their child from useless treatment. With these thoughts in mind, the physician should be ready to include parents in the decisions concerning the terminal care of their child when medical knowledge has nothing left to offer but comfort and support.

R. A.'s parents had a strong faith in God. This sad, sick child was no longer their fun-loving son, and they hated watching him suffer. They expressed their belief in an eternal life in heaven and felt deeply that when R. A. finally died, the loss would be theirs, not their son's. This is in sharp contrast to cases of extreme parental despair at their child's death.

Although grief is normal and unavoidable under these circumstances, there is a pathological grief, extreme in nature, which immobilizes people and prevents them from performing daily activities. This needs to be diagnosed and treated whenever possible.

Abnormal patterns the physician should look for in bereaved parents include such things as: 1) delayed reactions, when grieving doesn't take place until long periods of time after the death has occurred, 2) acute changes in the parents' behavior, including an increase in psychosomatic complaints and overactivity and, 3) abnormal social adjustment that might be characterized by hostility, isolation and, at times, frank psychosis (16, 27).

Sensitive management of the parents' grief reaction can, however, help prevent these types of problems from occurring. The physician should encourage the family to begin to resolve emotional ties with the dead child and establish new relationships. This can be accomplished by the physician encouraging the parents to verbalize their feelings and helping them understand the intense emotions they are feeling.

One of the most important concepts for the physician to remember is that oversedation of the parents at this time represses feelings and prevents them from having the opportunity to begin working through their grief immediately.

R. A.'s family had a belief structure that worked for them, that made sense out of death as well as life. And so they were able to accept R. A.'s death without feeling that death had cheated them or that God had dealt with them unfairly.

One of the things that makes death so difficult to accept in our day and age is the prevalence of agnosticism which leads us away from any system which we can use to make sense out of life and death. Whether God is perceived as the first principle or a contrivance of human beings, agnosticism offers neither rationale or relief. "As a result, that final event in our lives becomes," as Herman Feifel has said, "less and less an opening to the future and more and more a wall into which we collide." People must have some structure they can use to make sense out of life and the power of death (4).

R. A. lived for four days after he was hospitalized. Sometimes he was coherent, but most often he was comatose. He wanted his back rubbed, and he wanted to play with his toy dog. Sometimes he cried out in pain. The night before he died he cursed his family in a last expression of anger for the loss of everything he loved. The family stayed close, realizing his anger was not meant for them personally. They reassured the child and loved him. It is not known whether R. A.'s parents were counseled about the meaning of this anger or whether their sensitivity to their son was such that they understood, but their perception certainly made a difficult time a more positive experience for everyone.

In the days before his death, R. A. asked a heart-rending question, "Daddy, will I die?" His father answered, "No, son, you will be fine." This is an understandable answer to a very difficult question, and physicians do not always agree as to the approach one should take in answering it (11). It is difficult to talk to children about their own death no matter who initiates the conversation. However, children have a need to discuss their feelings relative to death. In Koocher's study (32) that included 75 healthy children from 6-15 years old, all of the children were able and willing to talk about death without any evidence of anxiety. He indicated that children less than eight years of age need simple, direct answers about death that extract as much as possible from the child's own daily life. Also, children of all ages can be helped to correct their misconceptions about death by asking them to explain back again what they have been told. This would help prevent unspoken fears and ideas of fantasy from playing upon the child's imagination.

Death should be discussed with children, particularly those who make specific inquiries. The issue should be straight forwardly addressed, and questions should be specifically answered without allowing explanations to go beyond what the child has really asked. If they are unable to discuss their feelings, they are forced to deny them and retreat into the loneliness of their personal loss, without emotional support from those they love. As was mentioned before, it is beneficial for children to be able to talk about their death and thus freely grieve the ominous and total loss it will bring (14).

After R. A.'s death the family continued to experience a great sense of loss. He was their only son and was named for his father. They took effective measures to fill the void. Family traditions were altered: When a sit-down holiday dinner was usual, they went on a picnic; for Christmas they vacationed away from home. Another way they handled their grief was to help others. They developed a book for parents of children with leukemia containing practical information explaining everything from chemotherapy to the importance of record keeping for insurance and income tax purposes. They were instrumental in obtaining a book about bereavement for other families. They continue to attend meetings for families of children with cancer. This sharing of grief by people who have been through this difficult situation has proved helpful to families who are dealing with their own personal grief.

Re-entering the world of the living after a child's death is a difficult experience. It is a help to parents if they are counseled by the physician as to what are normal grief reactions, what activities will be difficult to participate in, and generally, what pitfalls await them as they attempt individually to relate once again to each other, their other children, friends, a job and the daily tasks of living.

Functioning after the death of a child is not easy, but there are attitudes that can be learned and certain activities that can be structured to make the transition smoother. This particular family is a good example of the steps a family can take after the death of a child to resume a normal life style.

Some parents report that starting out small with essential everyday tasks helps, being sure to always complete the projects they start. The next step is to begin to enjoy some small pleasures such as buying new clothes. Then the parents must begin to restrengthen the family unit by doing something with the family members such as taking a vacation. It is good to restructure but continue holiday festivities, as R. A.'s family did. Many people also turn to creative endeavors such as writing, music or art to help them return to a normal level of functioning. Still others turn to philanthropic activities (22). All are attempts by the parents to resolve the grief they feel for their loss and to re-establish a normal life style, just as R. A.'s family did in such an effective way after his death. None of these efforts will be easy to initiate, but it is important for those who are bereaved to take some steps to restructure their lives without waiting until they feel like it. The physician can, with sensitivity, encourage the parents in this direction. Edna St. Vincent Millay captures the almost robot-like conduct that might well be necessary at such a time in her poem, "Lament:"

Listen children:
Your father is dead.
From his old coats
I'll make you little jackets . . .
Life must go on,
And the dead be forgotten;
Life must go on
Though good men die;
Anne, eat your breakfast;
Dan, take your medicine;
Life must go on;
I forget just why.

Case 5

Baby Boy R. was a premature infant who weighed 1250 grams at birth. The pregnancy was complicated by high blood pressure, edema and seizures in the mother, and the child was delivered by Caesarean section after thirty-two weeks gestation.

The baby was placed on a ventilator shortly after birth but only required minimal respiratory support initially. Over the following few days the child's condition worsened, and he required increasing ventilatory support. This worsening was thought to be secondary to a patent ductus arteriosus, and at five days of age, the child underwent surgical correction of this congenital heart disease. Although it was hoped that the child would improve after surgery, his condition continued to deteriorate. By ten days of age, the child was being treated for collapse of both lungs. This trend continued until the child had received five chest tubes to re-expand the collapsed lungs. During this time the child required maximum ventilator support with only minimal improvement in his arterial blood gases. He also experienced episodes of low blood pressure and slow heart rate.

Despite these difficult problems, the child survived to two months of age before he died.

Discussion

This case points out not only the parents', but also the physician's problems in dealing with a child who is dying. As physicians we experience grief over the loss of patients with whom we have become involved. Often we do not permit ourselves to get close to a patient because we are taught that to show emotion is to lose objectivity and so to be ineffective in taking care of our patient's medical problems. This approach, however, overlooks the physician's need as a human being to develop meaningful relationships with other human beings. It also overlooks the patient's need to relate to someone whom they can feel secure with and trust. These necessary, warm relationships cannot develop in an atmosphere of emotionless objectivity. The physician, therefore, in order to meet the total needs of the terminally ill patient, must be involved with the child in more than a superficial manner. This means that the physician will also go through the grief process when an especially close patient dies. This grief will be similar to the family's, though less intense. To be any other way would compel a physician to take an insensitive, matter-of-fact approach to patients. Physicians need to be taught how to empathize without losing perspective and how to express sorrow and grief in ways that will be supportive and sensitive to the family (25).

In this case the physician started out being emotionally distant from the patient. The more she took care of him, however, the more involved she became, even to the extent of feeling jealous of the parents' visiting privileges. Often she would sit at the bedside touching the baby or talking to him. Soon she found herself staying late in the evening and coming in on her days off to be with the baby. The bond between physician and patient grew quickly, and the physician discovered herself in a close relationship with the patient. She then found it necessary to work through the grief process herself, just as the parents were doing.

An example of bargaining was evident when the physician bought the child an outfit of clothes. On the one hand she wanted him to have the outfit in case he died so he could be buried in it. On the other hand she used the outfit as a bargaining tool, feeling that he wouldn't die if he wasn't given his burial outfit.

As the patient continued to experience major setbacks medically, the physician began to withdraw emotionally from him, knowing that his death was imminent. As described earlier, this is a common behavior during the period of defeat (10) and during the period of anticipatory mourning (14, 16). The physician went back daily to the nursery to visit the baby, but she was reluctant to increase her involvement with the family. It should be remembered, though, that during this time the parents look specifically to the physician for help. It is from the physician that they will accept explanations that will relieve their fear, guilt and anxiety, and it is with the physician that they have established a relationship of trust and confidence (36). Therefore, the physician must be careful not to withdraw so as to be difficult to be communicated with by the parents.

The other significant aspect of this case is the effect of a neonatal death on the family. Some people feel that because an infant's life is so short, there is not enough time to form a strong bond between the baby and the family. In reality, attachment to the baby usually begins when the mother feels the fetus move and when the father places his hand over the mother's abdomen and also feels the fetus move (28).

Experiencing a neonatal death is a particularly difficult situation for the parents, however, because physicians portray conflicting viewpoints to them. On one hand the parents are encouraged to bond to their baby, while on the other hand they are encouraged to withdraw from the baby in preparation for the child's death. It is necessary, though, that physicians encourage both attitudes at the appropriate time. Forming some attachment with the baby makes it easier for parents to work through their grief (37) as does preparing the parents for the child's death and encouraging anticipatory mourning and detachment before the child actually dies (15).

In this case, the parents were both in their mid-teens. The father worked as a logger, and the couple lived with the mother's family. Early on in the child's care, the mother asked all the questions and held the baby, while the father supported the mother emotionally. As the mother became physically stronger post-delivery, she assumed a stronger role with the baby, and the father retreated to the background, visiting less frequently, reading a book during visiting hours, and leaving all phone communication with the nursery up to the mother. The father also started drinking heavily during this period of time. This retreat of the father is not an uncommon happening in families with fatally ill children. Often the mother becomes the one involved with the sick child and displaces the father who is then viewed as disappearing into the background of the child's care (33).

Because of the importance society and the medical profession place on the maternal-infant relationship, it is not surprising to see a devaluation of the father's role relative to the dying child. Only recently have investigators begun to explore the father-child relationship and the responses of the father to the sudden loss of his child. In one study (38) fathers of infants who died suddenly were evaluated for the way they responded to grief. Certain patterns of behavior common to these men included the need for increasing amounts of work to keep busy, feelings of diminished self worth, guilt over not being more involved in the child's care, and an inability to ask for help. It was not clear whether this inability to ask for help was because of the father's inadequacy or because of the physician's inability to recognize the father's need to talk. Sometimes these types of paternal behavior are unknowingly encouraged by physicians who try to help the father fulfill society's expectations of masculinity. Physicians should be aware of these problems and provide the opportunity for fathers of dying children to verbalize their feelings so they can constructively utilize support.

As the weeks passed, the family was warned daily of the baby's impending death by being given increasingly poor reports relative to his prognosis. This gave them some time to begin working through their grief.

CONCLUSION

When the physician attempts to meet some of the psychological needs of dying patients and their families, it places that individual in the dual role of doctor and counselor. Because of the relationships of trust involved and the characteristic respect held for the physician as the "last word," as well as because of the need to resolve personal disquiet, it is important for the physician to be as aware as possible of the most effective steps to take to meet the complex set of needs presented by the death of young patients.

Sometimes physicians hesitate to be involved with their dying patients in any capacity other than to treat their medical problems. This hesitation stems, at times, from a conviction that counseling the patient, developing a relationship of open communication in regards to the serious matters of life, is not the physician's role. Other physicians realize that this kind of relationship with a patient will require a certain amount of time and emotional investment and are unwilling or unable to make that kind of commitment to their patient. Then there are many physicians who simply feel inadequate to deal with the needs of their dying patients.

Feelings of inadequacy can be produced by a lack of training in the area of death counseling. With training in this area only recently becoming a priority, it is not surprising that in the majority of cases which we examined, the physician felt a keen sense of inadequacy in dealing with the dying patient and the family. However, no matter what classes may or may not be available in a particular medical school curriculum in regards to formal death education, there are seminars, meetings and books that can be taken advantage of by physicians who are interested in learning about the subject of death. The bibliography at the end of this chapter provides a list of some contemporary work that has been done in this area. However, no matter how many seminars or classes physicians participate in, these will be of little use if they have not resolved their own ambivalence toward death.

The way the physician responds to death and deals with personal feelings will affect how the family and the patient respond to death. In 1917, Freud said that grief is not pathologic. Grief is a normal process that "cushions the impact of the loss and leads toward an acceptance of what has happened" (19). If the physician wants to play a supportive role with the child and the parents, the normalcy of the grief process must be recognized, and acceptance must be the goal.

Finally, the physician must be able to accept that medical science has its limitations. There comes a time when those limitations have been reached, and there is nothing else that can be done for the dying child. At this point, in order for the physician to begin to deal with personal feelings of defeat about the child's death, that limitation must be accepted.

For every matter has its time and way, although man's trouble lies heavy upon him. For he does not know what is to be, for who can tell him how it will be? No man has power to retain the spirit, or authority over the day of death; there is no discharge from that war . . . (Ecclesiastes 8:6-8(RSV))

REFERENCES

1. Easson, W. M. The Family of the Dying Child. *Pediatr. Clin. North Am.* 19(4):1157–1165, 1972.
2. Schowalter, J. E. The Reaction of Caregivers Dealing with Fatally Ill Children and Their Families. In Sahler, Olle Jane Z. (ed.), *The Child and Death.* St. Louis: Mosby, 123–138, 1978.
3. Simpson, M. A. Social and Psychological Aspects of Dying. In Wass, H. (ed.), *Dying: Facing the Facts.* Washington: Hemisphere, 108–136, 1979.
4. Corr, C. A. Reconstructing the Changing Face of Death. In Wass, H. (ed.), *Dying: Facing the Facts.* Washington: Hemisphere, 5–43, 1979.
5. Paykel, E. S., McGuiness, B., & Gomez, J. An Anglo-American Comparison of the Scaling of Life Events. *Br. J. Med. Psychol.* 49:237–247, 1976.
6. Mauksch, H. O. The Organizational Context of Dying. In Kübler-Ross, E. (ed.), *Death: The Final Stage of Growth.* Englewood Cliffs: Prentice-Hall, Inc., 7–24, 1975.
7. Dickinson, G. E. Death Education in U.S. Medical Schools. *J. Med. Educ.* 51(2):134–136, 1976.
8. Kahn, G. S., Cohen, B., & Jason, H. The Teaching of Interpersonal Skills in U.S. Medical Schools. *J. Med. Educ.* 54(1):29–35, 1979.
9. Swain, H. L. Childhood Views of Death. *Death Educ.* 2(4):341–358, 1979.
10. Schowalter, J. E. Death and the Pediatric House Officer. *J. Pediatr.* 76(5):706–710, 1970.
11. Evans, A. E. & Edin, S. If a Child Must Die . . . *N. Eng. J. Med.* 278(3):138–142, 1968.
12. Pattison, E. M. *The Experience of Dying.* Englewood Cliffs: Prentice-Hall, 1977.
13. Rodabough, T. Alternatives to the Stages Model of the Dying Process. *Death Educ.* 4(1):1–19, 1980.
14. Kübler-Ross, E. *On Death and Dying.* New York: Macmillan, 1969.
15. Stillion, J. & Wass, H. Children and Death. In Wass, H. (ed.), *Dying: Facing the Facts.* Washington: Hemisphere, 208–235, 1979.
16. Benfield, D. G., Leib, S. A., & Vollman, J. H. Grief Response of Parents to Neonatal Death and Parent Participation in Deciding Care. *Pediatrics.* 62(2):171–177, 1978.
17. Lindemann, E. Symptomatology and Management of Acute Grief. *Am. J. Psychiatry.* 101:141–148, 1944.
18. Epstein, G., Weitz, L., Roback, H., & McKee, E. Research on Bereavement: A Selective and Critical Review. *Compr. Psychiatry.* 16(6):537–546, 1975.
19. Gilson, G. J. Care of the Family Who Has Lost a Newborn. *Postgrad. Med.* 60(6):67–70, 1976.
20. Grobstein, R. The Effect of Neonatal Death on the Family. In Sahler, O. J. Z. (ed.), *The Child and Death.* St. Louis: Mosby, 92–99, 1978.
21. Seitz, P. M. & Warrick, L. H. Perinatal Death; the Grieving Mother. *Am. J. Nurs.* 74(11):2028–2033, 1974.

22. Lewis, E. & Page, A. Failure to Mourn a Stillborn: An Overlooked Catastrophe. *Br. J. Med. Psychol.* 51:237–241, 1978.
23. Schiff, H. S. *The Bereaved Parent.* New York: Crown, 1977.
24. Grollman, E. A. *Talking About Death.* Boston: Beacon, 1976.
25. Friedman, S. B. Psychological Aspects of Sudden Unexpected Death in Infants and Children. *Pediatr. Clin. North Am.* 21(1):103–111, 1974.
26. Solnit, A. J. & Green, M. Psychological Considerations in the Management of Deaths on Pediatric Hospital Services. *Pediatrics.* 24(1):106–112, 1959.
27. Weston, D. L. & Irwin, R. C. Preschool Child's Response to Death of Infant Sibling. *Am. J. Dis. Child.* 106(6):564–567, 1963.
28. Dubin, W. R. & Wolman, T. Evaluation and Management of the Grief Reaction. *Pennsylvania Medicine.* 82(7):19–22, 1979.
29. Kennell, J. H., Slyter, H., & Klaus, M. H. The Mourning Response of Parents to the Death of a Newborn Infant. *N. Eng. J. Med.* 283(7):344–349, 1970.
30. Rowe, J. Clyman, R., Green, C. Mikkelsen, C., Haight, J., & Ataide, L. Follow-up of Families who Experience a Perinatal Death. *Pediatrics,* 62(2):166–170, 1978.
31. Spinetta, J. J., Rigler, D., & Karon, M. Personal Space as a Measure of a Dying Child's Sense of Isolation. *J. Consult. Clin. Psychol.* 42(6):751–756, 1974.
32. Hostler, S. L. The Development of the Child's Concept of Death. *In Sahler, O. J. Z. (ed), The Child and Death.* St. Louis: Mosby, 1–25, 1978.
33. Koocher, G. P. Talking with Children about Death. *Am. J. Orthopsychiatry.* 44(3):404–411, 1974.
34. Sanger, S. Honesty and Sensitivity in Managing Emotional Problems of the Child with Cancer. In Pochedly, C. (ed.), *Pediatric Cancer Therapy.* Baltimore: University Park Press, 275–290, 1979.
35. Woolsey, S. F., Thornton, D. S., & Friedman, S. B. Sudden Death. In Sahler, O. J. Z. (ed.), *The Child and Death.* St. Louis: Mosby, 100–112, 1978.
36. Foley, G. V. & McCarthy, A. M. The Child with Leukemia in a Special Hematology Clinic. *Am. J. Nurs.* 76(7):1115–1119, 1976.
37. Feifel, H. (ed.), *New Meanings of Death.* New York: McGraw-Hill, 4, 1977.
38. Morris, D. Parental Reactions to Perinatal Death. *Proc. R. Soc. Med. (London).* 69:837–838, 1976.
39. Adolf, A. & Patt, R. Neonatal Death: The Family is the Patient. *J. Fam. Prac.* 10(2):317–321, 1980.
40. Mandell, F., McAnulty, E., & Reece, R. M. Observations of Paternal Response to Sudden Unanticipated Infant Death. *Pediatrics.* 65(2):221–224, 1980.
41. Lansky, S. B. et al. Childhood Cancer and Parental Discord. *Pediatrics.* 62(2):184–188, 1978.

5

Helping the Dying Child

Practical Approaches for Nonphysicians

David W. Adams

INTRODUCTION

There is nothing more difficult for hospital staff than working with a child who is dying. In childhood cancer and other chronic and debilitating diseases, the child has often struggled through periods of remission and relapse and endured intense medical treatment complete with nausea, vomiting and physical changes before reaching a terminal care period. Many of the behaviors of the dying child and his or her family are repetitions of responses which have been learned during the course of the illness. Caregivers are thus faced not only with the challenge of providing excellent physical care but also with the need to understand the child and those who love him. This understanding must encompass knowledge of the child and his family, cultural and religious influences, the history of the treatment process, the dying child's developmental staging and the nature of the adaptation of both the child and family. This chapter will briefly examine these areas, discuss the behavior of the dying child and focus both on the impact of this behavior on us and on ways we can help the child. A brief section on home versus hospital care is included and the chapter closes with some issues to contemplate. It is important to stress that although this chapter focusses on the child with terminal cancer, there are many parallels which apply to children dying of heart disease, cystic fibrosis and other chronic diseases.

UNDERSTANDING THE DYING CHILD

The Family

Childhood cancer from the point of diagnosis on generates tremendous anxiety. Parents, time after time, refer to the diagnostic label as a death sentence for their child even though recent medical advances offer much more hope (1, 2). Despite the fact that the illness process creates an anticipatory grieving process complete with feelings of sadness, anxiety, anger and needs to deny, to seek information, to gain emotional support and even to rehearse the child's death, grounds for hope provide an aura of expectation that the child may survive (1, 3, 4). When the family's hopes are dashed by one or more relapses, the emotional impact is intense. As time elapses and treatment becomes less and less effective, the anticipatory grieving process intensifies. The child as a part of the process feels the change, knows about the change, and depending on age, will have some degree of conscious understanding of what it means (1, 5-7). Members of the family are the child's prime supporters and the major source of love, guidance and caring. When we encounter the child who is dying, we as part of a hospital team, must discern where the parents and other family members are in their cycle of adaptation to the illness, how much and in what way they support their child emotionally, how they communicate, and what their expectations are for terminal care. In addition, we must assess how much they can endure in the dying process.

Basic knowledge about the child's place in his family and how he is cared for may be obtained by the social worker, nurse clinician, or other staff with a primary interest in psychosocial care (1). In addition, use of the information gained from continuous contact can be of value to the total team in both outpatient and in-patient areas. To this information, we must add our knowledge of other key factors which affect children. These factors include the child's prognosis, the degree of involvement of parents in the care of the child during hospitalization, the existence of social problems, previous coping patterns of the family during crises, the family communication pattern and the amount of emotional support the family currently receives from the extended family and friends.

In his study in the mid-1960s Hamovitch found that the poorer the prognosis, the more difficulty families had in coping with the illness experience. He also found that the participation of parents in the care of their fatally ill child was a positive experience for both parent and child when the parents were able to do so with moderation. By participating, the parents could remain involved with the sick child and feel useful. When they could do so and still attend to the management of other children in the family and the problems of daily living at home, they avoided the problems experienced when parents left all of the care to hospital staff or became so involved that they were in conflict with nursing staff and smothered the child emotionally. Hamovitch also found that the existence of social problems such as alcoholism and difficulties in coping with past life crises inhibited a family's ability to cope with a fatal illness (8). In the writer's experience, most of Hamovitch's findings have been re-confirmed in clinical practice as have the work of Spinetta and his colleagues. Spinetta, in studying children ages 6 to 10 suffering from leukemia, found that in families who communicated openly with their child, the child was able to communicate both happy and painful feelings and anxieties and was thus able to cope effectively with both pleasant and unpleasant illness events. In such families, the child was able to be nondefensive, close to parents, content with himself or herself and able to express both negative and positive feelings within the family (6, 7).

In practical terms, the writer, like Hamovitch and Spinetta, believes that parental adjustment is the key to understanding how the child and family will cope. This is exemplified further by Townes and Wold in their study of siblings. They showed that the poorest adjustment of siblings occurred in families where there was little communication from the mother about the disease (9). Hamovitch's finding that single parents and parents who had experienced previous marriages had the greatest difficulty adapting to the stress of a child's illness and death also reinforces this belief (8). Indeed, the writer has found that one of the greatest problems in parental adaptation occurs with the single parent who often lacks emotional support from a partner, has socioeconomic problems and depends on the sick child for emotional support (1).

There is no doubt that in families where parents communicate openly, support each other emotionally, and have friends and relatives who care about them, the dying child has the best chance of receiving the warmth, security and healthy dependence required to face the death experience with minimal intervention from hospital staff.

Cultural Influences

Although it is virtually impossible to reflect in depth on a variety of cultural systems and how they affect the child, it is important to note that ethnic background and associated family behaviors have a marked influence on a child's adjustment. For example, the "stiff upper lip" behavior of some Anglo Saxon parents can dictate a closed communication pattern which is difficult for the child (10). Some Latin American and European cultures reinforce the need to pity the sick child and pity the mother. This leads to widespread grieving prior to death which can have a negative impact on a child by providing a funeral-like atmosphere. Such behavior can create problems in setting limits for the child's behavior and problems of overabundances of visitors and gifts which in turn can upset the child, the siblings and the hospital staff. Other cultures, like the Dutch Calvinist, have a closed family system in which the family is tied to the community and religion along with the emotional supports provided therein. This is often very positive and the child receives excellent family support but it can create a problem if the child's expression of feelings is inhibited.

In addition to the family and its cultural background, the child is part of the cultural setting provided by school and peers. The school represents the workplace for the child complete with achievements, failures, discipline, socialization and most important, a sense of belonging. For the dying child there is a need to be part of the class, to maintain contact with the teacher and to keep active as long as possible. Peers at school, in the neighborhood and in other settings, fulfill the child's need to be part of the group, to be recognized and to be seen as being just like other children. Terry, age 7, was a case in point. About 10 days prior to his death from leukemia, he had problems running and playing T-ball (a type of baseball); so, his father carried him to the ballfield where he still played as part of his team, striving to be like other children. A couple of days before his death, he insisted on being discharged from the inpatient unit to go to his class picnic.

In the hospital, a dying child's need to be connected to the outside world and friends there, remains. When this is not possible, a substitute culture with children his own age can partially meet the need. The inpatients' school, for example, frequently provides a bridge for the child to continue his schoolwork and socialize as well. Parties for children on the inpatient unit can also facilitate much needed socialization, generate new friendships and provide necessary and satisfying diversion.

Treatment Process and Disease

When the child with cancer has been ill for some time, a pattern of response has often been established which, apart from family support, is influenced very much by the means of administration of chemotherapy, the number of invasive procedures, the clinical setting including emotional supports provided, and the nature of the disease process. The negative impact of the illness process is illustrated by

Dafoe, in her study of hair loss of children ages 7 to 15. She found that the child's self-concept changes negatively after hair loss and that self-concept scores were lower for children who had relapsed. In addition, 82 percent said they were sick a lot, none indicated they were leaders in games and 64 percent said that they wanted to work on their own. This contrasted to a normal control group of whom none said they were sick a lot, 57 percent said they were leaders, and none wanted to work alone (1). Goggin and her colleagues found that children with malignancy tended to be more upset by strong emotional stimulation and more unrealistic in their thinking than normal children (11). Waechter found that the general anxiety level of children ages 6 to 9 with malignancy was twice that of normal children, even though only one-eighth apparently knew their diagnosis (12). Spinetta found that children with leukemia were much more anxious about bodily intrusion and aware of their illness than children who were normal or suffering from long-term chronic diseases (7).

In the writer's experience, this level of concern is demonstrated by Susie, age 11, who had leukemia, relapsed and was so fed-up with injections into her arms that she screamed and screamed. When the doctor told her that he would give the injections into her leg, she protested violently as she couldn't stand the idea that that part of her body would be mutilated as well. A day or two later, her parents observed her tying wool around her legs to imitate a tourniquet in order to get used to the idea that it was going to be necessary for the physician to use her legs. On her next visit, she complied. Another child, Roberta, age 11, asked why God must punish her and complained bitterly of needles. When approached about her questions of punishment, she turned up the radio to avoid discussing her feelings. Patricia, age 2, after experiencing many painful injections, would come into the clinic and upon seeing the dolls and syringes in the playroom would say "Ouch, Ouch." and poke the dolls numerous times. As these brief examples illustrate, the illness experience taxes the child regardless of age. As death approaches the accumulated impact of emotional trauma must be recognized and means provided to help each individual child. A more detailed discussion of the feelings and needs of dying children takes place in the sections which follow.

Developmental Staging and Anticipatory Grief

Although age-related responses are never cut and dried, there are some guideposts that can help us understand the child's response to illness and death. Both the child's awareness and beliefs about death, and the child's anxiety about life-threatening illnesses are linked. These factors are discussed briefly here and are dealt with in greater detail in another chapter in this book.

For the young child, from ages 3 to 5 or 6, death is an event which happens to someone else and is mixed in with fantasy life. A dead body can eat, sleep, see and move around. Death is associated with darkness, with being killed and with irrational objects or events so that wishes may not be distinguished from facts (6, 13-17). For example, Carol, age 5, whose sister was terminally ill was afraid her sister was going to die. She was petrified that death was going to hurt her sister a lot because death was like a train crash. In this age range as well, death tends to be mixed up with good and bad and with anxieties about aggression and retribution (6, 13-17). When children's lives are threatened by disease their major concern is the fear of being separated from their mother, and children readily sense and incorporate their mother's anxiety into their own worries (8). Morrisey in his study of leukemic children, noted that the youngest children frequently converted their anxiety into somatic disturbances and symbolism (18). Although the child may only manifest his fears of separation, other thoughts and fears such as those related to death can be integrated into the frightening process of hospitalization and illness.

As children grow older a transition takes place at approximately age 7, which parallels the development of rational thought processes. As children move away from the simple thinking of earlier ages, they begin to see death as relevant to their own bodies. Mutilation anxiety partially supplants fears of separation from mother and death anxiety tends to be channelled to fantasy life complete with wars and heroes (13, 14, 17). The child begins to sort out the meaning of heaven, of a possible life after death, and may become more covert about beliefs in magic and symbols. In her studies of fatally ill children, ages 6 to 10, Waechter found that they were isolated, lonely and preoccupied with death in fantasy, even though it was not expressed overtly (12). Spinetta and his colleagues support Waechter's findings and conclude that hospital-related and non-hospital-related anxiety was higher in children with leukemia than in children with long term chronic disorders (6, 7). They also suggest that despite attempts to keep the children with leukemia from knowing their prognosis, these children perceive that the illness is extremely serious and life-threatening. Children certainly realize that they have no ordinary disease (7).

Other studies of anxiety by Nagy (15), and Morrisey (18) and other researchers have shown that sick children ages 6 to 9 suffer from mutilation anxiety to the extent that they respond more severely than younger children to invasive procedures and to bodily changes such as hair loss and bloating. McCollum points out that a child may think of the skin as a wrapping and if it is slit, his insides may pour out (19). The writer has seen children worry about being drained dry by hemorrhage and be super-sensitive to the care of a surgical scar for fear of what would happen if it should open up.

As children grow closer to age 9 or 10 the universality of death and inevitability of their own death becomes a harsh reality (13, 14, 17). In the pre-teens and teens, death becomes the personal devastation of life's goals and dying a threat to independence, bodily integrity, sexual prowess and loss of friends and family (1, 17, 20, 21). For fatally ill children as Knudson and Natterson found in their study, death anxiety pervades at age 10 and beyond (5). As death approaches the fears of separation, of mutilation and blending of fantasy and reality all creep back into the thoughts and feelings of the dying adolescent, giving rise to the recognition that there is a cumulative effect of life experience as part of the process of anticipatory grief.

When we reflect on the importance of age as described above, we can readily understand why parents and hospital staff must struggle to find the most effective ways to care for dying children. The fears of separation of early childhood, later mixed with fantasy and feelings of retribution and omnipotence, succeeded by fears of mutilation and secretive anxieties about personal death, eventually replaced by the realization of universality and goal destruction, make the range of anticipative behaviors and problems assume major proportions. For example, it is no wonder that we question how much to tell a dying child about his or her illness, particularly the child at ages 7 to 10, because he or she has started to reason, to decipher the cues given by staff and family and to behave secretly, privately, and at times, quite independently. How do you keep a dying child from being alone and isolated?

THE BEHAVIOR OF THE DYING CHILD

As death becomes imminent the intensity of medical care and the likelihood of hospitalization increases. Intensification of medical care accelerates the child's fear of invasive procedures as final medical attempts to control disease and eventually to provide palliation are implemented. The blood transfusions used in the terminal period of leukemia or the chemotherapeutic agents which attack cancer cells, administered parenterally and used to reduce pain, can become overwhelming and intolerable. Fears of separation naturally precipitated by hospitalization may be increased by the child's physical deterioration and regression. Anxiety communicated by parents worried about their child's pain and how death will come can heighten the child's anxiety. Changes in their parents' behavior such as avoidance of visits to hospital or open demonstrations of sorrow can add to the child's uncertainty and enhance fears (1, 13).

As part of the hospital, those around the child also influence him. Staff and other patients assume new and greater importance. Vernick in his work on a cancer ward found that children ages 9 to 19 were concerned about their illness and the deaths of other children (22). In the writer's experience, Albert, age 12, and Anna, age 11, illustrated this concern when Paula, age 11, died. All three were cancer patients who knew each other in clinic. Albert was also terminally ill and was hospitalized during the same period but allowed to return home and come back for clinic visits. The return trips became upsetting for him because he had to pass the farm where Paula had lived. Anna, a patient in remission but with a very guarded prognosis, was tearful at Paula's death, became increasingly anxious about dying, began vomiting more and more during chemotherapy and experienced new behavior difficulties at school. She also became upset by Albert's physical appearance as medication had precipitated alopecia and his disease caused a severe ptosis leading to closure of one eye.

Children, like adults, experience not only anxiety about what is happening to them, but have a need to express anger, have a right to feel sad and will inevitably want to deny their illness and accompanying losses. The dying child may panic and use other emergency measures to cope with oppressive feelings. Defense mechanisms such as regression, rebellion, withdrawal, displacement, somatization and compensation are natural common measures the child invokes as a means of protection (1, 3, 6, 7, 13, 16, 17).

As hospital staff we face the challenge not only of understanding the dying child but also of helping the child cope with distress and what can be a devastating demise. The following section examines how nurses and other staff are affected by the dying child and how meeting the child's needs can provide the key to help us meet the challenge.

The Impact on Hospital Staff

The Nurse

When we interact with dying children and their families we experience a continuing and draining impact on our own emotional resources. For nurses, in particular, the challenge of relating to the dying child poses a major problem. This problem is related to the close alliance the nurse has with the values of the medical profession, to the role expectations others hold for the nurse and the social and emotional needs of the dying child which inevitably go beyond requirements for adequate physical care (23). In addition, nurses are the providers of care during the evening and night hours when anxiety of parent and child frequently rises (24).

Nurses, like physicians, expect to help patients experience hospitalization and recover. Many value the helping role and receive some intangible rewards from seeing patients recover and return to regular life practices. Death, particularly death of a child, is often upsetting and very taxing. As one staff member observed recently, at times of crisis some nurses must escape, get off the ward, find relief and perhaps temporary solace away from the strain of caring for sick and dying children. As in other staff, the proximity of death makes anxiety, guilt and anger surface in nurses. It is hard when you identify certain characteristics of the dying child with your own children, when you feel awkward when you are met with silence or hostility accorded by a child or parent or both because you are the new nurse or when you are frustrated because you can do so little to help and feel guilty about your ineffectiveness. The dilemma of prolonging agony which you would like to see end peacefully, the natural tendency to vent or direct hostility toward the physician who failed, the parent who interferes and even the child, who fails to cooperate, are all there. Some writers have observed that nurses and other staff avoid the dying patient (13, 23). It is certainly the most natural response to anxiety, albeit, of the least benefit to the dying child.

Parents and other hospital staff expect nurses to be able to cope, to care for the physical needs and to be warm and loving irregardless of the nurses' own emotions. It is no wonder then that avoidance creeps in or that hospital routine can be used at times as an excuse for attending solely to physical care. In the writer's observations, perhaps the greatest difficulty for nurses on an acute care ward is the necessity that they change gears suddenly, shifting from the need to help one child recover from an initial operation or transient illness, and accepting the dying child's needs for palliative care. This demands different goals and values as well as changes in the processes of care of the dying child and the family. Some nurses exemplify the problem of these new demands when they fail to recognize that medication must be given regularly to break the pain cycle. Even though a child is dying, nurses have expressed anxiety about addiction to pain-killing medication or about waking the child in order to administer medication which is required to keep the pain controlled.

When nurses are faced with a dying child, there are other factors which inevitably influence behavior. Traditionally, nurses are expected to be busy, to do procedures, to keep moving and to maintain nursing care of their patients. The reality of today, including pressure on hospital staff, often means that nurses are very busy and many hospitals limit staff severely. When this happens, there is a strong tendency for nursing practice to revert to procedural care and administrative as opposed to bedside nursing. Values on being busy and "doing" increase in such systems; time for sitting, talking, reading or playing with children become frills. The system negates not only the nurses' ability to relate to the dying child but also inhibits the nurse from gaining valuable knowledge about what the child thinks and feels. As one non-nursing staff pointed out recently, nurses do not play with the children when they are feeling good or have time to visit with them in their happier times, such as in the outpatient areas or inpatient playrooms. Nurses tend to see the children in their rooms when they are feeling rotten and for one reason or another, cannot interact with children who are up and about. Perhaps nurses feel most comfortable with this role because they must do something for the child. Even though they may not know a child really well and have little positive relationship experiences to draw on, at least their role is clear. Indeed, this may be the case and nurses feel less guilty if they are with the sick doing what they are supposed to do.

Other Hospital Staff

All staff who interact with the dying child are affected whether they are child life workers,* social workers, physiotherapists, school teachers, ward clerks, ward maids or other staff. The nurse simply exemplifies some of the behavior we all exhibit and portrays feelings that each of us has. We all have to guard against natural tendencies to meet our own needs. Perhaps it is keeping the patient captive in hospital longer than necessary, or adding to the gifts a child accumulates as part of the terminal period. As a social worker and team member, the writer has personally had to grapple with feelings of inadequacy at being unable to do something concrete to change a situation and has had to cope with the realization that anger associated with a dying child was displaced in some other form or to recognize than an overwhelming but passing feelings of sadness could be traced back to the death of a child. One child life staff member pointed out that she was less identified with medical values than the nurses or the writer, but that she felt the loss of the children because she had become attached to them. She found solace in good times spent in play relationships when the child was not in pain or semiconscious.

For each of us, there is also the need to avoid being entrapped by taking either the negative feelings of a dying child or parent personally. Although parents may be first in line to receive the brunt of the child's frustration, the staff and particularly, the nurses, are likely candidates. By the same token, fatigued parents displace and project anger onto hospital staff and it is taxing at times not to feel and express hostility in return (1, 5). If piqued sufficiently, it is even possible that staff may retaliate at the expense of both parent and child, even though such retaliation may not be rendered consciously.

As staff, we are also threatened in other ways. For example, at times it is hard not just for nurses, but for all of us, to relinquish care to a parent even though such care may benefit not only the child but the parents as well. A classic example occurred when a mother stood in front of a laboratory technician and a resident and said "No more, my child has had enough." She refused tests and further examinations and allowed only regular nursing care during the three days remaining in her child's life. Sometimes such behavior is needed. Even though it is important for us in hospital to maintain control of care, there are times when others must stand up for the rights of the child and help us recognize when we cease to be of value.

Pattison points out in his work with the dying, that he has learned that his own anxieties remain close to the surface (25). Encounters with dying children reawaken our own unresolved grief experience and generate new or reborn anxieties about our own ability to survive. This includes renewed recognition that we are vulnerable

---

*Child life workers are concerned about the "quality of life" of patients and have a "normative" view of child behavior. Their role includes child assessment and therapeutic play activity.

and will die as well. To work with dying children necessitates that we work through our own death—at least to have internally debated the issues involved and found some partial resolutions and comforts. By so doing, we gain at least some surface feelings of mastery and through new encounters with death, are able to cope more effectively ourselves and hopefully help others face death (13, 26).

When we reflect on our own experiences and our attempts to gain solace from the emotional wounds inflicted by past deaths, we can empathize with the panic of the young nurse or resident. The desperate struggle which surfaces in persons new to this work simply mirrors some conflicts which continue and are experienced at a deeper level by regular staff. In reality, each of us can identify with the nurse who at the time when death comes, feels wanted, is required to carry out valued procedures, and gains some fleeting freedom from the taxing job of meeting the emotional demands of the dying child.

MEETING THE NEEDS OF THE DYING CHILD

In reviewing the needs of children, Raths points out that a child needs love, a sense of belonging, a feeling of self-respect, an understanding of self, continuance of achievement and freedom from deep-seated feelings of guilt and fear (27). For the dying child, these needs are also appropriate especially when we add the need to feel secure and free from pain. For us, as hospital staff, the meeting of these needs encompasses a range of behaviors which can help the dying child through the terminal period.

Love and Security with Freedom from Pain

There is no need more fundamental than the need to be loved and to feel secure. For the young child the symbol of love and security is his or her mother. If we are to care for young children we must encourage and help administrative personnel value incorporation of help from the parent(s) into the child's care. For children under 5 and even up to 10 and beyond, hospital staff are poor substitutes for parents. Facilitating the mother's remaining with her child means that love and security can be readily provided. It is appalling to realize that there are still hospitals where the parent is sent away, particularly when we consider the emotional and physical strain which the dying child faces.

Helping the young child through the period of approaching death can be a very trying experience. When children are feeling ill and their sphere of activity is restricted, coping resources diminish as well. The world narrows down to the person who is closest—usually the mother or her substitute, or at times, a staff member or volunteer. This proximity not only taxes the loving or caring person, but readily develops into a type of symbiotic relationship which allows neither parent nor child freedom to relate to anyone else (1). This process makes a mother feel guilty about any type of abandonment of her child and results in intense fatigue of both parent and child. For the child and the nursing staff, the results can be equally crippling and can result in intense crying episodes and the child's withdrawal. At the hospital where the writer is based, the open visiting policy for parents and the addition of child life staff members who are geared to working with all ages of children who have all manner of disabilities or illnesses, have provided a much needed patient care dimension. Child life workers aid nursing staff by providing diversional and comforting activity, thus facilitating a break in an intensively difficult time when a parent or parents are not present. When parents are involved in the care of their child, diversional relief for them can facilitate a valuable change for the child and allows mother to eat, groom herself and perhaps go home for a few hours. Volunteers working under staff supervision can be extremely valuable as well. Often when parents remove themselves from the room, the child adapts to the new person quite readily.

As a major part of our contribution as staff members, we must recognize the benefits of a close relationship with the child. At the writer's home hospital, the ambulatory care staff continues to relate to the dying child during hospitalization. Continuing relationships with child life staff members and nurses, in particular, are invaluable because a degree of familiarity and trust which has already been established through time can be renewed and continued. Coupled with this relationship with ambulatory care staff, is the need for inpatient nurses to narrow the number of nursing staff who care for the dying child. Time after time, it has been observed that the child will identify with the most loving and caring staff members and relate to them regardless of age. The benefits of having the same social worker work with children with cancer should also be underscored as this leads to a continuing trust with parents and other family members including the dying child. This relationship can be invaluable when care becomes difficult on the ward.

In reflecting upon how a staff member can demonstrate love and care beyond providing for physical needs, one child life staff member said that it helps to think about the person or persons you remember who were kind and loving to you as a child and incorporate what you can into your approach. Loving and caring can be demonstrated simply by offering time to the child. Reading stories, talking and listening to music can be conducive to establishing relationships. When a child is suffering, the most valuable contribution given by staff members may be holding or stroking a child's hand or, as one colleague described it, offering a ministry of presence. How important it is for those who must perform procedures which hurt the dying child to find time to relate to the child as a person!

As part of the process of providing security comes the recognition that children need limits which clearly delineate behavioral boundaries. When children are seriously ill they still have the need to know where they stand and expect that some kind of rules and regulations will provide them with guidance. Those of us who have dealt with adolescent patients recognize that the need continues right into adulthood. As hospital staff we can play an important role in both recognizing the child's need for limits and in helping parents and ward staff provide them. In the writer's experience, one situation illustrates this need extremely well. Larry, age 5, had endured a lengthy illness from leukemia and his parents were extremely fatigued and uncertain about how to behave toward him as he was becoming increasingly irritable and demanding. Larry had begun to swear loudly and commanded that everyone do as he said. One day he even had his uncle waiting at the elevator for an hour to watch for his parents. Larry's dying had changed his parents' behavior so much that they were afraid to set rules and provide discipline. A session focussed on Larry's need for structure and security, his need for some discipline regarding appropriate language, and the implementation of other diversions directed toward helping him release his anger and frustration helped the parents renew their roles. The change in them effected a positive change in their son. The participation of parents in such limit setting offers reassurance of at least some degree of normality for the child. This reassurance helps provide much needed security and facilitates participation in much needed social relationships.

Along with this need for love and security must come the need for freedom from *pain*. Although there is considerable evidence pointing to the need to evaluate and understand its meaning to the child and family, there is also a need to control pain and where feasible to prevent it. The experience of pain and the behavior related to pain is amplified by cultural beliefs, by learning and by the physical and emotional state of children and their parents (10, 28). In the writer's experience, the commonest concern of parents is how a child will die—will my child be in pain? A few months ago, the writer was confronted by three mothers who were clustered in a corner of the waiting and play area discussing the recent death of a child. Each wanted to know if the child had suffered greatly and were comforted when they found she had not. For staff members, measures of pain control mean the need to give medications regularly and provide sensitive and sensible physical care. For nurses in particular, pain control signifies as well the need to use their resourcefulness in harmony with parents to comfort the child. Even a warm bath, gentle rubs, warm milk, a familiar story, clean sheets and good mouth care may make the difference to a child in pain (28-30). Experience at the writer's hospital suggests that parents take their behavioral cues from the child and vice versa. When pain is relieved and the child settles down, the parent or parents rest as well and what can be a difficult, and at times, a destructive anxiety-pain-anxiety cycle can be temporarily broken. In addition, even when pain is continuous children appear to have pain-free periods which allow them brief and often happy times (29, 30). These times can be a positive morale booster for the child, the parents and the staff members.

A Sense of Belonging

After a period of illness and gradual deterioration, hospitalization can be very isolating. Dying children frequently have an intense need to hang onto the relationship with school and neighborhood friends as long as they are able to do so. For example, one 9-year-old insisted on going to school and participating in a parade even though his knees gave out and he had to be carried by his teacher. In the writer's experience, this desire has often been related to a need to return at least briefly to school or to be part of a ball game or partake of some social event. As a child becomes sicker, however, continuance may become limited or impossible. Our treatment of the dying child in the hospital milieu and our sensitivity to the child's need for association with peers, albeit limited at times due to illness, is extremely important. It helps if we keep in mind that special measures like isolation techniques designed to protect the child from infection may be extremely punitive. For example, 11-year-old Donna pointed out that by being isolated she was being doubly punished. She felt illness was a type of punishment and that being isolated compounded it. Not only did she believe that God was punishing her but the doctors and nurses were trying to make her suffer as well.

A feeling of belonging does not simply mean association with other children but receipt of rights which accompany belonging. Often these rights are in keeping with sensible rules. If dying children are well enough, inclusion in events like planning a ward party, seeing films, making cookies, or by going to the playroom can all facilitate the feeling of belonging. Staff must recognize, however, that participation of dying children may be very limited and that they may become easily fatigued and require rest periods. Socialization in teen groups who listen to records, or make things, or help other children on the ward, all contribute to a feeling of being part of the ward process (31). Where suitable, dying children should be included.

Participation in ward events and a feeling of belonging also provide children with some sense of control of their own being and provide the child with an opportunity to be mobile. Being back in circulation when children are feeling well enough to be out of their rooms can be an uplifting experience worthy of our special recognition. Visits of siblings and the compansionship of family can help as well. Dying children seem to have a particularly intense need to keep in contact with other children and to see what's going on. The writer has encountered several children ranging in age from 2 to 10 years who demanded that their parents pull them around the ward in a wagon. Even though they were desperately ill, it seems to be intensely important not to be left out or isolated or forgotten. When no parents are available it becomes increasingly important for us to recognize this need and find ways to meet it, perhaps by using volunteers.

For older children, particularly adolescents, the value of the telephone, flexibility in visiting rules and allowances for short absences from the ward with family or friends must be considered. Most of all, teens value their mobility and their friends and although new associations help, time for sharing confidences from a dying adolescent's peer group may be the best tonic for a depressed and discouraged patient (1, 20, 21, 31).

A Feeling of Self Respect

Dying children, like dying adults, need to have a feeling of self worth and as hospital staff, we must be prepared to consider how to maintain the child's dignity in the face of continuing physical dependence. Children still need to have their privacy protected just as they would at home. One adolescent, age 17, exemplified this need in older children when she restricted visitors to a few staff, friends and family who could see her without her wig. As she had become thinner and more emaciated, her need to have privacy and maintain her dignity increased and staff respected her need. With younger children, nursing staff may have to consciously help the younger patient maintain this right.

Along with self respect and closely linked to it, is the matter of achievement. Protection of one's person is important but so also is the need to reinforce one's self worth by continuing to set goals which continue life and where feasible, result in even minor accomplishments. For example, Greg, age 13, maintained his scrapbooks until the day he died, and George, age 15, brought Christmas presents for his parents and worked hard to finish a model airplane. Ward staff can facilitate achievement simply by being attuned to providing experiences which bring about even the simplest accomplishment, whether it is making a Christmas card or going to a movie. The value of being able to be flexible enough to allow achievement and innovative to help the child determine ways of meeting even short term goals cannot be understated. This need must also be understood as part of the child's desire to deal with unfinished business and to be remembered. Many times children tie up loose ends which may or may not be related to short term projects. For example, Peter, age 11, was calculating the days to Halloween and planning how he could get out to see his neighbors in his wheelchair. He planned his life in days and not in weeks or months, and seemed to have an inherent need to see everyone who lived nearby and did so just before he died.

Freedom from Deep-Seated Feelings of Guilt and Understanding of Self

The process of self expression and self understanding in dying children is tied closely to the openness and honesty of both the child's family and staff involved in treatment. In effect, for ward staff, communication with the child is frequently influenced by their willingness to provide opportunities for discussion. In his work with leukemic children between the ages of 9 and 19, Vernick found that children knew about their illness, were concerned about other children on the ward and were more honest with certain staff than with parents (22). He advocated openness on behalf of staff and willingness to allow the child to interact freely, relate their concerns and receive honest answers. In the writer's experience, it is hard to disagree with Vernick's observations and their applicability to dying children and adolescents. It must be recognized, however, that at times adolescents need to use denial to protect themselves, particularly when they are not plagued by blatant and continuing symptoms of their illness (20, 21). For children under 10, however, indirect means of expression can be of tremendous value. At the writer's hospital, for instance, the child life workers have demonstrated continually the value of therapeutic play as a means of releasing anxiety both prior to and after painful procedures and in the face of other crises, including impending death. Therapeutic play facilitates the identification of misinformation, positive and negative thoughts and deep concerns and enables the identification of common themes (31, 32). As Green-Epner points out, when play can be provided as a means of communication and emotional release complete with insight into the dying child's feelings, thoughts and behavior, staff can plan care to meet the child's needs more effectively (13). Various media can facilitate such expression including doll play, art, clay, etc. In art, for example, dying children frequently convey a narrowing or darkening of their world or portray a feeling of entrapment (1). School teachers, who are key persons in helping children express their feelings in stories and poetry, and who help children continue to meet their needs for achievement, offer valuable support and assistance to both the child life and ward staff members.

When children are dying their most honest and open verbal expression may occur with a favorite nurse, perhaps at night, when the ward routine has slowed down and a child feels lonely. For example, about a week before he died, 12-year-old David, a child with leukemia, pointed to his fish bowl where a dead goldfish was floating and told the evening nurse that he would soon be like the fish. When she stopped to listen, he then related how he felt that death was most difficult for mothers and he was very worried about what would happen to his mother when he died. It was doubly important that his nurse listened because his own family wasn't able to share their thoughts and feelings openly with David or vice versa. Naturally, when families can be open with their child and parents can be helped to facilitate honest discussion it is highly desirable to have the parent speak with the child about death. For example, when dying became an issue for 11-year-old Hans, his minister came and talked to him and prayed as Hans had been accustomed to praying. When they were finished the minister realized the child had further needs and suggested to his mother that she discuss these with Hans. She was able to do it because the groundwork had been laid not only through the immediate discussion with the minister but by the openness of the family in their continued dialogue with Hans.

When children ask questions about death (and few do directly) it is important to find out what they are thinking and to respond to their questions simply, and with at least some hope (1, 33). Ideally, responses should come from parents but this is not always possible and the staff should be prepared to respond honestly in terms of what the child knows and understands. Howarth suggests that one technique which may help with young children when staff are concerned, is the telling of a story about a child in similar circumstances (33). If the staff are close to the child and play experiences are possible, staff concerns may be answered simply through the play experience. When older children are dying they are frequently guarded about expressing their feelings to more than one person. This person will be of their choosing and the timing will be set by the older children or adolescents in keeping with their trust and perception of who will answer them honestly.

When children are seriously ill, they, like adults, require times when they are allowed to withdraw and rest. Duff and Hollingshead, speaking of adults, suggest that withdrawal of chronically ill and seriously ill patients is often related to a need to enable the body and mind to rest and conserve energy, interest and attention. They also point out that this withdrawal is frequently interpreted as denial, suppression, repression, rationalization, etc. In dying children the same phenomenon takes place. Too often staff become immediately anxious that withdrawal means the child is severely depressed and request an immediate psychiatric consultation. Unless such withdrawal is prolonged, the most valuable contribution that can be made is the provision of a protected period which allows for uninterrupted rest periods and temporary withdrawal from ward routine. This may not meet our needs but facilitates what may be a brief recovery period which enables the child to renew even briefly his struggle to live.

Another type of withdrawal has been observed in children with leukemia when death is imminent. Lourie describes the distancing of the dying child as a state of resignation attributed to cachexia (bodily wasting) (35). Spinetta and his colleagues found that although this state occurred in most dying children, the distancing was less pronounced in families who communicated openly with their child (7). As death approaches this distancing must be understood. There is little that can be done when the end is so near except perhaps to reassure the concerned parent of the fact that this is a natural phenomenon. The most important contribution that can be made is in facilitating whatever closeness the child allows. Frequently staff must give parents additional encouragement and support to stay by their child quietly so that their child can continue to be comforted and his/her physical needs met.

Insight into their own behavior can be valuable for teens and pre-teens, and the social worker and other team members can be very helpful in enabling dying adolescents to understand their feelings. Along with this insight and as part of the exploration of thoughts and feelings can come an understanding of parental and staff behavior complete with a sense of relief. Sometimes facilitating dialogue between adolescent and parent can be the most valuable contribution possible. This dialogue can help parents understand and accept the adolescent's needs, especially his or her need to express feelings. The encounter can also begin recognition of the inevitable need for the adolescent to rely more and more on parents as death approaches (21).

If, however, staff are to bear the brunt of a child's anger and if expression of frustration is a continuing need, it is important to understand the source of the frustration and evaluate whether or not expression should be facilitated differently. Is the child really afraid to lash out at the parents? Is the child just feeling physically ill? Is the child depressed due to boredom? Is the expression of anger physically really a useful release or can we find other ways for the child to express it? The writer believes that at times children will release anger not just because they are frightened of parental retaliation but because they are familiar enough with staff to realize that staff will understand their feelings. Knowing the child and taking the time to determine why the child behaves as he does is crucial.

Throughout all of our interaction with dying children, regardless of age, there is the need for us to recognize that a child must mourn for the loss of what he was before. Children have every right to be sad and to feel cheated and lonely. There are times, however, when we observe behavior which we should not only understand but be prepared to help the child modify if we can. For example, 9-year-old Derrick had terminal osteogenic sarcoma and was in extreme pain. He was a pleasant child but became not only overly polite to his mother but apologetic as well. Because of his pain he became increasingly anxious and eventually would not move. The writer discussed reasons for his apologetic behavior with his mother, pointing out the possibility that he was probably feeling guilty about being a burden on his mother and he was definitely anxious about what was happening to him. It may well be that he had also endowed his mother with a supernatural controlling function in hopes that she could save him. Added reassurance was given to Derrick by his mother about her continued desire to care for him and the staff tried hard to be reassuring about the control of his pain. The mother prepared herself to answer any further questions he might ask about his illness or his impending death. Derrick died quietly in his mother's arms, without asking more questions and still legitimately worried about his pain. Derrick's anxiety about pain and death were real. He knew about his illness, had seen what it had done to his emaciated body and to his life. He mourned for his losses and his generalized anxiety led to suppression of normal feelings of anger and frustration. Helping his mother understand him and continue to relate to him with reassurance and honesty helped reduce at least slightly Derrick's need to apologize. Reassurance and gentleness from the nursing staff facilitated his comfort. Although Derrick died before the full impact of his mother's understanding could be evaluated in terms of changes in his case, this example illustrates how education and emotional support of the parent and emotional support of the dying child can be increased positively. When our observations signify that children may be blaming themselves for their plight and feeling guilty or believing that they are paying for past misdeeds, immediate attention should be directed to alleviating as much of the child's anxiety as possible. As staff we must also be able to recognize that what we say and do may be misconstrued and add further to the anxiety. A good example of this occurred in Peter, age 12, whose condition was deteriorating. He was taken off medication due to side effects and was told he was going home. He became very upset and tearful because he thought the doctors were giving up on him and he was being sent home to die. In effect, at the time this was not the case as there was still hope. Explanations carefully carried out can lead to alleviation of this type of anxiety, clarify any misunderstanding on the child's behalf and add to the child's ability to have some control over what is happening.

THE MILIEU: HOSPITAL VERSUS HOME
AS A SETTING FOR TERMINAL CARE

As this chapter illustrates, meeting the needs of the dying child, and those who love him, demands considerable knowledge and understanding. The availability of a variety of disciplines from both an ambulatory and inpatient base can provide added depth to a hospital staff's ability to provide high quality care. In the writer's experience, psychosocial care provided by physician, resident, nurse, social worker and child life worker enhanced by other staff such as the physiotherapist, occupational therapist, chaplain and psychiatric consultant far outweighs individualistic efforts of isolated disciplines (1, 23). The skills available from a team facilitate the provision of surrogate parental roles where necessary, deepen understanding of child and parental behavior and provide much needed staff relief and support. When ambulatory and inpatient care is integrated the care provided enables a continuance of trust and understanding built up through months or years. In recent years, however, it is recognized that although the hospital offers much, the home environment may offer more to both the dying child and his family.

Kulenkamp, a parent of a child who died, points out that care at home is less disruptive to the child, provides the comfort of familiar surroundings, enables interaction with the whole family including pets, allows access to the child's friends, makes parents feel their inadequacies are less visible and enables even brief escapes to pleasant places more readily than the hospital (36). In the writer's experience, if the family wants the child at home, and can cope with the anxiety related to the child's actual death, then the experience can be reassuring and comforting. But, not every family can cope with the responsibility (30, 36). In his experience, de Veber suggests that families appear to mourn less intensely and recover better when children die at home rather than in the hospital. Although this area requires further study, the writer would not disagree with de Veber's observations (37). From his experience, the writer believes that parents and other family members are able to grieve more openly at home. Often more time for terminating and separating are provided as well. Family members can hold the dead child and do whatever is necessary to realize that they must part with the body. Often an external support system including a family physician or hospital or home care staff members can assist with this process as sometimes helping the parents is too great a burden for the extended family due to their emotional investment with the parents, siblings and other relatives.

As hospital staff, it is our responsibility to see that the child's needs are met first whether at home or in hospital. This responsibility implies continued linkage directly with the family and with other agents in the community including family physician, home care program, clergy, etc. Meeting the child's social and emotional needs may mean facilitating regular home contact between home and hospital, provision of help to parents related to diversional activities for the child and continuance where feasible of the trusting relationship which has linked the child and selected staff members during earlier phases of the illness experience. Providing the same type of behavior interpretation and understanding for parents as they would receive in hospital and developing their understanding of the meaning of pain and pain control may be the two most important additional contributions we can make. Availability and and accessibility around the clock, seven days a week can make home care both a comforting and beneficial experience.

In closing, it is worth noting that both health professionals and the general public are ill prepared for death experiences, let alone the death of a child. Publicly, the expectation that children will die has been removed by advances in medical care and even though death has been rediscovered through the works of Kübler-Ross (38) and other public figures, the ability to educate children about death and understand their reactions to death is severely limited. Consequently, not only should opportunities for public education be pursued but as hospital staff we must recognize that children who enter our care often have had little exposure to, or understanding of, death. Often the parents are in a similar situation. When death is a possibility, education of parents who can in turn educate the sick child, should become a priority. By the same token, greater attention should be given to students from the health and health-related professions who are directing their studies toward care of the seriously ill in pediatric settings. Today many students do not even experience the death of an adult patient let alone benefit from working with a dying child. Our ability to use audiovisual resources, to provide seminars, and where possible, practical experiences should be taxed to the fullest to enable our students to have at least some beginning understanding of what is involved in this complex and taxing patient care experience. Furthermore, as health care practices continue to change and increasing numbers of children who die do so at home, it is important that we develop the type of home care programs which link family, hospital and family physician to ensure continuous medical and psychosocial care. Within this context we must provide new challenges and experiences for training our future practitioners in various disciplines in ways which facilitate learning but meet the needs of the child and the family and protect their rights to the privacy and protection of the home environment.

REFERENCES

1. Adams, D. W. *Childhood Malignancy: The Psychosocial Care of the Child and His Family*. Springfield: Thomas, 1979, pp. vii–12, 26–46, 131–148.
2. D'Angio, J. J. Health Memorial Award Lecture presented at Symposium "On the Curability of Childhood Neoplasms," M. D. Anderson Medical Center, Houston, Texas, February, 1980.
3. Langford, W. The Child in the Pediatric Hospital—Adaptation to Illness and Hospitalization, *Am. J. Orthopsychiatry*, 1961, 31:667–684.
4. McCollum, A. T. & Schwartz, A. H. Social Work and the Mourning Parent, *Soc. Wk.*, 1973, 17:25–36.
5. Knudson, A. G. & Natterson, J. M. Practice of Pediatrics: Participation of Parents in Hospital Care of Fatally Ill Children, *Pediatrics*, 1960, 26:482–490.
6. Spinetta, J. J. Communication Patterns in Families of Children with Life-Threatening Illness, Paper presented at Postgraduate Symposium, "The Child and Death," University of Rochester, Rochester, New York, September 15, 1977.
7. Spinetta, J. J. Communication Patterns in Families Dealing with Life-Threatening Illness, in *The Child and Death*, edited by O. J. Sahler. St. Louis: Mosby, 1978, pp. 43–46.
8. Hamovitch, M. B. *The Parent and the Fatally Ill Child*, City of Hope Medical Centre, Duarte, California, 1964, pp. 19–76, 110–121.
9. Townes, B. D. & Wold, A. A. Childhood Leukemia, in *The Experience of Dying*, edited by E. M. Pattison. Englewood Cliffs, N.J.: Prentice-Hall, 1977, pp. 138–143.
10. Mennie, A. T. The Child in Pain, in *Care of the Child Facing Death*, edited by L. Burton. London: Routledge and Kegan Paul, 1974, pp. 49–58.
11. Goggin, E. I., Lansky, S. G., & Hassanein, K. Psychological Reactions of Children with Malignancies. *J. Am. Acad. Child Psychiatry*, 1976, 15:314–325.
12. Waechter, E. Children's Reactions to Fatal Illness, in *Death and Presence*, edited by A. Godin, Brussels: Lumen Vitae, 1972, pp. 155–168.

13. Green-Epner, C. S. The Dying Child, in *The Dying Patient: A Supportive Approach*, edited by R. E. Caughill. Boston: Little, Brown, 1976, pp. 125–156.
14. Grollman, E. A. Explaining Death to Children, in *Explaining Death to Children*, edited by E. A. Grollman. Boston: Beacon, 1967, pp. 3–27.
15. Nagy, M. The Child's Theories Concerning Death. *J. Gen. Psychol.*, 1948, 73:3–27.
16. Rochlin, G. How Younger Children View Death and Themselves, in *Explaining Death to Children*, edited by E. A. Grollman. Boston: Beacon, 1967, pp. 51–73.
17. Schowalter, J. E. The Child's Reaction to His Own Terminal Illness, in *Anticipatory Grief*, edited by B. Schoenberg, A. C. Carr, A. H. Kutscher, D. Peretz, and I. K. Goldberg. New York: Columbia University Press, 1974, pp. 193–208.
18. Morrisey, J. R. Children's Adaptation to Fatal Illness. *Soc. Wk.*, 1963, 8:81–88.
19. McCollum, A. T. *Coping with Prolonged Health Impairment in Your Child*. Boston: Little Brown, 1975, p. 66.
20. Kagan, B. Use of Denial in Adolescents with Bone Cancer. *Ped. Clin. N. Amer.*, 1976, 20: 965–973.
21. Plumb, M. M. & Holland, J. Cancer in Adolescence: The Symptom is the Thing, in *Anticipatory Grief*, edited by B. Schoenberg, A. C. Carr, A. H. Kutscher, D. Peretz, and I. K. Goldberg. New York: Columbia University Press, 1974, pp. 193–208.
22. Vernick, J. Meaningful Communication with the Fatally Ill Child, in *The Child in His Family*, edited by E. J. Anthony and C. Koupernik. New York: Wiley, 1973, pp. 105–119.
23. Gordon, B. An Interdisciplinary Approach to the Dying Child and His Family, in *Care of the Child Facing Death*, edited by L. Burton, London: Routledge and Kegan Paul, 1974, pp. 141–150.
24. Duberley, J. The Role of Nursing Staff in Helping the Hospitalized Child, in *Care of the Child Facing Death*, edited by L. Burton. London: Routledge and Kegan Paul, 1974, pp. 122–126.
25. Pattison, E. M. (editor) *The Experience of Dying*. Englewood Cliffs, N.J.: Prentice-Hall, 1977, pp. 69–101.
26. Rothenberg, M. B. Problems Posed for the Staff Who Care for the Child, in *Care of the Child Facing Death*, edited by L. Burton. London: Routledge and Kegan Paul, 1974, pp. 39–44.
27. Raths, L. E. *Meeting the Needs of the Children: Creating Trust and Security*. Columbus, Oh.: Merrill, 1972, p. 25.
28. Graner, A. The Effects of Pain on Child, Parent and Health Professional, in *Home Care for the Dying Child*, edited by I. M. Martinson. New York: Appleton, 1976, pp. 61–69.
29. Craig, Y. The Care of Our Dying Child—A Parent Offers Some Personal Observations Based on Recollection, in *Care of the Child Facing Death*, edited by L. Burton. London: Routledge and Kegan Paul, 1974, pp. 87–98.
30. Wetzel, D. Meri: Recollections of a Father, in *Home Care for the Dying Child*, edited by I. M. Martinson. New York: Appleton, 1976, pp. 38–40.
31. Oremland, E. K. & Oremland, J. D. (editors) *The Effects of Hospitalization on Children and Models for Their Care*. Springfield: Thomas, 1973, pp. 193–266.
32. Petrillo, M. & Sanger, S. *Emotional Care of Hospitalized Children: An Environmental Approach*. Philadelphia: Lippincott, 1972, pp. 99–132, 205–247.
33. Howarth, R. The Psychiatric Care of Children with Life-Threatening Illnesses, in *Care of the Child Facing Death*, edited by L. Burton. London: Routledge and Kegan Paul, 1974, pp. 127–136.
34. Duff, R. S. & Hollingshead, A. B. *Sickness and Society*. New York: Harper and Row, 1968, pp. 268–305.
35. Lourie, R. S. The Pediatrician and the Handling of Terminal Illness. *Pediatrics*, 1973, 32: 477.
36. Kulenkamp, E. Eric: A Mother's Recollection, in *Home Care for the Dying Child*, edited by I. M. Martinson. New York: Appleton, 1976, pp. 15–27.
37. de Veber, L. L. Families, Children and Death, Lessons We Have Learned. *University of Western Ontario Medical Journal*, 1978, 48:18–20.
38. Kübler-Ross, E. *On Death and Dying*. New York: MacMillan, 1969.

6

Helping Parents Cope

A Model Home-Care Program for the Dying Child

*Patricia Carlson, Marian Simacek, William F. Henry,
and Ida M. Martinson*

with Kathy and Jay Montgomery

INTRODUCTION

While advances have been made in the medical and surgical treatment of child-hood cancer, families with a child who has cancer or other serious life-threatening illnesses face multiple stresses resulting from the ongoing treatment and, in some instances, the eventual death of a child member. Investigators have discussed the many psychological adjustments of families related to the anticipated loss of a member and vicissitudes of remissions and relapses of the disease. If the parents could be assisted in making these adjustments and in dealing with the disruptions associated with the course of the disease and its treatment, perhaps some of the stresses associated with life-threatening illness in childhood could be brought closer to manageable levels.

The primary disruptions for the family of a child with a life-threatening illness are the separation forced by hospitalization, the stresses attendant with hospitalization including loss of control, and the additional nonmedical expenses encountered by the family.

Separation of the family members has been viewed as a threat to family integrity (1–5). Family activities are terminated or curtailed when one or both parents are at the hospital with the ill child and the siblings remain at home. If one parent goes to the hospital and the other remains home, the parents have fewer opportunities to communicate and, in addition, have to cope with the stress of assuming additional unfamiliar roles and activities. Heightened marital discord has been reported by Lansky (6) as a byproduct of childhood cancer.

Parents are not the only ones impacted by the hospitalization of the child with cancer or other terminal disease. Siblings are subject to parental anxiety, repeated separations from the parents, and possible displacement to other homes or care-takers (3, 4, 7). The sick child is separated as well from the usual sources of support and comfort of familiar surroundings.

Martinson and Janosik (5) discussed the sometimes inflexible institution as making the family dependent on professionals, losing autonomy and control of parental functions. Children are subjected to separation, restrictions in the hospital, and the difficulty of maintaining normal activities.

To prevent weakening the family unit, parental participation in the care of the sick child has been advocated as a measure to increase involvement, to decrease separation fears for parent and child, and to help resolve guilt feelings (5, 8, 9). Siblings have also expressed the need to participate and be involved in the care of the ill child (2, 3). These positive measures can be difficult to apply when the treatment center is at great distance from the home. Along with the isolation of family members, abandonment by extended family and friends (6) as well as by hospital staff (10) has been observed.

Accompanying the hospitalizations and separation, the family of a child with cancer faces additional and sometimes extensive nonmedical expenses which are not reimbursed by third party payment. Lansky (11) found transportation, loss of pay, and the cost of housing and meals when the child is hospitalized to be major factors in adding stress to the already burdened family.

When the child is in the terminal phases of illness and no further cure-oriented treatment is expected, a return of the family—including the sick child—to the home can, in some measure, reduce some of the disruptions just described. With this objective in mind, a home care alternative was designed.

HOME CARE FOR FAMILIES WITH A DYING CHILD

The model for home care for children described in this chapter was developed by the Home Care for the Child with Cancer Project (DHEW, National Cancer Institute, CA 19490) at the University of Minnesota School of Nursing. The purpose of the project was to examine the feasibility and desirability of home care for children dying with cancer. In this model of care, the family is the primary provider of care for the child, the home care nurse is the major source of direction of the care and is available on a 24-hour basis, and the child's physician serves as consultant to the care providers. During the first phase of the Home Care for the Child with Cancer Project (1976-1978), 58 children received care through the project and died; during the second phase (1978-1978) health care institutions were assisted in adopting the model developed in Phase 1 and provided care to another 18 children who died.

The development of the home care model, the dynamics of the care provided, the process of institutionalizing that model and the desirability and feasibility of home care have been extensively reported elsewhere (12-16). The purpose of the present chapter is to view home care of a dying child as an active coping strategy by the parents and to examine the process of care and the parents' involvement from that perspective. The following section very briefly describes various elements of family stress and coping and relates these elements to an illustrative home care case. The next sections give numerous examples of home care experiences and present information from many of the families who received home care. Our goal here is to develop a broader view of the nature of the coping strategies involved. The final section of the chapter is a personal account of the coping value of home care written by the parents of a child who received home care and died during Phase 1 of the project.

ASPECTS OF FAMILY STRESS AND COPING ADDRESSED BY THE HOME CARE MODEL

Overview

While there were no "typical" families who entered home care (many levels of education, income, socioeconomic status and family structure were represented), one family has been chosen to illustrate the various aspects of family stress addressed by the home care model. The Holmes family (name changed to protect their identity) was chosen for this purpose because they were involved in home care for $3\frac{1}{2}$ months and because of their manifest good adjustment two years after the death of their 7-year-old daughter, Anne. Data on this family (and on the other families discussed in the following section) were obtained from the structured interview conducted with all families in the project 1, 6, 12 and 24 months after the child's death as well as from interviews with siblings, grandparents, nurses and physicians and from notes kept by the home care nurse.

Anne Holmes was diagnosed as having acute lymphocytic leukemia and was hospitalized five times for a total of 132 days in two and one-half years. The hospitalizations (at a regional cancer treatment) brought separation for the family because Mrs. Holmes stayed at the regional treatment center with Anne. Mr. Holmes would frequently join her there, leaving the two older girls (12 and 14 years) at home with the grandmother. When cure-oriented therapy was discontinued, the parents and Anne decided to return home—Anne did not wish to be in the hospital and the parents wanted the family reunited. Anne was expected to live for only a few days after leaving the hospital. However, she lived for three and one-half months, during which time she went camping with the family and enjoyed other family activities outside the home. It is possible that Anne's home environment was able to accomplish what Kastenbaum (9) has described as an extension of survival in dying patients through the continuation of interpersonal support.

After Anne's death, the family adjusted well. Two years after the death, the family had resumed former social activities and had begun some new ones. The siblings continued to do well at school and in relationships with peers and had no continuing somatic complaints. While the parents described the family as "always close," the siblings stated they felt even closer as a result of their experience. Also, at 24 months after Anne's death, her parents took the SCL-90-R (17), a symptom checklist used to measure stress. They scored at the mean (relative to a "normal" group of parents) on the Global Severity Index of the SCL-90-R. This index is a composite of the distress inherent in the symptoms reported. The parents' scores indicate they are not extraordinarily distresssed.

Parental Stress Resulting from Home Care

Beyond the stress inherent in the family's anticipation of the death of their child, home care itself could be viewed as a stressor because it demands considerable changes in family roles and relationships. Potential sources of stress include uncertainty about what to expect and about how to care for the child and the assumption of full responsibility for the child's comfort. Thus, the child and family were not "taken care of" in hospital but the family must develop the necessary skills and resources to care for the child at home. Chief among the resources needed is information. The Holmes family actively sought information from their home care nurse, from physicians and other health professionals involved in Anne's care and from other families who had undertaken home care.

Friends, relatives and other sources of social support may withdraw from the home care family either because they do not understand home care or because they are afraid to approach the family. In the case of the Holmes, the family's relatives lived far away and the family did not count heavily on friends during the home care process. However, the home care nurse was able to provide major relationship support for the family. It should be noted that withdrawal of family and friends may also occur when the child is cared for in hospital, especially when the hospital is remote from the family's home community.

Because the costs of home care are not always fully covered by insurance, some families might suffer additional financial hardships. However, because the care was provided free of cost under the grant, no costs were experienced by the family. Moreover the Holmes family was adequately covered by insurance and were not concerned about the expense.

Even though care functions were shared by parents and siblings, fatigue might be considered as an additional hardship. Mr. Holmes took extra time off from work and the family cut down on social activities. However, it is highly likely that these events would have also occurred had Anne been hospitalized.

Because home care always included the option for the parents to readmit their child to hospital, an additional hardship might result from the child's return to and death in the hospital—especially if the family had developed expectations for the child's death at home. In addition, unmet expectations concerning a "peaceful death" might add an additional burden. While Anne's death was not peaceful (she had been restless and had bled from the nose and had trouble breathing) interviews with the family indicated that they had worked through their disappointment by six months after her death.

Finally, to the extent that the family desired support from familiar hospital personnel, the withdrawal of that support (by virtue of the distance from the medical center) may be a stressor in home care. In this instance the family was visited by a pediatrician and several of the hospital nurses, so support by such personnel was maintained.

Coping Potential in Home Care

As described by Pearlin and Schooler (18), home care itself might also be considered an active coping response. Rather than the helplessness described by families in hospital (5, 9), home care families are not only able to do *something* for their child, but something that they perceive as *good*—they became "active participants" as advocated by Knudson and Natterson (9). In this instance, the Holmes family took the initiative in establishing a relationship with the home care nurse and with the support of education, supplies and equipment, was able to carry on a variety of normal family activities. During home care, the Holmes' met most of the definition of Pratt's (19) "energized family": they actively interacted, maintained contacts with other groups, actively coped, where flexible, and promoted autonomy.

The family also fits Kaplan's (20) description of "adaptive coping": they understood that the leukemia was serious, an inordinate amount of time was not spent on blaming selves or others and the nature of the disease was communicated within the family. The siblings were told that Anne's prognosis was poor and that she did not have long to live. Anne was able to discuss the fact that she was dying. The family did not seem to project blame at themselves or others and felt that this was "God's will." Self esteem of all members of the family was enhanced by learning new tasks involved in Anne's care. As was true in Iles' (3) study, the siblings were anxious to contribute to Anne's care.

A major benefit of home care is that the sick child is in better control of herself at home. For example, during home care Anne's food preferences and requests were honored repeatedly even though she was not to stay in her bedroom alone. To increase her comfort, she occupied the family's living room for the first part of home care and later was able to be cared for in her own bedroom.

Religion was a major asset used by the Holmes family in coping during home care. They viewed Anne as someone who was given to them by God to bring them closer together as a family. Both parents and siblings said that her death was more acceptable because she would "be with Jesus who died for her sins." In each interview with the family, faith was stated as the key factor that enabled this family to take care of Anne at home and bear her death.

Open communication about the disease and dying has been found to be a positive factor in successful adjustment of parents and siblings because it allows them to express their grief openly, validate ideas about the cause of illness and share important information (2, 21-24). The Holmes' maintained open communication with Anne and her siblings about the process of Anne's disease and her prognosis. In one instance, Anne's 12-year-old sister was concerned that she might have leukemia when she experienced a nosebleed similar to those Anne was suffering. However, through the family's open communication pattern, she was quickly reassured.

Cobb (25) has described social support as including emotional, esteem and network support and as decreasing the family's vulnerability to stress. Social support has also been viewed as a positive factor in recovery (26). Parent groups have been advocated as an effective form of social support (10, 27), as have religious communities (26), although Cobb (28) found religious rituals useful on allowing expressions of grief and in publicizing and formally establishing the new status of the family.

Provision of such social support is a major consideration in home care. The Holmes family used their religion for emotional and network support. Also, the home care nurse provided esteem support through encouraging parent participation and control. While in the hospital, the parents found it helpful to meet other parents of children with leukemia but did not like to participate in the parent support groups. They stated that the meetings merely turned into gripe sessions. Two years after Anne's death, they said they would not seek out a grief support group now, but would be willing to talk individually with families experiencing similar crises.

The medical center staff provided additional emotional, esteem and network support through their visits to the family. The support the family appreciated in the hospital was continued to a limited extent at home.

An event defined as serious may make the family more vulnerable (29), but the process of defining an event as serious is viewed by Kaplan (20) as adaptive coping which later affects adjustment. As the home care family reached the decision to take the child home, the family must realistically consider the responsibilities involved and appraise their resources to meet those responsibilities. If the family defined the child's care as a burden or anticipates it to be beyond their ability, then that "seriousness" makes them more vulnerable. If home care is viewed as a challenge, and as a way of helping the dying child and family to stay together, then vulnerability is not increased. It is apparent that the Holmeses approached home care as a benefit for Anne and also as a serious undertaking for them. They put a good deal of thought and effort into their decision and carefully weighed the anticipated difficulties against their own abilities.

During the home care experience, the Holmes family drew closer together and subverted individual needs to the tasks at hand. After Anne's death they reverted to a level of cohesion more common for a family with adolescents—after the death, the siblings were able to concentrate on individuation through friends and school activities and were thus less involved with the family. During however the family was able to admit the nurse into their unit, but were able to function well when she was not around. The Holmes family shares a close emotional bond, but gives room for individual differences.

While it was important to the Holmeses to limit their outside activities to share in Anne's care, they were able to resume normal activities three to four months after Anne's death. The mother again became involved in church activities and the girls participated in more activities in school (although they had maintained some participation while Anne was at home). Having activities outside the home helps to fill the gap after the death of the child. If too much is given up for too long a period of time, it is possible that the adjustment process would take longer.

In summary, a fundamental contribution of home care is that, while it does not protect the family from pain, it allows the family to experience sorrow fully, while dispelling feelings of total helplessness. The parents and siblings actively contribute to the well being of the dying child and to each other's adjustment. The home care nurse provides emotional support and material resources during home care and after the death.

The major strengths of the Holmes family included strong religious beliefs, open communication, interaction with the community and continued family activities even though Anne was dying. The family "pulled together" to care for Anne and did not fall apart afterwards. There was an absence of psychosomatic symptoms and a return to activities with friends. The father stated, "Don't get the idea that this was easy." While it could never be easy to lose a child, the Holmes family managed their resources and relationships well, defining their situation as one which would bring them closer together.

OTHER EXAMPLES OF COPING DURING HOME CARE

The following are brief case histories of families who have cared for a dying child at home in this project.

> When the nurse was first referred to this family, she found that they were not enthusiastic about receiving any help. They had been caring for their child during her three years of illness and were working things out quite well for themselves. However, the family appreciated the nurse's efforts in obtaining a hospital bed and in regulating the child's diet and fluid intake. The nurse also facilitated the administration of intravenous fluids and helped the family become very adept at these procedures—as the father stated: "I can do that; I watched them in the hospital and there's nothing to it." He then regulated the flow and phoned the nurse whenever it was time to change the bottle. During a visit when the nurse was assisting with the intravenous equipment, she observed the progress of a birthday party being held for a younger brother of the dying child. The brother and his friends continually looked in on the child and actively included her in their festivities.
>
> Another family derived a great deal of satisfaction in caring for their teenage son in their home where they felt more relaxed and comfortable than in hospital and where the boy's friends could visit freely. The mother was proud of her idea to use the boy's grandmother's walker to help him get around. Even during times of extreme illness he continued to participate in his own care and the mother encouraged this independence.

At times this was very difficult (as when she waited twenty minutes for him to swallow)—however, the nurse gave the mother encouragement and support in her patience. Because the child was concerned as to how his death would affect his siblings, he and his parents discussed this concern and were able to relieve much of his anxiety.

A firm religious faith was of value to many families in home care. One family was happy to have their son at home so that family, neighbors and friends could assist with their prayers and visits. The parents felt comfortable with providing physical care and comfort measures and the other children were reassured by their presence and by frequent visits to the ill child's bedside. As the mother stated, "Our base is God's help, and prayer helped me to do what was needed." The nurse mentioned that the home was filled with pleasant conversation, soft religious music that was the child's favorite, and a quite congenial atmosphere. In another family, the child herself was able to use her faith to help the family cope. She took the younger children aside and talked to each one about her dying. She reassured them they they did not need to be sad because she would not hurt any more and she would be with Jesus. She let them ask her questions and she answered as well as she could. Until that time the children were having problems and reacting with resentment. After talking to her they were able to speak freely about her death and their feelings.

The home care nurse for the family of a small girl recognized the mother's increasing fatigue. She noted that the mother appeared "frazzled" with the care of the younger children as well as the constant attention to the dying child. The nurse volunteered to take all the children for car rides, as well as to babysit on occasion so the mother could rest. When the parents were rested they were able to cope more effectively with the care of all the children.

Many families involved the grandparents and others in the extended family in the child's care. In one family in which the final stages of the child's life extended over several weeks, both grandmothers lived in the home during home care. As the mother stated, "They are available 24 hours a day." The four adults did an exceptional job in providing care for the 10-year-old girl. All four were able to rest well and the parents were able to leave for short periods, such as to attend church services. In another family, the mother of a teenaged boy with cancer was divorced and the family felt she needed some extra help in sharing the responsibilities. Two older sisters learned to give injections and to assist in moving and bathing the boy. His mother moved home to assist with care and to give his mother time to rest. The brothers-in-law learned to handle oxygen tanks and to regulate the oxygen flow. The family planned their time to help with his care and to visit him. They felt the child did not want to bring up the subject of death to spare the family. During the last week they felt that he was at peace and this made it easier for them. In the process of providing care they felt they had learned their own strengths and what they could do for themselves.

Home care nurses frequently assisted families in discussing their feelings about the child's death. In one family, the nurse drew the two brothers, aged 11 and 12, into a conversation with their father. They discussed death, and how the ill child and their parents were feeling. She advised them to cry if they felt like it and not keep it inside. They discussed how they felt about the illness and about the time spent in the care of the child. They agreed that, with the nurse's help, they would be able to get through the coming days. They also said they would think about the child's death and bring any questions to her. The father told the nurse later that it was beneficial to him to know he could cry if he felt like it. He had always been taught that men must be brave and not cry, and this made him feel much better. In another family, the home care nurse was asked during her first visit to assist the parents in discussing the child's impending death with her younger sister. The two extremes of telling the child everything or telling her nothing were confusing to the parents. The nurse talked about the need to be honest with the child and suggested answering direct questions but not overloading her with information that was not really being requested. The nurse also supported the mother by indicating that simply giving the idea some thought and facing the problem was helpful.

The words "beautiful" and "peaceful" were frequently used by parents to describe the death of children in home care. In the case of one four-year-old boy, his parents and grandparents sat by his bed, he squeezed his parents' hands. His mother whispered in his ear that it was time for him to go. She said later that at this point she was able to *"feel fear leave the room."* *The boy's father said the room seemed to be "full at one moment and empty the next." Although these parents were angry at the beginning of home care and had denied the fact of the child's impending death, they gradually came to accept the facts and coped with the death. They attributed this change to the support offered by their religion, home care, and relatives. In another family, during the treatment stages the small child found it very hard to let his parents leave the hospital. Because he would cry when they left, even though he realized they would return, it became increasingly difficult for the parents to leave him. While in the hospital, he would murmur a final "good night" to his parents, but he never said "good bye." When he came home, he was less anxious and more reassured by his parents' presence. Several nights after returning home, he prepared for bed and then carefully said "goodbye" to his sister, his baby sitter, his stuffed animals and his parents. Later his mother and father discussed the fact of his imminent death and the fact that a three-year-old child could be aware that he would die soon. During the night the child died in his own crib and the parents were perhaps better able to cope with his death because they were able to say "goodbye" earlier in the evening.*

BEREAVEMENT AFTER HOME CARE

Two questions asked during the interviews conducted with parents 24 months after the child's death provide information on the duration of the parents' bereavement. The first question asked parents if they felt they had returned to their normal life style. Of the 82 parents responding 68 (83 percent) replied that they had returned to their normal life style. Comments made by the 14 (17 percent) parents who replied in the negative included the following:

> *We're back to the routine but not the normal, because your life is never the same. You're not the same person because so much has happened to us.*
> *No, I don't think so. It's too deep in my soul and myself. He had changed my whole life and my perspective in life.*
> *I don't think you ever do. There's always kind of something missing. I think you live more in the past than you ever did because you want to think of things you did in the past.*

The second question asked parents to identify when the most intense time of their bereavement was over. Again, responses to this question (shown in Table 1) indicate wide variation across parents. Over one-fifth of the parents replied that the most intense time of their bereavement was not yet over at 24 months after the child's death. Another one fourth- of the parents replied that the most intense time of their bereavement was not over until 12-18 months after the child's death. In addition, there is some difference between mothers and fathers in their responses to this question. Fathers were nearly twice as likely as mothers to reply that the most intense part of their bereavement was over within a few weeks to one month after the child's death.

Responses to these two questions further support the assertion that there are wide differences across these parents in how they respond to their child's death. Clearly, for a substantial portion, these parents' intense bereavement is a long-term process and includes some disruption of the family's normal routine. Also, fathers and mothers appear to respond to their loss differently.

When asked 24 months after their child's how they felt they had adjusted, 68 (85 percent) of the 80 parents responding said they had adjusted fairly well—that they had accepted their child's death. The remaining 12 (15 percent) parents felt

Table 1 Phase 1 parents' responses 24 months after the child's death to question: "When was the most intensive time of your bereavement over?"

	Mothers		Fathers		Total	
	Number	Percent	Number	Percent	Number	Percent
First weeks	5	9.8	4	23.8	9	11.3
1 month	2	3.9	5	17.2	7	8.8
3 months	6	11.8	4	13.8	10	12.5
6 months–1 year	7	13.7	0	–	7	8.8
1–1½ years	13	25.5	7	24.1	20	25.0
Not yet over	12	23.5	5	17.2	17	21.3
Unsure	6	11.8	4	13.8	10	12.5
Subtotal	51	100.0	29	99.9	80	100.2
Not asked/not interviewed	7		26		33	
Not present during home care	0		3		3	
Total	58		58		116	

they had not adjusted well. Some of this latter group's comments include the following:

> We have a lot of trouble making decisions about anything. We listen to our friends and end up doing something we don't like to do.
> It just seemed like it was never going to end and it's never going to get better so I don't care. It's like you want to give into it and the heck with the whole world.
> I feel kind of an apathy for a lot of things that I used to have more spirit for.

During the interview 24 months after the one child's death, parents were also asked to rate their present level of coping with their grief. They were asked to use a scale ranging from 10 (best coping) to 1 (complete distress). There was some variation in how parents rated their coping, but ratings are generally on the upper end of the scale—71 percent of the parents rated their coping as 8, 9 or 10. There was very little difference between mothers' and fathers' ratings of coping.

Parents' were also asked whether there was anything they could not do 24 months after the child's death. Fifty-five (67 percent) of the 82 parents responding to this question reported there was nothing they couldn't do. Four parents said they could not go to the hospital where their child had been treated, other said they couldn't attend funerals (one of these specifically mentioned funerals of children), three others said they could not prepare or eat some foods that the deceased child had enjoyed and three parents said it was difficult to look at pictures of the child. One mother said it was difficult to visit the child's grave and another said she couldn't decide whether to have another baby. Two couples referred to difficulties in going out with other couples—however, one couple said they couldn't go out with other couples (because of conversations about children) while the other said they could only go out when other couples were present. Five other parents each said they couldn't do specific things that were closely related to the deceased child. These ranged from caring for the child's horse to reading a diary kept during the child's illness.

Again, these data leave the impression of adequate coping by a large proportion of the parents and wide variability among the group who express some difficulties.

During the interviews 24 months after the child's death, parents were asked whether their grief had interfered with their ability to function in their daily activities (i.e., their job or their management of the home) in the 12 months preceding the interview. As in other questions, a sizable proportion—84 percent of the 81 parents interviews—answered that their grief had not interfered in the past 12 months. Also as in other questions, there was variation among the responses of the 12 (16 percent) parents who answered affirmatively. These included the following comments:

> I don't have an interest in anything anymore. Everything seems like it's such a hassle.
> We had trouble making decisions in our daily life. It was hard to manage our house or to work.
> I'm not as good a mother or a housekeeper because I just don't feel like getting things done. I have all these feelings inside me.

Several questions related to the effect of the parents' grief on their employment. Only 6 (7 percent) of the 81 parents responding said there had been days in the 12 months preceding the interview when they could not go to work. Even among these 6, only one parent indicated they had missed more than one or two days in the preceding 12 months because of their grief. However, one-third (33 percent) of the parents said there had been days when they went to work but didn't get much done because of their grief. Finally, during the interview 24 months after the child's death, parents were asked whether they had had a change in employment in the preceding 12 months. While 23 (23 percent) of the 100 parents on whom data are available changed employment, there were no cases where anyone had to stop working as a consequence of their grief. Except for one father who retired and one mother who quit work because she had a baby, all other changes were the result of improving jobs or of entering the labor market. In particular, 10 mothers had begun new part- or full-time jobs in the previous 12 months.

Parents were also asked whether their children had missed school or play activities because they were distressed by their brother's/sister's death. In none of the 51 families who were interviewed was this reported to have occurred.

APPENDIX: THE PERSPECTIVE OF PARENTS
WHOSE CHILD HAS DIED AT HOME:
Kathy and Jay Montgomery

We were among the 7300 families each year whose child is diagnosed with cancer. We have found in speaking with numerous other parents in the same position that there is a remarkable commonality to the experience and the feelings that transcend any of the particular individual situations. Our son, Seth, was diagnosed at a very early age (4 months) with acute myelogenous leukemia, one of the childhood cancers that so far has proven to be fairly unresponsive to available treatments.

Whereas a large number of parents of children with cancer can anticipate a 50–80 percent likelihood that their child will be disease free and finished with treatments in three years, we knew that Seth would probably die within two years. To be specific we were *told* that—we did not "know" it. Actually we couldn't "imagine" it—and couldn't "believe it" initially. But that is only the beginning of the experiences which characterize parents and families in this situation.

Our story begins with our seven-week-old son, Seth, and a three-year-old daughter, Leah, being packed for a job-induced move from St. Paul, Minnesota, to Washington, D.C. Within a few weeks of the move, before we had really finished our unpacking, Seth developed a slight fever and became rather fussy, a change for our otherwise healthy and cheerful baby. We had been to the pediatrician just a few days earlier for a routine check-up for Seth who according to the doctor was a "very healthy baby." As survivors of one infancy, we were quite comfortable with our new pediatrician's declaration of "childhood virus." As the days and fever continued, Seth's appetite dropped dramatically. Our concern increased and we made several visits to the pediatrician who assured us nothing serious was wrong and soon Seth would get better. Despite the doctor's pronouncements Seth did not get better—he got worse. He was able to sleep only for brief periods (we hadn't had any decent sleep in days either) and was not drinking fluids at all. By now we were no longer just worried; we were panicked! Despite the fact that one of the physicians told Kathy she was reacting like an "hysterical mother," we insisted the pediatrician examine Seth again. Exhausted, and with our confidence in ourselves and in our pediatricians badly eroded, we again brought Seth to the doctor. This time blood tests were done. The results were not good, and we rushed Seth to the hospital. The hematologist called in on the case wanted to do a bone marrow aspiration "to rule out leukemia." When the results came back, written on our hematologist's face, the world, at least momentarily, came to an end for two exhausted parents. The unthinkable, the unbelievable had happened—our baby had leukemia, and needed to be started on induction chemotherapy immediately. The world, for us, was suddenly out of control.

As the shock and numbness began to settle in we made our way home that evening without Seth. It felt awful to leave him in the hospital—alone. As we talked and cried, we began to make some tentative decisions. We decided that one of us would stay with Seth at all times and the other parent would attempt to spend as much time as possible with our daughter. Jay's mother would be arriving the next day to take care of Leah, but still we worried. How would all of this affect a three-year-old still adjusting to the birth of a sibling, to say nothing of a move to a new location?

The next day at the hospital one of the ten nurses asked us if we would like to speak to a parent from Candlelighters, a support group for parents of children with cancer. She said parents in this group had indicated a willingness to talk with parents of newly diagnosed children. We both indicated our interest.

Somehow the idea of talking with another parent of a child with cancer struck a chord. We couldn't remember ever having felt so alone. It seemed all the other children in the pediatric ward had nothing more than severe diarrhea or hernia repairs. And no matter how understanding and comforting the nurses and doctors tried to be, at that time we felt a huge emotional distance from them. After all, we thought, it was probably easy for them to offer words of assurance. They really didn't know how it felt; it wasn't their child.

Later that evening, one of the parents from Candlelighters, a father, came to see us. Neither of us can remember exactly what he said. Maybe it's because we were in shock. And maybe it's because it wasn't so much his words as his presence that mattered. Kathy just recalls not feeling so alone. Jay remembers being impressed by the fact that this man was still walking around—functioning—in spite of what he had been through. He was living proof it was possible to survive this agony.

As the shock wore off we became more interested in the care provided Seth and developed a voracious appetite for information relating to the disease and treatment processes. Our physicians gave us a hematology textbook which we devoured. As we began to understand better what we were fighting and our odds of success, we became astute and critical observers of the care process.

We learned a lot in those days which followed the diagnosis. We learned that when we held Seth for the IV (intravenous) and bone marrow aspiration procedures that we not only felt better but that Seth was more cooperative and quieted down far more easily when we could comfort him immediately afterward. We learned that we could do many of the nursing functions as well as the nurses could and that they were very willing to teach us if we asked. And when the day finally came when "good" white cells began to propagate Seth's blood, we started to learn how to give injections for his chemotherapy as we had already decided that to the extent possible we would treat Seth at home. We learned that no matter how good the hospital was, how caring the staff, that home was where Seth belonged.

When the bone marrow tests came back showing Seth was in remission we packed up and headed home. Seth needed a lot of care. He needed his chemotherapy injections and pills on a regular basis and the resulting nausea, vomiting, and alternating diarrhea and constipation were never-ending problems. Seth also had developed a serious infection in his left buttock in the hospital and he needed meticulous and time consuming care to help this area heal. It wasn't easy but we had him home and that's what really mattered. It seemed like a miracle to us.

We began attending Candlelighters meetings on a regular basis. Once-a-month educational meetings were held at which physicians, nurses, and other professionals involved in the treatment of pediatric cancer patients were invited to speak. Small support groups also met monthly. These were very informal sessions held in one of the parents' homes. The goal of these meetings was simply to share and support. Common topics included what to tell the child with cancer, effect on brothers and sisters, stress on marriages—the grief as well as the joy, the fear, the guilt, and the hope. Not all of us felt the same, or took the same approach to coping with the diagnosis of cancer in one of our children. However, we came to realize that that wasn't necessary or perhaps even helpful. By sharing our various views and feelings with others, we seemed better able to come to grips with what we were comfortable with—what we wanted for our son. Above all, participating in the small groups got us talking with each other. It sounds simple, but when each individual feels crushed by the weight of his own personal grief, communicating is difficult.

Our real test came eight months later when Seth relapsed. The relapse was a shattering of all of our dreams. The miracle had escaped us. For the first time the reality of his leukemia hit us on a gut level and we began to face the probability of his eventual death. Now, more than ever, every minute with Seth was precious. With full cooperation from our physicians we attempted this second round of induction chemotherapy on an out-patient basis.

Seth became terribly nauseated from new drugs being tried to get him back in remission. We would barely make it home from the doctor's office before the horrible vomiting would begin. But our decision to attempt the chemotherapy on an out-patient basis instead of the hospital would be rewarded about 8 hours later when the nausea would decrease and Seth would suddenly slap a smile on his face and be off and running. Out came the cars and trucks and we were back to normal. And while this may have been the best part, we were not unaware that during this found of induction therapy we had slept with some regularity and Leah had remained part of the family.

Seth did achieve another remission and when the opportunity came to move back to Minneapolis we didn't hesitate. We all had our fill of Washington and, knowing what we were going to have to face in the months ahead, we felt a strong need to go back to familiar territory with family close by. Seth got a "clean" bill of health before we headed west. Two days on the road and we noticed the first bluish patches on his skin. After arriving we immediately visited our new physicians and our fears were promptly confirmed. Seth was in relapse again.

We consulted with the doctors about chemotherapy. Within days Seth went into a "blastic crisis." Even if we were successful in pulling him out of the crisis, we were told it was probably only a question of months. The doctors wanted to hospitalize Seth immediately. We took him to the hospital where he stayed two hours during which time they tried unsuccessfully to get and keep an IV in him. He was hysterical.

Finally, we could take no more. We had often talked about what we would do when this moment came—we decided to suspend treatments of any kind and take him home with us. The doctors were more supportive of our decision and offered whatever help was necessary. We were frightened but above all else wanted our son to die, if it must be, in the warmth and security of his home.

We had been told about a special nursing project at the University of Minnesota which provided home care for children with cancer. A friend contacted the group and the next afternoon a nurse came out to our home. She immediately put us at ease. She offered to help with anything from pain relief injections to babysitting Leah. She emphasized she was available 24 hours a day and not to hesitate to call day or night. It was just the reassurance we needed. We felt we were doing the "right" thing but definitely needed the support and encouragement to actually carry it through.

We called the nurse the first time around 2 a.m. Seth was in pain and we felt he needed something stronger. She arranged for the prescription and brought it over. It was wonderful not having to use up such precious minutes with those time-consuming details. We had Seth in bed between us and held and comforted him as best we could.

The next morning we brought Seth down to the living room and started a big fire in the fireplace. We took turns holding him—the way he seemed most comfortable. This was the hard part—watching him suffer and feeling so helpless. Yet there was no question in our minds that home was where he wanted to be.

The nurse came for another visit. Shortly after she left Seth slipped into a coma. We knew it wouldn't be much longer. Kathy's sister had been taking care of Leah at her house. We called her and she brought Leah home for final hugs and good-byes.

At around 4 p.m. Seth died—with privacy and dignity in the arms of his parents in the warmth and security of his home. It was not morbid, as some people might think, but beautiful and peaceful. Three years later, we continue to grieve for our son. However, the memories of those final days remain a source of comfort to us that is immeasurable.

Although Seth's peaceful death was a great source of comfort to us, we discovered in time that we still needed to confront the reality of his death in terms of what it means to each of us as individuals and as a family. For two years Seth's cancer had been the center of our lives. We had a lot of "left over" feelings to catch up on.

Again we turned to a group—a grief group for parents who had lost a child. Here, again, we found support from others who had had a similar experience. We attended the group on and off for about six months, tapering off our attendance after that to visits on special anniversary occasions such as his birthday, Mother's Day, the day he died, etc.

It has been over three years since Seth died. At times the pain of losing him is as sharp as ever. One *never* "gets over" the loss of a child. But we are a family still and life is good. We both work full time and spent a lot of time doing volunteer work in the area of childhood cancer—something we feel has been a constructive outlet for our grief. We get tremendous satisfaction out of watching our daughter grow up. We try to spend time together as a family for we have a heightened sensitivity to the fragility of life. For the most part, we feel we have regained control of our lives.

REFERENCES

1. Cobb, B. Psychological impact of long illness and death of a child on the family circle. *Journal of Pediatrics, 49*, 1956, 746–751.
2. Craft, M. Help for the family's neglected "other" child. *MCN, 4*, 1979, 297–300.
3. Iles, J. Children with cancer: Healthy siblings' perceptions during the illness experience. *Cancer Nursing*, October 1979, 371–377.
4. Kaplan, D. M., Grobstein, R., & Smith, A. Predicting the impact of severe illness in families. *Health and Social Work, 1*, 1976, 71–82.
5. Martinson, I. & Janosik, E. Family crisis intervention. In J. Miller & E. Janosik (eds.), *Family-centered care*. New York: McGraw-Hill, 1980.
6. Lansky, S. B. & Lowman, J. T. Childhood malignancy. *Journal of Kansas Medical Society, 75*, 1974, 91–94.
7. Wold, D. A. & Townes, B. D. The adjustment of siblings to childhood leukemia. *The Family Coordinator, 18*, 1969, 155–160.
8. Kastenbaum, R. In control. In C. A. Garfield (ed.), *Psychosocial care of the dying patient*. New York: McGraw-Hill, 1978.
9. Knudson, A. & Natterson, J. Participation of parents in the hospital care of fatally ill children. *Pediatrics, 26*, 1960, 482–490.
10. Heller, D. & Schneider, C. Interpersonal methods for coping with stress: Helping families of dying children. *Omega, 8*(4), 1978, 319–331.
11. Lansky, S. B., Cairns, N. U., Clark, G. M., Lowman, J., Miller, L., & Trueworthy, R. Childhood cancer: Nonmedical costs of illness. *Cancer, 43*, 1979, 403–408.
12. Martinson, I. M., Armstrong, G. D., Geis, D. P., Anglim, M. A., Gronseth, E. C., MacInnis, H., Kersey, J. H., & Nesbit, M. E. Home care for children dying of cancer. *Pediatrics*, July 1978, 106–113.
13. Martinson, I. M. & Henry, W. F. Some possible societal consequences of changing the way in which we care for dying children. *Hastings Center Report, 10*(2), April 1980, 5–8.
14. Moldow, D. G. & Martinson, I. M. From research to reality—Home care for the dying child. *MCN: The American Journal of Maternal Child Nursing, 5*, 1980, 159–166.
15. Martinson, I. M., Moldow, D. G., & Henry, W. F. *Home care for the child with cancer: Final report: Grant CA 19490, HHS, National Cancer Institute*. Minneapolis, MN: University of Minnesota School of Nursing, 1980. (offset)
16. Moldow, D. G., Armstrong, G. A., Henry, W. F., & Martinson, I. M. The cost of home care for dying children. *Medical Care, 20*(11).

17. Derogatis, L., Rickels, K., & Rock, A. The SCL-90 and the MMPI: A step in the validation of a new self-report scale. *Brit. J. Psychiat., 128*, 1976, 280–289.
18. Pearlin, L. & Schooler, C. Structure of coping. In H. McCubbin (ed.), *Family stress, coping and social support.* New York: Springer, in press.
19. Pratt, L. *Family structure and effective health behavior.* Boston: Houghton Mifflin, 1976.
20. Kaplan, D., Smith, A., Grobstein, R., & Fischman, S. Family mediation of stress. In C. A. Garfield (ed.), *Psychosocial care of the dying patient.* New York: McGraw-Hill, 1978.
21. Binger, C., Albin, A., Feuerstein, R., Kushner, J., Zoger, S., & Mikkelsen, C. Childhood leukemia: Emotional impact on patient and family. *New England Journal of Medicine, 280*(8), 1969, 414–418.
22. Spinetta, J. Communication patterns in families dealing with life-threatening illness. In O. Sahler (ed.), *The child and death.* St. Louis: Mosby, 1978.
23. Stehbens, J. & Lascari, A. Psychological follow-up of families with childhood leukemia. *Journal of Clinical Psychology, 30*(3), 1974, 394–397.
24. Vollman, R. The reactions of family systems to sudden and unexpected death. *Omega, 2*, 1971, 101–106.
25. Cobb, S. Social support and health through the life course. In H. McCubbin (ed.), *Family stress, coping and social support.* New York: Springer, in press.
26. Murawski, B., Penman, D., & Schmitt, M. Social support in health and illness: The concept and its measurement. *Cancer Nursing,* October 1978, 365–372.
27. Fischhoff, J. & O'Brien, N. After the child dies. *Journal of Pediatrics, 88*(1), 1976, 140–146.
28. Krupp, G. Maladaptive reactions to the death of a family member. *Social Casework, 53*, 1972, 425–434.
29. Burr, W. Families under stress. In H. McCubbin (ed.), *Family stress, coping and social support.* New York: Springer, in press.

7

Helping Siblings and Other Peers Cope with Dying

Frederick W. Coleman
Wendy S. Coleman

A family practitioner in Indiana as a routine part of his evaluation of a new family has at least one long interview with the entire family together to evaluate family patterns and interactions, with the belief that these will vitally influence the health and illnesses of all members of the family over time. A family therapist dealing with a patient with a major mental illness has sessions with the entire nuclear family, and at times even sessions with both sets of grandparents or other members of the extended family. An oncologist chooses always to discuss initial diagnosis, and any major new information with a patient and spouse together, to insure clarity of understanding and family communication. A parents group is set up for the parents of children with leukemia to meet and share their experiences, not only with their ill children, but also of the effects on themselves, their marriages, and their other children. At one medical center, whenever a child is dying, an attempt is made to meet at least once with the entire family to assess how all members are handling stressful events. Hospice programs stress the family as a unit of care during a terminal illness, and meet with them as a whole during the bereavement period to watch for problems that any family member might be having. In the last decades, practitioners of all kinds within the American medical care system are showing an awareness that illness, dying and death happen to individuals in the context of a larger family and social network where interventions can be both immediately beneficial and preventive of longer term problems. This awareness has developed over the past several decades as a counterpoint to the increasing technology of hospital based care, with its possibility of increased efficacy of treatment and risk of depersonalization. As with the development of any new perspective, it is a rediscovery of things long known, paired with a broadening and deepening of new insights, which only gradually win acceptance.

The dying of a child has long been perceived as one of the most painful of familial experiences. Our current rediscovery of this truth as reflected in the professional literature began in the 1950s with an emphasis on the impact on mothers. Interestingly, this seems to have been considered in some detail even before the reconsideration of the impact on the child. At a time when a clear majority of clinicians still closed their eyes to how much their child patients knew and experienced of what was happening to them, it was clear that the mothers who came with them into the clinics and hospitals were showing signs and symptoms of distress which could not be overlooked. With the 1960s and a new look at the child's conceptualization of death and a growing awareness of the impact of dying on adult patients, the dying child was more closely observed. By the end of the 1960s fathers were rediscovered as the whole issue of the effects of terminally ill children on the stability of marriages was raised. Finally, as the last decade has passed, more serious consideration has been given to the dying child's siblings, who had previously remained in the background (and occasionally other peers, wardmates and schoolmates). At present our knowledge is based on clinical reports, impressions, and small-scale retrospective studies and is filled with many interesting but untested assumptions.

This chapter will review the limited literature that deals expressly with the siblings and peers of dying children. It will be clear that there are few attempts to describe the whole range of phenomena which can be observed in these children. In part this results from the lack of a well-defined evaluative framework for considering the whole experience of the child. We will therefore provide a detailed description of the range of assessment which we find clinically useful in thinking about such children. A series of clinical vignettes will be provided to illustrate the areas of concern which we have encountered as we work clinically as a pediatrician and a psychiatrist. Finally we will pose several questions for research which may only be answerable with well-controlled, longitudinal, prospective studies. In particular, we must address the difference between naturally occurring, nonpathological phenomena and symptoms which justify active intervention.

REVIEW OF THE LITERATURE

One means of assessing the impact of the dying and death of a sibling is to study the correlation, if any, between sibling loss and later psychiatric illness or symptomatology. Blum and Rosenzweig (1), Pollock (2) and Rosenzweig and Bray (3) all note the presence of reported sibling loss in the backgrounds of psychiatric patients of varying diagnoses. None of these studies provide adequately controlled data to assess the comparative incidence or the likely import of these findings. Hilgard (4) goes into much more detail in presenting both case material and some hypotheses. This paper, one in a series dealing with anniversary reactions to a number of different types of major loss, includes four cases. The first, a case of Wilhelm Stekel's, depicts a family in which there had twice been the birth of a baby with the death of another child in the family on the same day. The boy in the case develops a strokelike picture following the birth of yet another child. A brief intervention returns the child to normal function. The second case is an $11\frac{1}{2}$-year-old who presents with a picture of a degenerative neurological disease at the same age at which a sister had earlier died. Brief intervention is successful. The third case is an adult who commits suicide at age 43, when his son is 12. The patient's older brother had died the day after the patient's twelfth birthday. The parents treated the patient as a replacement for his older sibling, placing an overwhelming set of expectations on him. The fourth case is a 34-year-old woman who becomes acutely psychotic at the time of surgery for her younger son who markedly resembles her brother who had died of a ruptured appendix at age 10. From these cases Hilgard abstracts four phenomena, the influence of a family saga, the issue of replacement children, the development of excessive guilt, and the presence of parental suffering at a time when their own children reach a critical age, reminding the parent of critical events of his or her own childhood. She includes no data on the incidence of such anniversary reactions, and adds a caution not to overinterpret as there are anniversary events which bear no clear relationship to current symptoms.

Cain et al. (5) provide a far more detailed listing of observed disturbed reactions to the death of a sibling. The sample for the data is entirely of psychiatric patients with no control population. There is no attempt to draw inferences regarding the frequency of such reactions in the general population at risk, or even to specify the frequency of many of the various specific problems in the population studied. Roughly one-half of the cases showed guilt reactions. These included "suicidal thoughts, depressive withdrawal, accident-prone behavior, punishment seeking, constant provocative testing, exhibitionistic use of grief and guilt, massive projection of superego accusations, and acting out." One-third of the cases involved situations where the surviving sibling had actually had some responsibility for the death, and had to face the problems of parentally enforced silence engendered by the parents' own struggle with anger and guilt. A number showed either superego projections of anger or fear of losing control of anger. Slightly less than one-quarter of the cases had experienced parentally enforced guilt for not mourning in an approved fashion. There were a variety of distortions in conceptions of illness and dying, with almost one-third equating growing up and dying. This often led to regressive behavior, fright of minor illness, or problematic attitudes toward doctors and hospitals. Some 40 percent showed immediate, prolonged or anniversary identification with symptoms of the dead sibling—hysterical pains, pseudoconvulsive states, asthma, etc. Death phobias were noted in some, with talion fantasies, and some measure of identification with the dead sibling. One-fifth noted some treatment by parents as a substitute child for the deceased. One-half found themselves subject to unfavorable comparisons with the deceased. About 15 percent showed some major distortion of cognitive function. Family variables included changes in sibling relations, parent-child relations, pathological parental mourning, and protracted mother absences during illness of the sibling prior to death. A lengthy but partial list of determinants of the type of reaction includes the nature of the death, the age and characteristics of the child who died, the child's degree of actual involvement in the sibling's death, the child's pre-existing relationship to the dead sibling, the immediate impact of the death on the parents, the parent's handling of the initial reactions of the surviving child, the reactions of the community, the death's impact on the family structure, the availability to the child and the parents of various "substitutes," the parents enduring reactions to the child's death, major concurrent stresses on the child and his family, and the developmental level of the surviving child.

Turning to studies which select on the basis of the presence of a dying child or a past death rather than the presence of psychiatric disturbance, we find a series where families are studied and siblings are considered to some degree. Cobb (6) notes that illness may lead to an extended absence of the mother from the home and that the parents will have to tell the siblings something after the death. Bozeman et al. (7) strongly emphasizes the impact of leukemic children on the mother. This, of course, provides an important part of the context in which the sibling experiences the dying of the ill child. In this study of twenty families the mothers show "a sense of guilt and responsibility for the illness, anger and hostility at physicians, anxiety at separation from the hospitalized child, problems accepting the reality of the diagnosis and prognosis, a later ambivalent acceptance of the diagnosis, conflict about ceding the maternal role of inpatient nursing staff, lack of extended family supports, ambivalent relationships with their own mothers and virtual absence of support from their own fathers, and lack of support from the group of other parents of children receiving care at the same time." Clearly, a variety of these issues reflect on hospital practices of the time regarding parental involvement in hospitalization, support groups, etc. A scant paragraph comments on the care of other children. The mothers' increased nervousness and irritability prevents them in many cases from carrying on normal activities with the other children. Five try to maintain the old balance of favors and discipline, ten clearly favor the ill child, three require special acts from the siblings, five felt that at some point they specially compensated the siblings. The siblings are noted to have some increase in school difficulties. Binger et al. (8) interviewed twenty families who had lost a child to leukemia several years before. At the time of illness, the families were in general protective of each other with closed communications systems, absenting fathers, and a primary unspoken fear of how and where the actual death would take place. Approximately 50 percent of the families reported one or more of their previously psychologically healthy children to have had one or more of the following—severe enuresis, headaches, poor school performance, school phobia, depression, severe separation anxiety, persistent abdominal pain, guilt, fear, or a sense of rejection by the parents. There is no clarification of how many of these siblings showed symptoms while the child was ill or dying, or only following the actual death. There is no data on how the families handled the siblings' problems although in eleven of the families some member was seen for psychiatric help. The only suggestion for intervention is the provision of "supportive therapy for parents and siblings."

Share (9) makes an attempt to review in some detail two divergent patterns of family communication. The protective approach is based on a belief that the exposure of the ill child or his siblings to any of the reality of the disease, diagnosis and prognosis except when absolutely unavoidable will be detrimental as it will be conceptually or emotionally too taxing (10, 11). Advocates of this approach may go beyond concealing knowledge from the child to actively encourage the child to deny. This approach runs the risk of children left in isolation, fearful of showing what they feel or asking what they wish. If they break the compact of silence, the adult world may reject them. In addition, this protection may leave them unprepared for the grief work which is to come when the sibling dies. The open approach implies a setting in which the siblings feel comfortable showing their concerns and asking the questions that occur to them (12, 13). This allows the child not to be isolated and to engage in the necessary work of reacting to familial change, which may include loss of attention, the physical absence of parents, role realignments, changes in valued family activities, and feelings of anger, fear and guilt (14). This approach runs the risk of overwhelming the child if indeed the conceptual and emotional stability or ability to engage in this psychological work and anticipatory grieving is not present. Share (9) comes to a final strong favoring of the open approach based largely on the apparent evidence that, given the opportunity to choose, most parents and children opt for open patterns and siblings demonstrate a great awareness of what is happening.

Heffron et al. (15) present data from group meetings for the parents of leukemic children held during the time of illness. As in other studies, almost all of the informants are mothers. All of this data is drawn from the fresh experiences when the child is ill or dying as opposed to the retrospective design of earlier studies. A number of the issues that emerge appear to have particular significance for other children in the family. The families are described as oscillating between the "sick world" and the well world with a marked change or dislocation in family activities consequent on the switch. A marked ambivalence toward God with a major questioning of previous religious attitudes and activities was often present. The mothers remarked on how important it was to share experiences with someone else who really understood out of their own similar experiences. The ill children set up informal groups as a communication network for their own experiences (16). Only siblings in large families have a chance among themselves for such a reference group. The mothers reported a recurrent frustration with the periods of increased depression or dependency in the ill child. Finally, it was clear that if any other family member became ill, the anxiety level and the stress experienced by the entire family markedly increased. Obviously this may relate to the mother's increased problems dealing with dependency needs of any member of the family when her reserves are stretched quite thin. The siblings were noted to be caught between the pain of potential loss and the anger at the special privileges often granted to the ill child. There was often some jealousy and teasing with a consequent guilt for the mistreatment. The general stance of the caregivers and the families in this study was one of open communication, with a shared belief that siblings' behavior changed if they better understood the events. A sweeping statement is made that "if handled openly there were no instances of a sibling using this information to hurt the child with leukemia during arguments."

Kaplan et al. (17) also discuss the family effects of stress during the illness, with data derived from interviews with 56 families of leukemic children from diagnosis to two months post death of the child. There is no indication of the structure of these interviews, how they were presented to the families or who among the family members was interviewed. The authors report an 87 percent failure to adequately cope based on their definition of appropriate coping. This may represent an over-pathologizing of the families as one of the criteria for adaptive coping is to reach an understanding of leukemia as a serious, ultimately fatal disease, often within a few days of diagnosis. This leaves little leeway for the family that for any dynamic or historical reasons has a much greater struggle with this new reality. More appropriately, they emphasize open communication and sharing of family grieving as an adaptive attribute. Although once again there is some rigidity in the notion that workers in the health and social service fields realize "what patients and family survivors 'must' experience to accept fatal illness and death." Two reactions which are seen as inhibiting open discussion are a fear of some unknown resultant disaster which openness might bring and the inability to deal with the diffuse hostility which family members feel. The result is garbled communications which disrupt the process of individual grieving and weaken family relationships. A set of guidelines for treatment proposed by the authors include—physicians as the pivotal figures in management, the need for the physician or social worker to "share the anguish, grief and fear" by simply listening, a gentle but persistent probing of any denial, and conserving energy for the long course of the disease by not making sudden energy consuming changes such as pregnancy, divorce, remarriage, job changes, and moves.

Lansky et al. (18) review the available data on the specific effect of childhood cancer on marital relationships. Hamovitch (19) noted a 10 percent incidence of marital problems during the illness or post death. Oakley and Patterson (20) studied 15 families eleven months post death and found no separations or divorces. Stehbens and Lascori (21) noted that twenty families seen at six months to three years post death reported no divorces or separations. Kaplan et al. (22), looking at forty couples three months post death, found 5 percent divorced and 18 percent separated. Lansky et al. (18) report on 188 of 259 families returning a questionnaire, and an additional 28 for which ancillary data provided information regarding marital status. Thus, based on a 83.4 percent of the total sample, they found a 1.19 percent person year divorce rate compared with the 2.03 percent rate for the population at large in the same state area. This study has the virtue of larger numbers and an attempt at controls. Unfortunately, the missing portion of the sample could easily have been unreachable in part because of major marital change, and the control group is by no means a matched one. At least they do question the earlier clinical wisdom that the death of a child with cancer leads to a high incidence of separation and divorce. In addition they report on 38 intact couples with a child in treatment for cancer who show comparable levels of stress to the parents of hemophiliac children and less stress than couples in marriage counselling, based on the Arnold Sign Indicator, a derivative of the MMPI.

Those reports which focus on the siblings as the primary subject of study as opposed to the focus on mothers or marital relationships do not shed much further light on the problems they encounter. Lindsay and McCarthy (23) differentiate between babies (age range ?) who are most vulnerable to loss of attention, toddlers who feel bad at decreased attention and regress with sleep disturbances, aggression, and digestive problems, and older children who understand but are angry. Symptoms include regression with increased daydreaming, psychosomatic symptoms including accidents, anxiety with vague fears and phobias, and reaction-formations to earlier rivalries with siblings. Lavigne and Ryan (24) compared 62 three to thirteen-year-old siblings of pediatric hematology patients with siblings of cardiology patients, plastic surgery patients and healthy children. The only clear increase in pathology is in the three to six-year-old siblings of the plastic surgery patients. Unfortunately, information on the healthy controls was obtained by mail, as opposed to the hospital-based interview study of all ill-child families, which may yield a difference of both frankness and type of information. Also important with the leukemic families, there is no indication of the relative health of the children. Early treatment and the time of dying may present quite different stresses to the family. Cairns et al. (25) note that siblings of children with cancer show similar levels of anxiety and fear for their health as their ill siblings, greater levels of social isolation, an angry concern with parents' over-indulgence and protectiveness, and fear of failure (older siblings). On at least one measure (their "family relations fear") however, the siblings do not differ from healthy children coming for visits for routine health care. The authors' recommendations are to include siblings in a family conference with physicians, help the family be attentive to their needs, and follow-up on possible stress-related physical complaints. Grogan (26) provides a much later follow-up of siblings at an average 13.5 years post-diagnosis. Thirteen siblings ranging in age from eight to twenty-eight, from eight families, were interviewed. At the time of interview none of them reported memories of having felt abandoned, some remembered an increase in rivalry for parental attention, and only rarely had guilt played an important role in the intervening years. The small sample, the informal, non-objective nature of the data, and the lack of any data concerning symptoms at the time of illness, make conclusions difficult. At most, one can say that some children may experience little if any long-term distress related to the dying and death of a sibling.

Besides the previous writings almost entirely about children with cancer, only one terminal illness of childhood has been looked at in much detail. Meyerowitz and Kaplan (27) looking at familial responses to cystic fibrosis noted two stress-related factors. Stress was increased in children who were aware of the sibling's diagnosis or if there had been a prior sibling's death. Tropauer et al. (28) reviewed twenty families and noted complaints of psychosomatic illnesses, school adjustment difficulties, learning problems and delinquency among the siblings of cystics, with no quantification or controls. McCollum and Gibson (29) summarize findings from 56 families based on questionnaires, interviews and parent groups. They note a variety of parental reactions and problems of the ill children but have no comment regarding siblings. There is also no discrimination of problems arising during a terminal phase of the illness. McCrae et al. (30) report a low rate of divorce and separation among the parents of children with cystic fibrosis. Allan et al. (31) discuss fifty families with a child currently or previously in treatment for cystic fibrosis. They note the material effects of the prolonged illness. The siblings are noted to suffer from lack of attention. Forty-one of the fifty families had one or more unaffected children. One-third of these mothers reported one or two normal children with overall behavior problems; including "soiling, stealing, fire-setting, abdominal pain." Only one was seen at a psychiatric clinic. There is no control population and no indication of incidence of specific problems or when in the course of the illness the problems developed. Kerner et al. (32) in a retrospective study noted that three of thirty-three siblings in thirteen families had problems with one receiving psychiatric care, one having poor school performance, and one with psychosomatic illness. In sixteen families there was one divorce and one threatened separation, which was felt to be a low incidence. Psychiatric care was provided at some time to 25 percent of the families. Data were based on home interviews an average of two and one-half years after the death of the affected child. There was no control comparison. Clearly, the problems of families with a cystic child overlap with the problems of families with other chronically but not necessarily terminally-ill children. It is not within the scope of this chapter to review that literature (see 33-36).

There are a number of authors who without studying a particular population have written about the evaluation of the family with a dying member and types of intervention. Many of these concentrate on the family with an ill adult (37-40). Others which consider the family of the dying child (34, 35, 41, 42) have little or no comment on the particular problems of siblings. Petrillo and Sanger (33) consider problems related to the dying child as one among many issues relating to the emotional care of hospitalized children. They indicate the need to help parents prepare siblings for the death with information and explanations. Three phases of sibling reactions are noted. From birth to five years the child reacts to changes in the parents with a sense of loss and withdrawal; from five to ten, with concern about the implications of the illness and fearfulness for self, and from ten to fifteen with generally supportive actions. Feinberg (43) presents a detailed description of a lengthy intervention with two siblings of a dying child. He identifies a series of principles to guide such work. A forthright approach with an attention to reality is necessary to show a readiness to respond to the child's concerns. Discussions about previous severe losses can have an immunizing as well as educational aspect. Time is needed for catharsis of anger and resentment. A general orienting to the reality of events with instruction about illness and medical care provides a basis for understanding future events. Finally, the therapist may need to help initiate the process of mourning/remembering.

Two other sets of peers of the dying child should be briefly considered here. These include the clinic and wardmates of the child and the friends and schoolmates. Natterson and Knudson (44) extend the rule of concealment and closed communication to the wardmates as a recommendation procedure, while Vernick and Karon (12) attribute the same problems of isolation to these peers as to siblings. Bluebond-Langner (16) depicts clearly how much the children in this situation are aware of what is going on and that if silent, they remain so to follow the adult rules. Schowalter (45) comments on the indirect communications which may be made to other children on the ward by such practices as openly posting a danger or critical list, with consequent unspoken anxiety. Petrillo and Sanger (33) describe a case of roommates who show varying degrees of guilt and anxiety and require brief intervention, as one member of a foursome is removed to critical care to die. Fredlund (46) in discussing the viewpoint of the school setting notes that, given one in twenty persons losing a mother, father or sibling by age twenty, not considering the deaths of significant relatives or friends, the school cannot avoid the presence of death in the children's lives. She recommends an honest openness in the classroom and continued contact with the family. Kaplan et al. (47) note problems which may occur leading to the expulsion of the ill child from the school, or a lesser withdrawal of contact, commenting that these actions are often to protect the adults involved and do not put the needs of the children first.

The preceding review leaves us with few acceptable generalizations. Siblings may be seriously affected in almost all cases or very rarely. The level of distress may be serious or similar to healthy children under mild stress. There is no diagnostic set of symptoms to indicate immediate turmoil or to predict long term serious consequences. The net effect of the research literature may even leave some readers wondering if there is a problem worthy of study. To explore this we will turn back to more direct clinical experience. A familiarity with issues not covered in the review but dealt with at length elsewhere in the book will be assumed. The growing understanding of the development over time of the child's ability to conceptualize death (Chap. 2), the capacity of the child to mourn and how this changes with age (Chap. 9), the more detailed understanding of the impact on the parents and consequent change in family context for the siblings (Chap. 6), and the role of education within the school (Chaps. 15 and 16), are all necessary bases to understand the particular experience of the siblings and peers of the dying child.

FRAMEWORK FOR EVALUATION

To understand case material presented by any particular clinician it is essential to understand the conceptual framework he or she uses for viewing specific symptoms, behavioral disturbances or complaints. As a psychiatrist and a psychiatrically-oriented pediatrician, we have come from separate perspectives to share a common approach to the evaluation of problems faced by the siblings and peers of the dying child. The individual child can be seen at the center of a series of concentric circles of influence. These will be discussed in order from individual-to family-to school (peer)-to extended world. This sequence does not indicate a step-wise grading of importance, e.g., there is no implication that family variables should be included only if the individual ones are not sufficiently explanatory. Systems' theory leads us to see a constant interaction among levels of explanation with events at each level spreading to shape and change events at all others. We are frequently dismayed to find clinicians or theoreticians speaking and writing as if some event was solely an intrapsychic, family structural, subcultural or developmental one.

At the individual level there are important issues related to both developmental stage and past experience. Analytic theory provides one approach to developmental stages. Intrapsychic function whether psychosexual or ego structural offers insights and controversy. There is not even clear agreement on whether mourning can occur effectively in a four-year-old or not until the end of adolescence (48). The extrapolation from hidden events to external behavior is always fraught with ambiguity. More formal cognitive theorists from Piaget on present observations concerning the child's behavioral relations with various aspects of reality, though at times losing touch with the meaning of the experience for the individual. The child also lives in an expanding social network in which observations take on new meanings. In addition, as Chess and Thomas have described, each child has both characteristic qualities of temperament from birth and a developing set of individual personality traits. A four-year-old showing early oedipal conflicts, delayed development of time concept with consequent difficulties with delayed gratification, frequent play with a next-door neighbor of the same age with some clear appreciation for rules, a history of temperamental irritability, a low threshold for change with a high activity level and another four-year-old still struggling with phallic issues, but having an early sense of time and some mastery of delayed gratification, rare contact with children of the same age with consequent greater dependence on the mother, and a temperamental history of passivity, slow and less marked response to changes, with a low level of activity will show markedly different responses to the dying of an older sibling and the temporary loss of maternal attention which is a likely concurrent event. Beyond the various developmental patterns which must be considered, there are particular past experiences which are pertinent. Most obviously, any past occurrence of the same behavior or symptomatology which now brings the child to the attention of the parents or the caregivers must be established. Further, a particular history of past experience, normal and abnormal, with separation, loss and grief are of importance. This may include a maternal hospitalization at a particular age with consequent behavioral reactions, the manner in which the child handled the first day in nursery school, or witnessing the death of a pet in a car accident.

Family therapists such as Minuchin and Nagy attend closely to the structuring and restructuring of families. Others such as Watzlawick concentrate on patterns of communication. Whitaker has helped us in understanding the flow across multiple generations of deeply experienced patterns of irrational behavior which often cannot be dealt with at a simple cognitive level. In addition the work during the past decade on stages of development in adult life is beginning to be employed by family therapists and theorists to evaluate possible stages of development of family life. The basic structure of the family unit actually living together is a starting point. This involves some understanding of the roles filled by each member, patterns of both verbal and non-verbal communication, and the experienced but unspoken myths which may permeate a family unit. The broader context expands to include at least a three-generational history of important physical and psychological events, with an understanding of this moment in the history or development of a unit of a larger family tree.

The child also has a social context which includes both the peer group of friends at play, and classmates at school. Each individual will have a current level and history of performance in the academic tasks of school life. In addition the socialization of the child as demonstrated in interpersonal skills with age mates is both a forum in which problems may arise, and a source of support and strength when the underpinnings of life in the family are threatened by the presence of serious illness and death.

The extended world may be used as a catchall category for a range of variables including sociodemographic (urban/rural, social class, economic), cultural, and institutional (the particulars of the system of care in which the dying child, parents and siblings are enmeshed). The meaning of differences in many of these areas are even less well established in terms of their effect on the siblings and peers of a dying child than the more easily observable ones of the previous levels of evaluation. Nevertheless we try to bear them in mind for the insights which they may bring us in the process of clinical intervention.

Finally, to mention the obvious, besides considering each of the above as broad contextual background for the symptoms or behavior that the sibling or peer is showing, one must take into account any concurrent stressful events. Is the child in the midst of a physical illness of his or her own? Has the mother's father had a massive heart attack? Do financial considerations in the community lead to a decision to close a child's school, pushing him into a strange new environment? Does a major recession further threaten family economic resources already strained to the breaking point?

An attempt to gather exhaustive information at all levels described above in every case presented to the clinician would clearly demand a level of grandiosity to which few of us aspire. Pragmatically, the demand on the clinician is to take seriously the challenge to the broad, systematic view of the possible levels of explanation. This allows pursuit of understanding at all levels necessary for effective explanation and intervention in each individual case.

INTERVENTION—AREAS OF CONCERN

The physician, nurse, psychiatrist, social worker or other health professional who works with dying children and their families, need only keep an open ear and he or she will hear about the siblings. They will be mentioned by the parents, by the ill child or speak for themselves in the waiting room or the clinic or the wards of the hospital. Their speech may be words, drawings, or other behavior. The following clinical anecdotes are taken from events seen by us or our colleagues[1] or reported to us by family members. They will be presented in abstracted form both to insure the confidentiality of families and to allow the discussion of how different the meaning of an event can be, when it occurs in different individuals or families.

---

[1] Dr. Patricia Joo and Dr. Dorothy Ganick.

Child's Definition of Sick Role, Dying and Death

A four-year-old with leukemia is the youngest of five children, 4, 5, 6, 8, 9. The six-
year-old becomes seven in the process of treatment. He is preoccupied with bodies and
what happens to them, and will not sleep alone at night without a light on after doing
so the previous three years. He is more upset than the other children if injured in any
way, and has more difficulties with doctor visits.

The evaluation of the child indicates that he has begun to grapple with the cognitive notion of death as a separate entity. He has developed a belief that it is a ghost-like figure likely to appear at night. Without having received much explanation from his parents he conceives of the hospitalizations of the sibling as an attempt to protect her from death in this personified fashion. Never having been really ill, he has very little conception of the process of physical medical treatment. The family, coming from a strong religious background, has turned to their church and explanations of God's action to understand why the disaster of this illness has befallen them. Thus the parents much like the child are struggling with understanding at a level beyond the immediately apparent or physically visible. The marital pair has placed responsibility for the well-being of young children on the mother, who because of her own at times distant mother has developed an intrusive, overprotective style with her children. Father comes from a family that highly values independence at an early age, particularly in boys. The six-year-old has just begun first grade and is showing a marked reluctance to play in some of the more physical playground games. An intervention must take into account the level of understanding the child has of events, the parental conflict over encouraging regression or demanding independence (light on or off at night), the increased visits by mother to the pediatrician to make sure that this child is healthy, and the teacher's lack of awareness of events. One or two sessions with the child in a play therapy setting may be sufficient to communicate some stage appropriate information regarding illness. A session with the couple can explore the family roots of their conflict. The teacher can be reached either by the mother or a social worker and given some brief consultation in handling the classroom situation of the child as the sibling's illness progresses.

A set of twins are followed from the age of 3–5, one with ALL. One day as the two of
them are drawing pictures together in the waiting room of the clinic, the healthy child
draws a picture of herself and her sister. When the staff hematologist enters, she colors
out her sister's face with black. Four to five months after her sister's death, she develops
an identical set of symptoms—tiredness, leg pains, loss of appetite.

The evaluation of the healthy twin indicated a clear level of identification with her sibling, unsurprising in identical twins. Her perceptions did not really include a notion of her sister having an illness which was continuing over time. She seemed most aware at the time of the picture-drawing that after a visit to the clinic, and receiving chemotherapy from the hematologist, her sister felt bad. She was noted to have distinct anger and aggressive wishes towards the doctor, and projected onto him an anger or wish to hurt her sister. The mother had regularly made an attempt to treat the two of them as individuals, not as interchangeable twins. The healthy girl clearly resented increased attention from other family members which was being given to her ill sister. In the week previous to the picture, a playmate had gone to a hospital emergency room to have a laceration sutured, and had talked about how it hurt. The later development of symptoms like her sister's occurred at a point when the mother was moving beyond her most intense grieving and beginning to reach out into the outside world for social contact with friends she had not seen. The surviving daughter experienced this as in part a pulling away from her, at a time when she was struggling with her own internalization of memories of her sister. A chance for both girls to play with the doctor equipment and dolls in the ward playroom during a hospitalization allowed the exploration of caring and hurtful medical roles, with the expression of fear and anger. An extended family conference helped a number of relatives to see the importance of providing attention to both girls. Finally, reassurance of the mother that her second daughter was not also developing leukemia, combined with a joint session (mother and daughter) talking about the daughter's needs for attention and how hard it was at times to deal with memories of the dead sister, led to a rapid resolution of the physical symptoms and a completion of the initial mourning for both.

Child's Internal World—Responsibility, Guilt, Anger, Anxiety

A boy with ALL from age 2-5, and older brother age 6-9. The older sibling demands to get in parents' bed whenever he wants, just like the sick child. He teases his younger brother and is overheard saying "Ha, ha, you are going to die." During the last hours of the sibling's life at home, he watches TV and will have nothing to do with the process. After the death is announced he runs around the house joyfully.

Billy, the older brother, has been a temperamentally very high intensity child since birth. He may indeed be hyperactive, though does not clearly have any deficit of attention span. In his first three years, he was a constant trial to his parents. The younger brother was born with a placid and pleasant temperament. The parents without consciously meaning to are far more rewarding to the younger child, simply because he is so much easier to live with. The rivalry between the two has therefore been couched in terms which Billy can never win without becoming another person. Both parents come from "good" families, in which overt expression of anger is muted, and expression of painful emotions such as grief is encouraged in a contained and respectful fashion. Billy's father, however, as an adolescent went through three years of somewhat stormy rebellion against his parents, before settling back into the family mold. During the last year of the illness, Billy has become progressively more aggressive in school, particularly with any children who he sees as well-liked by the teacher. On both individual and family evaluation, Billy is seen to be almost overwhelmed with his anger. Intervention in this case, if accepted by the family, will involve long-term (possibly several years) family and individual therapy. Billy has shown a style which has grown more pervasive with time and creates almost continuous conflict within all major spheres of his life. Untreated, he can easily be seen progressing to full blown characterologic problems as an adult.

C is a 6-year-old leukemic. She receives a bone marrow transplant from her 18-year-old brother. Over the next years out of the home he has marked trouble with his own life planning. He expresses the feeling that he can never make plans, since he must always be available if she needs another transplant.

The brother is at a developmental stage where his main task is the major separation from home and the development of an independent identity which will allow him to function successfully in the adult world. Just at that moment he finds himself bound in a particular way to a sibling. His tie is in some ways quite different from that of the kidney donor of which more has been written. Potentially he could continue to be a donor, standing between his sister and death. The family is one that over several generations has not had members leave the immediate area, but has encouraged early marriages and settling within the same community, the pressure not to strain family ties will be increased. This brother had before his sister's illness demonstrated academic achievement beyond the norm for the family and had goals of professional training. In his first two years of college his work has been well below the standards that could have been reasonably expected. His father has been only mildly disappointed, having secretly hoped that the boy would eventually come back to farm with him as he had with his father. Furthermore, the brother has experimented with marijuana a couple of times on campus, but not discussed with anyone his fear that this may injure his marrow and "accidentally" make him no longer eligible as a donor. A brief session or two with the family to unravel some of the past demands and expectations can be followed by individual, and probably brief psychotherapy (6 months) enabling the son to focus on the costs to him, if he constructs a false barrier of his sister's illness, to avoid dealing with the internal conflicts of attachment/separation and dependence/independence from the family.

Ten-year-old twins, one with leukemia. There is the necessary match for a marrow transplant. The healthy sibling states "she never did anything for me, why should I do this for her?" When hospitalized for her donation, she is markedly anxious with vomiting and stomach pains. The transplant is later rejected, and the sister dies.

On evaluation of the healthy girl and family history it turns out that the two girls have actually been very close. They have had their share of fights and disagreements, but have always been each other's closest friend. A closer look shows that the parents have begun to worry that the girls are too close. This year in school they have encouraged them to develop more individual friends. Although the family and the treating institution have offered an open pattern of communication, the healthy twin has not during the course of the illness seemed to give any thought to the possibility that her sister could really die. Mother herself was a twin and has always felt a unique bond with her sister. They have ended up living at some distance from each other with a strong wish that it were not so. Part of the mother's encouraging the girls to decrease their dependency on each other is her hope that such adult separations will be easier. At school the ill twin has been the more socially at ease and often provided the possibility of entering new friendships to her sister who follows a step behind. At the time of the transplant the family has tried to push the healthy twin to realize that her sister might die without the operation. For the first time she faces the possible permanent loss of what is truly in some ways still a part of herself. Her physical symptoms in the hospital appear in later therapy to be an attempt to take on the illness as she gave of her health, to sacrifice herself for her sister, to whom she truly feels she owes "everything." She requires some lengthy intervention, to deal with the sense of failure which the marrow rejection brings.

A five-year-old is playing with his six-year-old brother and a six-year-old neighbor. There is a can of burning trash in the back yard. They take a pan full of gasoline which they have seen Daddy use to start fires, and try to throw it on the fire. The five-year-old is badly burned, spends six weeks in a burn unit, and dies. The sibling has nightmares, becomes withdrawn, teary, and loses his appetite.

The family has always been fairly arbitrary about discipline, with the children having a great deal of difficulty forming a coherent sense of what is right and wrong. One time a misbehavior may result in a physical beating by father, another time in no comment at all. The children are not closely supervised. Since the accident the father has begun drinking heavily, a pattern which has been there at previous times of stress. Grandparents live in two other sections of the country and are not a source of support to parents. Their finances are limited and frequent trips to the regional medical center are not possible. The parents are unable to express either their own feelings of guilt about the accident or to find a balance between rage at the remaining child and need to hold onto him as the burned child fails. Intervention both in the form of family therapy and individual sessions for the sibling are crucial. Although difficult to do in terms of available time, the sessions are vital in intervening in the massive guilt and depression experienced by the six-year-old. Without having had a stable pattern of psychological growth, and facing the erratic mood swings of the parents, he is at high risk.

Child's Family—Clarification of Communication and Roles

A 20-year-old is diagnosed with AML and spends a stormy five months getting a remission, with many close brushes with death. About two months after remisssion he has a fight with his 16-year-old brother. Both get drunk. The 20-year-old then overdoses on sleeping pills. The 16-year-old feels responsible.

A more detailed picture of the family shows a close knit, almost symbiotically close unit, including two older sisters and one older brother. The family runs a small farm. There is a tradition of heavy drinking. Father drank throughout his twenties, older brother is just tapering off at 28, the patient began in high school and his younger brother has just joined a beer drinking crowd at school. Father has developed progressive emphysema and has begun to rely more and more on the boys for assistance with the farm. The mother is very protective of and indulgent of all of the male members of the family. One of the sisters is a nurses' aid, the other a teacher. Both clearly have chosen helping professions. The sixteen-year-old had assumed that he would have several years in his late teens to be wild, as his older siblings had done. The combination of father's progressive illness and brother's acute illness has placed a demand on him to be responsible much earlier than is usual for men in the family. The family is seen for a series of sessions with all members attending. Several issues become apparent. Throughout the time the 20-year-old was in the hospital he received massive amounts of attention from the family. When he achieved remission, he expected some kind of celebration of his "return to life." The family still fearful of the return of the illness, facing that more realistically than he is able to, and exhausted by the ordeal, want to return to business as usual. The father expects that the son can drink if he chooses but should settle back in to work helping with the farm. The son refuses to work and carouses around the local countryside at all hours. The mother feeling that her caring has helped pull him through is intensely angry at his taking risks which may kill him even if the cancer is cured, but is unable to speak the anger, since that is not a permitted role for a "helpful woman." She can only nag. The sixteen-year-old ends up in the fight with brother out of his anger at being asked to grow up too soon, but also as a vehicle for the unexpressed anger of both parents. After a few sessions the family agree to hold a family party to celebrate the recovery of the 20-year-old from both the leukemia and the suicide attempt, bearing in mind that the future brings no guarantee of continued health. Father agrees to use some outside help while the 20-year-old is still recuperating from the effects of chemotherapy and the 16-year-old is finishing school. Mother steps back from the 20-year-old and agrees to try to see him as an adult, not a child of 10.

A child, originally diagnosed with leukemia at age 10, relapses at age sixteen. During those six years he is never really an adolescent but acts more like a young adult. A 2-year younger sibling enters adolescence and at age 14, the time of sibling's relapse, is reported by parents to have become uncontrollable, addicted, promiscuous.

The parents present as very emotionally controlled people. Father is a college professor, mother an elementary school teacher. Throughout the illness, overriding the recommendations of treating staff, they have continued to press for a pattern of closed communication. The word leukemia is never used. The younger daughter has been told that her brother has anemia. The daughter at age fourteen is found to be doing very well in school. She reports having smoked marijuana a couple of times, and having had some beer twice. Her boyfriend is 15, and has made some overtures to go beyond petting, but thus far has accepted her refusal. Apparently since the time of relapse the parents have become highly overprotective of both children. Mother began to demand answers from daughter regarding any sexual activity with boyfriend and any use of drugs. Daughter's embarrassment, having never spoken openly with mother about sexuality, and concern for her own separateness have been interpreted as admissions of guilt. The family has chosen a style of communication which works when things are going well. Now, with potential disaster having struck and denial giving way to anger and fear, there is no avenue for the expression of their inner turmoil. Mother has projected the chaotic feelings onto her daughter, and sought a less fearful disaster to struggle with. A dozen sessions into family therapy, with great difficulty, the family begins to speak more openly regarding the illness and their own fears. Both children acknowledge that they have known much more than their parents credited, and express relief. The new openness provides a ground for building new trust between mother and daughter although there are clear crises ahead as she pursues a more normal adolescence than her brother has had.

Three siblings are 11, 9, and 7 at the time of death of the 11-year-old who was originally diagnosed with leukemia at age three. All are boys. The youngest resembles the oldest physically. At a family meeting close to the time of death, the 9-year-old is noted to look very depressed, which mother denies.

A more extensive family evaluation at that time reveals a very secretive family. As one example the mother had a first pregnancy at which twins were born, one died immediately and the other was severely deformed and institutionalized. Father had the physician tell mother that there was only one child, who died. Mother has always blurred the boundaries with her ill child, speaking of him as we, or of our feelings. She has an image of the child as having been very popular in school, but being abandoned by friends when the final relapse occurs. The school gives a picture of the child as always withdrawn and never active socially. The second child has never had much attention since the diagnosis, while the youngest, due in part to a resemblance in both temperament and appearance, has been secretly regarded by the mother as a replacement child if the illness should prove fatal. The middle child although in some ways ignored by mother has had a good relationship with father, and has picked up some of his independence and socially out-going manner. As family therapy is begun it is felt that the sibling initially presenting as depressed is indeed showing a fairly normal anticipatory grief reaction, and the younger sibling is actually at greater risk. He has already been infantilized to a marked degree by mother. His psychodynamic growth is restricted by the symbiotic bonds of her overprotectiveness. The father is unwilling to interfere in any active way. He is too afraid of his wife's fragility to challenge her efficacy in the maternal role. A lengthy period of family therapy is necessary to have any chance at significant change.

> An 11-year-old girl is clearly dying, and continues to hang on past the expectations of the care givers. She is conscious, but has intermittently severe and distressing pain. After her absent 20-year-old brother returns from a distant college campus, the family spends one evening in the hospital with the brother playing guitar and singing songs, and the girl dies peacefully in her mother's arms.

The tenor of the foregoing examples indicates that the siblings of a dying child only come to our attention in troubled or symptomatic manners. This family, however, has shown a clear ability to handle the emotional turmoil of a terminal disease. The brother who was away at school had been very close to the ill child and they had talked comfortably on his last visit home. The family had been in contact with him, and left it up to him to come home if he felt the need to be there. He had felt that he and his sister had parted well after the last visit and had not planned to return home. It had been the mother's question to the ill daughter as she was grimly hanging onto life, "What do you need," that had elicited a request to see brother one more time. Here, the major contribution of caregiving staff was the provision of a unit which allowed this kind of family openness of communication, and supported them as needed, during the final days.

Child's Role in Treatment

> A 13-year-old girl with a ten-year-old brother with leukemia. A program of home care facilitates the ill child spending most of his final months of life at home. The sister at mother's urging becomes increasingly involved in the physical care of the brother. She begins to show marked signs of anxiety and sleeplessness as his death approaches.

A family history included the information that the mother had been swimming with a younger sibling when she was fifteen years old. The brother had drowned, despite her efforts to rescue him. She had always carried the belief in her mind that she should have been able to do something more. Over the years she has come up with many ideas for aiding him, and felt if she had only done some of them she would have felt less guilty about his death. The girl has no previous history of anxiety reactions to stress. Her psychosocial development has been unremarkable. She is a good student at school, and has friends. During the earlier two years of her brother's illness, even at times when relapses had been life-threatening, he had been treated in the hospital. At those times she had not been symptomatic. In a family session, the mother's experience with the death of her brother was discussed for the first time as a family. Then mother and daughter began to discuss the daughter's reactions to being involved directly in the care of her sibling. The daughter described her growing fear that she would do something wrong, and hurt or kill her brother. Mother had clearly held back from being supportive out of her own ambivalence and fear that she herself might fall short once again. The program of home care, which they had readily accepted as a means to maintain the closeness all family members felt and wanted, had brought old tensions of a generation before back to life. After open discussion with the support staff of the home care program, all family members felt freer to turn to each other and the program staff for reassurance when needed. The daughter found herself able to participate at an individually chosen, not maternally chosen, level in the care of her brother.

A ten-year-old sibling of a seven-year-old leukemic began to develop leg aches, insomnia and headaches like her brother had had immediately before a hospitalization. She seemed angry and irritable.

In an individual evaluation, the girl presented anger at her family, and a general feeling of being left out. When her brother was hospitalized, she received much of her care from a nearby aunt. Mother spent much of the time at the hospital, and father would go to support mother when he could get free from work. The girl presented no history of previous separation problems, had followed a normal course of development, and appeared to have good academic performance and social relations in school. The family was a close one, with many members of the extended family living in several small towns within 30 miles of each other. Special arrangements were made for the girl to come to the area of the regional medical center where her brother was being treated. During her visit of several days, she came with her mother to the hospital each day. She participated in some simple types of care for her brother, learning where to get water for him and how to rub his legs when they hurt. Mother and daughter developed a special closeness during this shared time. As the hospitalization continued the daughter returned to spend much of the time with her aunt, and in school. The mother continued to talk regularly with her on the phone. With her personal experience of the hospital, she could understand much more of the simple things the mother shared about the day's events.

Two brothers 10 and 13 are riding on the back of the family pickup truck. Both fall off. The 10-year-old is killed instantly. The 13-year-old is in intensive care with a head injury and may be dying. A five- and eight-year-old, also boys, were not along on the truck. The five-year-old becomes "hyperactive" and begins to talk about how if he had been there he would have held onto them and saved them. He also wants to go to the hospital and make his other brother get better. The parents come to have him evaluated psychiatrically.

The family had been asked by the intensive care unit personnel earlier if they wished to see a counselor but had declined. It was only when the five-year-old's activity level became intolerable for them that they followed up on the suggestion. A brief review of the five-year-old's individual history indicated no previous pathology. There had never been a major family disruption before. The accident had occurred secondary to another driver's actions which had resulted in a sudden stop, throwing the two boys from the back of the truck. Although the parents had at times questioned the safety of the boys riding there, it had not been a major issue for contention. The family style presented in the initial interview was a controlled, non-expressive one. Both parents acted as if they should simply proceed stoically with their lives. There was no previous experience in their families of origin of sudden death of children. The five-year-old, however, began to show a range of emotion from anger to anxiety to sadness and began to talk in the same grandiose way of the fantasies of saving both his brothers. He provided the spark which enabled the parents to begin sharing the massive grief, that they had barely revealed to each other. As their pain became more apparent the five-year-old's activity slowed to a reasonable pace. Only several sessions were necessary to get the family unfrozen and allow them to proceed with their grieving on their own. In this situation, the five-year-old simply acted as a bellwether for the distress of the family and provided the means for the already offered institutional care to be accepted.

Type of Illness—Chronic/Acute, Disease/Trauma

A holiday weekend car accident in which both parents, and 3- and 5-year-old siblings are killed. A 10-year-old is in intensive care with a potentially fatal head injury, a 12-year-old girl has broken ribs and a broken arm.

Unlike illnesses which may have had some chronicity before entering a terminal phase the results of accidental trauma happen suddenly with no preparation. A survivor may also face massive simultaneous loss of the family. Any talk of her reactions to the dying of her brother is so affected by the concurrent stress of losing all her family that it demands a different approach. Perhaps the most helpful guide is the literature on survivors of disaster-plane crashes, natural disasters and wars. Lifton's work on survivorhood is helpful in understanding the total numbness that an individual may show. The girl in the example given attended sessions of a ward group for all teenage patients able to leave their rooms. Meetings were held in a room used only for teen activities and meetings. During the hour meetings the teens were protected by a hospital agreement that there would be no interruption for procedures, tests, or other medical business. Although she rarely spoke, the meetings were a time with a peer group, with whom she spent little time outside of meetings. She was very reserved with any adults, as if she was temporarily cut off from an older generation by the loss of both parents. In the group she found norms which included the acceptance of silence. Some members spoke very little for many weeks. It was one of the only settings in which she seemed to make any real contact with other people during the first weeks after the accident. Later, she began to emerge from the numbness, first with a roommate and then with other teens on the ward. After several weeks she was finally able to pay some real attention to her brother's condition and ask about his chances of recovery.

A family has three children, girls, 14 and 8, and a boy 13. The 13-year-old is away for the day on a fishing trip with an uncle when the 8-year-old is hit by a truck. He returns to find her transported to another city to a regional medical center. He is first taken up to spend the night in a vigil with the parents and older sister, then sent back to the grandparents, then called back as the sister's condition fails the next morning.

Following sudden trauma and impending death, the surviving family is often thrown into chaos, with no one being able to coordinate necessary activities. A year after the death, the son who had previously had some psychosomatic symptoms, began to have a marked increase in symptoms, as an anniversary date came closer. The family showed no abnormal patterns, other than a marked hypochondriasis in one grandparent and some alcoholism. The boy has followed a normal course of development and has had no other developmental problems or psychiatric symptoms. The pattern that became apparent is that during the time immediately following the accident, the vigil drew the three family members who were present closer together. The son, because he was in and out of the mourning group, never felt the depth of shared experience. Thus, at times when an anniversary brought the pain back to all of them, he again felt isolated and left out. It is essential for someone, at the intensive care unit, the primary physician or a family friend to intervene in a timely fashion and help the family to function as a unit so that all members can draw on the support generated.

Peers other than Siblings—Wardmates and Classmates

As a well-liked teenager on an adolescent ward is dying, the weekly teen group reflects his impending death in a number of themes. There is a protest of too strict regulation, a wish to spend more time off the ward and to be aided in ordering out pizza every night if they like. Two teens recovering from back surgery and currently in Streiker Frames, talk in a very anxious fashion of their desire to be out of them soon.

One of the most significant peer groups of children who are dying is the cohort of patients with similar diseases who have been treated in the same clinic, e.g., leukemics, and the children on the same ward, if the dying child is hospitalized. Despite well-intentioned efforts by adults to conceal reality, children of ages at least above four and maybe earlier show a clear awareness, either in play or language of death as it visits others. The teen group described earlier was an important forum for this. The few overt discussions of death usually occurred when there was no terminally ill patient in the group, in the context of pre-surgical fears. The emotions stirred by someone actually dying on the ward more often appeared in covert fashion. Themes as noted above included power and control. Discussions of rules seemed to reflect a concern with whether those who made the rules really had the best interests of the teens in mind. If so, then how could they allow a friend or acquaintance to die. Those teens who were most dependent on staff, immobilized in Streiker Frames, seemed to experience waves of anxiety as they tried to cope with the uncontrolled specter of death. Interpretations which directed discussion too rapidly toward the fact that someone was dying on the ward, met with rapid evasions. Sometimes it was necessary to avoid overt mention at all in order to allow further discussion about anxiety and control. Individual patients who seemed particularly distressed were followed up by staff later, and in a more private setting voiced some fears that the group seemed unable to contain.

A leukemic child in a school system in a small town. The child diagnosed at 7 now 9, has been told little about his condition and his classmates nothing. He has been teased about his hair loss, puffy cheeks, tiredness, missing school, and slowed growth. One evening on a local television station, both he and a number of his classmates see an appeal for money for a fund to help pay for his care, so that he will not die.

Secrets do not always keep well, and the distrust engendered after concealment is broken can be very damaging. A child who suffers from a potentially terminal illness still has to live in the world of children. This includes the school where lack of knowledge can lead to unmeant cruelty. A teacher who hopes to help a class deal with the illness of a class member needs both an awareness of the needs of the particular child, learned from frequent communications with the family, and a willingness to face his or her own fears about death and dying. An early intervention, with the teacher sharing with the class some understanding of what being ill and being hospitalized exacts, might have spared a good deal of two years of social ostracism. Too much information could isolate a child as a curiosity or freak, too little can form a barrier of isolation from lack of understanding.

The preceding vignettes illustrate some of the issues that arise with the siblings and peers of dying children. The anecdotes at times combine material from several different families. Most of the symptomatic presentations have been seen in other children, for whom a different set of data from the various levels of evaluation, indicate a different etiology and type of intervention. Other families with similar individual or systematic patterns, came to our attention with different presenting symptoms. Actual intervention may be very brief or long term therapy. It may be done by any one of many members of the medical team. Clinically, the critical issue is the awareness that the siblings and peers do exist and may show effects from the experience of having a brother, sister, ward-mate, or class-mate dying.

ISSUES FOR FURTHER RESEARCH

The beginnings of understanding any human phenomena are to be found in the direct observation of the people who are involved. It is unfortunate that so much of what writing has been done about the siblings and other peers of dying children is based on second hand reports, often given months to years after the critical events. Our clinical material is an unselected population, seen because something has happened to engage a parent's or a caregiver's attention. A series of cases, in which the siblings were routinely observed alone and in a family setting and parents were interviewed, would help to specify the range of behavior to be studied. If observations were extended to include the time after the death, correlations could be drawn between coping with dying and abnormalities of the grieving process. Are there predictors of later maladaptation? A longer term follow-up would give us a better sense of any causal connections between events during the illness and death of the sibling and later psychopathology. We alluded earlier to another set of unasked questions about similarities and differences between the more often studied cancer and cystic fibrosis cases and the rarely mentioned traumatic injuries, accidental or otherwise. Finally our clinical experience leads us to believe in the value of therapeutic interventions, usually short term, but occasionally lengthy. Accepting the general difficulty of demonstrating the efficacy of psychotherapy, can we show a difference in the short and long term outcome for children who receive the types of help described earlier?

REFERENCES

1. Blum, G. S. & Rosenzweig, S.: The Incidence of Sibling and Parental Deaths in the Anamnesis of Female Schizophrenics, *J. Gen. Psychol.*, 1944, vol. 31, pp. 3–13.

2. Pollock, G. H.: Childhood, Parent and Sibling Loss in Adult Patients, *Arch. Gen. Psychiat.*, 1962, vol. 7, pp. 295-306.
3. Rosenzwerg, S. & Bray, D.: Sibling Deaths in Anamnesis of Schizophrenic Patients, *A.M.A. Arch. Neurol. Psychiat.*, 1943, vol. 49, pp. 71-92.
4. Hilgard, J.: Depressive and Psychotic States as Anniversaries to Sibling Death in Childhood, *Rept. Psychiat. Clinics*, 1969, vol. 6, pp. 197-211.
5. Cain, A., Fast, I., & Erickson, M.: Children's Disturbed Reactions to the Death of a Sibling, *American Journal of Orthopsychiatry*, 1964, vol. 34, pp. 741-752.
6. Cobb, B.: Psychological Impact of Long Illness and Death of a Child on the Family Circle, *J. Pediatrics*, 1956, vol. 49, no. 6, pp. 746-751.
7. Bozeman, M., Orbach, C., & Sutherland, A.: Psychological Impact of Cancer and Its Treatment, III, The Adaptation of Mothers to the Threatened Loss of Their Children Through Leukemia: Part I, *Cancer*, Jan-Feb 1955, pp. 1-19.
8. Binger, C. M. et al.: Childhood Leukemia, Emotional Impact on Patient and Family, *N. Eng. J. Med.*, 1969, vol. 280, pp. 414-418.
9. Share, L.: Family Communication in the Crisis of a Child's Fatal Illness: A Literature Review and Analysis, *Omega*, 1972, vol. 3, pp. 187-201.
10. Plank, E.: Death on a Children's Ward, *Medical Times*, 1964, vol. 92, pp. 638-644.
11. Evans, A. E.: If a Child Must Die, *N. Eng. J. Med.*, 1968, vol. 278, pp. 138-142.
12. Vernick, J. & Karon, M.: Who's Afraid of Death on a Leukemic Ward, *Am. J. Dis. Child.*, 1965, vol. 109, pp. 393-397.
13. McCollum, A. T. & Schwartz, A. H.: Social Work and the Mourning Parent, *Social Work*, 1972, vol. 17, pp. 25-36.
14. Wiener, J.: Reaction of the Family to the Fatal Illness of a Child, in *Loss and Grief: Psychological Management in Medical Practice*, Schoenberg et al., New York, Columbia Univ. Press, 1970.
15. Heffron, W., Bommelaere, K., & Masters, R.: Group Discussions with the Parents of Leukemic Children, *Pediatrics*, 1973, vol. 52, pp. 831-840.
16. Bluebond-Langner, M.: *The Private Worlds of Dying Children*, Princeton University Press, Princeton, 1978.
17. Kaplan D. et al.: Family Mediation of Stress, *Social Work*, 1973, pp. 60-69.
18. Lansky, S. et al.: Childhood Cancer: Parental Discord and Divorce, *Pediatrics*, 1978, vol. 62, pp. 184-188.
19. Hamovitch, M. B.: *The Parent and the Fatally Ill Child*, Los Angeles, Delmar Publishing Co., 1964.
20. Oakley, G. P. & Patterson, R. B.: The Psychological Management of Leukemic Children and Their Families, *N. C. Med. J.*, vol. 1966, vol. 27, p. 186.
21. Stehbens, J. A. & Lascari, A. D.: Psychological Follow-up of Families with Childhood Leukemia, *J. Clin. Psychol.*, 1974, vol. 30, p. 394.
22. Kaplan, D. M. et al.: Predicting the Impact of Severe Illness in Families, *Health Soc. Work*, 1976, vol. 1, p. 71.
23. Lindsay, M. & MacCarthy, D.: Caring for the Brothers and Sisters of a Dying Child, in *Care of the Child Facing Death*, L. Burton, Routledge & Kegan Paul, Boston, 1974.
24. Lavigne, J. V. & Ryan, M.: Psychologic Adjustment of Siblings of Children with Chronic Illness, *Pediatrics*, April 1979, vol. 4, pp. 616-627.
25. Cairns, N. et al.: Adaptation of Siblings to Childhood Malignancy, *The Journal of Pediatrics*, September 1979, vol. 3, pp. 484-487.
26. Grogan, J. L. et al.: Childhood Cancer and Siblings, *Health and Social Work*, 1977, vol. 2, pp. 42-57.
27. Meyerowitz, J. H. & Kaplan, H. B.: Familial Responses to Stress: The Case of Cystic Fibrosis, *Soc. Sci. Med.*, 1967, vol. 1, pp. 249-266.
28. Tropauer, H. et al.: Psychological Aspects of the Care of Children with Cystic Fibrosis, *Am. J. Dis. Child*, 1970, vol. 119, pp. 424-432.
29. McCollum, A. & Gibson, L.: Family Adaptation to the Child with Cystic Fibrosis, *The Journal of Pediatrics*, October 1970, vol. 77, no. 4, pp. 571-578.
30. McCrae, W. M. et al.: Cystic Fibrosis: Parents Response to the Genetic Basis of the Disease, *Lancet*, 1973, vol. 2, pp. 141-143.
31. Allan, J. et al.: Family Response to Cystic Fibrosis, *Aust. Pediat. J.*, 1974, vol. 10, pp. 136-146.

32. Kerner, J. et al.: The Impact of Grief: A Retrospective Study of Family Function Following Loss of a Child with Cystic Fibrosis, *J. Chron. Dis.*, 1979, vol. 32, pp. 221–225.
33. Petrillo, M. & Sanger, S.: *Emotional Care of Hospitalized Children*, J. B. Lippincott Company, Philadelphia, 1972.
34. Debuskey, M. & Dombro, R.: *The Chronically Ill Child and His Family*, Charles C. Thomas, Springfield, 1970.
35. Cava, E. et al.: *A Pediatrician's Guide to Child Behavior Problems*, Masson Publishing USA, Inc., New York, 1979.
36. Anthony, E. J. & Koupernik, C.: *The Child in His Family*, John Wiley & Sons, Inc., New York, 1973.
37. Cantor, R. C.: *And a Time to Live*, Harper & Row, New York, 1978.
38. Barton, D. (ed.): *Dying and Death: A Clinical Guide for Caregivers*, The Williams & Wilkins Company, Baltimore, 1977.
39. Orcutt, B. A.: Stress in Family Interaction when a Member is Dying, in *Social Work with the Dying Patient and the Family*, E. Prichard et al., eds., Columbia University Press, New York, 1977.
40. Rosenbaum, E. H.: *Living with Cancer*, Praeger Publishers, New York, 1975.
41. Easson, W. M.: The Family of the Dying Child, *The Pediatric Clinics of North America*, Nov. 1972, vol. 19, no. 4, pp. 1157–1165.
42. Futterman, E. H. & Hoffman, I.: Crisis and Adaptation in the Families of Fatally Ill Children, in *The Child in His Family: The Impact of Disease and Death*, (vol. 2), E. Anthony and C. Koupernik, eds., John Wiley & Sons, New York, 1973.
43. Feinberg, D.: Preventive Therapy with Siblings of a Dying Child, *J. Amer. Acad. Child Psychiatry*, 1970, vol. 9, pp. 644–668.
44. Natterson, J. M. & Knudson, A. G.: Observations Concerning Fear of Death in Fatally Ill Children and Their Mothers, *Psychosomatic Medicine*, 1960, vol. 22, pp. 456–465.
45. Schowalter, J.: Anticipatory Grief and Going on the "Danger List," Chapter 22 in *Anticipatory Grief*, Schoenberg, ed., Columbia Univ. Press, New York, 1974.
46. Fredlund, D.: Children and Death from the School Setting Viewpoint, *J. of School Health*, Nov. 1977, pp. 533–537.
47. Kaplan, D., Smith, A., & Grobstein, R.: School Management of the Seriously Ill Child, *J. School Health*, 1974, vol. 44, pp. 250–254.
48. Furman, R. A.: A Child's Capacity for Mourning, in *The Child in His Family: The Impact of Disease and Death*, (vol. 2), E. Anthony and C. Koupernik, eds., John Wiley & Sons, New York, 1973.
49. Binger, C. M.: Childhood Leukemia–Emotional Impact on Siblings, in *The Child in His Family: The Impact of Disease and Death*, (vol. 2), E. Anthony and C. Koupernik, eds., John Wiley & Sons, New York, 1973.
50. Begleiter, M. L. et al.: Prevalence of Divorce Among Parents of Children with Cystic Fibrosis and Other Chronic Diseases, *Soc. Biol.*, 1976, vol. 23, p. 260.

8

Staff Stress in the Care of the Critically Ill and Dying Child

M. L. S. Vachon and Ed Pakes

The care of the seriously ill and/or dying child can evoke significant emotional stress in the caregivers who attend to them. Since most members of the healing professions receive their greatest gratification from patients who get better, it is not surprising that the treatment of these children can result in the caregiver's feeling anxious, frustrated and guilty (1). These feelings may be openly acknowledged or more covertly expressed through behavior or symptom formation. The resulting stress responses may in turn affect patient care and staff relations as well as the caregivers' mental and physical health and family relationships.

Too often this stress of caregivers is unacknowledged because of the concern we feel about the dying child and his or her family. However, if staff stress is unrecognized and no attempt is made to decrease it, then the stress of caregivers may come to parallel or even supplant that experienced by patients and their families (2). When this happens the caregivers can no longer care effectively and patient/family care deteriorates and may become dehumanized.

This chapter will attempt to analyze staff stress in the care of critically ill and dying children. The authors' assumption is that by conceptualizing staff stress in component parts it can be seen as being less overwhelming and therefore more amenable to change.

To this end the chapter will include the following: an overview of the concept of stress, using an evolving model of staff stress previously reported by one of the authors (3); the identification of specific stressors related to the type of illness, the pattern of the dying process, the environment in which the caregiver functions and occupational role responsibilities; personal, interpersonal and intrapersonal factors which may mediate the impact of such stressors; some manifestations of staff stress and ways of preventing or coping with job stress.

The data presented in the paper are gathered from the authors' clinical experience of the past several years in dealing with staff stress in adult (Vachon and pediatric (Pakes) settings; in-depth interviews with several individuals of widely

The authors wish to express their appreciation to Adrienne Sheldon and Susan Erle for editorial and typographical assistance. In addition the insights gained from caregivers proved to be most valuable. We are most grateful and appreciative of the help we received from: Shirley Avery, Eileen Goodin, Cathy Hann, Charmaine Marshall, Liz Nichol, Carol Puterbough, Julie Robertson, Carol Shepard, Nancy Shostenberg, Carmelle Simon, Marian Stevens, and Drs. Irwen Gelford, Mark Greenberg, Hanna Kocandrle, Peter McClure, and Lee Piepgras.

varied backgrounds and levels of experience who are working with critically ill and/or dying children and a review of selected literature. In no way does this chapter purport to be comprehensive for any specific type of illness, treatment setting, or professional group, rather, it attempts to provide a working model within which to view some of the stressors common to those who care for seriously ill children. While the primary but not exclusive focus in the chapter is on physicians and nurses, it is hoped that other professionals will be able to identify with some of the stressors and suggestions.

THE CONCEPT OF STRESS[1]

The concept of stress is probably one of the most ill-defined in the biological and behavioral science literature. According to Levine and Scotch (5), it has been used for a number of divergent dimensions ranging from the stimuli or stressors that lead to changes in the organism; to the outcome from such stimuli, to the emotional state or experience accompanying a changing social or personal situation. In this chapter stress will be used to refer to the emotional state brought about by exposure to stressors and manifested in a variety of individual behaviors and group interactions.

Much of the current interest in stress can be dated to the research of Hans Selye who in 1956 articulated his biological concept of stress as the "general adaptation syndrome," a set of non-specific physiological reactions to various noxious environmental agents (6). More recently, the Dohrenwends have translated Selye's paradigm into social and psychological terms (7). The authors' adaptation of this model can be seen in Fig. 1. In this model the severity of stress is dependent on the duration and intensity of the stressor as well as certain factors in the individual and social system which serve to mediate the degree of stress experienced. These may include the meaning of the event to the individual (both cognitively and emotionally) and the social support available (8). These factors may serve to increase or decrease an individual's vulnerability to the stressor thereby predisposing him to an adaptive or maladaptive response to stress. In an adaptive response, stress has a positive outcome and the individual may grow personally and professionally through exposure to the stressor. However, the response to stress may also be negative and may overwhelm an individual's capacity to cope, thereby predisposing him to a maladaptive outcome to the stressor.

[1] This section is adapated from earlier work by one of the authors (4).

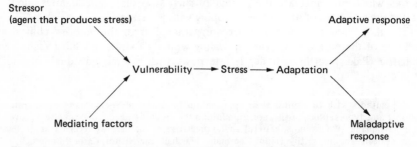

Figure 1 Adaptation of Selye's paradigm into social–psychological model.

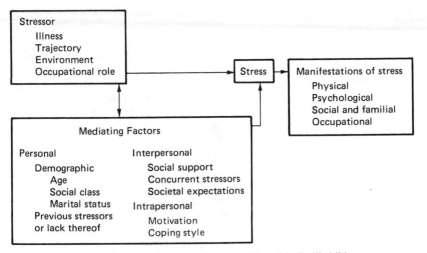

Figure 2 Working model of staff stress in the care of the critically ill child.

This maladaptive response may result from the overwhelming nature of the stressor, deficiencies in one's support system or a combination of these or other factors. Whatever the cause of the maladaptive response, however, it can be reflected in physiological, psychological (8), social (5) or occupational (3) difficulties.

Figure 2 provides a diagram of how these concepts might interact to produce a stress response in those caring for the critically ill or dying child. Such a model can be used to delineate the stressors which can and cannot be altered; to identify those who may be at risk of developing maladaptive stress responses at certain points in time; and to describe the ways in which stress can be manifest so that appropriate supports can be built into the system to facilitate coping, mastery and adaptive responses to stress.

STRESSORS FOR THE CAREGIVER

This section will discuss some specific occupational stressors to which the caregiver may be subjected. The following specialties will be dealt with: Neonatal Intensive Care Units, Intensive Care Units, Cardiology, Oncology, Bone Marrow Transplants, Cystic Fibrosis, and Muscular Dystrophy. By focusing on these areas the authors hope to show the differences in the stressors to which staff members are exposed in a variety of situations ranging from short-term acute life and death situations to longer term illnesses.

The Neonatal Intensive Care Unit

The stressors which impinge on staff members working on a Neonatal Intensive Care Unit almost defy description. The caregivers must monitor and care for defenseless, machine dependent fetuses hardly ready for birth yet exposed to the elements in an environment which was never seen before the last few decades.

Working with these infants in cramped and noisy quarters, the staff members must become used to the many machines which keep their tiny patients alive, a very heavy workload with frequent admissions to this referral center from peripheral centers, and functioning in a "fish bowl environment" in which everyone can see and hear what you do and say. It has been noted that the census is high on these units and the intensity of care increases yearly. The staff must work with successive waves of the sickest infants, with little opportunity to see the good results of their work (9). These units are usually large referral centers, drawing patients from a wide geographic area. In Toronto, for example, the NICU has 65 beds with an annual census of 3000 children of whom 300 will die, some quickly and some after many days, weeks, or months of intensive investment on the part of the caregivers.

One study from Tennessee (10) showed that the major stressors on the ICU included transport arrival when the unit was already full, heavy work load, a sense of responsibility for the infant's ultimate outcome, a maldistribution of nurses among shifts and a sense of discrepancy in the nurse's personal evaluation of her responsibility versus her competence. The experienced nurse in this setting may know as much or more about infant care as the resident physician, while the new nurse may feel called upon to function far beyond her level of expertise. The role of the nurse on the NICU is constantly evolving and consequently "not clearly delineated" (10). Nurses may head the transport team which brings critically ill neonates into the NICU; and it has been suggested that nurses will assume increasing responsibility for the running of these units, as physicians are not being attracted to the specialty (9). The nurse may be open to considerable role conflict and ambiguity in relations with parents and physicians. The situation may be compounded by feelings and attitudes on the part of some staff when these competent specialists feel that the problems they are called upon to treat may be iatrogenic, that is caused by physicians. The problem of blaming is common, even if it is not always true. It is especially common if the etiology of the disorder is unknown. One of the authors has previously noted a tendency for scapegoating in 90 percent of parents who "blame" the primary physician in cases of childhood cancer (11). Whether the phenomenon found on the NICU is scapegoating or an accurate assessment, nonetheless it serves as an important stressor in this setting and may result in an unresolved psychological wound which impairs "caring" on the part of the professionals and parents as well. One staff member said:

> You know that these were potentially healthy children who had a birth injury. The family often doesn't know what happened. You know that no matter what you do some of these kinds will be "out to lunch" because a local obstetrician made a mistake and know the parents will never know why the child has a problem. The staff then have trouble dealing with these parents as they don't know what to say or how to answer their questions.

Other situations may also cause problems between nurses and parents. Nurses often receive their major satisfaction from caring for these infants to whom they may give amusing or pet nicknames. The babies become like their own, sometimes almost to the exclusion of parents who may be seen as intruders into the nurses' territory. The parents, in turn, may view the staff members as holding their baby hostage in a totally alien environment. Nurses can come to resent the presence of parents on the unit and may be upset at discharging "their patients" to the care of parents whom they feel are not deserving of the infant.

Staff members who feel totally in control of their environment may resent those parents who belong to the new wave of demanding consumers who insist upon knowing exactly what is going on with their child. This type of conflict may become particularly acute when there is pre-existing friction between physicians and nurses regarding information exchange and certain types of treatment. The nurse may disagree with the physician but feel a professional obligation to uphold his or her judgment. Thus, for example, when parents question the use of frequent x-rays, the nurse may agree with the parents' concerns but not acknowledge this, saying instead "It's all being done for the baby's good." The physician may sense the hostility from the parents and nurses which adds to his or her sense of isolation in making decisions and prescribing innovative treatments which may cause long-term problems while meeting current needs.

Physician-nurse conflict may become acute around information exchange and role responsibilities. Beaton (12) has noted that a lack of communication around pertinent information and decision-making may lead to anger and resentment between staff members on an NICU. Such conflicts may occur because of the varying role responsibilities held by team members. The physician's primary role may be a commitment to research while the nurse's commitment is to care for the child. Thus the nurses can come to resent the physician's research protocols. When these discussions take place in a noisy, cramped, fish-bowl with critically ill infants, tempers may flare or silent resentments begin to mount.

Perhaps this situation is most acute when life and death decisions are being made by physicians but nurses are left to carry them out. The following quotation from a physician illustrates this well:

> The medical staff are the decision-makers ... They determine whether a baby can be offered any meaningful life. Once that determination is made, however, the nurses have to deal with the consequences. One hour they're fighting for an infant's life, and the next they're asked to pull back and allow the infant to die comfortably. (9, p. 40)

One of the most important concepts of this chapter is the fact that the stressors to which staff members are exposed vary in part, because of the designated occupational role of the caregiver. The authors take the position that it is not better or worse, easier or harder to be a nurse, physician or other caregiver. Rather, the roles and some of the stressors to which the professions are exposed are different and the ways in which the resultant stress may be manifest may therefore vary.

In the setting of the NICU when staff members are feeling conflicted about the many stressors to which they are exposed, they may sometimes develop a brittle shell and escape into the technical aspect of their work to protect themselves from openly confronting the emotional and ethical issues. It has been found in some instances that when NICU nurses were helped to confront some of these psychosocial issues, they became increasingly overwhelmed and guilty (10).

In concluding this subsection the worlds of one participant-observer on an NICU seem most appropriate. Speaking of the emotional responses of both parents and staff members, Beaton observed "... That sense of impending loss, or grief for what might have been, was at times almost too cruel to watch" (12).

The Intensive Care Unit

Speaking of the daily stressors on a pediatric Intensive Care Unit one nurse said:

> One hour the child is fine. The next hour he's critically ill or dying with tubes coming out of all orifices. It's one shock on top of another for parents who are already distraught.

They must deal with the impact of the accident, all the machinery and the Intensive Care Unit environment . . . We can get involved in dealing with the child and all that needs to be done for him. It's not that hard on us in many ways because never having met the child before he was dying you don't know him. You're removed from him. The parents are more difficult though, you can put yourself in their position, and feel their guilt and pain.

Anyone walking into the hectic unit can observe staff and visotors wearing isolation gowns; surgeons, anesthetists and nurses walking around with intense expressions on their faces; parents sitting by the beds of unconscious or critically ill children attached to ventilators and monitors with intravenous lines and catheters in place. On some beds there are a few cherished toys and perhaps a photograph of the child before his or her recent trauma. As one nurse said "While it's good to have the pictures there, sometimes it's hard as I'm not sure I really want to know what the child was like before."

A physician, speaking of his days on the ICU, said:

. . . the ICU is a narrow slice of life. You never see a child as a child, but rather, as a laboratory preparation. In some ways it didn't make a difference if they lived or died— except that if they lived it was like model building. You put the pieces together and it turns out the way it's supposed to at the end.

Learning to deal with the equipment can be a significant stressor on the ICU. Many young nurses said they came into this setting because they liked the technical challenge and enjoyed functioning under a high degree of stress. They found the early months on the unit both frustrating and challenging and were able to say that much of the time during those early months was spent learning how "to nurse the machines." As they became more comfortable with the machines they seemed to almost abruptly realize that these machines were attached to children and these children had families. Some of these young nurses said they felt as though they were suddenly exposed to a whole new set of stressors for which they were ill prepared.

A physician, speaking of the reliance on machines in preference to human judgement, said "The culpability and environment of accusation in which you function makes you feel responsible for everything . . . Those bloody machines . . . It's gotten so that if something goes wrong it can't be the machine, it's got to be you . . . You're responsible for everything."

Not unexpectedly, death is a major stressor on the ICU. Staff members report that some of the most stressful deaths are the ones "who are there one minute and the next they're gone. There's no time to prepare the family." Or the child "who has been around for a long time and you really got to know him (her). Especially some of the cardiac surgery children we've known for a long time, maybe over several hospitalizations." Worse yet "abused children . . . what do you do with the feelings you have towards the abuser."

Staff members also suffer conflict over the mode of death on the ICU. Staff may feel that parents should be there when a child dies, sometimes disconnecting a child from machines to allow the child to die in a parent's arms. But this isn't always possible. A child suddenly takes a turn for the worse; the code is called; parents are ushered from the room as everyone works to save the child. Then, as one nurse said "You get a sick feeling when you know you can't do anymore. You don't want to have to face the parents . . . I take a few moments to myself . . . then I go out."

Despite the problems that death brings to staff members on an ICU, it is some-times almost more difficult to deal with the stressor of the child who will live but may have severe brain damage. As one nurse, the mother of a severely retarded child, said "there are worse things than death . . . sometimes death is cleaner than living with a chronic problem like this."

Multiple deaths on an ICU can be another major stressor. As one staff member said "We need some light days once in a while to recuperate. You need some time to fool around and laugh. We haven't had it in a long time and we're really feeling it. There are too many sick, sick kids and too many deaths."

The final stressor which will be discussed is conflicting role expectations. Cassem and Hackett (13) describe the role of the nurse in a somewhat similar setting as being one wherein the nurse "bears the awesome responsibility of performing chores that are at one instant perfunctory and at the next heroic. Throughout she must be supportive, understanding and caring" (p. 1430). Vreeland and Ellis (14) say "The stresses in the minute-to-minute, day by day contact with patients whose lives depend upon the nurse's knowledge, alertness and skill are compounded by problems encountered working with a wide range of technical equipment purported to be life-saving or labor saving or both. Moreover maintaining smooth working relationships and effective communications with many different members of the health team and visitors moving through a relatively small physical space creates other tensions" (p. 332).

Like the NICU nurse, the ICU nurse is expected to function at a high level of professional competence—there isn't much room for error in this setting. Several nurses reported feeling that the closeness on the ICU team was important. Doctors and nurses usually worked well with and supported one another as has been noted previously (15). But there can be problems with role overlap and over-stepping what might be seen as role boundaries.

The nurses still had some feelings about an anesthetist who on completing his month on the unit had left with the comment "You're the most castrating bunch of females I've ever met." The comment hurt although they knew it was in part a tribute to their competence and a reflection of his feelings of inadequacy.

To sum up this subsection, it can be said that work on an ICU—and on an NICU—involves constant exposure to critically ill infants and children and their distraught parents in an atmosphere of ever-increasing technological change re-quiring constant professional learning. Staff conflicts often add to the pressures inherent in the environment as role boundaries blur and role conflict ensues.

But the ultimate rewards can be great when the NICU babies and children return on Clinic Day or as an ICU nurse described it:

> *Having a child come down to see us right before discharge is incredible. Last week a little girl we never thought would make it came running into the unit just before going home. There wasn't a dry eye in the place and that included the doctors. It makes everything you're doing so worthwhile and gave us what we needed to carry on because three other children died that weekend.*

Cardiology

The problems of pediatric cardiology may pose great technological challenges, and at times it may seem as though the emotional needs of patients, families and staff are ignored. One physician summed up his feelings about some of his colleagues in the following way ". . . as your involvement with patients is increasingly superficial, the more you can afford to go deeper . . . The ultimate achievement is to crack open a chest and put in a valve . . ."

A nurse described caring for a twelve-year-old boy who was dying of heart disease. He had been admitted a few weeks earlier with what appeared to be a virus but it quickly became obvious that he was in congestive heart failure. He developed a pulmonary embolism and was found to have clots in both ventricles. He was told he would die soon and asked for his family to come in and to contact his father who had abandoned the family five years earlier. The staff was very drawn to this boy and his family "who tried to catch up on time when the clock was running out."

The boy died and the nurse who cared for him needed time to grieve but as she said:

He died, another patient came back from having a cardiac catheterization and my transfer from ICU just arrived. Fellow staff members pull together for an hour to get you out of the crisis then it's business as usual with no acknowledgement that you need time. Sometimes we talk about taking time to deal with our feelings but the question is should we do it today or tomorrow? Then you're off for three days and you no longer have the same feelings. What happens to us though when these feelings are constantly left unresolved?

Another stressor voiced by nurses working in highly challenging areas was of being "dead-ended." "You move from being a staff nurse to a team leader or teaching position. But where do we go from here? Many of us aren't happy with what we're doing or with the return from the job. But the question becomes what do you do about it?"

Some nurses in cardiology work a twelve hour day to get more time off to pursue interests away from nursing. One staff member voiced concern about this saying, "You're tired before you start. It becomes like a marathon and very little care is given between 5:00 p.m. and 8:30 p.m., the time when families are there and really need you. There's so much time off that it almost feels like a part time job . . . You just blank out the days you work and struggle through them."

Other stressors in cardiology come from the nature of the disease and the uncertain trajectory following surgery. As one caregiver said:

How do you deal with a dying child on a ward with similarly vulnerable children. How do you maintain the ward atmosphere when everyone knows when some parents have received bad news or just finally begun to "put the pieces together" and realize their child will die. There's little privacy for families, therefore all families and staff must cope together, while struggling not to betray a family's privacy.

The issue of environment keeps coming up again and again with comments such as "with kids with like disorders everyone feels vulnerable. It's like working in a goldfish bowl. The majority of children come in and have surgery and it's successful. These children go on to have a normal life. But when death comes it's hard, everyone knows it and it always seems to come in runs."

Staff members can also experience stress from prolonged exposure to parents who are from out of town and staying with their critically ill children. These parents, most often mothers, may become close to other parents with whom they share their traumas and anxiety. In these situations the nurses sometimes feel the need to protect parents from the collective grief to which they are being exposed.

Staff members can also identify with parents to the point of "adopting" them, spending off duty time providing support, entertaining parents and showing them around the city. This can become a stressor in that the parents can come to expect increasing amounts of time and support from staff members who may then find themselves withdrawing in response.

Finally, again, the issue of role conflicts can develop. In one setting known to the authors, the staff cardiologists rotate through the service monthly and patients and families are expected to relate to whomever is on duty that month rather than expecting to be seen by the private cardiologist they see when outside the hospital. The parents and staff are expected to transfer authority for decision-making to a different physician every month which can serve as a major stressor as there can be conflicting treatment philosophies. In addition, this type of rotation system serves to minimize involvement with the cardiologist on-duty who maintains distance from the children and parents as this is only a temporary assignment. Other staff members may feel obligated to provide the continuity of care which may prove to be an unrealistically high expectation, thus posing still another stressor. As one doctor said "You don't hear us talking about getting burned out because we can always walk away from the bedside when it gets too hot. It's the nurse who gets left behind to deal with the problems."

Nurses often feel that they're always the ones left behind:

Trying to be all things for all people. There's a lack of support beyond the eight hour day. Social work, the dietician and most other staff only work 9:00 a.m.–5:00 p.m. Who do you call for help? An on-call system for social workers didn't work out, clergy aren't available and there's no one on call for Psychiatry. The nurse is left holding the bag. We don't get any support, but then again maybe we pick up the slack too readily.

"Picking up the slack" can be particularly difficult when the nurse feels obligated to do this following medical rounds. This is described as a time when the entourage of physicians enters the rooms which may have four patients, various family members and staff. "The children become 'teaching cases' they need to have their hearts listened to there and then, and then the doctors discuss exactly what's going on, using their medical jargon and oblivious to the fact that everyone is listening in and becoming increasingly more anxious." The non-medical staff feels obliged to be available following these rounds to defuse some of the anxiety the families feel. When nurses tried suggesting alternative arrangements for rounds such as having the discussions held in conference rooms the idea was met with resistance. The physicians' response was that rounds would continue and perhaps the parents would be asked to leave and be spoken to later. This option negates the anxiety generated in the children who quickly become quite sophisticated in understanding at least some of their cardiac problems and become concerned when they know they are not improving. Nurses feel they are left to deal with these feelings.

To summarize this subsection on cardiology, this type of setting where the illness trajectory may be quite uncertain, can pose a number of different stressors for staff members. Chief among these are functioning in a "fish bowl" environment with patients and families there together for an extended period of time.

Staff emotional investment in patients and families may be quite high and when patients die staff members grieve. But this grief may often be unrecognized and unresolved because of the legitimate pressures of the environment. Nurses especially, feel vulnerable in such a situation because they often feel that they are left "holding the bag" especially when major problems occur outside of the traditional 9–5 work day. Add to this the impact of very competent staff members feeling dead-ended in their jobs, fatigued from working twelve hour shifts, and the stage is set for significant job stress which may be reflected in interpersonal conflicts.

Oncology

In our language and minds cancer has been represented as a crab "eating" away at someone's insides. Through the efforts of medical pioneers this image has gradually evolved into that of a less ominous being which it might be possible to catch before "he devours his host." Nonetheless the many unknown factors in childhood cancer can lead to a considerable amount of fantasy weaving on the part of the child, parents and even caregivers. The situation is further complicated by the fact that the diagnosis of childhood cancer may be difficult to make. One of the authors interviewed the families of children with cancer and found that 90 percent of them blamed the original physician in some way for the child's illness. They accused him of either delaying the diagnosis or not telling them the whole story. A "scapegoating" phenomenon occurred which left the parents angry at the physician. The doctor was exposed to the stressor of feeling helpless to intervene because a specialist took over his patient and he lacked the skill to help the family resolve the grief and anger involved in the initial stages of diagnosis (11).

New drugs mean that a physician can no longer indicate how long a child might have to live. This uncertainty of care may add an undefined anxiety for the parents as well as the caregivers, some of whom have difficulty tolerating chronic uncertainty, whereas they might better be able to manage a predictable death (1). This problem is well illustrated in the following clinical example:

> The staff on the hematology unit became particularly distressed with a family whose 3-year-old son had been "routinely" diagnosed as having acute lymphocytic leukemia. Michael had peculiar reactions to the induction medication and almost died, but was revived by the ICU team.
>
> Michael was the only child of parents in their mid-30's who had been investigated for infertility for 7 years prior to his conception. Father was an only child whose mother used to tell him "If you worry a lot about something it will turn out ok." He became a computer technology expert whose job was to deal with "problem" computers. His son's disease became a non-statistical phenomenon that could not be put into computer terms.
>
> Additional anxiety was provoked in the father, which spread to his wife and the staff members, because the parents were told their son had a 50-50 chance. A computer gets indigestion with this kind of data and so did the father and staff. Fifteen or twenty years ago the physician was certain about stating that the child would die in two years. Now the uncertainty about the outcome of the illness affects some families more adversely than if the child were to clearly die.
>
> It is like living with a bomb which may or may not explode. The anxiety can become contagious and staff members can easily find themselves caught up in it.

Speaking of some of the pressures this type of situation puts on staff members, a nurse said:

> With improvements in prognosis you come to hope, but without too much conviction, that maybe they'll make it. If someone you really worked with and didn't expect to make it, does live, then you become upset if they don't come in to see you when they come to clinic.

They don't want to see us because we're a reminder of bad times, but we really need to see them to keep going with the sick ones in the ward.

Problems may develop for the caregiver who comes to hope that a particular child will be an exception and will live where others have died. When such a child dies the results on staff members can be devastating, perhaps more so than when they simply assumed that these children would die.

A nurse said "I knew it was time to get out when I felt a strong desire to go up to a new parent and say "Why bother, it's not worth it. Your child will just die too, like all of these others who dared to hope."
I could work with the dying children because I had a sense that I'd made a commitment to them a long time ago but I couldn't get involved with one more child who might die, so I left the field.

A physician tries to avoid making implicit promises about prognosis by spelling everything out to families in the early stages of the disease.

I try to lay it all out to the parents in the first couple of interviews so they know what they're up against. I say "with this type of treatment 30-40 percent of kids will have five years or more." I let them know what this means and what they can expect . . . Then I talk about the other 60 percent, where we'll try to get a second remission using second line drugs and the remission will be shorter. Then we talk about what will happen when we run out of drugs.

Elsewhere one of the authors has written of the various stages the medical team may go through in working with children with cancer (16). These are based on the Kübler-Ross stages (17) and while one can dispute whether such stages exist, they provide a framework within which to view the process of adaptation to cancer which staff members may follow. These stages are summarized in the following example of an oncologist's possible reactions:

Shock—"Here's another case. How shall I handle it"
Denial—"Maybe I'm wrong about my diagnosis. I'll show the slide to my colleague"
Anger—"Why are they being such difficult parents? I've worked hard on this case. They have no right to be angry. They probably didn't give the medication I ordered . . . I always get the most difficult patients"
Bargaining—"I promise to read my journals every night, just don't refer another cancer case for a while."
Depression—"I wonder why I feel so low today. All my patients are dying. The statistics I read from other centers are better. Are we doing enough?"
Acceptance—"I've tried my best. It's a difficult disease to treat."
Hope—"That was a great remission. I hope it lasts. I heard about a new drug. Maybe we should try it on our patients."

Each staff member may at times go through their own version of this progression (16). Because children with cancer often live for many years, the staff members come to know them quite well. Watching the progress of their disease, which may end in death becomes very difficult. An experienced oncology nurse said:

It's so hard to watch them come in with their curls, knowing that they'll soon be bald and crying about having another I.V.

You become attached to them. They creep into different corners of your heart. The problems come when it becomes evident they're going to die, particularly if it goes on too long. You struggle to care for them through pain and wondering how much they really know. They make comments like "why do you bother, I'm going to die anyway" or "I'm sorry I'm dying because I know you wanted me to get better"; or "I know things are bad because I hear the doctor's voice outside my door. She won't come in because she doesn't know what to say."

Participating in helping the children to handle their deaths in their own way can present a challenge almost beyond the comprehension of someone who has not done this type of work. This closeness to a young person struggling to maintain a sense of control over a premature death proves to be a major stressor for many staff members although it simultaneously provides an incredible sense of meaning and accomplishment in what they are going.

A nurse reminisced about many of the children she'd worked with who died. She spoke of the little girl who said "I know I'm going to die because everybody looks so different." This same child refused to have anything to do with her father after he'd cried about her death.
A ten-year-old boy knew he was dying and told his mother to send for the ambulance. When it arrived he said "I won't need the stretcher I can walk this last time." He arrived at the hospital and when it was clear that death would come within a few minutes the nurse said she'd call his mother. The boy's response was "she's been with me all along. She doesn't have to be here to see the end."
A child said "You're giving up on me." The nurse responded "All we can do is support you." The child answered "That's enough. I don't want to hear anymore."
A teenage boy whose parents were separated worried about his family and asked "Who will take care of Dad after I've died." He died very slowly and finished making a handbag for his mother with the nurse just before he died.

The same nurse said that being honest with the children is easier because there are no questions in the air. The loss is shared and time is used productively as the child sees fit. This may include making out wills and making funeral plans with young children. She said:

They've taught me a lot. They're very strong. They cope with it in their own way but often with more strength than adults. The lessons they've taught us stay with us. We remember the patients after they've died and we talk about it. If it's bad we'll make tea and share it together.

Contrast this with the isolation found on some of the other units and one gets a sense of the strength that can come from sharing the load. Another stressor in childhood cancer is an alteration in the expected trajectory of the illness. A staff member said:

One of the worst deaths was that of a young girl who died in the operating room during a routine staging procedure. No one knew what to do, so they brought her back to the ward. We gave her family a private room and let them spend time with her. What was hardest on us was watching her father brush her hair—tears streaming down his face.
We all gathered around them and tried to do what we could. We cried with them because we all felt so bad even though we didn't really know the family . . . The doctor even drove them home because we feared for their safety driving and wanted to do something.

In the "ideal" death the staff have time to prepare the family. Death occurs smoothly on schedule and with symptoms under control. When symptoms aren't under control, staff members can have trouble as voiced by one doctor, "I still have trouble with the death of one young girl. I promised her that she wouldn't die in pain and she didn't . . . but she died with uncontrollable seizures and I still feel guilty."

The involvement with families which may go on for years after death with considerable role blurring, can be another stressor for staff. In one situation a four-year-old was involved in caring for his brother who had a hereditary tumor and the mother was so involved in her child's care that she had access to the unit's locked medicine cabinet. Two years after the child's death the mother was embarassed at having usurped the nurses' role. Fulton (2) has noted that this role blurring may extend to the extreme of having parents assume the medical role of reading journals for the latest research findings and realizing the child will die because they see the progression of the disease, whereas staff members become the surrogate grievers who have difficulty accepting the child's death and have trouble dealing with the parents' lack of visible grief. One nurse went so far as to suggest that if parents didn't grieve more appropriately (e.g. openly) the staff would have to restrict their attendance at funerals.

Most staff members do not involve themselves to this extent, however, and are able to distance themselves and witness the parents' sorrow, knowing that it is not their own. They make comments such as:

Death is different with children. There's a different intensity of feeling. The staff feels the agony of the parent's loss which is untimely and unacceptable. There's a grim despair.

When a baby dies there's a raw grief, particularly in men. The women seem to be most devastated by the "mothery" things that are denied to them, especially if they have older children and know what they're missing.

With prolonged illness there's a tremendous void and a colossal loss. Death is a release for the children but a tremendous sorrow for the parents even though there might have been very little quality of life for a long time.

Bone Marrow Transplants

One of the authors (Pakes) has worked extensively in pediatric oncology and has taken a special interest in bone marrow transplants. This is a last-resort, experimental procedure for the treatment of leukemias and aplastic anemias that have not responded to conventional treatment. The patient's immune system is suppressed with massive doses of radiation and chemotherapy, following which they are given bone marrow infusions from a compatible blood relative. To reduce the possibility of infection the patients must remain in reverse isolation until there are clear signs that the bone marrow has taken or that the procedure has failed and may be repeated.

The stress, particularly on nurses, is most extreme because a breakdown in the procedure, especially the sterile environment, might "cause" the patient to die. With the patient's defenses against any infection absent, those entering the isolated system take the risk of aborting the experiment in renewing the life of the patient.

Sources of stress might be outlined as follows:

1. The questioning of new and experimental procedures which (some staff feel) may shorten life rather than prolong it.
2. The treatments producing psychiatric sequelae in patients, family and staff.

3. Patients in reverse isolation may suffer from sensory deprivation unless an "artificial normal" environment is created; parental or substitute parental figures are provided and teenagers are allowed to have access to an active line to the outside world via peers.

4. Families actively involved in the treatment may be exposed to a "non-stop soap-opera phenomenon" in which the parents are the main actors. In their intimate and often prolonged involvement on the unit their family life is over-exposed to the staff. They feel imprisoned, physically vulnerable and emotionally exhausted; reluctant to express negative feelings to the staff because they are dependent upon them to sustain life.

5. Staff, particularly nurses on the front line, may feel they are and often are, the life sustaining force for the patient; may feel conflict over how much to involve the parents and may have to watch deteriorating marital relationships between tense parents even to the extent of having to respond to sexual propositions from the fathers involved.

6. Staff must also practice constant vigilance to avoid being responsible for a break in sterile technique. While the job is life-sustaining, it may also be boring as it is more a matter of preventing an illness rather than treating an acute emergency.

Cystic Fibrosis

Easson (18) has suggested that when a child or adolescent begins to die the staff member's unconscious response may be "How dare this patient die, after all we've done for him." Another response is to forget that the disease often has a fatal outcome and to feel a sense of personal failure. As a physician working with children with Cystic Fibrosis—a hereditary disease with evidence of celiac syndrome and chronic lung disease (19)—said "when someone dies I always have a sense of failure and ask what went wrong, what can be improved the next time." While it is good medicine to constantly question, it can also serve to increase the sense of failure and unrealistic expectations which the staff caring for terminally ill children may have for themselves. A physician who works with chronically ill children, many of whom will die of their disease, tries to integrate a scientific and humane approach to his care of dying children. He says that in such situations one must alter one's criteria of success.

I see myself dealing with a spectrum of differing qualities of life. I hope that the children I work with, while living with an impairment, will have a better quality of life than if I weren't there. There comes a time when I know that I can no longer offer quality of life. At this point my criterion for success is making living more palatable for a longer or shorter time. I try to decrease problems to a manageable size and aim for quality in dying. I say to the parents then that the time has come when I can't offer quality of life. I told you that when all I could offer with treatment was pain and discomfort then I'd aim for quality of death.

In the case of children with cystic fibrosis the prognosis formerly was certain death by age 5. In one large Cystic Fibrosis Clinic the staff were among the first to begin to see their young patients live into their adolescence and beyond into their twenties when they began having children. The disease came to be seen as chronic, rather than potentially terminal, and the staff geared the children for living a reasonably normal life. They spent a considerable amount of time with one another not only in the clinic and in-patient setting, but as well at summer camp, to which patients and staff would go together. In the last few years many of these children have begun to die of infections that were not previously problems. Staff members now feel not only that they are losing their close friends, but that these losses are totally unexpected. Subsequently, they search frantically for an answer to their problems. At the same time they must continue to work with the other patients who ask "why didn't you tell me she died?" "When will it be me?" "I'm healthy, It won't happen to me . . . will it?"

As with any chronic illness, there have always been problems with a lack of compliance on the parts of both parents and children but this open acknowledgement of death in a setting where patients are so close and have followed one another's progress for so many years can serve to escalate non-compliance. There can be a sense that if it happened to Sue who always did her treatments it can happen to me too.

Staff members also have difficulty when there is a rapid succession of deaths where death used to be a rarity. As one nurse said "I came to work with cystic fibrosis because kids didn't die of it. Now look what's happening."

Muscular Dystrophy

With some diseases death is a certainty from the time of diagnosis. In such instances, the time of diagnosis is often the most difficult for the caregiver who feels he/she is sentencing the child. A psychologist who works with children with Duchenne Muscular Dystrophy, a degenerative muscular disease which always ends in death, says:

> *The deterioration is harder than death. There's a relief with death even though I miss them. Watching a child gradually deteriorate from a healthy two- or three-year-old through to be a severely distorted, shriveled adolescent who has only enough energy to move the "joy stick" on an electric wheelchair is hard. When the diagnosis is made we as staff tend to telescope things. We're not just looking at this seven-year-old child, we're projecting what he'll be like at seventeen.*
>
> *The staff in the Outpatient Department who work with children with a variety of problems say that the Muscular Dystrophy Clinic is the hardest to work in. It goes on and on and never gets any better. For twelve to seventeen years you see the same child continually getting worse.*

Muscular dystrophy progresses in a fairly predictable pattern and so staff members are exposed to having to help parents adjust to each new stage from needing braces to spinal support, to transfer to the special school for children with muscular dystrophy, to getting an electric wheelchair. "The more equipment they need, the more real the disease becomes. Getting a new electric wheelchair involves facing the fact that things are worse. I try to present it in such a way as to get families to incorporate the wheelchair as another family member."

Staff members must also deal with very intense emotions from children and parents who are constantly witnessing the deterioration of other children and know that their turn will come. Some parents consider murdering their children rather than watching the disease progress. Occasionally adolescents with M.D. will suicide to avoid the stages yet to come. In addition parents must be counselled about future pregnancies in what may be a hereditary disease. This is difficult in view of the parents' need to produce a healthy child to replace this sick one.

As in some of the other situations, staff members are also confronted with a need to deal with the death of patients with other children who know it's just a matter of time for them. Staff members sometimes use denial rather than dealing with the children about a peer's death but this just increases the children's sense of isolation. As one young boy said in such a situation "When I die nothing will happen. It will be as though I never lived. No one will acknowledge it."

The final stressor in dealing with children with muscular dystrophy is one common to some other areas of work with critically ill and dying children. That is, the stigma attached to the disease. As one staff member said "The disease is stigmatized and so in turn am I. Few people will talk to me about what I do, including my mother, therefore I feel that I constantly need to contain my feelings about my work."

This section has attempted to identify the stresors inherent in work with critically ill and dying children. These are related to the illness process, the dying trajectory, the environment in which care occurs and the occupational role the staff member occupies. As was obvious to the reader, no one disease has been handled in great depth and many of the stressors mentioned under certain sections could have been dealt with equally well elsewhere.

The following stressors have emerged as potentially causing staff stress:

Illness specific
>   Constant exposure to ever sicker children as new advances are made in perinatal care, surgery, chemotherapy and technology and children are kept alive who would never have lived previously.
>   Exposure only to children who are critically ill with little chance to see those who've done well on follow-up.
>   Dealing with iatrogenic disorders induced either through possible medical error or as the result of new treatment and research approaches.
>   Being involved with families from the time of diagnosis, through phases of hope, to relapse, deterioration, death and possibly beyond.
>   Getting close to children who share their feelings and ideas about their impending illness and death.

Trajectory Specific
>   Sudden and unexpected death
>   The unanticipated trajectory, whether too long, too short or uncontrolled
>   Learning to live with children who would previously have died but are now living with a completely unknown prognosis
>   Death of the "special" patient
>   The impact of diagnosis as a long-term death sentence
>   Organizing "a good death"

Environment Specific
>   High technology with the constant need for developing new skills
>   Trying to deal with children and parents in a "fish bowl" environment in which everyone knows who's doing well and poorly.
>   Depersonalization of the child whether by technology or medical treatment
>   Constant demands with no time to relax because of large numbers of sick patients and deaths.

Occupational Role
Isolation
Needing to function above or below level of expertise
Dead-ended positions
No time to grieve because of constant demands
Need to re-define areas of job satisfaction and ideas of "success"
Staff conflict
Role overlap, conflict, ambiguity and strain
Scapegoating
Need to come to terms with one's feelings regarding disease, disability and death
Stigma
Dealing with parents—issues of involvement, control, information exchange, sexuality
Communication problems
Care versus cure versus research dilemmas

MEDIATING FACTORS

The previous section has identified a number of potential stressors in the care of the critically ill and dying child. It is obvious, however that all caregivers are not equally susceptible to such stressors and that a given individual's susceptibility may vary over time. This section will briefly identify some of the factors which serve to mediate the potential impact of the stressors, thus increasing or decreasing a caregiver's vulnerability to a stress reaction in response to a specific stressor.

As seen in Fig. 2, these mediating factors can be divided into three types: personal, intrapersonal, and interpersonal. The personal variables include: age, social class, marital status and previous stressors, or lack thereof. The intrapersonal include: motivation, and coping style, while interpersonal includes: social support, concurrent stressors and societal expectations.

Personal

Age

Easson (18) has written that when staff are involved in the care of dying children their response may be determined by their normal age-appropriate emotional defense around the anxieties aroused by the death process. He suggests that the response of the medical team be as follows:

The young resident may feel the normal rage of the young adult. Death is seen as the destroyer which must be fought. Therefore, the resident may tend to "overtreat," assaulting the patient with every possible treatment in an attempt to prevent death. This denial of death may extend to a hesitancy to prescribe adequate narcotics for dying children in the belief that they might become addicted. Young and idealistic individuals may also be particularly susceptible to burn out because of unrealistic expectations which are untested against reality (20). In addition they may have had minimal prior exposure to death. Speaking of nurses on a Neonatal Intensive Care Unit, one caregiver said "It's hard when you're only 19 with little or no psychiatric expertise or personal exposure to death, to work on a unit where 300 newborns will die a year."

The younger professional is not the only one who finds it difficult to deal with dying children. Easson states that the middle-aged person may experience an intellectual acceptance while emotionally denying the meaning of death. Easson suggests that the physician in this age group may arrive to see the patient when the child is sleeping, the doctor then withdraws, rationalizing that the child would rather be left alone. "In the natural, human over-reaction of intellectualization, the doctor may repeatedly examine and submit the dying patient to a multitude of diagnostic procedures, in an understandable attempt to reduce this insoluble, emotionally unbearable problem to the level of an intellectual exercise" (18, p. 66).

In the elderly physician the increased personal acceptance of death as a natural life process may lead to an insensitivity to the normal tensions in patients, families and staff leading to a lack of recognition of the problem that death presents to this younger group (18).

Finally, it must be noted that any caregiver can have trouble when the dying child is the same age as his or her child. One physician said "I just realized that the reason I can't go into Tommy's room is that he looks so much like my son did at the same age." A nurse said: "Ever since my children became teenagers I have much more difficulty dealing with adolescents with osteogenic sarcoma. I'm so aware they could be mine."

Social Class

The issue of the importance of the social class of caregivers has not received much recognition other than the acknowledgement that the superior social status of the physician may cause communication barriers with families of a lower social class.

Much more research needs to be done in this area but a few issues which may tend to increase the stressors in the care of the dying child might include the following:

1. Parents of equal or higher social class than the caregivers which might simultaneously cause an identification with the family and an increased awareness of the vulnerability of the caregiver. This may result in favoritism or withdrawal.

2. The threat of superior knowledge of educated consumers whose awareness of medical treatment and corresponding demands may threaten the caregivers' sense of competence.

3. The belief that families of a different social class or ethnic background do not place the same value on an individual child. The message is almost "they have so many, what does one more or less matter."

4. Difficulty understanding the values of families of a different social class or ethnic background. For example, staff members in one hospital had considerable difficulty in relating to an Italian family who began to dress in black from the time their son was diagnosed as having cancer.

5. Problems with single parents or reconstituted families, particularly if of a different social class. Staff members don't know what to say to which family member, who should be allowed to visit and who should be informed when death is imminent.

Marital Status

The caregivers interviewed for this chapter agreed that their marital status often had a significant impact on their capacity to deal with the ongoing stressors of their job. Marital status itself is perhaps, however, too narrow a concept. The critical variable here may well be the presence of a confidant. Brown et al. (21) found in a large community survey of women that those who had a confidant (defined as a person, usually male with whom the woman had a "close, confiding, intimate relationship") were at less risk of developing psychological impairment when exposed to a serious life stressor. They found that those women who experienced severe life events and lacked a confidant were roughly ten times more apt to be depressed than were the other women in the study.

While similar studies have yet to be published with regard to the issue of staff stress, the authors' observations tend to substantiate the notion that a supportive relationship can sustain and refresh the caregiver who is being exposed to a number of job stressors.

Such a person can serve a number of functions from the psychological "He draws me out when I get quiet and mopey" to the practical "If I've had a bad day he'll cook even if it's not his turn." However, all spouses are not equally helpful. One psychologist said "It would be hard to do the kind of work I'm doing without a spouse but no spouse would be better for me than one I'd have to protect."

Many caregivers spoke of the fact that spouses or boyfriends encouraged them to leave their job when the stressors were extreme. This often created a situation where they were hesitant to speak of their job at home because of frequent comments such as "Why do you continue working there, do you really enjoy watching all those kids die?"

Previous Stressors

Past losses, especially if unresolved, can lead to difficulty when one is constantly confronted with death. Such losses might include the death of parents, siblings or friends, particularly during one's early formative years, or the death of one's own child or spouse. Such experiences can predispose one to develop depression when exposed to later loss situations. In addition, unresolved grief can lead to a delayed grief reaction which can be triggered quite unexpectedly, particularly in circumstances similar to the first loss.

However, lest there be an over-emphasis on the problems associated with previous stressors, it should be mentioned that a person who has never suffered any losses or had to test his/her capacity to cope under adverse conditions may experience great distress when confronted with the many stressors associated with the care of critically ill and/or dying child.

Intrapersonal

Motivation

Elsewhere one of the author's (22) has documented some of the ways in which one's motivations to work with the dying might lead to stress reactions. If, for example, one chooses such work in order to resolve past losses; to relieve feelings of guilt; because of a special sense of calling; to prove that one can care for the dying better than others cared for one's dying relative; or in order to do research to cure the disease or disorder that caused the death of a family member; then there might be particular risk in situations which thwart these intentions and threaten to upset personal equilibrium.

In addition, it has already been noted that some caregivers entered their jobs because they like excitement and a highly stressful environment. When such staff members adjust to the technological demands of the job situation, they may find themselves unexpectedly in the situation of having to deal with the reality of emotional involvement and investment in dying children.

The problems which ensue may be quite baffling to others in the hospital setting. One administrator, for example, presumed that nurses working in a highly stressful setting would be mature women who had already raised a family and woule be able to tolerate the strain imposed by the job. He was shocked to observe that these units attracted young, single, adventuresome nurses who became turned off of the idea of motherhood because of their experience in an ICU setting.

Coping Style

One's previous method of coping with stressful situations can cause additional stressors when children are dying and this reality threatens to break down these defenses.

Because the subject of coping will be dealt with in depth in the final section of the chapter it will not be elaborated on in this section. The person who has developed a wide repertoire of coping skills through exposure to previous life stressors, both personal and professional, is probably best equipped to deal with the care of the dying child. The professional who deals with feelings of helplessness and passivity by excessive intellectualization, flight into activity, denial (1), projection, rationalization or withdrawal is going to experience personal distress as well as finding himself/herself in the middle of considerable staff conflict.

Interpersonal

The following factors are somewhat different from the preceding factors which may predispose one to increased job stress. A lack of social support and concurrent stressors can be seen as vulnerability factors which may be transient and therefore more amenable to change. The onset of difficulties in these areas may however be unexpected, thereby leaving the individual unprepared for the effect they may have on changing susceptibility to pre-existing job stressors. These factors vary from time to time in everyone's life. Depending on how they are operating, one may have a greater or lesser tolerance for job stressors.

Social Support

If one enters a highly stressful job situation without a good support system she/ he will probably be especially susceptible to job stressors as there is nowhere to unload the tensions experienced in daily work. Furthermore, this lack of support may be indicative of long-term interpersonal difficulties and an inability to maintain an adequate social support system.

Concurrent Stressors

When someone is experiencing personal or family problems the capacity to cope may well be diminished. During this time a caregiver may be particularly vulnerable to a stress reaction and therefore may need to be protected from certain stressors inherent in the work situation by taking on a decreased work load.

Societal Expectations

The final mediating factor which predisposes caregivers to increased vulnerability to certain job stressors is the rapidly changing societal environment in which we live. Families have changed, more mothers of young children are working, the extended family resources have weakened, divorce is on the increase and the critical illness of a child can impose an incredible stress on a very vulnerable family structure. The caregivers live in such an environment as well and experience similar pressures in their own family lives. As well they are subjected to changing expectations in their professional role wherein they are expected to integrate an ever-escalating level of technological expertise with the warmth and caring of the old family doctor. Needless to say significant role strain may result as caregivers try to meet these apparent conflicting demands.

These are also other expectations which the caregiver may have adopted, often without too much thought, as caregivers are also members of the society in which they live. These expectations might include the following beliefs:

1. That significant advances in medical technology should prevent the death of children.

2. That the physician is omnipotent and omniscient, therefore capable of preventing death (23).

3. That all caregivers are beyond the normal human emotions of depression, anger, frustration and despair and are always patient and understanding.

4. That all caregivers should be able to relate equally well to all patients and families.

5. That all caregivers are capable of separating the stressors of their personal and professional lives.

6. That all caregivers will always be completely up to date with the most recent technological advances.

To summarize, this section has presented a working model of staff stress which shows the way in which the stressors inherent in one's work situation including the illness, trajectory, environment and occupational role can be mediated by certain personal and interpersonal factors which may alter the vulnerability of the staff member. In the next section the authors will delineate some typical manifestations of staff stress and will then present some ways of preventing and/or coping with staff stress.

MANIFESTATIONS OF STRESS, PREVENTION, AND COPING STRATEGIES

Before beginning this section it is worth noting that the field of occupational stress is still fairly recent and much has yet to be learned in the area. No one can prescribe sure-fire remedies for all stressful job situations. Rather, the authors wish to make some suggestions which have proven helpful for preventing and dealing with some of the manifestations of staff stress which they have observed. In so doing, they urge the reader to utilize our suggestions as they seem appropriate, but more importantly, to use them as a basis for extending his or her own ideas for coping strategies and techniques in the particular environment in which the reader functions.

In this section the authors will present typical manifestations of staff stress and suggestions for prevention and coping strategies in a tabular form. The intention behind this format is to attempt to continue our process of breaking staff stress into component parts in the hope that it can thereby become more manageable.

The underlying assumptions in this section are as follows:

1. All caregivers will occasionally suffer from at least some degree of job related stress. It is naive to attempt to prevent this entirely as that would imply that the caregivers are automatons.

2. Stress can be productive and conducive to growth when used effectively, or it can be maladaptive leading to physical, psychological and interpersonal difficulties.

3. In caring for the critically ill and/or dying child it is essential that the caregiver maintain a high degree of knowledge and expertise in his or her given profession. Developing an awareness of psychosocial needs of patients and staff should in no way be an excuse for allowing deterioration in physical care for patients.

4. There may come a time in the care of the critically ill and/or dying child when active treatment aimed at prolonging survival is no longer appropriate and treatment aims should then shift to symptom control and allowing death to occur (24).

5. Support systems for dealing with staff stress must be built into the organizational structure of the institution and not simply be regarded as luxuries.

6. The nature of this work requires that it not be done in complete isolation. Caregivers need a balanced workload with some exposure to healthy children; contact with professionals in similar positions outside of their own institutions; and access to other experts as needed.

7. Much of the work with critically ill and dying children is still in the pioneering phase. It must be acknowledged that caregivers with an innovative, sometimes evangelistic pioneering mentality will be attracted to this type of work but such people may soon "burn-out." The middle phase of technological development may require a different type of individual who may be less innovative but more mature and steady.

8. Caregivers need the option of leaving this type of work without it being seen as an admission of defeat.

9. If caregivers develop serious maladaptive symptoms their colleagues have a responsibility to help them to decrease the exposure to stressors by a temporary removal from the job situation and/or the provision of outside support. A psychiatrist or other mental health professional should be available for crisis intervention and support.

On this basis, in the remainder of this section we will consider the following types of stress manifestations, together with recommended prevention and coping strategies: physical symptoms, psychological symptoms, social and family symptoms, and occupational symptoms.

Physical Symptoms*	
Manifestations of Stress	Prevention and Coping
The signs and symptoms of physical problems which may or may not be related to psychological problems may include the following:	A good physical examination from a competent physician can help to ascertain which of the symptoms are primarily physical and which are of psychological origin and primarily a response

(See footnote on page 173).

Physical Symptoms*

Manifestations of Stress	Prevention and Coping
Chronic fatigue Headache Stomach pains Frequent colds and flu Frequent somatic complaints Increased use of sick days Weight problems	to stress. Appropriate treatment should then be undertaken. Taking care of oneself physically is the first step to acknowledging that caretakers like patients and families, need and deserve care. Learn to know your body's responses to stress and when you get the signals you're in "stress overload" take a break and get some extra rest, even if only a few hours.
Poor eating habits including overeating, undereating, or poor nutrition.	A well-balanced diet with regularly scheduled meals eaten in an unhurried fashion helps to decrease some of the manifestations of stress. Such a diet might aim at weight control, reduction or maintenance and should have controlled use of caffeine, cholesterol and unnecessary of carbohydrates to allow the energy necessary for work and play.
Lack of physical exercise	The avoidance of regular physical exercise is often a reflection of a lack of interest in oneself. Taking care of everyone else at the expense of yourself is self-destructive. A successful stress reduction program includes the use of scheduled exercise such as walking, running, squash, tennis, swimming, etc.
Sleep disturbances	Proper sleep habits should be established and maintained. Shift work, frequent night calls, and twelve hour shifts, may result in chronic sleep derivation which may lead one to develop physical or psychological illnesses. Rotation of shifts should be scheduled to allow ample time for adaptation to altered sleeping patterns.

*Parts of this and following table are adapted from (25).

Psychological Symptoms

Manifestations of Stress	Prevention and Coping
Depression can be evidenced in feelings or behavior patterns such as apathy, isolation and withdrawal and low self-esteem; lack of interest in work and other people and a sense of anger towards others in the environment. A more severe clinical depression may result in symptoms such as early morning wakening, decreased libido (sexual energy), weight loss, constipation and a feeling that life is hopeless or meaningless. Of most concern should be thoughts of suicide	Depression may result from a major loss or a series of minor losses which threaten one's sense of self. Take the time to think through and explore the reason for the depression and attempt to resolve this. For example, if depression is the result of many deaths then it's time to look at what these deaths mean to you. Are they significant because of your personal involvement with the deceased? If so, take the time to grieve, remembering the deceased, assessing what your relationship was—how you helped and didn't help—and try to bury the

Psychological Symptoms (*Cont.*)

Manifestations of Stress	Prevention and Coping
or frequent thoughts of death as an increasingly attractive option.	person psychologically instead of carrying them around with you forever. This will take a shorter or longer time depending on the degree of emotional involvement.

Is the depression the result of feeling a failure professionally? If so take the time to evaluate your professional goals. You cannot cure everyone. For some people assisting them to die in the best possible way is the most appropriate form of treatment. When this has not been possible the talking to experts in symptom control may be an effective step to decreasing your sense of powerlessness the next time.

A balanced approach wherein one deals with children who will survive as well as those who will die can be an effective antidote for depression.

Depression may result from a chronically low sense of self-esteem. Give yourself credit for at least one good thing you did each day. By thinking of the positive aspects of your job and personal life, rather than constantly dwelling on the negative, one can gradually develop an increased sense of self-esteem and mastery.

Depression may also be thought of as anger turned in on the self. Try to assess the root of this anger. For example is it the result of constant put downs from colleagues or family members? If so, taking an assertiveness training program may be helpful.

Is it the result of long-buried anger towards someone who died and/or abandoned you? If so try to resolve this loss either on your own or with professional help.

Physical exercise has also been found to be helpful in dealing with depression in some people.

Finally, if the symptoms of a clinical depression, most particularly suicidal thoughts and a preoccupation with death occur, then the depression is severe enough to require professional help which should be readily available. Get yourself to a psychiatrist or if these symptoms develop in a colleague recognize that it's a crisis situation and requires consultation and referral.

Frustration   Evaluate your goals. Are they realistic or are you trying to be all things to all people. Divide the tasks up by taking small realistic steps towards meeting your goals.

Psychological Symptoms (*Cont.*)

Manifestations of Stress	Prevention and Coping
Denial	Healthy denial is good for your mental health. Occasionally we all need to "just forget about it all" and do something else.
	Denial becomes unhealthy when people come to believe in an evangelical way that they have the answer for everyone. Contact with others who will help with reality testing thereby breaking down denial is helpful.
Anxiety	By definition anxiety is not knowing what you're afraid of. Take the time to try to assess the cause of the anxiety and get it to a level where it's working for you. Anxiety may have its source in a fear of death, sexual conflicts, or identity confusion among other issues. There is also the societal expectation that the modern person has to always be technically competent and able to function on his or her own. Realize "no man is an island" and we need to function together in this work and not in isolation. Feeling you're not in it alone can decrease anxiety.
Conflict-laden dreams	These often reveal repressed anxiety or depression of which the person is not consciously aware. Caregivers reported that such dreams often focused on fears about technical competence, identification with patients reflected in dreams of being tied up to machines or developing leukemia, or fears of the responsibility of work (e.g., dreams of disconnecting patients from dialysis machines or monitors). Realize that your dreams are telling you about your unconscious areas of concern and begin to work on these conflict-laden areas by developing increased technological expertise, and talking about your concerns.
Over-identification with patients	Over-identification with patients can be decreased through the realization that in the long-run your over-identification will not be helpful to you or them. Remember that your time to need help will come someday (26) and if caregivers over-identify to the extent of not being able to meet your needs your care may be jeopardized. The same holds true for your patients.
Anger, projection and displacement (27)	At the unconscious level many of us struggle with the concept that anger can kill. As one young boy said "no one dies, they're 'deaded'." Anger is often manifest in critical care situations with projected blame for incompetence which often reflects anger that death intervened and made us feel incompetent. Try looking at the source of your anger and begin to realize that none of us is omnipotent or omniscient.

Psychological Symptoms (*Cont.*)

Manifestations of Stress	Prevention and Coping
Constant awareness of one's vulnerability because of constant exposure to death.	The intellectual insight that it's not yet your turn but yours too will come is often helpful for helping you to carry on today without survivor guilt (26).
	This feeling also requires exposure to healthy people. Shift into more positive areas in your personal and professional lives. Professional responsibility for dying children must be shared. Team work with the approach consistent, rather than always having consistent people can help. Try to combine clinical work with research: work with dying children with those who'll live. Realize that it is possible for healthy children to be born and to stay healthy and enjoy them.
Alcohol and drug abuse	Be aware of the risks of trying to blot out personal and professional problems with drugs and alcohol. While the use of these substances is sometimes healthy to defuse job stress, their overuse can be a hazard. In general it is better to talk through conflicts using people rather than pills.
Dehumanization of self-feeling too mechanized, or organized to the point where it becomes self-defeating and you feel like an automaton who is unable to feel.	This is a crisis point. You need a break and outside help if it continues.
Chronic unresolved grief for patients, often accompanied by frequent dreams or hallucinations of the deceased.	The opportunity to grieve at the time of death needs to be built into the system. In areas where there are many deaths some staffs have found it helpful to have periodic "wakes" where they remember the deceased, but then go on to enjoy themselves together. This alleviates some of the survivor guilt with the recognition that they do have a right to go on. They are not "responsible" for all the deaths.
	Occasional attendance at the funerals of patients may also be helpful but there must be the conscious recognition that staff members should not become the surrogate grievers whose grief supplants that of the family members who are then expected to care for the caregivers (2).
	Follow-up of families whose child has died is often most helpful because the staff members see that the family survives and is often appreciative of what you did. This follow-up should not be the responsibility only of individual practitioners but should be built into the system through bereaved parents groups etc. so staff members don't feel the responsibility for dealing with their current patients as well as all the survivor families.

The best way to deal with psychological disturbances is to avoid their occurrence. This can be done in a number of ways as follows:

Take one hour a day to pursue something which really interests you. Read, bird watch, walk, mediate, engage in physical activity, listen to music—whatever gives you pleasure. This refreshes you, restores some of your decreased energy and reflects the fact that you deserve some of your own time. Despite constant attention to the dying you are still living and must be cared for accordingly.

Have personal and professional goals beyond getting to work today. By working towards something, be it a research study, a paper, an improved scheduling pattern, better patient care etc., one is identifying with a broader goal which mitigates some of the stress of daily stressors. In addition easy access to psychological support through structured group meetings or the presence of a consultation-liaison mental health professional may be helpful.

Social and Family Symptoms	
Manifestations	Prevention and Coping
Constantly bringing job tensions home.	This type of work is not usually an 8-hour day, 5-day-a-week job which can be left behind when one leaves the hospital. However, constantly bringing home the tensions of the day and expecting emotional refreshment from those with whom one lives is unrealistic. In general, an attempt should be made to get some support from the others with whom one works; from others in similar roles or from a outside therapist. Another option is to schedule some physical activity on the way home from work to defuse some of the stress one is experiencing— swimming, squash or walking may be helpful. The provision of a few minutes of "quiet time" before beginning dinner or attempting family interaction may also be helpful.
Decreased sexual energy or its converse, greatly increased libidinal drive.	The former is usually a sign of depression, anxiety or overwork—try dealing with these as already suggested. Constant exposure to dying children may also cause one to feel that such "life-affirming" behavior as sexual intercourse is inappropriate (increased libidinal drive may be a counterphobic activity aimed at warding off this anxiety by the continual reaffirmation of life). A more clear-cut distinction between work and personal life is to be advocated with exposure to healthy children, involvement in outside activities and possibly a decreased work load.
	If decreased libidinal drive persists then a mental health professional should probably be consulted.
Fear of pregnancy	Constant exposure to critically ill and dying children may result in young women deciding never to have children because they are sure that such children would be deformed. More common is the situation where the caregiver will get pregnant but be inordinately worried during the pregnancy that the child will die, be deformed, or develop a serious illness. This concern often

Social and Family Symptoms (*Cont.*)

Manifestations	Prevention and Coping
	extends to colleagues and some staff members tell of returning to work after the birth of a healthy child only to be quizzed by colleagues about whether the child is really healthy.
	Considerable exposure to healthy children is helpful and some caregivers choose to leave high risk units before becoming pregnant to avoid getting caught up in this negative thinking. Leaving the unit also minimizes the transference problems with the parents of patients who may have trouble dealing with the pregnancy of staff members when their child is dying.
Constant awareness that one's children are susceptible to all of these diseases.	Looking at statistics helps sometimes. One comes to think that all children develop cancer, muscular dystrophy, etc.–some reality testing may be helpful. Contact with healthy children is also important.
No time for friends	The development of a good outside support system is of considerable value. Forming relationships with people outside of your own profession can often be refreshing, informative and enriching.

One must assess priorities and determine the value of work versus home life. If the priority is career advancement one might decide to forego marriage and/or children which may/may not lead to later regrets and a sense of emptiness in life. Should one decide that a career has absolute top priority, but that nonetheless one will marry and have children then there is the risk of marital breakdown, family problems such as adolescent drug abuse, and resentment from children as evidenced in the words of one's physician's daughter who developed cancer– "You've never been here for the good times, so I don't want you here now."

If a relationship and/or children have priority then time must be organized for the nurturing of such relationships. This may include the structuring of nightly family dinners with ample time to share the day's happenings; refraining from evening work or scheduling it late so as not to interfere with home life; family activities and holidays; and/or refraining from weekend work.

In dealing with occupational symptoms, one of the best ways of decreasing staff stress is through the appropriate selection of caregivers. Pre-employment interviews should focus on the individual's reason for choosing this type of work. Employers should realize that there may be an increased risk of a stress reaction in individuals who have experienced a recent bereavement or major life change such as divorce. Those with a poor outside support system and few outside interests may be at risk as they have no place to let off frustrations at the end of a day. Young caregivers with no prior loss experiences may also have to be watched for a stress reaction because of their previous inexperience (28).

Orientation for new staff members should include the physical, technological and psycho-social problems with which the new staff member will have to grapple. They must be assisted to develop the necessary skills through the use of a "buddy system" and/or the provision of competent role models who can teach and provide support.

More experienced caregivers of all disciplines need ample opportunity to keep up-to-date through educational programs research opportunities as well as attendance at workshops and conferences (28).

Occupational Symptoms

Manifestations	Prevention and Coping
Unrealistic expectations	Staff members of all disciplines must come to accept the fact that medical science has not yet progressed to the extent of being able to cure all of these diseases. Death must be seen less as a medical or technological failure and more as reflection of the state of medicine. While we can strive to push back the frontiers of science through research and clinical caring, we are not yet at the stage of eradicating death.
Work overload with ever-increasing amounts of time being spent at work or on work-related activities.	Staff members of all disciplines may be guilty of taking on ever-increasing work responsibilities and constantly increasing patient loads. This is often a reflection of an inordinate "need-to-be-needed," guilt over other "failures" (27) or a desire to show that one is the most competent person in the group.
	This type of overload can be helped through the more effective use of multidisciplinary teams. Although it is often difficult to share responsibilities, an effective multidisciplinary team can result in the more even distribution of caring, responsibilities and decision making. Such a team can be helpful in setting realistic limits on the involvement of individual team members, and provide for coverage and time off to permit the maintenance of family relationships and outside activities.
Feeling completely overwhelmed by job responsibilities.	Step back, assess goals and establish priorities. Break the tasks to be done into smaller component parts (if necessary making a list of these parts so they can be checked off, showing yourself that you really have done something; accomplishment of many small tasks or resolution of many small problems adds up to progress towards a goal (29).
Inability to detach one's self from the job	This may be the onset of a serious stress reaction. Schedule time for outside interests and family and take the time to meet these obligations. At this point a change in lifestyle must be treated as a medical prescription. Time away may be needed.
Repetitive accidents or impaired work performance.	This is a crisis situation. Time away is essential. Professional help is probably warranted.

Occupational Symptoms *(Cont.)*

Manifestations	Prevention and Coping
Over-involvement with patients and families.	While this is still a comparatively new area in which firm guidelines cannot be set, caregivers must become aware that if they develop personal relationships with patients and families outside of the work situation then care may be jeopardized because of impaired judgement. One can come to be resentful of the increasing expectations and non-reciprocal relationships which may develop with patients and families outside the work context. Sexual liaisons sometimes occur (or are suggested) between the parents of dying children and caregivers. This may seem to be a reflection of the intense relationships which develop in the critical care situation. However, it is often a transference/ countertransference relationship in which the parent unconsciously looks to the caregiver to "give life" and create a healthy child and the caregiver responds out of guilt and/or a sense of failure.
Withdrawal from, dehumanization of or cynicism about patients.	This stage often occurs as a reaction formation following intense involvement or identification with patients and families which overwhelmed the caregiver. The best treatment is time away from patients with an opportunity to get refreshed. If the symptoms are not too severe this time away can be attendance at a meeting, a holiday or a few days off. In more severe cases a temporary transfer to another job may be helpful or it may be time to change jobs. Sometimes these feelings can be avoided by exposure to children who have done well. Pictures of "success stories" can adorn the walls of the Neonatal ICU, and ICU. Pictures of chronically ill children engaging in normal activities can be helpful in oncology, cystic fibrosis or muscular dystrophy units. Having children who are doing well visit the unit also helps to increase staff morale.
Role ambiguity, role conflict and role strain.	This type of work is best done by a multi-disciplinary team, so that no one is working in total isolation. Getting and keeping such a team working is difficult however. Roles are often ill-defined and ambiguous and conflicts develop over professional responsibilities. While it may seem simplistic, it is worth mentioning that if the patient/family needs are kept primary and it is acknowledged that different staff members can meet varying needs with different patients then fewer conflicts ensue. It is probably unrealistic to have clearly defined role boundaries, for example: The doctor treats and cures The nurse cares and coordinates

Occupational Symptoms (*Cont.*)	
Manifestations	Prevention and Coping
	The social worker copes with problems The chaplain prays The physical therapist exercises
	Significant role strain ensues with the rigid adherence to such roles, nevertheless some teams have found it difficult to function without some type of role clarification. This may need to be done in the early phases of team formation but hopefully over time mutual trust develops and roles can be more flexible. Frequent staff meeting with a focus on patient care, informal conversations about management, the use of consultants and some outside socialization often prove effective in the maintenance of effective team relationships. This makes decisions about treatment—particularly shifting goals—somewhat easier.
Decreased role satisfaction	This can sometimes be alleviated by acknowledging expertise and providing for the assumption of new role responsibilities, e.g. doing research, joining the transport team, becoming a team leader, etc. Whenever possible these role changes should be accompanied by a salary increase. In some situations of high stress "front line pay" might be helpful.
Role reversal with parents	Try to set realistic goals for the involvement of parents in treatment programs so that staff members avoid assuming the major parenting roles for most children. The use of parent support groups and bereaved parent groups is often helpful for sharing the load.
	In addition these groups provide the reinforcement that parents survive even when their children die—reinforcement that parents and caregivers both need.
Fish bowl environment	Private space for caregivers and parents is essential. When a caregiver has been directly involved in a death experience she/he needs time away from the bedside to grieve and work through the experience.

SUMMARY

This chapter has provided a theoretical model of staff stress in the care of critically ill and dying children. The stress that staff members experience is a reflection of stressors inherent in the patient care environment as well as those mediating factors which the individual brings into the work setting from his or her personal life. These factors may either strengthen the individual in a stressful situation or may make the caregiver more vulnerable to a stress reaction. Stress may be manifested in physical or psychological symptoms or in difficulties in the person's social, family or occupational life. Specific suggestions were given for coping with some of these manifestations of stress.

REFERENCES

1. Pakes, E., The Dying Child and His Family, in *Psychological Problems of the Child and His Family*. P. D. Steinhauer and Q. Rae-Grant (eds.), Toronto: MacMillan of Canada, 1977, pp. 347–360.
2. Fulton, R., Anticipatory Grief, Stress and the Surrogate Griever, in *Cancer, Stress and Death*. J. Tache, *H. Selye and S. B. Day* (eds.), New York: Plenum Medical Book Co., 1979, pp. 87–93.
3. Vachon, M. L. S., Staff Stress in Hospice Care: A Theoretical Model, in *The Hospice* (2nd ed.). G. Davidson (ed.), Washington, D.C.: Hemisphere Publishing Co. (in press).
4. Vachon, M. L. S., *Identity Change Over the First Two Years of Bereavement: Social Relations and Social Support in Widowhood*. Toronto: York University, unpublished doctoral dissertation, 1979.
5. Levine, S. & Scotch, *Social Stress*. Chicago: Aldine Publishing Co., 1973.
6. Selye, H., *The Stress of Life*. New York: McGraw-Hill Book Co., Inc., 1956.
7. Dohrenwend, B. S. & Dohrenwend, B. P., Class and Race as Status–Related Sources of Stress, in *Social Stress*. S. Levine and N. A. Scotch (eds.), Chicago: Aldine Publishing Co., 1973, pp. 111–140.
8. Rabkin, J. G. & E. L. Struening, Life Events, Stress and Illness, *Science*, 194(3 December 1976):1013–1020.
9. Price, M. E., Why NICU Nurses Burn Out and How to Prevent It, *Contemporary Obstetrics and Gynecology*, 13 (March 1979):37–46.
10. Schmidt, C., Emotional Stress in the NICU, P/N November and December, 1977, pp. 37–44.
11. Pakes, E. H., Physician's Response to the Diagnosis of Cancer in His Child Patient, Mimeo, 1979.
12. Beaton, J., The Neonatal and Pediatric Intensive Care Units–Impact on Parents and Providers, paper presented at The Canadian University Nursing Students' Association, National Conference, Winnipeg, Manitoba Feb. 8, 1980 (mimeo).
13. Cassem, N. H. & T. P. Hackett, Sources of Tension for the ICU Nurse, *American Journal of Nursing*, 72:1426–1430, August, 1972.
14. Vreeland, R. & G. L. Ellis, "Stresses on the Nurse in an Intensive Care Unit, *Journal of the American Medical Association*, 208:2:332–334, April 14, 1969.
15. Quint, J., Awareness of Death and the Nurses' Composure, *Nursing Research*, 15:49–55, Winter, 1966.
16. Pakes, E. "Care for the Care-Givers." Paper presented at Conference on Children and Death. The University of Chicago, March 17–19, 1978.
17. Kübler-Ross, E., *On Death and Dying*. Toronto: Collier-Macmillan, 1967.
18. Easson, W. M., Care of the Young Patient Who is Dying, *Journal of the American Medical Association*, 205:63–67, July 22, 1968.
19. Osol, Arthur (ed.), *Blakiston's Gould Medical Dictionary*. New York: McGraw-Hill Book Co., 1972.
20. Storlie, F. S., Burnout: The Elaboration of a Concept, *American Journal of Nursing*, December, 1979, pp. 2018–2011.
21. Brown, G. W., M. M. Bhrolchain, & T. Harris, Social Class and Psychiatric Disturbance Among Women in an Urban Population, *Sociology*, 9:2:226–254, 1975.
22. Vachon, M. L. S., Motivation and Stress Experienced by Staff Working with the Terminally Ill, *Death Education*, 2:113–122, 1978.
23. Knapp, R. J. & L. G. Peppers, Doctor-Patient Relationships in Fetal/Infant Death Encounters, *Journal of Medical Education*, 54:775–780, October 1979.
24. Mount, B. M., The Problem of Caring for the Dying in a General Hospital: The Palliative Care Unit as a Possible Solution, *Canadian Medical Association Journal*, 115:119–121, July 17, 1976.
25. Vachon, M. L. S., Care for the Caregivers, The Laura Barr Lecture, Presented at the Registered Nurses' Association of Ontario, Annual Meeting, Toronto, 2 May 1980.
26. Weisman, A., Personal Communication, 1974.
27. Redding, R., Doctors, Dyscommunication and Death, *Death Education*, 3:4:371–385, 1980.
28. Vachon, M. L. S., Staff Stress in Care of the Terminally Ill, *Quality Review Bulletin*, May 1979.
29. Weisman, A., Address at Princess Margaret Hospital, May 1980.

III

BEREAVEMENT

Bereavement as it relates to childhood and death can take many forms and involve many kinds of people. We are beginning to realize, for example, that there are many more dimensions and responses to loss than was believed earlier, and that grieving—the emotional response to a recognized loss—can begin well before death and continue (for survivors) long afterwards. Pre- and post-death grieving cannot be kept apart if we are to understand them properly. As the following chapters demonstrate, we do have a good knowledge base of this subject. But there is much yet to learn about the process of mourning or working through grief, and about anticipatory grieving both in itself and in relationship to the grieving that follows a death. The aim of this section is to gather together what has been learned about the central features of post-death bereavement as it applied to childhood and death, to complement what has already been set forth in Part II, and to indicate additional ways to assist those who must struggle with this side of death.

Perhaps the first thing to say is that many people can be caught up in bereavement. They include children, parents, family members, friends, and caregivers. In each case, the nature, intensity, and length of the mourning process will depend upon the previous relationship with the dead person, the manner of the death, the individual's own abilities to cope with or adapt to stress, and the kinds of external support that are available. The four chapters that follow explore the principal variables among these many factors. Of course, individuals must be expected to mourn in their own particular ways. But we can understand and help them better the more we know about general patterns of bereavement in childhood or of adult bereavement as that relates to the death of a child.

In Chap. 9, Erna Furman provides the necessary theoretical basis for this section through her definition and elucidation of the concept of mourning. As she draws out the import of this concept, we can see: 1) why losses resulting from death differ from other sorts of losses—which may be either partial or reversible; 2) why losses through death may differ among themselves; and 3) why the parent-child relationship may specially influence mourning. An account of mourning as a threefold task and of five central factors which may influence the way in which children meet these tasks carries us forward into a fuller description of functional modes of mourning and some preventive measures against aberrations. What comes across throughout this discussion is the author's confidence in the naturalness of mourning and her sensitivity to its nuances as a process in childhood. The moral for adults is to help our children mature and grow in meeting the sadness of bereavement, and in so doing to grow with them ourselves.

Furman has in mind particularly, but not exclusively, the child in bereavement. The other side of this coin is represented by families and other individuals who are mourning the death of a child. In Chaps. 10 and 11, common problems faced by this latter group are addressed by a pediatrician and a pediatric nurse, Morris Wessel and Margaret Miles. As experienced clinicians and educators, Wessel and Miles offer both insight and advice. Wessel speaks more generally of families as a unit and of children or other individuals within that context; Miles explores the special burdens of parents and, more briefly, some aspects of mourning in grandparents. Both authors include caregivers within the scope of their remarks. In harmony with principles outlined in the previous part, Wessel advocates that support for bereaved persons properly arises from those who are nearest and most available, whoever they may be, and he recommends that where possible support is best given through parents and the family unit to those of its members who are in mourning. This may seem to impose an additional burden, e.g., on a bereaved parent, but in fact it also reflects a need and an opportunity to turn outward and to share in ways that are usually conducive to the individual's own successful grieving. For her part, Miles adapts some ideas from Colin Murray Parkes to the construction of a model for understanding adult—especially parental—grief occasioned by the death of a child. The limitations of such a model are evident, but its heuristic value is great. Here it is particularly helpful in identifying components of such grief, in drawing out multiple types of guilt that can enter into such mourning, and in guiding those who would help with such bereavement.

Surely all deaths in childhood are and have been painful experiences for survivors. But death does not occur in a vacuum, nor is the manner of death irrelevant. In Chap. 12, Glen Davidson takes up both of these considerations. First, he shows how changes in societal expectations, in environmental context, and in modes of care all seem to contribute to greater disorientation in our society following the death of a child than was true years ago when such deaths were more common. Second, Davidson illustrates his point through an analysis of three kinds of infant death: stillbirth, neonatal death, and sudden infant death syndrome (SIDS). In each case, the mode of death and its incidence in the United States are defined, an example illustrates common qualities, and particular points of disorientation are noted. While it is undeniable that these are selected circumstances of death, Davidson's analysis defines many of the central elements of the impact of childhood death in our time. We can never wholly avoid that impact, but we may lessen its blow if we consider its import before it descends upon us or upon those whom we love or serve.

9

Children's Patterns in Mourning
the Death of a Loved One

Erna Furman

INTRODUCTION

Death impinges on us in different ways and at different times. Some of us were touched by it early on in our lives and have suffered hard-to-heal wounds and lasting tender scars. Others have encountered death repeatedly and may even now be in anguish, struggling to cope with dying or bereavement. And others yet are fortunate in having been granted a briefer or longer period in our lives when we can healthily deny the everpresent shadow of death. Absorbed in the business of living, we manage not be affected significantly by the evidence of death around us because it does not immediately befall ourselves or our loved ones. Such temporary disregard for death is then inevitably shattered when suddenly death comes very close and demands that we come to terms painfully in a new and different way. Over 20 years ago, this happened to our group of 14 child psychoanalysts at the Cleveland Center for Research in Child Development and Hanna Perkins Therapeutic School (1), and prompted us to embark on our research on mourning.

In the present sharing of our experiences and findings, the reader's old scars or new wounds of bereavement may be touched inadvertently. Things may be said that reawaken pains or cause them to hurt more. Even those may experience distress who are not personally afflicted but who, in reading this material, have offered their empathy and rendered themselves vulnerable. I therefore sincerely apologize to the reader in advance for inflicting unintentional upset and extend to him or her my warm sympathy. Would that it were possible to spare each person's feelings; yet we have found no way to grapple with the problems of death and bereavement intellectually without the inevitable and necessary emotional involvement.

This proved true for the stricken as well as for those who would assist them. However well and courageously bereaved children or adults may master their situation, they cannot avoid periods of deep distress. Likewise, professional mental health workers cannot meet their obligations to their bereaved patient unless they allow themselves to empathize appropriately with each client's specific feelings and experiences and come to terms within themselves with the limitations imposed on us by being helpless in the face of death. It is a difficult task, never completed and fully renewed with each bereavement and with each bereaved patient because no two deaths and no two bereavements are alike.

The events which shook our small professional community were the deaths, within one year, of two young mothers whose children were then attending our Hanna Perkins Nursery School and Kindergarten. The tragedies descended unexpectedly on the families concerned, on the classmates of the bereaved children, and on the staff of analysts and teachers who worked with them (2-10). During the subsequent months and years, as our efforts focused on understanding and mastering our patients' as well as our own varied responses, we realized that encounters with death and experiences of bereavement are much more common in the lives of children and young families than we had previously acknowledged.

As consultants to social agencies, nursery schools and day care centers, we had frequent opportunities to assist children with their losses through death of parents as well as siblings, grandparents, friends, relatives and pets. Through our own observations, and those of parents and educators, we came to appreciate also how often young children notice and puzzle about deaths which do not affect them personally—dead animals, killed insects or worms, funeral processions, cemeteries, ambulances, news reports in the media. We became especially aware that many of our own patients had significant experiences with death and bereavement. Some of us were currently treating orphans and, within the next few years, several more such cases happened to come to us for therapeutic help. It is noteworthy that we never sought cases of bereavement nor did the patients seek us because they wanted help with their losses.

We had no preconceived research project on mourning. Our decision to compare our data, to pool our findings, to formulate our conclusions, in short, to utilize for research purposes what we learned from our bereaved patients, grew spontaneously from the wealth of new material and fresh insights which each of us gathered through our psychoanalytic work with our patients and their families and from the emotional stress we experienced in empathizing with them. We felt that in sharing with one another our intellectual understanding and feelings, we would be better able to master our professional task of helping our patients, to develop our grasp of general aspects of bereavement, and, perhaps, to outline some prophylactic measures. Although we included in our thinking our professional work with death and bereavement in all forms, we decided to focus our detailed study on children who had suffered the loss of a parent through death and who had been treated intensively and longterm by one of our 14 participating child psychoanalysts. Our reason for focusing on parental bereavement lay in its special impact on the developing personality. Our choice of psychoanalytic data was determined by their unique propensity to yield insight. The specific requirement of psychoanalysis for daily sessions over several years provides, in itself, an unusually intensive and extensive means of investigation. Time, however, is only one factor. The psychoanalytic method is not only a form of therapy but a unique research tool. It enables the patient and therapist to uncover unconscious mental contents, to trace their causal connections and to relate them to past and present experiences. With the help of these previously unknown "missing pieces" the puzzle of the patient's difficulties can be solved and he or she can gain new conscious mastery through understanding.

There were 23 such children; the earliest bereaved was a girl whose mother died when she was 10 weeks old, the latest a boy whose father died when he was 13 years. Fourteen of them received individual psychoanalytic treatment and were seen 5 times weekly in 50 minute sessions for periods of 2 to 6 years. The rest were young children who were treated via the surviving parent, or parent substitute, while attending the Hanna Perkins Nursery School and Kindergarten. There they were observed daily over periods from 2 to 3 years by analysts and analytically trained teachers while the parents were assisted in their therapeutic work with the child by weekly meetings with the analyst. Since every family's payments at our Center and School are adjusted to its income and range from full fees to nothing, our group of 23 children had very varied socioeconomic backgrounds and also differed racially, ethnically, culturally, and in religious affiliation. In addition to their parental bereavement, some had suffered other losses through death, separation or divorce and many had endured other hardships. Their symptoms at the time of referral however in no way distinguished them from other patients and varied widely. There were difficulties with eating, toileting and sleeping, fears and obsessions, social problems with peers and adults, learning troubles, stealing and truanting, conflicts over sexual identity, behavioral disorders manifested in aggressiveness or withdrawal, and many more. With 8 of the children, the parent died during the course of their treatment, an event that had not been anticipated at the start of therapy. With the others, the parent's death had occurred earlier and the family did not relate the children's difficulties to their bereavement. In some cases, the death of the parent was mentioned only incidentally as a part of the child's personal history. The causal connection between the bereavement and the later difficulties revealed itself only in the course of treatment.

In the years since the completion of our research we have treated many more bereaved children. Some patients came because they or their families suffered a bereavement and some were, for this reason, referred by physicians, agencies or private individuals who had learned of our work and had come to recognize the importance of early help. We have thus had much opportunity to check our earlier findings against newly accumulated data. Although this ongoing study has deepened our understanding and refined as well as extended it in some respects, we have not yet found evidence to alter our earlier conclusions and suggestions (11-14). They form the basis for my attempt, in this chapter, to share with the reader some of what we have learned.

WHAT IS MOURNING?

The term "mourning" is used variously. It is often applied to a wide spectrum of mental states connected with different forms of loss, for example, "He mourned the death of his spouse; the passing of his youth; the destruction of his home; the infantile closeness with his mother; the loss of his fortune; his absent father; his shattered ideals; his biological parent whom as an adopted child he never knew; the loss of his vision through illness; his leg which had to be amputated; the healthy baby he had expected instead of the defective one that was born." Although these and many more forms of loss have some aspects in common, we learned that the realities they represent, and the inner psychological mastery they require, differ so greatly that we cannot treat them as identical experiences.

"Mourning" is also often used synonymously with "grief" which denotes the painful, sad and anguished feelings accompanying loss. This use of the term we found to be too narrow because the emotional aspects of loss represent but one of several mental processes which make up mourning.

It has seemed most accurate and clinically helpful to define mourning as *the mental work following the loss of a loved one through death.*

Does It have to be a Loss through Death?

Work with our patients showed that death is a reality which implies a special finality. Unless this unique reality is perceived, comprehended and acknowledged, mourning cannot begin. The mental work of mourning is set in motion by the bereaved person's appreciation of the death and serves as the means of adapting to the specific reality of a loss through death.

By contrast, partial losses in which aspects of a relationship are lost (such as the loss of bodily closeness in the later mother-child relationship) or separations (be they short, long or even permanent) are not experienced as total losses. We cannot accept these losses as irrevocable because as long as there is life there is hope. Also, whereas death excludes hope, threatens us and leaves us helpless, separations usually imply a degree of human power. In that sense they tend to inflict the hurt of rejection, "He could come back if he really wanted to," "She would not have gone away if she really loved me." Death, if properly understood, never implies a rejection. Even suicide is not "willed" but results from mental disturbances which affect a person's normal judgment and feelings. This makes death harder to cope with in some ways and easier in others. Some of our patients lost one parent through death, another through divorce. Mourning the dead parent was very diffi-cult but possible; coming to terms with the ongoing feelings of frustrated hope and rejection in regard to the unavailable divorced parent often proved impossible.

In instances where the loved one died but the bereaved does not know it for certain or cannot understand it, the loss is perceived as a separation and mourning cannot take place. With adults this happens, for example, when soldiers are missing in action. Children are often in this unfortunate position when they are not told about a death truthfully or are not helped to understand what dead means.

Does Mourning Follow Only the Loss of a Loved One?

There are two other kinds of losses, those of inanimate objects (losses of money, home, country or even of a beloved jacket) and those of a part of one's self (loss of limb or bodily function, restrictions and deteriorations due to ageing or illness, and mental losses, such as hopes, ideals and expectations). Such losses cause a change in what we are or how we appear, in what we own or regard as ours. Such changes require that we adapt our self-image to the new reality. Depending on the significance and magnitude of the loss—and it is usually of a diminishing or detri-mental nature—it may be very difficult or even impossible to master. It affects primarily our self-love, self-esteem and sense of well-being.

In relationships we not only love, we are loved back. This special mutuality, the salient feature of every meaningful relationship, is absent from our attachment to things as well as from our investment in ourselves. For this reason, the loss of a loved and loving being affects us differently and deprives us of different satisfac-tions. Our data show that the mental processes by which we cope with the loss of a loved one differ significantly from those which we use to adapt to the other losses.

There is, however, one kind of relationship in which the partner is both a loved person and a part of oneself, namely the parent-child relationship. The uniquely close and long-term bodily and mental interdependence between parent and child expresses itself in this special bond. During his earliest life the child does not know where he ends and the mother begins. For many years the parent functions in part for the child and, through their special relationship, gradually fosters the development of the child's independent personality. Although the parent's functioning does not depend on his/her child, the parent appropriately also regards the child as a part of himself. When a child loses a parent or, to a less significant extent, when a parent loses a child, the bereaved is faced with a double loss—loss of a loved one and loss of a part of oneself. This immeasurably complicates the survivor's task of mourning and accounts for some of its special features and hardships (15, 16).

All losses of loved ones through death are not the same. Even a consideration of mourning in our narrower sense points up at once the fact that our relationships vary. We cannot equate the relationship with a friend, spouse, parent, or sibling. Each relationship implies a different closeness and intensity, different kinds and amounts of love, frustration, gratification and anger. Moreover, relationships change with time and the number of relationships we maintain affects the significance of each. Mourning differs considerably, in form and intensity, according to the particular relationship that was lost through death.

The relationships of child and adult also differ greatly, in that the adult usually maintains several meaningful relationships (spouse, parents, relatives, friends, children, colleagues) whereas with children, and especially young ones, the relationship with the parent is paramount and all his other relationships pale by comparison. For this reason too, a child's parental bereavement constitutes an incomparable loss and the mourning task is especially difficult.

WHEN CAN A PERSON MASTER A BEREAVEMENT?

When we lose a loved one through death we are faced with a threefold task: 1) to understand and come to terms with the reality and circumstances of the death, 2) to mourn, and 3) to resume and continue our lives, which in the case of the child, implies appropriate progression in the development of his/her personality. Each of these tasks makes special demands on us. Difficulty encountered with one impedes resolution of the others; for example, some of our patients developed symptoms only years after their bereavement when they failed to cope with the demands of a new developmental phase or when they could not adjust to the newly constituted family with a stepparent. In many of these cases the trouble lay primarily with their earlier unobserved difficulties in comprehending the circumstances of the parent's death which, in its turn, prevented mourning.

Several factors proved important in enabling a bereaved to address himself to these tasks.

Emotional Health and Specific Personality Factors

In coping with a stress we stretch our resources to their utmost. The greater our strengths and the more reserves we have available, the better our chances of tackling the task at hand. The stress of bereavement tends to call on all our functions. In dealing with it, every area of health is an asset. Our weaknesses, perhaps unnoticed or of little consequence at happier times of inner equilibrium, tend to be revealed and prove a handicap. We found that emotionally healthy children and adults could cope with their bereavements better than those who suffered long-standing difficulties.

Mary's father died of a heart attack when she was 8. She had a long-standing difficulty in coping with frustrations. This affected her learning (she expected immediate success and quickly gave up trying) and her relationships (she was intolerant of others and lashed out angrily when they disappointed her). Mary had unusual difficulty in accepting the reality of the death and in mourning because she had so little capacity for bearing the inherent frustration and associated feelings of helplessness, pain and sadness.

Bodily and Mental Well Being

When we are ill or in danger of losing our job and home, our energies have to focus on self-preservation and cannot be devoted to other tasks. At a time of bereavement it is especially important that we feel assured of our own capacity for survival, of our own needs being met. The death of others implies a threat to our lives ("Could it happen to me?") and mourning which serves to relinquish our inner ties to the deceased, can be undertaken only when our lives promise to hold enough satisfaction to make it worth continuing without the dead loved one. Adults often plan for such contingencies, in wills or insurance policies, to provide economic support for the surviving family. In case of need, the bereaved adult at once directs his energies to finding alternate sources of income and turns to friends and relatives for help and comfort.

The child's only means of support are his parental figures. Unless he feels assured that they will continue to supply all his needs, he cannot address himself to the bereavement task. A child's urgent demands for bodily and mental satisfactions may seem selfish ("I want hamburgers like we always have on Sunday," "You have to take me to the library," "Won't you play ball with me?"). They are, however, the child's way of checking whether and how his or her needs will be met and, in this sense, the demands are merely the equivalent of the adult's "selfishness" in figuring out how he or she will make ends meet and on whom he or she can count as a friend in need.

Adequate assurance of bodily and mental well-being is a prerequisite for undertaking the task of mourning.

Lack of Additional Stresses

All additional stresses complicate, or even jeopardize, a person's capacity to master his bereavement. Some such stresses are unavoidable, for example one mother's death in a car crash involved also the death of one of her children and severe injuries to the surviving child; in another case, the death of an older brother happened when the younger child was hospitalized for pneumonia. Many additional stresses, however, are unnecessarily and unwittingly inflicted on children in the aftermath of a death in the family.

Whereas some bereaved adults find relief in actively changing their life styles and distancing themselves from reminders of the past, children of all ages rely on the continuity of their remaining relationships and draw comfort from their familiar environments. Separations and other losses are therefore especially taxing for them.

Bobby's father died from a debilitating illness when the boy was 2. The mother at once sold their home and took up full-time work. Bobby was sent to a day-care center. His 6-year-old sister had to change schools and stayed with neighbors during the late afternoons. The partial loss of the mother, loss of home, school and friends, as well as the need to adjust to so many new people and places proved too much to handle. Both children failed to cope with their bereavement and developed emotional difficulties.

By contrast, Jennifer's mother appreciated how important she was to her children at the time of their father's death and how much they depended on the safe familiarity of their surroundings. Although her financial means were very meager, she decided to keep their home intact and to work only part-time. During these few hours her toddler was cared for at home by a retired friend and 4-year-old Ray attended nursery school. As Mrs. S. put it, "We haven't eaten a real piece of meat in a long time but we've had each other."

Developmental Stage of Personality Development

In evaluating children's capacity for mourning it is important to distinguish whether they are required to master a parental bereavement or the loss through death of other loved ones—siblings, grandparents, peers, teachers, or pets. As mentioned earlier, the loss of a parent poses special problems for the child of any age because the parent is the main recipient of the child's feelings, fulfills the child's needs, represents a part of the child's personality, is instrumental in the further development of the child's personality and, last but not least, needs to help the child with the bereavement as he helps him with so many of his other activities.

In spite of these major complications, the work with our patients showed that, from nursery school age on, children were capable of mastering even the death of a parent with appropriate help from the surviving parent or parent-substitutes. This help was crucial for the pre-schoolers, very necessary but not so extensive for the school-aged children, and helpful to the adolescents. For example, pre-schoolers needed help to comprehend sufficiently what dead means, what caused the death, and how we dispose of the dead. School children needed help in understanding the cause of the death but had already formed a basic concept of death and burial. Teenagers were helped by talking these matters over with their parents to clarify details.

The difficulty of the younger child is directly related to the relative immaturity of his personality, limited experience, and emotional dependency on his loved ones. But it does not follow that the older a person gets, the better he can mourn. Some of our 4-year-olds could master their bereavement. Many older children could not do so, nor could many of the adults. Personality difficulties, special circumstances related to, or coincidental with, the specific loss, lack of other continuing relationships, were among the factors which interefered with their bereavement work. A child's efforts at mastery were also thwarted by the adult's inability to cope with the bereavement since children, and especially the younger ones, need the surviving parent's "permission" as well as help with mourning. I am not thinking of verbal permission, although that can be of some help, but of the many non-verbal ways by which adults convey their innermost wishes and attitudes and which children sense, respond to and comply with. When the surviving parent cannot address him/herself to the mourning task, the child is implicitly not expected to do so either. However, we worked with a number of adults who appeared to mourn quite adequately themselves, yet stood in the way of their children's mourning. Sometimes they deliberately wanted to "spare" the child (thus hoping to spare a part of themselves), at other times they were unaware of the subtle ways in which they showed their reluctance to support the child's grieving. There were also parents who welcomed and appreciated some aspects of the child's struggles, for example sadness, but shirked from others, such as concrete details of the death, angry feelings, or painful truths about the deceased.

Among our patients were some advanced older toddlers, around two years of age, who could mourn under special circumstances. Babies and young toddlers, however, although deeply affected by a bereavement, were too immature to cope with it by means of mourning. We shall discuss their situation at a later point.

Assistance by Surviving Parent(s)

It should not be surprising that children's ability to cope with a bereavement depends so closely on the parents' help and that the continuing relationship with them is so important. This does, however, place a special responsibility on the parents at the very time when they are grieving and, usually, also dealing with other stresses. When a child loses a parent, it is the parent's spouse; when a sibling dies, it is the parent's child; when a grandmother dies, it is the parent's mother. The parent's and the child's bereavement are never identical but involve a person significant to both. Even in mourning the same person they mourn different relationships.

Some people wonder how a parent could possibly fulfill his or her special role with the child at such a time. It is indeed difficult but many parents we worked with felt that their gains made the hardship well worth while. The parent's helplessness as a bereaved is, to an extent, constructively counteracted by actively helping the child. Self-esteem, often lowered by a bereavement, is immeasurably enhanced by the feeling of being a good parent. And the need for continuing relationships, which is also an adult's need, is satisfied through the parent's deepening relationship with his child. Children often are good companions in grief and so, in many ways, the child also assists the parent.

UNDERSTANDING AND ACCEPTING THE DEATH
OF A LOVED ONE

The importance of this first phase of the bereavement task is often not fully appreciated and the adults' need to help children with it is most frequently neglected. In part this is due to the fact that grown-ups may not realize the big difference between their own and children's grasp of real events, in part it lies in the adults' own unmastered fear of death. By failing to explain the upsetting realities and sidestepping the stress of coping with children's questions, we succeed in protecting our own sensibilities rather than the children's feelings. Since most of us have not quite come to terms with death, and many of us have "hang-ups" about some aspects, we are rarely comfortable in helping our children with it. We need not pretend that the topic is easy for us. When we are taken aback by their questions, we can say, "It's hard for me to talk about this. Let me think about it and I'll get back to you later," or, "I'm afraid I have trouble with talking about death, but I'll do my best to help you and I hope you will learn to do better than I," or, "I did not tell you the whole truth the other day because it's so difficult for me but I'd like to correct my mistake now and explain things better." It is more helpful to our children to see us as honestly struggling to cope with a difficult topic than to have them copy our avoidance or to perceive us as pseudo-perfect. A loved parent's halting piecemeal explanations are preferable to a stranger's "perfect" ones. Children are very understanding and sometimes help us out by their more matter-of-fact approach to death.

"What Is Dead?"

We learned that young children first need to understand the concrete reality of death in terms they can perceive, i.e., the dead do not move, sleep, feel pain, eat, talk, hear, see, or, as one toddler added, do BM's, and that they never will have these functions again. Children are helped to understand the death of a loved one when they can relate it to previous observations of death, e.g., "Do you remember when we found the dead bird? It did not fly or chirp. It couldn't do anything. That's the way grandpa is dead."

"What Made Him Be Dead?"

Deaths due to old age or special and unusual illnesses, are often easier for adults to talk about than deaths caused by violence (accidents, murders). Although it is always important for children of all ages to learn the real cause and circumstances of the death, it is possible to inform them in such a way as not to overwhelm them. Our patients were helped when they heard the news from the parent(s), when the account was fairly calm and simple, and when it was made clear that "we will talk about this many times because it is so hard to understand and makes us all so sad and worried. You will want to know many things about it. I hope you will ask me."

In many instances children made their own observations before the parent could talk with them, e.g., they witnessed a sudden death, or noted the debilitating changes of sickness which signalled its approach; they heard the news from other sources, or experienced the household stress and changes in routine accompanying the alarming event. It therefore helped to ask them about their own observations and to remind them of what they had perceived. Sometimes children misinterpreted their observations.

Seth saw a police car outside his home on returning from nursery school. When he learned that his father died on the way to the hospital, he assumed that the police had shot him. He was relieved when his mother told him that the police were called to get Dad to a doctor fast because that was one of their jobs.

Suicide is perhaps the hardest death to explain, especially when it occurs without a preceding period of observable mental illness. Several of our patients were helped by being told that a "mind sickness" (so different from the unhappiness, disappointment or troubles most of us have) caused the parent's thinking and feeling to be muddled and made him make himself dead by taking too many pills, or by jumping from a window, or by shooting himself.

The forms and causes of death among the loved ones of children are often especially frightening because they are untimely. Adults and children may take months to cope with the sheer impact and to grasp the sequence of events.

"Where Is He?"

Young children usually know little about our ways of disposing of the dead. Their repeated "Where is Daddy?" does not indicate that they do not know he is dead. It means literally "Where is his body?" They cannot complete their grasp of any aspect of the death unless they are helped to learn about burial. They may feel upset by the thought of the coffin in a hole in the ground but they also feel reassured by the fact that there is a concrete place for the body. Later visits to the cemetery serve to confirm the reality and to think it through. The grave is the end of the event of death. Young children find burial easier to understand than cremation.

Funeral services and customs are also an important part of coping with the concrete aspects of death (17). Children are helped by knowing what their families' rites of death are and, from school age on, they usually benefit by sharing in them. Preschoolers may attend funerals if they can count on the parent's emotional and physical availability throughout—a reassuring hand to hold, a whispered question answered, a puzzling sight explained. When the parent cannot prepare and assist his youngsters in this way they are better at home with a familiar adult and feel included by knowing where the family is and what they are doing.

At the time of a death in the family, the adults are so busy that it is tempting to relegate the children to the care of others and to postpone talking with them. Yet at this time of stress and confusion the children's questions are most urgent and they depend most closely on their surviving loved ones. Also, the sharing of facts and feelings during the initial days sets the tone and forms the basis for the long work of mourning that lies ahead.

Karen, aged 10, spent the day of her father's funeral at the zoo. Her mother had hoped to spare her daughter hardship. She succeeded only in erecting an emotional barrier between them and within the child which subsided much later during therapy.

Concrete explanations of death, of its causes, and of burial are often side-stepped in favor of religious or philosophical beliefs, "He is in heaven," "God took him." Preschoolers are usually frightened and confused by such concepts. Older children can use them only *after* they have developed a solid grasp of the concrete realities. When their younger children heard about heaven from others, many parents told them, "When you are older you will understand what we and others believe. Right now you need to learn what 'dead' means."

"Can It Happen to Me or to You?"

These questions inevitably arise in all of us when we learn of a death and they are especially scary for bereaved children—in part because they are for the first time confronted with the threat of death, in part because their personalities are not fully differentiated from those of their loved ones. What befalls them is felt as befalling oneself. The ability not only to understand but to accept a death, depends very much on a person's assurance that his and his surviving loved ones' fate differs from that of the deceased. The fact that all of us will die some time is not as helpful as the knowledge that we will not die now. When children ask these questions it indicates that they are progressing in their mastery of understanding death. We need to assure them that we and they are not now threatened and expect to continue our lives for a long time. We may add that people usually die only after they have been grandparents, or even great-grandparents, and that earlier deaths are very unusual.

"Who Will Take Care?"

Since children depend so closely on their loved ones, the question of who will care for the bereaved is very urgent and its reassuring answer is very crucial to the child's ability to accept the death.

After the mother's death, a father put it to his young sons this way, "Grandma and I will take care of you. We will make sure that we do all the things that Mommy used to do—cook, shop, read bedtime stories—but we will all also miss Mommy very much because nothing can make up for the way she loved us." In time, many children are helped by sharing in the carrying out of mommy's tasks as they are in sharing the missing of her.

THE PROCESS OF MOURNING

Two steps forward and one step backward is the normal rate of progression with all psychological developments, including the task of coping with a bereavement. The difficult job of understanding and accepting a death and its circumstances is intermittently set back by disbelief and confusion. As mastery gradually wins the upper hand, mourning begins—silently, unnoticed, not willed. It consists of two opposite but complementary processes: detachment, which serves to loosen our ties with the deceased, and identification, which enables us to keep aspects of the deceased forever by making them a part of ourselves.

Detachment is the anguished process by which we remember and intensely relive each memory connected with the loved one, long desperately to be with him or her and reach out to continue the joint experiences. When the empty reality fails to respond, we resign ourselves to the inevitable and withdraw our emotional investment from what is no longer there. Here all our feelings are engaged—fury, pain, guilt, sadness, helplessness, even joy and excitement related to past happy times. Our emotions do not necessarily show. Some people cry, rage or lament only when they are alone, and some never express their feelings overtly but bear them inside.

The process as well as the feelings it engenders are activated whenever the bereaved person's mental turning toward the deceased is met by the reality of his permanent unavailability. It may arise from within ("I have to tell her what happened at school today") or from without (seeing the empty chair at the dinner table). It is likely to be almost constant in the initial weeks, especially when the parent and child used to live together, and more intermittent later when special occasions call forth the need for the loved ones and memories of them, e.g. holidays. However, since we can bear only so much and also need to keep life enjoyable enough to make it worth continuing, we pace our mental work of detachment. We go about our business, we succeed in absorbing ourselves in it at times, we even manage to have some fun, and we stay away from some of the places or occasions that would remind and upset us.

When our mind keeps these confrontations too much at bay, we are in danger of not detaching ourselves or of being taken unawares and overwhelmed.

Roger burst into inconsolable tears on a visit to the museum. The last time he had been there with his now-dead father. Roger had avoided thinking and talking of his father and therefore could not absorb the longing and disappointment gradually.

Children, especially the younger ones, are helped with detachment by concrete reminders of the deceased, such as photos and belongings, and they also tend to remember in action and feeling rather than in thought and word.

Ian, $2\frac{1}{2}$ years old, used to enjoy watching his Dad shave. For many weeks after the father's death, Ian walked into the father's bathroom every morning, tinkered with father's toothbrush and shaving bowl and put the towel on the sink as he used to hand it to his Dad. His mother had thoughtfully left everything in place but she also appreciated his need to share his feelings and to learn words to help him master them. She therefore sometimes stood by him, told him how well she too remembered his happy times of watching Dad and how much both of them missed Dad.

The surviving parent's acknowledgement and tolerance of the child's feelings are especially necessary when the child shies away from bearing them.

Ann, a 3-year-old, announced happily that Mom would have dinner with them tonight. Her father replied, "You and I both wish that, but we really know that Mom is dead and cannot be with us. That makes us both sad."

Unhappy and angry times are remembered as well. It helps to acknowledge these feelings too and to support a realistic concept of the deceased, including his weaknesses and the frustrations they caused us. We need to mourn the good as well as the bad sides of the past relationship.

Identification, by contrast, proceeds altogether unconsciously and engenders no feelings. At best, we select and take into ourselves those aspects of the dead loved one's personality which represented the best of his and are most suitably integrated into our own, for example his interests, hobbies, values. Many a widow takes over her husband's activities or some of his likes or habits. Children sometimes experience difficulty with this process and need adult help. Sometimes they "select" unhealthy or unhappy attributes. They may have been so impressed with the parent's terminal illness that they identify with some of its manifestations.

Rose suffered from stomach aches and nausea following her mother's death of cancer of the liver. She was helped by her father's pointing out, "Mom often felt sick to her stomach before she died. Perhaps your tummy aches help you keep Mom with you, but you can be like Mom in other ways, ways that she liked better and that will make you feel better. Do you remember how she loved feeding the birds and what a good cook she was? It would be nice to be like her in these ways. I'll help you grow up into a nice lady like Mom without her sickness." It is sometimes thought that such unhealthy identifications can be prevented by not talking with children about the deceased person's cause of death or about his/her undesirable qualities. The reverse holds true. The better children understand a dead loved one's personality and cause of death, the less likely are they to identify with unhelpful aspects.

Some children are so afraid of dying like the deceased that they fear taking in any aspect of their personalities.

Four-year-old Jennifer often played lovingly with her doll but became furious when anyone called it her "baby." Her father understood her upset well. He told her that her Mommy had nicely cared for her and that she could grow up and be just as nice a mommy without having to die. Most mommies don't die. Thet get to be grandmas and live a long time. Jennifer hugged her Dad and said, "Yes, and then they wear a shawl like my Grandma."

Mourning never ends. Its acute stage usually subsides after 6-18 months but it continues intermittently, triggered, for example, by anniversaries. For children the loss is also revived with each developmental step—birthdays, report cards, onset of menarche, graduation, wedding, becoming a parent oneself. The loss can be mastered so as not to jeopardize a child's development but it cannot be erased.

As mentioned earlier, when a child loses a parent he also loses a part of himself. This aspect of the loss is experienced as a diminution in self-worth which, like the loss of a limb, causes one to feel different from and inferior to others. It is not coped with by means of mourning but complicates it by delaying and intensifying detachment (to keep the parent longer) and by increasing premature, often ill-adapted, identifications (to keep more of the parent inside). The continuing relationship with the surviving parent or substitute and his/her help and understanding are therefore especially essential.

RESUMING AND CONTINUING THE COURSE OF LIVING

When mourning has proceeded far enough to loosen some of our ties to the deceased and to free our energies for renewed investment in people and activities, we begin the third part of the bereavement task. Depending on their personalities and the nature of the loss, adults resume their work and interests, find new pleasures, and may commit themselves to new relationships or forego them, e.g., a widower may not remarry. When children lose a parent, their situation is different.

Bereaved adolescents, developmentally at the point of leaving the parents, may experience difficulty in "moving away" from the surviving parent or in following the dead parent's path into adulthood. However, they rarely search for a new parent. Often their mourning of the deceased and developmental step toward independence from him/her coincide and speed the adolescent's reaching out for new and different relationships outside the family.

Younger children still need and want both parents but cannot provide them for themselves. They often turn to older siblings, adult friends or relatives whom they can love, admire and emulate and who reciprocate their feelings. Relating to a stepparent is, however, different. Although ideally a stepparent meets the child's needs best, he/she is hardly ever chosen by the child and may enter the child's life too soon or too late because the course of the surviving parent's mourning may differ from that of the child. Even in fortunate cases where the child has known the stepparent all along and where he/she has actually cared for the child, the stepparent is not automatically related to as a parent. We find that the relationship with such a caretaking adult exists side by side with the continuing inner attachment to the deceased parent and serves to sustain the child while he is coping with his bereavement.

When the child has mourned sufficiently to be ready to relate to a new parent he/she either turns to a newly arrived stepparent or begins to view in a different light the relationship with the caretaking adult. In either case this step temporarily reactivates the mourning for the deceased as comparisons are drawn and old loyalties threatened. A heretofore harmonious relationship may appear to worsen at this point and a beginning relationship with a newcomer-parent may experience rough going.

Stepparents help children most and stand the best chance of ultimately receiving the children's genuine love, when they make it very clear in word and deed that they respect the attachment to the dead parent and do not seek to replace him/her in the children's affections. Actually, the bond which best unites stepparent and child is their shared thinking and talking about the deceased and the stepparent's empathy and support for the child's feelings and conflicts ("I can understand that you liked your Mommy's cake better than mine. I'm glad you remember her. Perhaps you'll feel like having some of this cake even if it doesn't taste so good," or, "I'm so glad you had fun shopping with me. I am sure your dead Mommy would have liked to see you having such a good time.") A child who maintained a satisfying relationship with the deceased parent and who is not forced to relinquish it prematurely, will eventually invest similarly rich feelings in the relationship with the new parent.

The surviving parent plays an important part in this period of readjustment. After their loss, parent and child often grow closer through their shared experience and dependence on each other. The stepparent may be felt to intrude upon this exclusive relationship and the child, who has already lost one parent, is threatened by "losing" the remaining parent to someone else. The surviving parent needs to help build a new family triad which still appropriately includes the memories of the earlier lost one.

Adults are sometimes so affected by the child's distress at the loss that they want to provide new parent-figures quickly in the hope of filling the gap and avoiding the pain.

Anthony's mother made a point of spending the weekends with friends so that her 4-year-old could enjoy the company of daddies and participate in the activities of these families. At first Anthony appeared to like these outings and played with the men much like their own children, but later on he begged, "Let's not go to the S's. I used to pretend that Mr. S. was like my daddy but looking at him just reminds me that he isn't. I want to be home." The mother realized that it was she and not the boy who could not bear the burden of pain. They stayed at home more and were a help to each other until the time came to make genuine new investments.

Resuming and continuing life is as slow and difficult as the preceding aspects of the bereavement task. However, obstacles that manifest themselves at this stage deserve careful scrutiny because they may stem from inadequate mastery of the earlier understanding and accepting of the death and/or of mourning.

ASSISTING THE YOUNGEST CHILDREN WITH BEREAVEMENT

Babies and young toddlers are most vulnerable when their primary caretakers, i.e. usually their mothers, die. The very young not only invest in this relationship almost all of their love. It also meets all their needs and sustains their personalities and its developing functions. As Winnicott (18) said, there is no such thing as a baby—only a mother-and-baby. The mother's continuous loving care and the relationship that develops around it, assure the baby's physical and mental survival.

As adults we may discontinue some of our activities following a bereavement because the pleasure has gone out of them, e.g., we may no longer go to the theater if we used to enjoy it as a shared hobby with the deceased loved one. With school-aged children many activities depend on the shared enjoyment with the parent:

Eight-year-old Ricky had been a very good and conscientious pupil but, following his mother's death, his work deteriorated and he failed to complete his assignments. In discussing the poor report card with Ricky, the father felt that the schoolwork had lost interest when there was no Mommy to show it to and to share with the pleasure of achievement. The father helped Ricky by telling him how much he cared about his boy's learning. He also reminded Ricky how much happier he would be with himself if he continued the good work he and Mommy used to enjoy so much.

With young toddlers much more essential achievements, such as walking, talking, self-feeding, may be given up when they are deprived of the mother's pleasure in them. With babies the most basic functions may be affected—eating, sleeping, experiencing bodily well-being, and the capacity to form stable relationships.

It is therefore not sufficient merely to fulfill a baby's bodily needs. The mothering person has to "care" in the fullest sense, i.e. be emotionally invested in the child and offer him a consistent relationship. Spitz (19) has shown that some babies who are well provided physically but lack the opportunity to relate in an ongoing way with a loving human being, actually die. Under less extreme conditions, for example when loving persons are available inconsistently, the youngsters may not thrive well and/or their personality development may be severely impaired.

May was 10 weeks old when her mother died suddenly. She was first cared for by her grandmother, then by her aunt and, during her second year, by another aunt. May's many difficulties included frequent stomach aches, obesity, and a pervasive inability to "feel good." These responded only partly to intensive therapy.

During a mother's terminal illness it helps when the future mother substitute gradually shares in the baby's or toddler's care to avoid a sudden interruption. With unexpected deaths it helps when the new permanent substitute takes over at once. Alas, this simple advice is so difficult to put into practice because even devoted fathers and grandmothers rarely can approximate a mother's round-the-clock care.

The death of family members other than the mother tends to affect very young children in a different way. On one hand they lost the father, sibling or grandparent with whom they had made a beginning relationship; on the other hand they lose the mother who, under the stress of her bereavement, may become physically and/or emotionally less available.

When 11-month-old Robin's brother died, she looked for him everywhere and became alarmed when her sister briefly left home. Above all she clung to her mother who understood Robin's concern. The mother left Robin as little as possible and helped her distinguish permanent from temporary absences with simple words, "Johnny dead, not come back." "Mommy bye-bye, Mommy come back."

Robin's experience reminds us that the youngest are not safe from the effects of bereavement even if they keep their mother or can make a gradual transition to a mother substitute. They suffer from the changes that often accompany a death in the family. They may be deeply affected by a mother's change of mood. They are inevitably exposed prematurely to the awareness of death. Even if they do not remember the lost loved one, they tend to hear about his/her death, pick up clues (e.g. from photos), sense the family's periodic distress (e.g. around anniversaries), or soon begin to puzzle why they lack certain relatives. Often they also feel left out of the memories other family members share. Some of our patients' families had taken great pains to protect the child from such knowledge but had only succeeded in exacerbating his inner confusion or in creating an emotional barrier. Families who did not avoid references to the deceased and used simple explanations at appropriate occasions, repeatedly noted more overt distress in their youngsters but better ultimate mastery and less interference in personality development.

Sandra's mother died suddenly 4 weeks after Sandra's birth. The maternal grandmother at once assumed full care of Sandra, supported by the father and grandfather. In spite of her grief and the burden of her unexpected task she helped the baby overcome her immediate distress and enjoyed her unfolding development. When Sandra began to notice pictures of the dead mother, grandmother said, "That's your Mommy." Following Sandra's first birthday, the anniversary of her daughter's death reactivated Mrs. A's mourning. Sandra was quite concerned about grandma's changed mood and occasional tears. She patted her and laughed in an effort to cheer up grandma. The latter gave Sandra a special hug and explained, "Sandra is a good girl. Grandma loves Sandra. Grandma cries for Sandra's dead Mommy. I'll be OK." This relieved Sandra as she sensed grandmother's empathy and reassurance. The words, though not understood at the time, formed a valuable basis for later ways of communicating.

EFFECTS OF BEREAVEMENT ON PERSONALITY DEVELOPMENT

We have already discussed the fact that the loss of the loved one may be followed by the loss of interests, activities and even basic personality functions. Children generally give up first what they acquired last, e.g. toddlers who were just beginning to talk may lose speech. These backward movements, or regressions, may be temporary or of longer duration, depending on the extent to which the child masters the bereavement task and on the nature of additional stresses in his life, especially the availability of continuing relationships.

Whereas these effects on the child's personality are readily noticed at the time of the bereavement or shortly following it, other forms may escape attention because they appear much later and are manifestly isolated from the bereavement. Among these are developmental arrests, impairments and deviations, leading to maladjustments and/or symptom formation.

Carl was 26 months old at the time of his mother's death. Like many toddlers he had not yet achieved toilet mastery and tended to be contrary and provocative. However, he did not seem very upset and did not mention his mother. When he was referred for help at age 7, he still wet and soiled quite often, argued with adults and fought with peers. His failure to master the bereavement showed itself in this partial arrest and linked him unconsciously to the relationship with the dead mother. What had been age-appropriate behavior then, now represented pathology.

Kathy, a well-behaved intelligent 8-year-old, suffered from a severe learning and sleep difficulty. Her father had been killed in a car accident 3 years earlier. She was an only child and the family had not discussed the circumstances of the death with her because they hoped to spare Kathy the upset of knowing that her father had been drunk. Kathy had obediently suppressed her curiosity and disregarded various clues. In time this prevented her from learning and remembering even what she should have known, namely her schoolwork. At the same time her own fantasies and unconscious bits of misinterpreted knowledge coalesced into a monstrous confusion which threatened to overwhelm her in dreams and caused her fear of falling asleep.

In some instances a bereavement may accelerate developmental processes. This also produces potential complications. Children between the ages of 4 to 7 years normally form their own conscience by internalizing their parents' rules and values. When one of the parents dies and is unavailable as a living model, this process tends to take place prematurely and the conscience may become excessively harsh and threatening. The child, as it were, takes in the parental injunctions earlier but, due to his/her immaturity and angry frustration, perceives the parent as more demanding and more punitive. Such a development is often marked by strong guilt feelings, fears and nightmares, low self-esteem, unrealistically high standards for oneself, reluctance to make mistakes and to compete or the reverse, namely an unrelenting drive to excel.

Some effects on the child's personality do not become evident until he/she needs to cope with a new developmental phase; for example, some of our patients who lost a parent around 6, did not experience serious difficulty until prepuberty. Their personalities could manage the ongoing daily life but were unequal to the new stresses and conflicts which progression brings.

Even this brief selection of the many varied effects of bereavement on children's personalities no doubt scares those who hope to help children. There is so much that can go wrong and so little we can do to prevent it. It is important to know our limits lest we overestimate or underestimate what we can and should do.

SOME PREVENTIVE MEASURES

The very magnitude of the potential damage to the bereaved child led us to ask ourselves what could be done to forestall or minimize the risk and, increasingly, parents have asked us, "What can we do to prepare our children?" Of course, a parental bereavement is such an enormous and unique stress that nothing can quite prepare a child for it. There are, however, some educational measures which can help children to develop the mental "muscles" which will stand them in good stead should they need to cope with the loss of a loved one through death, even the loss of a parent.

The first such measure is helping children to acquire a realistic concept of death, of some of its causes, and of ways of disposing of the dead. From toddlerhood on, children are exposed to many encounters with death. At first they may observe insects killed in the home, or find corpses of small animals outside. Later they may drive past cemeteries or meet a funeral procession. The news of death may reach them through adult conversation or via the media. The parents' or nursery school teachers' difficulty never lies in finding ways to introduce the topic but rather in making sure that ready opportunities are not avoided. How easily we deny what children see and hear about death! And how easily they adopt our implicit taboo. Just as we eagerly further their language development by naming every object the toddler reaches for, so we need to give him the word "dead" when they look at or touch a dead insect and explain that "dead" means lack of living function. "It won't fly," "It won't buzz."

With our help and words children gradually learn more of what "dead" implies, what causes living things to become dead, what we do with dead bodies. They will also note and take in our attitudes—that we do not kill needlessly, that we are neither horrified nor afraid of dead bodies, that we feel pity. Most young nursery school children we worked with knew that a dead bee would no longer fly, that it died of old age or by being killed, and that we would dispose of it as trash. Many also knew that a dead bird was old or had been hurt and would be buried. Their comments of "Poor birdie" would come side by side with detailed questions about its demise or decay. Although a young child's understanding is not established once and for all but needs repeated reinforcement and further clarification, the concept of death itself is not difficult nor is its extension to humans as long as it does not affect the child himself or his loved ones.

Yet, when the time comes to make this painful link, children are greatly helped by their earlier matter-of-fact knowledge. Religious or philosophical beliefs are not helpful to preschoolers but may be introduced to the school-aged child in addition to, not instead of, the concrete understanding of bodily death.

The second measure is to help children tolerate difficult feelings, especially those connected with separations—longing, anger, sadness. When young children experience age-appropriate separations from their parents, such as a few hours spent with a familiar babysitter or on entry to nursery school, these feelings are usually intense but masterable with the parent's help. Here again, the correct names for each feeling are important as well as the parent's acknowledgement of the child's experience. For example, in preparing for an evening out, mothers may say, "I guess you don't like it when I am not home. We'll miss each other but I know you'll be safe with Betty the sitter." She may pick up her child's bad mood or misbehavior and suggest he tell her that he is angry about her leaving and she may encourage him to tell the sitter when he feels lonely or sad. She will even return to the topic the next day, sympathize how hard it was, perhaps praise the child's ability to know what he felt. How often we try to spare us and our children such inevitable hard feelings! We call our children "good" if they neither complain nor cry. We hush over their potential pain by providing extra treats and excitements. We expect a sitter to amuse them so as to dispel their misgiving. Yet these brief exposures to separation feelings are our most valuable opportunities for teaching that such emotions are a natural part of life and can be borne safely. This gradually learned ability to recognize and tolerate difficult feelings is not equal to the strain and stress endured in bereavement but it is of immeasurable help.

Even the best intellectual and emotional stamina may falter at a time of bereavement and even the best intentioned and most conscientious parent may be unable to help his child with it as much as he would like to. This does not mean failure. To recognize one's limitations is a hallmark of good parenting. It prompts a parent to seek professional help as soon as possible. This step may indeed become another important prophylactic measure. Our experience with bereaved patients indicates that professional help to parent and/or child is most effective when it comes early.

REFERENCES

1. Furman, R. A. & A. Katan (eds.): *The Therapeutic Nursery School*. New York: International Universities Press, 1969.
2. Furman, R. A.: Death of a six-year-old's mother during his analysis. *Psychoanalytic Study of the Child*, 19:377-397, New York, International Universities Press, 1964.
3. Furman, R. A.: Death and the young child: Some preliminary considerations. *Psychoanalytic Study of the Child*, 19:321-333, New York, International Universities Press, 1964.
4. Furman, R. A.: Additional remarks on mourning and the young child. *Bulletin of the Philadelphia Association of Psychoanalysis*, 18(2):51-64, 1968.
5. Furman, R. A.: "Sally," in *The Therapeutic Nursery School*. Edited by Furman, R. A. and Katan, A. New York, International Universities Press, 1969, pp. 124-138.

6. Furman, R. A.: The child's reaction to death in the family, in *Loss and Grief: Psychological Management in Medical Practice*. Edited by Schoenberg, B, Carr, A. C., et al. New York and London, Columbia University Press, 1970, pp. 70-86.

7. Furman, R. A.: A child's capacity for mourning, in "The Child in His Family: The Impact of Disease and Death." *Yearbook of the International Association for Child Psychiatry and Allied Professions*, 2:225-231. Edited by Anthony, E. J. and Koupernik, C. New York, Wiley, 1973.

8. Barnes, M. J.: Reactions to the death of a mother. *Psychoanalytic Study of the Child*, 19:334-357, New York, International Universities Press, 1964.

9. McDonald, M.: A study of the reactions of nursery school children to the death of a child's mother. Psychoanalytic Study of the Child, 19:358-376, New York, International Universities Press, 1964.

10. McDonald, M.: Helping children to understand death. *Journal of Nursery Education*, 19(1):19-25, 1963.

11. Furman, E.: *A Child's Parent Dies*. New Haven and London: Yale University Press, 1974.

12. Furman, E.: Helping a child to mourn. *Pediatria—XIV International Congress of Pediatrics*, 6:168-173. Editorial Medica Panamericana, Piso, Buenos Aires, 1974.

13. Furman, E.: Bereavement in childhood, in *Social Work with the Dying Patient and Family*. Edited by Prichard, E. R. et al. New York, Columbia University Press, 1977, pp. 115-123.

14. Furman, E.: Helping children cope with death, in *Young Children*, 33(4):25-32, May 1978. Also in *Ideas That Work with Young Children*. Edited by Adams, A. and Garlick, B. Washington, D.C., National Association for the Education of Young Children, 1979, pp. 186-193.

15. Furman, E.: Newborn death: Care of the parents. Audio-Digest Foundation Continuing Education tape series. *Pediatrics*, 25(18), 1979. East Chevy Chase Drive, Glendale, Calif. 91206.

16. Furman, E.: Death of a newborn: Assistance to parents, in *Yearbook of the International Association for Child Psychiatry and Allied Professions*. Edited by Anthony, E. J. New York, Wiley, 1980. pp. 497-506.

17. Furman, E.: Commentary on how do children and funerals mix? *Journal of Pediatrics*, 89(1):143-145, 1976.

18. Winnicott, D. W.: *The ordinary devoted mother and her baby*. London, Brock, 1949.

19. Spitz, R. A.: Hospitalism: An inquiry into the genesis of psychiatric conditions in early childhood. *Psychoanalytic Study of the Child*, 2:53-74, New York, International Universities Press, 1945.

10

Helping Families

Thoughts of a Pediatrician

Morris A. Wessel

INTRODUCTION

One evening in 1968 I learned of the sudden death that late afternoon of a beloved first grade teacher at a school where I was serving as pediatric consultant. I phoned the principal of the school, suggesting that it might be helpful for me to meet with the class the next morning to provide the children with the opportunity to discuss their feelings about this tragic event. He readily agreed.

The principal and I walked together to the classroom the next morning. He introduced me, saying "You all know Dr. Wessel. He's going to talk about what happened to Mrs. Smith yesterday. He wants to make you feel better." He then left the room!

I remember all too vividly my anxious feelings as I faced the twenty first-grade children who looked up at me with bewildering facial expressions. Some of the children were unaware of Mrs. Smith's tragic heart attack and death shortly after school the day before. I struggled for appropriate words to help them understand and grapple with the loss of a teacher they all loved. I was unprepared for this awesome task. I had little knowledge of the various religious beliefs regarding life and death of the families of these children.

I began by saying, "One of the sad facts we have to accept is that many times even doctors can't save people who have heart attacks. This is what happened yesterday."

"When someone dies," I continued, "We always feel sad and lonely. Each person has his own way of reacting when he or she feels sad. Some like to cry; some like to listen to music; some like to be alone; some like to be with someone else whom they love. What do you feel like doing?"

The children knew quite well what they wanted to do:

"We must write to Mrs. Smith, or go see her." . . . *"Will you take us?"* . . . *"She must be somewhere—maybe she's in Heaven . . . that's where people go when they die"* . . . *"Oh, no . . . that isn't so . . . they throw you in the ground"* . . . *"That's not true about Heaven . . . you know the cemetery across the street? They put you in a nice box and bury you there . . . I have seen them do this lots of times."*

I was struggling to find an appropriate comment when Patty, a seven-year-old girl with shining eyes and black hair, said very seriously, "I don't think it would do

205

any good if we did see Mrs. Smith. When my dog was hit by a car last week, I found him lying by the road; he was stiff and cold. When I tried to pet him, he didn't even know I was there. I think that if we saw Mrs. Smith, she wouldn't know we were there." Thanks to this little girl, I now had one bit of reality to deal with—that of the inaccessibility of a deceased individual. We continued the discussion, agreeing that it would be helpful to think of the things we liked about Mrs. Smith. We decided to write these ideas on the blackboard and then send a copy to her husband. I think that this decision made the class feel better. It certainly made me feel better (1, 2).

The principal's interest in the session resulted from his awareness of my involvement in the initial planning phases of The Connecticut Hospice, which recently opened in Branford, Conn. With the rapid proliferation of hospice programs and courses in death and dying throughout the country, the taboo nature of discussion of death is diminishing rapidly. Physicians, teachers, nurses, and clergy must be ready to meet demands of frequent requests to participate at moments of stress which children experience frequently (3).

This classroom session stimulated me to consider in greater detail than I had previously how professionals, relatives, and friends might be constructive to adults and children at the time of the death of a beloved person who plays an important role in a child's life.

We must not underestimate the need to consider this problem. No matter how much we wish to protect children or adolescents from having to cope with the loss through death of someone they know and love, the fact is that frequently deaths of members of the family, of friends, of teachers or recreation leaders do occur. Patricia Ewalt, in a recent study of high school students, reports that 93 percent had seen a dead person, 84 percent had experienced a significant loss, and 10 percent had lost a parent through death (4).

We cannot shelter children or adolescents from these tragic life experiences. Our only choice is how we will help children and adolescents cope with these tragic losses. Neglecting this responsibility leaves young individuals desolate, lonely and frightened to grapple simultaneously with the mysteries of life and death, his or her own fears of death, and the loss of someone they love and who has loved them.

I have reached two major conclusions as I have considered how we might help children who are coping with this tragic loss of a loved one.

My first conclusion relates to Patty's remark about the dog. Children who have had previous experiences which establish in their mind the distinction between *being alive* and *being dead* are better able to understand, grapple with and cope with a tragic loss than other children who have never had this experience.

Second, I believe that the most important people to help a child cope with a loss are the adults who have nurtured him or her and have thus developed a long-standing basis of mutual trust. The efforts of professionals and friends are most effective when supporting adult members of a family who take on the important and crucial task of comforting a bewildered and frightened child who tries to grasp the reality of the tragedy and the feelings of loss. We must realize that this is a formidable task for adults. Each step in assisting a bereaved child becomes constructive only when it grows out of full acceptance and respect for the facts and feelings that comprise a specific child's unique situation. There is no exact formula as to how a child should or should not act during this stressful experience. Any death in a child's circle of relationships is stressful. However, death of a parent is particularly overwhelming because of the fact that a child invests so much of his feelings and capacity to relate to his parents. A parent, particularly the mother, is not only a loved person, she is an integral part of a child's personality (5).

THE CHILD'S CONCEPTUALIZATION OF DEATH

At what age can a child begin to grasp the difficult concept of what is alive and what is dead? At a much earlier age than many adults realize. Preschoolers understand that furniture and toys are inanimate objects, while worms and pets are alive and have feelings. Nursery school teachers and parents often utilize the opportunities which arise, such as the finding of dead insects, birds or the loss of a parakeet, dog or cat, to help a child conceptualize the meaning of being alive and being dead. A very young child comprehends with ease that a dead goldfish no longer swims, a lifeless bird no longer sings or flies, and a dead cat or dog is no longer able to romp and play in the yard. Educational colleagues throughout the country are now concentrating more than ever before on developing appropriate curriculum for discussing the meaning of death at various age levels (6).

Pediatricians and teachers urge parents to use these common experiences to help a child develop understanding of the meanings of life and death. A preschool child often grasps this meaning with unusual clarity. Dr. Robert Furman reports a two-year-old who, after being told, "When someone is dead and is no longer alive, she will no longer eat or sleep or run or play or feel or be sad or happy or angry." The wise two-year-old who had just mastered the important task of toilet training put this explanation in terms that were developmentally appropriate for him by saying, "He won't do wee-wee or BM anymore either" (7).

Although it is advantageous for a child to have learned about life and death as it applies to a pet or animal, there is, of course, an enormous difference in dealing with the reaction of a child losing a parent, close relative or loving friend. The prior experience, however, provides a base for initiating the process of understanding the finality of death and facilitates the child's capacity to begin the process of adapting to the loss of the loved one.

A FATAL ILLNESS IN THE FAMILY

When a family member suffers a serious illness, it is inevitable that adults in the household become preoccupied with concerns related to the person who is ill. Children have the right to know what is going on. They are quick to sense the preoccupation of the adults who care for them. If it is a close family member who is ill—a mother or father or other person who had been involved intimately in the child's care—they feel overwhelmed and frightened. They must cope with the fact that the person is less and less available to them, in essence, has deserted them. Children have difficulty grasping why the individual who usually provides for much of their care is acting so strange and appears to care less. A child may think, "What did I do to deserve this treatment?" A child also resents the amount of time the adults in the family spend in the hospital with a sick family member. Therefore, a child loses the attention of the person who is sick, and also loses considerable attention from the rest of the family who are preoccupied with meeting the needs of the sick person (8).

When it is a sibling who suffers an illness, well children often react to the fact that the sibling seems to be getting an inordinate amount of care and attention from the parents. At times, well children become angry at the sick sibling because of the high priority parents place on meeting his or her needs. Ida Martinson noticed that in her experiences in a home care program for terminally ill children, a frequent comment of the well siblings when a child is returned home in the terminal phase relates to their appreciation for the fact that finally their mother will have more time at home (9).

The definitive diagnosis of a fatal disease in a child inevitably evokes a series of reactions in the parents. All health care professionals are in a unique and important position to be helpful to parents and siblings as the disease progresses.

Parents have a difficult, two-fold task as they struggle to maintain their equilibrium. They need to love and care for their sick child, yet at the same time they must deal with their intense feeling of despair as they anticipate the inevitable loss in the future. Usually parents of seriously ill children seeking medical consultation suspect the critical nature of the sickness. The persistence of symptoms such as weight loss, pallor and disinterest in normal activities suggest a dreaded disease. The physician who shares concern and diagnostic impressions, and in due time the confirmative laboratory findings, usually substantiates the parents' worst fear. Parents are stunned, even though they acknowledge their fears, often remarking, "I was afraid of this." Often, however, they are unable at first to grasp the full implication of the diagnosis. Later, in another conversation, often with a person other than the doctor, for example with a social worker, nurse or clergy person, they begin to discuss their feelings of bewilderment and inevitable guilt. They often wonder if they had sought medical care earlier whether their child would have had a better chance for survival.

The initial treatment for malignant conditions, often producing temporary remissions, may intensify the parents' feelings of disbelief. They may say, as did one patient, "Part of me believes there is nothing wrong with him . . . but there's a little part of me deep down in my heart that knows that there's got to be something there. I'm sure you're not lying to me."

The remissions and exacerbations during the course of chemotherapy and radiation treatment of malignant diseases offers repeated episodes of alternating periods of hope and despair in parents. As time progresses, the impending loss of the child begins to sink in. Some parents even begin to mourn in advance and withdraw from the child, often at the consternation of the nurses and other personnel on the ward. However, in spite of frequently grieving in anticipation as the reality of the eventual loss becomes increasingly apparent, most parents demonstrate remarkable capacity to continue to assume responsibility for work, home, and for the care of the patient whether at home or in the hospital. The efficient manner in which many parents assume these responsibilities is often interpreted as the denial of the tragic reality. Yet, this is rarely true. The daily parental tasks of being a homemaker and caring for their child provides parents with a specific role and purpose while underneath they are struggling to adapt to the inevitable loss.

An increasing number of home care programs throughout this country and Canada provide a unique and satisfying opportunity for professional health caregivers to offer a support system which enables many families to summon up extraordinary capacities to care for terminally ill patients at home. This fulfills the patients' wish to remain at home amidst family surroundings and people who love them. This experience also can, in many instances, facilitate children's and adults' ability to adapt and cope with the reality of the loss when death occurs. It somehow helps bring the family together in the final phases and they are more likely to grieve together because of their cooperative endeavors in the final days of their loved one's life (9).

WHO HELPS THE DOCTOR?

The responsible physician, as for example an oncologist, cannot be expected to take on single-handedly the complicated role of meeting all the needs of a family at this stressful time. The motivation for a doctor's professional choice involving long and arduous training results in a human being whose highest priority is to provide compassionate and technical care with the hope of curing his or her patients. The sense of failure experienced by physicians when the patient reaches a terminal phase is inevitable. Most physicians, struggling with these intense and complex personal feelings, provide care to the end. However, I am firmly convinced that it is important for other professionals, such as the family's personal doctor, social workers, nurses or clergy personnel, to share this heavy burden of providing professional care for the family. These colleagues, free from the decision-making responsibilities for the patient's daily care, often find it a less arduous task than does the responsibile physician to take on the task of supporting and comforting the members of the family as they express their anger and bitterness over medicine's failure to cure their loved one (10).

For some parents, religion offers solace and comfort; yet to others it is of little help. Clergy personnel should always be available to offer a supporting role. All of us who wish to help families during this stressful time must learn to individualize our approach and be available to them during this anticipatory phase of grieving. We must always respect the manner in which each person adopts what is, for him or her, a satisfactory means of coping with the tragedy at hand. There is no single formula for dealing with these crises. All professionals can really do is stand by, supporting and comforting grieving and bereaved individuals as they work out in their own way the best possible means for them to meet the task at hand.

A CHILD AND THE DEATH OF A LOVED ONE

It is important to remember that the death of a loved one is difficult and painful for any human being, adult or child. Nothing can reduce the pain, anguish, and longing for a person who has played an important part in one's life. Grief, mourning, and bereavement are normal human reactions to a loss. These processes are hard work. They involve the detachment of one's feelings from the person who is no longer available as a focal point for one's attachment. Adults wishing to help bereaved individuals—adults or children—by supporting and comforting them during this inevitable sad and difficult struggle will find it exhausting and debilitating. The death of a child's parent may recall our own painful losses during childhood; or evoke fantasies of how one would have felt if the death of a parent had occurred in our own childhood; or how one might feel momentarily about dying and leaving one's own children. These reactions make it extraordinarily difficult for professionals and other adults to comfort and support a child who is struggling to adapt to the loss of a beloved family member. Too often, adults assume that a child is "too young to understand," and that he or she cannot grasp realistically the finality of the loss. This assumption permits one to avoid the poignancy of a child's struggle which is painful to observe. It is, however, grossly unfair to the child.

How much adults in a bereaved family can provide for a child is variable. Professionals and others with a close relationship to a family can be most helpful by supporting the adult members so that they, in turn, can nurture, comfort and maintain a child as he grapples with the reality and deals with his feelings of being hurt and angry at the loss of a loved one. Nothing can prevent a loss from being troubling to a child. However, as Erna Furman (5) points out, whether there remains an unmasterable burden interfering with a child's psychological development, or whether it becomes a stress a child experiences, copes with and adapts to, depends to a great extent on how adults who care for a child provide sustained understanding, support and comfort over time. The task for adults is enormous. The challenge is not to protect a child from sadness for the loss is very real. A child *needs*, above all, and has the right to be supported and comforted in his or her sadness during his struggle to deal with a loss. How do we help any person who is caring for bereaved children? First of all, it is important to remember that frequently a physician, particularly an oncologist or cardiologist, is likely to be preoccupied with duties and responsibilities for many critically ill patients. After the death of a patient, it is too much to expect him to be continually available to the grieving family. Other members of the health care team, such as primary physician, pediatrician, nurses, clergy personnel or social workers, can and should play helping roles at this time.

Some member of the health team, and if at all possible an individual with a long-standing relationship with the family, should specifically be asked to assume the responsibility of making sure that the adults place appropriate priority on the needs of the children. Unfortunately, adult family members, preoccupied first with meeting the needs of a terminally ill patient and their own feelings of grieving, and then later in the midst of bereavement, often fail to attend to the care of the children.

No matter how difficult it may be, even a very young child can be helped to understand the confusing mood of the household by being told, "You know ――― is very sick. The doctors and nurses are doing all they can to help." Towards the end of the illness, as the family members begin to grieve in advance, it is wise to add, "――― is getting sicker and sicker; he may die soon." Whether or not the child really understands, the fact that one has been open and honest provides a basis for further discussion.

Whisking children away from their home and familiar environment by sending them to a strange home of well-meaning neighbors or friends is bewildering and disconcerting. Despite the turmoil as illness and eventual death of a loved one occurs, children of all ages find it easier to cope with stresses while they have the supporting affect of their family, their familiar toys and furniture, and the surroundings of their own home. They should be allowed to participate in the household activities, even though there is much turmoil and grieving. When it is a mother or other primary parenting person that is ill, it is important that, if at all possible, a relative or housekeeper be involved increasingly so that the children are assured that at least *one* person will be providing for their basic nurturing needs during the stressful time and after the death occurs.

A quiet oppressiveness inevitably invades a household when the moment of death occurs. It is imperative at this moment that someone of the health care team take on the responsibility of reminding some responsible adult in the family, preferably a parent or other close relative with a long-standing relationship with the child, to discuss with the child that the death has occurred. This important task is too often forgotten in the confusion at any moment of tragedy. Careful choice of words is important. The discussion should be honest and factual, for example, "——— has been very sick and has died. It is very sad. He was too weak to live. He's resting, no longer breathing, moving, thinking or feeling. There is nothing you could have done to save him, and there's nothing that you did that caused him to die. The doctors and nurses did everything they could to help him and make him comfortable." Care must be taken to avoid the use of the word "sleeping" to indicate the deceased state, for this can easily lead a child to develop additional anxieties over the possibility that the child, too, might die in his or her sleep.

Families differ considerably in their beliefs about a life hereafter. Again, one must be honest in one's discussion; children are quick to sense deceit. Explanations involving a description of God's needing the deceased to work in Heaven or God's coming down to take one to Heaven may offer comfort and solace to religious adults; however, to a young child who wants his beloved relative right here and now, this explanation is likely to encourage distrust and hatred of the God who swoops up a beloved adult to Heaven, leaving the child deserted.

For families with religious and philosophic beliefs of life hereafter, it is wise to suggest phrasing explanations with, "I like to believe . . ." or "We Catholics like to believe . . ." that the body of the dead person is buried in the cemetery and the spirit, that part of the person that we love and remember is far off in Heaven where there's no pain, suffering, hunger, war—just peace and quiet.

I'm reminded of a panel discussion on children and death held in Waterbury, Conn. in 1977, at which Sister Mary Malinowski of Boston described a little boy who had attended a funeral and evidently had listened carefully. He remembered the line from Genesis, "Dust thou art, and unto dust shall thou return." Looking under his bed that night and noting a large accumulated pile of dust, he screamed out, "Hey, Mommy! Am I coming or going?"

The "I like to believe" approach shares with a child what adults believe. It does not force a child to accept the same beliefs which may be incomprehensible at his or her particular stage of cognitive development.

Every child is quick to sense dishonesty and insincerity. A disbelieving adult who presents a concept of life hereafter, hoping that somehow this will aid a child, only creates confusion and stimulates distrust. It is far better to say, "I do not know exactly what I believe happens after death, but all I know is (whoever it is) will no longer be available for us to talk with and to visit with.

A child may not grasp the full meaning of the loss of a beloved person at this tragic moment, but honest and open discussion, even with a preschool child, forms a basis for the child to begin to grapple with the tragic event in the difficult times ahead and provides future opportunity for a child coping with the help of his trusted adults with his feelings of his loss.

All human beings, adults as well as children, long for the return of a beloved deceased person (11). Children, feeling deserted, wonder whether anything they did could have caused the beloved one to desert them. Children recall episodes when they were angry, for one reason or another, at the deceased individual. They often conclude that these thoughts and feelings in some magic way were responsible for the disappearance of the beloved person. This very common reaction is often unrecognized in the midst of the family turmoil when the death occurs. It can be alleviated somewhat if someone—doctor, nurse, clergy person—suggests that a parent or other close family member sit down with the child and say, "I know you must wonder why ——— died. He was very sick or hurt very badly or had a disease we could not cure. There was nothing you said or did that caused him to die."

Parents often ask whether a child should attend a funeral. A child of four or older can make this decision for himself. One should describe the type of services to be held and that relatives and friends who attend will be very sad and crying. An appropriate way of presenting the opportunity is to say, "We will all be very sad because we miss ——— so much. I will be sad, too; I may be crying. There will be music and prayers. Our minister (rabbi, priest) will talk about ———. If you would like to be there, I'll ask (a relative, close friend, babysitter) to come with us. If you would rather stay home, that's all right, too. She will stay here with you."

A child may look forward to the gathering of the family and friends and the ritual of the service may be supportive. On the other hand, a child may sense that the experience is more than he can cope with, and wisely decide to stay at home. When the child does attend the funeral, it is imperative that he be accompanied by a friend or babysitter, particularly one who is not intensely grief-stricken. This adult companion should be ready to leave with the child should the experience become overwhelming. Nothing is sadder than a bewildered, grief-stricken child standing alone during a funeral service while adults are preoccupied with their own grief (10).

Intellectually knowing about the death, being told about the death, and even participating in the funeral still may fail to help a child completely grasp the reality of what has taken place. Accepting the permanence of the loss of a loved person is not an instantaneous process for adults or children. Longing, wishing, hoping, imagining that the deceased person is still present, thinking "It can't be," hallucinating in which the bereaved sees or hears the deceased in familiar activities, are common experiences in the early phase of bereavement.

Mourning, that is, giving up one's attachment to a loved one, is always a slow and arduous and exhausting task. Many bereaved adults, and an even larger number of bereaved children, fail to complete this task. Adults must recognize that as we share our honest sadness with children and encourage them to participate in family and ritualistic activities at the time of death, we are setting the stage for even very young children to initiate the difficult task of grappling with the reality of the loss and beginning to mourn in their own individual manner. Visits to the grave site, making mention of the deceased's birthday or anniversaries of the death can be constructive ways of dealing with the need for all human beings to deal with the sad reality which stimulates one to mourn and "let go" over a period of time. Young children need time to work on these processes, particularly if the deceased is a close family member who loved them and whom they loved dearly. At times, it is important to reassure a child that his nurturing needs will be met, but that at the same time he will miss the deceased person very much. This is particularly important to do when it is the mother who has died. A child needs much more time than adults to begin to work on this process. One may anticipate that a bereaved child will regress during this stressful period to behavior which the child had formerly abandoned. The child may become anxious at bedtime, experience nightmares, and be fearful of leaving home; the child may even lose urine and bowel control. He or she may generally be restless and out of sorts. Poor school attendance due to bodily complaints and a decrease in ability to meet educational challenges are common symptoms (7).

Bereaved children constantly dread illness, even a minor one. They imagine that they may be about to die, hence every call to a physician concerning a child's symptoms merits prompt response and careful consideration. This reassures both the child and the adults in a family. Also, one must bear in mind that illnesses in bereaved children do occur. Gastrointestinal complaints during the stress of bereavement may reflect an early phase of malabsorption syndrome, peptic ulcer, or ileitis. Diabetic or thyroid conditions have been reported to become clinically symptomatic during the stress of bereavement.

It is important, however, to remember that bereaved children who present behavioral symptoms as they grapple with the loss may be far healthier than children who deny the loss completely and are unable to deal with it in any manner whatsoever.

The death of a parent during adolescence has unique effects because of this particular developmental phase of life. At one moment, healthy adolescents are extremely independent, setting off with great determination to make their own way in the world. They discontinue many old associations and seek new relationships. At other times, particularly after a stressful period, adolescents often revert to a less mature state, seeking considerable parental care, sympathy, and advice, quite in contrast to the behavior during the independent phase. Such fluctuations between independence and dependence would be considered highly abnormal at any other time of life. Vascillation and restlessness are expressions, during adolescence, of the normal process of maturation. The normal family constellation with two parents allows the adolescent to break away gradually on a trial basis, and to thrive at activity outside of the immediate family setting. Yet, during these phases of intense independence, when the adolescent is often critical and at times openly hostile to parents, there still remains the comforting fact that the option exists to return to home base and be taken care of as in former years. Even during intense bursts of independence, an adolescent often lives at home, or if living away, returns home periodically to enjoy his or her parents and the opportunity to be cared for.

These alternating ways in which a young person relates to parents must be considered as an adolescent copes with a tragic loss of a parent. It is one experience to be struggling to free oneself and to become independent, knowing that both parents are available when needed. It is quite a different experience when death removes a parent in the midst of this struggle for emancipation (12).

Bereaved children, and adolescents particularly, even more than young children, do dread any illness, even of a minor nature.

SOME SOCIOLOGICAL ASPECTS OF STRESS OF BEREAVEMENT

Family members suffering from the death in a family, and women, particularly, suffering from the death of a husband, soon discover the painful fact that community responses are relatively minimal. Neighbors and friends, church and synagogue groups, after a brief period of intense involvement immediately following the death, all too often tend to withdraw from the scene. A woman suffering the death of her husband often discovers the painful fact that her social network revolved largely in the circle of friends related to her husband's occupation. There are, fortunately, a few outstanding exceptions to this unfortunate state of affairs. Phyllis Silverman, a social worker in Boston, has single-handedly mobilized synagogue personnel to extend outreach programs to bereaved families in that area. In the United Kingdom, CRUSE, the organization for widows and children provides effective resources, particularly when a husband and breadwinner dies (11).

There are many reasons for this tendency for the most well-meaning individuals, professionals, relatives and friends to withdraw. First of all, it is painful for anyone to be in contact with a grieving person. The magnitude of the bereaved person's distress and their need to share these intense feelings with anyone who will listen, taxes even the individual who is confident in his or her ability to cope with this distress. Close friends are often embarrassed, strained and ill at ease when in the presence of grieving individuals. It is important, however, to remember that participation as a professional, relative or friend is very helpful to suffering individuals during their period of grieving and mourning. We cannot diminish the anguish and course of grieving, but we can comfort, support and nurture people in this difficult transitional phase. There are many ways those of us concerned with bereaved families and children and adults can be of help. Food—casseroles, baked breads, desserts—are always welcome. Offers to take children to swimming lessons, nursery school, recreational activities are simple contributions of one's time and energy which are often so simple that they are overlooked. Professional members of the health care team may be unable to take on these tasks. However, professionals, particularly nurses and religious personnel, can often help mobilize friends and relatives to arrange to provide some of these very necessary specific services.

The person who is most valuable to bereaved individuals is not always the one who expresses repeated sympathy, but rather the one who "sticks around," quietly taking on some of the daily tasks of living. Friends, relatives and professionals who remain involved must anticipate the fact that normally bereaved individuals often verbalize intense anguish and anger. We must remember that we become the recipients of these bitter feelings. They in no way should be considered as a personal attack. Doctors and nurses who have spent endless hours and efforts on the care of a patient need to be reminded that these repeated outbursts indicate that the bereaved relatives have considerable trust in them and feel that they will be understood in their need to vent anger and bitterness.

Many hospital pediatric social service departments, many community agencies, and in some instances parent groups, arrange for continued group meetings of bereaved individuals when a child dies. These gatherings provide opportunity for mutual support during the period of acute grief. The very fact that the bereaved individuals have the opportunity of sharing with each other and to learn that anger, bitterness, sleeplessness, weight loss, apathy and lethargy are common symptoms in all grieving individuals helps many to cope during this stressful period (13).

One of the most difficult tasks for bereaved parents is trying to help siblings of a deceased child. The understandable preoccupation which adults have in their own grieving often leaves them with little energy or ability to deal with their children.

Harriet Sarnoff Schiff, in "The Bereaved Parent," states this very well in her report of a conversation with a woman in her late forties. "I kept looking for some help from my mother after my brother died," said a women in her late forties. "Although he died when I was sixteen, I'll never forget that feeling of aloneness—or how frightened I was because neither my mother nor father seemed reachable. I really don't remember them trying very hard to help me. They were too busy with their own grief—I was angry with them because they made me feel I was being shoved aside just when I needed them the most. I see now that they were incapable of giving me any more than they did" (14).

It is inhuman to expect bereaved adults to be able to function in a parental role as if no tragedy had taken place. However, parents should be encouraged to openly share the sadness with their children. This often leads to the growth of a supporting relationship in which all members of the family benefit. Nothing is sadder in my pediatric practice than to have adults share their memories of losses in childhood in which they describe hours of crying under the bed clothes, being fully aware that a parent was doing the same thing in another room. Everyone wanted to protect the other one from knowing that they were in tears.

Initially, denial of the reality of the loss of a loved one is to be expected in young children. It is expressed by comments, "Will Grandpa be back for my birthday? For Christmas?", etc., or by the child who sets the table including the dead person's place.

Adults, at moments like this, often conclude that a child is too young to understand and may turn their back and withdraw from any attempt to continue the communication with the child. Children are grappling to hold onto the image and presence of the deceased so that they will not be obliged to cope with the reality of their loss. No matter how difficult, it is at moments like this that a trusted adult with a long-standing relationship should be encouraged to comfort the child. One might say, giving the child a firm hug, "I guess we will miss ——— very much. It will be sad without her. I, too, wish she would return, but that's impossible. I guess we'll have to remember all those happy days when she was here." Such an approach is not easy for an adult, particularly one suffering with his or her own bereavement. But to offer a child less is unfair. He needs comforting in his struggle to deal with his loss, not withdrawal of trusted adults when he seeks their comfort amidst his sad thoughts and feelings as he struggles to grapple with the meaning of the loss of his loved one.

If the adult bursts into tears as he or she attempts to comfort the child, I believe that no harm is done. Indeed, a child seeing an adult cry may sense that it gives him permission to be sad also.

Adults and children mourn at different paces. Quite frequently, a parent may mourn completely over time, and be free to remarry, while a child or adolescent is still dealing with the separation process. A new wife who assumes the maternal role with warmth and love may be unprepared for the reactions of the child who, once he appreciates the extent and depth of his new mother's warmth and caring, may for the first time be free enough to openly express his sadness over the loss of his natural mother. Such behavior on the part of a bereaved child reflects the success of a new wife's assumption of the parental role. It should not, as is often the case, be considered any failure on her part. Health care personnel should share this point of view with families when appropriate, for this information can be very helpful for both husband and wife.

THOUGHTS ABOUT STAFF

The increasing sensitivity towards the needs of terminally ill patients and of families before and after the death necessitates consideration of the inordinate stress placed upon nurses and physicians and other health care professionals who choose or are assigned to work with dying patients. Nurses and physicians choose to work in this field for many different reasons. Some choose the care of cancer patients because of the fascination of the disease process. Others are drawn to this field because of the widespread current interest in thanatology and the conviction that caring for dying patients offers unique opportunities and professional satisfaction in improving the life until the end. Others are drawn to hospice programs because of the charismatic leaders who lecture and conduct stimulating seminars at medical and nursing meetings; others have a religious calling to work in this field.

Whatever the motivation, health care professionals working with dying patients and their families often work beyond their physical and psychological capacity. A healthy balance between work and outside life must be established. The individual who constantly "needs to be needed" by the patients and family members will soon be "burned out." Doctors and nurses must have support systems while at work, and also outside of the work setting. This is often difficult to achieve because of the intense desire on whatever basis of many doctors and nurses to try to meet *all* the needs of the patient and *all* of the needs of the relatives *all* the time. This can only lead to ultimately undue stress causing depletion of physical and psychic energy to the extent that the health care worker can no longer function.

When stress becomes overwhelming, professionals become argumentative and often become either over-involved or tend to withdraw from patients. Nurses find fault with doctors, and doctors find fault with nurses.

It is imperative that health professionals work in teams, with definitive arrangements for time off. Although many patients may have individual favorites among the doctors and nurses, I am firmly convinced that adequate time off and coverage arrangements are acceptable to patients and families. Appropriate sensitive care for terminally ill patients can only be achieved when well-selected staffs have appropriate training, supervision, and adequate time off to utilize outside life experiences to help them maintain their equilibrium. Without these considerations, the stress on the caretakers ultimately exceed their capacity to work, and they will find it necessary to change jobs (15).

Elie Weisel, in his novel *The Accident*, quotes a physician as saying, "My victories can only be temporary. My defeats are final" (16). Physicians, health care givers, and family friends who feel despondent and discouraged by the death of a patient or friend can often find personal and professional satisfaction in comforting the family as they grieve, mourn and regain equilibrium. Bereaved adults and children need to know that their physicians, the children's teachers, and friends really do care about them at this tragic moment.

REFERENCES

1. Wessel, M. Death of an adult—and its impact upon the child. *Clinical Pediatrics*, 2:28,1973.
2. Wessel, M. A death in the family: The impact on children. *J.A.M.A.*, 234:865, 1975.
3. Wald, F., Foster, Z., & Wald, H. The Hospice Movement as a health care reform. *Nursing Outlook*, 28:173, 1980.
4. Ewalt, P. & Perkins, L. The real experience of death among adolescents: An empirical study, *Social Casework*, 60:547, 1979.
5. Furman, E. *A child's parent dies—Studies of childhood bereavement*. New Haven: Yale University Press, 1974.

6. Mills, G., Reisler, R., Robinson, A., & Vermillye, Q. *Discussing Death—A guide to death education*, An Etc Publication, Homewood, Illinois, 1976.
7. Furman, R. The child's reaction to a death in the family. In *Loss and Grief: Psychological Management in Medical Practice*. Schoenberg, Edited by Schoenberg, B., Carr, A., Peretz, D., & Kutscher, A., New York: Columbia University Press, p. 70-86, 1970.
8. Futterman, E., Hoffman, I., & Sabshin, M. In Schoenberg, B., Carr, A., Peretz, D., & Kutscher, A. (eds.), *Loss and Grief: Psychosocial Aspects of Terminal Care*. New York: Columbia University Press, p. 243-274, 1972.
9. Martinson, I. *Home care for the dying child*. New York: Appleton-Century-Crofts, 1976.
10. Wessel, M. The primary physician and the family during the terminal illness and afterwards. In Sahler, O. J. (ed.), *The Child and Death*. St. Louis: C. V. Mosby, p. 72-82, 1978.
11. Parkes, C. *Bereavement studies of grief in adult life*. New York: International University Press, Inc., 1972.
12. Wessel, M. The adolescent and death of a parent. In Gallager, R., Heald, F., & Garrell, D. (eds.), *Medical Care of Adolescent*. New York: Appleton-Century-Crofts, 1976.
13. Fischoff, J. & O'Brien, M. After the child dies. *Journal of Pediatrics*, 88:140, 1976.
14. Schiff, H. S. *The bereaved parent*. New York: Crown Publishers, p. 84, 1977.
15. Rogers, J. & Vachon, M. Nurses can help the bereaved. *The Canadian Nurse*, 71:1, 1975.
16. Wiesel, E. *The accident*. New York: Avon, 1970, p. 70.

11

Helping Adults Mourn the Death of a Child

Margaret Shandor Miles

The death of an infant or child was once such a common occurrence that people accepted it rather naturally. The death of children in modern society, however, is not seen as a natural part of life. Because of our modern health technology, the majority of infants and children who are born have the opportunity to live long and productive lives. But, children do die. Some parents still experience the death of an infant from stillbirth, prematurity, Sudden Infant Death Syndrome, and a variety of birth defects or acute illnesses. During the preschool and school years, children also die from cancer and other chronic diseases, acute illnesses, or complications of surgery. Children of all ages die of accidents which are the leading cause of death in childhood (1). In addition, an alarming increase in the number of children dying from suicide and homicide has been noted recently (2).

The death of a child, no matter if the child is an infant or teenager, is one of the most traumatic experiences his family will ever have to endure. Children are in many ways extensions of their parents. They represent the beginning of life, the future, and in a sense, immortality. Having children provides parents with status, an opportunity for growth, a sense of personal competence, and continuity with life (3). Children also bring many worries and problems. They are expensive, noisy, time-consuming and dependent. During the adolescent years, children and parents often have very stormy relationships which are important in the establishment of independence and self-identity for the child. In addition, since not all children are planned and wanted, ambivalent feelings about a child's birth and life may cause emotional stress.

When a child dies, then, the parents, many family members, and friends, experience painful and difficult emotions which continue for months and even years following the loss. An important source of help for bereaved parents, family members and friends during this period may include professionals who have either worked with them during the child's illness or at the time of death, or who have become involved with the family during the period of grief. Another source of help may be friends and relatives or other bereaved parents who either knew the parents before the death or who have come in contact with the parents through a mutual self-help group. To be an effective helper to the parents, however, helpers must be knowledgeable about the grief process, the effects of the grief experience on the family, and the kinds of intervention that are helpful throughout the course of the grief experience. In addition, helpers must be in touch with their own feelings and reactions to the death of a child including helplessness, fear, death anxiety, guilt, and anger (4). Helping grieving parents is not easy and has a tremendous impact on the helper.

The purpose of this chapter is to discuss the emotional, behavioral and cognitive manifestations of grief that may be experienced by parents as well as grandparents and other relatives and friends during the phases of the grief process. Intervention strategies useful in helping parents throughout each of these periods will be emphasized. In addition, the feelings and needs of grandparents, other adult relatives, friends, professional and other helpers working with bereaved families will be discussed.

The model for parental grief used in this chapter was developed by the author and is based primarily on the works of Parkes (5-8). (See Fig. 1.) In this model, the grief process is divided into three phases, which have previously been suggested by a number of authors (5, 9-11). These phases include: a period of numbness and shock, a period of intense grief, and a period of reorganization or recovery. It is

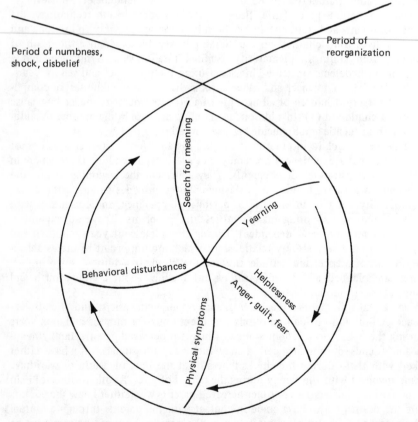

Figure 1 A model of parental grief.

the author's belief that the grief experiences and coping behaviors of bereaved parents and significant survivors are too individualized and unique to fit into a "stage model" of grief. The broad categorizations of the grief experience into three phases, however, allows for a better understanding of the grief manifestations, for assessment of the bereaved, and for intervention. The period of numbness and shock, depicted on the left side of the model seen in Fig. 1, first occurs during the period immediately after the child's death. The symptoms, however, can continue for weeks and months and serve to protect the bereaved from intense pain which occurs in the phase of active grief. During the phase of active or intense grief a wide ranging variety of emotions, symptoms, and behaviors occur. Many authors have attempted to place these reactions into a staging process wherein the symptoms are hypothesized to occur in a specific order (5, 9-13). Parkes, however, cautions that transition from one stage to another is seldom a distinct process because symptoms from one stage may persist into the next (5). It is my belief that these feelings, symptoms, and behaviors may occur at any time, may occur simultaneously, and may reoccur many times during this period. In Fig. 1 they are depicted as a "wheel of reactions" which may be continually experienced during this period. For purposes of discussion, they have been clustered into several groups of grief manifestations including: yearning, helplessness, physical symptoms, behavioral changes, and the search for meaning. The period of reorganization is depicted as the phase when the symptoms of active grief begin to subside and the bereaved parents begins to reenter into their usual life activities and patterns. The model in Fig. 1 indicates that although most bereaved parents find themselves in this period at the same level of growth and development as before the loss, some parents may grow while other parents may deteriorate in their status.

PERIOD OF NUMBNESS AND SHOCK

Many authors, including Parkes, have described the reactions of the bereaved during the first few hours and days following the death of a loved one (4, 6, 7, 14, 15). The major reactions mentioned are feelings of numbness, shock, disbelief, denial, and unreality.

Parents, describing their own feelings at the time they learned of their child's death, often describe it as a time when they were in a fog or as a time they can hardly remember. Others have described a feeling of unreality or a feeling of denial that the child had really died. This shock reaction helps to cushion the impact of the tremendous loss they must face and gives the parents time for the reality to seep slowly into their awareness. For some parents, the shock leads to an immobilization in which they simply cannot function and make decisions. For others, the shock, denial and numbness may cause them to behave as if nothing really happened. Such parents may demand over and over to see their child so they may take him home. When a child has died of a long-term illness or has been critically ill in an intensive care unit for days, parents may also experience fleeting or frank feelings of relief because the child is no longer suffering.

Parents may also be flooded with feelings of anger, helplessness, rage, frustration, and guilt. Those feelings lead to a wide variety of behavioral reactions including hysteria, crying, wailing, hitting, or physical acting out. The behavioral reactions of parents may vary widely and depend on many variables including the suddenness of the death, the way in which the parents are told about the death, and the personality and role of the parents which may affect their ability to express very painful feelings.

Not all family members will react in the same manner. It is not unusual for one or more of the family members to act as if they were "strong" in order to help the rest of the family and to make the decisions that must be made. Recently, after telling a couple and the maternal grandmother that their newborn infant was not going to live, the two women sobbed and talked about their pain. The father sat off to the side looking sad but saying nothing. Finally, the grandmother said, "He has to be strong for both of us." I intervened at that point and said, "Perhaps, but I know that fathers have lots of tears and many sad feelings, too. It's okay if he isn't strong for you. You can all grieve together." At this point, tears came to the father's eyes and his wife reached out to him. Fathers, then, are often put in the role of the strong one, even though they have the same painful and sad feelings. The same thing may happen to grandparents who feel responsible for helping their children through the crisis, even though they themselves are in deep grief.

The most important need of parents and grandparents at this time is caring, and human contact so that they feel someone understands and cares. Nonverbal communication is extremely important. Sitting silently with a family, touching them at appropriate times, or just simply getting them coffee are actions that communicate caring concern. A private room where families can feel free to express their feelings and ask their questions is also important. Remember, however, that some parents need time to be alone together, while other families need continual support by professionals and should not be left alone.

Many families are not ready to talk about their experience at first. As the shock wears off, open acknowledgement of their stress, listening to their pain and sorrow and answering questions become important. Eventually, parents may ask about the events surrounding the death. Most of all, they need to know that everything possible was done to save the child's life, especially in the case of sudden death. Parents who remain numb and silent may need assistance to help them talk about their experience so that they can get in touch with reality and put the experience into focus. Simple words can be used to convey to them that they are indeed experiencing a terrible blow which is difficult to face.

Dealing with parents who openly express rage and anger and who exhibit other overt behaviors may be more difficult than working with quiet, withdrawn families, as it is hard for health care professionals and other helpers to deal with persons who are out of control emotionally. The helper needs to be in touch with his own reactions to the parents' behavior and find out why the parents are reacting in this way. Otherwise, a helper can too quickly retaliate with angry remarks, hush up a parent's expression of anger, or sedate the parents too quickly thereby delaying their grief reactions. Learning to stay with a person who is out of control and who is expressing deep pain and anger is extremely important for professionals who work with parents during the immediate period of bereavement.

Parents also need practical help; a problem-solving approach should be used whenever possible to help them decide what needs to be done, how it should be done and who should do it. Some of the decisions that must be made include deciding who to notify of the death, who to have with them at this time, whether an autopsy should be done, and what funeral home to notify. The latter two points are extremely painful and should be approached only at the parents' readiness to face such issues. Asking parents about permission for an autopsy when they have not yet fully realized that their child is dead will only result in more pain and a negative reply. Similarly, parents cannot think about a funeral home until the reality of the event has begun to take hold.

Before leaving the hospital, parents should be offered the opportunity to see their dead child. Seeing their child after death can help them to face the reality and to say "good bye." Although parents may be reluctant to ask, many of them want this time together with their child. After preparing parents for what the child will look like, the individual needs of the parents should be considered. Some parents will prefer to be alone, while others will be too uncomfortable to be alone and will need the supportive presence of the professional. The length of the visit should also be left to the parents. Some will want to stay only a few minutes, whereas others may want to stay with their child for a long time. There will also be parents who will be too uncomfortable to see their child at all. Their needs should be respected and accepted although it is good to offer them the opportunity more than once since the feelings of parents are in a great state of flux.

When asking parents about seeing their child, it is important to ask each parent the question separately. One parent may want to see the child while the other parent may be appalled at the idea. In addition, one parent or the grandparents may try to "protect" the parent who wants to see the child by making the decision for everyone. I always make it clear that each person must make his own decision and that their needs may be different. Each parent then needs to be supported in this decision.

Recently, a child at our hospital died of an anesthesia reaction. The death shocked everyone involved. When the parents were asked, after a long period of crying, talking, and planning, whether or not they wanted to see their daughter, the father immediately said, "No." But the mother just as immediately replied, "Yes." Each parent was supported in their decision. The mother was accompanied upstairs to see her daughter by one nurse while another nurse stayed with the father.

Leaving the hospital after the death of a child may be very difficult for parents. They may stall around for hours until the staff becomes uncomfortable and wishes they would leave. Leaving the hospital may represent the final reality of the child's death. It may also represent the loss of many, supportive persons, especially if the child had a long-term illness. It is helpful if someone they trust can accompany them to the door.

PERIOD OF INTENSE GRIEF

As mentioned by Parkes (14), the overall level of affective disturbance may not be at its peak during the period of numbness because that protective shield may persist for hours, days, or weeks. As the numbness lifts, parents begin experiencing increasing episodes of pain, panic, and depression. Harriet Schiff in her book, *The Bereaved Parent*, has described this pain as, "a deep, slashing, gouging pain that knifes right through you upon awakening in the morning, while trying to fall asleep, and sometimes all day long" (16). This deep pain symbolizes the period of intense, active grief which Bowlby also called the stage of developing awareness (9).

During this period, parents experience a wide ranging variety of emotions, symptoms, and behaviors which may occur at any time during this period, may occur simultaneously, and may reoccur many times during the period of active grief (see Fig. 1). For purposes of discussion, the reactions have been clustered into several groups including: yearning, helplessness, physical symptoms, behavioral changes, and the search for meaning.

Yearning

It was Bowlby who first identified the symptom of yearning as an important component of the grief process (9). Parkes subsequently built upon the ideas of Bowlby as he evaluated the grief reactions of widows and widowers during the first year of bereavement. Parkes describes the yearning or searching behavior as a strong urge on the part of the bereaved to recover the lost person. The mourner finds himself pining for the loved person, and subsequently, becomes preoccupied with remembrances. He begins to direct his attention to places and objects in the environment that may be associated with the person who died. The mourner may continually go over the events leading up to the final illness and death, or may go over other events of the past. As a "perceptual set" is developed for the lost person, the mourner may begin to have clear visualizations of the person; he may see the person in dreams, hear the person talking, or see the person in a crowd (5, 14). Davidson comments that unlike the previous period when stimuli were rejected, the mourner now becomes acutely aware of stimuli that remind them of the loved person and may even search for such sights, smells, and sounds. He found this symptom to be strongest from the second week through the fourth month of grief (17).

For bereaved parents, the symptom of yearning begins with an intense sense of loneliness and emptiness, accompanied by a deep, aching desire to physically hold, touch, or see their child again. The emptiness and loneliness is especially difficult for the mother who carried the baby through nine months of pregnancy or who spent the major part of the day caring for the child. It is also difficult for parents who spent many years caring for a sick child, as in giving medications and treatments around the clock, and for fathers who spent many hours with a child in a sports activity or business venture.

Deep loneliness and emptiness lead to the yearning and searching behavior described by Parkes and Davidson (5, 14, 17). Parents become preoccupied with the thoughts of the child who died. They may mull over the pregnancy, birth, life, illness, and death of their child. Some parents may find themselves needing to return to the hospital ward, intensive care unit, or emergency room where their child died. One mother who was critically injured in a car accident which killed her son, came to the intensive care unit where her son died as soon as she was able to be up in a wheelchair. It was important for the nurses to discuss her son's injuries and his death with her so she could perceptually understand and accept what happened. Because of this need to relive and rediscuss the child's life, illness, and death, it is a good idea for health care teams to make routine appointments with parents after the child's death for the purpose of discussing these areas and to discuss the child's autopsy if one was done. If distance makes such an appointment impossible, letters and phone calls can be helpful. Some parents, who are not contacted by health care professionals after their child's death may need assistance by a helper in asking for such an appointment. Parents whose children have died suddenly in an emergency room or intensive care unit may have a difficult time in knowing who to contact for assistance in discussing the death since they may have little relationship with the health care providers. A professional helper can assist parents to relive the experience in counseling sessions. This kind of intervention can be very profound and should only be done within the confines of an ongoing counseling relationship. During such a session, a parent may need to have the opportunity to "talk:" to their dead child to resolve differences and to "say goodbye."

Bereaved parents also find their attention drawn to the environment where the child played and lived. The child's toys, clothes, special collections, and pictures may become very important to some parents who find it extremely difficult to pack these items away. Other parents find these items painful reminders of their emptiness and loneliness, and attempt to quickly remove them from the house. A helper working with bereaved parents should bring up the issue of the room and belongings, help the parents discuss their feelings and needs, and assist them in making the right decision about the child's possessions at the time right for them. In addition, the right time for the father may not be the right time for the mother; the helper can assist them in problem solving and compromise.

If a parent did not have an opportunity to see and know the child whom they lost, as in a stillbirth or death of a small infant, they may spend much energy during this period in determining more about the child. Davidson poignantly describes a mother who alternatively rocked and held a cucumber and a rolling pin as she attempted to imagine what her baby whom she never had a chance to see would be like (17). Even if parents have seen their infant, the memories are so few that they soon begin to fade, and this becomes very distressing. Many professionals are now encouraging the staff of nurseries and neonatal intensive care units to take pictures of the stillborn infant or the sick neonate. These mementos become extremely important to bereaved parents.

Visualizations and hallucinations of the beloved person, described by Parkes (12) also happen to bereaved parents. It is not unusual for parents to think they hear their infant cry, to think they see their child in a crowd, or to feel their child's presence in some way. In addition, parents often find themselves getting up in the middle of the night to give a treatment or medication, going into the baby's room to change a diaper, or setting the child's place at the table. The professional or lay helper working with bereaved parents should encourage them in both accumulating and sharing these mementos.

The desire to be close to the child, the continuing feeling that one needs to nurture and protect the child, and the fleeting feelings that the child is still alive may also cause parents to visit the cemetery frequently, or to take toys and other items to the grave. One mother made a coverlet of flowers for her daughter's grave so that she would be protected from the snow.

The experiences of yearning and searching can be extremely frightening to parents who may not feel free to discuss them easily with anyone. Other parents find them comforting but are still reluctant to discuss them with others. In addition, Davidson has mentioned that our society is poorly prepared to tolerate the characteristics of yearning and searching, and thus friends and relatives may not readily listen to parents when they try to share their experiences (17). This reluctance on the part of the bereaved and of society may serve to intensity the loneliness which has already been felt keenly by the parents.

Thus, professions and other helpers working with bereaved parents during this period of active grief should attempt to help the parents discuss their child's life, illness, and death and their feelings of loneliness and emptiness. Eventually, as trust with the helper is developed, parents, may begin to share their experiences of yearning and searching. They often need reassurance from others that such behavior is not crazy but is a normal part of grief that has been experienced by thousands of other bereaved parents. When working with bereaved parents, it is helpful to mention that such visualizations can occur and can be frightening. One mother thought she was going crazy because she woke up consistently at 3:00 a.m. to give medications and treatments to her dead child. When reassured about the normality of this experience by the helper, she was greatly relieved.

Helplessness

The death of a child, whatever the cause, leaves parents with a deep sense of helplessness. This feeling comes primarily from the fact that as protector of the child, the parents could do nothing to prevent the death. Helplessness, in turn, causes feelings of anger, guilt and fear.

Anger has been identified by many authors as an emotion commonly experienced by bereaved individuals (5, 6, 13, 15, 19). Parkes mentions that anger in widows and widowers changes in form and focus with the passage of time and may be directed at people who were perceived as offending either the bereaved or the dying person. This can include health care professionals, ministers, or relatives. Anger can also be focused on the person who died. Parkes also said that the most frequent form of anger was a general irritability and bitterness (5).

Anger is a common emotion felt by bereaved parents at some point in their grief process. The intensity of anger and the focus of the anger, however, varies greatly depending on the cause of death, the personality of the bereaved parents, and the experiences of the parents at the time of death. Anger in bereaved parents can be focused on the health care system, relatives, other children, each other, their dead child, and God.

Anger toward the health care system is a complex problem for parents. If the child had a long-term or acute illness, most parents probably had some degree of trust in the health care providers that they chose to care for their child. The failure of the system to save their child may have been a big disappointment. As their anger emerges, they may focus on specific persons whom they perceived as non-helpful or they may focus more generally on the system that did not provide the kind of physical care or emotional support they deemed important. If the child died rather suddenly as in the case of an accident or sudden, acute illness, the parents may have had no previous relationship with health care providers. The latter can then more easily become the target of the parents' anger and frustration. This is especially true if the care given the child and family was not perceived as humane and supportive.

Anger toward relatives is often focused on their lack of support or on the expectations which they have laid on the bereaved parent. Sometimes the anger is focused on grandparents or other relatives who try to take over the parental role by making important decisions and telling everyone what to do.

Anger with other children may come because the parent fleetingly questions why they survived when this special child died. Some parents become irritated because the siblings are not grieving in a way considered appropriate by the parents or because parents have little energy to meet their many demands and needs.

Bereaved parents can also find themselves angry with each other. This anger may focus on many complicated issues including previous marital problems, the previous relationship with the child who died, and the behaviors exhibited during the grief process. Some of these issues are explored later when discussing marital communication problems during bereavement.

Although many parents turn to religion and God for support during the grief crisis, some become angry and alienated from God or church. Some parents feel betrayed by God for not answering their many prayers. Some become disillusioned with religion generally because their minister and church community were not very helpful. Anger with religion and God is a very difficult emotion for the bereaved to face and may cause many dilemmas.

Another difficult kind of anger is anger that is directed toward the child who died. Parents may feel anger toward the child for past problems in the relationship, for behaviors of the child which contributed to the death, for the amount of time spent in caring for the child during a long illness, or for just leaving the parent through death.

When the source of the anger has not been clearly identified or the emotion itself has not been faced openly by the bereaved, it is often expressed in a general sense of irritability. The bereaved parent may find himself snapping at the other children, getting irritated with the boss, or yelling at his spouse for some insignificant thing.

Because anger is such a common aspect of grief and can have long-term ramifications, it is important for the professional and other helpers working with bereaved parents to be alert for the symptoms and help parents express anger. Since anger is not a very acceptable feeling in our society, bereaved parents may need help in sharing angry feelings and in getting in touch with the sources of anger. An open-ended statement such as "sometimes parents feel angry toward everyone, even God, after a child dies," will allow parents to share angry feelings when ready.

When anger is expressed, it may be explosive and heavy. It is important for the helper to remember that some of the angry feelings may be related to real events they experienced, while other aspects of the anger may be irrational. For this reason, the helper should listen to the outbursts without either agreeing or disagreeing with the parent regarding the source of the anger. The primary need of the bereaved parent is the presence of another person who will listen without prejudice (18). In time, some parents may need help in forgiving and forgetting. Hanging on to bitterness and resentment can prolong adjustment and delay recovery.

At some point, the professional may become the target of the angry feelings, especially if he was associated with the health care institutions where the child died. Since it is difficult for parents to express anger toward someone who is also perceived as being helpful, signs of such anger such as cancelled appointments, decreased contacts or snappy communication should be explored. If anger is vented to the professional, or other helpers, it is important not to take it personally and not to retaliate or withdraw. Rather the helper needs to develop an attitude of understanding acceptance and compassion.

The deep feelings of helplessness caused by a child's death may also contribute to a variety of *guilt* feelings as parents begin to explore why the event occurred. Guilt has been identified by a number of authors as an emotion experienced by the bereaved (5, 6, 11, 18, 19). Lindemann (19) found a strong preoccupation with guilt in the bereaved people he studied. Parkes, however, did not find guilt a prominent feature in his studies of widows and widowers; when present, he felt it was an indicator of poorly resolved grief (5). Because of the dependency of a child on his parents and society's expectations that a parent be responsible for a child's well being, guilt can play a very prominent role in the grief of parents. The circumstances surrounding the death and the individual parent's personality are important variables affecting the type and severity of the guilt feelings. It has been this author's experience that there are at least four types of guilt which bereaved parents and sometimes grandparents experience: causation guilt, cultural guilt, moral guilt, and survivor guilt (8).

Causation guilt occurs when parents begin to explore the cause of the child's death. During this process, they often think about ways in which they may have caused or contributed to the death by sins of omission or commission. For example, they may feel guilty because they did not notice the symptoms of the illness earlier, because they did not check on their infant in the middle of the night, or because they signed the operative permit thereby giving sanction to the operation which led to the child's death. When an infant dies at birth or in the first few months of life, mothers may explore their behavior during the pregnancy searching for something that they might have done (or neglected to do) which contributed to the cause of death. Parents even blame themselves for such indirect actions as giving the child permission to have the car the night of a fatal accident.

Cultural Role guilt comes from feelings of "ought" and "should" which are based on the cultural myth of parents as superhuman beings—always sacrificing, giving, loving, listening, accepting, pacifying, and protecting. A parent experiencing cultural guilt feels inadequate as a parent in some way. For example, a mother who became angry at her screaming infant in the middle of the night may feel extremely guilty after finding her infant dead from Sudden Infant Death Syndrome. Fathers may feel guilty because they did not spend enough time with the child or infant who died. Parents of teenagers who are in the midst of the parenting conflicts may feel very guilty because they were unable to resolve these normal conflicts. Other examples of experiences that may cause cultural guilt include not attending a child's special school program, not taking a child to a special place as requested, or not making the child's special dinner when asked. In addition, working mothers often feel guilty because of not staying home and caring for the child as society expects mothers to do. Sometimes the cause of cultural guilt is as simple as "I wish I had loved her more!"

Moral guilt is caused by thoughts that the death was somehow a punishment for past sins or transgressions. This type of guilt is most often experienced by parents with a strict conscience or parents with a religious background that focuses on guilt. Examples of experiences which may cause moral guilt include: pregnancy before marriage, extramarital affairs, poor church attendance, marriage outside of religion, or having had an abortion.

Survival guilt, first identified in survivors of World War II concentration camps (18), is experienced when parents and especially grandparents face the fact that they have survived their child or grandchild. This experience has been eloquently described by Johnny Gunther's mother at the end of the book *Death Be Not Proud*:

> *I think every parent must have a sense of failure, even of sin, merely in remaining alive after the death of a child. One feels that it is not right to live when one's child has died, that one should somehow have found the way to give one's life to save his life . . . (20, p. 160)*

Although it is considered unatural in our society for a parent to bury a child, new demographic facts leave us with a unique version of this problem of survival guilt. Many adult children, especially men, may die before their aging parents. This leaves a surviving bereaved parent who can also be facing many other losses and problems such as illness, loneliness, and poverty.

Sources of guilt generally come from within the individual parent, but significant others may contribute to these feelings. Grandparents, friends, and even the other parent may increase guilt feelings by making comments about the cause of death or about the care the child received during his lifetime. Often the comments are not meant to be accusations but are interpreted as such by the bereaved parent. The comments may be made as a defense against feelings of helplessness and pain that are often felt by close friends and relatives. Wanting to say something to relieve their own distress, they may say something that causes guilt. For example, one mother of an infant who died of congenital heart disease became very distressed when her aunt reminded her, after the infant's funeral, that she had commented on the baby's cold feet when the baby first came home after birth. This comment created both intense feelings of guilt and some degree of anger towards the aunt who was only trying to be helpful.

One of the most important ways of alleviating guilt feelings is to be able to share them with others. Thus, when parents and grandparents begin expressing their feelings of guilt to a helper, it is important for the intervener to truly listen. One has a tendency to want to step in and take away the burden of guilt from the grieving parent by negating what they are saying, but this may not be appropriate. It is hard enough for a parent to begin sharing these feelings; it is harder still to find someone who does not put them down or try to take them away. Let parents share all of their guilt feelings. Reinforce the idea that guilt feelings are commonly experienced by grieving parents so they do not feel odd or crazy. When they have shared many of the causes of their guilt, then help them explore the reality of the situation and the irrationality of their guilt feelings. One mother, for example, felt that her child's sudden death from congenital heart disease was her fault because she didn't notice the symptoms early enough and didn't get the infant to a doctor. When it was pointed out that the symptoms the child had were very subtle and difficult for a lay parent to detect and that earlier care would not have prevented the child's death because of the severity of the heart defect, she immediately felt relieved of her guilt feelings. A father felt guilty because he felt he was too busy at work and hadn't spent enough time with his son. Together with the helper, however, he began to rationalize that his son admired his professional role and that the income he provided had permitted his son to have many enjoyments including a trip to California, a special ten-speed bike, and private music lessons. In cases such as accidents, where the guilt is not irrational but real, help the parent rationally examine their strengths and limitations as a parent. A mother expressed her profound feeling of guilt because she had planned the celebration event for her son's birthday that ended in his tragic death. During the process of sharing her guilt and rationalizing, she became aware of the fact that she was trying to be a good parent when she planned the event as her son had been so pleased with the celebration plans. In addition, parents may need permission to forgive themselves for perceived past transgressions, since long-term continuation of guilt feelings may seriously delay the resolution of grief. The helper can encourage parents to forgive themselves by writing a letter to the dead child or by writing a journal about their guilt feelings and their desire for forgiveness.

The helplessness that is felt by parents, and the deep pain they are feeling, can lead to a pervasive *fear* that something else might happen to hurt them again. This fear is especially present when the child died suddenly as in Sudden Infant Death Syndrome or accidents. Parents report waking up in the middle of the night with a sense of panic and a fear that someone else has been injured or has died. One mother reported getting up at night to see if her husband was breathing after her infant died of crib death. Following car accidents, parents have reported being in a state of continual anxiety when another child uses the car. In the case of chronic disease, parents may begin to fear that a sibling has the same disease if he develops similar symptoms. One mother whose daughter died of Cystic Fibrosis reported feeling very frightened when her remaining child developed a chest cold. Another mother whose child died of leukemia panicked when her child developed a large bruise following a bicycle accident. Health care professionals and other helpers working with parents who are experiencing such fears regarding fatal illness in other children should be alert to these fears. They are often manifested in frequent phone calls to the doctor or nurse about minor ailments in a surviving child. Intense fears for the safety of other children can be manifested in overprotection of these children—not allowing them to go out on dates, keeping them home from school for minor colds, or checking on their activities at all times.

It is important for professionals and others working with bereaved parents to be alert to the specific fears the parents may be feeling, help them discuss the fears openly, and assist them in determining how these fears may affect the present and future needs of the remaining children. Most parents do not want to harm their other children by being overprotective, and with support can gradually make the necessary adjustments needed to allow them the freedom they need.

Fears can also affect plans regarding future pregnancies. This is especially true for the mother who may develop fears not only about the specific problem that caused the child's death but about anything that might go wrong during pregnancy, birth, and infancy. Such fears can make it very difficult to make a decision regarding another pregnancy. Professionals and others working with the parents during this time should help them discuss these fears, support them and help them in making a pregnancy decision, and support them through the next pregnancy and delivery.

Physical Symptoms

Physical symptoms and medical problems have been identified in many studies of bereaved widows and widowers (5, 14, 19, 21, 22). Although few studies have focused on morbidity in bereaved parents, several authors have found some indications of physical ailments or illness in grieving parents (23, 24). The physical symptoms experienced by bereaved parents may include poor appetite, insomnia, dizziness, fatigue, irritability, headaches, muscular pains, abdominal pain, and digestive disturbances. Parents who have a history of past physical problems may find this problem getting worse. Some parents may develop medical problems such as pneumonia, hypertension, diabetes, ulcers or arthritis, after the child's death.

The relationship between these somatic complaints or illnesses and the grief has not been clearly identified. One can, however, hypothesize several interrelated causes: 1) the impact of emotional stress on the body as identified by Selye (25); 2) the lack of attention to such basic needs as rest, nutrition and rest in the bereaved; and 3) the fact that the sick role may legitimize a bereaved parent's need to withdraw or his need for extra attention (17).

An additional physical problem which can occur in bereaved parents is the abuse of drugs and alcohol. Both drugs and alcohol can be used initially to avoid the painful symptoms of grief. Eventually, higher doses may be needed to numb the pain, which can lead to serious addiction and may delay the resolution of grief for years.

When working with bereaved parents, then, the helper should assess both their physical symptoms and their health. Attention should be paid to their basic needs, eating, sleeping and exercise. The importance of eating routine nutritious meals, however small, should be emphasized. Planned exercise can serve to meet basic physical needs and can serve as a positive coping behavior when under stress. One bereaved father, for example, who expressed his grief by quiet withdrawal was assisted in planning to take a daily mile long brisk walk before coming home from work. Not only did this help him feel physically strong, but it also gave him a time when he could gather his thoughts about his dead son and later share them with his wife. Sleep habits should be discussed along with an exploration of ways that might help the parents to sleep better. Going to bed later than usual, physical exercise before sleep, and relaxation techniques can be useful. While mild sedation for short periods of time might be needed, solely for the purpose of helping parents to rest, other types of tranquilizers should only be recommended with caution because of the dangers of addiction and blocking of the pain. Likewise, the helper should be aware of signs that parents may be using alcohol as a crutch and refer them for appropriate help.

Behavioral Changes

In addition to the symptoms already mentioned, bereaved parents may also experience many changes in their usual behavior patterns. Parkes, Lindemann, and others have identified restlessness and tension as a common experience for grievers in the first month of grief (5, 11, 14, 17, 19). In my experience, the changes in behavior involve many other areas of life and occur much later in the grief process than others have identified. These behaviors include: inability to concentrate, disorganization, disorientation, confusion of thought processes, and a tendency either to withdraw or to become hyperactive. Parents may experience these symptoms one at a time or they may experience them all at once. A mother may report that she cannot get her housework done even though she tries each day to get organized. Another may report sitting at the table and staring at the floor for days. A father may have a hard time concentrating on his work and may thus become frustrated when he cannot keep up with his regular work load. Parents may also report that they start one thing, and soon find themselves doing something else without finishing what they started. They do not remember when or why they stopped the first project. Sometimes, they report memory losses even during a conversation. "I was going to tell you something but now I can't remember." During this period of disorganization, helpers should assist bereaved parents in finding ways of getting themselves organized such as making lists or developing daily and weekly plans.

These behavioral reactions may become very difficult for a parent who must return to full-time work soon after the child's death. The difficulties with concentration and confusion of thought processes can make it hard to keep up with the usual work load. Yet, most organizations do not recognize that a grieving employee may not be able to produce as much as before the tragedy and thus do not reduce their expectations of that person. A helper might need to assist bereaved parents who find themselves in such a position to be more open and assertive about their grief experiences and the ensuing problems at work.

Sometimes parents become extremely busy in a wide variety of activities that serve to keep their minds off their deep pain. Some pour themselves into getting themselves and everyone else organized. Such activities may help them to maintain some control over their emotions and behavior at a time when they feel vulnerable. If a helper observes bereaved parents who are manifesting such "busy" behavior to the point that it is both interfering with their ability to face their grief pain and with their family's needs, it should be pointed out to them in a gentle, caring manner.

Because of the irregularity of behavior and the difficulty in thinking things through clearly, decision making may be very poor at this time. It is very important that parents be cautioned not to make important decisions unless necessary for six months to one year.

These symptoms of disorganization frequently lead parents to have feelings of depression and lowered self-esteem. They may begin fearing that they are crazy. It is not at all uncommon for a grieving parent to report their secret fear that they are "nuts." Intervention with grieving parents must center around the normality of these behavioral experiences and their fears of going crazy. One mother who experienced the death of her child from Cystic Fibrosis was interviewed one year after the death. As she poured forth her feelings and cried, she softly mentioned that she sometimes thought that she was going crazy because of all these symptoms and feelings she was experiencing. When told that her feelings and symptoms were normally experienced by all grieving parents, she sighed deeply. It was the first time that anyone had told her about normal grief symptoms, had helped her share her feelings, and reassured her that she was not crazy.

Search for Meaning

No event in life has more impact on the search for the meaning of life than the death of one's child. In her opening essay in the book, *Death Be Not Proud*, Mrs. Gunther clearly describes this experience:

> *Death always brings one suddenly face to face with life. Nothing, not even the birth of one's child, brings one so close to life as his death .... The impending death of one's child raises many questions in one's mind and heart and soul. It raises all the infinite questions .... What is the meaning of life ... ? (20, p. 155)*

As the course of the grief process progresses, many parents spend much psychic energy searching for a meaning to their child's death both for themselves as individuals and for human beings in general. For some the answer is found in a religious meaning as they think of their child as an angel or united with God in a peaceful setting. Others may think of the death as the end of the child's special time on earth for a reason only God knows. Some parents may find meaning in a philosophical sense by focusing on the many people who were influenced by their child or on the many things they had learned from their child's life, illness, and death. Sometimes parents focus on the other children who may be saved because of what was learned from their child's illness and death. This is especially important when an autopsy is done or when experimental drugs are used. Thus, giving parents information about the autopsy findings is extremely important.

Whatever the answer, this search for some purpose or meaning in the event may be an extremely important exercise which eventually helps bereaved parents come to grips with the loss in a meaningful way. When parents begin sharing this search with a helper, it is very important to be nonjudgmental and accepting especially if the meaning assigned to the death differs from the professional's own values and philosophy of life. If parents do not seem to be entering this search for meaning, the helper may need to encourage such exploration. In doing this, the helper should not imply that the loss of their child was planned so they would find a meaning in the loss. Rather, the idea that the loss occurred and was a tragedy for them should be emphasized first, and then discussion should focus on what that event has meant to them—both positively and negatively.

Because religious values are so profoundly affected by the death of one's child, religion is a very important part of the search for meaning. If a helper does not feel comfortable in dealing with this aspect of grief counseling, parents should be referred to a minister with training in grief counseling.

Parents can also be helped to find meaning in their child's tragic death by providing help to others, by creating a special memorial or scholarship fund, or by getting involved in an organizational activity designed to prevent such deaths in other children.

Additional Interventions

This period of active grief, then, can be the time of greatest need for bereaved parents. It is also the time when fewer people are reaching out to listen and to help (17, 26-28). Davidson, in a study of mothers who experienced neonatal death found that almost all the mothers felt as though they were left "helpless" in trying to find emotional support from others. He suggests that society generally thinks that grief ends after about two weeks (17). Even though grieving parents have great needs during this period, they are not apt to seek help unless they are experiencing extreme difficulty. Thus, it is important for professionals and other helpers who have had contact with the family to reach out to them during this period.

Generally the goals of counseling should include: permitting the parents to talk about the illness, death, and special meaning of their dead child; facilitating the sharing of feelings and concerns; assisting them in understanding the normal course of grief; and assisting parents in communicating with and understanding the reactions and needs of all family members. The particular focus of each contact, however, should be guided by the special needs of the parent at that time, as feelings in grief are very fluid and the focus of problems changes rapidly. In addition, the helper should gently convey to parents hope that they have the inner strength to "make it." Positive reinforcement is important in helping them see each improvement in their status. At the same time, parents should be prepared for the usual ups and downs which can be expected to occur, especially on anniversaries, birthdays, and holidays. The helper should emphasize frequently the need to have patience—patience with oneself and patience with one's family.

Some parents find it very helpful to find appropriate reading materials which enable them to accept the normality of their own experience and to feel that they are not alone in what they have experienced. A wide variety of reading materials are available and all professionals working with grieving parents should be knowledgeable about these pamphlets and books (16, 18, 29-32).

Another important intervention for families, is helping them find the social support they need so badly from others. Cobb has emphasized the importance of social support in the resolution of family crisis (33). Helping bereaved families find sources of social support also helps to reduce dependency on professionals and thereby promotes healthy growth. Some parents find it very helpful to know of grief support groups where they can meet other parents who have been through such experiences and who will listen and understand. At the present time, there is a growing movement toward mutual self-help groups of bereaved parents. Self-help groups such as Compassionate Friends, National Sudden Infant Death Foundation, Candelighters, and Mothers-In-Crisis can be extremely important referral sources. An excellent summary of such resources can be found in a recently published annotated resource guide (34).

PERIOD OF REORGANIZATION

When working with bereaved parents, one can begin to suspect that they are entering the phase of reorganization when they begin to speak enthusiastically about other aspects of their lives. Davidson (17) suggests that reorganization can be measured by four criteria: 1) a subjective feeling of release from the loss; 2) renewed bursts of energy; 3) greater ease in making decisions and in handling complex problems; and 4) a return to usual eating and sleeping patterns. At this point, parents begin to notice that the good days outbalance the bad days, to enjoy aspects of their lives that were fun before and to plan for the future. The child can be remembered with more emphasis on happiness and less emphasis on the pain and suffering. In addition, instead of idealizing the child, he can now be remembered as a person with negative as well as positive traits. By this time, decisions will have been made about the disposition of the child's toys, clothes, and room. An appropriate method of memorializing the child's memory will have been completed such as a special album or a scholarship fund. Parents will also have less difficulty interacting with their child's peers or other children of the same age.

It is important to remember, however, that reorganization is not recovery, for parents say that they never recover from the loss of a child. They are never their old selves again, but face life as a different person. The pain, which has become much less intense, is still there and can be evoked easily, although it generally doesn't last as long. As one father put it so poignantly, "I can still feel the pain just as intensely as I did eight years ago when she was killed by the car, but I have more control over when I experience it and how long it will last."

Predicting or defining the length of an appropriate grief reaction is very difficult and perhaps inappropriate since there is little data to underpin any prediction. There are many viewpoints on how long grief should last. Lindemann (19) in his classic paper on grief suggests that four to six weeks was sufficient time to settle all but the most complicated or distorted of grief reactions. His viewpoint may have been influenced by crisis theory which suggests that a crisis will resolve itself in about two months. Parkes and others suggest that grief must be measured in years rather than weeks when a spouse dies (5, 6). Davidson suggests that it takes between eighteen and twenty-four months for reorganization to occur (17). Several authors who studied parental responses to the death of an infant have suggested that grief reactions continued well beyond the first year (36-38). Parents interviewed by DeFain and Ernst said that it took them over fifteen months to regain their previous level of personal happiness after the death of an infant from Sudden Infant Death Syndrome (36).

When a professional or other helper is working intensively with bereaved parents, it is easy to try to rush their entry into the period of reorganization because their continued sharing of deep pain and frustration can become very draining. In my own counseling with bereaved couples. I can recall frequently becoming very discouraged with their lack of progress and my perceived lack of skill in helping them during the period between eight and fifteen months following the death. Patience, supervision, and an awareness that this phenomena can occur will assist the helpers to stay with the parents through the entire phase of active brief.

As parents enter into the reorganization period, helpers need to be aware of the potential occurrence of a new source of guilt feelings—recovery guilt. Parents may report feeling bad because they had a good time, went on a vacation, or enjoyed a good book. They may need to hear from a outsider that it is fine to learn to enjoy life again and that their child would have wanted this for them. During this period, helpers also need to plan a gradual termination with the parents. Hopefully, if the parents have begun to get reinvolved in their past activities and/or are involved with a parent self-help group such as Compassionate Friends termination will occur naturally and with few problems. Parents also may need help in terminating from a self-help group. If they perceive that the group helped them in a significant way to deal with their crisis, they may feel disloyal when they want to terminate from group activities which they no longer need for support.

Parental grief which is either delayed or exaggerated may prolong the length of grief and make the entry into a phase of reorganization very difficult. Delayed grief may be seen in parents who attempt to deny the reality of the loss on some level and, thus, delay the expression of their deep pain and sorrow. Exaggerated grief can be seen in parents who seem to get stuck on one component of the grief process, especially anger and guilt. If parents continue to be deeply angry or profoundly guilty years after the loss has occurred, they may need professional help to identify the sources of the anger and guilt and to deal with them directly. Parents who may be a risk for delayed or exaggerated grief include those who have experienced many major losses in a short period of time, parents who have a history of mental illness, parents who had a profoundly difficult and unresolved childhood experience with loss, parents with little social support, and parents who are facing many additional life stresses at the time of the loss. Helpers who are working with such parents need to be alert to their need for more in-depth therapy and refer them to a mental health professional with skill in working both with emotionally disturbed clients and with the bereaved.

FAMILY CONSIDERATIONS

One of the major differences between the grief of the widowed and the grief of parents is the close interaction between the bereaved mother, father, and grandparents. Each of these adults brings into the grief process their own personality, past experiences, patterns of emotional expression, coping skills, and self-concept. In addition, each marital couple has their own unique system of interacting with each other, with their children, with their extended family, and with the larger community. All of these factors affect both the individual and interactional aspects of the grief experience. Although the parents and grandparents may be drawn closer together during the initial phase of grief, during the active grief period they may begin drifting apart and fighting (8, 15, 16, 26).

THE MARITAL RELATIONSHIP

One of the major causes of stress between parents may develop because the two partners are experiencing their grief at different times, expressing their grief in different ways, or coping with their pain differently. For example, one parent may cope with the death by reliance on religious beliefs including the idea that the death was God's will. If the other parent feels alienated from and angry with God and religion, a conflict may ensue. If another parent is coping with the death by continually eulogizing the dead child while the partner is coping by trying to forget him or her, difficulties may arise. If one parent needs to visit the grave frequently while the other partner feels an aversion toward going near the cemetery, they may argue about which behavior is appropriate. If one parent withdraws during his grief while the other one is coping by keeping very busy, their needs may clash.

Generally, difficulties between parents arise when one parent expects the other partner to behave and grieve in the same way and at the same time. Misunderstandings also occur when one partner feels unsupported by the other. This problem is especially evident when one partner needs to express his or her pain and sorrow and the other partner doesn't want to listen any more. In many instances, the mother is the one who needs to emote and talk about the child, while the father copes by holding his feelings inside and acting strong. Fathers may do this because of the strong cultural messages they get about not crying and being brave and strong. However, the mother may become very angry when he tells her she's crying too much and needs to get over it. The crying of the mother, on the other hand, may be difficult for the father to handle because it gets too close to his own feelings of sadness or because he is worried that she may be having serious emotional difficulties.

There are other interpretations about the causes of marital stress during bereavement. One bereaved mother mentioned to me that she and her husband were in a sense competing with each other to see who was grieving the hardest. Another idea mentioned by Schiff (16) is the fact that it's difficult to lean on something that's already wavering because of the burden it's carrying. In other words when one's partner is having a difficult time with her grief, the other partner may feel a need to protect her from his grief and pain. Conversely, an overwhelmed mourner doesn't want to take on more pain and may withdraw from a tearful spouse.

Conflicts may also arise over many other issues such as deciding whether or not to discuss the dead child, what to do with the toys, what to do on his birthday, and whether or not to have another child. In addition, problems may arise in the sexual relationship. Little research has been done regarding the impact of parental grief on the sexual relationship. It is possible that one partner may want to cope with grief by sexual intimacy, whereas his partner may find interest in sexual aspects of marriage diminished. If the woman is concerned about another pregnancy or if the death is somehow connected in their minds with sexuality, the desire for and interest in sex may be altered for a long time and this may create marital problems.

For many reasons, then, irritations between marital couples may begin building up as the partners begin getting impatient and angry with each other. It is vital that professionals and others working with bereaved parents help them discuss the reactions of and relationships with their spouse, help them understand the grief reactions and coping behaviors which their spouse may be exhibiting, help them keep open the lines of communication, and help them understand the normality of these marital problems. If the helper is involved primarily with only one of the parents, attempts should be made to see them as a couple. One mother whom the author was counseling expressed deep anger because she felt that her husband did not care about the baby's death because he did not seem to be grieving. Furthermore, he did not seem to care about her grief and pain for he constantly cut off her attempts to share it with him. In meeting with them as a couple, her concerns and anger were shared. The father then began to sob and told us both of his deep feelings of loss and pain and of his attempt to hide his pain from his wife because he wanted to protect her and to act as a role model. Once his feelings and behavior were understood by his wife and her needs were made clear, the couple learned to grieve together.

Grandparents

The needs of grandparents and other close adult relatives during this period of active grief are rarely discussed and little research has been done in this area. Yet, grandparents and sometimes other relatives suffer a sort of double grief. They are grieving deeply for the child and, at the same time, grieving for the parents who are in great pain. Though their pain is great, grandparents and other relatives often have a hard time knowing with whom to share their grief and knowing how to help their grieving child. Some grandparents work very hard to hide their grief because they feel they must be an example to their children. Grandfathers can have an especially difficult time in sharing and facing their pain because of the male stereotyping of their generation in which men were not supposed to cry or share feelings (39). Yet, grandparents may experience all of the previous mentioned symptoms of grief. They may exhibit the yearning and searching behavior such as hearing the baby cry or seeing the child in a crowd. They may need to review the meaning of the child's life, illness and death. Feelings of helplessness may occur when grandparents feel excluded from the grieving family or when their attempts at helping meet rejection. The helplessness may lead to feelings of anger, guilt, and fear. Survival guilt may be especially difficult for grandparents as they search for reasons why their grandchild died instead of them, in addition the grief over the loss of their grandchild can reactivate past unresolved losses or can cause an overload because of many present losses in their lives.

Behavioral disturbances such as disorganization, disorientation, and poor decision making can already be problems if the grandparents are elderly. These symptoms, then, can become exaggerated during grief and can be profoundly difficult to cope with. Similarly, physical problems which already have been experienced may become more problematic and new ailments may occur.

Communication problems with the grieving parents can also occur. Although grandparents can be extremely important sources of support to bereaved parents, communication problems can also occur. The causes may be similar to those discussed earlier in relationship to husband-wife problems: fear of mentioning the child because of not wanting to upset the parents, conflicting expectations on the part of either party regarding behavior during grief, and the use of vastly different coping behaviors to cope with the pain. Additional sources of conflict can occur when grandparents, in their attempts to help the bereaved parents in some way, offer advice which is promptly rejected or misunderstood by the parents (39, 40). The result of such communications can lead to what Bowen has called the "conspiracy of silence" (27).

Unfortunately most professionals working with bereaved families do not routinely include the grandparents. Planning family sessions in which the grandparents are included should be an important goal of parental grief counseling since the grandparents can be an extremely important resource for the bereaved parents. Such counseling can also serve to strengthen the family system. Bereaved grandparents should also be included in the self-help groups for bereaved parents. In these groups, grandparents and parents can be helped to share and help each other.

CAREGIVER

This chapter has focused primarily on the grief reactions of parents and grandparents since they are the adults most affected by a child's death. There are, however, many other adults who experience grief when an infant or child dies. Among these many adults are the professional caregivers who may have had a long-term relationship with the child and his family or a very intense short-term experience. In addition, professionals and other helpers who have follow-up contact with bereaved parents can become very involved with the loss. Some of the professional caregivers who may be affected by a child's death can include nurses, physicians, respiratory therapists, social workers, ministers, and psychologists. Lay helpers include other bereaved parents, friends, and relatives.

The intensity and duration of the caregiver's grief is generally not the same as that of parents and relatives but it can be complicated by other factors. Wallace and Townes suggest that the grief of staff can be complicated by the fact that they are often expected to play the dual role of comforter and bereaved (41). This can also be true for family, friends and other bereaved parents. In addition, like grandparents, caregivers often grieve both for the child and for his parents whose suffering they have observed. Caregivers can also be faced with a high frequency of loss experiences, especially in settings where many children die each month or in which many bereaved parents are seen. One grief experience can thus build on top of another grief experience eventually causing a major grief reaction.

Although there are many articles that focus on the stresses associated with caring for sick and dying children (40-45), little has been said about the specific grief symptoms that professionals can experience after a child dies. Some of the emotional reactions which are common include: denial, shock, disbelief, helplessness, anger, guilt, fear, anxiety, disorganization, depression, and somatic complaints (40, 41, 44, 45). The specific emotional reaction and the depth of the grief depends on many variables including such things as: the past history and personality of the caregiver; the quality and length of the relationship with the child and family; the type of illness and death (sudden versus expected, painful versus peaceful); the caregiver's sense of adequacy as a professional; the amount of unresolved grief from past experiences; and the amount of institutional conflict and stress at the time of the death.

Professional caregivers and other helpers who do not receive support and help in dealing with their grief and who have many unresolved experiences with childhood death, can find themselves reaching a state of "chronic grief" or emotional drain in which they feel generally depressed, numb, and unable to respond to the emotional needs of others. In order to prevent this kind of "burnout" from occurring, caregivers need help in facing and sharing their own grief reactions. This can be done by both individual and group sharing of experiences between caregivers so that they realize they are not alone in their grief. In addition, caregivers may need help in developing their philosophy of life and death so that the death of a child can be accepted as a part of life, and the helping role they provide as an important way of meeting societal needs. All caregivers who work routinely with dying children or grieving parents should take care to vary the amount and type of this work so that not all of their energy is focused on grief. They should use breaks, vacations, and time-outs whenever needed to do other creative activities. They should learn to separate their personal and professional lives enough that their time away from work becomes a time of renewal, rest and refreshment.

SUMMARY

When a child dies, the circle of adults who are affected in some way is indeed large. Although parents are the adults most centrally affected, grandparents, other relatives, church members, neighbors and professional caregivers all can be profoundly influenced by the loss. All of these adults can experience a variety of emotional and behavioral symptoms commonly called grief. The intensity and duration of the grief response depends on many variables including the specific relationship of the adult to the child, past experiences with death, and the personality of the adult. The grief process for parents and close relatives may last for several years. Although professional grief is generally of shorter duration and less intensity, repeated experiences with child death can eventually lead to a major grief response in the caregivers. For all grievers left behind when a child dies, the most significant human need is caring, that is, human contact with at least one other person who shows understanding and patience. Sheldon Kopp has summarized this need succinctly when he said "We have only ourselves and one another. That may not be much but that's all there is" (46).

REFERENCES

1. *Promoting the Health of Mothers and Children.* U.S. Department of Health, Education, and Welfare, Maternal and Child Health Services. Rockville, Maryland, U.S. Government Printing Office, 1972.
2. Suicide Rate up for Young. *Kansas City Times,* Sunday, May 26, 1979.
3. Berelson, B. The Value of Children: A Taxonomical Essay. In N. Talbot (ed.), *Raising Children in Modern America.* Boston: Little Brown and Company, 1976.
4. Miles, M. S. S.I.D.S. Parents are the Patients. *Journal of Emergency Nursing,* 3:29–32, 1977.
5. Parkes, C. M. *Bereavement: Studies of Grief in Adult Life.* New York International Universities Press, Inc., 1972.

6. Glick, I. O., Weissman, R. S., & Parkes, C. M. *The First Year of Bereavement.* New York: Wiley Interscience, 1974.
7. Miles, M. S., Mattioli, L. M., & Diehl, A. M. Psychological Support of Parents of Children with Critical Heat Disease, *Journal of the Kansas Medical Society*, 48:124-126, 151, 1977.
8. Miles, M. S. A Model of Parental Grief. Paper Presented at the Forum for Death Education and Counseling Conference, Orlando, Florida, 1979.
9. Bowlby, J. Processes of Mourning. *International Journal of Psychoanalysis*, 42:317-340, 1961.
10. Gorer, G. *Death, Grief, and Mourning.* Garden City, New York: Anchor Books, 1967.
11. Maddison, D. The Relevance of Conjugal Bereavement for Preventive Psychiatry. *British Journal of Medical Psychology*, 41:223-226, 1968.
12. Engel, G. L. Grief and Grieving. *American Journal of Nursing*, 64:93-98, 1964.
13. Kübler-Ross, E. *On Death and Dying.* New York: MacMillan, 1969.
14. Parkes, C. M. "Seeking" and "finding" a lost object: Evidence from recent studies of the reactions to bereavement. *Social Science in Medicine*, 4:187-201, 1970.
15. Friedman, S. B. Psychological Aspects of Sudden Unexpected Death in Infants and Children. *Pediatric Clinics of North America*, 2:103-111, 1974.
16. Schiff, H. *The Bereaved Parent.* New York: Crown Publishers, 1977.
17. Davidson, G. W. *Understanding Death of the Wished-for Child.* Springfield, Illinois, O.G.R. Service Corporation, 1979.
18. Simos, B. G. *A Time to Grieve: Loss as a Universal Human Experience.* New York: Family Service Association of America, 1979.
19. Lindemann, E. Symptomatology and Management of Acute Grief. In H. J. Parad (ed.), *Crisis Intervention.* New York: Family Service Association of America, 1965 (1944).
20. Gunther, J. *Death Be Not Proud.* New York: Harper & Row, 1949.
21. Parkes, C. M. Effects of Bereavement on Physical and Mental Health: A Study of the Medical Records of Widows. *British Medical Journal*, 2:274-279, 1964.
22. Clayton, P. J., Halikes, J. A., & Maurice, W. L. The Bereavement of the Widowed. *Diseases of the Nervous System*, 32:597-604, 1971.
23. Cornwell, J. et al. Family Response to Loss of a Child by Sudden Infant Death Syndrome. *Medical Journal of Australia*, i:656-658, 1977.
24. Kerner, J., Havery, B., & Lewiston, N. The Impact of Grief: A Retrospective Study of Family Function Following Loss of a Child with Cystic Fibrosis. *Journal of Chronic Disease*, 32:221-225, 1979.
25. Selye, H. *The Stress of Life.* New York: McGraw-Hill Book Company, 1956.
26. Miles, M. S. (ed.) *Mental Health Aspects of Sudden Infant Death Syndrome.* New York: National Foundation for Sudden Infant Death Syndrome, Inc., 1975.
27. Bowen, M. Family Reaction to Death. In P. Guerin (ed.), *Family Therapy Theory and Practice.* New York: Gardner Press, 1976.
28. Helmrath, T. A. & Steinitz, E. M. Death of an Infant: Parental-Grieving and the Failure of Social Support. *The Journal of Family Practice*, 6:785-790, 1978.
29. Grollman, E. A. *Living When a Loved One Has Died.* Boston: Beacon Press, 1977.
30. Jackson, E. *You and Your Grief.* New York: Channel Press, 1964.
31. Miles, M. S. *The Grief of Parents When a Child Dies.* Oak Brook, Illinois: The Compassionate Friends, P.O. Box 1347, 1980.
32. Westberg, G. E. *Good Grief: A Constructive Approach to the Problem of Loss.* Philadelphia: The Fortress Press, 1962.
33. Cobb, S. Social Support as a Moderator of Life Stress. *Psychosomatic Medicine*, 38:300-314, 1976.
34. Wass, H., Corr, C., Pacholski, R. A., & Sanders, C. M. *Death Education: An Annotated Resource Guide.* Washington: Hemisphere Publishing Corporation, 1980.
35. Clayton, P. J. The Depression of Widowhood after Thirteen Months. *The British Journal of Psychiatry*, 122:562-566, 1973.
36. DeFrain, J. D. & Ernst, L. The Psychological Effects of Sudden Infant Death Syndrome on Surviving Family Members. *The Journal of Family Practice*, 6:985-989, 1978.
37. Cullberg, J. Mental Reactions of Women to Perinatal Death. In N. Morris (ed.), *Proceedings of the Third International Congress of Psychosomatic Medicine in Obstetrics and Gynecology.* New York: S. Karger, 1972.
38. Rowe, J. et al. Follow-up of Families Who Experience a Perinatal Death. *Pediatrics*, 62:166-170, 1978.

39. Hamilton, J. Grandparents as Grievers. In O. J. Z. Sahler (ed.), *The Child and Death*. St. Louis: C. V. Mosby, 1978.
40. Gyulay, J. *The Dying Child*. New York: McGraw-Hill Book Company, 1978.
41. Wallace, E. & Townes, B. D. The Dual Role of Comforter and Bereaved. *Mental Hygiene*, 53:327–332, 1969.
42. Luckner, K. R. Stress in Neonatal Intensive Care Units. *Issues in Comprehensive Pediatric Nursing*, 2:20–35, 1977.
43. Surveyer, J. A. The Emotional Toll on Nurses Who Care for Comatose Children. *Journal of Maternal Child Nursing*, 1:285–290, 1976.
44. Kavanaugh, R. E. Dealing Naturally with Dying. *Nursing '76*, 6:23–29, 1976.
45. Rothenberg, M. B. Problems Posed for Staff Who Care for the Child. In L. Burton (ed.), *Care of the Child Facing Death*. Boston: Routledge and Kegan, 1974.
46. Kopp, S. *If you Meet the Buddha on the Road, Kill Him*. New York: Banton, 1976.

12

Stillbirth, Neonatal Death, and Sudden Infant Death Syndrome

Glen W. Davidson

Loss of a baby may be less common today that it was forty or eighty years ago, but it is no less painful. In some ways, it may even be more disorienting. At least three factors suggest the possibility: change in expectations, change in context, and change in care.

Changes in societal expectations have been so gradual that they have occurred unnoticed to many people. But a review of notions about ideal family size illustrates one change of expectation. In 1900, physicians were just beginning to make progress in reducing deaths of mothers in childbirth, yet many a man would still expect to have at least two wives during his lifetime, and to sire at least six children with a little over half of them surviving into adulthood. By the 1940s, maternal death had become uncommon and, with the options for birth control, ideal family size was reduced to four children. By 1980, infant mortality had become uncommon and the ideal family size had been reduced to two births. Today, parents in particular and society in general do not expect children to die from disease. Similarly, they do not expect to have numerous births.

Old assumptions are revealed in language. When a child does die, both relatives and members of the health care professions are heard with great frequency assuring bereaved parents that "You're young, you can have another baby." "You'll forget this one when the next comes along." It is uncertain whether such cliches were ever comforting, but in today's mindset the cliches are disorienting. They do not speak to parent's expectations to have few births. Consequences of large birthrates, which disrupt vocational and social expectations, and experience with high death rates among children, which violate deep-seated notions of personal and family continuity, are unexpected.

Change in the context where many child deaths occur also has added to parent's disorientation today. At the turn of the century, births and deaths occurred in homes. Familiar surroundings there—be they objects or persons—helped couples reorient themselves when momentarily disoriented by either dramatic change. By 1940, most expected deaths still occurred at home, but not births. And by 1980, the overwhelming majority of both births and deaths occurred in hospitals.

For parents not acquainted either with hospitals or the people who staff them, institutional care can be very disorienting. A review of public relations literature from the 1940s shows extensive efforts being made to lift shrouds of mystery about hospitals and institutional care. Hospitals and their staffs were approached with awe. Patients' rights were uncertain at least in the minds of patients. Violations of good patient care often went unchallenged. The first successful malpractice suit which held a hospital accountable for conduct of its staff was in 1965 (1). Patients and their relatives were too unfamiliar with this relatively new context to know whether their expectations for care were realistic. They did not have traditions to guide them in what is right and proper for themselves or for the people assisting them in the name of professional competence.

Subtle cues, many held at the unconscious level, are used for day-to-day orientation. Rituals of daily living and habits for protecting survival needs are absent in new environments. Hospital specialists had to be trained in patient education to orient patients to institutional settings and treatment.

Like language, architecture, too, is a repository of old assumptions. For example, in 1900, little was understood about bonding relationships between parents and children. It was unquestioned and therefore not understood. Nurseries and children's wards were organized so that children could not see their parents. When mothers and fathers visited during very restrictive hours, they had to peer through small one-way windows. Child-maternal staffs believed that excitement expressed by a child upon seeing his parents, and the subsequent clinging and crying behavior, was unhealthy for the child and very disruptive for the staff. It seemed to be good practice to keep the child subdued through care by strangers, with lengthy hospital stays, until it was discovered to lead to "hospitalism" which today is called "failure to thrive."

By the 1940s, with the support of an extended family often absent, researchers in child development could begin to see the unique and vital process of bonding between the child and a significant other, most often the mother (2). Architecture of children's hospital units began to reflect the assumption. Gone were the one-way windows. The more progressive hospitals instituted physical changes in which parents and siblings could play with the patient, visiting hours were liberalized, and hospital stays kept to a minimum.

By 1980, the most progressive children's hospitals not only permitted parent and sibling involvement with the ill child, but fostered it by providing family quarters in the unit, established parent care responsibilities in tandem with staff care, and organized visiting hours according to the individual patient's needs. Today, the effect of disrupted bonding *on the child* is generally understood. Not well understood, or at least practiced by either family units or health care professionals, is the effect of broken bonding *on parents*.

The changes in context where many child deaths occur have revealed, in part, the changes in institutional care for critically and terminally ill children. But change is also reflected in the training of health care professionals. Hospitals with special units for child care need staff with special sensitivities and experiences with children. Special care units are equipped with specialized tools. Special tools require special staff training and accountability. Justification for use of specialists and highly expensive technology is based on the assumption that high risk patients can be stabilized and their symptoms reversed.

Specialized care for the critically and terminally ill baby tends to foster a contradiction between theory and practice. In theory, active involvement of parents in care of the baby, whether in the hospital or at home, is highly desirable in order to promote and protect child-parent bonding. However, unless specialists are very careful to behave in such ways as to include nonspecialists, of which parents are part, they promote exclusive care. Definitions of professional competence are made by the professions out of the acute care experience. In logic, this means that competent care is generalized from the standard procedure to its particular application for the patient. Staff are rewarded on the basis of adherence to standards of competence. But staff who relate to a terminally ill child and his parents as though competent care is dictated by goals for reversing his prognosis create only frustration and disorientation for all concerned. Paradoxically, that definition of competence for care to reverse pathological symptoms becomes a definition of incompetent care when applied to the terminally ill. In many institutions, it has been found necessary to retrain specialists, particularly physicians and nurses, to meet the unique needs of children with terminal prognoses.

Of all the changes which have occurred within North American society since the turn of the century, however, perhaps none has been as significant as the move from caring for babies and small children as though they are "little adults" to the realization that they are quite different, physically and emotionally, from adults. This change in understanding is often antithetical to the common sense or wisdom of grandparents who in traditional societies are the great stabilizers in crises. Death of the wished-for child is uncommon both in the frequency it was experienced in the past, and in the expectations, contexts, and care in the present. Three circumstances of loss illustrate my thesis that parents who lose children today suffer not only from the loss of a child but also from disorienting circumstances unique to our society. The three circumstances are: Stillbirth, Neonatal death, and Sudden Infant Death Syndrome.

STILLBIRTH

A definition of "stillbirth" is "fetal death." Because the term also has technical connotations, some of which are now in transition to avoid confusing spontaneous abortion with elective abortion, pediatric literature and even medical dictionaries are making the following distinctions: "Early fetal death" refers to spontaneous loss of the fetus prior to the twenty-first week of gestation. "Intermediate fetal death" refers to spontaneous loss between the twenty-first and twenty-eighth week of gestation, and "late fetal death" refers to loss after the twenty-eighth week, or during the last trimester of pregnancy (3). Use of these terms also replaces "miscarriage" which connotes to many that the mother had a misadventure and thereby is to be held accountable for the loss. The mother often is held responsible for fetal death but it is an assumption seldom justified.

There are approximately 40,000 documented cases of "late fetal death" in North America each year (4). The figure is misleading, however, since so many fetal deaths occur with mothers who either do not receive professional maternal care or are attended in clinics which do not give high priority to careful record keeping. Fetal deaths prior to the last trimester often go unrecorded regardless of the mother's economic or social status.

Regardless of the period of gestation, however, "stillbirth" refers to the failure of a newborn to give evidence of respiration, heartbeat, or definite movement of a voluntary muscle after having been expelled from the mother's uterus. Death may have occurred *in utero* or during delivery.

To the uninformed, it may seem that loss of a fetus at any stage of gestation, and even including birth, is a difficult event but one of little consequence. This assumption holds a notion of "humanhood" which begins only with a live birth. It does not assume that bonding for the mother which occurs prior to delivery. And it gives no credence at all to studies of human cognition and psychological development which discovered that orientation, even for the most mature adult, is an on-going process.

For a woman, awareness of pregnancy begins the process of bonding. As she adjusts to differences in feelings of her body, she is emotionally, and then intellectually, preparing herself for motherhood. Most women will mourn if their pregnancy is terminated prematurely at any point. On the basis of research presently under investigation, it appears that the degree of disorientation following loss of a fetus is in direct proportion to the length of the pregnancy. The longer the gestation period, the greater the grief reaction. And, it is assumed, that the cause of mourning is both physiological and situational. Our emotions are reflections of our body chemistry, and we react with emotion to change in our environment and to disruptions of our expectations.

For both the woman and man who want a pregnancy, and thereby have begun to organize their lives on that expectation, disorientation is associated with loss of a fetus at any point of gestation. This suggests that bonding is part of the orientation process for both genders even though for the male they may be based more on emotional expectations whereas the female's is based on both emotional expectations and physiological changes.

Case Illustration

Jane and Pete were expecting their second child. The first had been born without incident. Jane had had very little difficulty with the first pregnancy, but when she wanted to become pregnant the second time it took her a long time. That pregnancy was terminated by spontaneous abortion in the second month. After becoming pregnant again five months later, she experienced extreme morning sickness. The symptoms subsided somewhat in the second trimester, and by the third trimester her pregnancy seemed normal. The date of delivery came and went, however. Her obstetrician became concerned because the fetus seemed subdued. Vital signs were weak. He decided to have an x-ray performed and found the fetus was anencephalic.

He showed the x-ray to Jane and Pete as a means of preparing them for possible stillbirth of their child, or for death very soon after birth. Jane remembered very little of what the physician said, except that "there was a possibility that the child would be dead." She had heard about such circumstances from friends in the community. She remembered how one of her friends had a baby who died *in utero* two weeks before birth. That woman had terrible nightmares and feelings of contamination about carrying a dead fetus.

Whatever the cause, Jane's blood pressure became elevated into the range of high risk. The obstetrician decided to induce labor. Jane remembers what she interpreted to be fetal movement before her labor began. She was placed under general anesthetic and when she awakened she was told that her daughter had been born dead.

Jane never saw her daughter. She was moved to a different ward where she would not be among mothers and newborn babies. The physician encouraged Pete to make quick funeral arrangements. Pete and the funeral director made all the decisions about the funeral which was held the day following delivery. Jane was told very little about the details even when she asked.

Two months after their stillbirth, Jane and Pete moved to another community. Six months following the stillbirth, Jane sought out another obstetrician to complain that she was having severe difficulties healing, both physically and emotionally. She felt as though she still had a fetus in her uterus. She was being awakened every night by phantom crying from the dead baby, and she was haunted about whether the dead baby was warm enough in its grave, since her husband was unable to tell her whether the funeral director had fully clothed the body. Her blood pressure remained elevated. Jane was referred to a specialist in grief reaction.

Analysis

Analysis of this case, typical of the many I have followed, reveals at least five points of disorientation for the parents: at the time of birth, in their interactions with health care staff immediately following the stillbirth, during the period when the husband made funeral and other arrangements without the wife, when the wife returned home, and when the wife met with other people during the year following the stillbirth (5). Ways other people interacted with the couple and the way the couple was made to feel, had a determinative effect on their orientation (6).

Birth under the best of circumstances is a time of extreme exertion for the woman and high emotion for all family and close friends. High anxiety is kept under control by focus on the baby and by caring activity for the mother. Under the worst of circumstances, when stillbirth occurs, there is no baby for focus of emotions and there is a tendency to avoid the mother. High anxiety is then out-of-control for those most vulnerable—the parents.

Some of the women I followed report that when they became aware that "something" was wrong, it was very difficult for them to focus on any one thing long enough to complete an action. Rather, as one woman put it, "my mind jumped from one thing to another so rapidly, I just felt incapable of doing anything." This is the basic characteristic of high anxiety. For women who were aware that there was no longer fetal movement or who had had their fears confirmed by x-ray or sonogram, feelings of contamination tended to dominate their awareness. "Can't you imagine," one woman asked rhetorically, "what it is like to have your baby die in your own body and then have to carry the corpse around until labor begins?" All of the women in the study expressed strong feelings of guilt, which in turn were translated as confusion: "What went wrong?" "Was it something I did?"

With nothing positive on which to focus their swings of emotions, the women experienced what many called "being crazy." In the case of Jane, and many other women, the mother was not permitted to see the body of her child even though she may have asked. Unable to perceptually confirm who it was that she had been feeling during the pregnancy, she was left to her imagination.

Imagination is one of the most important means human beings have for orienting ourselves to survival needs. By playing out in the scenarios of our imaginations what consequences may come from a specific course of action, we have a better idea of what will and will not work. In the case of mothers whose expectations of a living baby are not met, there is the playing out in the imagination what possibilities have led to the unwanted consequences.

Imagination can become tyrannical and misleading when we fear that by omission or commission we have been irresponsible. Without being able to perceptually confirm the reality of our fears, we are left at the mercy of our suspicions. In the case of mothers who have lost their newborn babies, they are left with feelings of confusion which cannot be subdued. They then become victims of their own paranoia.

For women who have been encouraged to see the body of their baby, and have done so, there is far less likelihood that they will be subject to bizarre grief reactions. They have a higher probability of adapting to their loss. In Jane's case, however, episodes of phantom crying began soon after delivery. As a means for helping her focus her feelings, she was shown pictures of anencephalic infants. Rather than being repulsed by their appearance, she responded by saying, "Why, this is a beautiful baby!" To members of the health care staff who perceived anencephalic bodies as repugnant and viewing as inappropriate for the mother, another woman retorted: "Compared to the image of my imagination, what I see now is beautiful and precious." Thus far, no one has found a means for stopping unrelieved phantom crying other than use of pictures. Perceptual confirmation allows the mother to bring her obsessive suspicions under control.

How parents are reoriented by health care professionals in the first hours of loss seems to be decisive for adaptation to loss. The tendency of staff is to "make believe" by covering up as much as possible those things which make them uncomfortable. They can even "mislead" the couple by offering advice to unasked questions. Whether done with the best of intentions or not, those attitudes and behaviors which undermine the couple's sense of judgment and decision-making often leave unresolved conflicts. Examples of inappropriate staff behavior are: moving the mother from the delivery room to an area away from the nursery without asking her; refusing to adjust to a woman's request to be moved to an area away from the nursery if she has first asked to be cared for in the maternity area; offering sympathy by use of cliches like "you're young, you can have another baby," refusing to permit the parents to see the body of their baby; refusing to permit the mother to be part of decision-making about her own care, such as whether to take drugs which will thwart lactation.

Basic reorienting procedures call for us to help the disoriented to recover their perspective by giving sympathetic and accurate interaction. Appropriate interaction may require as basic a response as giving the time of day, the day of the week, the place the patient is located, and one's own name. Usually, however, far more sophisticated reorientation procedures are called for such as helping the mother and father to clarify their own questions by open-ended communication techniques.

Planning the disposition of the baby's body is a third point of frequent disorientation, particularly for the mother. As part of the tendency to keep all things unpleasant away from the mother, both care staff and relatives make decisions without the mother's involvement and may even hold the funeral without her. Such behavior reflects far more the anxieties of the staff and family than the needs of the mother. Seldom is disposal of the body required to be performed so rapidly that the funeral cannot be postponed or held in the hospital so that the mother can attend. Because mothers are often excluded from being part of planning, they interpret their exclusion as further proof of their worst fears about what they birthed and lost.

A fourth point of frequent disorientation is what is done for, and to, the mother upon her return home. Most of the families I have followed thought it very important to clear away all evidence that a baby had been expected. The baby's room was repainted and turned into a sewing room. The baby's furniture had been sold or put in storage. The baby's toys were thrown out or hidden. The impact on the woman was to return to a home not her own. It had been made to appear as though no baby were expected or wanted. Some of the women I have followed became desperate under these circumstances and frantically tried to find some evidence that the family had expected the baby. Upon finding some artifact, like a rubber doll, they found themselves clinging to it tenaciously.

Far better for relatives and friends to be with the mother upon her return to a home she organized and to be with her as she, herself, finds the emotional capacity to put nursery supplies away. At her speed and in her ways, she is then able to keep track of how she is adjusting to the loss of her wished-for child.

In their eagerness to relieve the young mother from suffering, family members often begin to push upon her an agenda for new pregnancy. While the intention may be well-meant, the impact is to make many mothers feel as though the lost baby was unimportant. For some women to become pregnant before completing the mourning process over the dead baby is to lead to inappropriate and hostile bonding with the new baby. In any case, it leads to chronic disorientation which interferes with the woman's efforts to put the loss of a child into meaningful perspectives.

The fifth point of frequent disorientation is the way other people act around the woman in the year following her loss. Many people do not understand that a stillborn child is a real person to the parents. They therefore pretend that nothing important has happened to the couple. Women in my study report going shopping and seeing good friends cross the street to avoid meeting them. There is a failure to keep asking how the bereaved mother is doing, a resistance to call the deceased baby by name, and a failure to recognize that mourning for the mother of a stillborn is as intense as for a mother who loses a much older child.

If a woman is to recover her sense of orientation, she needs a nurturing social context by which to test out her feelings and perceptions. If others convey to her that her feelings are unacceptable and her perceptions are unrealistic, she is left with reinforced feelings of failure. Rather than help the mother process her grief honestly, they force her to mourn privately and thereby be vulnerable to her suspicions of failure. Neither being busy at home nor engrossed in work can compensate for that kind of reorientation which is needed from exchanges with other persons about perceptions of loss.

NEONATAL DEATH

"Neonatal" is defined as the first four weeks of an infant's life. Neonatal deaths are on the increase. The trend to delay pregnancies into the 30s of a woman's life has brought with it an increase of both infertility and high risk babies. The total number of birth defects has tripled since World War II, now affecting one in seven persons including those who do not become aware of congenital defects until they, themselves, become parents. Geneticists estimate that fifteen percent of the 3.2 million births in 1979 involved congenital defects.

In addition, more teenagers than ever are having babies and they are at high risk because of inadequate prenatal care, improper nutrition and consumption of drugs and alcohol. The rate of birth defects for women in the 18 to 30 age group is one per 1000 live births. For teenagers, the risk increases to one in 400 births, the same risk ratio for women 31 to 37 years of age. For women between 38 and 42, the risk jumps to one in 50 live births.

In 1977, seventeen percent of all pregnancies were among women under the age of 19, twenty-one percent occurred to women over the age of 30. And for the first time, the statistical majority of births occurred among women older than 25 rather than among those younger.

Mention of change in ideal family size has already pointed to one factor of disorientation for parents who lose a baby. The change in age of mother at time of conception has led to heightened risk for losing a baby.

For babies born with respiratory distress, symptoms of cardiac malfunction, physical anomalies, or life-threatening internal obstructions like duodenal atreasia, intensive care is standard treatment in areas where neonatal equipment and specialists are available. But because specialized care is so expensive, neonatal intensive care units (NICUs) are limited in number and tend to be located in teaching hospitals in large urban areas. Some states have zoned health care delivery and intensive care is distributed more equitably.

When seriously ill babies are delivered in rural, small town, or suburban areas that lack intensive care units, they are transferred quickly by special ambulance or helicopter. Such a move may not be that disruptive for the family if the unit is located in the same city, but it is for families in less populated areas.

When a high risk baby is born, the physician and maternal care staff, in keeping with priorities established several decades ago, give highest priority to stabilizing the child's vital signs. Sometimes, however, staff anxiety may be so high that the baby is whisked away from the mother without her being able to see or touch the baby, which has longterm consequences for her.

In the 1970s, an increasing body of literature began to be published on the importance of mother-child contact during the first hours and days of the baby's life (7, 8). Separation during the baby's critical first hours impedes development of the bonding relationship between mother and child, and places the mother at considerable risk as to degree of disorientation about her delivery and the child, particularly if the child then dies in a NICU some miles away.

Case Illustration

Rebecca was 16 years old when she became pregnant. She had been sexually active for a year and because she had not become pregnant earlier had assumed that she did not need to take preventive measures. Besides, at times she felt strongly that she would enjoy having a baby and if she were to become pregnant she would not object. She, herself, had three half-sisters and a half-brother, all with different fathers. Much of her life she remembered as being lonely. She hoped that by having a baby of her own to raise she would no longer be plagued with the feeling.

Rebecca had dropped out of school two years before becoming pregnant. She smoked heavily and drank large amounts of both coffee and beer. When her son was born prematurely, he weighed 1500 grams—a high risk baby. The baby was flown by helicopter from Rebecca's small community to a neonatal unit 60 miles away. She remembers having caught a glimpse of him, but the staff seemed so intent on getting him to the high risk center they failed to let her touch the baby or to hold him. Some of the staff also seemed to have strong feelings about an unmarried teenager having a baby. One nurse was explicit: "She doesn't deserve a baby!" Perhaps Rebecca's baby was separated from her so swiftly in part to punish her.

Rebecca was placed in a four-bed unit for convalescence. She eagerly observed the other three women as they nursed and fondled their babies and she became quite aggressive about holding the babies herself. When she began to lactate, she wanted to nurse the babies indiscriminately, but this upset the other mothers and the nurses. Rebecca's physician gave her a drug which would help dry up her milk and he suggested strongly that she would have to endure the discomfort of inflamed breasts. Rebecca was released from the hospital on the third day.

Staff at the neonatal center phoned Rebecca soon after her son had arrived and encouraged her to come to the center to see him as soon as she was able. They expressed concern about the baby's survivability. Rebecca gave some thought to going to the center when she was released from the hospital, but had difficulty arranging transportation. The baby died on the fourth day before she managed to get to the NICU.

Several weeks after the baby's death Rebecca had the compulsion to relive the week of the birth and death of her son. Somehow in the confusion of that week, she remembered that the neonatalogist had asked permission to take pictures of her son. She wanted to see them. She wanted to see how high risk babies are treated, or more specifically, how her son had been treated. And she wanted to be where her son had been. She felt that if she could retrace and relive that week of being a mother it would make her "feel better."

The neonatalogist met with Rebecca for approximately one hour. He gave her pictures of the baby, explained procedures of the NICU, and offered to answer any of her questions. He remembers her as having been quite "talkative."

Six weeks after Rebecca's visit to the NICU she could not remember much of what the neonatalogist had told her, but she did remember feeling like she may have "touched" her son, "at least in my heart, but only for a moment." She appreciated the attention she received at the NICU and felt like the physician and nurses there had "really loved my baby." But her memories did not satisfy her compulsion of reliving the first week and she had great difficulty in clarifying her confusion about her pregnancy and her loss. Of one thing she was certain, however, she now felt extremely lonely and made the decision that she would become pregnant again as soon as possible.

Analysis

There are those who argue that the context in which most births in North America occur and the attitudes of the institutions' staffs have a profound and negative effect on mother-child health. It is the attitude which suggests that the birth of a baby is primarily a matter of medical specialists treating an illness (9). And when that illness is a high risk crisis, the priority goes to the most physically vulnerable.

There is no question that the lives of many babies are saved by neonatal intensive care. But one is left to wonder how much the decision to separate mothers from their newly born babies is based on judgments which consider consequences for both baby and mother and how many are based upon staff anxieties, or staff impulse, or, as in Rebecca's case, possible staff vindictiveness. Whatever the possibility, the relational bonds between mother and baby have not, until recently, been given much priority. Like Rebecca, the mother is seldom consulted about whether a baby with marginal prognoses should be transferred to an intensive care unit. The predictable consequences of maternal disorientation are seldom considered.

For many North Americans who worship the gods of progress and specialization, even to question this kind of decision is blasphemy—a supposed violation of the specialist's authority. "Even if the baby's prognosis is slim, and we have the technology available, then we should use it," I was informed by a neonatalogist recently. Fortunately, such mindless decision-making in the clinic is being increasingly challenged in the obstetric and pediatric literature.

Precisely because of the reduction of both maternal and neonatal morbidity and mortality, we are less skilled today to handle the crises of neonatal death. New studies of home delivery in North America, and of birth settings and rituals in traditional societies, help us see the contrast between what was common in 1900 and what is common today. Attachment phenomenon begins between the woman and her baby as soon as she becomes aware of the pregnancy. She begins the difficult and lengthy process of organizing and orienting herself for motherhood. In many traditional societies, rites of transition are organized by grandmothers or mothers. They will be the midwives at delivery. They instruct the novice in ways which have been successful for previous generations of mothers. They instruct her in the skills of coping effectively.

When the baby is delivered in traditional settings, it is usually placed in the arms of the mother as soon as she is ready. The family observers continue to give instruction and encouragement, orienting her to the new experience. One midwife with extensive experience notes that members of the family who observe labor and birth seem to be more attached to the baby than those who have not. Kennell and Klaus believe that this phenomenon, in the past, served the essential function of ensuring a substitute mother if the mother should die (10). It also ensured that the mother would be joined by fellow mourners should the baby die, a ritual process as instructive and encouraging to the mother and father as are the rituals of birth (5).

Recognizing the importance of bonding between mother and newly born child, and understanding the need for reorienting a mother who becomes disoriented when the expectations of birth are violated by death, maternal-child specialists are beginning to reinstitute some of the traditional ritual process into the context of institutional care. The neonatal staff, in Rebecca's case, began to establish communication with her as soon as the baby had been transferred to the NICU. Their encouragement to her to come to the unit as soon as she was able was in recognition of her need to continue the bonding process which had begun in pregnancy. The neonatalist's interview with her after her baby's death, the sharing of pictures of her baby, and the tour of the neonatal unit were all done as means of helping her with reorientation. But what the neonatal staff could not provide was continuing support throughout her period of mourning. From whom could she learn those skills necessary to cope?

When the environment in which we have learned to meet life's crises changes, we are either left with the need to learn new skills or to be subject to the distresses of incompetence and disorientation. For some, the distress is sufficient to cause chronic disorientation. In my own study of mothers who lost their babies in the neonatal period, women whose loss occurred as long ago as 1936 still found themselves disoriented on days which reminded them of their lost child and they were more vulnerable to depression and accidents on those days.

In some communities, a new context is being created for couples who have lost children. Self-help groups, composed of those who have experienced loss of infants meet with the newly grieving. Some groups use appropriate specialists to help them develop better skills for coping with their disorientation. Other groups choose to admit only those who have suffered the crisis first-hand (11). Whichever approach, the first task is to help the newly bereaved to discover that they are not alone in their crisis, nor must they invent coping skills for the first time in human existence. One woman put it this way: "After I lost my baby, I felt like I was the only one in the world to whom this ever happened. My mother, my husband or my friends, I thought, couldn't understand. When I discovered that I was not alone in my experience, I was not only able to begin getting organized, but I was able to understand that they needed me as much as I needed them. But we had to learn how to help each other."

SUDDEN INFANT DEATH SYNDROME

Sudden Infant Death Syndrome (SIDS) is a poorly understood phenomenon which claims approximately 8000 infants each year and accounts on the average for two out of every thousand live births. It is the leading cause of death among infants between the ages of one month and one year (12).

The first symptom of SIDS is death. Its occurrence is neither predictable nor preventable. However, epidemiological studies have pinpointed common circumstances which surround SIDS. First, SIDS babies usually give every appearance of being healthy until they are found dead. Some have had minor colds, but seldom is there a history of serious upper respiratory infection. Second, in most cases, death occurs while the infant is asleep. Third, while SIDS is the leading cause of death between the ages of one month and one year, most SIDS deaths occur between the ages of two and six months. Fourth, SIDS deaths occur more frequently among babies of low income, non-white families, with highest risk among those who live in crowded dwellings. Fifth, low weight babies and male infants are at higher risk. Sixth, most SIDS deaths occur between the months of November and March. Seventh, twins may have increased risk, as do infants born to teenaged mothers. As informative as these circumstances are, it should be noted that the generalizations are based on statistical methods and all have exceptions. No race, social, or economic class is exempt (13).

In external appearance SIDS victims are usually in a good state of hydration and nutrition. Although the child may be small for his age, he appears well-developed. There may be white or blood-tinged froth around the mouth or nostrils, caused by pulmonary edema which occurs with muscle relaxation. Similarly, vomitus may be found on the face, having been forced up from the stomach when the body relaxed. Because of normal muscle spasm following this, bedclothes and linens may be in disarray and the body may appear in an unusual position. Bruise-like marks, sometimes called "lividity," may be found on head and arms from blood pooling. Infants' faces may seem flattened because of general relaxation of body tissue. Because rigor mortis sets in quickly in infants, usually within three hours, the body's appearance may suggest parental neglect.

In the few cases when a SIDS death has been observed, the normal breathing infant stopped respiration, went limp and turned blue. There was no struggle and no cry. Vital signs could not be restimulated, even when a physician has been present.

SIDS has generated many misconceptions. Many people still speak of the phenomenon as "crib death" or "cot death." Based on what we now know, it is understandable how people thought that the baby had been suffocated by bedclothes. Others have argued that SIDS is caused by unsuspected illness, allergy to cows milk, freezing, air pollution, or sibling or parental abuse—all of which have been disproved. At this time there is no known method for either predicting or preventing SIDS.

Case Illustration

When Sandra and Tom brought their healthy baby boy home from the hospital they felt like their fondest hopes had been fulfilled. Having had three daughters, this baby was to be Sandra's last pregnancy. When the baby was three months old, Sandra had taken him to their pediatrician for his well-baby checkup. Getting him cleaned, bundled up and through the clinic had taken most of the morning. Soon after lunch she put him down for his nap. He seemed a bit more tired than usual. Sandra attributed this to the morning's adventure.

Later in the afternoon, Sandra noted that the baby was sleeping beyond his usual wakeup time but decided to let him sleep. When Tom came home from the factory, following the 3 p.m. shift, he wanted to play with his son. When he went into the nursery he found the baby dead. Froth appeared at the mouth. Bedclothes were messed up. The baby was on his stomach and his face appeared slightly flattened. A dark ring appeared around the spot where the baby's face had been pressed into the covers. Tom screamed for Sandra and when she ran into the nursery, his first question to her was: "What did you do to him?"

The police rescue truck was called and upon arrival the officers began to ask questions which indicated that they suspected possible foul play. Relatives and neighbors came quickly and stood around in disbelief.

For some time in Sandra and Tom's community there had been a campaign to acquaint people with the rising incident of child abuse. The legislature of their state had appropriated major funds in order to educate both members of the helping professions and voluntary organizations about child abuse, its causes, and ways of prevention. The baby's appearance, to the eyes of the police and the relatives, seemed to fit what they had been told about child abuse.

Tom's first question to Sandra haunted her. She became genuinely frightened by the policemen's line of questioning. Even Tom's mother wondered out loud about whether Sandra had been distracted and had not been taking proper care of the baby. In Sandra's own mind, she wondered whether her youngest daughter had done something to the baby because that child had expressed jealousies since the baby had been brought home.

When the coroner came to Sandra and Tom's house, his line of questioning took a different turn. Not only had he been trained about child abuse, but he had also participated in the state-sponsored SIDS training for medical examiners and coroners. To confirm his suspicions, he took the body to a pathologist who had also been part of the SIDS training program. The pathologist was able quickly to determine that the dark ring on the baby's face was caused by blood pooling, not from trauma which would have caused hemorrhage. He estimated that the baby had been dead for two hours before discovery and this accounted for the baby's facial appearance. In order to counter the destructive suspicions of relatives and friends, he advised the coroner to return to the family and explain the preliminary findings which suggested SIDS. He notified the SIDS center of his state, which responded by requesting a specially trained public health nurse to visit the family.

Because of the necessity to prove SIDS by negative findings, it took approximately six weeks for the autopsy report to be completed and returned to Sandra and Tom. In the meantime, the State SIDS center had phoned a couple who had had a similar experience in order that they could make a visit of consolation. In what could have been a highly destructive experience as a result of lay interpretation of SIDS death, Sandra and Tom were able to focus their grieving appropriately. Every year, however, several couples with similar experiences have not been so lucky. In some instances, one or both of the parents have been jailed on suspicion of committing homicide.

Analysis

In one of the early studies of SIDS (14), it was found that 14 percent of the parents in the study said that they had not been told why their infants died, 50 percent felt that they were not given an adequate explanation of the cause of death, and 83 percent were told that death was caused by a disease that was different from the cause listed on the death certificate. The same study indicated that few communities are organized to collect appropriate data about SIDS. If efforts to adapt to the loss were to be appropriately focused, if measures to prevent SIDS were to be developed, then it became imperative to get correct statistical data.

As early as 1960, SIDS parents began to organize into groups to address the kinds of problems they had encountered and to provide information to newly bereaved families, educate the general public, support research, and facilitate change in the way communities responded to the problem.

Extensive research is being conducted into the causes of SIDS. Most researchers agree that SIDS is probably the result of a series of physiological events rather than a single cause. Areas such as infection, immunology, and the mechanisms which regulate heart and respiration are being investigated. Over 100 hypotheses have been formulated and investigated. Some important areas of current research include studies related to prolonged sleep, apnea, chronic oxygen deficiency, and enzyme abnormalities (15, 16).

The National Foundation for Sudden Infant Death was organized and launched a compaign to "humanize" management of SIDS in the United States. A four-point program advocated: autopsy of all infants dying suddenly and without explanation, prompt parent notification of autopsy results, use of the term SIDS on death certificates instead of other appellations, such as "crib death," and followup information and counseling for all families provided by knowledgeable health professionals.

The Sudden Infant Death Syndrome Act of 1974 was passed following hearings before the United States Congress in 1972 and 1973. The Act directed the Department of Health, Education and Welfare to fund a number of SIDS projects around the country through the Bureau of Community Services, Maternal and Child Health Services. SIDS projects were to organize community resources and to provide counseling services to families who have lost a child through SIDS and to educate the general public. Special attention was to be given to "first respondees"—police, physicians, funeral directors, emergency room personnel, ambulance drivers, clergymen, pathologists and others who are likely to be directly involved with SIDS parents.

Typical of the projects is that established by the State of Illinois which established a SIDS office in the Department of Public Health for the purposes of acquiring better data, supporting basic research, training professional staff, and providing support for parents who have suffered the SIDS death (17). "First responders" have had state sponsored training seminars on SIDS. Medical examiners and coroners have been provided model protocols appropriate to meeting the objectives of the Project. A preliminary diagnosis is called for, and when through negative findings, SIDS is suspected, the family is informed promptly. Explanation is given for need of an autopsy and the family's immediate grief reaction is assessed. Next, the family physician is notified of the infant's death. The coroner or pathologist notifies the State Department of Public Health SIDS Project Office. The SIDS Project Officer sends a letter to the family expressing sympathy and offering the assistance of the SIDS Project Office. A local counselor, public health nurse, or parent support groups are notified in order to provide immediate support. A meeting with the family is arranged by the counselor in which the couple is offered options of no further followup, referral to a SIDS parents or other self-help group, or referral to mental health professionals. What traditional societies provided as reorienting rituals and coping skills to parents who lost their babies, the state and the professional specialists are beginning to provide.

CONCLUSIONS

What orients us is not always obvious or conscious. We often don't discover what we have used to organize our sense of *who* we are, *where* we are, and *when* we are until, through loss and hindsight, we discover what we expected, where we assumed we were, and who we counted on for support.

Similarly, what disorients us is not always predictable or obvious until, in the crisis of loss, we find our expectations violated, our context unfamiliar, and our support systems failing. Even for those parents who have anticipated death of a child, there is the added anguish of surprise that while death may have brought relief from suffering it also imposed upon them that confusion which they felt as despair and interpreted as senselessness or meaningless.

The work of reorientation, what the psychologist calls "adaptation," is incomplete until we are able to place our experiences of life, including loss, in a context of meaning. What makes sense, what is perceived as reality, what is felt as authentic is what we call "meaningfulness." The good clinician learns to assess quickly a patient's sense of person, place, and time. But the assessment is nothing more than a formal procedure which we all do when we test our sense against another's.

A couple may symbolize their move from the disorientation of their crisis to reorientation of their life's values in many ways, but usually they will tap the resources of meaning which are part of their cultural traditions. The British psychiatrist, Emanuel Lewis (6), tells of a cactus in the Far East with fragrant flowers which bloom for only a few hours on the occasional year. Good fortune comes to the family which mediates visibly on the brief birth and death of the flower. An Oriental couple gave the name of this cactus to their stillborn baby. Deep was the pain of loss. Brief was the relationship, but the bond between them and their baby was not without profound meaning for their lives.

When parents' resources for meaning that had been part of cultural tradition no longer apply to changed expectations about birth and death, to the context in which these changes occur, and to the care given to them, they are left disoriented. For some parents, this causes more suffering than the pain of losing their child.

REFERENCES

1. *Darling vs. Charleston.* 33 Ill. 2d 326. (1965)
2. Bowlby, J. Psychopathological Processes Set in Train by Early Mother-Child Separation, in *Proceedings of Seventh Conference on Infancy and Childhood* (March 1953). New York: Josiah Macy, Jr. Foundation, 1954.
3. *Dorland's Illustrated Medical Dictionary*, 25th ed. Philadelphia: W. B. Saunders Company, 1974.
4. *Monthly Vital Statistics Report.* H.E.W. Publication No. (PHS) 79-1120, vol. 26, 1978.
5. Davidson, G. W. *Understanding Death of the Wished-for Child.* Springfield, Ill.: OGR Service Corporation, 1979.
6. Lewis, E. Mourning by the Family After a Stillbirth or Neonatal Death. *Archives of Disease in Childhood*, 54:303–306, 1979.
7. Klaus, M. H. & Kennell, J. H. Mothers Separated from Their Newborn Infants. *Pediatric Clinics of North America*, 17:1015–1035, 1970.
8. Kohlsaat, B. The Psychosocial Impact of Tertiary Care. *Quality Review Bulletin*, 4(9): 28–29, September 1978.
9. Bibring, G. Some Considerations of the Psychological Processes in Pregnancy. *Psychoanalytical Study of the Child*, 14:113–121, 1959.
10. Klaus, M. H. & Kennell, J. H. *Maternal-Infant Bonding.* St. Louis: Mosby, 1976, p. 47.
11. Lieberman, M. A. & Borman, L. D. *Self-Help Groups for Coping with Crisis.* San Francisco: Jossey-Bass, 1979.
12. "Facts About Sudden Infant Death Syndrome," Health, Education and Welfare Publication (HSA) 78-5259, 1978.
13. Beckwith, J. B. *The Sudden Infant Death Syndrome.* Washington, D.C.: U.S. Government Printing Office, 1975.
14. Bergman, A. B. "A Study in the Management of Sudden Infant Death Syndrome in the United States." Baltimore: Central Maryland SIDS Center, 1973.
15. Weinstein, S. E. Sudden Infant Death Syndrome's Impact on Families and a Direction of Change. *American Journal of Psychiatry*, 135(7):831–834, July 1978.
16. Schiffman, P. L., Westlake, R. E., Santiago, T. V., & Edelman, N. H. Ventilating Control in Parents of Victims of Sudden-Infant-Death Syndrome. *The New England Journal of Medicine*, 302:486–491, Feb. 28, 1980.
17. "Sudden Infant Death Syndrome: A Guide for Nurse Family Counselors," Illinois Department of Public Health, 1980, pp. 27–29.

IV

SUICIDE

The subject of suicide among children and youth is traumatic for most adults. We have great difficulty acknowledging that the phenomenon exists and even greater difficulty absorbing the fact that the incidence of child and youth suicide has increased enormously over the past two decades. Suicide in all of its aspects deserves much more extensive and intensive study than has hitherto been given to it in order to provide improved understanding and more effective preventive and interventive action.

In Chap. 13 Cynthia Pfeffer examines one of the least well-developed facets of this subject: suicidal fantasies and behavior in pre-teenage youngsters. As Pfeffer shows, many adults believe that a child below the age of 10 or some other arbitrary age level is unable to understand death and is therefore incapable of suicidal behavior, i.e., behavior consciously intended to end his or her life. Adults are often unwilling to categorize the death of a young person as a suicide because of social stigma or other undesirable consequences that may accompany such labeling. Unlike Sudden Infant Death Syndrome (SIDS), for example, calling the death of a child a suicide seems to add to, rather than mitigate, the grief and guilt of survivors. For these and other reasons, we have very little reliable knowledge about suicide in particular or life-threatening behavior in general among children under the age of 12. Nevertheless, it would be wiser to accept the possibility of suicidal behavior in such children than to ignore this possibility. There is no specific threshold after which suicide suddenly emerges. If we are wrong in accepting the possibility of childhood suicide, we have only made a conceptual mistake. But if we reject that possibility out of hand, we may be turning away from children who very much need our attention and assistance. That price is too high to pay, even if the group of children involved is relatively small.

Pfeffer reviews the limited body of literature on this subject and draws on her own clinical experience with suicidal children to conclude that suicidal behavior is more likely to be underestimated than overemphasized. She puts this subject in the larger context of childhood fantasies about death and identifies the key elements—family context, adaptive capacities, and sources of external stress—that underlie such feelings, thoughts, and actions. This suggests a posture for intervention and further study that may help to diminish the potential for suicide in children, to improve the quality of their lives, and to foster more constructive interactions with death.

In Chap. 14 Michael Peck draws upon the more recent literature and his own professional experiences with suicidal youth as Director of Youth Services at the Los Angeles Institute for Studies of Destructive Behaviors and the Suicide Prevention Center to provide a succinct treatment of the problem of suicide in adolescence and youth. Peck presents the alarming statistics as well as a thoughtful analysis of the increase in self-destructive behavior over the past 20 years or so. His discussion of some of the distinctive psychodynamic profiles and presentation of a number of non-traditional categories of youth suicide currently used at the Los Angeles Center combined with case illustrations may help not only those directly involved in suicide prevention and intervention but also suggests the broader social contexts, milieus, and support systems that enable young people to grow toward healthy, integrated adulthood.

13

Death Preoccupations
and Suicidal Behavior in Children

Cynthia R. Pfeffer

A child's obsessions with death are compelling and disturbing concerns for those who know the child well. Such a situation becomes transformed into a devastating event when the child has successfully taken his own life. This tragedy leaves the survivors in a state of profound shock, remorse, disbelief, and guilt. Such occurrences must be prevented.

Unfortunately, children's warning signs of potentially suicidal actions are often not sufficiently heeded, recognized, or acknowledged by those who are intimately involved with the child. A lack of early response to such distress in children is based upon many facts, misconceptions, and social restraint. Furthermore, to date, the childhood suicidal phenomenon is relatively poorly understood by clinicians and even less well studied. The dearth of comprehensive knowledge about suicidal children, who are between 6 and 12 years old, is fostered by several existing dilemmas.

First, the incidence of suicidal behavior among latency-age children has not been completely established. Contributing reasons for this are beliefs that suicidal behavior does not exist in young children because young children cannot comprehend that their actions may result in an irreversible fatal outcome. In addition, it is thought that children are not physically or intellectually mature enough to be able to plan and carry out life threatening actions. Other reasons are that the United States Office of National Vital Statistics does not catalogue suicide as a cause of death in children less than 10 years of age. Furthermore, there are relatively few reports that attempt to determine the incidence of children with suicidal threats and attempts.

Second, even if statistics were more readily available, they would probably reflect gross under-estimates of incidence. Social restraints due to family secretiveness about cause of death, community political pressures that may influence documenting the real cause of death, and spiritual and philosophical belief systems that create taboos in acknowledging a suicidal death, contribute to the motivation for not accurately reporting a death as suicide.

Third, the determination of cause of death is frequently difficult and not precise. One study points out the discrepancies that often arise in diagnosis. McIntire and Angle (1) evaluated 60 consecutive patients ages 6 to 18 years who were treated in two poison control centers and found that the hospital reports documented accidents in 42 percent of the cases and suicidal behavior in 58 percent. However, the researchers concluded that 4 percent of the cases were accidents, 70 percent were suicidal gestures, 2 percent were suicide attempts, 22 percent involved intoxications, and 2 percent were homicides. In like manner, it is a fact that accidents are the leading cause of death in children but it is not clear how accurate or comprehensive the evaluations in determining the cause of death have been for deaths of children that are reported as accidents. Perhaps many of the reported accidental deaths may be suspected suicides.

Fourth, the degree of anxiety generated by clinical work with such children often has precluded widespread research. Self-directed death preoccupations in children create such an impact on a therapist's own psychic equilibrium that these self-directed actions generate intense thoughts about one's own life and death fears and wishes, one's philosophical principles about encouraging or discouraging another person's death urges, and one's ambivalent feelings of love and hate. As a result, many clinicians are overtly anxious in working with a potentially suicidal child. Such issues are vividly exemplified in the statements of one child psychoanalyst who said "a child's vehement expression 'if I'll die they'll start loving me' makes me shudder, and I feel safe only after this phase has subsided; (2, p. 838).

Fifth, among the clinical investigations of suicidal latency-age children, many reports have been anecdotal and based on only a few examples (3, 4). There have been only a few systematic studies (5-11). However, among studies of suicidal behavior of children, not only have the methodologies varied but many of the studies were retrospective (9, 12), lacked comparison groups (6, 9), or used only a small number of children (6). Noteworthy, is that additional systematic investigations are critically needed.

Sixth, many issues relating to the characteristics and dynamics of suicidal behavior of children have been neglected. Among the understudied issues are the developmental and phenomenological features of death thoughts, fantasies, fears, and wishes of suicidal children. Clarification of these issues may promote progress in early recognition or prevention of suicidal behavior of children, therapeutic interaction and treatment of suicidal children, and research of the predominant factors contributing to childhood suicidal behavior.

These considerations highlight the problems that currently hamper more accurate understanding of the suicidology of children. In this chapter, I will utilize a psychoanalytic and developmental approach to explain features of childhood suicidal behavior. I will endeavor to provide an overview of many aspects of current knowledge of suicidal latency-age children, who are 6 to 12 years old. Utilizing this overview, I will attempt to integrate knowledge about death concepts and preoccupations of suicidal children. The chapter will conclude with several statements about important principles of intervention with suicidal children.

INCIDENCE OF CHILDHOOD SUICIDAL BEHAVIOR

Completed suicide in children under 12 years old is considered rare (13-15). However there has been concern about the apparent increase of suicides among the younger age groups. For example, among children 10 to 14 years old, the total number of suicidal deaths in 1975 was 170. The rate has tripled from 1955 to 1975. In 1955, the suicide rate for children 10 to 14 years old was 0.4 per one hundred thousand population annually but in 1975 the rate was 1.2 per one hundred thousand population annually. In contrast, the number of suicides for 15 to 19-year-olds in 1975 was 1594 and this reflected a 15 times rate of suicide for the 15 to 19-year-old group than the 10 to 14-year-olds.

In an attempt to be more specific about clarifying the trends for completed suicide in young children, Shaffer (15) studied all the recorded suicides among children ages 14 or under in England and Wales between 1962 and 1968. There were 31 such deaths. Data was accumulated from coroners' records, school reports, medical, psychiatric, and social service records. The results of the study indicated that none of the children was under 12 years and the rate of boys to girls was 2.3 to 1. The most common methods used were carbon monoxide gas (43 percent), hanging (17 percent), drug overdose (13 percent), and firearms (10 percent). Furthermore, there was marked sex difference in relation to suicidal methods. More girls took an overdose of drugs and only boys hanged themselves. This finding is similar to that reported by Hollinger (14) in which suicides by firearms, hanging, and poisoning with gas has been carried out predominantly by males. Shaffer (15) noted that the circumstances which seem to have led to the suicidal act were most commonly disciplinary crises between the child and parents or teachers. Of special concern was that 46 percent of the children had threatened or attempted suicide previously.

The incidence of children who threaten or attempt suicide has not been determined with great validity. This is because existing reports have focused on only small population sizes or unique settings which may have excluded categories of children. It has been more recently recognized that suicidal threats and attempts in children are not uncommon (8, 10, 11, 15, 16). However, among the early reports that focused on observations of suicidal behavior of children, Bender and Schilder (6) recognized the clinical evidence of suicidal behavior among 18 children under 13 years of age out of a total of 2000 admissions of children and adolescents to the children's service of Bellevue Psychiatric Hospital. They noted that suicidal behavior in children under 13 years old was much more common among boys. Ackerly (5) reviewing published reports stated that it seemed that between 1 and 5 percent of children brought to child psychiatry facilities present with suicidal histories. However, Lukianowicz (16) noted that approximately 8 percent of children referred to two child guidance clinics in Northern Ireland either attempted or completed suicide.

Recent surveys indicate that incidence of childhood suicidal threats and attempts are higher than previously reported. In a sample of 58 latency-age children admitted to a large municipal hospital's child psychiatric ward, 72 percent had suicidal ideas, threats, or attempts (10). Furthermore, among 100 children referred to this hospital unit, 33 percent showed suicidal behavior (17). Among a sample of children seen in the outpatient clinic of the same municipal hospital, 33 percent had suicidal ideas, threats, or attempts (11). This increased incidence may be due to an actual increase in suicidal ideas, threats, and attempts among children that is similar to the increased rate of completed suicides. Another explanation for this may be attributed to more thorough clinical observation and psychiatric assessment of children coming for psychiatric evaluations.

The methods of suicidal threats and attempts of children vary widely. Children utilize jumping, ingestion, hanging, burning, running into traffic, and stabbing (9–11). There have been no reports in the literature of children shooting themselves. Jumping from heights seems to be the most common method of latency-age boys and girls (6, 10, 11). Unlike older age groups, there does not seem to be a sex difference in the type of method used (10, 11).

DYNAMIC AND INTRAPSYCHIC COMPONENTS OF CHILDHOOD SUICIDAL BEHAVIOR

Psychoanalytic theory proposes that motivation for behavior is based upon an individual's wishes, fantasies, fears and prohibitions. Most of this doctrine stems from work with adults. However, in children, although fantasy is a very strong motivating factor for behavior, the assessment of fantasy of children must be considered within a holistic context of the child's level of developmental competence in cognitive, motor, and ego functioning spheres. Therefore, a child's fantasy life must be viewed as a reflection of and determined by the child's perceptions and interactions within his environment and his unique degree of developmental maturity. As an example, a child with specific maturational lags in the motor sphere may succumb to a special type of fantasy elaboration. As maturation progresses, however, the fantasy complex may also change. Similarly, the child with perceptual motor disabilities may exhibit profound anxiety, compensation via wish fulfillment and repetitive fantasy elaboration. If the disability endures, the fantasy theme may become a fixed feature of the child's character structure. Therefore, in order to understand suicidal behavior in children, it is mandatory to focus upon the complex constituents that eventually combine to create the acting out of suicidal tendencies. These constituent features are the building blocks of each person's individual psychology. They consist of the child's involvement in the dynamics of family life, ability to endure external stress and frustration, ability to assess reality, degree of affect display and modulation, and unique capacity for object relations. In addition, in order to understand the role and significance of a suicidal child's death fantasies, wishes, concepts and behaviors, it is essential to have knowledge primarily about the child's family, external stress factors and level of ego functioning.

The Family Situation of Suicidal Children

Several family disruptions such as separation, divorce, death, parental psychopathology and family violence have been associated with the suicidality among children (8, 12, 15, 18, 19). However, many of these features may not be unique to childhood suicidal behavior but rather are contributors to a diverse spectrum of childhood psychopathology. Nevertheless, empirical studies have demonstrated that certain of these factors do have a special role in promoting suicidal behavior of children.

In a study of 60 abused children, 30 neglected children, and 30 normal children, there was a significantly higher incidence of self-destructive behavior such as biting, cutting, burning, hair pulling, head banging and suicide threats and attempts among the abused children (18). It was noted that self-destructive behavior was precipitated by parental beatings or in response to a separation from the parent. It was suggested that the parental violence produced in the child a wish to escape from the intolerable interactions of his parents. In addition, the observations of the study revealed that the children seemed to imitate the parent's aggressive behavior as well as to identify with the parent's hostility and criticism of himself or herself. As a result, the child regards himself as bad, hostile, destructive, and worthless.

Such parental repetitive and traumatic violence towards the child depicted in the child abuse syndrome is one severe external stress that may cause in the child severe ego deficits of reality testing, impulse control, and affect regulation. In addition, fixed self images of badness and worthlessness are ingredients to form destructive wishes and fantasies. Fear that these fantasies may be acted out may form the nucleus for intense death preoccupations.

Akin to the rejection and hostility noted for abused children Sabbath (20) postulated the "expendable child" concept. He based his conclusions on clinical observations of suicidal adolescents. However similar dynamics apply to younger children. This concept supposes that "a parental wish, conscious or unconscious, spoken or unspoken that the child interprets their desire to be rid of him, for him to die. The parent perceives the child as a threat to his well being and the child sees the parent as persecutors or oppressors" (p. 273). This idea was expressed by one adolescent girl who said "my parents wanted to make me perfect; they failed, and therefore they want to get rid of me" (p. 274). The girl could not recognize any positive feelings of her parents. For example, she could agree that her mother loved her but said that "it's because I am her daughter, not because I'm me" (p. 274).

In another case described by Sabbath (20) death wishes toward the adolescent were direct. One mother, when angry at her daughter, told the girl to "drop dead" (p. 279). The mother was unable to tolerate her daughter's defiance and wanted her to leave the house. As a result, the girl felt that she was the most dispensable member of the family. The suicidal behavior became a compliance of her mother's desire to have her out of the house and for her to drop dead.

Dynamics of the expendable child produce a patterned family system in which the child feels intense loss and abandonment. As a result, states of helplessness and worthlessness are produced. These feelings may generate wishes and fantasies of being somewhere else such as in a peaceful state of satisfaction. Death may be considered to provide such a blissful state. Therefore, these fantasies may be a strong element of death seeking desires.

A highly specific family factor for risk of suicidal behavior of latency-age children is parental depression and suicidal behavior. In a study of 58 psychiatrically hospitalized latency-age children, Pfeffer and colleagues (10) documented that there was a significant correlation between parents who were depressed and suicidal and the degree of dangerousness of suicidal behavior of the children. In the entire population of these children, 13 (22 percent) mothers had suicidal ideas, 10 (47 percent) mothers attempted suicide and 2 (3 percent) mothers committed suicide. Among all the fathers, 2 (3 percent) had thoughts of suicide, 3 (5 percent) attempted suicide and 1 (2 percent) committed suicide. The findings of this study lead to the hypotheses that the children identify with their parents' states of helplessness and worthlessness. In addition, the incidence of parental suicidal behavior provides an actual experience for the child with threats of death. The identification of the child with the parent's fantasies of death may enhance the child's suicidal potential.

All of these studies share a common trend which points out the great importance of parental attitudes and emotional states. Parental actions, feelings and affective states influence the child and produce in the child lasting identifications which, in turn, become apparent in the child's perceptions and fantasies of himself and others. States of helpless despair and worthlessness produce intense psychological pain which must find an immediate release. Suicidal behavior may be one drastic mechanism for the unburdening of intolerable feelings.

Ego Functioning of Suicidal Children

During the long process of development, a child's mechanisms of adaptation that include the sensory, motor, cognitive and interpersonal functions are changing and becoming fixed characteristics of each person's unique style of responses. Not only are the biological influences significant but environmental experiences maintain as much force as the innate and constitutional. The eventual effect can be observed in the type of ego functioning that evolves. The paramount components of ego functioning are the degree of reality testing, capacity for affect regulation, intellectual and cognitive functioning, ability to tolerate frustration, and quality of interpersonal and object relations. Each component of ego functioning can be operationally defined so that it may be evaluated and compared. For example, reality testing is the capacity to respond appropriately to internal and external stimuli and situations. Affect regulation denotes the quality, intensity, and timing of display of such affects as joy, pleasure, anxiety, aggression, sadness, and depression. The intellectual and cognitive functions are a whole set of apparatus that interact to maintain one's sense of comprehension of circumstances, information storage of experiences, level of academic achievement, intelligence, and integration of perceptual and motor stimuli. The ability to tolerate frustration consists of an individual's sense of tolerance for frustration, capacity to delay action to a future time, ability to make decisions, and sense of planning for the future. Interpersonal and object relations implies a person's style of relating to others as well as his inner sense of identity.

Relatively little systematic clarification exists about the quality of ego functioning of suicidal children. However, there have been several beliefs that are maintained or questions that have been raised. These issues must be rigorously tested to see what degree of validity exists about them. For example, it is said by some that suicidal behavior of children is an impulsive action (7, 21). Others, basing their statements on clinical case evidence, indicate that suicidal behavior although it may superficially appear to have an impulsive quality, is actually not impulsive but rather the culmination of severe long standing family or other enduring external conflicts (22). Unfortunately, by indicating that suicidal behavior in children is impulsive, it has hampered a more systematic approach to clinical evaluation especially regarding the factors that may have promoted the building up of suicidal tendencies. Therefore, caution is required in concluding that childhood suicidal actions occur precipitiously or in an unexpected fashion.

The issues have been raised as to whether suicidal children are more seriously disturbed than nonsuicidal children. Additional systematic studies using large numbers of suicidal and comparison groups of nonsuicidal children are needed to clarify this issue. A strong proponent of the belief that suicidal children have severe emotional disturbances is Ackerly (5). He studied clinical cases of 31 suicidal latency age children who either threatened or attempted suicide. He believed that a child's suicidal threats are prompted by complex interactions between a child's aggressive drives and narcissistic orientation to life. However, children who attempt suicide seem to be in a psychotic state with massive disruptions of adaptive mechanisms and a withdrawal of interest in the world.

Ackerly (5) therefore, believed that children who threaten and those who attempt suicide represent two distinct groups of children. In contrast, I believe that, at present, there is no proof that children who attempt suicide or threaten suicide should be considered as two distinct groups (10, 11). Suicidal behavior is such a complex symptom involving multiple factors that it is premature to dichotomize suicidal behaviors. Instead I prefer to consider suicidal behavior of children as a continuous spectrum of behavior ranging from nonsuicidal, to suicidal ideas, suicidal threat, suicidal attempts, and completed suicides. I have documented that there was no difference in diagnoses along the spectrum of severity of suicidal behavior. Therefore, it cannot be clearly stated that suicidal attemptors are in more of a psychotic state than those children with suicidal ideation or threats. In a similar manner, Mattsson (8) studying suicidal and nonsuicidal child and adolescent emergency cases found no differences between the primary diagnoses of the two groups of emergency patients.

The role of defense mechanisms in maintaining psychic equilibrium has a central place in the psychoanalytic theories. The defenses are important to modify expression of feelings, fantasy and behavior. They balance and integrate one's perception of reality, one's ability to delay impulse discharge, and one's vulnerability to intense affect. It is believed that the capacity for defenses to function is important as the preventative force for expression of self-destructive impulses. However, there are relatively few studies addressing this issue. Pfeffer and colleagues (10, 11) tried to clarify the role of ego defenses for childhood suicidal behavior. Among a sample of 58 suicidal and nonsuicidal psychiatrically hospitalized latency-age children, it was documented that denial, projection, introjection, repression, and displacement were ego defenses commonly noted in this population of children. However, the ego defense profiles were not different for the suicidal and nonsuicidal children. This report serves as an example of the type of systematic studies that are still needed to definitively understand the operations of the defense mechanisms in relation to childhood suicidal behavior.

Another component of ego functioning is the regulation of affect expression. Such regulation includes a variety of affects that are displayed, the timing of when they are evident, and the degree of intensity they are manifest. For example, if a child feels sad and responds to a disappointment, the intensity and timing may range from a transient state of unhappiness that lifts when he realizes that he or she can endure the disappointment to a lengthy display of intense depression because of a feeling of hopeless resignation. Of course, assessment of the child's capacity for appropriate affect regulation is a key element in understanding suicidal behavior of children.

Depression has been implicated as the most significant of affects of suicidal behavior of children (8, 10, 11, 23). Unfortunately, there has been great controversy about the existence of and the signs and symptoms necessary to diagnose childhood depression. There are some who believe that depression cannot exist in young children because the children have not matured intrapsychially to be vulnerable to depression (24). This argument focuses primarily on the component of guilt and superego development. The postulate is that depression is a manifestation of aggression turned inward and directed at internalized bad objects. It is considered that guilt arising from primitive superego functioning is the key mechanism that causes aggression to be turned against the self. This argument, however, is not in keeping with observable phenomena in infants, toddlers or latency-age children. For example, classic studies of Spitz (25) using hospitalized infants, pointed out that during the first year of life, infants, when abandoned by their mothers, are vulnerable to anaclitic depressive reactions. Such reactions are observable in infants as not eating or sleeping properly, susceptibility to illness and weight loss, lack of appropriate development and lack of joy, energy or interaction with others. Among toddlers there have been accurate observations and descriptions of depressive reaction (26, 27). Furthermore, among a study of 100 latency-age children who were treated psychoanalytically at the Hamstead Child Therapy Clinic, London, England, it was discovered that many children showed depressive reaction to a wide range of internal or external precipitating circumstances (28). The children showed tendencies to regress, disturbances of sleeping and eating, and autoerotic repetitive activities. These children showed sadness, unhappiness and depression. They withdrew and showed little interest in anything. Not only were the children discontented, not easily satisfied, and had little capacity for pleasure, but they communicated a feeling of being rejected, unloved and disappointed. As a result, they were unable to accept help. Sandler and Joffe (28) were emphatic in their statement about these children that the depressive reaction in children "can be of a long or short duration, of low or high intensity, and can occur in a wide variety of personality types and clinical conditions" (p. 90).

Although it seems clear to the majority of researchers and clinicians that childhood depression is an existing entity or syndrome, it is still contended as to what signs and symptoms constitute a diagnosis of depression in children. Some diagnosticians contend that depression in children may manifest itself in a wide variety of symptoms that can be considered depressive equivalents (29, 30). The symptoms are thought to mask the underlying or true depression. Such symptoms include temper tantrums, boredom, restlessness, hypochrondriasis, truancy, disobedience, delinquency, learning disabilities, hyperactivity, aggressive behavior, psychosomatic illness, and self-destructive behavior. Others believe that depression can be conclusively diagnosed in children by the presence of depressive themes in fantasy, dreams and verbal expression. Such themes include ideas of mistreatment, blame, criticism, loss, abandonment, personal injury and death. Verbal expression of depressive ideas also includes a sense of hopelessness, helplessness, guilt, being unloved, worthlessness and unattractiveness (31). In keeping with these controversies, other researchers prefer to diagnose depression in children when explicit signs and symptoms similar to those observed in adult depression exist (32-34). These symptoms include changes in affective, vegetative, and psychomotor functioning, motivation, self regard, and cognition. Required criteria for diagnosing childhood depression, by these standards, would include a duration of at least 2 weeks of dysphoric mood such as depressed, sad, blue, hopeless, irritable, and at least five of the following signs of change of appetite, and weight, sleeping problems, loss of energy, psychomotor agitation or retardation, loss of interest or pleasure, feelings of self reproach or guilt, decreased ability to concentrate, recurrent ideas of death or suicide.

As can be noted, specific themes and fantasies are associated with depressive reactions. These themes are also central to the elaboration of intense death preoccupations noted for suicidal children. Furthermore, although many depressed children may exhibit suicidal ideas or behavior, not all depressed children show suicidal symptomatology. Additional clarification is needed to understand the nature of suicidal behavior among depressed children.

Another issue in need of additional study is the relationship of other affects such as aggression and anxiety to suicidal behavior in children. Several investigators have remarked that suicidal children frequently show marked dangerously aggressive behaviors towards others (6, 8, 35). Despert (36) studying suicidal children commented that the children he studied showed no evidence of depression but rather definite signs of aggressiveness and impulsive behaviors. However, in view of these observations, it is essential that aggressive tendencies as they relate to suicidal behavior of children be studied systematically.

Death Fantasies and Concepts of Suicidal Children

Fantasies are one of the unique aspects of man's existence. They derive from the earliest experiences with one's environment, physiological functions, and sensory perceptual stimuli. The integration of these broad occurrences lead to the specific nature of fantasy. Fantasies usually change as one matures. They acquire more complexity and serve to foster adaptive functioning. In children, fantasy may be obvious in play, verbalization, poetry, art, and music. These avenues for fantasy expression help the child gain mastery over new, frightening, or challenging experiences. They help a child turn passive feelings into activities, help to diminish anxiety, and helplessness by the elaboration of control and mastery through fantasy. In some, fantasy provides for the central characteristics of individual personality formation.

The previous sections of this chapter have pointed out important issues and variables that have been found to be relevant to childhood suicidal behavior. Other significant features are the child's preoccupations, experiences and concepts of death. This essential component to understanding childhood suicidal behavior derives from the effects of the interactions of the other variables of ego functioning, developmental phase maturity, and actual and imagined experiences. Unfortunately, relatively little has been studied in relation to death concerns in regard to childhood suicidal behavior. This section will briefly highlight the clinical investigative work that has important bearing on death issues in childhood suicidal behavior.

In order to comprehend the suicidal child's concerns about death, it is essential to understand not only their emotional backgrounds of conscious and unconscious experiences but also the types of age acceptable concerns about death of children in general. Caprio (37) contends that the inevitability of death exerts a profound influence on all human beings and that ideas about death are found in everyone. Furthermore, it is accepted that death attitudes are formed chiefly by experiences in childhood and are often the expression of a child's conscious and unconscious death ideas directed toward the parent (38, 39).

Among children, death is conceived of as a disappearance and is associated with loneliness (40). Anthony (40) noted that in children, death is a sorrowful separation and a "fear bringing thing" that results from aggression. He noted that children associate death with themselves and their experiences with the elderly and observations of animals. The child soon realizes that he or she is getting older and will eventually die. Chadwick (39) emphasized that fear of death in children represents a simultaneous loss of power or a state of helplessness and also a paradoxically diametrically opposite gain of power or triumph. It must be noted that these seemingly contradictory feelings are important influencing factors on suicidal children.

In an attempt to further understand children's reactions to death, Caprio (37) studied the childhood death memories of 100 adults. It was observed that among the majority of persons death was associated with fear, morbidness and sadness. It was noted that children tended to deny death and believe in their own immortality. The memories seemed to indicate that children associate death with punishment, mutilation, and retribution, and that sleep problems may be caused by the identification of sleep with separation and death.

Among one of the earliest empirical studies of children's theories about death, Nagy (41) attempted to decipher what a child between ages 3 and 10 years thinks death is and what themes they elaborate to explain death. She based her findings on written stories, drawings, and interviews of 378 children. She found that children less than 5 years do not comprehend death as an irreversible event. They equate death with sleep or even deny death. Between ages 5 and 9, she discovered that children personified death and think of it as a continuous process with life. That is, death is temporary and can alternate repeatedly with life. The personification of death is apparent as an identification of death with a distinct personality who is invisible and carries people off. Another concept is the identification of death with the dead. After the age of 9, death is conceptualized as an irreversible process that is a universal phenomenon. These developmental schemata are important in relation to suicidal children. Among suicidal children, there tend to be fluctuations in their concepts of death. These fluctuations are influenced by the degree of stress the child is experiencing and the capacity to maintain stability in ego functioning.

One example will illustrate the fluctuations and death concepts and ego functioning in a 7-year-old suicidal boy. Allen attempted to kill himself to relieve his confusion resulting from his desperate home atmosphere. His grandfather, who was the most satisfying support for Allen had just died. Previous to the death, Allen understood that death was a final occurrence. In addition, Allen believed that bad people are prone to die more readily than nice people who he believed live to an older age. However, after his grandfather died, Allen repeatedly stated that death is not final and that his grandfather might someday return. In addition, he altered his statements about death and bad people and now talked about death as a pleasant place where good people go. In this child, the developmental processes were fluid and the child was prone, under stress, to show regression in some of his understanding of death.

Von Hug-Hellmuth (42) gave a detailed acount of a young boy's evolving concepts about death. Death concepts of this child were shown to have arisen from the child's experiences and served as commentaries of his interactions with the world. For example, the little boy expressed wishes that he could be free from his mother's prohibitions. He decided this was possible as soon as "she is shot dead" (p. 503). However, later his conscious and unconscious death wishes against his mother became a source of pity and regret. Other illustrations were given of how the child identified the dead with the self and how the child's death fantasies were connected with the strong sadistic tendencies. The evolution of each individual's child's understanding of death is strongly influenced by his experiences and availability of supportive adults who can interpret real events. For many suicidal children, experiences have been traumatic, violent and lacking in supportive ego strengthening adults who are able to help the child cope with his circumstances and fantasies about death. Instead, such children are often alone to develop their own idiosyncratic explanations of what they witnessed and imagined.

An empirical study of 41 school children, ages 3 to 12 years, pointed out that while children's concepts of death generally mature with age, children by no means are identical in this process of development (43). It was noted that among those 21 children who expressed realistic concepts of death, 2 were between 4 and 5 years of age, 1 was between 5 and 6 years, and the remainder were older than 6 years. Therefore, in work with suicidal children, it is essential to systematically and intensively interview the child in order to understand his specific beliefs about death rather than to make assumptions about these concepts.

In another empirical study, 75 children, ages 6 to 15 years, were grouped according to Piaget's schemata of preoperational level, concrete operational level, and formal operational level. The mean ages of these groups of children were 7.4 years, 10.4 years, and 13.4 years, respectively (44). It was observed that children's answers to questions about causes of death were related to the child's level of cognitive development. Age alone did not appear to be a sufficient basis upon which to classify or group responses. These findings strengthened the clinical concern for the necessity of thorough clinical evaluation of death concepts when interviewing suicidal children. Koocher (45) emphasized that there should be "no unspoken barriers" in talking with children about death. He noted that "children are capable of talking about death and seem to want to do this" (p. 410).

The brief description just offered highlights several facts. First, more empirical data is necessary to understanding children's beliefs about death, their coping styles when confronted with these issues, and methods of interviewing distressed children. Second, while normative data is slowly accumulating about children's beliefs about death, relatively little is known about suicidal children's understanding of this issue. Unfortunately, many assumptions have been fostered which are based on a lack of sufficient data. Third, methods of relieving clinicians' inhibitions in talking with children about death must be developed. This may be readily accomplished when knowledge and techniques of interviewing about death for children are improved.

Suicidal children, unlike most children, are actively confronting all possible concerns about death. Obviously, their behavior may lead to death or serious injury. However, their motivations for this form of action may vary from child to child. Very little has been defined about the latency-age suicidal child's concepts about death.

Lourie (46) attempted to explore the nature of death wishes that school children have toward themselves. In speaking with 100 school children with emotional problems, 70 percent reported thoughts and wishes of their own death. Sixty-nine children stated they had consciously wanted to die at one time or other. In a comparison group of 50 normal school children, 54 percent had consciously thought of killing themselves. The children stated they hoped to achieve an escape from terrible situations, retaliation toward those who were unjust to the children, and love from others by sacrificing themselves. A few children, 5 percent of the normal children and 12 percent of the disturbed children, admitted using death threats for manipulation.

In comprehensively understanding suicidal behavior of children, it is important to realize that a child's concepts of death are one ingredient in this type of dangerous behavior. Concepts of death include the child's cognitive and affective orientation to death. Concepts of death may include fantasies of what death may be like. It may include repeated thoughts or preoccupations of one's experiences with death. These issues are somewhat different than the fantasies of the suicidal child which includes the goals and aims of what suicidal behavior may accomplish. Such goal related ideas may be called the suicidal fantasies or motivation for suicidal behavior. Considering this clarification, the suicidal child's cognitive concepts of death will be discussed and then types of suicidal fantasies will be characterized.

Pfeffer and associated (10, 11), attempting to determine high risk variables for childhood suicidal behavior, focused on aspects of latency-age children's concepts of death. Systematic interviews with 58 psychiatrically hospitalized children, ages 6 to 12 years, involved questions focusing on the child's preoccupations with death that included thoughts of the child's own death, the death of relatives, dreams about death, and fears about death. The child's actual experiences with death were examined. These experiences included knowledge of one's death, attendance at a funeral, and involvement with serious physical illness of self or relatives. The child's cognitive understanding of finality of death was explored. Similarly, the child's affective orientation toward death was determined. This included estimates of whether the child considered death to be a pleasant, peaceful wished for state or a horrible, frightening, warded off state. It was determined that the suicidal children significantly more frequently were preoccupied with thoughts of their own death than nonsuicidal disturbed children. The suicidal children intensively wished to die. They viewed death as a pleasant state in which problems would be absolved. Furthermore, the suicidal children more often believed that death was reversible. They saw death as a temporary and pleasant solution to their immediate and chronic problems. Suicidal children seemed to have more real experiences with death. They often knew someone who was dying from terminal illness or knew of relatives or family friends who had died. Many of the deaths were by suicide. Almost no latency-age suicidal child knew of the death of an age mate by a suicidal action.

These intense death preoccupations and definite concepts about death have marked relevance for clinical evaluation and intervention with potentially suicidal latency-age children. For example, one 9-year-old boy who I saw in consultation because of his severe behavior problems at school told me during his first interview about worries that his relatives were dying. He was concerned that his mother would be devastated if her sister was sick and would die. The fact was that this aunt did not have a life threatening illness. The child continued to tell me about another aunt who died three years previously. I asked the child what his beliefs were about death. Although he seemed to have a realistic impression that death was final, I was alerted by his intense preoccupations with death. I questioned the child about possible thoughts of wishing he were dead or ideas that he wanted to kill himself. Relieved by my initiating these questions, the boy told me that three months before he considered suicide by threatening to jump out the school window. At that moment in our discussion, the child felt the sense of grief unburdening his thoughts that were troubling him.

Other investigators suggested that the suicidal behavior of children may be partly attributed to the child's view of death (47). An idiosyncratic distorted view of death in children with psychopathology or under severe stress may facilitate suicidal tendencies. Orbach and Glaubman (47) illustrated this in two suicidal girls who considered death as another form of life and a need fulfilling state. These authors hypothesized that suicidal thinking evokes defenses that may result in distortion of the meaning of death. This may eventuate when the emotional pressure endured by the suicidal child may affect his still fluid cognitive structure in the direction of wishful thinking. In their empirical study of interviews about this with 21 school-age children who were divided into 6 suicidal children, 14 aggressive children, and 19 normal children, it was determined that suicidal children attributed cause of death to suicide and considered that there is a life after death (48). However, the aggressive and normal children emphasized the finality of death. In addition, normal children attribute cause of death to natural causes, while aggressive children attribute cause of death to brutality. Orbach and Glaubman (48) concluded that a child's concepts of death is an integral part of his entire personality and reflects his life experience and internal dynamics. Furthermore, they state that the evidence of their study lends support to the notion that the suicidal child's distorted death concepts are a reflection of a defensive process. That is, by choosing suicide as a solution to a troubled life, the suicidal child is maintaining that death is another form of life and that he might return to the present life after his death. This protects the suicidal child from actually confronting the realization of death finality. Both Pfeffer and associates (10, 11) and Orbach and Glaubman (48) agree that suicidal children view death as a pleasure and a need fulfilling state, and that these concepts actually facilitate the suicidal behavior. They agree also that attempts to promote an aversion of death is one means of fostering a deterrent mechanism to suicidal action in children. Orbach and Glaubman (47) also observed that suicidal children's distortion of death involves only beliefs about the child's own death but not so much the child's belief about other people's death which in many cases is conceived of realistically. It was therefore concluded that this makes it more likely to propose that the suicidal child's idiosyncratic ideas of personal death serve a defensive function with denied personal death.

Assuming that these death concepts are one component factor to promoting this suicidal behavior, it may now be possible to integrate these underlying concepts of death with the understanding of the child's intense motivation toward self-inflicted death. Remembering that suicidal children often view their own death as temporary and a need fulfilling state may help understand various fantasies associated with suicidal behavior. Therefore, a schema can be conceptualized that integrates various types of beliefs and fantasies. The suicidal fantasies are those ideas that propel self-destructive actions. The death concepts are beliefs about personal death and are ingredients of the suicidal fantasies.

The Suicidal Fantasies of Children

A common attribute of most suicidal fantasies is that they serve as a communication. Their origins are based upon the child's perspective of his real or imagined situation. One function of suicidal fantasies is to be a wish fulfillment. In addition, the suicidal fantasies have a quality of being action oriented and they attempt to transform the child's perception of his passivity to one of active mastery. Often several suicidal fantasies coexist and are maintained within a single child. However, the timing of their expression may be determined by conscious and unconscious processes. The ultimate aim of the suicidal fantasies is influenced by intense affect, concepts of death, and narrowing or deficits in ego functioning. The ultimate aim is to propel the child toward suicidal action. It must be underscored that the fantasies in and of themselves do not lead to suicidal behavior. These fantasies must be combined in the complex fashion with a specific combination of intrapsychic and external variables. To emphasize this concept, Ackerly (5) pointed out that the complex forces involved in promoting suicidal behavior include the child's aggressive drives, his narcissistic expectations, his archaic superego, his withdrawal of libido from objects, his alternation of ego by identification, his disappointment at not being able to achieve the aspirations of his ego ideal, his loss of sense of well being or ideal self, his struggle with his early emerging concepts of death, and his attempt to overcome his helplessness by means of wishes or fantasies of reunion with an all giving parent. Furthermore it must be noted that suicidal fantasies, when considered by themselves may be observable in other types of child psychopathology.

Bender and Schilder (6) were among the first clinical investigators to describe fantasies for suicidal motivation. They noted that suicidal children are reacting to a perceived deprivation of love by means of aggressive action which punishes the parent. The child views death as an escape from an intolerable situation and a chance to experience a more peaceful state. Unconsciously, such a fantasized peaceful condition stands for the reunion with an idealized nurturing parent. One can see in these dynamics of this type of suicidal fantasy, that death concepts become an integral aspect of the suicidal fantasy. The escape is considered possible only through the act that will inflict death. Such a child rarely sees other alternative means of handling his or her distress.

Ackerly (5) believed that childhood suicidal behavior is based upon a regressive state of ego functioning. Apparent in this ego state is the elaboration of suicidal fantasies which Ackerly called a phoenix motif. This type of suicidal fantasy is the spinning out of the child's wanting to return to early childhood when he is ideally nurtured by an all giving good mother. Ackerly (5) sees suicidal behavior as a striving to return to the state of primary narcissism or oneness with an idealized mother. Such reunion fantasies are definitively observable in suicidal children who have lost a parent through death and occasionally loss inflicted by separation or divorce. Intense longings to rejoin the lost parent have profound impact on the mourning process as well as to increase the child's vulnerability of succumbing to psychopathological reactions.

Several other common suicidal fantasies were noted as "a cry for help," an act of revenge, and a release from inner turmoil in psychic pain (8, 12). A cry for help is the child's desperate attempt to dramatically highlight his plight of helplessness resulting from overwhelming external stress. Usually this phenomenon is associated with such environmental stresses as family chaos, physical illness and school problems.

The act of revenge or manipulative suicidal fantasy is aimed at teaching a hated parent a drastic lesson. The child uses suicide as a means of gaining what he or she wishes. Often the desire to actually die is minimal. However, this form of suicidal fantasy must be taken with great seriousness especially since the child is fully capable of succeeding at his own actions.

The wish for relief from inner turmoil and psychic pain is often apparent in extreme case of confusion, panic or psychosis. The inner suffering is so great that suicidal behavior is an attempt to remove this type of distress. Death is viewed as a peaceful alternative and resolution to this intense inner suffering.

It must be emphasized that these suicidal fantasies are strong motivating factors for suicidal behavior. However, they are important catalysts only when the right combination of ego functioning and stresses are such that they potentiate the possibility for acting out upon wishes and impulses. Therefore, a critical mechanism of acting out upon suicidal tendencies rests with the balance of various ego and defensive mechanisms. The suicidal fantasies will help intensify the potential shift of ego devices toward more ease of acting out that will include suicidal actions.

COGENT PRINCIPLES OF INTERVENTION

Much more is to be learned about treatment of suicidal children. As the etiological, natural history, and characteristics of this disorder are explicated, treatment directions will become more focused, intensive and potentiating of cure.

The first principle of treatment is establishment of an accurate diagnosis. The diagnosis entails not only an assessment of the quality of suicidal behavior but also the type of constitutional developmental, personality structural, and environmental organization that exists for the child. Therefore, a holistic approach is required for evaluation and subsequent treatment planning.

The establishment of a diagnostic formulation regarding the suicidal behavior requires an interviewing technique of the child that would be facilitating in uncovering of information about the child's potential for suicidal ideas, threats, attempts, or completed suicide. Ideas about methods of enactment of this behavior, concepts about death, and ability to be motivated for assistance. Such an assessment might be more complex in children than in adults because of children's reticence and lack of facility with language. Therefore, it is imperative to gather history and observations of the child's behavior, communication and feeling states from adults who are clearly in contact with the child. Parental and school reports are primary avenues to pursue in data gathering. In addition, interview techniques of children must be tailored to ease communication between the child and the therapist. Methods of interviewing suicidal children should include such modes as talking, playing, and drawing.

It has been noted, for example, that suicidal children's play may have specific themes that may provide clues of potential suicidal action (49). One theme of the potentially suicidal child is of dealing with the developmental issues of separation, loss, and autonomy. This may be illustrated in such play as throwing and dropping objects and dolls from heights so that they would be found and rescued. Another manifestation in play of a potential clue to suicidal behavior is repetition of dangerous and reckless behavior. This may represent attempts to cope with intense stress by direct motor discharge. A third clue to suicidal behavior is the repetitive misuse and destruction of toys, throwing objects out windows or throwing objects at others. This destructive treatment of play materials may represent a confusion between self and objects in which aggression directed toward the objects actually represents aggression directed towards the self. Another indicator in play of potential suicidal behavior is the repetitive unrealistic acting out of omnipotent fantasies of being superheroes. In this play, the child attempts feats that would actually be dangerous. The need to pretend to be a superhero and to do dangerous things may represent the child's attempt to diminish intense feelings of helplessness and vulnerability.

Once the diagnostic assessment indicates that a child is at serious potential risk, interventions must be immediately planned. The primary concern ought to be in providing the child with immediate constant protection from harm. This may be accomplished by intense observation at home only if it is possible to diffuse suicidal tendencies rapidly by acute outpatient intervention. However, often it is too risky to chance this approach and it is questionable if external supports are reliable and effective or if the child is able to form a quick, intense, therapeutic alliance with the distinct motivation to seek alternative means of coping with his or her discomfort. Therefore, acute psychiatric hospitalization may be the choice intervention to ensure protection from harm and then to provide additional diagnostic assessment and treatment (35).

As a means of protecting a child from harm and of unraveling and remedying the family turmoil that may have contributed to the child's suicidal behavior, it is mandatory to work with the child's family. It is inconceivable in working with acutely suicidal child not to immediately involve the child's family. All too often this treatment task is overlooked. Morrison and Collier (22) provided further insight into the value of family intervention in crisis treatment of suicidal children and adolescents. These authors noted that suicidal behavior is not only a symptom of individual upheaval but also of long standing family disruption which may be related to forms of threatened or actual separation. They postulated that "if the individual and his family can be seen promptly, the episode can be used in working with them to bring about increased openness of family communication and therapeutic movement within the system" (p. 141). They advocated a diagnostic interview with all family members which should be maintained with regularity as long as acute suicidal symptoms last and until the crisis has been settled. This, of course, can be carried out in conjunction with individual sessions between the therapist and the child. The goal of the family meeting was to identify external situations that provoke the crisis and to clarify the family's internal susceptibility, development of symptoms, and means of resolution of these problems.

Another aspect of intervention involves the associated symptoms of the child. These may be related to constitutional, reactive, or characterological concerns. Interventions must be geared specifically to their amelioration. Treatment may include various forms of psychodynamic approaches, medication and academic remediation. No specific one of these forms of intervention is unique to the suicidal child. A note in this regard involves the use of medication which may include any number of types of drug management. For example, a psychostimulant may be indicated for an attention deficit disorder, an antidepressant for severe depression, a major tranquilizer for psychotic behaviors and so forth. Wise and judicious use of medication is most recommended.

Finally, treatment of suicidal children entails a long term approach. Often children must be seen intensely for a period of years. The goal is to channel acting out of suicidal tendencies into verbalization or other symbolic expression. Through this process of treatment, eventual removal of all suicidal impulses can be hoped for. Future follow-up is extremely helpful in providing clues of early warning signs of need for resumption of treatment and also to learn about the long term natural course of this disorder.

REFERENCES

1. McIntire, M. S. & Angle, C. R. Psychological biopsy in self-poisoning of children and adolescents. *Amer. J. Dis. of Children*, 126:42–46, 1972.
2. Lowenthal, V. Suicide, the other side. *Arch. Gen. Psychia.*, 33:838–842, 1976.
3. Aleksandrowicz, M. K. The biological strangers: An attempted suicide of a seven and a half year old girl. *Bulletin of the Menninger Clinic*, 38:163–176, 1975.

4. French, A. P. & Stewart, M. S. Family dynamics, childhood depression, and attempted suicide in a 7-year-old boy. *Suicide*, 5:29-37, 1975.
5. Ackerly, W. C. Latency-age children who threaten or attempt to kill themselves. *J. Amer. Acad. Child Psychiat.*, 6:242-261, 1967.
6. Bender, L. & Schilder, P. Suicidal preoccupations and attempts in children. *Amer. J. Orthopsychiat.*, 7:225-233, 1937.
7. Gould, R. E. Suicide problems in children and adolescents. *Amer. J. Psychotherapy*, 19: 228-245, 1965.
8. Mattsson, A., Seese, L. R., & Hawkins, Suicidal behavior in a child psychiatric emergency. *Arch. Gen. Psychiat.*, 20:100-109, 1969.
9. Paulson, M. J., Stone, D., & Sposto, R. Suicide potential and behavior in children ages 4 to 12. *Suicide and Life Threatening Behavior*, 8:225-242, 1978.
10. Pfeffer, C. R., Conte, H. R., Plutchik, R., & Jerrett, I. Suicidal behavior in latency-age children: An empirical study. *J. Amer. Acad. Child Psychiat.*, 18:679-692, 1979.
11. Pfeffer, C. R., Conte, H. R., Plutchik, R., & Jerrett, I. Suicidal behavior in latency-age children: An outpatient population. *J. Amer. Acad. Child Psychiat.*, 18:703-710, 1980.
12. Toolan, J. M. Suicide and suicidal attempts in children and adolescents. *Amer. J. Psychiat.*, 130:719-723, 1962.
13. Fredrick, C. J. Current trends in suicidal behavior in the United States. *Amer. J. Psychotherapy*, 32:172-200, 1978.
14. Holinger, R. C. Adolescent suicide: An epidemiological study of recent trends. *Amer. J. Psychiat.*, 135:754-756, 1978.
15. Shaffer, D. Suicide in childhood and early adolescence. *J. Child Psychol. & Psychiat.*, 15:275-291, 1974.
16. Lukianowicz, N. Attempted suicide in children. *Acta Psychiatrica Scandinavica*, 44:415-435, 1968.
17. Lomonoco, S. & Pfeffer, C. R. Suicidal and self-destructive behavior in latency-age children. Presented at American Academy of Child Psychiatry Annual Meeting, 1974, San Francisco, California.
18. Green, A. H. Self-destructive behavior in battered children. *Amer. J. Psyciat.*, 135:579-582, 1978.
19. Shaw, C. R. & Schelkun, R. F. Suicidal behavior in children. *Psychiatry*, 28:157-168, 1965.
20. Sabbath, J. C. The suicidal adolescent: The expendable child. *J. Amer. Acad. Child Psychiat.*, 8:272-289, 1969.
21. Bakwin, H. Suicide in children and adolescents. *J. Pediatrics*, 50:749-769, 1957.
22. Morrison, G. C. & Collier, J. G. Family treatment approaches to suicidal children and adolescents. *J. Amer. Acad. Child Psychiat.*, 8:140-153, 1969.
23. Toolan, J. M. Suicide in children and adolescents. *Amer. J. Psychotherapy*, 28:339-344, 1975.
24. Rochlin, G. N. *Griefs and Discontents: The Forces of Change*. Little Brown, Boston, 1965.
25. Spitz, R. "Hospitalism": An enquiry into the genesis of psychiatric conditions in early childhood. *Psychoanalytic Study of the Child*, 1:53-74, 1945.
26. Freud, A. The concept of developmental lines. *Psan. St. Ch.*, 18:245-265, 1963.
27. Mahler, M. Thoughts about development and individuation. *Psan. St. Ch.*, 18:307-324, 1963.
28. Sander, J. & Joffe, W. G. Notes on childhood depression. *International J. Psychoanalysis*, 46:88-96.
29. Glaser, K. Masked depression in children and adolescents. *Amer. J. Psychotherapy*, 21: 565-574, 1967.
30. Toolan, J. M. Depression in children and adolescents. *Amer. J. Orthopsychiat.*, 32:404-415, 1967.
31. Cytryn, L. & McKnew, D. Factors influencing the changing clinical expression of the depressive process in children. *Amer. J. Psychiat.*, 131:879-881, 1974.
32. Carlson, G. A. & Cantwell, D. P. Unmasking masked depression in children and adolescents. *Amer. J. Psychiat.*, 137:445-449.
33. Cytryn, L., McKnew, D. H., & Bunney, Diagnosis of depression in children: A reassessment. *Amer. J. Psychiat.*, 137:22-25, 1980.

34. Puig Antich, J., Vlau, S., Marx, N. et al. Prepubertal major depression disorder: A pilot study. *J. Amer. Acad. Child Psychiat.*, 17:695–707, 1978.
35. Pfeffer, D. R. Psychiatric hospital treatment of suicidal children. *Suicide and Life Threatening Behavior*, 8:150–160, 1978.
36. Despert, L. J. Suicide and depression in children. *Nervous Child*, 9:378–389, 1952.
37. Caprio, F. S. A study of some psychological reactions during prepubescence to the idea of death. *Psychiatric Quarterly*, 24:495–505, 1950.
38. Bromberg, W. & Schilder, P. The attitudes of psychoneurotics toward death. *Psychoanalytic Review*, 23:1–25, 1936.
39. Chadwick, M. Notes upon the fear of death. *International Journal of Psychoanalysis*, 10: 321–334, 1929.
40. Anthony, S. *The Child's Discovery of Death*. Harcourt-Brace, New York, 1940.
41. Nagy, M. The child's theories concerning death. *J. Genetic Psychology*, 73:3–27, 1948.
42. Von Hug-Hellmuth, H. The child's concept of death. *Psychoanalytic Quarterly*, 34:499–516, 1965.
43. Melear, A. Children's conception of death. *J. Genetic Psychology*, 123:359–360, 1973.
44. Koocher, G. P. Childhood, death and cognitive development. *Developmental Psychology*, 8:369–375, 1973.
45. Koocher, G. P. Talking with children about death. *Amer. J. Orthopsychiat.*, 44:404–411, 1974.
46. Lourie, R. S. Clinical studies of attempted suicide in childhood. *Clinical Proceedings Children's Hospital of D.C.*, 22:166–170, 1966.
47. Orbach, I. & Glaubman, H. The concept of death and suicidal behavior in young children: Three case studies. *J. Amer. Acad. Child Psychiat.*, 18:668–678, 1979.
48. Orbach, I. & Glaubman, H. Suicidal, aggression, and normal children's perception of personal and impersonal death. *J. Clinical Psychology*, 34:850–857, 1978.
49. Pfeffer, C. R. Clinical observations of play of hospitalized suicidal children. *Suicide and Life Threatening Behavior*, 9:235–244, 1979.

14

Youth Suicide

Michael Peck

Each year, in the United States, more than 5000 young people aged 24 and under commit suicide. It is suspected that these official figures are an understatement and that the actual numbers are much higher. For 15-24-year-olds, suicide is now the third leading cause of death, preceded only by accidents and homicides. Among white male youths, suicide is the second leading cause of death. Before 1965, the suicide rates in the United States and in much of the world increased directly with age. Thus, the lowest suicide rates were among the young; moderate suicide rates were among those in their middle years; and the highest suicide rates were among those in their older years (1). In the late 1960s, the suicide rate among young people began increasing. These increases, which have continued until the present, changed those earlier relationships. Suicide rates now generally increase rapidly in the teen years, reaching a peak sometime in the 1920s; taper off and drop slightly in the 1930s and 1940s, and then go up higher again in the 1960s and 1970s (2). As one can see by Fig. 1, the relative rate of increase and decrease by age varies also by race and sex.

From the years 1961 through 1975, suicide rates among 15-24-year-olds increased 131 percent, while the suicide rate of the population as a whole increased only 22 percent (3). Even the very young, those 14 and under, showed a dramatic rise of 150 percent during this period. Holinger (3) points out that the suicide rate of young men in the United States in the 15-24 age group was four times higher than the rate for female youngsters, and the suicide rate for whites was consistently higher than that of blacks and other nonwhites. This is in contrast to an earlier finding in California (4, p. 40) showing suicide rates among female youngsters rapidly approaching those among male youngsters, while suicide rates of young blacks were as high or higher than those of white youths. More recent data appear to suggest that the rise in suicide rates for youth was a short-lived phenomena of the early 1970s and that suicide rates of female youngsters and nonwhite youth are again lower. A recent finding by this author (5) suggests that the suicide rate of young Hispanics in the Los Angeles area is considerably lower than that of the black or white youth population. It would appear that the rate is less than one-half that of the other ethnic populations in Los Angeles County. If, in fact, for whatever reason, young Hispanics have a lower suicide rate than the general population in the United States, then this would artificially decrease the suicide rate of the white

Reprinted from *Death Education*, 6:29–47, 1982. Copyright © 1982 by Hemisphere Publishing Corporation.

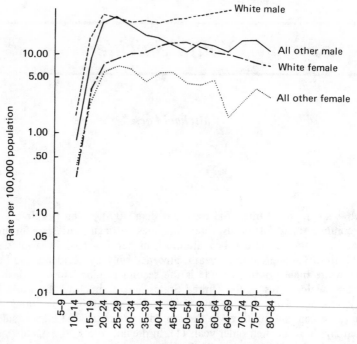

Figure 1   Suicide rates by age, color, and sex: United States, 1977.

Anglo population in the United States. This is because the more than 20 million Hispanics in the United States are not counted as a separate ethnic group as far as vital statistics mortality data are concerned, although Hispanics are designated separately in census data. It is possible, therefore, that if Hispanic suicides were identified separately in the mortality statistics, the suicide rate of young, white Anglos would appear even higher.

It is likely, based on the clinical observations and research of many suicidologists, that people who commit suicide and who threaten and attempt suicide come from two different populations. At best, they are on some continuum separated by a quantitative distance of lethality and desperation. Suicide attempters and threat- eners represent a considerably larger group than those that actually commit suicide. For example, the total number of committed suicides in the United States, among those age 24 and under, is probably close to 5000. The ratio of those who attempt suicide to those who commit it appears, both from clinical and research observa- tion, to be much higher for young people than for older people. For people in general and those in the older age group, that ratio is probably somewhere between 5:1 and 10:1; for adolescents it may be as high as 25:1 or 50:1. It is possible that there are as many as 250,000 suicide attempters in the United States each year under the age of 25. In addition, there are larger numbers of people who never attempt suicide but think about it and talk about it. The ratio here is unknown, but is is safe to say that *each year*, in the United States, for this age population, around a million or more children move in and out of suicidal crises, thoughts, ideations, episodes, and so on. We do know that, whereas male youth commit suicide two to three times as often as female youth, in attempted suicides, the sex ratio is reversed. Many more adolescent girls than boys attempt suicide.

With increased suicide deaths come increased suicide attempts. There are more youngsters thinking, obsessing, and worrying about suicide than ever before (6). The author's own observations and surveys (7) suggest that up to 10 percent of the youngsters in any public school classroom may be considered at some risk for suicide.

This might seem like a startling statistic. It means that, in the average high school or junior high school of 2000 or 3000 students, as many as 200 or 300 students may be walking around with suicide on their minds. The potential not only for disaster but for a wide-ranging impact on teachers, family, and friends is enormous. In addition, the students become nonfunctional; their grades become poor; relationships with friends and parents become poor; and they may suffer emotional setbacks and require a very long rehabilitation process.

How is it that such a large number of youngsters become suicidal? There are two factors involved: (a) the tendency in general for the rise in youth suicide, unhappiness, and self-destructive equivalents and (b) a factor discussed by Litman (8) that centers on the concept of suicide zones. People move in and out of periods of suicidal risk, ideation, and thought, some for very brief periods, some for moderate or long periods. During this time suicide is on their minds, and they are at risk for suicide. It is likely that the 10 percent of youngsters in the classroom that have suicide on their minds fit this description. Some of the youngsters move out of periods of unhappiness rather rapidly; others linger longer, while new people move into that zone. With this increase of suicidal activity, there must be a concomitant increase in worry, upset, confusion, and disruption in the lives of the family, friends, schools, and other institutions closely associated with these youthful suicides.

ANALYSIS OF THE INCREASE

The problem that behavioral scientists interested in the youth culture and self-destructive behavior are faced with is to understand various trends among young people and various factors in the youth culture that contribute to an increase in self-destructive behavior. A number of complex variables may have contributed to the increase of youth suicide in the last 15–20 years. Peck and Litman (2) relate the population explosion of the late 1940s and early fifties to the youth suicide phenomenon. Children born between 1950 and 1955 passed through their teens and early 20s during the period the suicide rate was rising most rapidly. The population in this age group was higher than it had ever been before and was certainly out of proportion to other age groups in size. It is possible that an overcrowding phenomenon occurred in this generation that resulted in too many young people wanting too many things that were not available, contributing to an increased feeling of anonymity and alienation.

Coleman (9) refers to the same phenomenon, the postwar baby boom, which he believes weakened family ties and accelerated a breakdown in family relationships. This resulted, according to Coleman, in a greater problem of emotional identity among youth and a trend to greater isolation.

Many social changes occurred among youth in the middle-to-late 1960s and early

1970s that appeared to be dramatic departures from the past. These included greater activism, particularly in the antiwar movement; an increase in youngsters dropping out of both school and society; and a dramatic rise in the use of drugs and, more recently, alcohol. The mid-1970s also saw a dramatic increase in crime committed by young people. It may be that some of the variables that contributed to the increase in suicide rates. The author has observed (5) that many suicidal youngsters abuse alcohol and drugs and become involved in criminal activities as a defensive system and coping mechanism against their unhappiness and depression. The increase in these kinds of youngsters who become suicidal may, in part, account for some of the increase in suicide from the early 1960s to the early and middle 1970s.

Hendin (10) has described much of the behavior among young people as a flight away from emotional commitment or depth of feelings. In talking about the problems young women face, he states:

> More and more young women today see life as fatal to the woman who is not inpenetrably cool. The women students I saw are determined to be overwhelmed by experience, but in the search for the antidote to emotion, they often find they have killed their power to care deeply for anyone. (p. 354)

In describing the young men that he studied, Hendin goes on to say:

> Nothing distinguishes this generation of young men more than the degree to which they are irresistibly drawn to killing feelings as a means of survival. Working at making life not matter may be intended simply to remove the depressions, the hurts, the angers that afflict, leaving only the better emotions, yet the habit of detachment, once acquired, leads inevitably to a general numbing in the face of all experience. Belittling people to cut down their importance, attempting to control the flow of experience, concentrating only on one's personal gratification without any concern for anyone elses, are defensive maneuvers that inescapably squeeze the juice out of life. (p. 354)

Certainly, in this description, there is a clear sense of isolation, alienation, and meaninglessness that correlates highly with suicide.

Another way of trying to understand the increase in suicide among the young comes from Weisman (11) and Solomon and Hellon (12). Solomon and Hellon pointed out that—when we consider that the risk for committed suicide is high among suicide attempters, particularly in the first two years following the suicide attempt—then as more young people who are attempting suicide enter high-risk suicide ages, the result could be a higher suicide rate. Solomon and Hellon continue that their own data of attempted and completed suicide suggest that people who commit suicide are younger than in the past, and that to the extent the suicide committers and suicide attempters resemble each other in age, the risk of completed suicide increases.

One explanation for the tendency for youngsters to be attempting and committing suicide at younger and younger ages has been put forward by Ishii (13). He suggests that the data indicate that youth suicide is primarily a phenomenon associated with postpuberty and that, in fact, the age of puberty has been dropping by approximately 1 year every 10 years. Ishii, therefore, reasons that it would be understandable that suicidal youngsters should be getting younger and younger.

A number of other factors of importance have been discussed by a variety of researchers. Farberow (14) reviews some of these major factors:

1. The previous history of suicide attempts or threats were significant in determining the outcome of current suicidal behavior.

2. Depression characterized by sleep disturbance, eating disturbance, trouble with concentration, and tiring easily are frequently identified as important factors.

3. A disturbed relationship with parents was crucial, as was frequent quarreling and actual physical assaultive behavior between parents and children. Family alcoholism was another factor mentioned, as was loss or threatened loss of a parent or a love relationship. Withdrawal and isolation, accompanied by poor interrelationships, were among the most frequently mentioned social characteristics related to youth suicide.

One of the earliest discussions of social isolation and withdrawal in relation to youth suicide was by Jan-Tauch (15) in a study of New Jersey school children who had committed suicide. He reported that the youngsters had no close friends with whom they might share problems or receive psychological support. He also observed that differences between those who attempted suicide and those who committed suicide centered on the former having had a close relationship that played some role in their rescue. Schrut (16) pointed out that, if the history of the youngster is one of progressive or continued isolation in early childhood, the prognosis for suicide is more serious than if the history includes the ability to have some relationships, at least early in college. Peck and Schrut (17), in studying a sample of college students suicides, described the students who committed suicide as being more hopeless, more isolated, and less likely to communicate to others that they need help.

The author has observed some shifts in the clinical population in the last 15–20 years, that, on some reflection, may well be related to increases in youth suicide. While most people generally expect suicidal behavior to be linked with frustrations, hurts, and losses, as in fact it often is, a surprisingly large amount of suicidal behavior, in particular among adolescents, tends to be linked with a lifestyle that can best be described as without goals, direction, or substance. The youngster grows up with little clear-cut guidance, confused or absent values, and a sense of floating along in time without direction. Clinical observations suggest that this kind of syndrome, which is frequently described in the psychiatric literature as a borderline personality disorder, has increased in the last 15 years.

One of the factors that may be associated with the increase centers around the value of the home, the family, and parenting. Many adolescents who have experienced traumatic divorces and separations in their families describe what might best be called a narcissistic do-your-own-thing upsurge among parents. That was almost unheard of in previous generations. The 13-year-old who is told by his father that he is leaving the family and getting a divorce because he has to "do his own thing" or find himself experiencing the father's revelation as clear-cut rejection. What it feels like to the 13-year-old is that his father is being even more irresponsible than he is, while *he* is being told to grow up rapidly. This scene is being repeated by mothers and fathers more frequently today than in previous generations, and the impact on the children is often devastating. In addition to the trauma of divorce, the general narcissism and self-obsession that has infiltrated the American family has really communicated to the youngster, "I come first; I have to take care of all my needs and pleasures, and then if I have some time and energy left over, I'll try to teach you how to grow up." These characteristics, at least in a clinical sense, may well contribute to the rising total of adolescent suicides.

SOME PSYCHODYNAMIC OBSERVATIONS

According to this author's work (5, 7), children who commit suicide find that their efforts to express their feelings of unhappiness, frustration, or failure are totally unacceptable to their parents. Such feelings are ignored or denied, or they are met by defensive hostility. Such a response often drives the child into further isolation, reinforced by the feeling that something is terribly wrong with him.

The author found certain specific, clear-cut differences at the Los Angeles Suicide Prevention Center between the committed-suicide group and the other groups of suicidal adolescents. Greater frequency of psychiatric hospitalization, combined with a higher rating of emotional disturbance and fewer prior suicide attempts, marked the history of the adolescents who committed suicide. These findings suggest a higher incidence of diagnosed psychotic disorders in the committed group compared with the other groups.

From work done at the center, there is some clinical evidence that a suicidal person who is also diagnosed as psychotic is a higher suicide risk than a suicidal person not so diagnosed. There is evidence that the adolescent who commits suicide has a greater predisposition toward self-destruction and therefore requires less overt stress than his colleagues to initiate the suicide act. This evidence was confirmed in some degree by the fact that the loss or threatened loss of a loved one operated less often as the precipitating stress or "trigger" among those in the committed-suicide group than it did in the attempts of those in the suicidal groups. While this particular example may be an artifact of other data (e.g., those in the committed-suicide group are more likely not to have a loved one to begin with), stress was reported to be higher among persons who attempted suicide. The reaction of the latter groups was to communicate their suicidal intent openly—verbally or behaviorally—to let others know the psychologic pain they were experiencing, and thus ultimately to reduce the stress they were feeling.

The author's previous work continues:

> The psychodynamics of the adolescents who attempted suicide differed, in relation to their childhood experiences with their parents, from those of adolescents who committed suicide. Attempters may have seen their parents as being unresponsive to their needs rather than as denying their needs and may have used their parents as fantasized projections of themselves to the extent that they would become unconscious projections of their parents. The parents of the suicide attempters were seen as more passive and as having relatively little in the way of concrete goals for their children. These parents tend simply not to respond supportively or enthusiastically to the success or failure of their child.

Although there are many ways to view adolescent suicide, at the center we have found it useful to attempt to group suicidal adolescents by the way they present themselves in relation to certain kinds of activities. Such things as the nature of their relationships, major impairment in functioning, and certain life events form the basis for these groups. In developing these categories, we have decided to overlap the most traditional of all categories, that of suicide attempt and suicide ideation on the one hand, and committed suicide on the other. The distinctions between the traditional categories are, of course, still useful and meaningful, but they do not form a basis for categories in this analysis. These categories cut across traditional diagnostic categories.

CATEGORIES OF YOUTH SUICIDE

The Very Young

In the age group 10-14, the actual numbers of suicide are low in comparison to older age groups. The rate has jumped by 33 percent from 1968 to 1976 (National Center for Health Statistics). To understand the psychodynamic reasons for suicide in this age group better and to help clarify some of the possible reasons for the increase in this young age group, the Los Angeles Suicide Prevention Center engaged in a pilot study reviewing 14 suicide deaths that had occurred between the years 1975 and 1978 with victims under the age of 14. Before this study, we had observed that many youngsters in this age group had suicidal ideation centering on the loss or fantasized loss of a parent and the expressed wish to die to join the parent (7). The most outstanding thing that we were able to learn in this more recent study was that 50 percent of the 14 cases had been diagnosed as having a learning disability. The actual diagnoses that were mentioned were hyperactivity, perceptual disorder, and dyslexia. The surprising aspect of this is that, in most school districts, the actual percentage of this is that, in most school districts, the actual percentage of youngsters labeled "learning disabled" is below 5 percent (17), although some estimates go as high as 7 or 8 percent. The suggestion, therefore, is that the process of being "learning disabled" may bring with it such extreme feelings of loss of self-esteem as to place rather young children in an at-risk category for suicide.

A typical case example of a youngster in this category is that of 12-year-old Donald, the youngest of three children, living in an intact family in a middle-class neighborhood in Southern California. Donald was a sixth grader with a history of inability to relate to peers and equally poor relationships with adults. In the third grade, Donald was diagnosed by the school as "hyper-kinetic" and was placed on Ritalin and treated in a special program within the school. That helped somewhat with his wild, disruptive behaviors, but his attention span was still poor. Donald was described as having a poor frustration level, and when annoyed or bothered by his peers, he would physically lash out in anger. From the third grade on, he was teased by his peers for his poor temper control, his sloppy habits, and his lack of coordination. At age 11, he expressed over and over again his feelings of unhappiness and his wish not to continue living. After similar continuing frustrations, he hanged himself on a tree in his backyard. Although Donald had received considerable attention by significant others and school authorities for his learning disability and his disruptive behavior, there was little attention paid to his painful unhappiness. This suicidal type includes large numbers of youngsters who threaten, attempt, and think about suicide, as well as those who commit suicide.

The implications of these findings for parents, teachers, and any other people who work with youngsters are most important. The first and most vital issue centers on the fact that youngsters as young as age 9 and 10 can, and do, commit suicide. These very young people enter into periods or episodes of suicide and threaten and attempt suicide. These are very real dangers and need to be taken seriously. Further implications suggest that there are particular kinds of characteristics that are linked with higher vulnerability to suicide in this young age group. It is of great importance that parents and those of us who work with young people pay particular attention to youngsters who have recently lost a parent and to youngsters who suffer from learning disabilities. That they are at greater risk for suicide is becoming more and more apparent.

The Loner

The "loner personality type" begins to emerge at age 14 and 15 and has been described in our previous studies as fitting a clear-cut symptom pattern (2, 17). Characteristics associated with this kind of person center around loneliness, isolation, lack of friends, and poor interpersonal communication with peers and parents. Most often, youngsters who are described as "loners" come from intact families with relatively normal parents. From close analysis of these families, it appears as though the parents have some difficulty with their image of themselves as parents and are constantly concerned about making mistakes and not being good parents. They interpret their child's complaints about problems, unhappiness, or general life difficulties as a statement of their lack of competence; therefore, in a defensive gesture, they often insist to the child that he really is not unhappy or really has nothing to complain about. In these families the child usually learns at an early age that what he thinks of himself and what his parents think of him are different, and he comes to distrust his own thoughts and feelings. His solution is often not to communicate this unhappy thoughts and feelings to anyone. This builds up in the later teens to a youngster with a high potential for suicide.

This type can be illustrated by presenting the case of Art. Art was a 17-year-old white youth who lived at home with his mother and father and older sister. He was a senior in high school, where he did not distinguish himself with either grades or extracurricular activities. Art had no friends with whom he would spend evenings, afternoons, or weekends with outside of school. He was very much afraid of girls and felt too shy to talk to them. Although he was urged to attend college away from home by his parents, he was terrified by the thought. His parents, on the other hand, genuinely believed Art had many friends and many interests in and out of school and that he was looking forward to going away to college. His acquaintances in school had no idea why he would take his own life, and one of his teacher's comment about him was that she could not remember what he looked like. It seems safe to assume that Art's isolation reached the point where he could not share his fears, unhappiness, and the terror of growing up into an unknown world. He felt he was not suited to the task and that he never would be. His sense of hopelessness was a major variable in his shooting himself with his father's gun two weeks before his 18th birthday.

Unlike most of the other categories, the "loner" represents a kind of suicide in which suicide deaths may occur with relatively greater frequency than suicide attempts. This may be related to the paucity of clues emitted by this group. The "loner" is most commonly diagnosed as a schizoid personality, in a borderline state, depressive-reactive, or—nonclinically—most often as "shy."

Those Who Act Out Depression

Suicidal thoughts and attempts are most common among those who act out depression. The number of youngsters that fit this category appears to have begun increasing in the early 1970s and the category was introduced by us in an earlier paper (2). The increase in suicide in this group may, in fact, largely account for the increase in suicide in general among young people. Although there still may be more white male youth in this group, there are a larger proportion of ethnic groups and female youth than in the aforementioned categories. These youngsters are characterized primarily by behaviors that are seen by others as illegal, dangerous, disruptive, harmful, or hostile. The major symptoms represented by people in this category are drug and alcohol abuse; running away; petty crimes like shoplifting and joyriding; assaultive behaviors, frequently with family members; and occasionally, serious violence.

Psychodynamically, these youngsters most often experience, in their early teens, surges of depressive feelings that they are unable to understand, explain, or cope with. They often experience and interpret these feelings as painful boredom; and frequently, through role models in their nuclear or extended families, they decide the most effective way to cope with these feelings is through some form of action. The action, which often includes substance abuse, typically helps them get through the most difficult part. They keeping doing it as long as it works. Often these people get in trouble, however, particularly with the authorities. The authorities tend to treat them as delinquents rather than as depressed youngsters, which adds to their sense of despair. These children often come from broken homes, where chaos, inconsistency, and substance abuse are not uncommon. Learning to use alcohol and drugs as a solution to their problems is very frequently something that comes directly from a parent or older siblings.

A case in point is Linda. Linda began treatment at age 17, at which time she was heavily addicted to barbiturates, Quaaludes, and alcohol. Her mother and father had been divorced since she was 9, and her two stepfathers would frequently beat her, her mother, and the other two children. On one occasion, at age 13, the stepfather sexually molested her in front of her mother, who was too drunk to do anything about it. She began using pills at 14 and dropped out of school at 15, when she was too "stoned" to function. Linda made her first suicide attempt at age 16, was found quite by accident, and was rescued. Most of her peer relationship choices were extremely harmful to her and would often lead to her feeling overwhelming pain and despair, which would be followed by larger amounts of pills and alcohol. After a suicide attempt at age 19, she remained in the hospital until she was detoxified and then joined Alcoholics Anonymous. When she was really free from drugs and alcohol and had a clear sensorium, the degree of severe emotional pain she had been suffering became most obvious, both to Linda and to the therapist. At that point, however, her depression could be dealt with directly, and with some success. Young people in this group are frequently misdiagnosed as cases of sociopathic character disorder, when in fact, they are depressed.

The Psychotic Suicide

The psychotic suicide category of youth suicide is somewhat smaller in numbers than the others. These youngsters are very difficult to work with therapeutically and have a most guarded prognosis. The symptom picture often includes delusions, hallucinations, and occasionally, direct messages from voices to kill themselves. Much of the fantasy and some of the behavior of these youngsters would be considered violent and, occasionally, bizarre. The suicidal behavior itself is often bizarre.

These youngsters most often come from single-parent families or at least families in which only one parent is psychologically present. Occasionally, the parents are grossly psychotic, alcoholic, or both. Sometimes, the behavior patterns are quite varied and they resemble other categories of suicidal youngsters, but the decision to place the youngster in the particular category of the psychotic suicide is determined by the bizarre symptomatology combined with suicidal behavior.

An example of this kind of profile is that of Laura, a 16-year-old girl, who had made nine suicide attempts since the age of 14. In each case, the suicide attempt was of low lethality. In each case, the mother, who had raised Laura herself when she was not residing at the local state hospital, queried Laura as to why she had done that and always accepted Laura's bizarre answers. Her answers included: "Because I wanted a new hairdo and you wouldn't let me have it," or "My eyeglass frames are ugly," or "You don't let me wear lipstick," or something in a similar vein. Finally, Laura made a suicide attempt that included the ingestion of ground glass and then running away. When she was finally located and hospitalized, the juvenile authorities entered the case and arranged for Laura's hospitalization and placement out of her mother's reach.

The Crisis Suicide

Youngsters who evidence suicidal behaviors and symptoms who fit into the crisis category probably represent less than 15 percent of all suicidal youngsters. The major findings among these kinds is that there is an apparently normal premorbid personality, no history of severe emotional trauma, and a reasonably stable family pattern. A typical pattern is that an adolescent reaches a point in his or her life where he or she becomes aware of, or has inflicted on her or him, sudden traumatic changes. The changes may include the loss of a loved one or the loss or threatened loss of status in school, through academic or athletic failure. Subsequently, the youngster undergoes sudden and dramatic changes in behavior that may include loss of interest in things that were previously important; sudden hostile and aggressive rejecting behaviors in a previously placid youngster, or signs of confusion and disorganization. There is typically an inability to concentrate and frequently a series of classical depressive symptoms.

An illustration of this kind of case is that of John, an 18-year-old youth who was a center fielder on his high school baseball team. The expectation that he had of himself, and that his friends had of him, was that his senior year would be an outstanding one, that he would be an all-city baseball player and sign a pro contract. Instead, he had just an average year, hit under 300, and performed no outstanding feats. Not only did he not make all-city; he was not even invited to any professional baseball team training camps. While John was struggling with feelings of despair related to this major failure in his life, his girlfriend told him that she no longer wanted to go steady and thought it was time that they each started dating others. John immediately went into a severe depressive crisis, began talking about suicide and making suicide threats, and stopped going to school. He had difficulty eating and sleeping and, for all practical purposes, became nonfunctional. The depression lasted three weeks, during which time intensive crisis therapy and support by his family prevented a suicide attempt. His own emotional resources were shored up, and this eventually led to a remission of symptoms and a return to normal functioning. These suicidal young people are typically diagnosed as reactive depressions.

Those Whose Suicidal Behavior
Is a Form of Communication

The final category, those for whom communication is a major factor in their suicidal behavior, focuses on a rather large number of suicide attempters and threateners. It is a much less frequent category when examining suicide deaths. In these cases, the person becomes suicidal when more common avenues of expression of frustrated feelings become blocked, interrupted, and stymied. This is not to say that the young suicidal person who is communicating through suicidal behavior is doing so in a calm, rational manner. The experience of the person is usually one of desperation, unhappiness, and great upset. But the lethality of the behavior is almost always low. The ultimate purpose of the behavior, in a posthoc analysis, seems to be to clear the way, to open up, to break through the barriers, so that the significant others will know how desperate or how unhappy the person feels. This represents the classical "cry for help." This suicidal youngster does not necessarily have a history of severe disturbance or prior suicidal episodes, although they may be present.

A typical case illustration is as follows: Barbara is a 15-year-old girl entering high school, who swallowed a handful of medicine-cabinet pills, in the presence of her parents. After she was treated medically and received the physician's recommendation that she get help, her stepfather brought her to a therapist. After considerable inquiry and probing, the girl broke down sobbing. She stated that what was troubling her was the fact that her mother was terminally ill, and the whole family had long ago decided that no one was allowed to talk about it. She was frightened that her mother would soon die and also frightened that her stepfather would not have her live with him after her mother died. She feared she would have no place to go, and didn't even know how to discuss it with anyone. The therapist, in spite of the stepfather's resistance, opened up the entire issue with the mother, the daughter, and the stepfather, forcing a resolution and forcing the subject to be discussed openly. The girl's suicidal symptoms quickly abated and did not even return after her mother's death, although she required additional therapy to deal with her grief. It was clear, in understanding this particular case, that suicidal behavior occurred to her as a measure of her desperation; but the goal, in a functional way, was to open up the lines of communication.

Although suicidal communications that have as a goal to change the nature of relationships between people and open up lines of communication are often of low lethality, there is no question that fatalities can also occur, even though sometimes by accident. These kinds of behaviors frequently occur in troubled families or in relationships where serious difficulties are emerging but have not been dealt with. The most important result of the suicidal behavior is for every to recognize that serious trouble has occurred and that communication must be opened up and remedies need to be proposed. Often, this kind of low-lethality suicide behavior is met by defensive hostility on the part of parents or significant others. Statements such as "He really didn't mean to do it," or "All she wanted was attention," or "He's just trying to manipulate me to get his own way" are not uncommon from parents of adolescents who have made a suicide gesture. They reflect on the insecurity, anger, and helplessness of the family member who has just experienced suicidal behavior of a child and are meant somehow to minimize and defuse the situation by implying it is not important or dangerous. The helping professional must be acutely aware of this kind of parental reaction and be ready to intervene actively, because, where this attitude is allowed to persist, the suicide risk increases, and the next suicide attempt by the youngster would be more lethal.

CONCLUSION

This attempt to look at youth suicide from a different point of view has as one goal to make current intervention and treatment approaches more efficient. Identifying a suicidal youngster and then connecting with that youngster in a therapeutic manner represents one of the major ways of saving lives. Those at the center hope their current efforts will serve to promote this end.

REFERENCES

1. Seiden, R. Suicide among youth: A review of the literature, 1900–1967. *Bulletin of Suicidology*, 1969, December supp.
2. Peck, M. L. & Litman, R. E. Current trends in youthful suicide. In J. Bush (ed.), *Suicide and blacks*, Fanon Research and Development Center, 1975, pp. 13–27.
3. Holinger, P. C. Adolescent suicide: An epidemiological study of recent trends. *American Journal of Psychiatry*, 103:416–422, 1978.
4. Allen, N. H. *Suicide in California, 1960–1970* (State of California, Department of Public Health Monograph). Sacramento, State of California, 1973.
5. Peck, M. L. *Suicide consultation in the schools*. Book in preparation, 1980.
6. Howze, B. *A Cross Cultural Approach to the Study of Predisposing Characteristics to Suicide in a Group of Urban Detroit Youth*. Unpublished manuscript, 1979.
7. Peck, M. L. Categories of adolescent suicide differentiated. *Roche report: Frontiers of psychiatry*. World Wide Medical Press, 1980, in press.
8. Litman, R. E. Personal communication, 1976.
9. Coleman, J. S. *Science*, 182:141–145, 1973.
10. Hendin, H. *The age of sensation*. New York: Norton, 1975.
11. Weisman, M. M. The epidemiology of suicide attempts, 1960–1971. *Archives of General Psychiatry*, 30:737–746, 1974.
12. Solomon, M. I. & Hellon, C. P. Suicide and age in Alberta, Canada, 1951 to 1977. *Archives of General Psychiatry*, 37:511–513, 1980.
13. Ishii, K. Adolescent self-destructive behaviors and crisis intervention in Japan. *Journal of Suicide & Life Threatening Behavior*, in press.
14. Farberow, N. L. Adolescent suicide. In Golombek (ed.), *The adolescent and mood disorders*, in press.
15. Jan-Tauch, Studies of children, 1960–1963. In *New Jersey Public School Studies*. Trenton: State of New Jersey, Department of Education, 1963.
16. Schrut, A. Suicidal adolescents and children. *JAMA*, 188:1103–1107, 1964.
17. Peck, M. L. & Schrut, A. Suicidal behavior among college students. *HSMHA Health Reports*, 86:149–156, 1971.
18. Lerner, J. W. *Children with learning disabilities* (2nd ed.). Boston: Houghton Mifflin, 1976.

V

DEATH EDUCATION

Education is essentially another mode, along with caregiving and counseling, of constructive human interaction with children. When we teach, support, or treat children, we merely employ different ways of serving the same primary purpose of maximizing their well being and quality of life. Thus the fundamental principles that have been seen in the foregoing parts of this book apply also when we turn to more specific educational contexts. Furthermore, with appropriate adaptations, these principles can be expected to apply to healthy children just as they do to dying or bereaved children. That is, children do not stop being children when they encounter dying or mourning. If we believe that they should be helped in the latter situations to deal constructively with death, then there is every reason to do likewise before such situations arise. In fact, to incorporate death-related education within the general process of nurturing and educating children is the best preparation for meeting particular problems. More important, it is a necessary part of preparation for dealing with life in all of its aspects. For death is a part of life; encounters with limitation and loss occur through living and, when properly handled, they can be indispensable opportunities for growth and maturation in children.

In this section, we address three major educational contexts: the home, pre-school and elementary school settings, and secondary schools. This runs the gamut from birth through colleges and universities. Our authors—Joan McNeil, Ute Carson, and Darrell and Dixie Crase—draw upon personal experiences, formal research, and relevant literature to identify and to demonstrate how we might satisfy needs and interests that children in these settings have for death-related education. The unifying aim is to show where opportunities exist and how our responsibilities might be met. In each case, there is an awareness of the role of developmental factors and of the impact of environment in regard to death-related thoughts and feelings in children. Only on that basis, as these authors realize, can one lay out a program of practical pedagogy, whether of a formal or informal nature. Teaching children about death is both desirable and feasible with this preparation and with some forethought. The chapters in this section set out the groundwork for that task.

All of our authors agree with Erna Furman's remark (p. 201) that children will benefit from being given a chance to develop their mental "muscles" in more or less "safe" encounters with death before they are required to deal with more powerful and demanding experiences. The normal course of everyday events usually provides such opportunities; our task is to exploit their constructive potential. This beings in the ongoing socialization processes within the home. Joan McNeil recognizes these fundamental and many-sided modes of interaction and locates them in the context of communication within family systems. This means that whether or not we acknoeldge it, adults *are* already teaching children lessons about death, just as life does without first asking our permission. In fact, however, McNeil's own research suggests that more parents than might be expected are aware of death as a topic of concern in children, do recognize their role in teaching about this aspect of life, and are appreciative of guidance in fulfilling that duty. Such positive attitudes together with obvious failings and deficiencies in many adult interactions with children, are all the more reason to marshal resources and to draw up guidelines for improving death-related education. McNeil is aware that her research is a limited initial inquiry into this subject and that there is no single "right" way to teach children about death. But she points us in the proper direction and her call for aiding parents in this area is well put.

In quite a different way, Ute Carson sketches a program of death education for pre-school and elementary children based on teachable moments occasioned by "small deaths." At this level and in the home, the most appropriate forms of education are those which emerge naturally from life events. We need not merely blunder into such events; our actions can influence their character and likelihood. But however they arise, we will do well to seize upon them in ways that are attractively modeled in Carson's vignettes. The range of these vignettes is particularly noteworthy: from fairy tales and stories, through plants, animals, and pets, to creative literature and human death they reflect the diversity within the worlds of children. Carson wisely respects the value of temporary denials, the uniqueness of individual development, the truth (if not the reality) of fantasy, and the expressiveness of an attentive silence. By sharing words, actions, and pictures of children, she confirms our conviction that death education is a cooperature project in which children can help themselves and their adult supporters. This applies to the sad times as well as to the happy moments of life, and it is one reason why constructive death education is a healthy, rather than morbid, undertaking.

When we turn to older children, these principles and practices are not abandoned, but it seems proper to shift our emphases somewhat to more formal or structured forms of death education. In Chapter 17, Darrell and Dixie Crase offer a rationale for death education at the secondary school level, which envisions close cooperation among educators, parents, and society, as well as among teachers, counselors, and administrators within the school system. Their aim is not to preempt responsible roles of those outside the schools, nor to burden overworked educators with ever-increasing obligations. Rather, death education is properly a part and an extension of a curriculum that enhances life. It requires specific competencies, which the Crases set forth, and an appreciation of the audiences to which it is addressed. But, as with younger children, the goals we seek are multifaceted and they can be achieved in a variety of ways. Thus, well-prepared educators are free to exercise their creativity within a framework of accepted needs and governing principles.

15

Death Education in the Home

Parents Talk with Their Children

Joan N. McNeil

Most of the questions children ask about death make parents uncomfortable. It is often thought that there is no appropriate answer that would not be alarming or threatening to children. Therefore, the subject of death is mostly evaded entirely or fantasized. (1, p. 15)

INTRODUCTION

"I try to give realistic answers," said a father recently in a parent workshop, "but death is a subject I'd prefer to shy away from."

Other parents agreed. "I guess I do want my children to ask me about it—but I'm not sure I can make them understand," a mother confessed.

"I don't know what to say and what *not* to say," said another woman. "My daughter tends to magnify things—could my statements make her worry?"

"They ask such impossible questions!" exclaimed a third mother. "And I don't want to frighten them, or make them think death is such a big deal!"

A young father cleared his throat and frowned. "Well, isn't it?"

The group was silent for a moment then, in shared acknowledgment that death is, after all, a significant part of living, which we can neither escape nor change, and which must be dealt with at some time or other in the lives of all family members, parents and children alike.

As many writers have pointed out, any preparation for understanding and dealing with the experience of death and dying ought to begin in the home, with a helpful and natural understanding of death as a part of the life cycle (e.g., 2-5). The child's first experience with talking about and coping with death should not be upon the death of a loved person (6). Children do learn about death in many ways, and can have some ideas and concerns about it very early in life, but their attitudes are colored by what they also learn about avoidance or acceptance of this topic in the family. Kastenbaum (7) believes that how children interpret death is influenced by their developmental level, their individual personalities, their life experiences, and finally, the general pattern of communication that has been established especially with their parents.

It is this last area of influence on children, *communication with and support from parents*, on which this chapter focuses. More specifically, it considers some of the ways in which children are socialized in families to learn what is expected of them in American culture, and what families as "systems" are like, including the ways parents and children communicate in normal families and what happens when death is a topic of concern. Finally, this chapter describes a study by the author of young mothers' styles of discussing death with their children, and suggests some general guidelines for what parents need to know and how they might go about learning it.

THE SOCIALIZATION PROCESS

The key role of the family in the physical, emotional, and social well-being of the young child has long been recognized (8). From the beginning of life, what children learn is grounded in what parents teach. But the skills for this task have radically changed over the years, and at an accelerating rate. As Pickarts and Fargo (9) have pointed out, it is no longer possible for parents to concern themselves simply with their children's nutrition and general health, to see to it that they play well with their peers, and to trust they will follow in their parents' footsteps. The socialization process is far more complex today than ever before.

Today's "knowledge explosion" deeply affects children growing up in our society. They are bombarded with such a confusion of vivid and varied experiences that they cannot, without their parents' help, understand what those experiences mean or how to relate to them. Values have also become diffuse and conflicting, so that "parents must provide a clear, personal ethic to guide the child's own growing search" (9, p. 23).

It is not a new idea that the parent teaches the child, even without being aware of it. Parents are transmitters of the culture. They are the instructors and models for a vast range of attitudes, behaviors, values, and ideas that reflect both the cultural norms and their unique responses to their experience. What is somewhat new is our understanding that the *way* in which they teach has a pervasive effect not just on what children learn, but on how they view their experiences and how they use it. Grollman's statement (10, p. 6) emphasizes this point: "What is said is important, but *how* it is said has even greater bearing on whether the child will develop anxiety or fears or accept, within his capacity, the fact of death."

Social and behavioral scientists have long been interested in the effects that different child-rearing practices have in shaping a child's personality and behavior. Underlying this interest is the assumption that all parental actions, whether intentional or not, play a part in fashioning a child's potentialities (11). Researchers have attempted to identify the aspects of parental behavior that are especially influential. Three major dimensions repeatedly emerge from this research:

1. The warmth or hostility of the parent-child relationship (acceptance/rejection)
2. The control or autonomy of the disciplinary approach (restrictiveness/permissiveness)
3. The consistency or inconsistency that parents show in using discipline

The primary theme of these dimensions is the discipline process in the rearing of children. While this theme may restrict our view of the entire picture of communication and interaction in families, it does give us some clues to ideas about parenting methods. For example, Schaefer (12) explored aspects of parental discipline, suggesting children's personality traits that are associated with four combinations of types of parenting. Using some of Schaefer's concepts, Wesley Becker (13) developed a general conceptual framework for categorizing parental discipline. He suggested that it be categorized by using three dimensions: warmth/hostility, restrictiveness/permissiveness, and calm detachment/anxious emotional involvement, and that these qualities of parenting produced specific child behavior and personality characteristics. Parental warmth, openness, and calm detachment ("coolness") will be discussed further in a study of communication and death.

However important these qualities may be, as Davis has commented (14), the presence of a single factor in parent-child interaction does not predict with certainty a specific outcome in child behavior. Parental behavior is multidimensional; a parent may be warm and affectionate while also controlling and restricting the child, for example. The entire constellation or pattern of parental behavior should probably be considered for a complete understanding of the child's experiences in the family—not an easy task for the researcher. Interactions and relationships among family members are dynamic and changing entities, as well. So "what is true at one point in time may not be true at another" (15, p. 4).

Another consideration in viewing the socialization process is the individual personality of the child. This process is far from simply "teaching the right things," or inscribing on a blank slate. What the child is taught is subjected to "translation, selection, misinterpretation, substitution, and distortion—all in accordance with the emotional preoccupations and ways of thinking of his particular personality" (16, p. 85).

As the child interacts with his or her parent, in unique ways, the parent's behavior can also be seen to adapt accordingly. Clarke-Stewart's studies (17) support this view. She points out that the child's biological characteristics and reaction patterns, along with early acquired characteristics and immediate physical state, greatly influence both the effectiveness of parent behavior and the form and likelihood of that behavior. Clarke-Stewart's investigations indicate that stimulating responsive maternal behavior significantly influences the child's intellectual development, especially in the area of language; whereas in the area of social relations, the child's behavior influences the mother.

Thus, in the complementary parent-child relationship, a great deal of information about the world is processed, with the parent playing a primary role in conveying data to the young child. The child learns what the world is like from the parent through the use of language. And the parent responds to the child's reactions to the world as he or she grows by attempting to provide what the adult perceives the child needs. Watzlawick, et al. (18), in their excellent studies of human communication, have called this process the "feedback loop," in which the behavior of each person affects and is affected by the behavior of the other person. Both stability and change are necessary in such relationships, and communication is an *interaction* process, not just a one-way phenomenon from speaker (parent) to listener (child).

The complexity of such interactions within a family has only recently been recognized and explored in studies of human development. The ecology movement has made us more aware of the interdependence of all living systems, the interconnectedness of life. Observers have begun to see each family as a *system*, which functions as a "whole" with its own structure, rules and goals. It is also an entity with parts (or family members), each member behaving in a predictable relationship with one another and affecting one another's behavior. The family systems concept, as Minuchin (19) has pointed out, gives us a method for understanding many different levels of relationships.

FAMILIES AS SYSTEMS

"Every family is a miniature society," state Napier and Whitaker (20, p. 79), "a social order with its own rules, structure, leadership, language, style of living." This complexity may not be obvious to others. Outsiders may find it difficult to enter into or even to perceive patterns and relationships that have grown up over years of living together. But this history of shared experiences and the interactions that follow upon them is nevertheless real. It defines each family as a unique microcosm. Thus attention to the social dynamics of each family system is indispensable in understanding the life of the family as a whole and the behavior of its individual members.

Much of the early literature on family systems has concentrated on families with disturbed members (schizophrenics or drug-abusers), contrasting their behaviors and relationships with those of so-called "normal" families, or families without major disturbances. Minuchin (19) reminds us that this extreme contrast has produced an idealized view of the normal family as living without stress. Despite serious studies of family life, he says (p. 51) that "the myth of placid normality endures, supported by hours of two-dimensional television characters. This picture of people living in harmony, coping with social inputs without getting ruffled, and always cooperating with each other, crumbles whenever one looks at any ordinary family with its ordinary problems."

Minuchin's research and clinical work with families has shown that "normal" families, in spite of their ordinary problems, do tend to handle real conflict well enough to maintain stability, are adaptable to changes, and allow their children to develop autonomy, competence, and interests outside the family. Another researcher, Blum (21) described what he called "excellent families," in which there is freedom to be oneself and to express innermost feelings. Such families were observed to express love and respect for those around them, both young and old. Odom and his colleagues (22) described what they called "democratic" families, which are characterized by a warm, accepting atmosphere, a high degree of communication among family members, and concern and tolerance for others. Mishler and Waxler (23), studying interaction in families, described the "normal" family's expressiveness as pervasive, with the prevailing family attitude as one of caring. There is clarity of communication in such families, personal autonomy is encouraged, and there is acknowledgment and acceptance of individual thoughts and feelings. In her summary of research on family interaction, Doane (24) found that "normal" families tend to have more flexible patterns of interacting than "disturbed" families, exhibit a greater level of harmony or closeness, and are able to function more effectively in a variety of tasks. Such families also tend to have similar values and preferences, and are actively supportive of one another.

From a Timberlawn Foundation clinical study comparing "healthy" families with those where mental illness was present, Beavers (25) describes various qualities of healthy families. The most capable families demonstrated open, direct expression of humor, tenderness, warmth, and hopefulness "to a striking degree" (p. 71). The prevailing mood of healthy families in this study was one of "warmth, affection, and caring, with a well-developed capacity for empathy" (p. 76). Beavers reports that children who had spent formative years in such a family had learned that it was safe and acceptable to talk about feelings. Although conflicts and anger were felt and expressed, there were many affectionate, loving messages. The freedom to be expressive was coupled with a sense of worth and value. Beavers emphasizes that "the ability to accept separation and loss is at the heart of all the skills of healthy family systems" (p. 69). Plainly, one of those skills is effective interaction among family members, for "healthy families communicate clearly" (p. 212).

COMMUNICATION IN FAMILIES

It seems an indisputable fact that the process of communication in families, complex though it may be, is a significant means by which parents and children influence each other's behavior. In fact, as Myers and Myers (26, p. 179) have pointed out, "we cannot *not* communicate. Interpersonal communication may not be conscious or intentional, nor successful, but it takes place." In other words, all behavior is communication.

Watzlawick and his associates (18) state that every communication has both a *content* and a *relationship* aspect. In their view, the relationship aspect, revealed through such nonverbal communications as body movements, facial expressions, and voice inflections, as well as through verbal cues, classifies the content (information) aspect, and is thus a metacommunication. In a parent-child interaction, the central functions of communication are not only to convey facts, but to offer each participant definitions of their relationship, and by implication, of themselves. Roles are defined through communication.

A very concrete way in which parents translate ideas about life and death is through their use of language. Language emerges during toddlerhood as a new tool for children in organizing experiences and for communicating inner states. As children grow, they learn to express and interpret their own needs and reactions to their surroundings, through language; while their parents influence the process of language acquisition and communication skills in a number of ways.

For example, some researchers have noted social class differences between families in the amount of verbal interaction and in the use of words. Hess and Shipman (27) report that middle-class mothers in their study were more effective teachers than were lower-class mothers. That is, they were more likely to offer explanations and specific information, to define tasks clearly, and to offer various kinds of support and help. They criticized their children as much as lower-class mothers did, but they also praised them more. Lower-class mothers had little success in teaching their children simple tasks required by the researchers. They had trouble getting ideas across because they were vague in instructions and in expectations. Furthermore, instead of encouraging their children to solve the problems, they stressed compliance and passivity, implying that the children were supposed to follow orders, unquestioningly. While other investigators have also claimed that language is used in a fundamentally different manner across social classes, careful examination of the use of language in diverse social classes suggests that these differences are only superficial. The dialect favored by lower-class persons tends to transmit the same information as that captured in the language of the middle- or upper-class person (28).

There is also research exploring the idea that parents (specifically, mothers) with high self-esteem, who value and respect themselves, have children whose emotional health is also good, and that mothers with low self-esteem tend also to have children with low self-esteem (29, 30). That mothers with high self-esteem are also good communicators, or vice versa, is indicated in these studies.

To summarize, parents evidently tend to demonstrate different skills in communicating with their children, depending on their social class and educational background, as well as their self-concept.

In addition to reflecting on the attributes of parents, one should probably also consider the task of learning language and communication skills from the child's point of view. An important theme in the functions of language for the child, according to Newman and Newman (31), is that language is more concrete, more specific, and more powerful for the child than for the adult. Children apply words to themselves in a very literal manner. Words with double meaning or words that sound similar confuse the young child. Such adult uses of language as sarcasm, punning, metaphors, or euphemisms are not easily understood by the youngster. One outcome of this characteristic of the child's language is that words can become hurtful, threatening, or destructive, as well as an essential element of the child's creative fantasy. Newman and Newman (31, p. 150) put it this way: "Words have magic. They can curse or cure, destroy or create." It is thus important for parents to clear up any misunderstandings their children may have about death-related subjects. One young mother told this story:

> *When my four-year-old told the neighbor children we're going to have a new baby, they said, "I hope it's not a boy, because a man comes along and kills all the boy babies!" They had heard this story in Sunday School, about King Herod and the Jews. My daughter cried and cried about this, until I found out and explained the facts to her. Kids do get some mistaken ideas!*

Communication habit patterns are learned early. The development of listener abilities, an important aspect of communication, was studied by Ironsmith and Whitehurst (32), who found that children have difficulty in detecting ambiguity in messages. Younger children (kindergarteners) displayed the greatest difficulty. The frequency of specific questions asked for clarification purposes increased with age (up to fourth grade), indicating that skills in listening and understanding of ideas are probably related to developmental and experiential differences. The investigators concluded that even though older children may be more capable of detecting ambiguity than younger ones, or formulating questions, they may not see the desirability of giving the speaker feedback about the adequacy of a message (or to say "I don't understand what you mean.").

A clear implication of these studies is that adults who discuss difficult or "taboo" topics like death with children must use simple, concrete terms that children can understand, and must encourage questions. Although most adults do tend to modify their speech somewhat when talking to young children, using more simplified, redundant speech patterns (33), they may find this task perplexing when dealing with a mystery they themselves do not comprehend fully. Thus they are likely to resort to ambiguities, or involved, abstract explanations, which are not only ineffective in conveying ideas to children (who are likely not to ask questions to clear up their confusion), but can also produce harmful misunderstandings. An example of this is using the word "sleep" when talking about death: "He looks like he's asleep." Children know that to sleep means to wake up, and may assume that death, too, is impermanent. Or they may assume that if they themselves go to sleep, they will die, and thus may refuse to sleep. Other adult references to "passing away," being "lost" or "expired" can confuse a child further, as Gordon and Klass point out (34, p. 27).

Farb (35) proposes that it is essentially through communication that we develop prejudices, assumptions, and outlooks on what life is like or ought to be like. But what do most parents actually want their children to believe about death?

This question was asked in a series of parent workshops (36), and the answers varied widely, as might be expected. Some parents specified that children must have *facts* ("I want them to know what death is, how it occurs, and why it is necessary"). Others emphasized *reassurance* as a theme ("I hope they can learn not be afraid or to worry about dying"). Still others insisted the focus should be *religious* in nature ("Death should be accepted as part of God's plan, as a natural end to life on earth, but there is hope in Heaven"). Many simply shook their heads at the enormity of the question, and said "I don't know what I want them to believe." Certainly these ideas vary as parents themselves differ in their beliefs, concerns, and value systems. Many may not have thought deeply about their own beliefs, and so will not appreciate their roles in communicating ideas and feelings about death to their children.

DEATH AS A TOPIC OF CONCERN

The commonness of the fear of death has been pointed out by various writers (e.g., 37, 38). Family researchers Napier and Whitaker (20, p. 89) state that "there is a greater fear in the family than the fear of losing one another, and this is the fear of immobility and stasis, which is really the fear of death. The awareness of death underlies all our experience, and this consciousness is a crucial family dynamic."

Verbally stated values (such as "I am not afraid of death") may have little to do with internalized values that dictate a person's behavior. Anxiety can also be communicated unintentionally, as Kalish (38, p. 223), observes:

To some extent, children develop their feelings regarding death from what they hear in their homes, from the tone of voice, the sentence broken off in the middle, the willingness to use the word death *instead of euphemisms, attendance at a funeral.*

Parent attitudes, then, are extremely important influences on children's understandings and concerns about death. Portz (39) interviewed three- to nine-year-old children and their mothers regarding death experiences and understandings. Age, varying kinds of experience with death, and specific approaches to presenting the meaning of death to the child, all related significantly to the child's conceptual and affective learnings about death. However, the most useful predictor of the child's reactions to the idea of death was the mother's attitude toward the child's curiosity about the meaning of death. Mothers who did *not* avoid their children's questions about death had children who showed more curiosity about the meaning of death. Where parental openness of discussion occurred, children had a more adequate death concept and relatively less separation anxiety. These children handled their anxieties over death more maturely, resorting less to the use of magical thinking and fantasy than did children not so well supported by their mothers.

"Avoidance of the topic of death on the part of parents is well intentioned," state Stillion and Wass (40, p. 210), explaining that most parents have a great need to shield their children from distressing realities of life and death. Not only their own anxieties about death, but their confusion about what to believe may prevent parents from explaining clearly what death is and what it means in our increasingly secular, technologically-based society. Gordon and Klass (34, p. 16) have noted a possible explanation for this: "Today's parents may have had no satisfactory childhood models to handle questions about death because of rapid social change, and so had no models to pass on to their children."

Communication in times of crisis is undoubtedly even more difficult for parents than handling children's day-to-day curiosity. Kingsbury (41) studied emotional responses of parents in stressful parent-child interaction situations, and categorized parents as "high withdrawing" or "high involvement." He found that "high withdrawing parents," when confronted by anxiety-producing situations (as we could assume a death experience in a family would be), tended to avoid the main issues and focus on irrelevant details, to display over-simplification in verbal explanations of the crisis, and to have difficulty separating reality from fantasy.

In another study specifically concerned with the effects of death anxiety upon communication behaviors of parents, Becker and Margolin (42) found that bereaved parents tended to insulate their young children from the painful aspects of loss, and to promote avoidance and denial of the finality of death and of feelings related to it. The small size of the sample (only nine parents were studied) indicates a need for further research of this question.

Family patterns of behavior are often reflected in the expression or suppression of feelings, especially strong emotions such as grief, according to child psychiatrist John Bowlby (43). He suggests that an important reason why some people find it difficult to express grief is that the family may be one in which the attachment behavior of children is regarded unsympathetically, and as something to be grown out of as quickly as possible. In such families, he says, to cry or otherwise to protest at separation is apt to be dubbed babyish, and anger or jealousy as reprehensible. The more children demand to be with mother or father, the more they are told that such demands are silly and unjustified; the more they cry or throw a tantrum, the more they are told they are babyish and "spoiled." Thus, when such children suffer a serious loss in their family, instead of expressing the feelings every bereaved person is filled with, they may be inclined to stifle them. And because their relatives are products of the same family culture, the person who most needs understanding and encouragement is the one least likely to receive it.

A poignant example of such unmet needs of young children in a time of shock and sorrow appears in descriptions of the thoughts and feelings of young Rufus and Catherine in James Agee's prize-winning novel, A Death in the Family (44). The children's fears, puzzlement and pain after their father's death were met with various responses by adults, but mostly with impatience or admonitions or hasty reassurances.

The whole problem of a wise approach to death in our culture is not a trivial matter, comments Edgar Jackson (45), who believes it may well be one of the major emotional concerns of our time. The ability to cope with deep feelings, to face the reality of loss, and to develop inner resources for meeting the experiences of life usually begins for children in the family.

The warm, open, and expressive family described by family specialists as "healthy," "democratic," "normal," or "excellent," appears to be more likely than the extremely inexpressive family to provide good death education on a continuous basis, as well as at a time of stress. As Kastenbaum has written (7, p. 26):

Constructive patterns of communication and support tend to pay off in crisis situations. The family that seldom takes a child's views and sensitivities seriously will find it difficult to change its ways when all are confused and frightened in the midst of a crisis.

Family communication patterns are important; and because they tend to have repeated themselves for generations, they may be most resistant to change. This is the challenge facing the death educator.

YOUNG MOTHERS' COMMUNICATION ABOUT DEATH WITH THEIR CHILDREN

Very little research has been done to show what parents actually say when their children ask about death. The prevalent view is, of course, that most American parents do not handle the death education of their children well, if they handle it at all. The assumption is that, along with questions about sex, most adults will respond to children's death-related questions with: (a) irrational fantasies (which they themselves may not believe); (b) anxiety expressed in over-protection or irritation; or (c) avoidance of the subject altogether in the belief that children are "too young to understand." Any awareness of the child's capacity to cope with death-related ideas, or of underlying worries about death, is also assumed to be lacking in the majority of parents in this society.

While there is some convincing evidence for these generalizations, their very broad nature causes some reservation, at least on this writer's part. For example, do *all* parents tell their children fairy-tales about death? Or does every adult believe the children in his or her world are unaware of death and unmoved by its mysteries? There has been a notable increase in the amount of information on death and dying poured out to the public during the past few decades; is it possible that this deluge of books, popular articles and television dramas could have escaped notice by all the parents of young children across the continent? This does seem unlikely! It seems that we might be doing an injustice to many parents, and in the process have made them feel unnecessarily guilty and defensive—which could prevent them from seeking appropriate advice on "how to talk about death," if that is our aim in offering death education opportunities.

Numerous conversations among groups of parents during the past ten years demonstrate their concern that they "do a good job" of parenting on many levels and their willingness to discuss their family experiences around the problems of life and death. Some tend to seek simple answers to complex questions, of course, but most appear to be aware that there is value in the questions and in consulting each other (as well as the "experts") for additional insights. In coming together, they find support while examining their own philosophies and the problems of parenthood, and gather the courage to help their children to deal more effectively with the real world.

In order to build a stronger conceptual basis for future death education programs for parents, and to investigate what parents really say to their children when they ask about death, a research project was designed that studied one hundred parents of young children in a five-county area of a Midwestern state (46). Although fathers are presumably key figures in families and contribute as well as mothers to the death education (or lack of it) of their children, only mothers were selected as a sample, in order to avoid the sex variable. Also, since most mothers tend to spend more time than fathers with their young children during any ordinary day, the mother-child interaction was chosen for investigation as providing more significant effect upon young children.

Generally, the study showed that the majority of women interviewed had dealt with their children's questions conscientiously, at least attempting to be aware of feelings and trying to offer clear, rational explanations. They often appeared eager to share their concerns about their children's learnings on the subject of death, although most (81 percent) admitted to feeling uneasy talking about death, and had seldom (29 percent) or only occasionally (44 percent) discussed death with family or friends. A large percentage of the sample (94 percent) had, however, experienced the death of someone close to them at some period in their lives, and 87 percent had had questions about death from their children, which indicated their strong need to discuss this subject with someone who might understand their concerns. Obviously, this interview gave them a unique opportunity to do so.

Individual Responses

Most of the subjects (81 percent) had not received or could not recall parental explanations of death when they were young, a finding similar to that of a nationwide survey (47). However, 60 percent of the sample could recall clearly their own first encounters with death when they were children, and described details of those events that were remarkably vivid, even after several decades. For example:

> A friend of my sister's was hit by a car and killed, when I was about 8 years old. I felt terribly guilty, because we wouldn't let her play with us. And I remembered the look on her face when we told her to go away, for a long, long time.
>
> I was close to my great-grandmother, who was blind. She told me that she wanted to die, and helped me understand that death wasn't so terrible, after all—although my parents thought I was too young to go to her funeral.
>
> My pet rooster died when I was about seven. I cried and cried and was mad at everybody for days.
>
> My grandfather died when I was nine or ten. Nobody explained what was wrong with him. I was terrified when we went to his funeral, because my sister and I were supposed to lay bouquets on the casket, but I was too scared to do it. I dreamed night after night that Grandpa came back, and woke up shivering and shaking.... But nobody talked to us children about it; it got about as much coverage as sex!

Obviously, the emotional impact of those childhood experiences has affected the attitudes and values of these young mothers, although precise effects are difficult to determine. However, several stated that they were determined to "help my children understand better than I did." As one mother remarked, "I don't want them to be afraid, as I have been."

Mothers in this sample have used their own early experiences with deaths of loved ones in answering their children's questions; and many of them have done so in spite of a lack of full support from their husbands. At least a third of these young women commented, with some understanding, on their husbands' inability to deal with difficult emotional issues. As one woman said, philosophically but a little sadly,

> My husband tends to hold things inside too much. I wish he'd talk about things that bother him instead of keeping them in and getting upset—but he has a fear of me think-

ing he isn't able to take care of things properly, the way a man should. It keeps him from sharing things with me and the children.

Many of the mothers in this sample have strong religious faith, as might be expected from participants in this predominantly rural area, and thus their death-related discussions with their children have often focused on interpretations of religious convictions, in addition to a frank acceptance of reality. These two themes are sometimes conflicting, however, as one mother revealed:

Since the children were at least three years old, they've asked what it means to die, where you go. I believe in being honest, with a religious viewpoint. I explained you go to Heaven, but then they asked, "How come you get put in the ground?" I tried to talk about the soul going to Heaven—but I get so tangled up! I told them I really don't know the answers. But I tried to let them know that people who die are not really gone. If you love them, they live within your heart.

Group Responses

Through the use of a set of tape-recorded Death Situations, in which a child's voice asks pertinent questions or reflects various reactions (curiosity, anger, fear, sadness, stoicism, and fantasy),[*] it was possible to sort the mothers' recorded responses into groups of both *content* and *style*, aided by judges who listened to the tapes and categorized them. However, while judges agreed very well on the type of *content* present in the women's responses (such as "religious," "factual," "philosophical," "concern for feelings," "fantasy," "avoidance," or mixtures of these), the responses were too individually inconsistent, and too widely spread across the entier sample to permit them to be placed usefully into groups.

Nevertheless, by noting the consistent patterns of types of style or relationship responses of the mothers to the Death Situations, they could be grouped according to the following simple "Communication Style" paradigm:

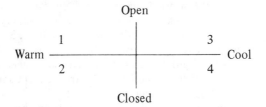

Thus, individual mothers in this study tended to use fairly consistent ways of responding to children's questions that revealed rather predictable *styles*, or methods of relating to a child, so they could be grouped under the following descriptive categories:

Style 1 ("Open-Warm") n = 26

In this group, the typical mother's first concern is the emotional content of the child's communication. She wants the child to talk about how he or she feels and what is bothersome, and listens supportively. Examples of this approach: "This

---

[*]Parent communication behaviors were expected to be influenced by the ways in which child behaviors were perceived.

really upsets you, doesn't it" or "Are you worrying about what Mom and Dad have been talking about?" She indicates her non-verbal behavior would be supportive (touching, holding the child), and while she would offer facts to set the child straight, she would state them simply and clearly, making sure the child understood and felt free to ask questions. One mother commented, "Children tend to accept what you tell them, so it's important to tell the truth. Of course, as they get older, it's not always so clear what the truth is, and it's harder to explain. But if you talk to them with love and understanding, they'll know you really care how they feel, and that's all you can do. Maybe it's enough." Another mother in the Open-Warm category was typical of this group when she stated in response to a tearful child, "I think what this child needs is just to be hugged a long, long time!"

Style 2 ("Closed-Warm") n = 11

In this group, the typical mother apparently perceives the child's emotional message first also, but reacts in an anxious way, tending to downplay realities to protect the child from difficult facts and to focus on the "positive" approach, to protect the child (and herself) from an upsetting emotional experience. She wants to make everything *right* again for everybody, and may simply avoid discussion by directing attention away from the subject at hand. A mother in the Closed-Warm category might say to a tearful child, "There now, don't cry—let me see you smile! Tell you what, you can come help me bake some cookies . . . and maybe later, Daddy will take us down and get a nice new puppy to love!" One mother told me that when her father-in-law died and her four-year-old son asked "Where's Grandpa?" she informed him that Grandpa had moved away, and was never coming back. "He's such an emotional child, I wanted to spare him," she said.

Style 3 ("Open-Cool") n = 36

In this group, the typical mother tends to focus on the child's cognitive message, perceiving her role as that of an instructor who sets the facts straight in a rational, objective manner. In the case of a pet that has died, she would point out clearly, "Yes, Captain is dead. He can't see or hear us any more. No, crying won't bring him back to life again; and the vet couldn't make him well . . . So we'll dig a grave for him in the back yard." The Open-Cool mother explains everything she can in a straightforward way, one might sometimes think in an unfeeling way, but she aims to help her child cope with the hard facts by facing them squarely. Her message might vary from religious or fanciful content to facts, such as "Grandpa's gone to Heaven to be with Jesus," or "What you see is just his body in a casket, there's no life in it." She might even say frankly, "I don't know, nobody does." While one might not always agree with the content of her replies, this mother's style is to encourage questions, and she is consistently open and honest with her child.

Style 4 ("Closed-Cool") n = 9

In this group, the typical mother is also straightforward in her answers to a child's questions, but her main concern seems to be her need to control the child's emotional reactions, and the appropriateness of his behavior. She might first make sure the rules are clear: "I know you're upset, but you mustn't let your teacher see you act like this," or "Settle down now and be good." In response to the situation about a dead pet in which the child reacted with anger and some hysteria, one Closed-Cool mother remarked, "If he was my kid, I'd give him a good smack! I can't stand tantrums!" Responding to a tearful child, this mother declared that she would leave the youngster alone, so as to learn to handle his or her own emotions. Thus she tends to avoid dealing with the real, death-related subject, as well as with the child's strong emotional responses, and strives to feel some sense of comfort in controlling the situation.

An additional "Mixed style" group ($n = 18$) was included in the categorization of subjects in this study. These were women whose style responses were inconsistent, with perhaps a clear "Open-Warm" answer in one death-related situation, and an "Open-Cool" answer in another. But this grouping was eliminated in the final analyses and comparisons of groups.

The largest of all the groups was the "Open-Cool" group (Style 3), with thirty-six of the mothers qualifying here. Second in size was the "Open-Warm" group (Style 1); third was the Mixed group (Style 5); fourth was the "Closed-Warm" group (Style 2); and smallest was the "Closed-Cool" group (Style 4). The significance of the group sizes was not explained by the data, but the voluntary nature of the sample may be primarily responsible. (Additional explanations are offered briefly below under "limitations of the study.")

What kinds of women were these? The next task, after placing them in the communication categories just described, was to try to discover some of the relevant background experiences and attitudes that might have influenced their replies. In the interviews, mothers answered questions which were later factor-analyzed for content; they also filled out four psychometric scales: the Collett-Lester Fear of Death and Dying Scale (48), the Rosenberg Self-Esteem Scale (49), a life satisfaction measure, and a parental role acceptance scale. Again, group comparisons were made so that some generalizations might be drawn about the different communication styles (Open-Warm, Closed-Warm, Open-Cool, and Closed-Cool).

One major determinant of the style categories was found to be the *type* of situation to which subjects responded. Most mothers tended to answer similarly to the "developmental" Death situations, in which a child displays simple curiosity about death. These two situations, recorded with a narrator and a child's voice, were:

Narrator: One night at bedtime, as he is being tucked in for the night, your six-year-old son suddenly asks you,
Child's voice: Are you going to die?

Narrator: While walking with your preschool daughter this morning, you come upon a dead bird lying on a neighbor's lawn. Your daughter stops and looks, then bends over to pick up the bird. As she does so, she says,
Child's voice: What's this birdie doing on the ground?

Probably due to the straightforward nature of the child's questions and the lack of emotional content of the situation, the majority of mothers gave clearly objective, factual responses. Generally, the judges categorized these answers as having an Open-Cool style with Factual content.

The remaining six situations involved deaths which were intended to be personally involving to the subjects, and which expressed emotional reactions of a child. These evoked a variety of communication styles and content. Clearly, to the degree that objectivity is a desirable characteristic of communication, it is far easier to display in situations which are not ego-involving. A related generalization is that most people are capable of, and can produce, objective responses to death if the situation is "right."

Among the five style groups of subjects (Open-Warm, Closed-Warm, Open-Cool, Closed-Cool, and Mixed), two strongly differentiating characteristics stood out. These were factors entitled "resistance to emotional discussion" and "commitment to education." They were lowest and highest, respectively, for the Open-Warm group, and highest and lowest for the Closed-Cool group and the Closed-Warm group.

An explanation of these two significant factors may be helpful here.

"Resistance to emotional discussion" described a group of interview responses that not only indicated comfort or discomfort in talking about death-related subjects, but also contained responses to questions about confiding personal feelings, worries or attitudes with husband or children, which gave a rough estimate of the mothers' patterns of self-disclosure (50). Another aspect of this factor was experience (or lack of it) in some parent education program.

"Commitment to education" described a group of interview responses having to do with experience with educational programs, both formal and informal, and the accomplishment of some amount of higher education. Mothers who were committed to the idea of education were more open and warm, perhaps because they benefited from the positive features of such programs, increasing their skills in interacting with others and broadening their understandings. On the other hand, it may be that warm and open people are more committed to education. The data were inadequate to disentangle this "chicken or egg" question.

Because there is a general consensus among authorities that both "open" and "warm" characteristics are desirable when communicating about a personally meaningful death, findings which differentiated these groups from "closed" and/or "cool" groups were of particular interest. Style groups were collapsed into groups with these particular characteristics to increase the stability of statistical estimates. The *Open* group could then be distinguished from the *Closed* group by a conglomerate of five characteristics. The *Open* group of young mothers was more committed to education, less resistant to emotional discussion, had higher self-esteem, was more accepting of the parental role, and was more experienced with death. Similarly, the *Warm* group was differentiated from the *Cool* group by displaying more commitment to education, less resistance to emotional discussion, higher self-esteem, less fear of others' dying, fewer family religious ties, and less family togetherness.

A brief explanation of each of these additional differentiating factors follows.

"Self-esteem" has often been stressed by authorities as significant in affecting social skills such as ability to communicate freely, spontaneously, and empathically (29, 49). Those persons with a less positive attitude toward themselves find communication more difficult, especially when some emotional aspect is involved. Predictably, Warm and Open groups of mothers in this study scored higher on self-esteem than did Cool and Closed groups.

"Acceptance of parental role" described attitudes toward parenting and family life which appear to define the *Closed* group of mothers as follows:

> *As adults, we have a responsibility to protect our young ones from frightening or morbid things like death (7, p. 22).*
> *When a child keeps asking questions about difficult subjects like sex or death, it is best to try to distract his attention to something else.*

The *Open* group responded negatively to those two statements, among others, and positively to such statements (51, p. 51) as:

> *Family life would be happier if parents let children feel they were free to say what they think about anything.*
> *Children should have a share in making family decisions just as the grownups do.*

"*Personal experience with death.*" Half of the Open-Warm subjects had lost at least one parent through death; Open subjects also had experienced the death of a parent more often than had Closed subjects. Perhaps experience produces understanding and dispels some fear of the unknown. That is consistent with the finding that Open and Warm mothers were less fearful of death of self and death or dying of others.

"*Family religious ties*" and "*Family togetherness.*" These two factors appeared as reversals of the expected trend, with *Warm* groups displaying *less* family togetherness and fewer family religious ties than *Cool* groups. Research in the measurement of family interaction may offer an explanation. For example, Olson, Sprinkle, and Russell (52) propose the concept of "cohesion" in families, which resembles and may be synonymous with "togetherness." Families displaying the highest degree of cohesion have more rigid rules; members tend to rely on ritual and structure as a way of defending the system against stress, and allow less opportunity for individual members to separate from the others. *Cool* mothers' families in the present study apparently fall into this category, while *Warm* mothers' families may have been more flexible, less emotionally "enmeshed" or entangled with each other, more open to change and more spontaneous in their relationships. The "family togetherness" displayed in constant sharing of all meals and all recreation in *Cool* families may also indicate high cohesion or enmeshment qualities. The strong emphasis on regular, frequent church attendance in such families can be interpreted similarly. The mothers who commented "We do absolutely everything together" or "We're extremely family-oriented" were most often found in the *Closed* groups.

Summary and Implications

To summarize the study, tentative answers to the question "How do mothers communicate with their young children about death?" can be offered on the basis of these findings:

1. At least four types of communication *styles*, and a variety of *content* types characterize young mothers who talk with their children about death. Style, or how content is communicated, appears to be the most significant way of classifying mothers in this area.

2. The patterns of communication tend to differ according to the situation. A majority of mothers react with logical, straightforward answers when children pose questions out of simple curiosity (those which lack personal involvement with death); yet they react in diverse, but relatively consistent ways when dealing with a death that is personally involving.

3. Background and personality variables related to young mothers' communication patterns are: commitment to education, resistance to emotional discussion, self-esteem, parental role acceptance (openness to family communication), personal death experience, family religious ties (or lack of), family togetherness (or lack of), fear of death of self or others, and fear of dying of others.

4. Parents *do* find the task of talking about death with their children to be a difficult one. They generally feel inadequate to provide helpful answers, and while many may prefer to "shy away" from the entire subject, they also feel a strong obligation to meet their children's needs in this sensitive area. They tend to welcome opportunities to discuss this challenge with other parents, and to acquire from knowledgeable resources some meaningful death education.

This investigation was, in every sense, a preliminary one. Limitations of the study may be found in the composition of the sample, the categorization of subjects, and the measurement of specific background and personality variables. First, the subjects were volunteers from those visiting the office of a pediatrician. The fact that they were volunteers means that they were probably more open to discussing the topic of death and children than the population at large. The fact that they visited a pediatrician's office suggests that they may be more affluent and perhaps more committed to parental responsibilities than young mothers in general. They appeared, on the whole, to be well-educated, with at least high school educations. Most lived in a Midwestern university community, or within twenty-five miles of that city in rural areas or small towns, so that cultural diversity was restricted. Although socio-economic status and race were not explicitly assessed, it appeared from husbands' occupations and education that the majority of subjects were middleclass, and only two subjects were black. Of course, the sample was limited to one sex, and to women with small children.

Second, in categorizing subjects by communication preferences, one structured system was arbitrarily selected (Open/Closed and Warm/Cool relationships). Other dimensions might also be investigated as meaningful. Validity of categories was assumed but not established, and inability to use cross-validation procedures limits the credibility of the findings.

Finally, none of the paper-and-pencil measures of attitudes was free of defects. Findings for the Collett-Lester Fear of Death and Dying Scale proved to be somewhat disappointing; however, deletion of several items improved the internal consistency of the scale. The other scales were shown to have acceptable reliability for group comparisons, but not for individual diagnosis.

The needs for further research in this area appear to be important and obvious. The present study offered considerable support to the idea that people can be meaningfully classified by their communication patterns. There is reason to believe these classifications have implications for the design and implementation of educational programs for parents. But there is a need to explore with considerable rigor the structure of communication patterns, especially in families with children. More heterogeneous samples of parents need to be investigated, with additional information gathered on background and personality variables as they relate to communication in families. More thorough and reliable measurement devices need to be created; the "Death Situation" tests used in this study appear to be promising, and even more complex versions, permitting multiple responses, should be explored. Another important need is to relate these understandings to educational challenges. There is a need to develop models of parent education which are consistent with theory and empirical results, as well as which address basic aspects of educational design.

PARENT EDUCATION

"Parents are blamed, but not trained," asserts Thomas Gordon, clinical psychologist and author of the Parent Effectiveness Training books and programs (53).

However, by becoming a parent, one automatically takes on a new function: the task of teaching. The parent teaches, as Pickarts and Fargo (9) have stressed, perhaps more significantly than those formally trained to teach. But parents are to a large extent thrown on their own resources. Generally, they do the best they can—teach what they know and translate to their children what their lives have taught them about the way things are.

The goal of parent education, according to authorities in this rapidly growing field, is to improve the quality of family life by encouraging individual decision-making, and by helping parents understand their own strengths and values so they can choose alternatives appropriate to their specific problems. Leviton and Forman (54, p. 9) have stated, "The need for death education as a part of a program of parent education is apparent. The goal would be to educate parents so that their children are reared with fewer anxieties and hang-ups than the previous generations."

What specific things do parents need to know? The literature contains a wealth of prescriptive advice to parents on the subject of death. Most well-known death educators have written articles or books containing excellent suggestions for parents to follow (cf., 1, 3, 4, 7, 10, 34, 40, 45, 54-67). A summary of their recommendations follows. A parent needs to:

1. Come to terms with her or his own thoughts and feelings about death, realizing how previous experiences may have influenced attitudes and beliefs, and what death means to her/him personally.

2. Understand the child's development in relation to knowledge and ideas about death, and respond naturally to any question the child has at any age.

3. Be aware of the child's emotional needs concerning doubts and fears about death, especially in time of loss and grief; and interpret the child's behaviors in light of those needs.

4. Practice good communication skills with the child at all times, employing complete honesty in facing facts about death, empathic and reflective listening, and warm reassurance and living acceptance.

5. Help the child to accept death as a natural part of life, with attention to beginnings and endings throughout many life experiences.

All these learnings should be incorporated into a carefully-devised program of parent education about children and death. In addition, results from the study just discussed suggest that a program for parents should be tailored as closely as possible to the needs, background experiences, and communication skills of the prospective participants, if they can be determined.

Adult education is traditionally voluntary. Therefore, one of the first tasks in creating a death education program for parents would be to plan a way to attract or recruit participants. Parents who already have good communication skills (who might be classified in the "Open-Warm" category, perhaps) will typically display interest in and commitment to education. They can be expected to be open to an invitation to take part in a special workshop or series of meetings on death education. However, special recruiting efforts may need to be made for parents who are not usually attracted to such programs, or who are less interested in or more threatened by a workshop that proposed to discuss the subject of death. Invitations would need to be personal, perhaps in the form of a phone call through agencies already familiar to the prospective participants, such as churches, schools, daycare centers, and the like. Emphasis should be made on the positive benefits of the program to each individual parent, as well as reassurance that other parents he or she knows will also attend.

In designing a program for a diverse group of parents, it would be wise to consider some of the characteristics of adult learners, as suggested by leaders in this field (e.g., 68, 69). They propose that adults who volunteer for educational programs have the following attributes:

1. They want practical solutions to specific problems.
2. They have expertise from life experiences which can be shared with others.
3. They are highly motivated to learn, but usually impatient with what they perceive as time-wasting experiences.
4. They have many distractions and other priorities which may prevent full concentration or consistent participation in a program.
5. They are self-directing in most instances, and tend to relate what they learn to their own needs.
6. Their competence in educational tasks and their self-esteem are very closely related.

The first step in presenting a death education program would be to provide some support for all parents' "inclusion" needs, as described by Schutz (70). Efforts should be made by a trained facilitator to help participants get acquainted with each other, and become comfortable with sharing experiences in the group. Each parent needs to feel that he or she is included in the group, that his or her contributions are especially worthwhile, and that he or she is accepted by others.

As part of the early informational aspect of the program, there should be recognition of the "language barrier" of death words and terminology (as discussed in 54). The degree to which the removal of the language barrier is accomplished will determine the success of any educational effort. The instructor or workshop facilitator should use such words as "death," "dying," and "dead" naturally and without undue emphasis, encouraging participants to do so and to avoid the use of popular euphemisms.

A death education program for a heterogeneous group of parents may induce more effective learning among participants if it combines didactic and experiential materials. Durlak's research (71) supports this view. He found that a death education program combining information presentations with experiential exercises in confronting and sharing personal feelings about death and dying was significantly more effective in changing attitudes than a totally didactic program.

Information can be supplied through short lectures, readings, special written assignments, field trips, panel discussions, and audio-visual presentations. Special exercises to help parents develop or improve communication skills would be a significant part of each program. As a way of provoking interest in the key issues of death education, and open sharing of ideas and concerns, "case study" stimulus exercises similar to the following have been used in many parent groups:

Case Study

Read this study aloud in your small group, and discuss the alternatives you might choose. Be sure to go over each of the questions. Then you will be asked to share your ideas with the rest of the larger group (20 minutes).

> *Your child attends a nursery school. One morning, someone comes and takes Mary Ann (one of the other children) home. The teacher informs you that Mary Ann's father was killed in an accident, and that she has not discussed the reason for Mary Ann's departure with the rest of the children. She would like the parents to talk to their own children before they return to school.*
>
> *How would you handle this situation with your child? What would you help your child to say and do when Mary Ann returns to school? Suppose you know the family— would you visit them? Or take your child to visit them? Would you take your child to the funeral? Why or why not?*

Discussions of this type of case usually tend to provoke sharing of examples from participants' personal experiences with their own children. Questions and ideas, feelings and beliefs all come freely, and help parents find support from each other as well as needed information.

An evaluation of the program would be a final, necessary step. Usually, if the events have been structured carefully, with no lags in the timing and everyone feeling "there wasn't quite enough time for everything I wanted to say!", participants will retain enthusiasm for what they have accomplished, and will tend to "spread the word" about future programs. Successful programs can build more successful programs. Of course, it is imperative that a program of this type for parents be planned and conducted by an experienced death educator. While good intentions and a certain amount of factual knowledge or teaching experience can be helpful, they may not be sufficient in dealing with this potentially sensitive topic.

In many ways, the challenge of helping parents to become better death educators is a basic goal, for we know the ability to cope with life and death issues is learned in families. So we need to help them discover the strengths they already have. And we need to ensure them that, even though they may feel inadequate at times, they *can* communicate with their children about death. There are no easy answers, of course. As Hedda Sharapan has written (67): There are no books that will do it for us and there are no magic "right" words to say. It's the trying, the sharing, and the caring—the wanting to help and the willingness to listen—that says "I care about you."

REFERENCES

1. Kastenbaum, R. The kingdom where nobody dies. *Saturday Review*, 1972, December, 15-19.
2. Peniston, H. The importance of death education in family life. *Family Coordinate*, 1962, *11*, 15-18.
3. Irish, D. Death education: Preparation for living. In B. Green and D. Irish (eds.), *Death education: Preparation for living.* Cambridge, MA: Schenkman Publishing Co., 1971.
4. Young, E. F. Preparatory understanding of death: The young child. In S. Cook (ed.), *Children and dying.* New York: Health Sciences, 1974.
5. Wass, H. and Shaak, J. Helping children understand death through literature. *Childhood Education*, 1976, *53*, (2), 80-85.
6. Furman, E. *A child's parent dies: Studies in childhood bereavement.* New Haven: Yale University Press, 1974.
7. Kastenbaum, R. Death and development through the lifespan. In H. Feifel (ed.), *New meanings of death.* New York: McGraw-Hill, 1977.
8. Mussen, P. H., Conger, J. J., Kagan, J., and Beiwitz, J. *Psychological development: A life-span approach.* New York: Harper and Row, 1974.
9. Pickarts, E. and Fargo, J. *Parent education: Toward parental competence.* Englewood Cliffs, NJ: Prentice-Hall, 1971.

41. Kingsbury, S. *Constructive use of emotions*. Berkeley: University of California Extension Media Center, 1970.
42. Becker, D. and Margolin, F. How surviving parents handled their young children's adaptations to the crisis of loss. *American Journal of Orthopsychiatry*, 1967, *37*, 753-757.
43. Bowlby, J. Foreword, in E. J. Anthony and C. Koupernik (eds.), *The child in his family: The impact of disease and death*. New York: John Wiley and Sons, 1973.
44. Agee, J. *A death in the family*. New York: Avon Books, 1957.
45. Jackson, E. N. *Telling a child about death*. New York: Hawthorne Books, 1965.
46. McNeil, J. N. *Young mothers' communication about death with their children*. Unpublished doctoral dissertation, Kansas State University, Manhattan, KS, 1979.
47. Shneidman, E. S. You and death. *Psychology Today*, 1971, June 43-45 and 74-80.
48. Collett, L. J. and Lester, D. The fear of death and the fear of dying. *Journal of Psychology*, 1969, *72*, 179-181.
49. Rosenberg, M. *Society and the adolescent self-image*. Princeton, NJ: Princeton University Press, 1965.
50. Jourard, S. M. *The transparent self*. New York: Van Nostrand Reinhold, 1964.
51. Hereford, C. F. *Changing parental attitudes through group discussion*. Austin, TX: University of Texas Press, 1963.
52. Olson, D. H., Sprenkle, D. H., and Russell, C. S. Circumplex model of marital and family systems. I. Cohesion and adaptability dimensions, family types and clinical application. *Family Process*, 1979, *18*, 3-28.
53. Gordon, T. *Parent effectiveness training*. New York: New American Library, 1970.
54. Leviton, D. and Forman, E. C. Death education for children and youth. *Journal of Clinical Child Psychology*, 1973, *3*(2), 8-10.
55. Grollman, E. A. *Talking about death: A dialogue between parent and child*. Boston: Beacon Press, 1970.
56. Wolf, A. W. M. *Helping your child understand death*. New York: Child Study Press, 1973.
57. Kübler-Ross, E. Facing up to death. *Today's Education*, 1972, *61*, 30-32.
58. Zeligs, R. *Children's experiences with death*. Springfield, IL: Charles C. Thomas, 1974.
59. Koocher, G. P. Talking with children about death. *American Journal of Orthopsychiatry*, 1974, *ee*(3), 404-411.
60. Crase, D. R. and Crase, D. Helping children understand death. *Young Children*, 1976, *32*, 21-25.
61. LeShan, E. *Learning to say good-bye: When a parent dies*. New York: Macmillan, 1976.
62. Mills, G. C., Reisler, R., Robinson, A., and Vermilye, G. *Discussing death: A guide to death education*. Homewood, IL: ETC Publications, 1976.
63. Bluebond-Langner, M. Meanings of death to children. In H. Feifel (ed.), *New meanings of death*. New York: McGraw-Hill, 1977.
64. Kübler-Ross, E. Helping parents teach their children about death and life. In E. E. Arnold (ed.), *Helping parents help their children*. New York: Brunner/Mazel, 1978.
65. Rudolph, M. *Should the children know? Encounters with death in the lives of children*. New York: Schocken Books, 1978.
66. Sahler, O. J. Z. *The child and death*. St. Louis: C. V. Mosby Company, 1978.
67. Sharapan, H. B. *Talking with young children about death*. Pittsburgh, PA: Family Communications, 1978.
68. Kidd, J. R. *How adults learn*. New York: Association Press, 1959.
69. Knowles, M. *The adult learner: A neglected species*. Houston: Gulf Publishing Co., 1973.
70. Schutz, W. *Joy: Expanding human awareness*. New York: Grove Press, 1966.
71. Durlak, J. S. Comparison between experiential and didactic methods of death education. *Omega*, 1978, *9*(1), 57-66.

16

Teachable Moments Occasioned by "Small Deaths"

Ute Carson

WHEN TO TELL, HOW TO TELL, AND WHEN TO BE SILENT

Eastern Airlines announces the final boarding call for the flight from Gainesville to Atlanta. My mother walks to the departure gate flanked by two of her grand-daughters who are both crying. "Why do you have to leave?" Claudia attempts for the last time to change the inevitable. My mother, herself in tears, explains and reassures, "I'll be back next year." "Next year?" Caitlin sighs, a promised reunion too remote for a ten-year-old. Cecile, our three-year-old, skips along with excite-ment. "You guys, you'll miss the plane," she reminds us. My mother proceeds through the checkpoint and waves to us again from the steps of the plane before she enters the aircraft and disappears from sight. We run outside to watch the plane taxi down the runway and take off. "Grandma flies up into the sky," Cecile shouts. We talk on the way home about the sadness of departures and I try to console the older girls with promises of future visits. When we return home we acknowledge that we are going to miss Grandma after a two-month stay. Cecile opens the guest room door and, twirling around to us, announces, "Grandma is gone." Then she begins to take off her clothes and, minutes later, is tucked under my mother's sheets. "I'm always going to sleep in Grandma's bed," she tells us. In no time she is asleep, taking the longest nap she has had for quite some time.

Children experience "small deaths" at all ages through separations from toys and pets and people. Life presents these situations to children and they develop mechanisms for coping with them. In the intimate family situation, as well as in the classroom setting, children need help in making sense of experiences of loss. We need to guide children without imposing an adult point of view. Children often see a loss through quite different eyes. They are ingenious in finding channels to work through a hurtful event. It is important that teachers have their own percep-tions about death, are comfortable with the subject, and able to answer questions honestly. But even more important is listening carefully to what children tell us about a particular experience. It is our task to hear children and to interpret for them and for ourselves what they are going through.

Children differ in their responses to loss. Some are more curious than others, some are timid and frightened. Children also react according to their level of maturity. Anna, seven years old, and Lisa, twelve, have just listened to their mother read them a story involving a death when the conversation turns to the possibility of their own mother's death. Their mother reassures them that she hopes to live a very long life but that death can occur at any time. Lisa breaks into tears and throws her arms desperately around her mother's neck. "No," she sobs, "you must never, never die, even when you are very old." After Lisa's outburst Anna smiles proudly at both and declares, "Mommy, when you die I'll bury you under the lilac bush in the garden. Won't that be a pretty place?" Lisa is no more sensitive a child than Anna but being in a stage of development where breaking into adolescence and independence is accompanied by the need for strong support, she cannot bear the thought of ever losing her mother. Anna, still anchored in a firm mother-child union, is not yet threatened by the possibility of separation.

As teachers we must keep attuned to children's emotional development. On the subject of death it is our task to listen for hidden questions, uncover buried fears, and clarify misconceptions. It may also be appropriate, on occasion, to leave children alone, if probing is apt to violate their privacy. Children need to learn to mourn and to find ways to recover, but the way is not always straight and there are temporary forms of denial which need to be respected. Aunt Hannah is known to me as a person who has weathered many losses in her life and has given comfort and strength to others bereft. Her story may exemplify the importance of letting children guide us in deciding how much to tell, when to tell, and when to be silent.

Aunt Hannah was born in a farm community at the beginning of this century. Babies were delivered in the home and people died there as well. A farm worker was hit by lightning during harvest time, a boy killed by a runaway horse, a mother died in childbirth. Numerous small gravestones told of the early death of children. Pets died and farm animals were slaughtered for consumption. Rabbits were hunted in the fields. When a person died, his body was laid out in the parlor for three days. Aunt Hannah recalls the odor of decomposition mingled with the fragrance of flowers surrounding the deceased. "The smell stays with you," she tells me, "like the sight of blood gushing from a butchered pig."

Aunt Hannah was ten when her grandmother died. It was customary to view the body and for the community to participate in the feast following the funeral. Children were not asked whether they wanted to take part. It was taken for granted. When the time came for the immediate family to take their place at grandmother's coffin, little Hannah refused to go. She had already wetted her pants and been scolded by her mother. "Let the child be," counseled the girl's visiting aunt. And since there was no opportunity for lengthy discussion, Hannah's mother dropped the matter. She grieved, too, but for her the loss was not unanticipated. She would miss her mother in many ways, not least as an extra hand around the house. Grandmother had helped with many household chores and done all the darning. That's how they had found her, slumped over in her armchair. Death had interrupted her, knitting a pair of woolen socks. Hannah's aunt took her for a walk that funeral day. They talked until Hannah's tight little fist finally relaxed under the gentle pressure of that adult hand.

In spite of the farm chores that needed doing, the graves at the cemetery were always tended by members of the family. It was weeks before Hannah's aunt returned to the farm. When she set out to pay her customary visit to the cemetery, she asked Hannah to go along. "That child hasn't been to her grandmother's grave once," her mother commented. Later at the burial place Hannah and her aunt set about pulling weeds, straightening tendrils of wild ivy. "I know you can't hear me down there, Grandmother," Hannah suddenly burst forth with anger, "but I don't like it at all. Now nobody tells me stories, and I have to feed the chickens all by myself."

Hannah frequented her grandmother's grave weekly from then on, and one day she was near tears. "I do miss you, Grandmother," she mumbled, and went on, "but Mr. McNeill said, if there are too many deer we have to shoot some or they will overpopulate the forest. Maybe it's the same with old people. It would be too crowded if everybody lived forever. I'll just come and visit you here." Several elements of denial as well as the beginning of a slow healing process are to be found in Hannah's recollections. Eventually Hannah came to terms with the finality of her grandmother's death. However, what helped her at this early stage was that she was neither confronted abruptly by facts nor pushed into a resolution of her grief by adults. Her aunt intuitively sensed that Hannah needed time to work through the loss on her own terms.

The teacher should, after the parent, be the second most important pedagogue in a child's life. Education involves the transmission of facts but, more importantly, the formation of children's attitudes. In helping children understand losses which they experience all along, we need to discern their perceptions before guiding them. Materials such as books, films and television, as well as children's own experiences, can be starting points for discussions and, to some degree, tools in shaping opinions. There should be no taboos on subject matter. What matters is the approach.

THE IMPORTANCE OF FANTASY FOR SMALL CHILDREN

It is important for the teacher to have a basic knowledge of the developmental stages according to which the average child perceives death. Also helpful is an appreciation of the importance fantasy plays for children dealing with separation and loss. In his book, *The Uses of Enchantment* (1), Bruno Bettelheim takes the fairy tale as the art form which best helps children to deal with problems of growing up and interpreting the world. "The child," he writes, "intuitively comprehends that although these stories are *unreal* they are not *untrue*; that while what these stories tell about does not happen in fact, it must happen as inner experience and personal development; that fairy tales depict in imaginary and symbolic form the essential steps in growing up and achieving an independent existence" (1). Bettelheim captures here some important meanings of fairy tales for children. We have learned from Piaget that the child's worldview remains animistic until puberty, and from Freud we know that it is the inner life that confronts the child with basic human predicaments. Only slowly, step by step, is the world outside incorporated and understood as a separate entity. Children need suggestions in symbolic form which help them transform their inner needs and struggles into thought and action in the outside world. According to Bettelheim, several characteristics of the fairy tale make this transition easier. The fairy tale states a conflict situation briefly and in simple terms. Since children are not yet equipped to handle ambiguity, the fairy tale simplifies dilemmas. The characters in a fairy tale are always either good or bad, beautiful or ugly, lazy or industrious. Choices are clear cut, nothing is ambivalent as in real life. "Presenting the polarities of character permits the child to comprehend easily the difference between the two, which he could not do as readily were the figures drawn more true to life, with all the complexities that characterize real people" (1, p. 9). The child can thus identify with a character in a fairy tale and learn to make simple choices which are based on the child's like or dislike and not yet on right versus wrong. The fairy tale is an art form tailored to the needs of children. Children will choose one particular story again and again over all others. Or they will choose the fairy tale which corresponds to their inner conflicts at a particular stage of development. Children do not themselves know why they are fascinated by a certain fairy tale because the struggle is carried on at an unconscious level. Bettelheim warns us repeatedly not to interpret for the child by pointing to hidden meanings. In doing so we risk destroying the enchantment the child derives from the story.

Fairy tales deal with the problems of life but they do it in a way that permits the child to cope and grow and not be unduly frightened. There are such problems as sibling rivalry, depicted in Cinderella; the changes of adolescence, as in Sleeping Beauty; separation from parents, as in Hansel and Gretel. The themes of marriage and old age and death are often dealt with in fairy tales.

From four until puberty what the child needs most is to be presented with symbolic images which reassure him that there is a happy solution to his oedipal problems. ... But reassurance about a happy outcome has to come first, because only then will the child have the courage to labor confidently to extricate himself from his oedipal predicament. (p. 39)

A fairy tale always has a good ending. This strengthens the child's budding ego and encourages him to take on the unavoidable difficulties of life. At a time when a more realistic viewpoint might undermine his still shaky self-confidence, it assures the child that everything will turn out alright in the end.

Many teachers are troubled by what seems to them the "unreality" of fairy tales. What is the difference, they ask, between a fairy tale and telling the child a lie, such as "Grandfather is in the flowers" when in fact he is dead and in the grave, or "The stork brought the baby," when the child has seen a picture of a baby being born? Besides being bothered about the veracity of the fairy tales, critics often charge that such stories inadequately confront the lived world of the twentieth century child. As Gloria Goldreich puts it, children today are "bereft of the shield of fantasy and heir to an age where reality and reason govern and penetrate every dimension of life" (2). Bettelheim responds that the problems of the inner life are timeless for children and that we are not lying when we allow them to develop according to their timetable. Children do not begin with an abstract understanding of things and acquire objective thinking over time. The emotions and the unconscious dominate the perceptions of childhood, and the world is experienced only subjectively at first. Allowing children to cope with unconscious pressures in a childlike way will enhance, not diminish, their chances of developing a rational explanation of the world when the time is ripe.

Fairy tales often begin with the death of a parent and almost always end with the line, "and they lived happily every after."

... An uninformed view of the fairy tale sees in this type of ending an unrealistic wish-fulfillment, missing completely the important message it conveys to the child. These tales tell him that by forming a true interpersonal relation, one escapes the separation anxiety which haunts him. (1, pp. 10–11)

"THE WOLF AND THE SEVEN LITTLE GOATS"

The following fairy tale was told to a class of three- and four-year-olds at the First Presbyterian Preschool in Gainesville, Florida. It was also told to a kindergarten class, a third-grade class and a fifth-grade class. Because it is not well-known to English readers, I will recount it here. A mother of seven goats has to leave them alone at home while she goes on an errand. She warns the little goats to play nicely and not to open the door to anyone except herself. After she leaves, the little goats occupy themselves contendedly until a wolf comes to the door and asks to be let in. Twice the goats reject his overtures because he cannot identify himself as their mother who has a soft voice and white hooves. The wolf's voice is gruff and his paws are brown and covered with coarse hair. The wolf seeks a disguise first from a druggist who gives him chalk to soften his voice, subsequently from a baker who sprinkles flour over his paws. When he comes to the door the third time the goats mistake the wolf for their mother and let him in. He swallows six of the goats. The seventh one, the youngest, hides in a grandfather clock. Seeing the door open upon her return and discovering none of her children inside, the mother goat despairs. The sound of the voice of the smallest goat revives her hope. She fetches the little one and together they search for the wolf whom they find sleeping under an apple tree. The mother goat cuts open the wolf's stomach and rescues her children. Together they fill the stomach with heavy stones. When the wolf awakes he goes to the well to slake his thirst and the weight of the stones topple him into the well where he drowns. Mother and children dance around the well, singing merrily.

Many of the symbols which appear in this story are discussed by Bettelheim. The figure of the wolf, as portrayed in Little Red Riding Hood and The Three Little Pigs is multi-dimensional. It is at once the stranger who beckons the goats to the door, the male seducer, the world outside the self and the home, the externalization of the badness the child feels when he does not obey. The wolf is the animal in all of us and, most important for our purposes here, the wolf is the bringer of separation from the parent. It is the one who tempts the goats to try independence and who finally brings death in the form of swallowing six of them. That death is not final here corresponds to the child's understanding. Factual death is not yet comprehended.

What is experienced by the child are forms of death—separation from the security and bondage of parents, and steps toward independence. The reunion with the mother at the end shows that independence is only slowly achieved and, if entered prematurely, can have grave consequences. The parent is still necessary as a shield and support in the maturing process. Death is seen here as a part of growing up. It is not the end of life in this story. Being cut out of the "womb" again, this time by the mother out of the wolf's stomach, means being reborn—entering a new stage in one's development. The wolf is punished at the end by drowning. In this way the child can externalize the guilt he may feel over his efforts at separation. The mother figure can also be understood at various levels. Suffice it here to say that she is a bridge for the child. She leaves the children because she knows that separation is necessary, but she also returns and lends her assistance as long as the children are small and need her. The youngest goat holds a special place in the story. His example shows the child that even if he is small, he can avoid the worst fate by being clever. It also shows the child that older siblings have to endure growing pains first. For the very young, the close tie to the mother is sanctioned.

Equipped with this "adult" interpretation of the story, I set out to test Bettelheim's assertion that "the 'truth' of fairy stories is the truth of our imagination, not that of normal causality" (1, p. 117), by telling the story, first, to the three-year-olds. I wish to stress that I am discussing the responses of school children to "small deaths" and not children's reactions to uncommon tragedy or the loss of a loved one.

The children listened attentively even though no visual material was used. Upon finishing the story I asked the following questions. Did you like the story? Was it a funny story? A sad story? A scary story? The answer most often given was that it was a bad story. Why? Because "the wolf came," or because "the wolf ate the goats." Whom did you like best in the story? All shouted, "the little goat." Why? "Because he is hiding." Could the wolf come to *your* door? This question brought the greatest response. All children said no. When asked why, one child answered, "there are no wolves in Florida." Where are they? "They are way down town." Another said, "we have two doors in our house. The wolf would come to the other door." Or, "we have a big, big house. He couldn't come in." Or, "we would lock the house up." A final answer was, "my father has a gun, and my brother would shoot him." No child had any cognitive awareness of his dealings with separation or any of the other meanings of the wolf. All was denial and defense against the wolf.

The pictures the children drew afterward tell a different tale. To the question, Do you think that the little goats did something wrong in letting the wolf in, there was an unequivocal "no." "We don't open the door to anybody." "A stranger might give us some poison candy." "We play nicely." "We do what mommy says." "My mom always stays with us and watches us." "We are with our mom." Children who stay with sitters gave similarly reassuring answers. There was no apparent awareness of guilt. Divided answers were given to the last question. Should the wolf have drowned? "Yes, because he eats goats." "Yes, because he is bad." Others felt, "no, because he was thirsty." Amplifying this last answer, one little girl said, "I'm getting a stomach ache." There was no mention of cutting open the wolf's stomach and filling it with stones.

Fourteen children drew pictures after answering the questions. Two could not remember the story well. Five children, all boys, painted pictures with the wolf at

Figure 1

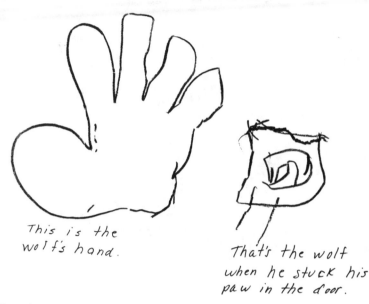

This is the
wolf's hand.

That's the wolf
when he stuck his
paw in the door.

Figure 2

the center (Fig. 1). The importance separation seems to play at this age, particularly for boys, is overwhelming. Only one boy drew the wolf in the water, which suggests that he has come to terms with the problem. At the other extreme was a boy who drew squares all over the page and pointed to every square saying, "there is the wolf, and there he is too." The most sophisticated picture was done by Josh (Fig. 2). Drawing the wolf's paw covered with flour and extended through the door opening shows that Josh unconsciously perceived the disguises a symbolic figure can assume.

The other children, all girls, had the mother goat and/or baby goat and the wolf as their theme. Girls at this age seem much less threatened by separation and still quite secure in the mother-child relationship. Jennifer's picture (Fig. 3) shows her to be bound to her mother in a secure way but unaware of the wolf. She drew mother and baby goat. Another girl drew only the baby goat, that is, herself. Two drew the wolf and the goats, which indicates the theme of being threatened and swallowed. Lara drew the wolf inside the house with the baby goat looming large above the scene. No mother goat is in sight (Fig. 4). As I learned later, Lara is going through the trauma of adjusting to the presence of a new baby sister. Cecile drew all three characters (Fig. 5). The picture shows the drowned wolf in the well (mastery of the conflict), as well as mother and baby goat (pointing out the mother-child tie still intact and secure).

There was some overlap in responses when I told the story to four-year-olds, but the older children gave more detailed answers. The discrepancy between the verbal response and the pictures was greater too. The children tried to outdo each other in answering the questions regarding how they themselves would handle the wolf, while in their drawings they concentrated on a variety of subjects. A slight but interesting shift occurred in that the children came up with very active defenses

Figure 3

Figure 4

Mother + baby goat

wolf in the well

Figure 5

against the wolf, ranging from "putting a mask on" to "going boo!" to "I would chop his head off." Some of the four-year-olds also responded to the question regarding their (the little goats') own collusion in the wolf's gaining entry by admitting that "the goats shouldn't have opened the door so wide," "they should have just peeked out," "they should have checked the wolf's paw more closely." Guilt first becomes conscious here. When I came to the question, Were you surprised that all the goats were alive? the children turned the question around and asked me "How did the wolf eat the goats?" or "Why were the goats not chewed up?" Regarding the question, Should the wolf have drowned? Should the goats have put stones in his stomach? they asked, "How did the wolf drown?" "Why didn't he swim?" And after coming up with answers themselves, connecting the drowning to the heavy stones, a girl volunteered, "The wolf should have used his sharp claws to scratch the stomach open and get the stones out." Questions about the father goat were asked by the children. In one of the drawings a boy placed the father goat inside the house with the little goats and the mother. Another boy said, "Father goat is at work." I learned that his father is away on business a lot and that the family spent a recent vacation on the beach without him. In all the answers and the drawings, reality (as the world "outside") is incorporated into the fantasy world of this fairy tale. One boy began, "The mother goat told all the little goats to get into the space ship to get away from the wolf" (Fig. 6). Another boy shows a police car waiting to pick up the wolf (Fig. 7). In another picture the well is a boat that tips over, drowning the wolf.

Details get mentioned and included in the drawings. The stones appear frequently in the pictures, as does the grandfather clock. One little girl insisted on having white chalk so that she could portray the mother goat accurately. More

Figure 6

Figure 7

children at this age use all three figures—the mother, the little goats, and the wolf. One boy used three devices to overcome the wolf problem (Fig. 8). There is the hiding place (the grandfather clock), the well water (which he wanted labeled "hot"), and the stones in the wolf's stomach. This is a child who had considerable difficulty adjusting emotionally to the nursery school and has only lately (mid-year) come to like it.

The next groups to hear the story were classes at J. J. Finley Elementary School in Gainesville, Florida. The kindergarteners gave answers not fundamentally different from those given by pre-schoolers, though the details become ever more elaborate as the children grow older. The discrepancy between the verbal accounts and the drawings also continues to widen. Verbally, the children in the early grades (through approximately grade three) jump on the bandwagon against the wolf, outdoing each other in their attacks on the villain. In their drawings, however, many children return to the mother goat and the baby goat symbols. One very bright kindergartener named the baby goat after herself and had the mother goat call that name repeatedly. The wolf gets drawn more and more expressively. One girl showed the wolf's mouth full of big teeth. Means to frighten the wolf from the child's environment are used again and again. Matthew had his dog chase the wolf away (Fig. 9). Children are convinced by this age that the wolf must be punished. They are as concerned about his disguises as they are about his devouring the goats. They also are more ingenious regarding ways in which the little goats might have identified the wolf. As one girl suggested, "They should have seen the flour dripping from his paw." Affections are divided between the littlest goat ("because he is smart") and the mother goat ("because she put stones in the wolf's stomach").

A big change in perception is noticed with the third graders. I added a question

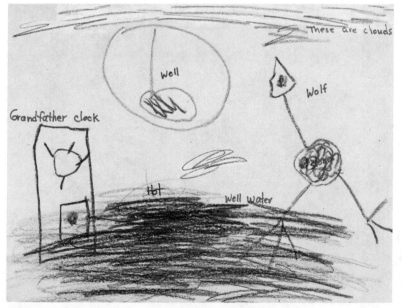

Figure 8

Figure 9

in my discussion with this group, asking them to describe what the wolf did and then to tell me what the wolf means. Most said simply "a wild animal" or "he's like a fox." Only three of the twenty-five children attempted to translate the symbol into reality. One girl thought "the wolf could be a person dressed up for Hallowe'en in fur." Two others likened the wolf to a stranger coming to the door. No child expressly identified the wolf as the bringer of death, but the wolf clearly meant for many the tempter, against whom mother has erected rules and commands. One child's picture was a sequence of the deceptions the wolf used, followed by the admonishments of the mother (Fig. 10). No child said the wolf is not real or does not exist.

About the drowning the children were divided. Many saw the stones as punishment enough. Old age came up at this point, one girl suggesting that "maybe the wolf was old and needed food and had to catch the goats." Another girl drew the wolf under the apple tree with its stomach opened, the mother (scissors in hand) standing there while one of the goats escapes (Fig. 11). I inquired of the teacher about this girl's apparent preoccupation with death and rebirth and learned that her grandfather had died only a week prior to my visiting the class. The happy ending was important to most third graders. "The story was sad, but I'm glad it had a happy ending." "The wolf ate the goats, but in the end they all got out alive."

After these conversations about the wolf and related matters I was most surprised when I saw the pictures. Fourteen children of twenty-five drew neither the wolf nor the mother nor the baby goat but the grandfather clock where the little goat is hiding (Figs. 12 and 13). One boy showed the little goat hiding in the television. A strong identification with the baby goat suggests that the self at this age has gained enough strength to overcome the close familial ties and is no longer

Figure 10 "The little goats make a mistake by opening the door to the wolf."

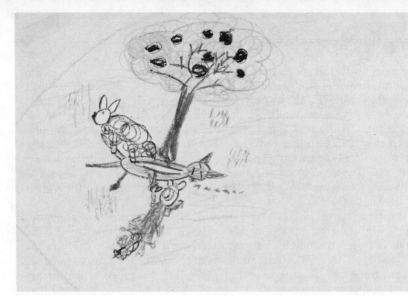

Figure 11 "The mother is cutting open the fox and the baby goats are coming out."

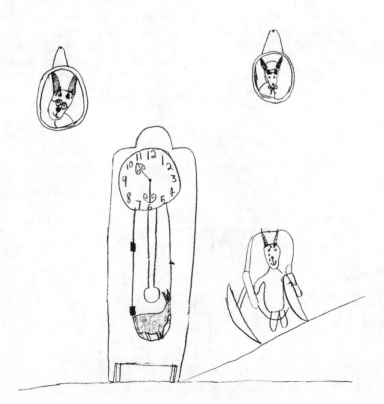

Figure 12

Figure 13

under the domination of the threat of separation. The outside world gets explored and takes on new importance. Friendships provide an alliance against being overwhelmed by the world. The little goat suggests to the child that he can master the challenges of the world, and that the wolf—danger, loss, temptation, and separation—can be outsmarted. Tears may be shed over the death of a beloved pet, but even greater sadness is experienced when a close friend moves away. The child is still vulnerable and needs protection (grandfather clock, or another friend), but death is not of primary concern when all energy is directed toward strengthening the self and establishing a secure place in a small community (classmates, friends) outside the family. By this age, the child is also beginning to comprehend others' problems, as one girl's picture suggests in portraying the little goat comforting a crying mother goat with the words, "Don't cry, mommy."

As I moved up through the grades, the fifth graders exercised increased control over the story. For example, they preferred to work with pencil over crayon in doing their drawings. Otherwise, there was little change in the responses except that they were reticent to talk about the story. I had to press them for answers. At this age peer pressure is very strong, with the result that the children fear giving a "wrong" answer and appearing foolish. There was, however, unanimous agreement that the goats were careless in admitting the wolf to their house. One boy cited the fact that a wolf does not have hooves like a goat and claimed that the little goats were negligent in not noticing this. For the first time a boy identi- fied the wolf as evil, saying that the wolf was not just a stranger or a deceiver but evil itself. Of the twenty-one children, six identified with the little goat, as shown in their drawings. Two girls drew the little goat outside the protection of the grandfather clock. One drew it outside the house. Both girls, I learned, had recently had to work through the breakup of a friendship which had left them quite vulnerable. All other pictures show the wolf very much at the center of things. The wolf is the tempter and the wrongdoer, as shown in Andrea's picture (Fig. 14), where the wolf knocks at the door of the peaceful home of the little goats. Or he is the deceiver, as shown in a picture of the wolf with a white paw (Fig. 15) and in another of the wolf entering the house (Fig. 16). But the com- ment on this drawing is also revealing. Even though the wolf is present and eats the goats, the smart mother punishes the wolf by putting rocks in his stomach. In

Figure 14   "The wolf knocks at the door of the peaceful home of the baby goats."

Figure 15

Figure 16   "I thought the part in the story where the mother goat put the rocks in the wolf's stomach was pretty smart on behalf of the author."

yet another picture the mother is an ally. She arrives at the sleeping wolf's side with a pair of scissors ready (Fig. 17). Birth and death symbols are mixed in several of the pictures. The wolf (the bringer of death), slumbering in the shade of the apple tree, looks quite pregnant (Fig. 18). This symbolic ambiguity should remind us of the perceptions of the three- and four-year-olds for whom the wolf first played a central part in their attempts at independence. Here, as there, he is the severer of ties, but now in a different disguise and inhabiting a more complex world.

"MOTHER MOUSE IS DEAD"

The unconscious and the emotions govern a small child's life, but reality does exist even if separated only in part from the inner world. The older the child, the more reality gains the upper hand. Mrs. Lenox did not intend that the little book, *Year In and Year Out With Pixie and Mouse*, should turn into a lesson about death for her kindergarten class. Each day Mrs. Lenox reads aloud to the class about a particular month of the year. January is about snow and an underground burrow for the mouse family. July brings a harvest of apples and peaches. About November she read

What does this mean?
The autumn crocuses ring.
Mother Mouse died today.
Did she have a stomachache?
Or did she catch a cold
So late in the year?
The animals of the meadow mourn
And the mouse child shudders.
Because she is without her mother
Everybody cries.
The November fog is damp.
Let's light our lanterns.

When Mrs. Lenox begins to read about December and Christmas the next day, Jennifer interrupts, "Read us about Mother Mouse is dead again." The rest of the class crowds around Mrs. Lenox and demands the same page be read again and again. The children are drawn to the subject but there are no questions at first, only the repeated demand that the poem be read. Recess brings some help. Stephen finds a dead beetle and starts poking it with a stick. The children congregate around. "Ooo," someone yells. "Leave it alone," another interjects. "It's dead." Cheryl curls up her nose, "Look at all the ants eating it." The children are simultaneously repelled and fascinated.

"It's time to come in," Mrs. Lenox calls to her class. The dead beetle and the poem about the mouse elicit a variety of reactions from the children. "Mrs. Lenox, what is 'dead'?" Erica asks. Before she can answer, Eric mumbles, "Don't be stupid. When ants eat you, you're dead." "Is the Mother Mouse dead?" Erica continues. "Yes," Mrs. Lenox confirms. "But when will she wake up again?" "She won't, Erica." "Did she eat something bad?" It is still Erica, pressing. "Yes, perhaps she ate something that made her very sick." "But now the little mice are without their mother." Erica becomes agitated. "That's right, Erica, and that is very sad. Fortunately it doesn't happen very often. Most mothers die only after

Figure 17   "It was nice to listen to a fairy tail instead of a composition."

Figure 18

they have lived a long time." "How long?" John wants to know. "Until their children are grown up and can live without them, maybe even have children of their own." "How will I know when I'm dead?" Linda whispers. Mrs. Lenox explains, "Your heart will stop beating." She puts her hand over her heart. "Now," she instructs the children, "put your right hand on the left side of your chest. Feel it? It goes thump, thump. That's your heart." She goes from child to child, helping them feel their heartbeat. "When your heart stops beating, you are dead." The class is excited. "How does my heart beat?" Eric is back with his down-to-earth questions. "Let me show you." Mrs. Lenox goes to the basin and fills it with water. The group gathers around her. "Your heart is a big strong muscle about the size of your fist which opens and closes. The water is like the blood that is pumped from your heart throughout your body." "Even into my toes?" Eric looks quizzical. "Yes, Eric, into your toes and into every other part of your body." Mrs. Lenox squeezes the water out of her fist and opens it, letting water flow back in, then presses it out again. She lifts her hand from the water. "When your heart stops pushing the blood in and out, you are dead." "Like Mother Mouse?" asks Erica. "And like the beetle," Eric chimes in. "Death is disgusting," he goes on. "When you are dead, you look like a beetle." Erica seems exasperated with everyone, including Mrs. Lenox. "But I am asking you, when does Mother Mouse wake up again?"

The lines about Mother Mouse have stimulated the children to ask questions about death. The subject has aroused their curiosity, but the reality of death seems at best partially understood by most and pushed aside by others. But, most important, the subject of death was discovered by the children and carried by Mrs. Lenox as far as the developmental stage of the children permits her to go.

FACTS VERSUS EXPERIENCE

Mrs. Douglas likes to garden. Living in Florida she finds that she can grow vegetables and flowers all year round, so she starts her school garden during summer vacation. One of the projects for her first graders is to be a unit on health foods, good eating habits, and balanced meals. She is pleased to have peas ready to be picked by September, and the tomatoes are also ripe. When it comes time for the tasting party, her pupils are thrilled to harvest the vegetables themselves, and even the finicky eaters taste the pea they have popped out of its green casing. The garden serves many educational purposes. The children learn the parts of plants, they press leaves for their art collections, and Mrs. Douglas explains the natural cycle of living things from birth through growth to decay. A rose on her desk, into whose blossom every child has stuck his nose at least once to whiff the fragrance, begins to lose its petals. "The rose is wilting," Mrs. Douglas tells the class. "Losing its petals is the beginning of a dying process. Later the leaves will dry and their edges will wrinkle." She crumbles the dry, fallen leaves in her hand. "What do these leaves look like?" she asks the class. "Like Grandpa's tobacco," Raymond observes. "Like ashes," says Monica. "Exactly," Mrs. Douglas concurs. "And if we spread these ashes over some dirt, soon they will all be mixed together and we are back where the plant started, with the soil out of which a new seedling can grow."

When Mrs. Douglas plants her garden again the following year, she waits until classes have begun. She realizes that the children need more involvement from the start and more responsibility for the maintenance of the garden. The children derive satisfaction from digging up the soil and sowing seeds. They are thrilled when the first seedlings peek through the earth, and they faithfully water and weed the school garden. Again this year the harvest proves to be the high point for all the little gardeners. After that they pay less and less attention to the plants, even though Mrs. Douglas tries to show them the discoloration of the leaves and explains how the plant prepares for cooler times by withdrawing moisture from all exposed surfaces and finally sheds its leaves. The children have raked together a small pile. Following a rainy weekend the leaves have a strange odor and are matted together. Mrs. Douglas tells the class about decomposition, about the elements breaking down the structure of the leaves and the growth process coming to an end. She also assures the children that the bare bushes will bring forth new growth in the spring.

At home in the evening Mrs. Douglas looks through the pupils' notebooks. She ponders one drawing which bears this label in neat handwriting: "This is a dead plant." She is pleased at how much the children have learned about the life cycle of plants, but she cannot explain a feeling of slight dissatisfaction with her garden project. Clearly, the children have understood how a seed is put into the soil, grows, bears fruit, then wilts and decomposes. The children can all distinguish between a living and a dead plant. Why does she still feel something is missing? A chance incident clarifies her puzzlement.

After the vegetables are harvested, Becky brings some sunflower seeds to class. "Sunflowers," she tells Mrs. Douglas, "are my mother's favorites because they really look like the sun. Can we plant them?" A spot in the garden is readied. After all dead plants have been pulled and the soil turned over, Mrs. Douglas draws a line about two inches deep. Each child deposits a few seeds in a hole along the line several inches apart. They fill dirt in over the seeds and sprinkle water over them. As the sunflowers come up, each child watches over his own plant with particular devotion. Green and ready to bud, the sunflowers are greeted each day by the expectant youngsters. Then one afternoon the sun shines mercilessly on the fragile plants and by evening their crowns are drooping, their shafts bent sideways. Becky comes running in the next day. "Our sunflowers are falling over," she cries. "They are all dry." She grabs a paper cup and runs to fill it with water and bring it to her plant. Many other children follow suit. Too late is the attempt to revive, the damage has been done.

Mrs. Douglas stands before a disappointed group, explaining how the sun, which makes plants grow, can also kill them by beaming down on them too long. "No," she reassures the class, "it was nobody's fault. You watered enough. It was an accident. The hot sun destroyed your plants and your work." The children remain listless the rest of the morning, and after school many a child glances at the devastated little plot.

To restore faith in life's continuation, Mrs. Douglas starts a new project the following day. She hands out small flower pots and new seeds. Together they begin again, and soon the enthusiasm for planting and gardening returns. Mrs. Douglas discovered that death, even in its smallest form, must be experienced to have an impact. To learn the facts of the life cycle is one thing, but to live through and experience the loss of a plant into which effort and concern have been invested is quite another matter.

THE BIRD WITH THE BROKEN WING

"Mrs. Nelson, Mrs. Nelson, it's a bird. Come and look!" Peter's breathless outburst leaves little room for a reply. He is off, running back to the track field where he has spotted a sandy plumaged bird with a black crescent around the back of its neck, the right wing dragging like an anchor adrift. Mrs. Nelson glances at the power lines spanning the athletic fields before she clasps both hands around the bird whose attempts at freeing himself are feeble but frantic. "Peter, run ahead and get a cardboard box out of the front closet. Amy, Sue, Mike, help him cover the bottom of the box with kleenexes." She follows slowly, trying not to loosen her grip but careful not to squeeze. "It's a ringed turtle dove," she instructs the class while placing the bird in the box. Amy hands the teacher her loosely knitted sweater which she spreads over the box. The dove is unusually docile. They bring it water and dip its beak into it. It becomes frantic again and flutters around for a few seconds.

To fill the remainder of the hour Mrs. Nelson tells the class about different kinds of doves and pigeons, which are the larger members of the same species. But she cannot hold the class's attention for long. Again and again the children want to look at the dove, and they bombard their teacher with questions. "Can we keep it?" "Will the bird get better?" "Do you think it will fly again?" Mrs. Nelson has decided to stop at the veterinary hospital on her way home from school. She tells the class that the dove seems to have broken its wing when it struck the power lines above the track field. She hopes that Dr. Anderson can set the wing and tell them how to take care of the injured bird. "In any case," she instructs the class, "bring some small acorns and seeds tomorrow. Maybe we can start feeding it." "Let's name him," suggests Peter. " 'Little Dove'," Amy calls out. "No, let's call him 'Dovey'," is Sue's proposal. "Could it be 'Sandy' because of its color?" asks Mike. Mrs. Nelson writes the suggestions on the board and brings the decision to a vote. "The name of our little bird is 'Sandy'," she announces to the class. She is relieved when the school day has ended. The children, still in a state of high excitement, reluctantly prepare to leave for home.

Dr. Anderson is not able to offer good news about Sandy's condition. "It's not the wing alone, I'm sorry to say, Mrs. Nelson. The bird has suffered internal injuries as well. The kindest deed I can perform is to put it out of its misery." Mrs. Nelson, feeling miserable, nods her consent. "There will be no charge. I'm glad you brought it in." Dr. Anderson looks up questioningly: Why is that lady still standing there? "I need the bird back, when it's dead, I mean." Mrs. Nelson says this as someone who has made a decision which has not yet come fully to consciousness. Dr. Anderson's puzzlement about Mrs. Nelson heightens. He has treated many of her pets in the past and she always seemed a reasonable young woman to him. "Yes, I need the dead dove back," Mrs. Nelson says more steadily than before. "I left my class with the expectation of having a wounded animal to nurse back to health. I must not rob them of the only way I know to get them through their disappointment, and that is by having them take part in Sandy's burial." "It's up to you," Dr. Anderson replies. "If you'll step out into the waiting room, I'll hand you your box back in a moment. Remember, the bird will be stiff by tomorrow. You'll have some explaining to do." "I know. Thank you, Dr. Anderson."

It is not easy to face the class next morning. Mrs. Nelson waits until everyone is seated before bringing the box containing the dead bird into the room and placing it on her desk. Eager faces greet her and change expression as they discern some troubling news in her look. "Children, Sandy had to be put out of his misery. He had been hurt inside his body and he was suffering a great deal. He is dead now, and I know how sad this will make you. But if you try to think of Sandy first and then your own feelings, I think you will agree with me that putting him to death was the kindest thing we could do for him." After a moment of stunned silence Peter bursts forth, "Couldn't the vet have given Sandy a shot? Why did he have to kill him?" "Don't be angry with Dr. Anderson, Peter. I know that if there had been a shot that could have saved Sandy, Dr. Anderson would have given it to him. A veterinarian has chosen his profession because he cares about animals. He wants to help them get well. But he can't always do that." Heads sink to desktops, and a pin could have been heard dropping. "Would you like to see Sandy before we find a place to bury him?" Mrs. Nelson asks the children. They all file past the little box and take a glance inside. Amy asks, "May I touch?" "Of course," Mrs. Nelson replies, "that is a kind way to say goodbye." Amy's fingers glide over the dove's head and wings. "You expect it to move any minute, don't you?" "Yes, you do," is Mrs. Nelson's response, "but Sandy won't move anymore." "He won't be able to fly again?" Sue bursts into tears.

It is time to find a gravesite. Mrs. Nelson realizes that continuing to talk at this point will only heighten the tension and deepen the sorrow. The children walk out silently, but at the fence of the schoolyard they begin to argue over where the best place for Sandy might be. Mrs. Nelson wants to involve as many children as possible, knowing that participation will help them work through their sadness. One child holds the box, another digs the grave, another places Sandy in the excavated hole. Several place dirt back over the box, and then they are dispersed in several directions to find pretty objects such as flowers and stones to decorate the grave. "We won't forget you, Sandy," Mrs. Nelson closes their little ceremony. "Even though you were with us just a day, you made it a day that all of us will remember for some time to come."

The story of the bird with the broken wing does not end here. The bird's death stirred many questions in the minds of the children. The following morning Peter kicked over a box of study sheets standing next to Mrs. Nelson's desk. It was the kind of box the children had buried Sandy in. "I don't like it that Sandy is dead," Peter mumbled. Mrs. Nelson guessed that other children also felt this way and decided to devote some time to their concerns. "Write something, anything you would like to say, about Sandy," Mrs. Nelson instructs the class. "If you want to go to the library and look up details about the pigeon and dove family, you may do so." There were many moving accounts of Sandy's death, but Peter's story is representative. "Sandy was a dove that flew into our schoolyard and hit a high wire and broke a wing. I found him. I wanted to keep him and love him. Doves are birds of peace. In the dictionary it says they are gentle and pure. Dove is the emblem of the holy spirit. Sandy was a pretty bird. His color was like sand. If I were Sandy I wouldn't want to die. I am glad I'm not Sandy. I believe Sandy still flies through the sky." The children want to hear each other's stories and listen with great interest. Mrs. Nelson comments and explains, reassuring them that, for them, death lies in the distant future. Whereas she had previously found it necessary to convince the class that it was merciful for Dr. Anderson to put Sandy to death, she now had to shift attention back to Sandy and away from the children's identification with the bird.

Two other small episodes occur. Mrs. Nelson customarily observes the children at play and it comes as no surprise to her to see Rachel and Sarah acting out Sandy's death. Rachel, spread out in the sand, holds her fingers in a cramped position much the way Sandy's foot had looked. Sarah walks around her, gently straightening her arms and legs. When she succeeds, she exclaims joyfully, "You can move again." Watching the two girls, Mrs. Nelson is glad she did not suggest role playing, as she had contemplated. Children will act out events that are unconscious or too painful to express verbally. Or, as we saw earlier, they may draw pictures of what they cannot yet say. In playing out a drama, conflicts are made external, and once external, they become less threatening. Young children, who have difficulty putting themselves in someone else's place also play out fantasies in numerous ways. Mrs. Nelson remembers her own five-year-old stuffing a pillow under her playshirt and acting out fantasies of pregnancy and birth. The initiative for acting out inner events at an early age is best left to the child. Adult suggestions such as "Why don't you play the dead bird" or "You be Dr. Anderson" put an unduly rational frame on the child's imagination. At about the third grade level children begin to identify with others—close friends or a grandparent. But even such an identification is still largely a projection of self. The other person is primarily a support and buffer. At about the fifth grade level, children are capable of working through events by role playing suggested by adults. By this time children are able to empathize—to imagine someone else's experience for themselves.

When Mrs. Nelson catches Richard and Scott digging up Sandy's grave several days later, she can hardly hide her anger. Taking the two scoundrels by the scruff of the neck, she trots them back to the classroom, plants them in their seats and asks, "What were you two up to?" The rest of the class is suddenly very attentive. Wrongdoing creates an atmosphere of excitement. "What were you doing?" Mrs. Nelson becomes insistent. The two conspirators look sheepishly at each other, unable to suppress a smirk. "We wanted to see what Sandy looks like now," Scott confesses. "Ooo, gross," several disapproving sounds echo through the classroom. "You guys should be ashamed of yourselves," Amy admonishes. "And what did you find?" Mrs. Nelson asks, having regained her teacherly composure. "Goofy stuff and lots of tiny bones," Richard blurts out. Pride resonates in his voice at the discovery that has been made, and Mrs. Nelson does not fail to register the contentment in his look, a contentment that comes from having satisfied one's curiosity. "I could have brought some in, but you wouldn't let us finish," Richard continues. "The bones are smaller than chicken bones." By now it is clear to Mrs. Nelson that the two boys did not perceive digging up Sandy's grave as a defilement, as an adult might. She sees her role as teacher in two ways.

First, she must respond to the children's curiosity. So she gives a short talk on the durability of bones and how explorers sometimes find the bones of people of bygone ages in their excavations. "It is our bones and teeth that survive longer than any other parts of our body." She also has to explain a custom to the children that has been invented by society to protect the grave against the curious. She tells of grave robbers who wanted the jewels that had been buried with the dead and of bodies exhumed for medical study. She tells them about the sacredness of burial grounds in societies which believed that the spirits of the dead inhabited graveyards. "And even today," she continues, "the cemetery can serve people otherwise busily involved in everyday activities as a quiet place where they may go to think about someone who has died. Not that we should not think about the person wherever we may be, but the graveside is a special place at which to remember." "I know," interrupts Becky, "we visit my grandmother's grave. She made fresh brownies when she was alive." "Yes, Becky," Mrs. Nelson wraps up her little talk, "we remember people by the things we did with them or the things they did for us. Graves are just one possible place to recall them. We might think of Sandy when we see a bird flying, but it is also comforting to have a place where we know he lies buried." "Where his bones lie," Richard mumbles, a remark which Mrs. Nelson graciously passes over.

THE INSTRUCTIVENESS
OF IMAGINATIVE LITERATURE

School-related experiences provide ample opportunity for teachers to engage children's interest in death. Materials, such as books, films, and television, should not be overlooked. A well-wrought story can evoke empathy and understanding.

The Yearling (3), by Marjorie Kinnan Rawlings, is a book about relationships which range from little Jody's tie to a particular place in rural Florida, his attachment to his parents, especially his father, interactions with neighbors, his friendship with the crippled and demented boy, Fodderwing, his bond to the foundling, the fawn, Flag. It is also a story about growing up, and the title refers not only to the young deer but to young Jody as well, as a remark by the father to his son at the end of the book reveals. "You've done come back different. You've taken a punishment. You ain't a yearlin' no longer" (p. 403).*

For Jody, growing up means working through those many relationships and assessing their meaning. He experiences the value the land holds for him through hard, satisfying labor. He learns from his father through imitation, and their relationship goes through tests of trust. After a year of painful maturing, Jody is able to take his ailing father's place on the homestead. Through living and working with his neighbors Jody sees that even uncouth and rowdy folk are stricken by sorrow and hardship. Twice Jody must deal with the breaking of an important relationship—the death of Fodderwing, and the killing of his beloved fawn.

The tone of the friendship between the two boys resounds in the joy of one of their meetings. "Jody saw Fodderwing hurrying toward him. The humped and twisted body moved in a series of contortions like a wounded ape. Fodderwing lifted his walking stick and waved it. Jody ran to meet him. Fodderwing's face was luminous" (3, p. 45). Jody, who does not find his friend's body repulsive, is able to enter into Fodderwing's strange, wondrous world. Sharing a love for animals, they tend and play with the various pets Fodderwing has acquired. Then one day, when Jody comes to show Fodderwing his new fawn, his friend is dead. "Like as if you blowed out a candle" (3, p. 191), an older brother informs him. The sudden news numbs Jody and he feels nothing at first, "no sorrow, only a coldness and a faintness. Fodderwing was neither dead nor alive. He was simply nowhere at all" (3, p. 191). When he confronts his dead friend, laid out on the bed, he is frightened. He wants to escape the terrifying scene, because that waxen face does not belong to his Fodderwing.

Three experiences help Jody over the shock and sorrow. Fodderwing's brother encourages Jody to say something to his dead friend. "He'll not hear, but speak to him" (3, p. 192). Jody whispers "hey," and suddenly the paralysis is broken. Jody

*Exceprts from *The Yearling* by Marjorie Kinnan Rawlings are reprinted with the permission of Charles Scribner's Sons. Copyright 1938 Marjorie Kinnan Rawlings; copyright renewed 1966 Norton Baskin.

understands that "death was a silence that gave back no answer" (3, p. 192). But Fodderwing has become familiar again. Next, he is given a task—to care for Fodderwing's pets. Even though he does not feel the joy he felt at sharing the task with Fodderwing, he derives comfort from doing what his friend is no longer able to do. He is also instructed to help Fodderwing's mother with her household chores. The best comfort comes, however, from his fawn to which he briefly returns and for which he asks when it is his turn to sit the night vigil with Fodderwing. Once again Jody is near panic when he is left alone at the deathbed, but Flag keeps him company and Fodderwing is not so frightening to look at when an image occurs to Jody.

> When he leaned far back, Fodderwing looked a little familiar. Yet it was not Fodderwing who lay, pinched of cheek, under the candlelight. Fodderwing was stumbling about outside in the bushes with the raccoon at his heels. In a moment he would come into the house with rocking gait, and Jody would hear his voice. He stole a look at the crossed, crooked hands. Their stillness was implacable. He cried to himself, soundlessly. (3, p. 198)

After the burial, Jody is given "Preacher," the lame redbird, as a remembrance.

The death of Fodderwing is a sad experience for Jody, but the death of Flag presents an existential crisis. Flag is Jody's companion from the day he finds him, and even at night the fawn is at his side. As Jody put it, "he and Flag were free together" (3, p. 360). To Jody's mother, Flag was always a nuisance. Full of curiosity, he had often come to her table uninvited. As a yearling he is forbidden the house because he has grown too big and restless. Jody tries to keep the fawn out of mischief, but one night Flag tramples the tobacco seed bed. He swears to his angry parents that it will never happen again. Then one morning when Jody inspects the young cornfield, he sees that all the delicate sprouts have been pulled up. He detects Flag's sharp hoofprints and knows who is the offender. After a fearful debate, Jody's parents give him one last chance. Jody is allowed to build up the fence around the field and plant again. But after all the hard work, Flag clears the new fence without trouble and again pulls the shoots up by their roots. Jody's father tells him to take the yearling out into the woods and shoot him. It is a choice between that and going hungry. All day long Jody thinks of alternatives to killing his beloved deer but none are workable. He returns at night, having been unable to carry out his father's order. His father, who is bedfast, tells Jody's mother to shoot the deer. She aims, fires, and wounds the animal but does not kill him. Flag topples into the sinkhole, a familiar rendezvous point with Jody in happier days. Jody has to finish the botched job so that his fawn will not suffer. The deed accomplished, "Jody threw the gun aside and dropped flat on his stomach. He retched and vomited and retched again. He clawed into the earth with his fingernails. He beat it with his fists. The sinkhole rocked around him. A far roaring became a thin humming. He sank into blackness as into a dark pool" (3, p. 388).

Jody feels that his father betrayed him. Nothing matters now but getting away. His odyssey on the river is an exhausting one. He encounters loneliness and discomfort and terrifying hunger. Found unconscious from starvation, he is brought back to the shore of his island by a passing boat. Seized by homesickness, he makes his way back and is welcomed with relief and joy by his father, who knows what a despairing road his son has traveled.

> I've wanted life to be easy for you. Easier'n 'twas for me. A man's heart aches, seein' his young uns face the world. Knowin' they got to get their guts tore out, the way his was

tore. I wanted to spare you, long as I could. I wanted you to frolic with your yearlin'. I knowed the lonesomeness he eased for you. But ever man's lonesome. What's he to do then? What's he to do when he gets knocked down? Why, take it for his share and go on. (3, p. 404)

And in his exhausted sleep the first night back home Jody answers his father, in a way. "He did not believe he should ever again love anything, man or woman or his own child as he had loved the yearling. He would be lonely all his life. But a man took it for his share and went on" (3, p. 405).

It all depends on the relationship. Animals are not more important than human beings, but in this story the most significant relationship for Jody was with his deer. For the child even a small loss can be painful. This should stand as a warning against adult judgments such as "It was only a pet." Whatever binds us most deeply is worth being mourned when lost.

A FIFTH–GRADER IS KILLED

Most children relegate death to old age or at least to a distant time in the future. To have a death occur in their school, striking close to them, is a shocking experience for many. Thinking back on our own early school years, we tend to remember our friends but find that most other faces have faded from memory over time. Those few who died young are, by contrast, usually remembered well.

If you enter a school on a normal day and there is neither laughter nor mild mayhem, and every pupil walks the corridors silently, you know something out of the ordinary must have taken place. The news of Doug's death has preceded Mrs. Wright into her fifth-grade classroom. She has not yet heard when she stops in at the library to check out a book before going to her room. Miss Rex hands her the book without engaging her in the usual small talk. "What's happened?" Mrs. Wright inquires. "Doug Murphy, in Pat Smith's class, got killed in a car accident this morning. The sitter was driving a carload of children to school when a truck didn't stop at the intersection of Main and Fifth and hit the car broadside. All the children were injured, and Doug was killed on the spot." Mrs. Wright had not known Doug personally but she had seen him play ball occasionally. He was a strong looking boy with a mane of blond hair, a kid with a reputation of being a nice guy, an average student, good at sports, and not very well known around the school, except by his fellow soccer players.

The atmosphere of shock that has swept through the school affects Mrs. Wright too as she stands at her desk sorting through her notes for the morning's first class period. She stacks the notes to one side and watches the children come in and quietly take their seats. "You all, by now, have heard the sad news of Doug's death," she finally breaks the silence. Tears run down her cheeks, not because of any personal association with Doug but simply because, like everybody else, she feels a deep pain at the thought that so young a person has been killed, and in a stupid accident at that. A truck failed to stop! The teacher's tears bring release to pent up emotions, and several students begin to weep. Mrs. Wright sits down. There is nothing more to say or do except to allow time for sorrow's expression.

Mike comes up to Mrs. Wright's desk. "May I have permission to ask the class something?" "Of course," Mrs. Wright nods. "The funeral," Mike begins, "will be in three days. I think we should all go." "You should give that suggestion some thought," Mrs. Wright agrees. "Talk it over with your parents. Don't feel obligated to be there, but if you decide to attend as a class, I will of course go with you. How many of you have attended a funeral before?" Only three hands go up.

The principal announces over the loudspeaker that all students and teachers are to come to a short assembly. Students will be dismissed for the day on account of Doug Murphy's tragic death. Buses will be prepared to depart the school ten minutes following the assembly. Accompanying her class down to the auditorium, Mrs. Wright overhears several conversations. Students have turned to a reconstruction of the accident, to the details of how it happened.

The class's decision to go to the funeral was unanimous. Mrs. Wright studies the faces of the students as they listen to the eulogies and file by the closed casket, but she can only guess at some of the hidden emotions. At this age children guard their feelings. After the day of Doug's death, no more tears are shed in public. Only Pat Smith's class goes from the funeral to the graveside. They carry flowers. The other children get into the waiting cars to return home. The students Mrs. Wright drives home are silent. She prefers that herself. The last stop is Marsha's house. Marsha slouches in the front seat and hesitates to get out of the car. "He was just a boy," she bursts forth, "just a boy like Mike or Bruce. It could have been my brother, or a friend, or me. It scares me to think of it, but death can hit anybody out of the blue. A few days ago Doug was playing ball. Today he was buried. How can anyone be safe?" Mrs. Wright touches Marsha's arm. "Death is unpredictable and often, as with Doug, we are unprepared for it. We have no warning. But we cannot live our lives in fear that death might strike us or someone we love. There would be no joy in playing or working if we were that fearful all the time. Death reminds us that we will all die, but its presence must not make us so timid that we are afraid to live. We can only be grateful to be alive. And, dear Marsha, one way of expressing that gratitude is to stand by those who suffer the pain of loss. See you tomorrow. We'll talk about this some more."

Mrs. Wright starts her class the next day with a reminder of the day past. "I'd like to have your thoughts," she addresses her class, "on how we could be most helpful to Doug's family. They have suffered a deep loss and need our support. Does anyone know the family? Who was on the soccer team with Doug?" They tell each other what they know about Doug's family, about his working parents and his two smaller brothers. "The two little brothers are on the Little League soccer team. I played with Doug. I could be like a big brother, look out for them in a way," is Raymond's contribution. "I could just drop by and visit with his mother in the evenings. Murphys are practically neighbors down the street from us, and she likes to garden." Suggestions such as these spur other helpful ideas. "You see," Mrs. Wright says, "it will be important to keep up the help over the weeks to come. Right now, everybody feels for the family. Soon we will all be concerned with our own daily affairs and we'll think less and less about Doug and his family. But, for them, healing will take a long time." "I have an idea," Bruce is excited. "Each first Monday of the month we'll talk about new ways to help Doug's family." Applause from the class. "Great suggestion, Bruce, let's make that a promise, and I'll be responsible for holding us to it. But now we have to get to work. Get your workbooks out and begin the composition on pages forty and following."

LEARNING TO LIVE WITH LOSS

Children acquire the capacity to love another person through their early attachment to the person who mothers them. This early bond provides them with what

Erikson has called "basic trust," that is, the ability to relate to the world in a positive, affirmative way. The mother-child relationship establishes a pattern according to which children later model their relationships. Children who are fortunate enough to experience such a relationship start out with the confidence that life will be good and with the assurance that they can master the world. The roots of deep and lasting attachments lie in childhood. A person who has thus acquired an attitude of basic trust will not only be able to attach himself to another person, he will, generally, also be capable of living through the loss of a loved one and of establishing afresh another relationship once mourning is over.

In his work on separation anxiety, John Bowlby (4) makes a convincing case for attachment behavior being the corollary of separation anxiety. The fear of losing the mother figure or her love begins in childhood. Every mother knows that from about eight months through five years of age children show clinging behavior, ranging from a refusal to be put to bed at night to the demand, often following a joyful outing with playmates, "Pick me up, Mommy." Running back to the mother's open arms after exploring the outside world is a familiar pattern among small children. If the child does not find adequate assurances against his anxieties and also experiences the loss of parental love, the development of his personality can be severely dislocated. Bowlby describes three phases of separation anxiety: protest, despair, and detachment. Protest is characterized by outward distress-crying, searching for the lost person, accompanied by the strong expectation that the loved person will soon return. Despair is a slow withdrawal by the child in which he makes few demands on his environment but mourns the lost person. Detachment is an expression by the child of renewed interest in his surroundings with, however, diminished interest in attaching himself to a substitute person. Breaking through the wall of protection the child has built around himself during the phase of detachment requires both love and skill, and time must pass before he can regain the confidence to attach himself anew.

In our study of the reactions children had to the story of the wolf and the seven goats we learned that the basic anxiety of being separated from the source of love and security permeates every age level and is more or less well-handled at different junctures in growing up. How a particular child will master the death of a friend or relative depends largely on how much anchorage his family and school environment has provided him. The sorrow will not be less for such a child nor will there be a cushion against sadness, but he will not ultimately lose his trust in life so easily, even when confronted with death.

REFERENCES

1. Bettelheim, B., *The Uses of Enchantment: The Meaning and Importance of Fairy Tales.* New York, Vintage Books, 1977, 73.
2. Goldreich, G., What is Death? The Answers in Children's Books. *Hastings Center Report,* Jan 1977, 18.
3. Rawlings, M., *The Yearling.* New York, Charles Scribner's Sons, 1967 (1938).
4. Bowlby, J., Separation Anxiety. *The International Journal of Psychoanalysis,* 1960, *41*; Grief and Mourning in Infancy and Early Childhood. *The Psychoanalytic Study of the Child,* 1960, *15*; Processes of Mourning. *The International Journal of Psychoanalysis,* 1961, *42*.

17

Death Education in the Schools for Older Children

Dixie R. Crase
Darrell Crase

INTRODUCTION

One of the functions of formal education is to provide a forum for the examination and discussion of relevant and/or controversial issues. The examination of death and dying has become one of the latest concerns to surface in education. As Wass (1) has stated, "We as individuals as well as a society have problems with death and dying, and if our aim is to solve them, we must clearly identify these problems, then consider all the facts, and use this information in trying to find solutions" (p. xv). This chapter represents an attempt to examine the feasibility of death education for the pre-adolescent and adolescent age groups within the school setting.

Many thanatologists have spoken eloquently of the need for formal death education (2-5). Within the past 10-15 years it has become an aspect of educational curricula at all levels. Most courses have been concentrated at the college and university levels, however death education is now also taught in junior high and secondary school levels. Several examples of formal instruction at the elementary school level are evident (6, 7) while other instances of utilizing the "teachable moment" strategy are reflected through professional literature (8).

One of the unarguable facts about death, according to Knott (4), is that our society is recognizing the need to come to grips with mortality while we are still capable of affecting our behavior and course toward it. Like sex education, instruction for death education has been largely ignored both in the home (9) and within the school environment. Parents have not been capable of talking with their young children and adolescents nor have educators until recently seen the need for the inclusion of formal instruction in school settings. Today, death and dying instruction is being more widely accepted as a worthwhile and necessary phase of education.

Several developments are responsible for this increased interest. For example, the median age as well as the average life expectancy of Americans is on a gradual incline. With more Americans living longer—4000 to 5000 reach the age of 65 every day—and retirement ages remaining the same or even lowering there is more time to contemplate and to plan for one's eventual mortality. Due to advances in medical technology including new and improved emergency life-support systems and the reduction of death due to catastrophic diseases the chances of one dying slowly are increasing. The mass media, including television, newspapers, and the movies have contributed enormously to the interest in death and dying with numerous sensational stories of real life and imagined events. Interest in death and dying phenomena may also be heightened by the continuing threat of nuclear annihilation. Feifel (3) describes the dilemma as "the development of modern science to a level where fantasies of world destruction are recognized as real possibilities, and the recognition that all truth is germane to the exigencies of survival" (p. 5). Regardless of causation, there is ample evidence to suggest that developmentally appropriate death education should be included within the schools for adolescent age groups. In the worlds of Feifel (10): "The time is ripe for death education to assume a rightful role in our development" (p. 353).

RATIONALE FOR DEATH EDUCATION

Why should It Be Taught?

If education contributes to the ultimate goal of human happiness and overall well being then death education should be a part of the process. If, according to Leviton (11), appropriate death education potentially contributes to one's joy in living by reducing the fear of death; if attitudes toward death and suicide can be enlightened then formal death education is justified. Death education is as much a requisite for a complete education as education for human sexuality (3), nutrition education, environmental education, or drug education.

Ulin (12) presents a convincing argument for the inclusion of death education within the public school curriculum. He implies that parents generally fail in their responsibility to communicate with their children relative to sensitive issues. Even church groups do not appear to be too effective with this age group. Many young people are inclined to go elsewhere for help. The schools, then, must assume much of the responsibility for helping young students learn more about death and dying and for developing basic coping strategies. School-based death education for adolescent age groups should be viewed as the continuation of the developmental processes that begin with birth and continue until death.

Formal death education experiences seem uniquely suited to pre-adolescents and adolescents because of implications derived from the consequences of their health behavior. From all indications, including an analytical report by Wynne (13), adolescent suicide and homicide rates are increasing. There is also evidence to the effect that drug, alcohol, and tobacco use is on the increase among pre-adolescent and adolescent populations. Changes in youth sexual relations reflect an increasing tendency for teenage pregnancies, illegitimate births, pediatric abortions, and venereal diseases. In addition, one out of every 600 adolescents (10–24 years old) will die this year; 35 percent from motor vehicle and other accidents; 15 percent from homicide and suicide (14).

These data reflect a variety of self-destructive and other-destructive behaviors committed by young people of all races and social classes. They portray increased alienation and pose important questions about the continuing vitality of American society (13).

There is now considerable interest in the abortion issue, near-death phenomena, euthanasia, understanding death, grief management, and consumer rights of individuals. While research data are limited, death education for young people may conceivably reduce fears toward death, but more importantly it may provide them with skills that ultimately lead to less suicide and other self-destructive behaviors. Coping mechanisms that may be learned through classroom instruction should strengthen the young person's ability to deal with fears and guilt.

Unlike years ago when death was experienced in the home, many death experiences today have been removed from the home. Thus, the act of dying has lost much of its dignity and has become institutionalized, dehumanized, and mechanized and young people are omitted from the experience altogether. Gordon and Klass (15) have described children growing up in a world "when the sight of natural death has been banished from everyday living but in a time when the nuclear bomb and the Nazi holocaust have made death more familiar than at any time since the plague of the fourteenth century" (p. 75). This lack of participation by young people must be corrected if society is to retain a proper perspective toward the value of life and living (16).

Whose Responsibility for Death Education?

The responsibility for death education in the schools may be assumed in a variety of ways. Should all teachers be prepared to respond to child-initiated questions and/or expressed concerns? Which teachers should initiate consideration for death-related issues via readings, activities, field trips or special visitors to the classroom? How may teachers and parents cooperate in order to support older children who have experienced a significant loss in their lives? Is the school counselor to be viewed as children's and parents' primary source of help during troubled times?

A loose, unarticulated approach to death education may result in the "silent majority" and/or a few teachers or counselors following their own philosophy and guidelines. As schools recognize the significance of their role in meeting children's developmental needs, a more comprehensive approach to death education may be forthcoming. In some schools, administrators, counselors, teachers and parents are in the process of establishing a basic philosophy and subsequent policies and suggestions for approaching death education.

A university laboratory school of 500 children recently experienced the death of the mother of one child and the father of another child within a two-month period. One of the surviving parents encouraged the school to establish a "network" to help other children faced with death. Consequently, the principal, curriculum director, school counselor, and a committee of teachers initiated inservice sessions to explore basic attitudes, philosophy, and guidelines. This school's concern for children was eventually expressed as "Helping Children in Crises."

Administrators' increased sensitivity to crises in families is reflected in publications such as a special October 1979 issue of the *National Elementary Principal* entitled "When the Family Comes Apart: What Schools Need to Know." Counselors are recognizing that while death represents the ultimate form of loss, children may be "losing" parents due to divorce, separation, hospitalization, disability, or death. Coping with loss may be nothing new, but the rapidity and volatility of recent changes influencing the family seem to call for renewed attention to handling crises.

An articulated approach to death education may offer teachers an institutionalized network of colleagues, supervisors, conferences, and workshops in order to share and work through the feelings generated by their work with children (17).

According to Sutherland (18), this seems essential in the face of clinical and research evidence showing that adults who have the most trouble working with
children are those who have been cut off from the supportive peer networks of
the adult world.

As indicated in an earlier illustration, parents may initiate consideration of a
school's approach to death education. Wass and Scott's (19) study indicates that
middle school students of better educated families seem to have "certain understandings of the fundamental relationship of death to life and therefore have less
fear" (p. 11). On the other hand, many parents have difficulty communicating
about death with their own children. Children are too often given little information
and/or assistance in expressing their feelings partially because of parents' limited
understanding of death education. Furman (20) reports research indicating 41
percent of the parents studied told their children under 16 little about the other
parent's death. Wass and Scott (19) acknowledge the possible opposition of parents
to death education in the schools. Teachers who are relatively comfortable with the
subject are encouraged to proceed into various areas that do not intrude into the
realm of religion. A respect for parental values and beliefs at some point may have
to be balanced against older children's right to search for their own answers to
ultimate questions.

Gordon and Klass (15) note that death education may be met with individual
noncooperation, delay, or expressions of disgust by parents. One of the strategies
suggested by them in combating resistance is for teachers, when they introduce
the topic of death, to "assertively but gently address themselves to parents' and
colleagues' fears before those fears have a chance to turn into resistance" (p. 230).
Letters to parents telling them of the approach to death education in the classroom
may also serve to alleviate resistance.

Fear of parental opposition in reality may not be a major concern. At least one
teacher who included a unit on thanatology for 7th graders reported only two
negative experiences in six years. On one occasion, the class stopped for lunch after
a field trip to a funeral home and one student was unable to eat. The mother of
another child reported that her child had nightmares during the unit of study. The
teacher shared her impression that most students' fears are allayed by having
additional information about the process of embalming, burial, etc.

Direct Instructional Responsibility

Which teachers should assume primary responsibility for direct instruction of
pre- and adolescent-age groups about death and dying education? The answer is a
simple one: the person best qualified to work with the learner in light of the
students' developmental age and psychological needs. When the school assumes
responsibility for death education, it should be seen as an evolving kind of experience with many disciplines having input at various points in time. Death education is not the domain of any one discipline. If any course within the school setting
should be handled with an interdisciplinary flavor and utilize resources from across
the campus, thanatology should.

A course experience in death education should evolve around the theme of viewing death-related phenomena from several disciplinary points of reference including
religion, science, health, insurance, psychology, business management, and others.
Various perspectives from those areas should then shed light on death as an integral

part of life itself. Preparation for life cannot be taught in one neat, concise package, nor can death education (5).

Who, then, should assume responsibility for instruction? The best qualified person may be a teacher of biology, physical science, or religion. However, teachers of health education should possess competencies appropriate for dealing with personal and family life crises throughout the life cycle from sex education to drug education and should be capable of initiating meaningful educational experiences of an interdisciplinary nature dealing with death education. Since helping young people think about the reality of their own death, helping them to reduce fears about the death of others, and helping them to prevent the likelihood of suicide are a function of health education, perhaps the health educator should assume major responsibility for the development and coordination of the death education course. However, it can just as well be assumed by another specialist within another discipline depending upon the circumstances. Again, whoever assumes the responsibility for instruction should utilize a team approach in order to maximize the educational benefits for students.

TEACHER COMPETENCIES

Anyone who possesses certification in a specialized area can conceivably assume responsibility for teaching older children about death and dying education. As of now there are no certification standards that must be met nor is there a standardized curriculum that must be followed in becoming a thanatologist. Consequently, many of those who have taken on the serious responsibility of teaching about sensitive issues are probably unprepared in terms of formal training. Four concerns in the development of potential teachers are discussed: self-development of teachers, professional preparation, communications skills, and counseling skills for special needs.

Self-Development

Five general criteria have been identified by Johnson (21) that apply to the qualities of a sex educator. With some modification by Leviton (11), these criteria apply equally to the death educator. They are:

1. The teacher must have initiated the process of understanding his or her own death feelings, and to have admitted not only its existence, but to its full status in the dynamics of his total personality functioning.

2. The teacher needs to know about death and death education in order to teach it.

3. The teacher of death education needs to be able to use the language of death easily and naturally, especially in the presence of the young.

4. The teacher needs to be familiar with the sequence of developmental events throughout life, and to have a sympathetic understanding of common problems associated with them.

5. The teacher needs an acute awareness of the enormous social changes that are in progress and of their implications for changes in our patterns of death-related attitudes, practices, laws, and institutions.

In addition to the above criteria, three other competencies of death educators seem to be desirable:

6. The teacher of death education should be able to communicate with parents of adolescents in managing grief and bereavement and in handling other sensitive issues.

7. The effective teacher should be fairly sophisticated about counseling and crises intervention techniques (22). Teachers will encounter students who are seeking special assistance in coming to terms with death and dying.

8. Teachers of death education should possess evaluation skills in order to make assessments of students' progress in light of predetermined course objectives.

Professional Preparation

Most teachers of children and adolescents have engaged in limited professional preparation for the teaching of death education. The major reason being that formal preparation just does not exist in any particular organized fashion. Perhaps the most frequent type of preparation for the prospective teacher comes through enrolling in a university-level death education course that may or may not be well taught. Death education courses have become quite prevalent on college and university campuses according to various surveys, and many teachers certificated in other areas are undoubtedly gaining some expertise in death education in this way.

Several workshops and symposia are now being offered across the country providing excellent opportunities for would-be teachers and/or counselors. For example, in December of 1979 and October of 1980, the Forum for Death Education and Counseling sponsored two excellent pre-conference workshops in connection with its national meetings for persons involved in teaching and counseling. These conferences ran for several days and were conducted by recognized professionals from throughout the country. Professional societies such as the Forum for Death Education and Counseling and the Foundation of Thanatology are providing additional experiences that are helpful in the area of staff development and improvement.

The array of professional media becomes a third source available for the self-development of teachers. Death and dying literature in the form of books, journal articles, and monographs has become abundant; it is growing daily. In addition, audiovisuals (film, cassettes, records), lists of bibliographies, mediagraphies, and reviews of existing sources are now available. The reader may wish to consult each issue of the informative international quarterly, *Death Education*, for an excellent and comprehensive media exchange.

In time, processes must be developed in order to insure a higher quality of instruction. Specific guidelines must be developed and initiated that will hold teachers accountable for their actions. At present, there is no such machinery.

Communication Skills

Effective communication in response to student-initiated questions or concerns is a significant responsibility of teachers. Appropriate communication depends in part on the teacher's ability to interpret what students want to know and then possessing sufficient knowledge in order to respond with ease and accuracy. It is important that the teacher first be a facilitator and a catalyst and second a subject matter specialist (23).

Much of the death education course experience for pre-adolescents and teen-agers will focus on the utilization of community resources. Classroom and community activities will ultimately be centered around the specific needs of the students. Thus, the death educator must possess communication skills for working with community resource persons such as morticians, cemetery owners, ministers and others.

Counseling Students with Special Needs

Teachers of adolescents must be prepared to assume roles other than those of a didactic nature in the classroom. Many students will enroll in death education classes in order to resolve conflict, to find out more about their impending mortality, or to attempt to resolve special problems they have encountered. The teacher may need to function in individual or small group counseling sessions with suicidal students, those who have experienced a significant loss of a parent or loved one, or those who have developed fears or guilt about some particular aspect of death. Unusual deaths may occur and thus the management of grief and loss may be exceptionally difficult for the older child. Teachers must attempt to deal effectively with these special concerns.

Preparation for working with students with special needs will come essentially through experience. Inasmuch as each case may be different and couched in a unique set of circumstances teachers will need to be knowledgeable and flexible and utilize a variety of resources within the counseling situation. Specialists outside the school environment such as pediatricians and other doctors, funeral directors, and religious leaders will of necessity be involved in a team approach in resolving special needs of students. Classroom teachers should facilitate these cooperative efforts.

CHARACTERISTICS OF ADOLESCENTS

Development of appropriate educational experiences for any audience is at least in part dependent upon an understanding of the age group. Death education for older children must take into account the characteristics of adolescents. With the onset of puberty, teens are catapulted into a world of change. Changes within their own bodies and minds, and in their relationships to peers, parents, and society require adaptation on the part of young people.

The significance of the adolescent years is being re-evaluated. Bronfenbrenner (24) suggests that the first six years of life have previously been identified as the most important in the life cycle. Today, more psychologists are recognizing the critical nature of early adolescence. Dobson (25) confirms that it is difficult to overestimate the significance of development during the thirteenth and fourteenth years. In fact, this may be the most challenging twenty-four months in life.

The most apparent, tangible change confronting the prepubescent child is the physiological development within his or her own body. In the prepubescent stage, the secondary sex characteristics begin to develop. Pubescence lasts about two years and ends in puberty, the point at which an individual is sexually mature and able to reproduce. Sexual maturation is accompanied by an unprecedented "growth spurt" in height and weight which contribute to the awkwardness of adolescence. Over the past century, each generation has been growing taller and heavier. This trend seems to be due primarily to higher living standards including better nutrition and is leveling off in most sectors of the nation.

The age of onset and duration of the growth spurt varies from one child to another. Thus a normal group of adolescents may differ dramatically in their physical development and appearance. Whether an adolescent is an early or late maturer may be of significance to the individual or his or her parents. Several studies suggest the advantages of early or average maturation for boys (26, 27). Potential problems of late maturing boys may be offset by appropriate guidance (28). The differences between early and late maturing girls seem not to be so clear (26, 29). However, early menstruation may complicate girls' development. Girls need help to complete the psychological tasks of childhood; to see menstruation as one episode in the long process of their psychological and sexual development.

Older studies (30) indicate that most young teenagers are more concerned about their physical appearance than about any other aspect of themselves. More recent studies confirm the long term significance of perceived attractiveness during the teenage years (31). The keen sensitivity to one's physical appearance helps to explain the traumatic effect of life threatening experiences. Loss of hair or other physical impairments resulting from treatment may seem to be more devastating than the ultimate consequences of disease or accidents.

Change is again the key word in relationship to adolescents' cognitive development. Before adolescence, a child is largely concerned with the here and now, with what is apparent to the senses and with solving problems by trial and error. The emerging capacity for formal operational thought changes the adolescent to one who formulates hypotheses, thinks more abstractly, and considers what might be rather than merely what is. This awareness of the discrepancy between the actual and the possible is at least in part responsible for the critical teenager. Deficiencies within existing social, political, religious and family systems are regularly critiqued.

Although adults may grow weary of the relentless attack on cherished values, the intellectualizing exercise seems to be an integral part of the teen's cognitive development. Elkind (32) regards the major task of early adolescence as "the conquest of thought" (p. 43). Intellectualization may be employed as a psychological defense by some adolescents to deal with troubling anxieties that may be too painful to deal with directly. According to Mussen et al. (33), intellectualization involves casting into an abstract, impersonal, philosophical form, issues that are actually of immediate personal concern. Thus, apparently impersonal, highly intellectual discussions of the role of aggression in human affairs, of responsibility versus freedom, of the nature of friendship, and of the existence of God may, in fact, more nearly reflect deep-seated personal concerns. Linked with the adolescent's development of a more mature understanding of time, may come the poignant awareness that everyone is caught up in the ongoing process of growth, aging, and death (34, p. 432).

A reading list for 12-year-old students at one school included *Death of a Salesman* and *Our Town*. Intellectual, unemotional discussions proceeded as book reports were shared in the classroom. However, one parent reported her daughter's fear of death being verbalized after the family attended a stage production of

Hamlet. The combination of "messages" apparently brought forth a personal fear of the child. The daughter quoted Emily in *Our Town*, "I can't. I can't go on. It goes so fast. We don't have time to look at one another . . . Take me back up the hill to my grave . . . Do any human beings ever realize life while they live it—every, every minute?" (35, p. 138).

Young children's moral judgment is likely to be based on avoiding punishment, meeting one's own needs, or gaining approval from an authority figure. Not until adolescence, do individuals have the mental capacities required for understanding universal moral principles. According to Papalia and Olds (36) advanced cognitive development does not guarantee advanced moral development, but it must exist for the moral development to take place. Postconventional morality indicates that the individual makes choices on the basis of principles that have been thought through, accepted, and internalized. Right behavior is the behavior that conforms to these principles, regardless of immediate social praise or blame. Obviously most adolescents, like most adults, conform to social conventions, and think in terms of doing the right thing to please others or to obey the law.

At no time in life is a person as likely to be concerned about moral values and standards as during adolescence according to Mussen (33). Discussions related to death often revolve around values. Moral education is not teaching what is right and what is wrong. It is helping the individual to recognize that moral choices exist. Kohlberg (37) is committed to the belief that adolescents can be taught to elevate their moral thinking when they are confronted with difficult moral dilemmas. Interactions with persons operating at a higher level of moral thinking are likely to stimulate advancement through the stages of moral judgment.

Erikson's theory of psychosocial development identifies the major task of early adolescence as establishing a sense of identity. Answering the perennial question of "Who am I?" consumes a lion's share of the young teen's attention. Answers do not come easily amidst the changing pressures within the developing self, and in response to expectations of peers, parents, and society. When a sense of identity has been successfully integrated, the older adolescent is in a better position to establish a sense of intimacy in a responsible way.

Peers play a central role in the psychological development of most adolescents as relationships with parents weaken. The prolonged dependence on parents is sometimes a source of conflict as teens strive for independence. Although the peer influence is often seen in opposition to parental values, this is the exception rather than the general rule. Adolescent friends often come from families with similar backgrounds and standards of behavior.

Although adolescence is characterized by rapidity of growth and unprecedented physiological and psychological changes within a complex world, most teens are reasonably mature, happy, responsible members of society. However, a significant minority of adolescents are not successfully accomplishing critical developmental tasks. Their failures result in headlines accentuating problems associated with teenagers including school dropouts, runaways, premarital pregnancies, venereal diseases, delinquency, suicide, and use of drugs and alcohol. Feifel (3) suggests that delinquency at times may reflect masked mourning. Indeed, some violence may well serve as an active response to unmastered anxieties about death.

At a time when teens are experiencing growth pains, their parents may be caught up in failing marriages, disillusionments on the job, aging parents, inflationary times, and their own mid-life crises. Some observers are suggesting that for many adolescents, the most regular, stable influence in their lives is the school. Schools, and teachers in particular, have been asked to do a lot of things and have been soundly criticized when they have failed. Can teachers take on additional responsibilities in terms of "parenting" young people? Is preparation for life, including death, within the realm of educators in middle schools, junior highs or high schools?

CURRICULUM

Goals of Death Education

Without attempting to be too global, perhaps the overall aim of all education is to improve the quality of life for the individual and society. The quality of life extends through death, therefore the quality of dying and bereavement then becomes a concern for the living. Leviton (38) has defined death education as "a developmental process that transmits to people and society death-related knowledge and implications resulting from that knowledge" (p. 44). Without taking issue with this definition or attempting to develop it further, let us now look at some attainable learning objectives applicable to the young adult population. These goals/objectives are summarized from the works of several authors.

Gordon and Klass (15) have identified death education goals directed specifically toward young children through adolescence. Overall, they would like children to be knowledgeable about death and the process of dying, to have the personal and emotional resources to cope with death in a healthy manner, to be able to make informed decisions about medical and funeral choices, and to be socially and ethically aware of issues relating to death and dying. Stated specifically, their four objectives are (p. 129):

1. To inform the students of facts not currently widespread in the culture
2. To help the student affectively deal with the idea of personal death and the deaths of significant others
3. To make the student an informed consumer of medical and funeral services
4. To help the student formulate socioethical issues related to death and define value judgments these issues raise

Examples are offered by which teachers may evaluate the extent to which these objectives have been met.

Berg and Daugherty's (39) objectives identify the need for developing a realistic mental framework toward viewing death as a universal phenomenon; development of an appreciation for literature relative to death; providing knowledge that leads to an understanding of biological, sociocultural, religious, psychological, and economic phenomena; understanding a variety of death-related viewpoints; and development of usable cognitive skills.

Leviton (38) has provided a very useful list of thirteen objectives many of which are appropriate in the instruction of school-age children. Obviously, as he implies, objectives vary according to the target population. Most notable among the objectives or goals are those which speak to the need for removing the taboo aspect of death language in order to facilitate communication; reduction of death-related anxieties through appropriate education; understanding and being able to react to a suicidal person; consumer education; understanding death and the dying process; and recognizing variations in aspects of death both within and across cultures.

Knott (4) focuses on what he calls a "triad of conceptual handles." The first is that of *information sharing* of relevant academic types of materials that deal with definitions, biomedical dimensions of death and dying, bio-statistics, and phenomena surrounding bereavement, grief, and mourning. The second concept, *values clarification*, offers the opportunity to examine values that determine one's lifestyle and deathstyle. Some of the more global aspects, e.g., nuclear holocaust, would be discussed in arriving at and in determining one's set of personal values. Knott identifies the third learning objective as *coping behaviors*. Here the learner analyzes coping strategies that are useful in managing loss, grief, and bereavement. The absence of "loss experiences" during the developmental stages punctuates the need for further study of self-help systems for the adolescent.

More specific learning objectives would be developed by the teacher in accomplishing the broader goals identified. These would be dynamic, reasonably attainable objectives so structured for local situations. An excellent model to follow in classifying specific objectives is that proposed by Stillion (40) and patterned after Bloom's well known work with educational taxonomies. The three dimensions that are helpful to teachers in planning a learning/teaching environment are the cognitive, affective, and psychomotor domains. The first two are pertinent to death educators. The cognitive domain includes those objectives that deal with the development of intellectual skills and abilities while the affective domain includes objectives that describe changes in attitudes, values, and appreciations. A thorough discussion relative to the implementation of this framework is presented in (40).

Content Areas

Death education can be taught (1) on a "teachable moment" basis void of any set structure, (2) as an integrated subject within the context of several courses, (3) as a specialized unit within a formal course such as biology, health education or home economics, or (4) as an autonomous offering within the broader curriculum. Utilization of the "teachable moment" strategy is more likely to occur with very young children, e.g., kindergarten through fifth grade. It is the major focus of the previous chapter. While definitive data are not available, it is assumed that teachers of middle school children would pursue death education on an informal basis or as a specialized unit within the context of an existing course, e.g., health education. Senior high students would be more likely to study death education as an autonomous offering. As Hardt (41) suggests, whether or not educators choose to include units or courses on death education in their school curricula partially depends on prevailing attitudes toward death inasmuch as attitudes play a significant role in learning and understanding. In other words, local environments will dictate directions curriculum planners should follow.

Public Law 94-142 and the mainstreaming of handicapped and terminally ill children into regular classrooms and the consideration needed for long-term, chronically ill students will require special attention by teachers and curriculum planners. The mainstreaming phenomenon should provide additional impetus for specialized counseling within school environments in addition to the need for some type of effective death education.

There is no standardized curriculum available for use with pre-adolescents and older children, nor is there any concerted pressure by any particular group to force standardization of death education curriculum within school systems. The subject matter that is taught and the methods utilized in teaching it are almost solely left to the discretion of a teacher and/or a particular school system. There are, however, several sources and/or curriculum guides (15, 23, 39, 42-46) available to educators undertaking death instruction that speak to content, curriculum designs, and principles of curriculum development. Other excellent sources such as those by Watts (47) and Grollman (48) offer helpful insights and suggestions for teaching and counseling young students.

Gordon and Klass (15) have developed one of the most comprehensive guides to curriculum development to date. It is a suggested curriculum by grade (nursery school through grade 12) and goal. Each of the curriculum units is centered around one or more objectives that are specific statements of the general goal (see goals identified in previous unit). Resources, e.g., literature and other media, available to students and teachers are suggested for each grade level. One example of one goal and one objective for grades 6 and 7 follows:

Goal One: To inform the students of facts not currently widespread in the culture.
Objective: Students study the various methods of body disposal.
Activities:
  1. Visit a funeral home and cemetery, family graves, mausoleum, columbarium.
  2. Ask a funeral director about methods of body disposition.
  3. Talk to a physician about organ donation and body donation.
  4. Students talk to parents and grandparents about funeral customs in their family and prepare reports in the form of a book, scrapbook, recording, and the like.
  5. Students research funeral customs in past and other cultures. Make bulletin board, class newspaper; spend class time in school library (pp. 169-172).

Specific student and teacher resources are then suggested that are pertinent and useful in achieving the objective.

The content of a death education unit or course will vary depending upon the developmental levels and ages of students, the instructor's knowledge of subject matter, and the students' particular interests. In a state-wide study of the non-parochial schools in Wisconsin, Price and Henke (49) determined that death education was most frequently taught at the 11th and 12th grade levels with units varying in length from one week to one semester, the most frequent being two weeks. The most frequently taught topics in descending order were terminal illness, management of death fear and suicide, euthanasia, abortion and bereavement, geriatrics, murder, and "other" category including war, manslaughter, disasters, religion, and death.

McMahon (42) offers a very practical curriculum guide suitable for advanced students capable of doing independent study at the high school level. The guide consists of behavioral objectives, questions to be answered, activities to be performed, and assessment tasks. Students study subunits on The Taboo of Death, Biological, Sociological, and Psychological Definitions of Death; The Crises of Man; Views on Death and Dying; Understanding the Dying Patient or Relative; Psychological Implications of the Funeral, Burial, and Bereavement; and the Understanding of Suicide and Self-destructive Behaviors. An example of one brief unit follows:

Definitions of Death: Biological, Social, and Psychological

Behavioral objective: The student will be able to differentiate between the biological, social, and psychological definitions of death. Students should answer the following questions:

1. What is the biological definition of death?
2. What constitutes social death?
3. What constitutes psychological death?
4. How do these definitions interrelate?

Student activities: Upon reading all required readings for this subunit, make a chart depicting the interaction and separation of each definition of death.
Assessment tasks:

1. Define biological, social, and psychological death as described by the various authors listed in the required readings.
2. Cite three case histories (can be hypothetical) that depict each type of death (p. 30).

In one of the earlier efforts, Berg and Daugherty (39) developed a teacher's resource book which gives the teacher specific procedures to follow in the form of daily lesson plans. The guide is merely suggestive and the teacher is free to alter or to make adaptations as necessary or desirable. Thirty daily lesson plans are provided that call for decisions on funeral customs, comparative religious viewpoints, psychology of grief and visits to cemeteries and funeral homes, and the utilization of several guest speakers. In addition, the authors suggest the writing of essays, role playing activities, and a final assessment.

Mills et al. (23) utilize a conceptual approach to the curriculum for ages 13-18. Major concepts represent typical content areas (e.g., life cycles, causes of death, attitudes, and death rituals) one would generally use in death education courses at the high school or college level. For each concept, several learning opportunities are suggested with objectives and activities being identified for each. The authors have also provided some helpful notes for teachers in facilitating the instructional process.

Student Activities

In a death education unit or course for young learners, a number of instructional strategies should be employed in addition to traditional didactic methods. As with any learning endeavor myriad experiences should be provided that meet the educational and personal needs of the learners. The possibilities are limitless:

1. Independent projects
2. Reading assignments (fiction, social sciences, autobiographies)
3. Field trips to cemeteries, crematoria, mortuaries, medical schools, hospice units, and emergency units of hospitals to name a few
4. Utilization of guest speakers, e.g., clergymen, lawyers, doctors, morticians, hospice workers, nurses, coroners, the widowed, and dying persons
5. Use of media including film, cassettes and records

6. Tape recording sessions
7. Film making
8. Small group counseling
9. Individual counseling
10. Written work that describes a loss in the student's life and his or her coping techniques utilized
11. Informal discussions
12. The writing of a daily journal

Resources

Numerous types of curriculum materials are now available to the death educator at the secondary level and they are growing daily. Both books and professional articles are vast in number though most textbooks have been written for professionals representing many disciplines and for students at the college and university level. Many excellent films, film strips, and cassettes have been developed during recent years and are available from various sources. Several bibliographies, mediagraphies, and curriculum guides have been published. One of the best and most recent resource guides (50) identifies, abstracts, and indexes books, journals, audiovisual media, published research, and professional organizations identified with death-related phenomena.

Evaluation

Both formative and summative evaluation should be practiced by the death educator. Formative evaluation should be undertaken to ascertain learning mastery during the formative stages of instruction and continued throughout the instructional unit. The main purpose is to determine what has been learned within individual units and what yet must be mastered. Formative assessment tasks could involve content-types of written or oral tests, written or oral reports, and a host of other techniques. Summative evaluation, on the other hand, takes place at the conclusion of a course and is usually more comprehensive. This method of evaluation is used to determine how well course objectives have been achieved and the degree to which they have been achieved.

Evaluation of death education experiences is difficult because teachers may have difficulty in establishing meaningful and attainable course objectives. That is, what are the behavioral and attitudinal changes desired from educating about death and dying (51)? Perhaps considerably more thought should go into pre-planning of death education courses for young adolescents and older children in order to achieve more precise operational definitions of learning behaviors. A second problem in evaluation emerges because of the impreciseness of measuring instruments. At present, there are few published assessment tools available other than a dozen or so attitude scales. Thus the evaluator is committed to the use of criterion-referenced standards of measurement—the degree to which the student has attained a particular standard—as opposed to norm-referenced standards that involve the hierarchial ordering of individuals.

In time, educators are going to be held more accountable for their actions; they will have to justify and more precisely articulate that which is to be accomplished through death education. More energy must be devoted to the development and utilization of specific evaluation techniques as well as overall assessment procedures for use in supporting death education rationale.

RESEARCH/ASSESSMENT

Those who teach death and dying concepts to older children, or to any population for that matter, can side with one of two alternatives regarding the research/assessment component. First, they can postulate that formal instruction is in the neophyte stage and sufficient structure and standardization have not yet accrued to facilitate accurate assessment of the effects of instruction. They would be partially correct. Or, death educators can move ahead and attempt to develop a scholarly data base that will support instructional efforts. At present, this is not being done on any consistent, widespread scale.

The 1975 editors of *Omega* (52) called for an accounting of death education experiences. They reported several attempts of researchers to evaluate the outcomes of death education. Since then, additional reports have been published in the periodical literature and some of these have been summarized in other publications (53, 54).

The major research efforts so far have produced results of limited use to the death educator. For the most part, researchers have focused on the assessment of attitudinal changes of students utilizing quasi-experimental research designs. The samples have usually been small and have come from more mature populations such as college and nursing students. The research format usually involves the identification of students, a control group and an experimental group; pretesting both groups with one or more of several existing attitude scales; applying the treatment (instruction) for a specified number of days or weeks; then posttesting using the same instrument.

While the tenability of the early research findings may be questioned, the following conclusions appear to have some support:

1. Favorable death attitude changes may be achieved from a relatively brief death education course.

2. Experimental groups tend to show a marked increase in thought about their own death.

3. Experimental groups tend to entertain more frequent thoughts of death and demonstrate greater amounts of interest in death-related phenomena than subjects in control groups.

4. Instruction in death and dying improves one's attitude about counseling or caring for dying persons.

The data on adolescent behavior are less abundant. Two recent studies have utilized older children as subjects. Perkes and Schildt (55), in determining sex-related attitudes, found that males and females differed significantly on several components. Females, more than males, were in favor of abortion, valued funerals, and were more concerned as to what might happen to their bodies subsequent to death. Some differences were found in attitudes about capital punishment and near-death phenomena. No significant differences were found on the fear of death component.

Bailis and Kennedy (56) sought to determine whether students experienced values. Never again will peer approval be so crucial. In the struggle for independence of thought and action, adolescents are often acutely aware of the reality of their prolonged dependence on parents. Helping young people to develop a consistent and meaningful lifestyle and deathstyle within these parameters is the challenge of death education in the schools.

Goals of death education are summarized from several sources. More specific learning objectives particularly suited to adolescent needs are suggested. Available curriculum guides vary in terms of objectives, student activities, and assessment techniques. The evaluation and selection of media should include such criteria as the multiple usage of media, accuracy and validity of information, guidelines for use, examination of references and bibliographies, quality and soundness of curriculum materials, media availability, past use of records and results, and the overall educational quality and application potential of media.

The need for both formative and summative evaluation of death education is noted. The difficulty in establishing meaningful and attainable course objectives is coupled with the impreciseness of measuring instruments. The ultimate strength and educational worth of death education for older children will depend upon a sound and useful research base.

REFERENCES

1. Wass, H. Preface. In H. Wass (ed.), *Dying: Facing the facts*, Washington, D.C.: Hemisphere Publishing Corporation, 1979.
2. Leviton, D. The need for education on death and suicide. *The Journal of School Health*, 1969, 39, 270–274.
3. Feifel, H. The meaning of death in American society. In B. R. Green & D. P. Irish (eds.), *Death education: Preparation for living*. Cambridge, Mass.: Schenkman, 1971.
4. Knott, J. E. Death education for all. In H. Wass (ed.), *Dying: Facing the facts*. Washington, D.C.: Hemisphere Publishing Corporation, 1979.
5. Crase, D. R. & Crase, D. Live issues surrounding death education. *The Journal of School Health*, 1974, 44, (2), 70–73.
6. Mueller, J. M. I taught about death and dying. *Phi Delta Kappan*, 1978, 60, (2), 117.
7. Maddocks, M. In Florida: A life and death class. *Time*, 1979 (December 3), 14–16.
8. Marlowe, J. Won't you come home John Dewey? *Phi Delta Kappan*, 1979, 60, (8), 603–604.
9. Stillion, J. & Wass, H. Children and death. In H. Wass (ed.), *Dying: Facing the facts*. Washington, D.C.: Hemisphere Publishing Corporation, 1979.
10. Feifel, H. Epilogue. In H. Feifel (ed.), *New meanings of death*. New York: McGraw-Hill, 1977.
11. Leviton, D. The role of the schools in providing death education. In B. R. Green & D. P. Irish (eds.), *Death education: Preparation for living*. Cambridge, Mass.: Schenkman, 1971.
12. Ulin, R. O. *Death and dying education*. Washington, D.C.: National Education Association, 1977.
13. Wynne, E. A. Behind the discipline problem: Youth suicide as a measure of alienation. *Phi Delta Kappan*, 1978, 59, (5), 307–315.
14. Alexander, A. Adolescent health: Challenge of the 80s. *The Journal of School Health*, 1980, 50, (1), 47.
15. Gordon, A. & Klass, D. *They need to know: How to teach children about death*. Englewood Cliffs, N.J.: Prentice-Hall, 1979.
16. Berg, D. W. & Daugherty, G. W. Teaching about death. *Today's Education*, 1973, 62, 46–47.
17. Fogel, A. Expressing affection and love to young children. *Dimensions*, 1980, 8, (2), 39–44.
18. Sutherland, J. D. The study of family relationships in contemporary society. In P. Lomas (ed.), *The predicament of the family*. London: Hogarth Press, 1972.

53. Crase, D. The need to assess the impact of death education. *Death Education*, 1978, 1, (4), 423–432.
54. Crase, D. Death education: Accountability through scholarly inquiry. *Journal of the American College Health Association*, 1979, 27, (5), 257–260.
55. Perkes, A. C. & Schildt, R. Death-related attitudes of adolescent males and females. *Death Education*, 1979, 2, (4), 359–368.
56. Bailis, L. A. & Kennedy, W. R. Effects of a death education program upon secondary school students. *Journal of Educational Research*, 1977, 71, 63–66.
57. Kastenbaum, R. We covered death today. *Death Education*, 1977, 1, (1), 85–92.

SELECTED RESOURCES

In this final section Charles Corr offers a short annotated bibliography of books for adults, Hannelore Wass a brief annotated list of books for children, while Richard Pacholski adds similar listings of organizational and audiovisual resources. Our aim is to point the way to further reading and to resources other than printed materials. In each case, these are selected from a much wider range of existing resources. For broader and lengthier lists of such resources, the reader is referred to the guides noted below that have been prepared by the same authors and their colleagues. It is enough to say here that there *is* available a rich spectrum of resources for use in connection with the many aspects of childhood and death. Not every subject is equally well treated or as fully developed as we might wish. If that were so, there would be no further fields to conquer. We do have much yet to learn, but we are also the beneficiaries of a large body of knowledge and insight that is already at hand. Our purpose in the present book has been to consolidate and to extend that accumulated wisdom insofar as that can be achieved within the pages of a single volume designed for a broad readership.

Books for Adults

Charles A. Corr

The following bibliography is meant to provide guidance for additional reading. It is a selected listing of 24 books about coping with dying or with bereavement as they relate to childhood. In each case, the annotation supplies a description of the contents of the book, together with some comments about background, strengths, and/or limitations. There is no need for a fuller bibliography because those who wish or need more can consult two other guides which are already available. *Death education: An annotated resource guide* by Wass and her colleagues (see below) is a full-scale directory to many types of resources in the field of death and dying. And *Helping children cope with death: Guidelines and resources*, edited by Wass and Corr (see below), contains a lengthy annotated resource section detailing books for adults and children, as well as audiovisual items, that relate to childhood and death.

Adams, D. W. *Childhood malignancy: The psychosicial care of the child and his family*. Springfield, IL: Charles C Thomas, 1979. David Adams is a Canadian medical social worker writing for caregivers who serve children with malignant diseases and their families. His book integrates a careful review of the literature, an awareness of recent changes in childhood malignancies and their treatment, first-hand experience, and personal insights. After describing the approach of a multidisciplinary team, the text proceeds from early family responses to their child's life-threatening illness, through impact of disease and treatment, to death, bereavement, and follow-up care. Difficulties are illustrated through concrete examples, and practical guidelines are offered for constructive intervention. The book lives up to its billing as "a major resource, reference and text" for caregivers. The author has also prepared a companion work, *The psychosocial care of the child and his family in childhood cancer: An annotated bibliography*, to accompany this book. The 92-page bibliography is available separately for $4.50 from Department of Social Work Services, McMaster University Medical Centre, 1200 Main Street West, Hamilton, Ontario, Canada L8S 4J9.

Anthony, E. J. & Koupernik, C. (eds.). *The child in his family, Vol. 2: The impact of disease and death*. New York: John Wiley and Sons, 1973. A large book of original contributions from invited international authorities respresenting different disciplines and cultures. Altogether there are 31 independent papers, 2 short symposia with discussions, a lengthy symposium on children of the holocaust with 7 principal papers and discussion, and 6 editorial comments. This volume boasts major contributors and a very broad reach; it is a substantial resource for professionals.

Burton, L. (ed.). *Care of the child facing death*. London & Boston: Routledge & Kegan Paul, 1974. Contains 17 papers mostly by British contributors divided into four groupings: general problems (the extent and nature of the subject, together with difficulties faced by parents, children, and staff); specific problems (the child in pain, the "doomed family," and coping with a difficult treatment regime); helping the child (observations from the perspectives of a parent, education, social work, nursing, and psychiatry); and helping the family (an interdisciplinary approach, the role of the physician, parents' groups, counseling grieving parents, and caring for siblings before death, bereavement and rebuilding of family life afterwards). Important and well worth reading.

Burton, L. *The family life of sick children: A study of families coping with chronic childhood disease.* London & Boston: Routledge & Kegan Paul, 1975. Many discussions of dying children seem to have in mind a short and relatively straightforward trajectory. To that extent, they neglect longer-term chronic illnesses, as well as the special characteristics that relate to hereditary and incurable disorders. The author, a research psychologist in Northern Ireland, corrects those deficiencies in this excellent detailed study of the family life of children suffering from cystic fibrosis. Burton sets himself the task of determining the nature of the problems posed by CF for families who live in a welfare state (and are therefore not burdened by additional financial worries). By interviewing all but one of the 54 known CF families in Northern Ireland, he builds a portrait of problems from preliminary symptoms and diagnosis through death and its aftermath. The concluding chapter evaluates some of the ways which parents and children developed to deal with stresses imposed on them. There is also a bibliography, and lists of helpful organizations in Britain and of CF organizations around the world. A model study.

Easson, W. M. *The dying child: The management of the child or adolescent who is dying.* Springfield, IL: Charles C Thomas, 1970. An early monograph setting forth in a clear and readable way the author's views on the following topics: how children react to the threat of death; problems involved in caring for preschoolers, school-age children, and adolescents who are dying; impact on the family; and effects on the treating personnel.

Furman, E. (ed.). *A child's parent dies: Studies in childhood bereavement.* New Haven: Yale University Press, 1974. The classic volume on bereavement in childhood from a psycho-analytic viewpoint. The editor provides here, on behalf of her colleagues, an introductory account of the study on which this book is based, theoretical insights on helping bereaved children, grief and mourning, the process of mourning, individual circumstances, differences between children and adults in mourning, effects of parental death on the child's personality development, and observations on depression and apathy, and a 64-page review of literature that relates this work to other studies. Meanwhile, nine lengthy examples by individual therapists appear through the text. Indispensable.

Gyulay, J. E. *The dying child.* New York: McGraw-Hill, 1978. This book is aimed primarily at members of the health care team; its author is a pediatric nurse. Four central parts discuss: concerns of the child—young children, older children, and special children, such as those who are physically or emotionally handicapped, mentally retarded, adopted, from one-parent families, of foreign descent, twins, or an only child; problems affecting the grievers—parents, siblings, and significant others (taken very broadly); phases of illness and death, from diagnosis through remission, relapse, the terminal state, or sudden loss, to the post-death period; and guidelines for nursing care of dying children. No references within the text, but an extensive bibliography at the end. Commendable for its broad scope. Otherwise not particularly new, but useful as a blend of existing knowledge and common-sense insights.

Haim, A. *Adolescent suicide.* Translated by A. M. Sheridan Smith. New York: International Universities Press, 1974. A comprehensive, theoretical account by a respected French scholar. Haim is concerned to show the uniqueness of his subject, both as a death-related event and as an event of adolescence. The successive parts of the book take up: notions of suicide and adolescence, and available statistical data; attitudes of adults and society toward this phenomenon; causes—Haim favors an association of factors rather than a single cause; and some hypotheses and conclusions to guide future caregiving and research. In general, Haim emphasizes how little we know in any rigorous way about this subject. His analysis is valuable precisely for that caution and for its thoroughness of detail.

Hamovitch, M. B. *The parent and the fatally ill child: A demonstration of parent participation in a hospital pediatrics department.* Duarte, CA: City of Hope Medical Center, 1964. A report of an early research project that "proposed to demonstrate that a hospital program that provides for full participation by the parents in the care of these children [i.e., children with a fatal illness, especially leukemia or sarcoma] can mitigate the traumatic effects of such a crisis upon the children and the parents" (p. 1). The study explored family adaptation during illness and following death, together with staff adaptations. Results demonstrate that a parent participation program of this sort is both feasible and effective.

Hollingsworth, C. W. & Pasnau, R. O. *The family in mourning: A guide for health professionals.* New York: Grune & Stratton, 1977. This 200-page book consists of 27 short chapters written by a total of 14 contributors. This total includes the two editors, who together prepared 19 chapters and individually participated in two more. The five principal parts of the book deal with the following topics: 1) a study of a family stricken with congenital cardiopathy from the viewpoints of cardiologist, nurse, social worker, psychologist, and psychiatrist; 2) how physicians should meet their responsibilities to inform families after various sorts of death; 3) observations on mourning by parents following the death of a child, by children following a death in the family, by a surviving spouse, after abortion or the birth of a handicapped child, and in cases of delayed grief or pathological mourning; 4) ways to help families in mourning; and 5) the role of liaison psychiatry in helping the helpers.

Martinson, I. M. (ed.). *Home care for the dying child: Professional and family perspectives.* New York: Appleton-Century-Crofts, 1976. This book is the most substantial publication to emerge from the Home Care Project at the University of Minnesota School of Nursing. Specifically designed for health professionals, the book brings together many viewpoints to describe this effort to assist parents who take their children with terminal illnesses home to die, the nursing care that is involved, impact on the family, technical and clinical aspects of care for children with cancer, and some theoretical considerations for health professionals. Martinson's project is in the best tradition of medical and nursing caregiving and it has much to offer to a limited population of families with a child facing a life-threatening illness. But while home care, dying children, and their families are the immediate context, the principles to which this book directs us are not limited to those circumstances. On the contrary, they have broad application for all who work with dying and bereavement.

Miles, M. S. "The grief of parents." Privately printed, 1978. Now available from The Compassionate Friends, Inc., P.O. Box 1347, Oak Brook, IL 60521. Ten pages of text plus a two-page bibliography; by a nurse educator who has specialized in the grief of parents after the death of a child. Describes typical experiences and suggests some guidelines for coping. Gentle and sensitive; ideal as a first piece of literature for those who are thrust into this sort of crisis, or for anyone assisting such people.

Moriarty, D. M. (ed.). *The loss of loved ones: The effects of a death in the family on personality development.* Springfield, IL: Charles C Thomas, 1967. There are two complementary parts to this book. Part I, written by Moriarty, provides case materials, analyses, and suggestions for limiting personality damage caused by the death of a loved one. Part II consists of eight chapters by a judge, two clergypersons, a sociologist, two child psychologists, a child psychiatrist, and an adult psychoanalyst, who were each asked "to write whatever their reactions were to the rough draft [of Part I] with the emphasis being on their personal ideas rather than any attempt to review the literature" (p. x).

Pattison, E. M. *The experience of dying.* Englewood Cliffs, NJ: Prentice-Hall, 1977. The effort here is to get beyond "staging dying" to a richer appreciation of different trajectories in the living-dying interval. Pattison provides a lengthy introductory overview and concluding synthesis of major themes related to dying, as well as a topical bibliography. The long middle of the book is given over to his contributors who offer 20 portraits and case studies of many types of dying situations across the lifespan from early and middle childhood, through adolescence, young adulthood, and middle age, to the elderly. There is no excuse for simple stereotypes about dying or about children after this book.

Reid, R. *My children, my children.* New York: Harcourt Brace Jovanovich, 1977. This history over the past 20–25 years of increased understanding (though the cause still remains unknown) and ability to anticipate through prenatal diagnosis the birth defect commonly known as spina bifida (myelomeningocele, and associated conditions of hydrocephaly or anencephaly) is a real-life drama that could hardly be exceeded by fiction. Here the story is told by a British journalist who names the principal scientists, physicians, and several of the parents who were actually involved. An engrossing tale of scientific, medical, moral, and human dilemmas and decisions.

Sahler, O. J. (ed.). *The child and death.* St. Louis: C. V. Mosby Co., 1978. Growing out of a 1977 symposium at the University of Rochester Medical Center, this book consists of 23 papers by professionals on the following general subjects: families and the death or fatal illness of a child, with some principles for helping; viewpoints and problems of those who care for dying or chronically ill children; survivors—of death or suicide, whether they be children, parents, or grandparents, and how some might be helped by bereaved parents' groups; and ethical and educational considerations, including issues for the clergy, the right to information and freedom of choice for dying minors, a program for death education at the high school level, and an annotated bibliography categorized by a modified Kübler-Ross schema. The book opens with a short Preface and Introduction by the editor, and a chapter on the development of the child's concept of death; it closes with two short personal statements by the mother and sister of a child who died at three months of age. Many good chapters for professionals, with some fuzziness in conception and unevenness in execution.

Schiff, H. S. *The bereaved parent.* New York: Crown Publishers, 1977. Parents who have experienced and survived the death of a child offer a unique reassurance to others who may be confronting "this most unnatural of disasters" (p. xiv). Harriet Schiff is such a parent and she has interviewed many others along with various experts to write this book. It is not an academic book full of references to the scholarly literature. But it does consider thoughtfully such topics as normal and abnormal patterns in grieving, guilt, funerals, effects on a marriage and on siblings, communication, and religion. *The bereaved parent* is the fullest discussion of this complex and difficult subject thus far available for lay readers. It has given help and comfort to countless people at a time of great trial. The hard lesson for Schiff herself was the most fundamental: "It was only when I could think 'Robby is dead' that I could also think 'but I am alive' " (p. 7).

Schulman, J. L. *Coping with tragedy: Successfully facing the problem of a seriously ill child.* Chicago: Follett Publishing Co., 1976. Most psychiatrists deal with people who tend to cope badly. This book is an effort by an American child psychiatrist to explore sources of strength in successful coping. Fifteen years earlier, the author had experienced the sudden death of his own five-year-old child, and it is with problems arising out of serious illness in childhood that he is here concerned. Each of the 29 chapters in the book consists of an edited transcript of an interview. In Part I the speakers are parents of children with leukemia, cystic fibrosis, spina bifida, and other serious disorders; in Part II we hear from five physicians and a chaplain. Intriguing and uplifting.

Sherman, M. *The leukemic child.* Washington, D.C.: U.S. Department of Health, Education, and Welfare, Publication No. (NIH) 76-863, 1976. Mikie Sherman is a writer whose seven-year-old daughter died of acute lymphocytic leukemia in 1972. She speaks here as a parent addressing other parents in order to offer information, support, and practical guidance. Treatments and cure rates have changed since the publication of this book, but stresses and problems for leukemic children and their families—whether in the hospital, at home, or in the community—remain much the same.

Stephens, S. *Death comes home.* New York: Morehouse-Barlow, 1973. Simon Stephens is an Episcopal priest who founded The Society of Compassionate Friends in 1969 in Coventry, England—a mutual- and self-help group for bereaved parents. In this little book he describes problems faced by a family after the death of a child. Special attention is paid to well-meaning outsiders who are unsure what to do or say and who therefore often withdraw and cease to mention the dead child, thereby further isolating the survivors and compounding their loss. The proper role for society at large and for groups like Compassionate Friends is identified in the following sentence: "Grief only becomes a tolerable and creative experience when love enables it to be shared with someone who really understands" (p. 53).

Wass, H. & Corr, C. A. (eds.). *Helping children cope with death: Guidelines and resources*, 2nd ed. Washington, D.C.: Hemisphere, 1984. This slim book is the most up-to-date handbook for adults who want to prepare themselves to help children deal with death. Three chapters provide guidelines to children's thoughts about death, to entering the world of a child encountering death, and to death education for helpers. The resources section includes: an annotated bibliography of 43 books for adults that complements the present listing (it emphasizes first-person accounts and discussions of developmental, educational, counseling, and bibliographical considerations); an annotated bibliography of 160 books for children; and an annotated listing of numerous audiovisual resources. Can be used independently or in conjunction with the present book.

Wass, H., Corr, C. A., Pacholski, R. A., & Sanders, C. M. *Death education: An annotated resource guide.* Washington, D.C.: Hemisphere, 1980. Intended primarily for those who teach in this area, but many sections will be valuable for others. Coverage includes: printed resources—books and articles describing death education for all levels and audiences, selected text and reference books, bibliographies, periodicals, and literature on research and assessment of death attitudes; almost 600 audiovisual resources of all kinds, together with distributors; organizational resources; community resources; and an appendix with last-minute entries.

Wolfenstein, M. & Kliman, G. (eds.). *Children and the death of a president.* New York: Doubleday, 1965. The assassination of President John F. Kennedy had a tremendous impact on many people. This book is concerned with reactions of children. Originating in a conference held at the Albert Einstein College of Medicine in April 1964, this volume is an instance of disaster research in the social sciences. It consists of nine papers employing a variety of methods (e.g., observations, interviews, clinical data, questionnaires, essays, and projective techniques) to study various populations ranging from young school children to college students and including both everyday settings and children in treatment centers. Three appendices reproduce a questionnaire used with primary and secondary school children, a number of short essays written by junior high school students, and a transcript of tape-recorded interviews with seven- to twelve-year-olds. Perhaps the most interesting overall result concerns differences in tempo of emotional response among the children and by contrast with adults.

Wolff, S. *Children under stress.* London: Allen Lane The Penguin Press, 1968. This book deals with children who need skilled psychological help because of the occurrence of a critical life situation or because of severe or persistent behavioral disturbance. The author is a British child psychiatrist and researcher on child development. For our purposes, the most interesting sections of the book are the fifth chapter on bereavement and perhaps also the fourth on illness and going to hospital (although the latter does not give special attention to terminal illness in children). The concluding part on treatment approaches is also of some relevance.

Books for Children

Hannelore Wass

Bernstein, J. E. *Loss and how to cope with it.* New York: Seabury Press, 1977. Nonfiction. Age 12 and over. In this book the author addresses older children and adolescents and discusses in a straightforward manner the responses of people to the death of a loved one, stressing that many reactions that are apparently bizarre, are actually normal and common. The author relates personal stories which serve effectively to make a point or convey a concept. Along the way much practical advice is offered to the reader. The book includes a list of other books on death and dying as well as some films and organizational resources. Valuable not only for children and youth, but for adults as well.

Bernstein, J. E. & Gullo, S. V. Photographs by Rosmarie Hausherr. *When people die.* New York: E. P. Dutton, 1977. Nonfiction. Age 6–10. This sensitive, beautifully written book explains honestly and at the same time reassuringly how people feel and act when a loved one dies and gently leads the reader through the grieving process, including shock and denial, physical distress, feelings of emptiness, anger, and isolation. The authors do not shy away from dealing with the biological and physiological aspects of death, decomposition, and body disposal. This book answers many questions children ask about death. The stunningly beautiful photographs by the young Swiss photographer add greatly to the value of the book. Particularly striking and poignant are the photos of the newborn infant who has just entered the world and whose wrinkled face expresses need for care, followed a page later by the beautiful face of an old woman (actually Mrs. Michaelson, a retired principal) whose wrinkles tell of the joys and sorrows of a long life well-lived and of wisdom and serenity achieved. A must.

Brown, M. W. *The dead bird.* Reading, MA: Addison-Wesley, 1965. Fiction. Preschool to age 8. A group of children find a dead bird in the park. They observe what "dead" is like by touching and looking. Then they decide to have a funeral, and bury the bird before resuming their play. Each day the children return to the bird's grave, put fresh flowers on it and sing to the bird. They continue this ritual of mourning "until they forgot." The final illustration depicts the children as they play ball with the bird's grave in the background. The author's insight and understanding of young children is evident. The story is straightforward, practical, detailed, and matter-of-fact, yet tender and caring. Valuable.

Dixon, P. *A time to love—a time to mourn. Original title: May I cross your golden river?* New York: Scholastic Book Services, 1975. Fiction. Age 14 and over. At 18, Jordon Phillips discovers he is slowly dying of the same muscular disorder that killed the famous baseball player, Lou Gehrig. The book vividly describes Jordon's and his family's reaction of shock, anguish, and pain. The reader is not spared details of the pain, and the progressive weakness that Jordon experiences, but the reader is also permitted to share Jordon's innermost thoughts and feelings and his interactions with his family and friends. The loving, caring support of his family helps Jordon to prepare himself and them for his death. This is a moving book by a gifted and sensitive writer that depicts masterfully a painful reality, but also portrays the power of love to help overcome fears and anxiety and cope with death at an early age.

These annotations are selections from an extensive annotated bibliography of children's books about death published in Wass, H. & Corr, C. A. (eds.) *Helping Children Cope with Death—Guidelines and Resources*, Washington, D.C.: Hemisphere, 1982.

Farley, C. *The garden is doing fine.* New York: Atheneum Publishers, 1975. Fiction. Age 6–8. This book describes the impact of parental death on a young child. Corrie's father is dying of cancer. Corrie and her mother refuse to accept this. Corrie recalls former happier times and is outraged at the injustice of her father's suffering. She prays for him and thinks of him often, but another part of her is also aware of boys, games, and school activities. Finally, when she can no longer deny the imminence of her father's death, she is consoled by the realization that his kindness and love will always be remembered and will live on through her memory.

Fassler, J. *My grandpa died today.* Illustrated by Steward Kranz. New York: Human Sciences Press, 1971. Fiction. Preschool to age 8. This beautifully written story is about a little boy David who, in narrative form, tells about his beloved grandfather's death and how he feels about it, how those around him feel, what they do, and particularly how caring and understanding they are toward David. David's grandfather had taught him many things, and had shared his thoughts about life and death. One day he had said: "David, I am getting very old now. And surely I cannot live forever . . . but I am not afraid to die . . . because I know that you are not afraid to live." With this memory, David is better able to cope with his grief and can get on with life. An essential part of this warm and comforting story are the exceptional illustrations that vividly depict in simple strokes the emotions of love, sadness, shock, the gentleness of comfort, and, yes, the joy of life. A must.

Grollman, E. A. *Talking about death—A dialogue between parent and child.* Illustrated by Gisela Héau. Boston, MA: Beacon Press, 1976. Nonfiction. Preschool to age 6. This is a new edition of the author's 1970 book by the same title. In this new edition the Parents' Guide is expanded to include various ways of using the book, of helping parents themselves come to acknowledge death and grief. This book is for children to read or to have read to them. The author discusses death in an honest, simple, straightforward manner. He insists that the reader understands that dead is *dead.* There is no flinching from the facts, no silence to the child's questions. At the same time, the book is warm, loving, sensitive, and tender. Gisela Héau's incredibly beautiful illustrations underscore the text and create a hopeful mood. This is one of the best nonfiction books about death for young children on the market. A must for parents with small children.

Hughes, P. R. *Dying is different.* Mahomet, IL: Mech Mentor Educational Publishers, 1978. Nonfiction. Preschool to age 8. This beautiful book by a gifted writer, artist, and psychologist, is intended to promote discussion of death between adults and very young children. The eighteen children's pages use drawings, strong colors, and poems to present a graduated succession of living and dead states in flowers, ants, fish, a cat, and a grandmother, followed by vivid thematic depictions of the inevitability of death, its justification, remembering, acceptance, grief, funerals, cemeteries, and the importance of love during life. An introduction and concluding remarks for parents and teachers suggest questions and guidelines for discussion. A very helpful resource for adult-child interactions, one that adults can read alone or share together with children. Available in both a large instructional edition designed to stand upright by itself and in a smaller personal edition in standard book format.

Langone, J. *Vital signs—The way we die in America.* Boston, MA: Little, Brown and Co., 1974. Nonfiction. Age 16 and over. In this documentary the author skillfully weaves together a variety of materials: classical quotations, scientific data, legal case material, news reports, and interviews with doctors, nurses, clergy, and dying persons, and their families. In doing this he shows startlingly facts about the way people die today. The reader is immediately involved in the current dilemma about the definition of death, in the depersonalization of contemporary dying, and the universal desire for dignity. This book is instructive and humanistic in its plea for greater empathy for the needs of dying persons. Indignant and compassionate. A valuable book for mature young readers as well as adults.

Lee, R. *The magic moth.* New York: Seabury Press, 1972. Fiction. Age 8–11. Ten-year-old Maryanne is the middle child in a family of five and she has a heart defect. Everything possible has been done, including heart surgery, but now the family is told that Maryanne cannot be cured. The story tells of the love, courage, strength, and support of the Foss family and the problems that had to be overcome in helping each other cope with Maryanne's impending untimely death. A moth bursts from its cocoon as Maryanne dies, and seeds sprout just after her funeral, symbolizing that "life never ends—it just changes," a belief that offers much comfort to both young and old readers. This is a touching story told in a straightforward and unsentimental manner.

Lee, M. S. *Fog.* New York: Seabury Press, Inc., 1972. Fiction Age 12 and over. This book deals with the grief and sense of loss that Luke experiences at the death of his father, as well as another kind of grief, hurt, and anger he feels when he and his girlfriend decide to stop seeing each other. The reader also struggles with the boy over his choice of a career and his feelings of guilt about the clubhouse fire. The language is contemporary and attractive to the reader. The characters portrayed are vivid and believable.

LeShan, E. *Learning to say good-bye: When a parent dies.* New York: Macmillan Publishing Co., 1978. Nonfiction. Age 10 and over. This family counselor and writer speaks to children in a simple, straightforward manner about the problems they face when losing a parent, and how these problems may be overcome. The main thrust throughout this helpful and comforting book is the acceptance of the griever as a person who is suffering much pain and disorientation but who is healthy and will be capable of coping by expressing and sharing his/her feelings in open communication with interested and caring adults. The book is well-written and examples are used amply to illustrate a situation or clarify a point. An informative, non-threatening, supportive book.

Shotwell, L. R. *Adam Bookout.* New York: The Viking Press, Inc., 1967. Fiction. Age 12 and over. Adam avoids acknowledging the deaths of his parents by pretending they are still alive. In his grief, he runs away from well-meaning guardians. When he reaches his destination, he meets a number of people from different backgrounds with many kinds of problems. He realizes that he is not the only one with problems. He learns, too, that problems are not left behind when people run away. Valuable.

Slote, A. *Hang tough, Paul Mather.* Philadelphia, PA: Lippincott, 1973. Fiction. Age 9–12. Paul Mather, a sixth grader, loves baseball, and he is good at it, especially pitching. But Paul also has leukemia and is in his third remission when the story begins. His parents have moved twice hoping to find the hospital that can cure their son. Now they have arrived in Michigan and the Little League of baseball teams in the new neighborhood need him. He is needed as a pitcher for the Wilson Dairy team, and when his parents refuse to give permission until he has seen his new doctor, Paul fakes his parents' permission and plays anyhow. His father is irate, his mother is frightened. Paul has trouble convincing his parents how much he needs to play baseball in order to keep up his hope. Paul's new doctor, Tom Kinsella, turns out to be of critical help. He is open, informal, understanding, and becomes personally involved. When Paul is hospitalized he visits three or four times a day. Twice, when Paul had vomitted, he helped the orderly clean up. But most of all, in Paul's own words "he knew how to break bad news better than any doctor I ever had." In this deeply moving book, the author tells of the courageous struggle of a young boy to cope with his illness, with his parents' protectiveness, and eventually with the knowledge that he has little time left to live. The author has an uncanny ability to evoke emotions by a style of writing that is full of understatements and has a simplicity that speaks eloquently. Inspiring.

Smith, D. B. *A taste of blackberries.* New York: Thomas Y. Crowell, 1973. Fiction. Preschool to age 6. A little boy is confronted with loss, grief, and guilt when his best friend, Jamie, dies from being stung by a bee while the two are picking blackberries. The feeling of guilt is natural enough. Jamie had a way of kidding around, so that when he rolled on the ground after the bee had stung, his friend thought he was only joking. After a time, the boy comes to accept his friend's death. This story is simply and sensitively written and richly illustrated. The book won a Child Study Association award.

Wersba, B. *Run softly, go fast.* New York: Atheneum Publishers, 1970. Fiction. Age 16 and over. David Marks, 19, has just returned home from his father's funeral. He hates his father and decides to write a journal about their relationship. He remembers that when he was young his father had been the most important person in his life. Slowly, his feelings had changed. This may have started when Dave discovered that his dad was having an affair with another woman; it may have been a reaction to his father's dislike of Dave's poetry and paintings; or it may have been when Dave realized what a ruthless businessman his father was. The final break came when his father accused Dave's best friend of "being a queer." Dave then moved out of the house to live in the "hip" community. He rarely spoke to his father. However, when his father was in the hospital dying of cancer, Dave came to visit him. Nearing the end of the journal, Dave recognizes errors in his recollections, gains a new perspective and now is able to perceive his father differently. A believable story to which young persons can relate well. It deals with the difficulties adolescents and youths have in accepting their parents as human beings with faults. Writing a journal helped David resolve his anger and facilitated his grieving for his father.

White, E. B. *Charlotte's web.* New York: Harper & Row Publishers, 1952. Fiction. Age 8–11. This beautiful and popular story is about Wilber, a pig, Templeton, a rat, and their friendship with Charlotte, a spider. Charlotte's death and the subsequent birth of her children help explain how the cycle of life continues through children. The story also describes the grief and sorrow one experiences after the death of a close friend and shows how memories of a dead friend can be kept alive in a healthy manner. A classic.

Whitehead, R. *The mother tree.* New York: The Seabury Press, 1971. Fiction. Age 8–12. When Tempe's mother dies suddenly, the ten-year-old girl quite suddenly has to take care of her four-year-old sister, Laurie, and help with the household chores. To make matters worse, Laurie continually asks "When will Mother come back?" Tempe's own impulses to play and be free of this burden of responsibility make her feel guilty. But the patience and kindness Tempe shows toward her little sister help Laurie to face the fact that her mother is dead and cannot return. At the end of a long summer, Tempe is rewarded by her father's praise and gratitude. This is a moving story.

Zim, H. & Bleeker, S. *Life and death.* New York: William Morrow & Co., 1970. Nonfiction. Age 9 and over. In this pioneering book the authors discuss in plain language the biological, physical, and chemical facts of life and death and the naturalness of the life cycle for plants, animals, and humans. In addition, the authors deal with people's attitudes toward death, with various death and funeral customs in different cultures and bring the reader up to the best definition of medical death then available. This is a scientific and dispassionate account, yet not at all insensitive. What impresses most is that this little book contains a great many of the answers to children's questions about death that often are not available to them through interaction with adults. This information-packed volume is most valuable because it will help to avoid misconceptions and fantasies about aspects of death that are unpleasant and distasteful to many adults. The book has a hopeful conclusion: It suggests that people who lead useful and happy lives are likely to come to an acceptance of all life, including its end. Outstanding.

Zindel, B. & Zindel, P. *A star for the latecomer.* New York: Harper & Row Publishers, 1980. Fiction. Age 12 and over. Brooke Hillary is 17 and lives on Long Island, but she commutes into New York City to attend a school for youngsters seeking a theatrical career. Her mother—who is 46 and has advanced bone cancer—wants Brooke to be something special, and Brooke tries hard to become a star before her mother dies. For herself, Brooke likes dancing, but she really would rather just have a boyfriend and be like other girls. This could have been little more than a tale of intergenerational conflict, but the authors know that real life is more complex than that. Mother and daughter do love each other, but each must seek her own freedom and fulfillment.

Zolotow, C. *My grandson Lew.* New York: Harper & Row Publishers, 1974. Pictures by W. Pene Du Bois. Fiction. Preschool to age 8. Four years have passed since Grandfather died. Now Lewis is six and suddenly tells his mother that he misses his grandfather. His mother had assumed Lewis had been too young to remember his grandfather. Now to her surprise, she finds that Lewis remembers many experiences with great clarity, such as the scratchy beard when Grandpa kissed him, the time he took him to the place that had many pictures to look at, and the time Grandpa let him warm his hand around the pipe. Lewis confides to his mother that he has missed Grandpa and has been waiting for him to return. Lewis' mother, in turn, tells the little boy that she has missed him, too. Sharing their memories of Grandpa make Lewis and his mother a little less sad. This story is a work of art in which each sentence is written with restraint and charm and provides evidence of the author's deep insight into the world of a child. Du Bois' pictures are vivid and project the same kind of warmth and love that characterizes the text.

Organizational and Audiovisual Resources

Richard Pacholski

ORGANIZATIONAL RESOURCES

Bereaved Parents

Candlelighters Foundation, 123 C Street, S.E., Washington, D.C. 20003. Formed in 1970, this is a loosely structured national federation of over 65 regional and local groups of parents with children suffering from or lost to cancer. While the member groups may have a variety of names and needs, the umbrella organization assumes larger tasks. It serves as a communications link among affiliated groups through newsletters, bibliographies, and other materials; helps in the formation of new local groups; sponsors regular gatherings of affiliates, many on the subject of new developments in research and treatment; conducts a parent-to-parent letter-writing program; and lobbies for increased federal funding for cancer research projects.

Teachers of death education, counselors and other professionals may establish contact with Candlelighters or with a local parents' group. These people are most happy to share, and are invaluable sources of information and insight. As noted above, group names may vary locally; for example, LODAT (Living One Day at a Time), IMPACT (Interested, Motivated Parents Against Cancer Today), CURE (Children's United Research Effort-St. Louis), COPE (Cincinnati Oncology Parents' Endeavor), PALMS (Parents Against Leukemia and Malignancies Society-Kansas), Living with Cancer, Inc. (Grand Rapids, MI), Parents Who've Lost Children (Tucson), First Sunday (Detroit). For information inquire at a local hospital, doctor's office, chamber of commerce, or write Candlelighters.

The Compassionate Friends, P.O. Box 1347, Oak Brook, IL 60521. The Society was founded primarily to provide one-to-one communication, counseling, and self-help for bereaved parents. There are nearly two dozen regional groups around the country. Besides organizing occasional conferences, the group publishes a National Newsletter and a number of filmstrip and audiocassette programs.

Cancer

American Cancer Society, Inc., National Headquarters, 777 3rd Avenue, New York, NY 10017. The very significant work of the Society cannot be adequately described in brief space, nor can its importance be over-emphasized. The Society makes available a wealth of printed and audiovisual material for the general public as well as for health professionals and educators. The topics include various types of cancers and their treatments, rehabilitation programs, caring for the terminally ill, and bearing and sharing grief. There are very helpful and informed staff members on the local level as well as associated professionals and volunteers. Operating under the sponsorship of or in cooperation with the Society are various other local and regional informational, self-help, and helping groups (for example, International Association of Laryngectomees, Reach to Recovery, and United Ostomy Association) for patients with particular diseases or with particular physical and emotional needs. The Society has divisional offices in every state and regional offices in many cities. The A.C.S. is one of the most valuable resource organizations.

Leukemia Society of America, 800 Second Avenue, New York, NY 10017. With affiliated organizations in each state, the Society provides help for needy leukemia patients, sponsors research, raises funds, and educates the public about the disease through a variety of publications and audiovisual materials. It is involved in professional education, sponsoring symposia and providing scholarships and awards. The Boston chapter sponsors a supportive program called OUTREACH for patients and family members that is typical of approaches used by other local affiliates:

O = Open doors of friendship
U = Unite patients and families
T = Trust one another
R = Reach out to understand others and oneself
E = Educate oneself to new ways of life
A = Approach life with new Awareness through sharing
C = Comfort one another at Crucial, Critical times in life
H = Hearing others talk about good days and bad days is how OUTREACH Helps
      families to cope

General

National Mental Health Association, 1800 North Kent Street, Rosslyn, VA 22209. With a million volunteers in over 900 state divisions and chapters, this is the only organization of its kind working on behalf of the mentally and emotionally ill. The national office sponsors research and is involved in legislative and governmental agency activities in all related areas. It publishes informational materials and sponsors educational programs. While the Association itself does not provide direct services, it works to ensure that quality mental health services are available to anyone who needs them. Locally, this goal means distribution of readings and films on such topics as aging, nursing homes, widowhood, suicide, mental retardation, and coping with deaths in the family. Local chapters also serve as referral centers and resource people to whom death educators and other professionals may turn for information.

Hospitalized Children

Association for the Care of Children's Health, 3615 Wisconsin Avenue, N.W., Washington, D.C. 20016. Founded in 1965 the Association "seeks to foster and promote the health and well-being of children and families in health care settings by education, interdisciplinary inter-action and planning, and research." Members are chiefly medical and administrative professionals, but interested parents are joining in increasing numbers. The Association's publications (a quarterly journal, a newsletter, various bibliographies, and other books) as well as its yearly conventions and study sections address themselves to a whole range of child-care issues, including, for example, the seriously ill child, the dying child, the child with cancer, and children in hospice settings.

Sudden Infant Death Syndrome

National Sudden Infant Death Syndrome Foundation, 310 South Michigan Avenue, Chicago, IL 60604. The major purposes of this group are to assist parents, to educate the public, and to promote research. It sponsors programs of professional counseling and, through its many local chapters, fosters parent-to-parent and self-help activities. It publishes a variety of educational and informational literature as well as a quarterly newsletter, and makes speakers available. Consult your regional or local chapter.

Suicide

American Association of Suicidology, 2459 S. Ash, Denver, CO 80222. The membership of this organization, the preeminent national group in the field, consists of nearly 600 professionals in various specialties devoted to the study of suicide and suicide prevention. The Association supports basic research, educational programs and activities, and sponsors various publications: a quarterly journal, "Suicide and Life Threatening Behavior"; a quarterly newsletter, "Newslink"; "Proceedings" of the annual meetings; a directory of suicide prevention centers; and a number of informative, low-cost booklets and pamphlets for general audiences.

AUDIOVISUAL RESOURCES

Bereaved Child

Children and Death. When children experience the death of someone close, their special needs demand knowledgeable and honest intervention. The topic is explored with an audience of parents, teachers, counselors, medical personnel, and clergy in mind. Wolfelt Productions, 814 W. Charles St., Muncie, IN 47305; color filmstrip (or slides) and audiocassette, discussion manual, 15 minutes, 1979.

Death in the Family. Eda LeShan, author of *Learning to Say Goodbye*, discusses the pain and the grief of survivors. Children, too, experience great suffering. Ms. LeShan analyzes their emotions and suggests ways of helping them cope. Psychology Today Cassettes, P.O. Box 278, Pratt Station, Brooklyn, NY 11205; audiocassette.

Reactions of Children to Serious Illness, Death, and Natural Catastrophe. This is a videotaped lecture to a medical audience by Dr. Howard Hansen. University of Washington Audiovisual Services, Seattle, WA 98195; 60 minutes.

Bereaved Parents

Dear Little Lightbird. The subject, an incurably ill "blue baby," is the 3-year-old son of the filmmaker. Viewfinders, Inc., Box 1665, Evanston, IL 60204; color film, 19 minutes.

Death and Dying: When a Child Dies. Dr. C. Charles Bachmann interviews a mother who has lost several of her children to a genetic disease. Communications in Learning, 2280 Main St., Buffalo, NY 14214; audiocassette, 43 minutes.

Death of a Newborn. Presented in this program is an interview with a young couple who lost their firstborn infant at age 4 weeks. Valuable insights are offered into parental needs, problems, grief and mourning, and into intervention techniques that do and do not work. Polymorph Films, 118 South St., Boston, MA 02111; color film or videotape, 32 minutes, brochure, 1976.

Death of the Wished-For Child. Glen W. Davidson, Professor of Thanatology at Southern Illinois University School of Medicine, interviews a mother who lost a wished-for child at birth and who developed emotional problems because of errors in intervention made by her caregivers. Dr. Davidson makes quite clear what should be done and said in such situations. O.G.R. Service Corporation, P.O. Box 3586, Springfield, IL 62708; or Professor Davidson, P.O. Box 3926, Springfield, IL 62708; color film, 28 minutes.

Grief Therapy. Originally produced as part of the CBS-TV "60 Minutes" series, this film presents several on-camera grief therapy sessions. Dr. Donald Ramsey leads a mother to "let go," to face the fact and separate herself from her daughter, whose accidental death she has been mourning intensely for over $2\frac{1}{2}$ years. Insights into the nature of grief are graphically presented. Carousel Films, 1501 Broadway, New York, NY 10036; color, 20 minutes, 1976.

Marek. Marek is a 7-year-old boy who must undergo dangerous cardiac surgery to correct a birth defect. The doctors advise the parents of the risks involved and counsel the family attentively. The surgery is performed but there are complications and Marek dies. The parents are then helped through the shock of the loss. Produced by BBC-TV, the film is well made and impressive. Time-Life Films, Time-Life Building, 1271 Avenue of the Americas, New York, NY 10020; color, 45 minutes, 1978.

The Syndrome of Ordinary Grief. In an interview, a sophomore medical student describes his reactions to the accidental death of his only child, a 2-year-old boy, some weeks earlier. Included is a scholarly paper on this case history. University of Texas Medical Branch, Videotape Library of Clinical Psychiatric Syndromes, Galveston, TX 77550; color videotape, 32 minutes.

With His Playclothes On. At 21 months Jerry dies suddenly of causes that, even after autopsy, are not completely understood. The immediate emotional responses of the parents and three older brothers are vividly presented. Two months after the death the family is still torn by unresolved shock, anger, and conflict, as the family members react on different levels and from incompletely shared points of view. This study of grief in the family, one of the best available on the subject, includes extensive analytical commentary by Dr. Glen Davidson, Professor and Chief of Thanatology, Department of Psychiatry, Southern Illinois University School of Medicine. OGR Service Corporation, P.O. Box 3586, Springfield, IL 62708; color filmstrip and audiocassette, 47 minutes, 1976.

Birth Defects

Mongoloid Infant: Should We Operate? A panel of doctors at the University of Virginia Medical School breaks this question down into its more specific medical and ethical components, and discusses the varying types of prognoses of mongoloidism, the "quality of life" concept, and the extent of parental rights in determining treatment. University of Virginia, School of Medicine, Charlottesville, VA 22904; black and white videotape, 60 minutes, 1973.

My Son, Kevin. Kevin, a "thalidomide baby," has no arms or legs, but he rises above misfortune to attend a community school and be a loved and loving person. This film would interest discussion groups on policies and attitudes toward malformed fetuses, abortion, and birth defects. Viewfinders, Inc., Box 1665, Evanston, IL 60204; color, 24 minutes.

A Question of Values. Down's syndrome is explained and moral issues related to keeping and caring for Down's syndrome and other handicapped infants are raised. Patients (three infants and three children, aged 5-21) and their families are introduced to illustrate commentary on the widely varying physical and psychological traits found in the D.S. population. This presentation tries to counter the film *Who Should Survive?* which presents the case of a D.S. infant, unwanted by the parents, who was allowed to die without corrective surgery. Edward Feil Productions, 4614 Prospect Ave., Cleveland, OH 44103; color film, 28 minutes, 1972.

Who Should Survive? The film opens with the birth of a baby, a diagnosis of Down's syndrome, the parents' refusal to permit life-saving abdominal surgery, and the subsequent starvation of the infant in the hospital. A 19-minute panel discussion then argues various legal, ethical, and scientific aspects of the case. A teacher's guide and bibliography are available. University of California, Berkeley, Extension Media Center, 2223 Fulton St., Berkeley, CA 94720; color, 26 minutes, 1972.

Cancer

American Cancer Society: National Conference on Childhood Cancer: Meeting Highlights. American Cancer Society, 777 Third Ave., New York, NY 10017; film, 2 hours, 1974.

Childhood Cancer: Emotional Effects. This videotape. is available for medical professionals. M. D. Anderson Hospital and Tumor Institute, Medical Communications Department, University of Texas System Cancer Center, Houston, TX 77025; color, 58 minutes, 1975.

Leukemia Panel Discussion. Parents of leukemic children and their doctors discuss the psychological and emotional effects of the disease on the families. Stanford University, School of Medicine, Division of Instructional Media, M 207, Stanford, CA 94305; color videotape, 32 minutes, 1975.

A Need to Know: A Family Faces Death. Part of the videotape series "Interventions in Family Therapy," this program presents an interview between Lois Jaffe, M.S.W., a leukemia patient herself, and the family of a child with the same disease. ETL Video Publishers, 1170 Commonwealth Ave., Boston, MA 02134; color videotape, 60 minutes, 1975.

You See—I've Had a Life. At 13 Paul Hendricks is diagnosed as having leukemia. After some initial attempts at denial, the parents decide to tell Paul. The whole family shares the experience with him, working to enhance the quality of his life in the time remaining. The film records Paul's continuing school and athletic activities, treatments by medical staff, the caregiving activities, and the personal reactions of the parents and of Paul himself. This is a moving, well-made story of one family's togetherness in the face of death and of one child's courage. The words of the title, which accurately suggest the essence of his character and the quality of his response to death, are spoken by Paul to reassure a friend who came to offer sympathy. Viewfinders, Inc., Box 1665, Evanston, IL 60204; black and white, 32 minutes, 1973.

Caring for the Dying Child

Counseling the Terminally Ill. Medical caregivers are the primary audience for this detailed film introduction to the physical and psychological needs of dying patients, both adults and children, in the clinical setting. The emphasis is on effective communication on matters of diagnosis, prognosis, treatment regimen, and involvement of family members. Write Charles A. Garfield, Ph.D., 106 Evergreen Lane, Berkeley, CA 94705; color film, 55 minutes.

Death and the Family: From the Caring Professions' Point of View. Professor Delphie Fredlund lectures on effective treatment of dying children and on the preparation and responsibilities of caregivers of the dying. The Charles Press, Bowie, MD 20715; audiocassette, 30 minutes, 1972.

Dying Child. Dr. Elisabeth Kübler-Ross addresses herself in this videotaped lecture to the problems and needs of dying children, their parents and caregivers. She offers several specific suggestions on ways of getting children to express their feelings about their deaths: poetry, play therapy, and art activities, for example. Medical College of South Carolina, Division of Continuing Education, 80 Barre St., Charleston, SC 29401; color, 42 minutes, 1975.

Nursing Management of Children with Cancer. The purpose of this film is to illustrate the skills, commitment, and rewards involved in pediatric cancer nursing. The procedures demonstrated include infusions, mouth care, control of infections and fevers, ostomy care, and play therapy. The need for emotional support for patients and their families is explained, as is the nurse's teaching responsibility in aiding parents to help and treat their children at home. Statistical information is provided that suggests that the prognosis of many childhood cancers is improving. American Cancer Society, 777 Third Ave., New York, NY 10017; color, 22 minutes, 1974.

Physician's Role with the Dying Patient. Three programs make up this series aimed at helping practicing physicians improve their work with dying patients. "Children Die Too" offers suggestions on treating dying children and relating effectively with family members. "Maintaining Integrity of the Profession" offers guidelines for physician-patient exchange at various stages in the dying process. "The Philosophy of Dying" discusses legal, social, and emotional factors in the dying situation. University of Arizona, Health Sciences Center, Division of Biomedical Communications, Tucson, AZ 85724; three color videotapes, 50-57 minutes each, 1974.

Death Education

See the commentary under the heading "Suicide."

General

Children and Dying Conference, University of Chicago, 1977: Proceedings. Audiocassettes are available on these topics: "Care for the Caregivers," "The Child and Sudden Death," "What Shall We Tell the Children?," "The Dying Child at Home," "The Dying Child in the Hospital," and "Parental Loss and Childhood Bereavement." Highly Specialized Promotions, P.O. Box 989, GPO, Brooklyn, NY 11202; available as a set or individually.

Sudden Infant Death Syndrome

After Our Baby Died: Sudden Infant Death Syndrome. This well-made, impressive film, winner of a blue ribbon in mental health at the 1976 American Film Festival, was created to help professionals and others who come into contact with SIDS parents to better understand the syndrome. Parents are interviewed, and offer telling lessons and insights for caregivers. Free loan from The National SIDS Foundation, Room 1094, 310 S. Michigan Ave., Chicago, IL 60604; color, 20 minutes, 1976. Write the Foundation for information on several other audiovisuals available.

Suicide

Suicide, of all death and dying topics, has been the most thoroughly explored in audiovisuals. We recommend that those interested consult *Death Education: An Annotated Resource Guide* (H. Wass et al., Washington, D.C.: Hemisphere, 1980), which describes in detail and cross-indexes nearly 100 audiovisual items on suicide.

Dozens of additional audiovisuals on all death, dying and children topics are also listed there. The book is a particularly rich source of information and resources on all aspects of death education, on which topic there are many, many audiovisuals, for all audiences and age levels. The resource guide describes and cross-indexes them by subject.

Index